MICROSOFT®
ACCESS
PROJECTS
WITH MICROSOFT®
SQL SERVER™

Microsoft®
.net™

Ralf Albrecht
Natascha Nicol

PUBLISHED BY
Microsoft Press
A Division of Microsoft Corporation
One Microsoft Way
Redmond, Washington 98052-6399

Library of Congress Cataloging-in-Publication Data pending.

Printed and bound in the United States of America.

1 2 3 4 5 6 7 8 9   QWE   7 6 5 4 3 2

Distributed in Canada by Penguin Books Canada Limited.

A CIP catalogue record for this book is available from the British Library.

Microsoft Press books are available through booksellers and distributors worldwide. For further information about international editions, contact your local Microsoft Corporation office or contact Microsoft Press International directly at fax (425) 936-7329. Visit our Web site at www.microsoft.com/mspress. Send comments to *mspinput@microsoft.com*.

Acquisitions Editor: David Clark
Project Editor: Lynn Finnel

Body Part No. X08-42089

Table of Contents

Part II   Forms and Reports

10   Forms   193

Part VI Transactions and Locks

Part VII Internet

Part I

Microsoft Access Projects and Microsoft SQL Server

This section describes the basics of setting up Access projects. Access projects differ from traditional Access mdb databases in that data and queries are managed and run with SQL Server and MSDE.

This section will explain in detail how SQL Server and MSDE manage data in tables and how they differ from Access mdb database tables. The SQL Server database diagrams correspond to the relationship diagrams in Access mdb databases for creating and documenting key relationships.

Queries are created with SQL Server or MSDE in the Transact-SQL programming language. Select queries can be defined as views. Entire program processes and action queries are implemented as stored procedures. You will learn how to create, edit, and run views and stored procedures from an Access project and will be given an overview of programming with Transact-SQL.

1

Introduction to Microsoft SQL Server and Access

Microsoft Access is the most commonly used product for desktop databases among beginners and professionals alike. However, Access has limitations when it comes to the administration of large amounts of data that many users access through a network.

Microsoft positions Microsoft SQL Server as a database server that can make large amounts of data available to many users at the same time. In addition, a SQL Server version is included with Microsoft Office Developer suites and Microsoft Visual Studio as a Microsoft Data Engine (MSDE) with limited functionality.

One goal of this book is to describe how Access and SQL Server or MSDE work together. Since the release of Microsoft Access 2000, it is possible to create Access projects. Access projects provide users and programmers with the usual Access development environment that includes queries, forms, reports, macros, and modules, with the data being saved on a SQL Server. Because this book focuses on creating Access projects (adp) and describing its new options and functions, the book does not cover the options of accessing SQL Server tables using Open Database Connectivity (ODBC) and so on using regular Access databases in .mdb format.

Access is a comfortable, high-performance development environment for the implementation of user-friendly applications. The second goal of this book is to demonstrate how you can retain Access as a development environment while using a high-performance server database at the same time. Access is often ridiculed as a "toy," with its usefulness limited to the implementation of a few small applications on desktop systems. However, by now, many Access programmers have proven the program's capability for handling medium-sized and large applications.

This book is based on working with software projects that utilized Access projects and SQL Server to replace existing Access solutions and original project developments that took advantage of SQL Server's performance features. Several version changes occurred while this book was being written: Microsoft SQL Server 2000 is the successor of Microsoft SQL 7, and Microsoft Access 2002 as part of Microsoft Office XP is the successor of Access 2000. SQL Server 2000 and Access 2002 feature a large number of improvements, particularly for tasks that require programming with Access projects. We have incorporated information about both new versions in the book and we discuss the problems related to version incompatibilities. For example, some Access 2000 project functions do not work while accessing SQL Server 2000.

Who Should Read This Book?

This book was written for readers who are familiar with Access, who have experience creating forms and reports, and who know how to program with Microsoft Visual Basic. This book does not cover the basic options available for creating forms and reports. Instead, it presents the differences between Access adp projects and traditional Access mdb applications.

Chapter Overview

The book's individual chapters are organized into parts for a clearer overview. The following summary introduces the topics covered in each chapter.

Part I: Microsoft Access Projects and Microsoft SQL Server

Part I teaches you how Access projects are structured and how to use an Access project to access SQL Server or MSDE databases. We explain the components of SQL Server or MSDE databases, such as tables, views, and stored procedures.

Chapter 2, "Access Projects," describes the basic properties of Access projects. We point out how conventional Access databases differ and introduce the various SQL Server and MSDE versions.

Chapter 3, "Installation," covers the SQL Server or MSDE installation process, both for version 7 and for 2000. We also discuss the different configuration options for transferring data between the Access client and SQL Server over the network.

Chapter 4, "Databases," provides an overview of SQL Server or MSDE databases and illustrates their structure. In addition, we introduce preinstalled sample databases, followed by a description of how to create new Access projects that access new or existing SQL Server or MSDE databases.

Chapter 5, "Tables in Access Projects," teaches you how to create tables in a SQL Server or MSDE database. We introduce the SQL Server data types and column properties for tables available in SQL Server or MSDE. The chapter also covers the creation of indexes, the definition of constraints, and much more. Next, you learn about how to work with tables in the Access datasheet view. At the end of the chapter, we briefly describe the system tables used by SQL Server and MSDE that can be found in every database.

Chapter 6, "Database Diagrams," is devoted to the definition of relationships among database tables. A database diagram lets you create well-organized graphical models that illustrate the tables in a database and the relationships among them.

Chapter 7, "Views," focuses on views. A view is based on a SQL *SELECT* command and corresponds to a select query in Access mdb databases. The chapter describes the query designer options for interactively creating views.

Chapter 8, "Stored Procedures," is an introduction to programming stored procedures. Stored procedures are routines written in the Transact-SQL programming language that you can use to query, add, edit, or delete data. We demonstrate how you can use variables and parameters in stored procedures and introduce the Transact-SQL Syntax. This chapter also covers how to create fundamental triggers, which are specialized stored procedures assigned to tables that are executed during the process of inserting, editing, or deleting the table's data. We address the process of debugging stored procedures in this chapter as well. We then move on to describe the user-defined functions that are new features in SQL Server 2000.

Chapter 9, "Transact-SQL," focuses on the Transact-SQL programming language. This chapter provides you with an overview on how to program with Transact-SQL and includes information about subqueries, temporary tables, and error handling.

Part II: Forms and Reports

Part II is devoted to forms and reports in Access projects. Note that the chapter does not cover all options available for creating and programming forms and reports. Instead, the focus is on those Access project form and report issues that are new or different from Access mdb database functions.

Chapter 10, "Forms," describes special circumstances related to working with forms in Access projects.

Chapter 11, "Reports," presents the changes and new functions available for creating reports in Access projects.

Part III: Programming with ADO

Part III is an introduction to programming the ActiveX Data Objects (ADO) data access interface. With conventional Access mdb databases, you could choose between the Data Access Objects (DAO) data access interface and ADO. In Access projects, however, you can only use ADO.

Chapter 12, "*Connection* Objects," teaches you how to work with *Connection* objects that specify connections between the program and the database server. We describe how to create new connections, particularly in Access projects, and how to use the Access project's connections.

Chapter 13, "*Recordset* Objects," details how you can edit, add, or delete data and introduces the most important *Recordset* object methods and properties. ADO uses *Recordset* objects to return a query's result sets.

Chapter 14, "*Command* Objects," is devoted to *Command* objects. The primary purpose of these objects is the execution of queries that edit, add, or delete data.

Chapter 15, "ADO Events," outlines the process of programming *Connection* and *Recordset* object events. Many of the objects' operations initiate events that you can capture and process with your own routines.

Part IV: Upsizing

Part IV consists of two chapters that provide helpful information on the conversion of existing Access mdb applications to Access adp projects.

Chapter 16, "Upsizing Wizard," presents the Upsizing Wizard that supports you during the conversion of Access mdb applications to Access projects. The Upsizing Wizard helps you transfer data from an mdb database to a SQL Server or MSDE database. On your request, the wizard attempts to transfer forms, reports, macros, data access sheets, and modules to an Access project.

Chapter 17, "From DAO to ADO," contains tips on how to use ADO to convert existing Access Microsoft Visual Basic for Applications (VBA) programs that use the DAO data access interface to Access projects.

Part V: SQL Server/MSDE Administration

Part V covers the different administration options for SQL Server and MSDE systems. We discuss using an Access project alone (particularly with respect to using SQL Server 2000 Desktop Engine and MSDE), as well as the use of the complete SQL Server version's administration tools.

Chapter 18, "Database Administration," teaches you how to create and administer SQL Server or MSDE databases with Transact-SQL commands and with the SQL Server Enterprise Manager.

Chapter 19, "SQL Server Tools," introduces additional SQL Server Enterprise Manager functions and describes the options available for using the SQL Server query analyzer, the OSQL program, and the SQL Server Profiler.

Chapter 20, "Security," is devoted to the methods for backing up your data on SQL Server or MSDE. SQL Server and MSDE let you set up users and user groups. You can then assign to the users or groups detailed access rights for tables, views, and stored procedures.

Chapter 21, "Data Backup Functions," discusses the different options for backing up and restoring your SQL Server or MSDE databases. You can use

Access project functions, SQL Server Enterprise Manager functions, or Transact-SQL commands.

Chapter 22, "Data Transformation Services," covers Data Transformation Services (DTS). With DTS, you can use object linking and embedding database (OLE DB) or open database connectivity (ODBC) to export data from your database or to import data from database systems. DTS supports the definition of transformations that perform conversion and transformation functions during the data import or export process.

Chapter 23, "The SQL-DMO Library," introduces the SQL Distributed Management Objects (SQL-DMO) library, which enables you to access SQL Server functions from your programs. We use examples to illustrate some of the options.

Chapter 24, "External Data Sources," describes how to access external data sources from SQL Server or MSDE. With OLE DB or ODBC, you can use Linked Servers to create links to external data sources, which means that you can then directly utilize these data sources in your queries.

Chapter 25, "System Stored Procedures," lists the most important SQL Server and MSDE system stored procedures. You can control or execute all SQL Server or MSDE functions with system stored procedures.

Part VI: Transactions and Locks
Part VI consists only of Chapter 26, "Transactions and Locking," which discusses the basics of SQL Server and MSDE transaction and locking functions.

Part VII: Internet
Part VII is devoted to Access project and SQL Server Internet functions.

Chapter 27, "Web Publishing with SQL Server," briefly introduces a few SQL Server Internet functions, such as time- or date-controlled generation of static Hypertext Markup Language (HTML) pages.

Chapter 28, "XML with Access 2002 and SQL Server 2000," provides you with an overview of the products' Extensible Markup Language (XML) capabilities. Access 2002 and SQL Server 2000/MSDE 2000 support the data interchange format, the importance of which has recently continued to increase, especially for Web applications.

Appendices
Appendix A, "Naming Conventions," contains the Reddick VBA Naming Conventions. These guidelines for naming variables can help support and standardize your programming. Appendix B, "Internet Addresses," features a list of interesting Web addresses. Appendix C, "SQL Server/MSDE Specifications," is a reference index in which you can look up some Access project and SQL Server specifications.

The Sample Database

We have made an effort to illustrate all examples with a manageable database example that asks simple as well as complicated questions. The advantage for you is that you do not have to familiarize yourself with a new data model every time a new example is presented. The sample database and installation instructions are included on the book's companion CD

We have selected Contoso, Ltd, which shows current movies on multiple screens. The sample database administers show schedules. Contoso wants to administer its movies, schedules, and theaters. For each calendar week, there is a list of movies playing during that week. Other information on the database includes how long each movie has been out, the movie's length, and the Motion Picture Association of America (MPAA) rating. Show schedules, admission prices, the theater where the movie is playing, the number of seats in that theater, and the turnaround time (the time needed to clear the theater and fill it up with the audience attending the next show) are also provided.

All details relating to a specific theater are saved in the table *tblTheaters*, shown in Figure 1-1. The *TheaterNumber* is the table's primary key (PK).

TheaterNumber	Theater	Seats	Turnaround	Note
1	Alpha	120	25	
2	Beta	150	30	
3	Gamma	90	20	
4	Delta	50	15	
5	Epsilon	90	20	
6	Omega	450	30	
7	Sigma	300	30	

Record: 8 of 8

Figure 1-1   Theater data

Detailed information about the individual movies is saved in the table *tblFilms*, and the primary key is the *FilmNr*, as shown in Figure 1-2.

FilmNr	Filmtitle	MPAANr	Length	Summary
1	The Perfect Sto	3	129	The movie is dr:
2	The Next Best '	3	107	Abbie and Robe
3	X-Men	3	97	Professor Xavie
4	Pokemon, the N	1	80	A Pokemon col
5	The Bachelor	3	101	In this update o
6	Gladiator	4	165	In the final days
7	Mission: Impos	3	125	Ethan Hunt leac
8	Dinosaur	2	90	The journey of a
9	The Patriot	4	160	Benjamin Martii
10	Hollow Man	4	135	Government res
11	Big Momma's F	3	90	FBI agent Malc

Record: 1 of 24

Figure 1-2   Movie data

The field *MPAANr* references the table *tblMPAA* (not shown), where the MPAA values *G, PG, PG-13, R,* and *NC-17* are listed.

Theater schedules are always created for one week, which means that a movie plays for the duration of one week. During that week, the movie can be shown in different theaters. On the weekend, for example, a specific movie might be shown in a large theater. The corresponding film number for a calendar week is saved in the table *tblWeeks*. In this example, a calendar week is identified by the date for the first day of the week. The table *tblWeeks* also includes a column named *WeekShown,* which contains entries that specify the number of subsequent weeks a movie is being shown. In our example, shown in Figure 1-3, the movie admission prices are determined by week.

WeekNr	Week	FilmNr	WeekShown	Note	Price
46	8/4/2000	10	0		$10.00
47	7/14/2000	4	2		$10.00
48	7/7/2000	14	1		$10.00
49	6/30/2000	24	0		$10.00
50	6/30/2000	13	0		$10.00
51	7/23/2000	16	1		$10.00
52	6/30/2000	11	3		$10.00
53	7/14/2000	14	2		$10.00
54	7/7/2000	11	4		$10.00
55	6/30/2000	16	2		$10.00
56	8/11/2000	10	1		$10.00
57	7/7/2000	13	1		$10.00

Record: 1 of 67

Figure 1-3 The *tblWeeks* table

The table *tblMovieSchedule* contains information about the specific days a movie is playing during the respective week and which theater is showing the movie, along with the showtimes. The *WeekNr* field is used to create a link to the calendar week, and thus to the movie. As shown in Figure 1-4, the *Theater-Number* column specifies which theater is showing the movie during the respective week.

ShowTimeNr	WeekNr	TheaterNumber	Day	Time	Note
1	79	6	5	8:00:00 PM	
2	89	2	1	5:30:00 PM	
3	89	2	2	8:30:00 PM	
4	89	2	3	1:15:00 PM	
5	89	2	4	1:15:00 PM	
6	58	5	6	1:00:00 PM	
7	63	4	3	2:15:00 PM	
8	63	4	4	2:15:00 PM	
9	63	4	3	5:15:00 PM	
10	63	4	4	5:15:00 PM	
11	63	5	7	8:15:00 PM	
12	63	5	7	1:15:00 PM	

Record: 1 of 217

Figure 1-4 Schedule data

The *Day* column specifies the day of the week. For scheduling purposes, Germany's cinema week begins on Thursday, meaning that new theatrical releases premiere on Thursdays.

The program now creates a record for every show. For example, if a movie's show time is Thursdays at 8 P.M., the entry in the *Day* column is 1 and the entry in the *Time* column is 8:00:00 PM.

If a movie plays every day of the week at 8 P.M. in the same theater, you must save seven records in the table. To limit data volume, conventions were created to summarize data.

For example, if a movie plays every day of the week at the same time in the same theater, only a single record with the value *11* is entered in the *Day* column. If a movie is scheduled to be shown on the weekend, the value *9* is entered in the *Day* column. Table 1-1 lists the relevant codes.

Table 1-1   Data Entry Conventions for Days

Number of Days	Description
1 … 7	Individual days (Thursday = 1 … Wednesday = 7)
8	Fri/Sat
9	Weekend Sat/Sun
10	Thurs/Mon–Wed (all days of the week, except weekends)
11	All days of the week

We also use the table *tblBoxOffice*, shown in Figure 1-5. The table is intended to provide information about how many moviegoers attended each show.

Figure 1-5   *tblBoxOffice* table

Figure 1-6 illustrates the relationships among the five tables. Note that the relationship lines do not run to and from the fields that are related to each other. Instead, the relationship lines simply end somewhere at the respective tables. The easiest way to discern the actual relationships is to look at the field names. For example, the tables *tblFilms* and *tblWeeks* both contain a field named *FilmNr*, which is used to create the foreign key (FK) relationship.

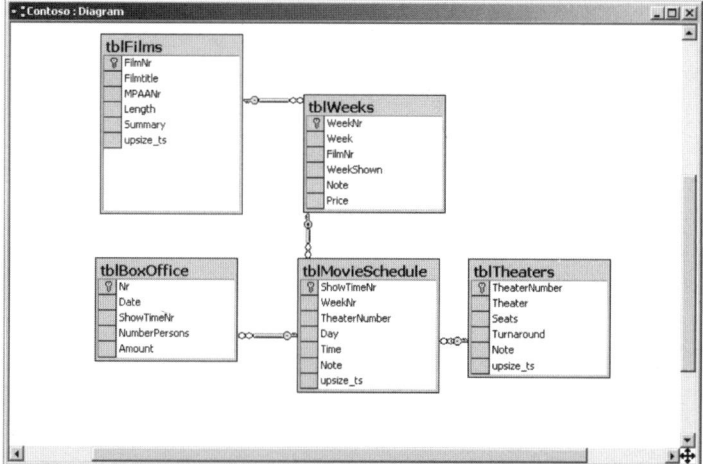

Figure 1-6   Relationships between the tables

System Requirements

Your companion CD includes the README.TXT file in the root directory of the CD. It will provide you additional information about the CD contents and support information for the book.

The following are the minimum system requirements for using the CD-ROM included with the book:

- PC with Pentium 166 MHz or higher processor

- Microsoft Windows 98, Windows Me, Windows NT 4.0, Windows 2000, Windows XP

- 32 MB of RAM for Windows 98, Windows Me, Windows NT 4.0

- 64 MB of RAM for Windows 2000, Windows XP

- Hard-disk space required:

    - 250 MB for a typical installation of SQL Server

    - 53 MB (minimum) for installation of MSDE

    - 40–100 MB for installation of Service Packs

- CD-ROM drive

- VGA or higher-resolution monitor required

- Display system capable of 800 x 600 or higher resolution.

- Microsoft Internet Explorer 5.01 or later to view the electronic version of the book

- Microsoft Access 2002

Support

Every effort has been made to ensure the accuracy of this book and the contents of the companion CD-ROM. Microsoft Press provides corrections for books through the World Wide Web at the following address:

http://www.microsoft.com/mspress/support/

To connect directly to the Microsoft Press Knowledge Base and enter a query regarding a question or issue that you might have, go to:

http://www.microsoft.com/mspress/support/search/asp

If you have comments, questions, or ideas regarding this book or the companion CD-ROM, please send them to Microsoft Press using either of the following methods:

Postal Mail:
Microsoft Press
Attn: *Microsoft Access Projects with Microsoft SQL Server* Editor
One Microsoft Way
Redmond, WA 98052-6399

E-Mail:
MSPINPUT@MICROSOFT.COM

Please note that product support is not offered through the above mail addresses. For support information regarding SQL Server and Access, please visit the Microsoft Product Support Web site at

http://support.microsoft.com

2

Access Projects

Microsoft Access was originally designed as a database for small-solution applications and desktop use. Consequently, database applications that use Access encounter difficulty when the application handles large volumes of data or numerous users access an Access database over a network.

With its simple yet powerful interface and the Microsoft Visual Basic for Applications (VBA) integrated programming language, Access creates an excellent environment for rapid application development; however, many programmers and database developers have undertaken large-scale projects using Access. In many cases, this approach has been successful, notwithstanding the extra efforts and workarounds required to compensate for the shortcomings of Access.

When large volumes of data are being handled, possibly involving multiple users at the same time, database management systems (DBMSs) like Oracle, IBM DB2, Informix, Software AG ADABAS, Microsoft SQL Server, and others are much more suitable than Access. Many businesses use Access as the front end client to these databases, but this is not problem-free either, as we discuss later.

For many years, Microsoft has been trying to get a foothold in the hard-fought database market with its DBMS product, SQL Server. Whereas most of the products, like those offered by market leader Oracle, originated on mainframes and large UNIX computers, Microsoft has taken a bottom-up approach.

SQL Server evolved from Sybase SQL Server, released in 1987. In 1988, Microsoft joined in the development of the product, which led to Microsoft SQL Server 4. Subsequently, Sybase and Microsoft parted ways after version 4, with Sybase further developing the UNIX versions of the product and Microsoft focusing on Windows NT versions. Microsoft SQL Server 6 was the first version to be completed by Microsoft alone. SQL Server 6.5 was released in 1996, and version 7 appeared in 1998.

With Microsoft SQL Server 7, Microsoft released a product that was more or less on par with established DBMSs. At the time of writing, Microsoft SQL Server 2000 holds several benchmarks, coming ahead of UNIX competitors.

Microsoft is trying to increase SQL Server's share of the market by positioning it as a database system for small to large applications, with Access serving as the front-end and development environment. A "scaled down" version of SQL Server called Microsoft Data Engine (MSDE database as part of SQL Server 7 release) is included with every Microsoft Office 2000 and Microsoft Office XP suite, the aim being to tempt Access users to migrate.

With Access, it has always been possible to attach tables from external database systems, ensuring that the data could be accessed. The connection to the DBMS is accomplished using open database connectivity (ODBC) drivers. Unfortunately, the ODBC connection approach is not very powerful and can lead to bottlenecks with large volumes of data. Furthermore, not all of the features offered by DBMSs can be exploited.

Access 2000 retains the method of attaching tables using ODBC. Among the new features are Access adp projects, which are special database projects for accessing SQL Server. Access 2002 offers numerous improvements and new features over Access 2000 projects such as Data Access Page Designer, PivotTables and PivotCharts, and XML Presentation Output, to name a few.

Interfaces

To program Access databases with Microsoft Visual Basic, a data access interface is required so that the data can be manipulated.

DAO and the Jet Engine

Conventional Access databases (mdb projects) use the Jet Engine to manage data. The Jet Engine, included in Access, is the database kernel through which all database operations are executed. Two versions of the Jet Engine ship in Access 2000 and Access 2002: Version 3.6 is in the "normal" version of Access, when the Data Access Objects (DAO) data access library is being used, and version 4 is used when gaining access with ActiveX Data Objects (ADO).

DAO is the original interface for database programming with Access, and it is sophisticated and stable. With the use of DAO, all the database functions provided by the Jet Engine can be programmed. However, DAO was designed and optimized for desktop databases, not for accessing server databases.

Accessing Oracle or SQL Server databases with DAO is very complex, often limits functionality of the underlying DBMS, and can be very slow, partly due to the fact that the ODBC interface is used to access the data. Furthermore, the Jet Engine is involved in all operations, even though this is unnecessary when accessing server databases. Since Microsoft Access 95, ODBCDirect connections have been available in DAO, permitting ODBC access while bypassing the Jet Engine. Although ODBCDirect improved access to server databases, it by no means solved all problems. SQL pass-through queries, which pass a SQL query directly to the database server for processing without involving the Jet Engine, are also supported.

For access to server databases, Microsoft offered Microsoft Visual Basic 4 for the programming environment and the Remote Data Objects (RDO) library for subsequent versions. RDO, however, is more complicated than DAO to program, requiring the programmer to become familiar with the ins and outs of the ODBC connection.

ADO and OLE DB

A new data access interface, ADO, was developed, and is still being improved with the latest version, ADO.NET. ADO combines the best of both worlds: the comfort of the DAO interface with RDO's access options and speed.

In Access 2000, Microsoft defined ADO as the new standard. DAO (and RDO in Visual Basic) were to be superseded by ADO. However, this has not yet been fully replaced in Access 2000 and Access 2002: DAO is still supported to ensure that the wide number of existing Access programs also run with Access 2000 and Access 2002. This interface coexistence can lead to considerable confusion for Access 2000 and Access 2002 developers, as DAO is mandatory for several functions in these programs. As a result, programmers have to master and use both interfaces. Within Access, too, most of the functions are still implemented using DAO; for example, in queries, forms, and reports. Access 2002 includes improvements, but there, too, DAO and ADO still exist side by side.

ADO is based on OLE DB, an interface to relational and hierarchical data, implemented as a Component Object Model (COM) interface as part of the Microsoft Windows Open Services Architecture (WOSA). OLE DB is a component of Microsoft's Universal Data Access (UDA) strategy.

Access programmers do not actually come into contact with the OLE DB interface, but use ADO instead. ADO hides all the details of OLE DB and facilitates use of the interface.

ADO-based access to a database system and files with data require an OLE DB provider. The provider prepares the specific data and services of the respective system so that they can be addressed with ADO.

In this book, the OLE DB provider for SQL Server is used and described almost exclusively, as this is the provider used by Access projects to access SQL Server and MSDE.

Access Projects

Microsoft developed Access projects for powerful and fast access from Access to SQL Server (or MSDE). Access projects use OLE DB and ADO. Figure 2-1 shows how Access and SQL Server work together.

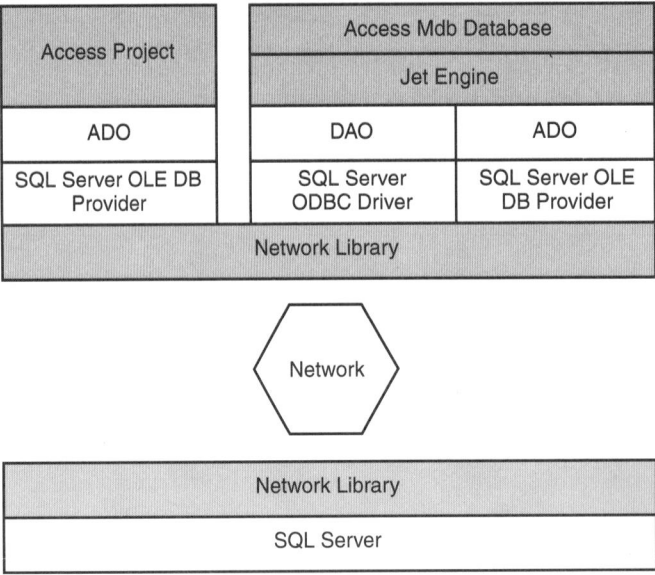

Figure 2-1   Access and SQL Server

Tables, database diagrams, views, and stored procedures are stored on the server. Forms, reports, pages, macros, and modules, on the other hand, are saved in the Access project file (with the filename extension .adp).

In Access 2002, views and stored procedures have been combined under the generic term *Queries*, as shown in Figure 2-2. In addition, user-defined functions (UDFs), a new feature in SQL Server 2000, can also be managed under *Queries*.

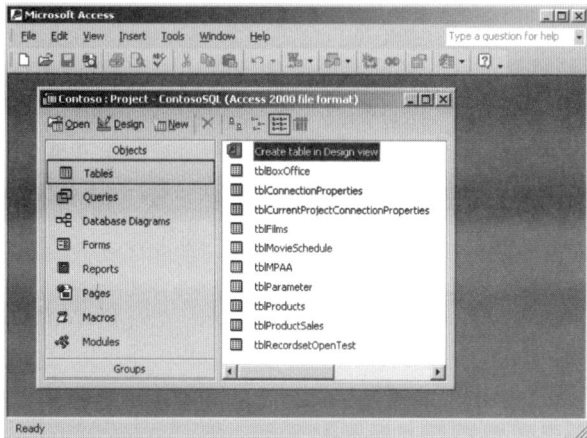

Figure 2-2   Access project in Access 2002

In Access 2000, views and stored procedures are managed in their own sections (see Figure 2-3).

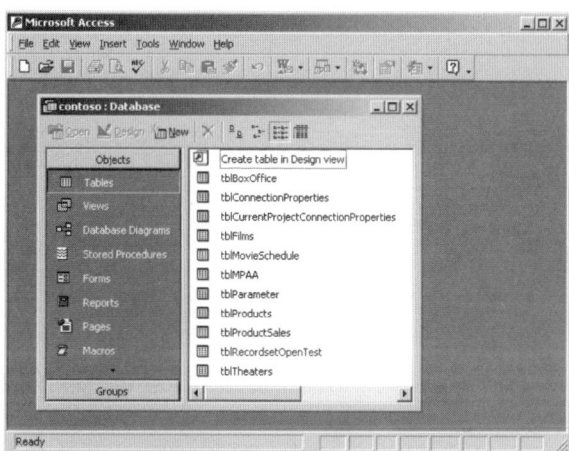

Figure 2-3   Access project in Access 2000

The term *Access projects* can be misleading. There are many projects for which you can use Access, but that doesn't mean that all of them are Access projects.

Note   References to Access databases in this book refer to mdb databases based on the Jet Engine.

Microsoft developed Access projects to work with only Microsoft SQL Server, although they could probably access other DBMSs using OLE DB.

SQL Server and MSDE Databases

SQL Server and MSDE can be used to manage an almost unlimited number of databases, each containing tables, views, database diagrams, stored procedures, user information, and rights. Databases are accessed by name. Internally, SQL Server and MSDE databases are stored in one or more files (usually as .mdf, .ndf, and .ldf), which can be distributed on one or more of the server's hard disks.

Every Access project establishes a connection to a SQL or MSDE server and a specific database. As soon as the connection is established, tables, database diagrams, views, and stored procedures of the connected database are displayed in the Access project.

When the connection is being established, the system checks to see whether you are allowed to log on to SQL Server or MSDE and are authorized to use the database in question. SQL Server and MSDE have a sophisticated, two-tier security system that is described in more detail in Chapter 20, "Security."

In SQL Server/MSDE and Access, data is saved in tables. All Access data types are mapped to SQL Server/MSDE data types. SQL Server/MSDE also support a wide range of additional data types, presented in Chapter 5, "Tables in Access Projects."

A view is based on a *SELECT* query, but with no sorting (that is, with no *ORDER BY*) and without parameters. It is basically the same as a *SELECT* query. SQL Server 2000 allows you to create *indexed views* that can be managed with Access 2002.

Database diagrams are the equivalent of relationship diagrams in Access mdb databases. As in the Relationships window, the relationships between the tables and views can be drawn using lines.

SQL Server and MSDE typically work with foreign key constraints that are defined as part of a table definition, known as declarative referential integrity (DRI). In contrast to Jet databases, DRI can be enforced (such as using Check Existing Data On Creation), but with SQL Sever 7 there is no capability to cascade update or cascade delete. With Jet tables, a cascading update causes the changes in the relationship field on the "one" side of a one-to-many relationship to be automatically made to all the records on the "many" side. The same applies for deletetions when cascade delete is activated.

Cascading updates and cascading deletes from Access databases can be implemented using *triggers*, which are stored procedures assigned to tables that can be activated when records are inserted, modified, or deleted (SQL 2000 also introduces *INSTEAD OF* and *AFTER* triggers).

> **Note**   SQL Server 2000 and MSDE 2000 handle cascading updates and cascading deletes without the use of triggers; however, this is not something that can be set directly from Access 2000. With Access 2002, DRI-based cascading updates and cascading deletes can be managed from within Access.

The capabilities of server programming offered by SQL Server and MSDE can be fully taken advantage of only with stored procedures, triggers, and, in SQL 2000, user defined functions, all of which are based on Transact-SQL and run on the server. This way, some of the data-intensive processing can run centrally on the server, resulting in a reduction in network traffic, among other things.

SQL Server and MSDE

Access projects from Access 2002 (part of Microsoft Office XP) work together with SQL Server 2000 and 7, as well as with MSDE 2000 and Microsoft Data Engine 1 (MSDE 1). You need to be aware of inconsistencies between certain releases, because a variety of versions and different releases of servers and Access applications need to talk to each other.

Access 2000 (part of Office 2000) can work with SQL Server 7 and MSDE 1. It also works, to a degree, with Microsoft SQL Server 6.5 (with Service Pack 5 installed), SQL Server 2000, and MSDE 2000. A service pack for Access that eliminates the problems with SQL Server 2000 and MSDE 2000 is available. Microsoft provides the Access 2000 and SQL Server 2000 Readiness Update at *www.microsoft.com/downloads*. You can find it by selecting Access 2000 from the Product Name list on the Microsoft Downloads Center page.

SQL Server

SQL Server 7 and SQL Server 2000 are offered in three versions:

- Microsoft SQL Server Enterprise Edition for single- and multiprocessor systems with up to 32 processors and up to 64 GB of RAM

- Microsoft SQL Server Standard Edition for single- and multiprocessor systems with up to 4 processors and up to 2 GB of RAM

- Microsoft SQL Server Desktop Edition or Microsoft SQL Server Personal Edition for single- and multiprocessor systems with up to 2 processors and up to 2 GB of RAM

The following operating systems are supported: Microsoft Windows 2000 Data Center, Microsoft Windows 2000 Advanced Server, Microsoft Windows 2000 Server, Microsoft Windows NT 4 Server, and Microsoft Windows NT 4 Enterprise Edition. The SQL Server Personal Edition also provides support for the following operating systems: Microsoft Windows 2000 Professional, Microsoft Windows NT 4 Workstation, Microsoft Windows Me, and Microsoft Windows 98. There is also a special version of SQL Server 2000 for Microsoft Windows CE.

> **Note**   The service packs provided by Microsoft for SQL Server 7 and SQL Server 2000 (Service Pack 3 and Service Pack 1, respectively at press time) can also be applied to MSDE. The latest service pack can be downloaded from *www.microsoft.com/sql/downloads*.

MSDE

MSDE is a full-featured but streamlined version of SQL Server 7 and SQL Server 2000, optimized for five users. MSDE and MSDE 2000 support databases up to 2 GB in size. Access projects developed to work with MSDE should also work with SQL Server 7 and SQL Server 2000 without requiring any changes.

MSDE is actually the desktop version of SQL Server without the following components:

- Enterprise Manager is a comfortable and extensive program for managing servers, databases, users, and so on.

- MSDTC Admin Console controls the Microsoft Distributed Transaction Coordinator, which is responsible for handling transactions involving several SQL servers.

- Profiler eases the monitoring and analysis of data traffic to and from the SQL server.

- Query Analyzer is used to run SQL queries, views, and stored procedures interactively.

- Online Documentation contains the complete documentation for SQL Server.

MSDE databases can be managed within Access projects, through external Enterprise manager consoles, or by using other programs, such as OSQL, available from the command prompt.

MSDE 2000 comes with Office XP and Access 2002, whereas MSDE ships with Office 2000 and Access 2000. Both versions have to be installed separately, as described in Chapter 3, "Installation."

Standalone, Network, and Client Server

In this section we discuss how Access databases differ from Access projects with access to SQL Server and MSDE and introduce some of the basic concepts involved.

Access as a Desktop Database

Access was designed as a desktop database, or a database in which the data and program are located on the same computer with only one user accessing the data. The Access database kernel, Jet Engine, is optimized for this type of access.

Access as a File Server Database

You can set up an Access database on a network file server using two different scenarios. In the first, the .mdb file with the data, queries, forms, reports, and modules is copied to the file server. Each user then activates the same Access database. In the second scenario, the data is placed in a separate .mdb file. This .mdb file, with the queries, forms, and so on, links to the individual tables. Each user can access the same program .mdb file or each user can have his or her own .mdb file with links.

In either case, the actual work on the database is carried out by the local Jet Engine. The following example illustrates this: An .mdb file with a table called *tblAddresses* containing 100,000 records is located on a network server. On the local computer, an .mdb file including a query to filter all records in *tblAddresses* with a surname that ends with "ly" is opened. As the query is processed by the local Jet Engine, all the records need to be transferred across the network to the user's PC. The desired records can then be filtered out.

Access to a Database Server

With a database server, not only is the data stored on the server, but it can also process there. To continue with the preceding example, the relevant command is transferred from the client to the server to filter out the addresses in which the last name ends with "ly." The server gets the records and returns the resultset back to the client.

This kind of processing reduces network traffic, optimizes data access on the server, and harnesses the server's computing capacity.

The most widespread command language for relational databases is Structured Query Language (SQL). SQL is standardized, although most vendors of database server software have adapted and expanded the language, as Microsoft has for SQL Server. Microsoft SQL Server and MSDE support SQL with the specific Transact-SQL (T-SQL) extension. Besides the standard SQL commands, T-SQL offers additional language components that enable developers to program complete processes with flow control, loops, and more on the server.

Data and Log

One of the main differences between desktop and server databases in the storage of data is that the database server usually logs all the database operations like insertions, updates, and deletions. Every database operation is known as a *transaction*, which can contain several database commands. Every transaction is recorded in a log file. Based on a backup strategy, if the actual data file becomes corrupted, the contents can be restored on the basis of the database backup and the transaction log.

With SQL Server and MSDE, therefore, each logical database consists of at least two files: a data file with the file extension .mdf and a log file with the extension .ldf. A SQL Server/MSDE database can be distributed across several data files and log files located on different drives. Many SQL Server installations keep the data and log on different hard disks for security reasons.

Should anything go wrong while you are writing to a database, such as a drive error, network failure, or power failure, the information from the transaction log is restored and the database is reverted to its last consistent state.

.mdf = data file
.ldf = log file

3

Installation

This chapter contains a short description of the installation process for Microsoft SQL Server and MSDE. Although the setup for the different SQL Server and MSDE versions is very similar, there are a few exceptions that must be taken into account. The following sections describe the setup for SQL Server 2000, MSDE 2000, SQL Server 7, and MSDE 1. Before continuing, please read the corresponding section for the relevant server, as well as the section titled "Running SQL Server/MSDE."

Installing SQL Server 2000

After running the setup program and a few initial screens, you will see the Computer Name dialog box displayed in Figure 3-1. You can install SQL Server on a local or a remote computer. For the purposes of this chapter, select Local Computer.

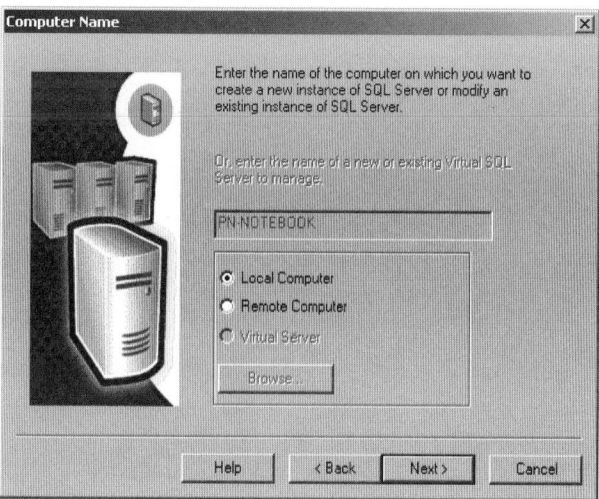

Figure 3-1 Specifying the destination computer

SQL Server 2000 allows you to set up several instances on one computer, so several SQL Servers can run simultaneously under different names on the same computer. Microsoft included this installation option for large server systems working for an entire company, so that SQL servers can be set up for each department, for example. Using a central server can save hardware and administration costs. For the purposes of this chapter, select the first option in the Installation Selection dialog box, shown in Figure 3-2.

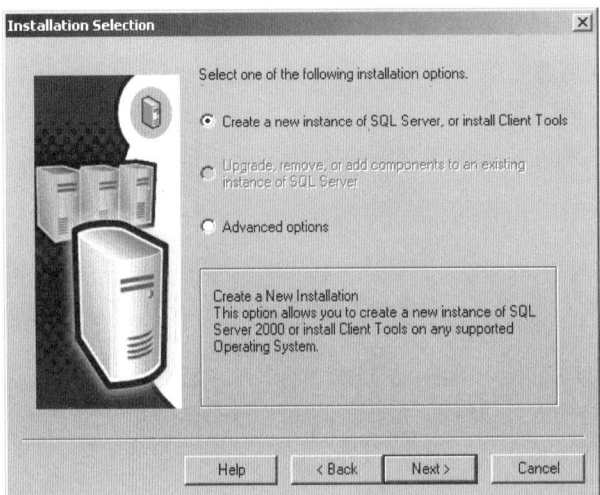

Figure 3-2   New instance or only client tools

By selecting Advanced Options, you can create a special file for an unforeseen server installation or you can reset the registry entries if a SQL Server installation is showing errors on the computer.

Select the type of installation you would like to perform in the Installation Definition dialog box, shown in Figure 3–3. The client tools are the SQL Server administration programs, as well as the drivers required to set up a connection with a SQL server.

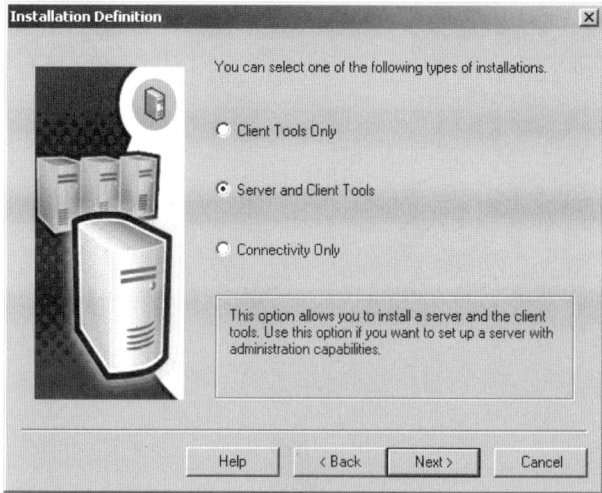

Figure 3-3   Selecting the installation type

In the Instance Name dialog box displayed in Figure 3-4, you determine whether you want to install the default server or an additional server instance.

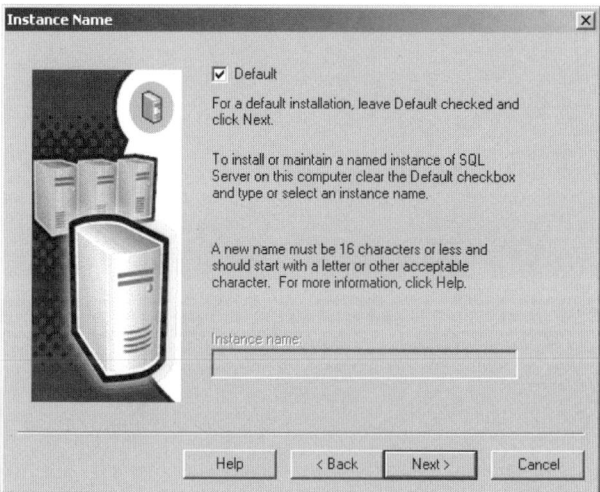

Figure 3-4   Select the default or new instance

In the next step, you determine the scope and destination of the installation. The components included with SQL Server 2000 are given in Table 3-1. You use the Custom option in the Setup Type dialog box, shown in Figure 3-5, to select components according to your requirements.

Table 3-1 SQL Server 2000 Components

Components	Subcomponent
Server components	SQL Server, replication support, full-text search, debug icons, counters
Administrative tools	Enterprise Manager, Profile, Query Analyzer, Distributed Transaction Coordinator (DTC) client support, conflict display
Client connectivity	Named Pipes, Multiprotocol Net-Libraries
Online documentation	Books Online on Disk
Development tools	Headers and libraries, Microsoft Data Access Components Software Development Kit (MDAC SDKs), application programming interface (API) for saving and restoring, debugger interface
Code examples (over 16 options)	ADO, DB-Library (DBLIB), Desktop, Data Transformation Services (DTS), Embedded SQL for C (ESQLC), Microsoft Distributed Transaction Coordinator (MSDTC), SQL Distributed Management Objects (SQL-DMO), SQL Namespace (SQL-NS) and XML Samples

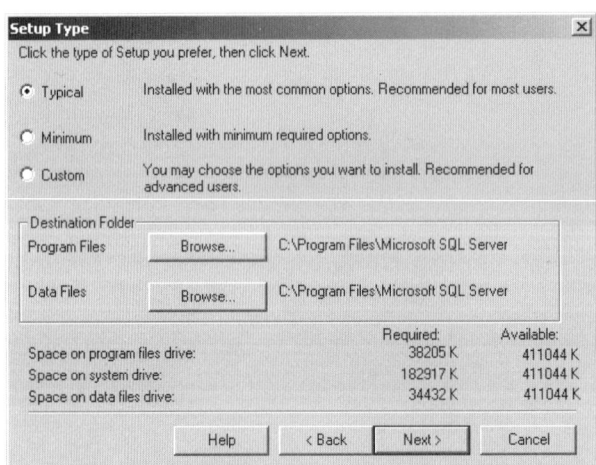

Figure 3-5 Selecting setup scope and destination

In the Services Accounts dialog box, shown in Figure 3-6, you specify the user account information to be used when starting SQL Server, or Microsoft SQL Server Agent (when running with Microsoft Windows NT or Microsoft Windows 2000). If you are working with several SQL servers in a single network, it makes sense to use a cross-domain user account so that data can be exchanged between the SQL servers; however, you should use unique domain accounts for SQL Server Agent so that each server can send and receive e-mail independently. If your SQL server is the only one in the network, select the Local System account. Usually, the same account is used for all services.

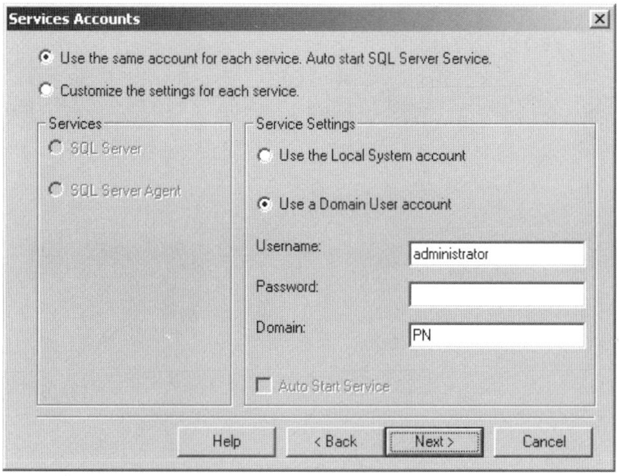

Figure 3-6   Services accounts settings

In the next step, using the Authentication Mode dialog box shown in Figure 3-7, you specify how user accesses are handled on SQL Server. If you select Windows Authentication Mode, then access is only granted to users that have been authenticated by a Windows NT or Windows 2000 server. In mixed mode (the second option), a separate SQL Server authentication is also allowed.

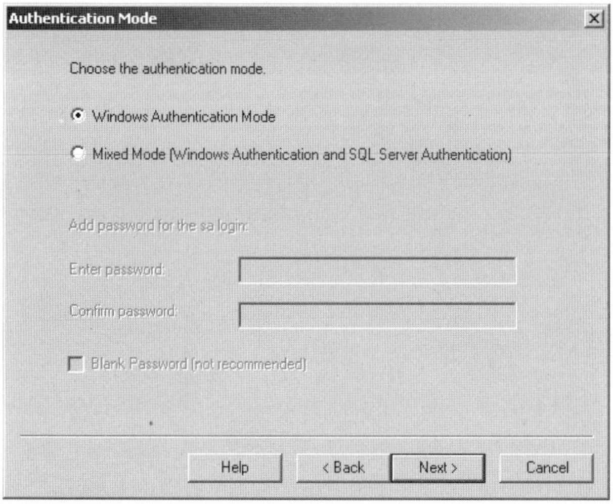

Figure 3-7   Authentication mode

When installing SQL Server 2000, the data access components of MDAC 2.6 are also installed. See the section entitled "Running SQL Server/MSDE," later in this chapter, for further information.

SQL Server 2000 recognizes two different types of license: per seat or per processor. In the Choose Licensing Mode dialog box, shown in Figure 3-8, enter the license variant that applies to you.

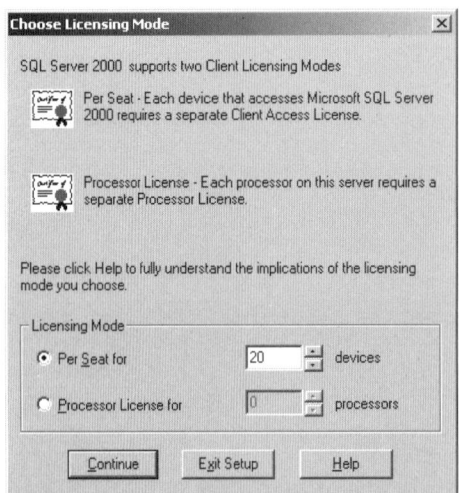

Figure 3-8   Selecting the type of license

You have now entered all the specifications required for installation, and SQL Server 2000 will now be installed. For more details, see "Running SQL Server/MSDE," later in this chapter.

Installing MSDE 2000

MSDE 2000 is part of Microsoft Office XP. If you install Office XP-MSDE-Version (\MSDE\Setup.exe), then you have no other configuration options. The Service Manager program call is included in the Start menu, under Programs, AutoStart. This calls the Service Manager automatically.

Installing SQL Server 7

You can start the SQL Server 7 installation process with the SETUP.EXE program in the file \Sql\x86\Setup or place the CD-ROM in your computer to start the installation program automatically.

After the initial screens of the setup program, you will see the Select Install Method dialog box displayed in Figure 3-9, where you select the required installation option. The Local Install option installs SQL Server on the computer from which the setup program was started. The Remote Install option allows you to install SQL Server on a remote computer.

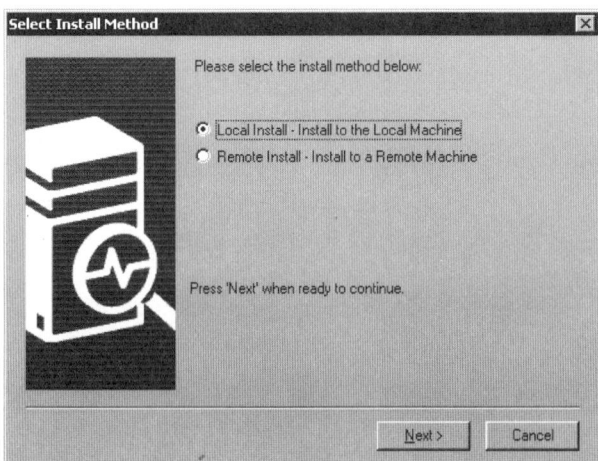

Figure 3-9   Selecting an installation option

In the next step, you determine the scope and destination of the installation using the Setup Type dialog box shown in Figure 3-10. The components included with SQL Server 7 are listed in Table 3-2. You use the Custom option to select them according to your requirements.

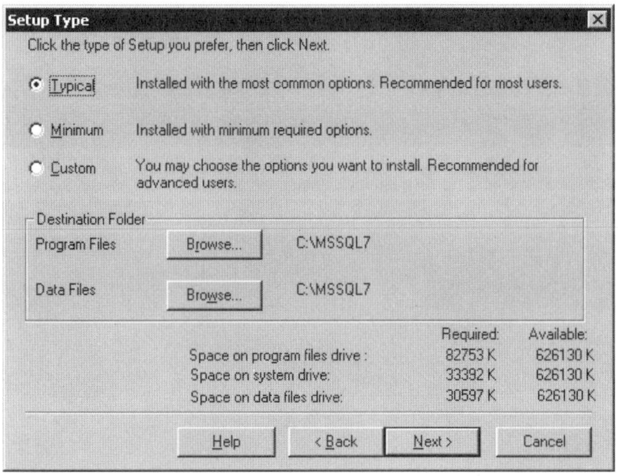

Figure 3-10   Scope and destination of the installation

By default, SQL Server 7 is installed in C:\MSSQL7.

Table 3-2   SQL Server 7 Components

Components	Description
Database server	Contains all basic components of SQL Server
Administrative tools	Contains administrative tools such as Enterprise Manager, Profiler, Query Analyzer, and so on
Client connectivity	Contains all the components needed by the client to set up a connection with SQL Server
Online documentation	Contains full documentation
Development tools	Contains support files for programming
Code examples	Contains example files for different programming options

In the Services Accounts dialog box shown in Figure 3-11, you specify the user account information to be used when starting SQL Server or SQL Server Agent (when running with Windows NT or Windows 2000). If you are working with several SQL servers in a single network, it makes sense to use a cross-domain user account so that data can be exchanged between the SQL servers. If your SQL server is the only one in the network, select the Local System account. Usually, the same account is used for all services.

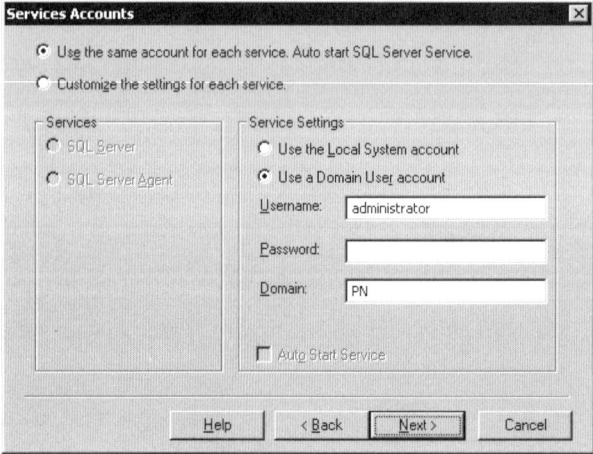

Figure 3-11   Selecting accounts

Installing MSDE 1

MSDE 1 is included with Microsoft Office 2000, but must be installed separately. To install it, start SETUPSQL.EXE in file \Sql\X86\Setup on the installation CD.

In the first screen of the MSDE installation program, you can select where you would like to install MSDE (see Figure 3-9) . If you select Remote Install, the installation program asks you to specify to which computer in the network you would like to install MSDE. You must also enter the user name and password for this computer to access it. For the purposes of this chapter, select Local Install.

By default, MSDE is installed to the \MSSQL7 folder, as shown in Figure 3-12. This is also the folder in which a complete SQL Server 7 installation would be saved.

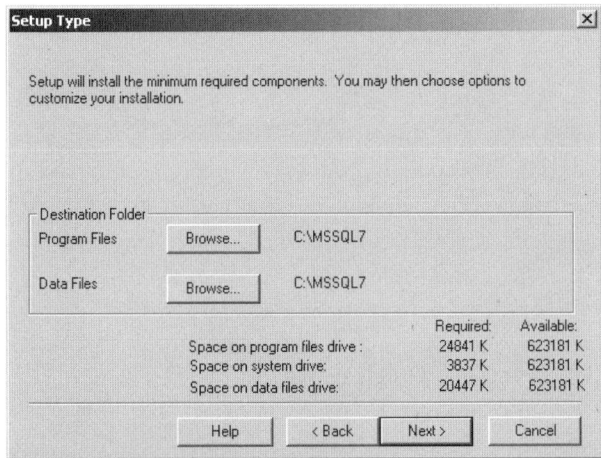

Figure 3-12   Selecting a folder

In the Character Set/Sort Order/Unicode Collation dialog box shown in Figure 3-13, you define the general settings for MSDE.

In the Network Libraries dialog box, shown in Figure 3-14, you define how clients access MSDE Server. In a pure Microsoft network, the settings are already sufficient. If you are using a Novell, Banyan, or Apple network, you must activate the relevant libraries.

> **Note**   Always reboot your computer after installation, even if the installation does not require it, to ensure that you will benefit from the full range of functions.
>
> See the next section, "Running SQL Server/MSDE," for further information.

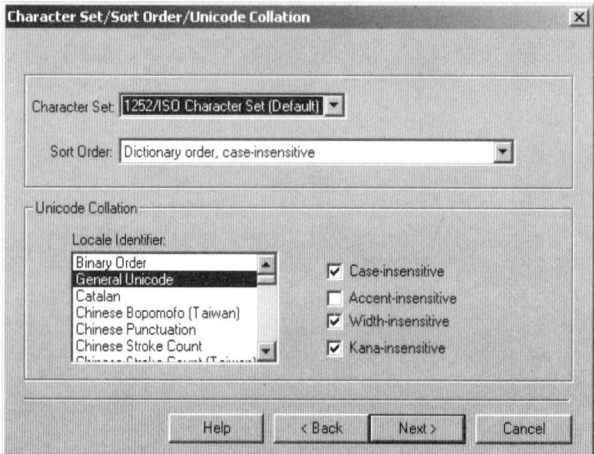

Figure 3-13 General settings for MSDE

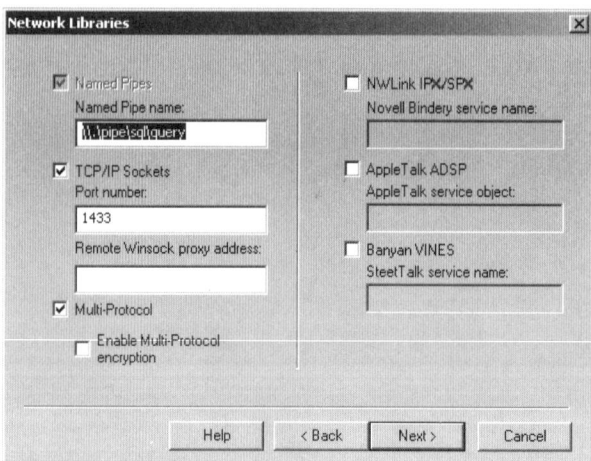

Figure 3-14 Network libraries

Running SQL Server/MSDE

The following sections describe programs and settings for operating SQL Server and MSDE.

The Service Manager

All SQL Server versions install the Service Manager tool, as seen in Figure 3-15, which is usually automatically placed in the Startup group. To start it, click Start, select Programs, select either Microsoft SQL Server or MSDE, and then select Service Manager.

Figure 3-15   SQL Server Service Manager

Every SQL Server/MSDE computer in the domain is referred to with a unique NetBIOS or Fully Qualified Domain name. The network name used is that of the computer on which SQL Server/MSDE is installed. SQL Server 2000 also provides the option to run several instances of the server in parallel on a single computer. Every instance receives a name preceded by the name of the computer (for example, SERVER/CONTOSO).

Select the Auto-Start Service When OS Starts check box to make SQL Server/MSDE available when the computer is started without having to call the Service Manager. The Service Manager is displayed when you select the icon in the taskbar. Double-click the icon to call the program. As well as SQL Server itself, you can also use Service Manager to start, pause, or exit the SQL Server-Agent, the DTC, and other related SQL Server services.

Network Settings

Communication between SQL Server and clients can be carried out with various network protocols. By default, the Transmission Control Protocol/Internet Protocol (TCP/IP) is used.

Server Network Settings

You can use the SQL Server network configuration program to configure the SQL Server/MSDE computer for data transfer to the client. If you installed SQL Server, then you can call the program using Start/Programs/Microsoft SQL Server/Server Network Utility. If you installed MSDE, you can find the corresponding program SRVNETCN.EXE in the folder \Mssql7\Binn or \Programs\Microsoft SQL Server\80\Binn.

SQL Server/MSDE can be configured for several protocols simultaneously. Figure 3-16 displays the network configuration program for SQL Server 2000/ MSDE 2000. Two protocols are configured here: TCP/IP and Named Pipes.

The protocols supported by SQL Server 2000 are on the left in the Disabled Protocols list box. The same protocols (up to VIA) can also be used with SQL Server 7. Remember that the operating system of the SQL Server/MSDE computer must be configured for the selected network protocol.

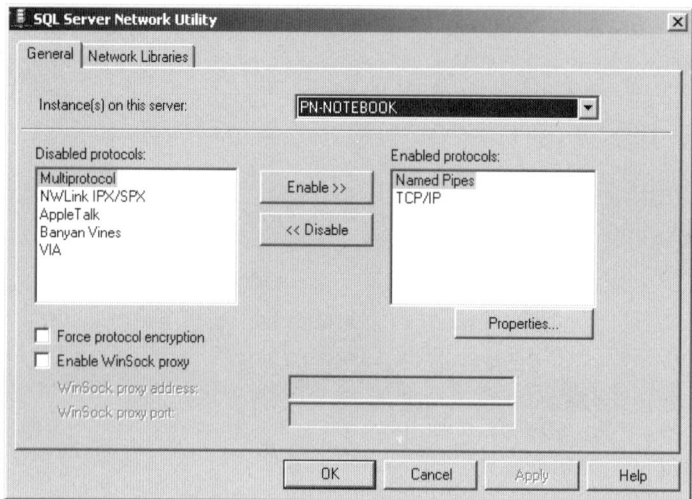

Figure 3-16   Server network configuration for SQL Server 2000/MSDE 2000

Client Network Settings

For a client to access SQL Server/MSDE, it must be configured so that it supports one of the protocols configured on the server. You can call the client configuration program using the Client Network Utility shortcut from the Microsoft SQL Server Group or using CLICONFG.EXE in C:\Winnt\System32 or C:\Windows\System.

Problems often arise when setting up a connection if SQL Server or MSDE is installed on a Microsoft Windows 95 or a Microsoft Windows 98 system. If clients attempt to access the network through the Named Pipes protocol, the system issues messages similar to "Specified SQL Server Not Found."

4

Databases

In this chapter, we describe how to create new Access projects. To use an Access project, you always need a database on a Microsoft SQL Server or MSDE computer. Thus, we first cover the basics of SQL Server and MSDE databases and then continue with a description of how to use Access projects to access these databases.

SQL Server/MSDE Databases

In Chapter 2, "Access Projects," we covered the basic differences between Access mdb and SQL Server/MSDE databases. We now more closely examine the SQL Server/MSDE structure and components.

The actual database server runs in the background as a process on the computer where SQL Server or MSDE is installed. Under Microsoft Windows NT or Microsoft Windows 2000, the SQL Server process is a service, and under Microsoft Windows 98 or Microsoft Windows Me it is a regular program that runs in the background.

The database server process manages the databases and answers calls that are sent to it, usually over the network.

Databases

The SQL Server/MSDE database names are used to access the databases. In contrast to Access mdb, you are not accessing the physical database file, but are using the database name managed by SQL Server/MSDE. SQL Server/MSDE abstracts the access to data through a database name that is stored in one or more of the physical database files; users or programmers do not need to know the names of the physical files.

In the process, a logical database name can refer to multiple database files, which may also be stored on different hard drives. The actual data files have names that end with .mdf extensions (or .ndf extensions, if data is stored across multiple files, as a secondary filegroup) and are stored by default in the \Program Files\Microsoft SQL Server\MSSQL\Data folder for SQL Server 2000 or MSDE 2000 or in \MSSQL7\Data for SQL Server 7 and MSDE 1.

There are also one or more log files with names ending in .ldf extensions that are associated with the data file(s). You can save these files in the same folder as the .mdf files. If you want to set up your SQL Server/MSDE to be particularly secure and scalable, the .ldf files should be stored on different hard drives than the .mdf files. Refer to Chapter 18, "Database Administration," for more information.

Predefined Databases

The predefined databases shown in Table 4-1 are available once you have installed a new SQL Server or MSDE.

Table 4-1   Predefined Databases

Database	Explanation
master	The *master* database contains system tables, with information needed to operate SQL Server, along with numerous system procedures.
model	The *model* database contains models used as templates for creating new databases.
msdb	The SQL Server agent uses the *msdb* database, which contains information about data backup procedures, replication, and so on.
Northwind	*Northwind* is a database that contains examples. This database is not required to operate SQL Server.
pubs	*pubs* is also a database that contains examples. This database is not required to operate SQL Server.
tempdb	*tempdb* is a database for temporary objects and data created during operation.

Note   Note that the *tempdb* database, where the system saves temporary data during operation, can grow quite large when the database is used intensively by several users at the same time. In one case, for example, a customer's system crashed regularly when creating complex online data. The reason was the hard drive's insufficient size: SQL Server was installed on the rather small C drive, with the database itself located on the D drive, where many gigabytes of disk space remained available. Because the system typically creates *tempdb* on the drive on which SQL Server is installed, this meant that the database was stored on the small C drive. This caused the system to abort complex operations because the insufficient space on the C drive caused a runtime error for *tempdb*.

Chapter 18, "Database Administration," and Chapter 19, "SQL Server Tools," describe how you can determine and edit the assignment of database names and files.

User Administration and Access Permissions

SQL Server and MSDE manage access and permissions for the individual databases. The system uses a two-step process: The first step controls access to SQL Server and MSDE, and the second step controls access to a specific database and the permissions within that database.

If the database server was installed on Windows NT or Windows 2000, SQL Server and MSDE can use the Windows NT or Windows 2000 access information for authentication in the first step. This means that a user who can successfully log on to Windows NT or Windows 2000 can also be authenticated against SQL Server, without necessarily having access to any of the databases.

Alternatively, when the database server is installed on Windows Me or Windows 98, you must use SQL Server's own security system. This means that you must enter a user name and password to access SQL Server and MSDE. SQL Server/MSDE stores its own account database with the user names and their passwords. Refer to Chapter 20, "Security," for a detailed description of the SQL Server/MSDE security system.

Creating a New Access Project

From the File menu, select New to create a new Access project. The new dialog box will open and offer you two options for creating a project: You can either create a new project with a connection to an already existing database, or you can create a new database for the new project.

Creating a New Access Project with a New Database

When you select Project (New Data) (or, in Microsoft Access 2000, select Project (New Database)), you must first name your new project before the system displays the database window. Next, the SQL Server Database Wizard opens, as shown in Figure 4-1, prompting you to specify on which SQL server to store the database. You are also prompted to enter the database name and the name of the user who wants to create the database. If SQL Server or MSDE is installed on the same computer as Access itself, you can also use (local) to specify the server name.

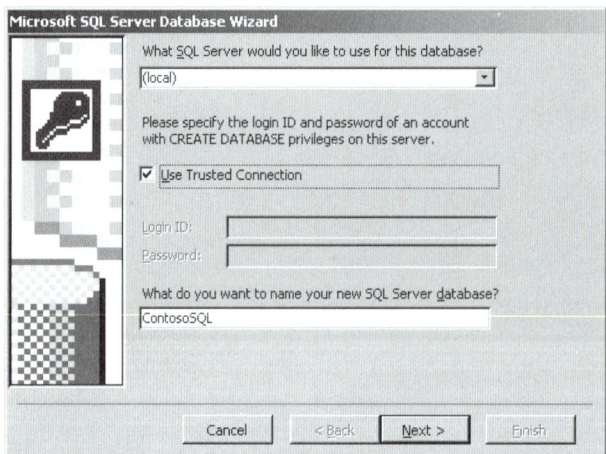

Figure 4-1   Creating a new SQL Server database

If SQL Server/MSDE is working with the Windows security functions, select Use Trusted Connection so you can omit the Login ID and Password entries, as the system uses your Windows user name to check your SQL Server/MSDE access permission.

To create a new database, you must have the relevant permission for SQL Server and your user name must be a member of the System Administrators or Database Creators *server roles*. See Chapter 20, "Security," for more information. System's accounts with rights of the local administrator account on Windows NT and Windows 2000 always has a System Administrator role.

During the installation process, all SQL Server/MSDE systems create the user name *sa* (system administrator), which belongs to the System Administrators server role. By default, if using Mixed Mode authentication, the system creates the *sa* user name without a password, but you should always specify a password for this user name.

Connecting a New Access Project to an Existing Database

You also have the option of connecting the new Access project to an existing database. Open the Data Link Properties dialog box shown in Figure 4-2.

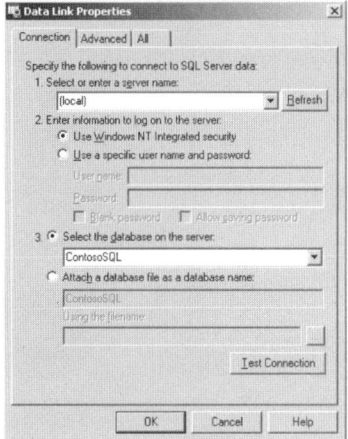

Figure 4-2   Connecting the new Access project to an existing database

First select the server on which the database you want to create a connection to is located. With Access 2000 or SQL Server 7/MSDE 1 you will have to type in the respective server name, as clicking Refresh does not display the expected list of servers. This problem is fixed in Microsoft Access 2002 and SQL Server 2000/MSDE.

Under the option group 2. Enter Information To Log On To The Server:, you can specify if you want to work with Windows NT or Windows 2000 integrated security (in which case the system uses your Windows logon information to log on to SQL Server as well) or if you want to use a specific user name and password to log on to the server when using SQL Server security.

If you select SQL Server security, the system enables the Blank Password and Allow Saving Password check boxes. The Blank Password check box does not affect SQL Server/MSDE access and the system does not save it. If you select the Allow Saving Password check box, the system saves the user name and password to the .adp file in unencrypted format.

> **Note**   If you select the Allow Saving Password check box, every user who opens the .adp file has access to the database because the system uses the stored access information when opening it.

Use the Combo check box to select the database name on the server to which you want to connect your Access project. Incidentally, the box displays all databases, even if you do not have access permissions to all of the listed databases.

Click Test Connection to determine if you can establish a connection to the specified database server. To open the Data Link Properties dialog box at any time, from the File menu, select Connection.

Attach Database File

The Attach A Database File As A Database Name option is rarely used, but it is useful, for example, if you are using a SQL Server computer as a test server for developing an application and you want to copy a database from the test server to the production server's SQL server. During the process, the database's .mdf file is transferred from the test server to the production server. On the production server, you must then create a logical database name and connect it to the existing .mdf file. You can use the Attach A Database File As A Database Name option to accomplish this task.

Enter the new logical name, as well as the .mdf filename and path, in the next field. If you confirm the dialog box entries with Connect, the system creates the database file on the server under the new logical database name and connects the Access project to the new database.

5

Tables in Access Projects

The previous chapter showed how to create a new database or use an existing one by creating an empty Access project. In this chapter you will learn how to create tables in the database.

Creating Tables

You create a new table by selecting the table object in the Database window and clicking New. The system prompts you to enter a name for the new table. We recommend that you follow the same guidelines that apply when naming Access mdb tables; for example, do not include spaces in the table name.

> **Note** Tables are created by Microsoft SQL Server/MSDE on a user-specific basis, that is, every user with the appropriate permissions can create tables in the current database. Different users can also use the same table names. In the Access Database window, tables for the current user are displayed with the table name only, and tables belonging to other users are displayed with the user name in parentheses.

Creating Tables with Microsoft Access 2002

The dialog box used to create tables in mdb databases is also used to create tables in Access 2002. The lower portion of the dialog box displays the available properties for the selected field, as shown in Figure 5-1.

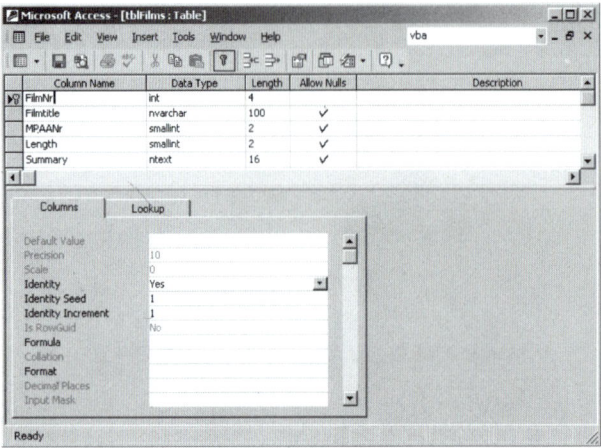

Figure 5-1   Creating tables with Access 2002

Access 2002 provides table fields with a range of properties that you will recognize from mdb databases such as *Mask* or *Input mask*. The properties available depend (among other things) on whether you are accessing Microsoft SQL Server 7/MSDE 1 or Microsoft SQL Server 2000/MSDE 2000. Figure 5-1 displays the properties available with SQL Server 2000.

Lookup Fields
Access 2002 and SQL Server 2000/MSDE 2000 also allow lookup fields as used in Access mdb databases. You can use a lookup field to look up values for a column in a linked table if a one-to-many relationship exists between the tables. The values found are then used to display tables, views, and so on.

Creating Tables with Microsoft Access 2000

The table design window in Access 2000 differs from the one that you know from Access, as displayed in Figure 5-2.

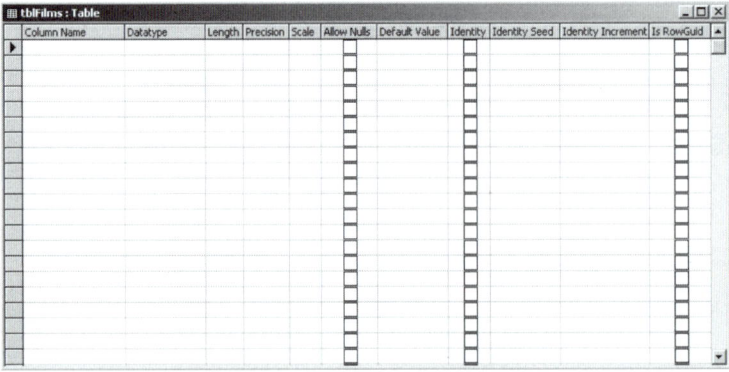

Figure 5-2   Table design view for new tables in Access 2000

The field names (displayed in SQL Server databases as columns) are entered on the left and their properties are entered on the right in Table 5-1.

Table 5-1   Properties of Columns in a SQL Server Database

Name	Description
Column Name	Name of column or field.
Data type	SQL data type.
Length	Disk space in bytes or number of characters.
Precision	Maximum number of digits (only for numerical expressions).
Scale	Maximum number of decimal places (only for numerical expressions).
Allow Nulls	If this field is activated, then a line can be stored with value *Null*.
Default Value	Default value for this column.
Identity	If this field is activated, unique values are created for this field automatically.
Identity Seed	Initial value for the automatically created identity value (default value is *1*).
Identity Increment	Increment for the automatically created identity value (default value is *1*).
Is RowGuid	Describes a column using the globally unique ID (GUID) data type, which uniquely identifies a record (for use with replication).

Data Types

Table 5-2 lists the data types that can be used and their validity ranges and memory size.

Table 5-2   SQL Server Data Types

Type of Data	Data Type	Validity Range	Memory Size
Integers	int	–2,147,483,648 to 2,147,483,647	4 bytes
	smallint	–31,768 to 31,767	2 bytes
	tinyint	0 to 255	1 byte

continued

Table 5-2 SQL Server Data Types *(continued)*

Type of Data	Data Type	Validity Range	Memory Size
	bit	0 or 1	Bit data types can be shared with other bit columns: 1 byte for up to 8 columns. If there are 8 or fewer bit columns in the same table, they are stored as 1 byte. If the table only has a single bit column, then this also takes up 1 byte.
Packed decimal numbers (exact numeric)	*decimal(p,s)* *p*: Precision *s*: Scale	$-10^{38} + 1$ to $10^{38} - 1$	2 to 17 bytes depending on the precision (*p*) specified (up to 38 places). $0 <= s <= p$
Floating-point numbers (approximate numeric)	*Float(n)* (precise to 15 places) *n*: Number of bits in mantissa	$-1.79*10^{308}$ to $1.79*10^{308}$	4 to 8 bytes
	real (precise to 7 places)	$-3.4*10^{38}$ to $3.40*10^{38}$	4 bytes
Character	*char(n)* (fixed length)	Correspondingly *n* to 8000 characters	1 byte per declared character
	varchar(n) (variable length)	Up to 8000 characters	1 byte per stored character. Declared but unused characters do not take up any disk space.
	text	Maximum $2^{31} - 1$ (2,147,483,647) bytes in binary data, variable length	
Unicode strings	*nchar(n)*	Up to 4000 characters	2 bytes per declared character
	nvarchar(n)	Up to 4000 characters	2 bytes per stored character. Declared but unused characters do not take up any disk space.

continued

Table 5-2   SQL Server Data Types   *(continued)*

Type of Data	Data Type	Validity Range	Memory Size
	ntext	Up to $2^{30} - 1$ characters (1,073,741,823)	
Currency values	*money*	−922,337,203,685,477.5808 to 922,337,203,685,477.5807	8 bytes
		Stored with precision of one ten-thousandth of a unit (4 decimal places)	
	smallmoney	−214,748.3648 to 214,748.3647	4 bytes
		Stored with precision of one ten thousandth of a unit (four decimal places). For display purposes, smallmoney values are rounded to two decimal places.	
Date and time	*datetime*	Date values from January 1, 1753 to December 31, 9999 Precision: 3.33 milliseconds	8 bytes
	smalldate-time	Date values from January 1, 1900 to June 6, 2079	4 bytes
		Precision: 1 minute	
Binary (fixed length)	*binary(n)*	Binary representation up to 255 bytes	*n* bytes
Binary (variable length)	*varbinary(n)*	Binary representation up to 255 bytes	Actual stored number of bytes

continued

Table 5-2 SQL Server Data Types *(continued)*

Type of Data	Data Type	Validity Range	Memory Size
OLE field	*image*	Maximum $2^{31} - 1$ (2,147,483,647) bytes in binary data, variable length	
Special types	*timestamp*	This value is used for internal processing. Only one timestamp can be defined per table (see "Timestamp Columns," later in this chapter).	8 bytes
Special types	*uniqueidentifier*	Globally unique identifier	16 bytes

Data Types in Sample Table *tblFilms*

The columns and data types that are used for the sample database (see Chapter 1, "Introduction to Microsoft SQL Server and Access") are listed in Table 5-3. Along with the movie number and movie title, each column also contains an entry for the movie age restriction, the length of the movie, and freely definable additional text.

Table 5-3 Columns and Their Definitions for the Sample Database

Column Name	Data Type	Length	Precision
FilmNr	Int	4	10
Filmtitle	*Nvarchar*	100	0
MPAANr	*Smallint*	2	5
Length	*Smallint*	2	5
Summary	*Ntext*	16	0

The value entered for *MPAANr* is a lookup for the table *tblMPAA* in which the Motion Picture Association of America (MPAA) ratings are listed. The length of a movie is measured in minutes.

bit Data Type vs. *Yes/No* Data Type

SQL Server/MSDE stores *bit* values of 0 and 1. In Access mdbs, however, *Yes/No* data fields are represented internally by 0 and –1. Also, bit fields created with Access cannot take the value *Null*, because the Allow Nulls option in the table design cannot be selected; this error was corrected as of Office 2000 Service Release 1.

Timestamp Columns

Including *timestamp* columns in your table allows you to accelerate the table update process. *Timestamp* fields are automatically generated binary numbers that are guaranteed to be unique within a database.

When the user wants to change a record, that record is copied to a buffer for processing by way of the client or the server. After the modification in the buffer is complete, this buffer is then copied back to the database. If several users in the network attempt to change the same record simultaneously, then SQL Server/MSDE must ensure that the users do not impede each other on saving. Consider the following posting procedure, for example: A stock-keeping table shows 20 units of a particular product available in the warehouse. Two users sell this product simultaneously. Both call the current record for the product to the client they are using. Both receive the information that 20 units are available for sale. The first user sells 15 units, which are then debited from the record. Shortly thereafter, the second user sells 10 units. This is not possible, however, because the warehouse now contains only 5 units. The system must now warn the user that this transaction cannot be carried out.

SQL Server/MSDE provides two procedures for checking whether another user has made changes to a record in the interim: Either all columns of a record are checked, or only the *timestamp* value, which contains the time recorded internally for the most recent update, is checked.

Including a *timestamp* field in your tables supports and improves the performance of SQL Server/MSDE. Furthermore, if you convert your tables from Access mdbs to Access projects with the aid of the Upsizing Wizard (see Chapter 16, "Upsizing Wizard"), it can be used to generate *timestamp* columns automatically for all tables.

User-Defined Data Types

SQL Server/MSDE allows the definition of user-defined data types (that is, you can create and name your own data type definitions). User-defined data types can be used to improve documentation if you use a user-defined data type name that is as self-explanatory as possible instead of a data type definition. An additional advantage is standardized definition of data columns, because all columns with the same user-defined data type will also have the same definition.

User-defined data types can only be created with SQL Server Enterprise Manager or directly using SQL, not with a standard Access project.

Allow Nulls   *Null = Value*

If you want to ensure that an entry is always made in a field, make sure that the Allow Nulls check box is cleared. We generally recommend that you do not permit *Null* values and define default values instead. *Null* values in a field can cause problems during queries. If, for example, you attempt to sum up values in a column that also contains *Null* values, then the total for all values will be calculated as the value *Null*.

In the sample database, *Null* is only allowed for the columns *Age Restriction*, *Length*, and *Summary*.

Default Values

You can use default values to specify values to be entered for columns when users do not enter a value. Make sure that you use the correct separator character (for example, an apostrophe ['] for text and date entries).

You also have the option to use SQL Server/MSDE functions when defining the standard values. For example, *GETDATE()* sets the current system date as the default value for a date column. You can find a complete list of all SQL Server/MSDE functions in Chapter 9, "Transact-SQL."

Identity

Tables can only contain one column in which the *Identity* property is activated. This kind of field can be incremented independently by SQL Server/MSDE while you specify the initial value and the increment. *Identity* columns are ideal for simple numeric fields, such as movie numbers, customer IDs, or similar purposes. This does not guarantee, however, that the values will be absolutely sequential. A value is treated as used as soon as a user edits a new record. If another user then creates a new record, the next highest number will be assigned automatically. If, for some reason, editing of the first record is terminated and the value is not saved, a gap will appear in the numbering that will not be filled.

If you want to fill in the gaps in the numbering later, either because they were not assigned or because records were deleted, you can deactivate the *Identity* property and enter the required numbers.

> **Note**   When you define the *Identity* for a column, it corresponds with the *AutoNumber* function in Access mdb tables, where SQL Server/ MSDE provides more flexible handling. The section titled "Reset the Identity Value" in Chapter 9, "Transact-SQL," describes a system function with which you can reset the identity seed value.

In the sample table, *Identity* is set for the movie number (see Figure 5-3). The default values were used for the *Identity Seed* and the *Identity Increment* columns.

Column Name	Datatype	Length	Precision	Scale	Allow Nulls	Default Value	Identity	Identity Seed	Identity Increment	Is RowGuid
FilmNr	int	4	10	0			✓	1	1	
Filmtitle	nvarchar	100	0	0	✓					
MPAANr	smallint	2	5	0	✓					
Length	smallint	2	5	0	✓					
Summary	ntext	16	0	0	✓					

Figure 5-3   Sample table *tblFilms*

CHECK Constraints

Right-click the table design and select Properties from the shortcut menu. In the resulting dialog box, shown in Figure 5-4, you can define certain restrictions, known as *CHECK constraints*, for the table. Click New to permit entries in the Constraint Expression text box, where you can enter the constraint.

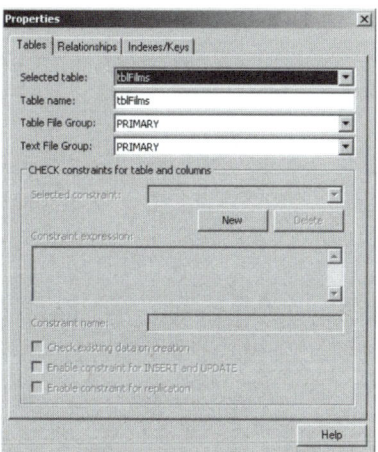

Figure 5-4   Defining constraints for tables

Generally, *CHECK constraints* can be expressed as follows:

```
{Constant | Columnname | Function } [[Operator | AND | OR | NOT}
{Constant | Columnname | Function } É]
```

You can use the operators described in Table 5-4.

Table 5-4   Operators That Can Be Used in *CHECK Constraints*

Operator	Description	Result Type
+	Addition of two numbers	Data type of higher-level argument
+	Positive value for a numerical expression	Data type is retained
+	String concatenation	Data type of higher-level argument
–	Subtraction of two numbers	Data type of higher-level argument
–	Negative value of a numerical argument	Data type is retained
*	Multiplication of two numbers	Data type of higher-level argument
/	Division of two numbers	Data type of higher-level argument; if an integer is divided by another integer, then an integer value is obtained (decimal places are truncated)
%	Remainder after division of two numbers (modulo)	Int
=, !=	Equal, not equal	Boolean
>, >=, !>	Greater than, greater than or equal to, not greater than	Boolean
<, <=, !<	Less than, less than or equal to, not less than	Boolean
<>	Not equal to	Boolean
BETWEEN	Between	
NOT	Not	

If several operators are used in an expression, they will be evaluated in the following sequence:

- + (positive), – (negative)

- * (multiplication), / (division), % (modulo)

- + (addition), + (concatenation of strings), – (subtraction)

- =, >, <, >=, <=, <>, !=, !>, !< (comparison operators)

- *BETWEEN*

- *NOT*

- *AND*

- *OR*

> **Note**   A constraint cannot contain references to other fields or subqueries.

Deleting Constraints

If you want to delete an existing *CHECK constraint*, reactivate the Properties dialog box for the corresponding table and click Delete in the Tables tab.

Checking Constraints

The Check Existing Data On Creation check box (activated by default) is used to check all future and existing values entered in the table. If you have already entered data that does not correspond to the defined constraints, the system issues an error message, displayed in Figure 5-5, when you close the dialog box using the cross on the title bar.

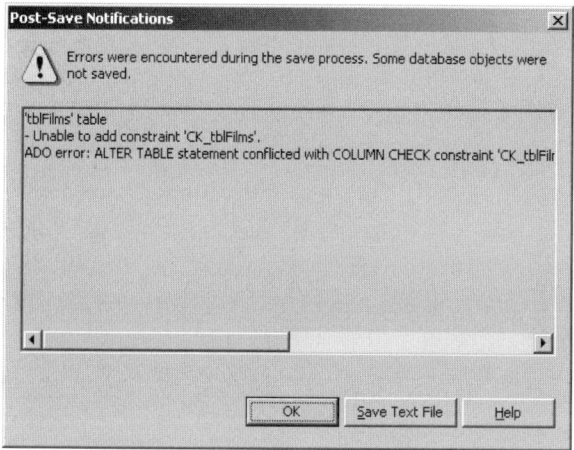

Figure 5-5   Error message

Clearing the Enable Constraint For INSERT And UPDATE check box allows you to enter data that does not meet the constraint requirements. This option can be used to enter data that is not to be checked by the constraint. For example, instead of only permitting up to 300 minutes for the movie length, you could allow longer running times to be entered.

Clearing the Enable Constraint For Replication check box removes the constraint for the purposes of replication. This ensures that data can be replicated from other data sources and copied into the table without impediment from the constraint.

Constraints for Sample Table *tblFilms*

In the sample table, the age restriction is kept at less than or equal to 18 years, and the length of the movie is set at a maximum of 300 minutes (greater values are likely to be the result of keying errors), as shown in Figure 5-6. Both fields also allow you to make no entry, as permitted by *Is Null*.

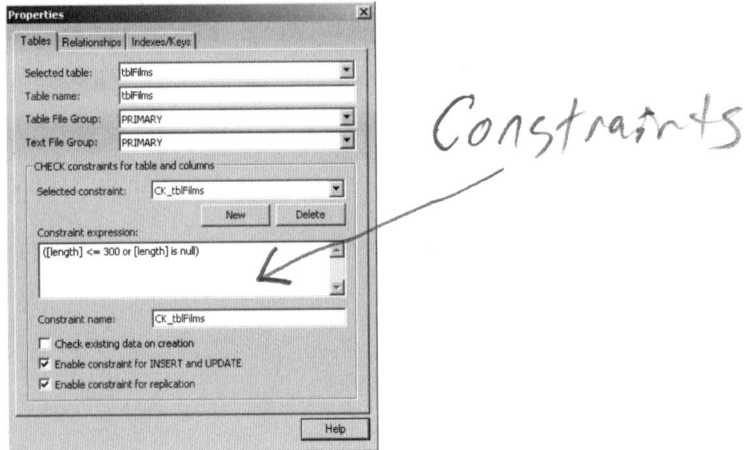

Figure 5-6 Inserted constraint

> **Note** Along with *CHECK constraints*, you can also use triggers for the purposes of validation. Triggers, described in Chapter 8, "Stored Procedures," are procedures that can be executed on insertion, change, or deletion of data in a table. You can also use triggers and their programming options to create complex constraints.

Defining Constraints with Access 2002

In Access 2002, the input fields for constraints have their own Check Constraints tab in the Properties dialog box, as shown in Figure 5-7. If the database is created in SQL Server 2000/MSDE 2000, then the Validation Text field is also activated for Access 2000 and SQL Server 7, where you can enter message text that is displayed to a user when a constraint violation occurs.

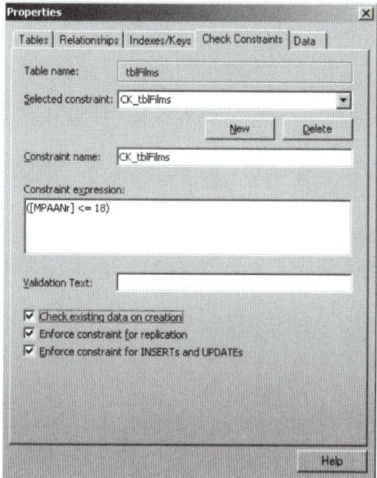

Figure 5-7   Definition of constraints with Access 2002

Indexes for Tables

Indexes can be defined for tables to significantly accelerate searching and sorting. The advantages of greater processing speed and improved data reading performance are offset, however, by increased administration time and greater use of disk space.

> **Note**   Chapter 19, "SQL Server Tools," describes index analysis by the Microsoft SQL Server Query Analyzer, as well as the Index Tuning Wizard for the SQL Server Profiler. You can use these tools to check your indexes and generate proposals for new indexes using the actual data used in the SQL Server/MSDE.

Creating an Index

Indexes are defined from the Indexes/Keys tab in the Properties dialog box for a table, shown in Figure 5-8. In the Selected Index text box, select an existing index to view and, if necessary, change the definition. Click New to create a new index, and define the name in the Index Name text box. Access proposes a name that you can then change.

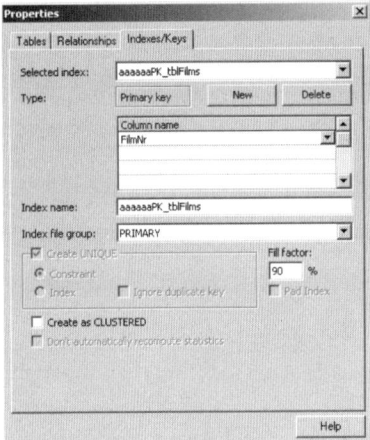

Figure 5-8   Indexes/Keys tab

> **Note**   Remember that the total size of all columns participating in an index cannot be greater than a total of 900 bytes. Columns with a defined length that exceeds this limit cannot be indexed. You can create up to 250 indexes per table, one of which can be grouped (see the "Comments on Clustered Indexes" section, later in this chapter).

Settings for Indexes

Table 5-5 displays the configuration options for indexes.

Table 5-5   Settings for Indexes

Property	Description
Index name	Freely definable.
Index file group	If you have created several file groups, you can select a configuration other than *PRIMARY*. File groups are not described in detail in this documentation. We recommend that you read more detailed materials on SQL Server.
Create UNIQUE	The column can only contain unique values.
Constraint	A constraint is used to ensure the unique status defined by *Create UNIQUE*.

continued

Table 5-5   Settings for Indexes   *(continued)*

Property	Description
Index	An index is used to ensure the unique status defined by *Create UNIQUE*.
Ignore duplicate key	Duplicated values entered for a column will not be indexed when using the *Index* setting.
Fill factor	Internal layout of the index. Changing this is not recommended.
Pad index	Available if you change the fill factor.
Create as *CLUSTERED*	A *clustered index* (a grouped index) can be created for each table. In a grouped index, the data and the index entry are stored in the same physical location, and the index determines the physical order of data in a table. This significantly increases access speed. Usually, the primary key is defined as a *clustered* index.
Don't automatically recompute statistics	The statistics for an index are usually updated automatically. This is required by SQL Server/MSDE Query Optimizer, so this setting should not be changed.
Validation Text	(Only with Access 2002 and SQL Server 2000/MSDE 2000) The validation text is displayed to the user when a key violation occurs.

Comments on Clustered Indexes

Clustered indexes are a special feature of SQL Server/MSDE, described as a procedure for improved performance. Microsoft recommends that you create a clustered index in every table, but only one clustered index can be created per table, for the reasons described in the following section.

Indexes in relational databases such as Access mdbs and SQL Server/MSDE are created as binary trees (B-trees). This can be illustrated by describing, for example, how an index for the *Filmtitle* field in the *tblFilms* table is handled.

A B-tree starts at the highest level with the root node. In this example, the first movie title in the table is "A Perfect Storm." The title is stored with the record number, 1 in this case. The second movie is created from the root node as follows: If the movie title comes before the root node, then a sheet is created to the left of the root node in the B-tree; if not, the sheet is created to the right. Therefore the second movie title, "The Next Best Thing," is placed on the right along with record number 2. Figure 5-9 displays the entire B-tree for the sample table.

Figure 5-9   B-tree for the index of part of the *tblFilms* table

If you search for a movie title in an unindexed table, the table must be searched from beginning to end. Searching with the aid of an index minimizes the number of comparisons that need to be made to find the title. If, for example, you search for *dinosaurs*, then the system must make seven comparisons without the index and only two with the index. Furthermore, SQL Server/MSDE uses lengthy processes, ensuring that a B-tree is well balanced (that is, evenly constructed).

In a normal index, the data and the index are stored separately. This means that after searching with the index, the database must be accessed again to fetch the corresponding record from the table.

In a grouped index, the number of the record is not stored in the corresponding node of the B-tree, as shown in Figure 5-10; rather the entire record is stored in the node. This means that it is not necessary to access the database to retrieve the record, saving considerable processing time for databases with extensive tables and many simultaneous users. This also explains why only one grouped index can exist per table.

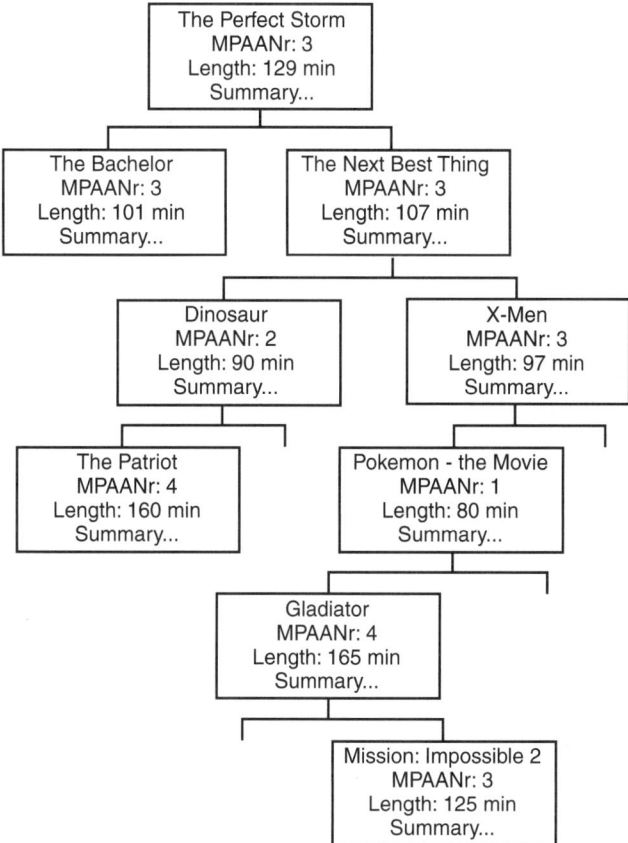

Figure 5-10   B-tree for grouped index

If a grouped index is re-created in a table, then all other indexes for the table must also be re-created because the grouped index copies the table data. This also applies when deleting a grouped index in a table with several ungrouped indexes. These ungrouped indexes must be re-created. The index is re-created automatically, which can take a very long time for large tables. Remember that when creating a grouped index, the data is copied and the database is enlarged accordingly, requiring sufficient disk space.

Combined Index

An index can be combined from several columns, as shown in Figure 5-11. Simply select the required columns in the Properties dialog box. Remember that the total length of index columns cannot exceed 900 bytes. You can combine up to 16 columns in an index.

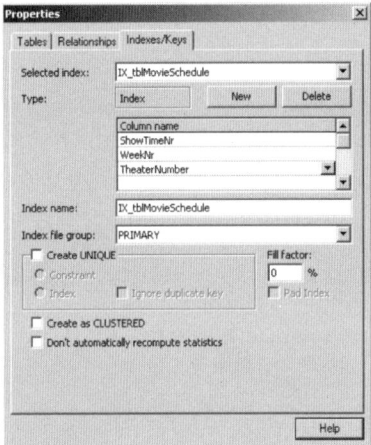

Figure 5-11   Combined index

Additional Properties with Access 2002

If you are accessing SQL Server 2000/MSDE 2000 with Access 2002, then you can access the Data tab of the Properties dialog box, as shown in Figure 5-12. This is where you can define settings for subdatasheets.

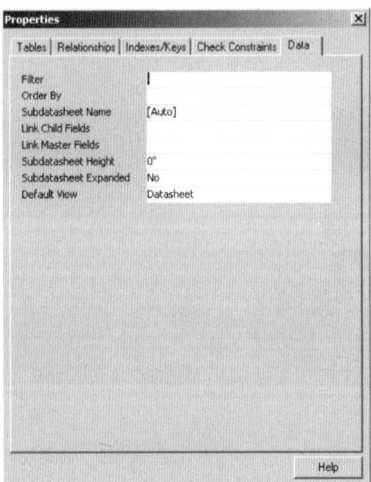

Figure 5-12   Data tab

Copying Tables

In Access projects, as in Access mdb database files, you can copy tables using the Windows Clipboard. Select the table to be copied, choose Edit, then Copy, and insert the copy choosing Edit, then Paste. The Paste Table As dialog box, shown in Figure 5-13, appears, in which you can enter a name for the new table.

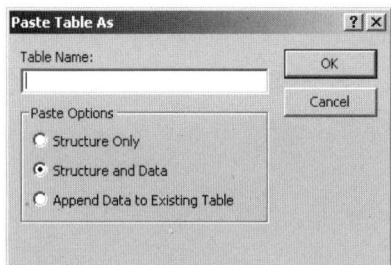

Figure 5-13   Pasting a copied table

Working with Tables

As in Access mdb database files, you can branch from the table design into the *Datasheet* view. This section describes some of the special features of the *Datasheet* view in Access projects.

If you call the *Datasheet* view for a table in an Access project, all lines in the table are transferred from SQL Server/MSDE to Access at the client. An Access project has a predefined restriction of 10,000 data lines (that is, only the first 10,000 lines of the table are transferred). This restriction was introduced to prevent extremely large tables with millions of records from overloading the server, client, and network when they are accessed.

The preconfigured restriction can be changed. Open the Options dialog box by selecting Tools, then Options. Click the Advanced tab and then change the Default Max Records option as required. Enter **0** if you want unrestricted data transfer.

In the *Datasheet* view, you can use the Maximum Record Limit button to display the dialog box shown in Figure 5-14. You can then use the slider provided to define the maximum number of records to be called by the server.

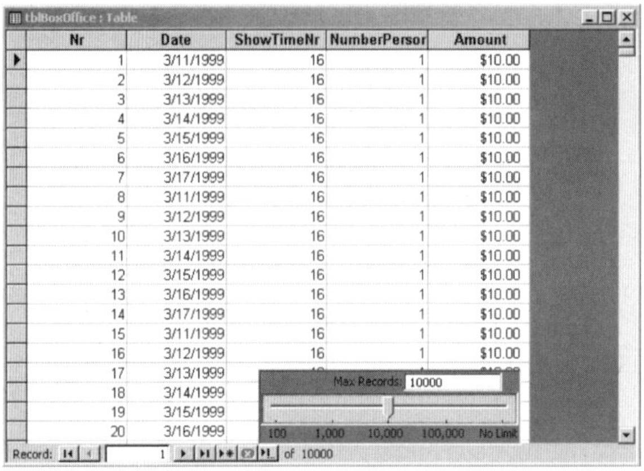

Nr	Date	ShowTimeNr	NumberPersor	Amount
1	3/11/1999	16	1	$10.00
2	3/12/1999	16	1	$10.00
3	3/13/1999	16	1	$10.00
4	3/14/1999	16	1	$10.00
5	3/15/1999	16	1	$10.00
6	3/16/1999	16	1	$10.00
7	3/17/1999	16	1	$10.00
8	3/11/1999	16	1	$10.00
9	3/12/1999	16	1	$10.00
10	3/13/1999	16	1	$10.00
11	3/14/1999	16	1	$10.00
12	3/15/1999	16	1	$10.00
13	3/16/1999	16	1	$10.00
14	3/17/1999	16	1	$10.00
15	3/11/1999	16	1	$10.00
16	3/12/1999	16	1	$10.00
17	3/13/1999			
18	3/14/1999			
19	3/15/1999			
20	3/16/1999			

Figure 5-14 Table in *Datasheet* view

If the Cancel Query button displays a red cross, then data from the server is currently being transferred to Access for display in the datasheet. Click that button to cancel the data transfer.

Subdatasheets

When used in combination with SQL Server 2000/MSDE 2000, Access 2002 can display subdatasheets, which you can use to include data from a table that has a one-to-many relationship with the displayed table. This functionality is already available in Access mdb databases.

System Tables

Every SQL Server/MSDE database contains a series of system tables that you can view in the Access Database window. Select Tools, then Options, then choose the relevant dialog box. Click the View tab and then select the System Objects option.

The names of system tables all begin with *sys*. Table *dtproperties* is an exception to this rule, as shown in Figure 5-15. This table contains information on the relationship diagrams (see Chapter 4, "Databases").

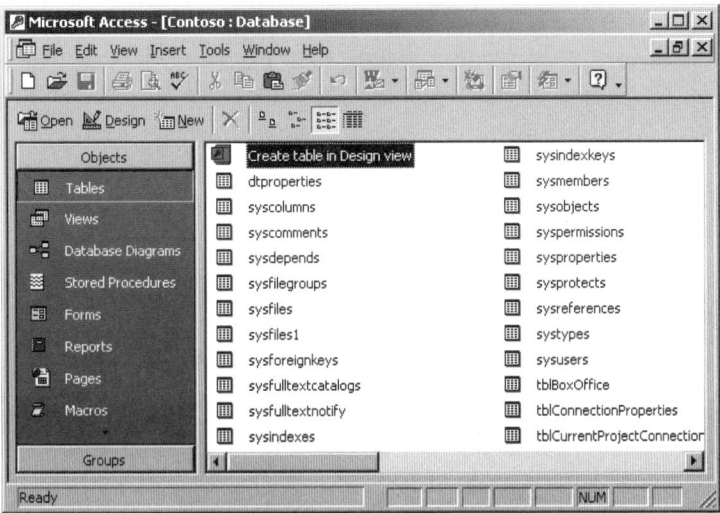

Figure 5-15   System tables

The information in the tables cannot be interpreted without precise knowledge of the internal structures. Even if, for example, you access SQL Server/MSDE as *sa* (system administrator), you should not make any direct changes to these tables (assuming that ad hoc changes to SQL Server/MSDE settings are allowed at all). You should always use system procedures (see Chapter 8, "Stored Procedures") to carry out modifications. Chapter 20, "Security," uses the tables *sysobjects* and *sysusers* in the program examples. *sysobjects* contains information on all database objects, and *sysusers* contains data on the users who are allowed to use the database.

6

Database Diagrams

You can use database diagrams to create and describe the relationships between tables.

Creating a Database Diagram

When you open a new diagram window, an empty window is displayed. As in the Access mdb Relationships window, you first need to drag the relevant tables into the window. Click Add Table to display the Add Table dialog box on the right, as shown in Figure 6-1. We have arranged four tables in the database diagram window as an example.

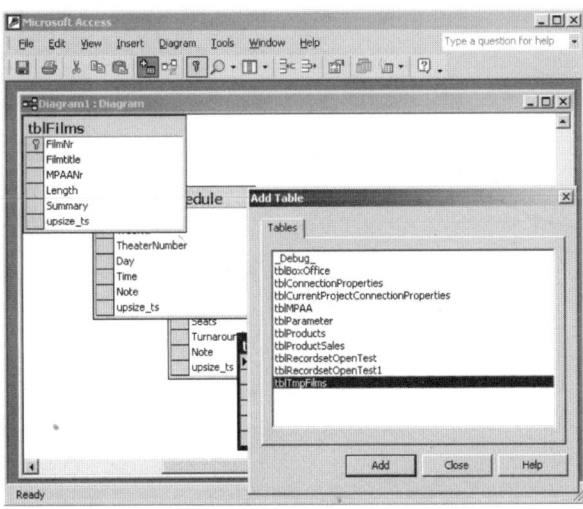

Figure 6-1 Database diagram in Access 2002

The design of the Add Table dialog box in Microsoft Access 2000 differs from that in Microsoft Access 2002. In Access 2000 you have to drag the table names from the Add Table dialog box to the diagram pane.

You can also create new tables directly in the database diagram window. Right-click the white background of the window and select New Table from the shortcut menu.

Saving the Database Diagram

When you save the database diagram, Access creates the appropriate SQL commands to modify tables and relationships. The database diagram is not saved if the new definitions cannot be applied to the existing data. With relationships, for example, you can specify whether existing data is subsequently to be verified or not and whether the new defined foreign key names are sufficient.

The definition of the actual database diagram is stored in Microsoft SQL Server/MSDE. A database can have several database diagrams.

Editing Tables

Tables can be edited directly in the diagram using the shortcut menu displayed in Figure 6-2. Select one of the following display options on the shortcut menu for a table:

■   Column Properties shows all the columns in the table design.

■   Column Names is the default shown.

■   Keys displays only the names of the indexed fields.

■   Name Only shows only the title bar of the table in question.

■   Custom View lets you assemble any design columns for display in the window.

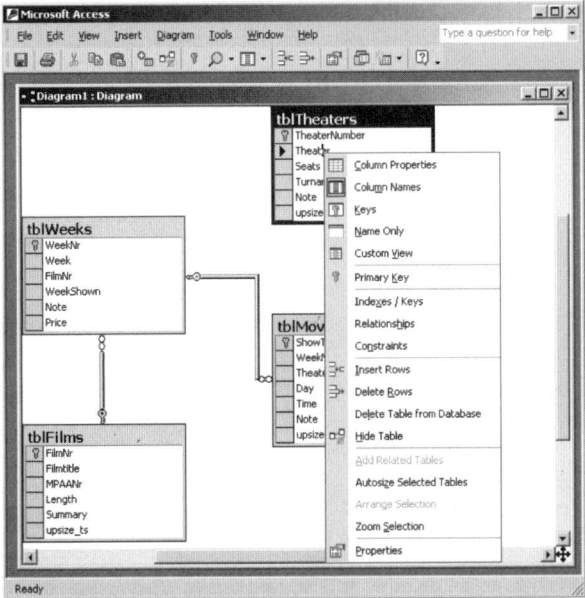

Figure 6-2   Selecting a display

All of the options described in Chapter 5, "Tables in Access Projects," are also available for editing tables.

Defining Relationships

The next step is to define the relationships between the tables; for example, by clicking the *FilmNr* field in the *tblWeeks* table and then dragging the cursor on the field with the same name in the *tblFilms* table. This displays the Create Relationship dialog box, which includes the details about the relationship definition, as shown in Figure 6-3. Existing relationships can be edited by selecting Properties from the relationship's shortcut menu.

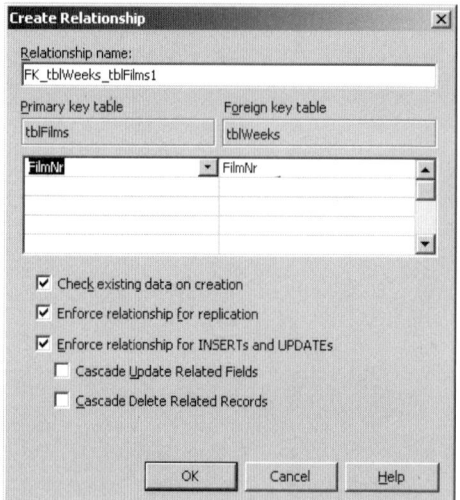

Figure 6-3 The Create Relationship dialog box

The relationship name is suggested by Access. It usually begins with the letters FK, which stand for *foreign key*.

If you select the Check Existing Data On Creation check box, SQL Server/ MSDE checks whether the foreign key relationship is valid, that is, if there is a corresponding primary key for each foreign key.

If you select the Enable Relationship For INSERTs and UPDATEs check box, the system will check if there is a primary key for the specified foreign key with every insert or update operation. When this check box is not selected, the relationship line between the two tables is displayed as a dashed line. In addition, this prevents rows in the primary key table from being deleted when matching rows exist in the foreign key table. In addition, please note that in contrast to Access mdb relationship lines, the relationship lines only run as far as the boundary of the table window without necessarily being on the level of the field to which the relationship line actually belongs, as shown in Figure 6-4.

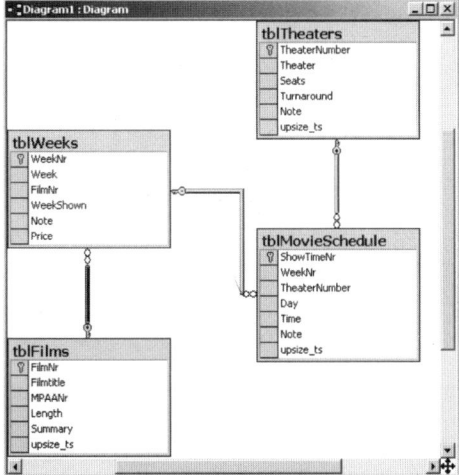

Figure 6-4 Relationship lines

Cascading Update and Delete

Microsoft SQL Server 2000 and MSDE 2000 support cascading update and delete without the use of triggers. When you create relationships in Access 2002, you can set this SQL Server 2000/MSDE 2000 function directly. Figure 6-3 shows the additional check boxes that are available in the Properties dialog box Relationships tab.

A cascading update updates all the foreign key values of a relationship when the value of a primary key changes; similarly, a cascading delete deletes all the lines with the corresponding foreign key value.

In Access mdb databases these functions are called *Cascade Update Related Fields* and *Cascade Delete Related Records*.

In Access 2000 and Microsoft SQL Server 7/MSDE 1, cascading updates and deletes are accomplished using triggers. More detailed information about triggers is provided in Chapter 8, "Stored Procedures," and Chapter 16, "Upsizing Wizard"

The Properties Dialog Box

Clicking Properties displays the Properties dialog box. In Access 2000 this dialog box includes three tabs, whereas up to seven tabs are provided in this dialog box in Access 2002. You can use the options in these tabs to determine settings for tables, indexes, relationships, and so on. The Properties dialog box was presented in Chapter 5, "Tables in Access Projects."

The Properties dialog box, shown in Figure 6-5 for Access 2002, displays information about the object currently selected in the database diagram. When the Properties dialog box is open, you can select an object, for example a table or relationship line, to view and modify its properties.

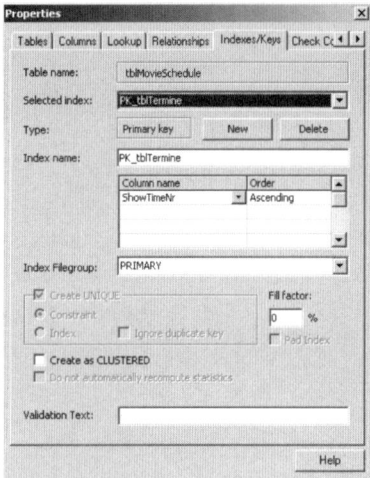

Figure 6-5 Access 2002 Properties dialog box

Diagram View

Database diagrams can be formatted and commented. The available commands are introduced in the following sections.

Diagram Formatting and Layout

If your database includes numerous tables, it can often help to use Zoom, from the View menu, to vary the display size.

With the from the Diagram menu, select Diagram Layout to tell Access to arrange your tables on the diagram so that as few relationship lines as possible overlap.

If you wish to print your relationship diagram, it is a good idea to view the page breaks on the screen prior to printing. From the Diagram menu, select View Page Breaks to view the breaks, or select Recalculate Page Breaks to have Access recalculate the page breaks so that the tables are rearranged, if necessary.

Labeling Diagrams

To better document your data models, you can type text directly in the database diagram. Right-click where you want to type your text and select New Label from the shortcut menu. Access displays a box in which you can type your text.

The labels can be arranged as needed in the relationship diagram. Labels can also be formatted as follows: Select a label, right-click within the box, and then select Font from the shortcut menu.

7

Views

A view defines a certain perspective for viewing data. A view's results are displayed in the form of a virtual table that you can use like a regular table. A view is based on a SQL *SELECT* command that collects data. You can also use *JOIN* to compile data from different tables.

You can use views to create simple representations of complex table structures by instructing the system to display only those columns you actually need or to transmit only those rows you actually need when you are dealing with large tables. You can also assign access permissions for views, so that, for example, users can access table-based data only by using views. Thus, for large Microsoft SQL Server installations in particular, users can always only access those columns they are directly authorized to use. All other columns that, for example, might contain additional information for certain programs are hidden from the users and programmers.

You can also use views to make complicated joins between tables easy to handle. This means that a query does not use the complete set of join instructions, but only the view that is based on them.

Views can be based on tables and on other views. You can create views with up to 32 nested levels. If a view is based on a table with integrity rules and constraints, those apply to the view as well, meaning that a view cannot override a table's rules.

There are a few minor differences between Microsoft Access 2000 and Microsoft Access 2002 with respect to creating views that this chapter points out.

> **Note** This chapter primarily describes how to use the query designer for Access projects. Refer to Chapter 9, "Transact-SQL," for detailed information about the many options associated with the *SELECT* command on which views are based.

Access Queries vs. Views

If you are familiar with Access mdb queries, you already know how to create and use views. However, there are a few restrictions that apply to views, as follows:

- Views cannot contain any parameters. You must use stored procedures to pass parameters (see Chapter 8, "Stored Procedures").

- In views, you cannot use any references to forms and report fields in the form of *Forms!Form!Control* (see Chapter 10, "Forms").

- Views can contain only *SELECT* statements. You cannot use *INSERT*, *UPDATE*, and *DELETE* in views.

- There are restrictions on the sort criteria that views can contain. This means that you cannot use *ORDER BY* when defining a view. This restriction, however, only applies to Access 2000 and SQL Server 7. With Access 2002, you can create and execute views with sort criteria.

Creating Views

To create a new view, proceed as you would using Access mdb: Click Queries in the Database window, and then click New. A New Query dialog box opens, in which you select which type of query you want to create. Select Design View.

In Access 2000 click the Views tab in the Database window, and then click New. The query designer opens, where you can assemble your view in a manner similar to using the Access query design view, as shown in Figure 7-1. Incidentally, Access projects do not provide wizards to support you during the view creation process.

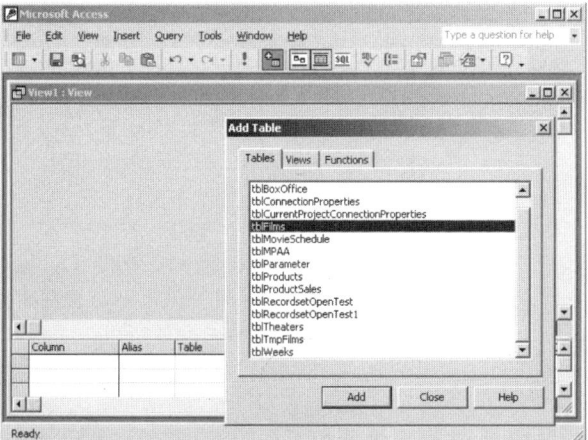

Figure 7-1   Creating a new view

If you want to edit or delete an existing view, open the view from the Database window in Design mode. Select Design View and then Delete from the shortcut menu or click DEL to delete a view selected in the Database window.

Note that Microsoft refers to the query designer as view designer elsewhere. Additionally, the Database pulldown menu refers to an editing mode of many database objects as a Design View, which is unrelated to database views.

> **Note**   To create views, you must be a member of the database roles *db_owner* or *db_ddladmin*. Members of the *sysadmin* server role or the *db_owner* database role can give other users permission to create views.

Query Designer Areas

With the query designer, you can display or hide three areas for displaying the view design, listed in Table 7-1. By default, the system displays the Diagram and Grid areas, which basically correspond to those of the Access mdb design view for queries. However, in the grid area, columns are defined one below the other, whereas the mdb design view positions them next to each other.

Table 7-1   Query Designer Commands

Text	Description
Diagram	Shows or hides the diagram display
Grid	Shows or hides the column grid
SQL	Shows or hides the SQL view

Displaying the query's SQL code (see Figure 7-2) lets you control SQL commands that were actually used for the view. You can directly edit the SQL command in the SQL area. However, for complex or UNION queries this can cause the query designer to no longer display changes to the SQL code in the grid area, even if the code is free of errors.

You should display the SQL area, because there you can see immediately which transformations the query designer is making, if any. For date values and the built-in SQL functions, in particular, the designer often inserts additional information in the SQL text.

> **Note**   With Transact-SQL you can add comments to the SQL commands. Please refer to Chapter 8, "Stored Procedures," and Chapter 9, "Transact-SQL," for a description of how to use comments. Theoretically, you can also add comments to your views, but only if you are not using the query designer. Unfortunately, the query designer removes the comments once you save the view.

Adding Tables or Views

To add tables or views in the diagram area, click Add Table or select Query, then Add Table from the shortcut menu. An Add Table dialog box opens in which you can select the tables or views to show.

> **Note**   In Access 2000 you can move tables or views in the query designer's diagram area only by using the mouse to drag them from the Show Table dialog box. The only option for using the keyboard to add tables or views to the diagram area is to enter the table or view names directly in the SQL area.

Microsoft SQL Server 2000 provides you with the ability to define user-defined functions. These are functions in SQL Server that are created using the Transact-SQL programming language that can return results. With Access 2002, you can create and edit user-defined functions, whereas Access 2000 only lets you execute such functions. However, you cannot interactively select them from the user interface.

Selecting Columns

You have the following options to select columns for your view:

- In the diagram area, select the check box of a column in the respective table or view window.

- Use the mouse to drag a column from a table or view window into the grid area.

- In the grid area, make an entry in the *Column* column, or make a selection in the combo box.

- Directly enter the *SELECT* command in the SQL area.

In Access 2000 you can use *IDENTITYCOL* in the diagram area's table window to select the table column for output for which an identity was selected. In the example shown in Figure 7-2, this is the *FilmNr* column, which is also the primary key. The column is then added to the SQL text as *Table.IDENTITYCOL*. Because there can be only one identity column per table, a reference to it is always unique. Unless you are familiar with the identity field from the table structure, there is no way to determine it in a view.

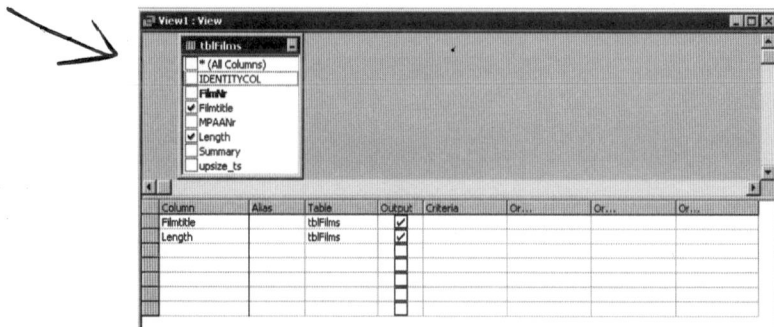

Figure 7-2   Query designer

Enter collective or calculated columns in the grid area's first column or directly in the SQL area's SQL text. The use of calculated columns is covered in the section "Calculated Columns," which appears later in this chapter.

Aliases

The following sections describe how you can assign aliases to columns, tables, or views.

Aliases for Columns

You can assign an alias to every column or, specifically, the column headline as it appears in the results display. Enter the alias in the *Alias* column in the grid area.

You can also assign aliases in the SQL area using the different types of syntax available. You can use an equal sign to place an alias for a column name in front of it, as shown here:

```
SELECT ProductNr, Net = SalesPrice / 1.07 FROM dbo.tblProducts
```

You can also enter the alias directly after the field name, as shown in these examples:

```
SELECT ProductNr, SalesPrice / 1.07 Net FROM dbo.tblProducts
```

or

```
SELECT ProductNr, SalesPrice / 1.07 AS Net FROM dbo.tblProducts
```

You can use *AS* to append the alias behind the field name. When saving SQL text, the query designer always sets the syntax option to the one using *AS*.

Aliases for Tables or Views

You can also use aliases for table or view names. For example, for the following code:

```
SELECT tblProducts.ProductNr, tblProducts.SalesPrice / 1.07 AS Net

FROM dbo.tblProducts
```

you can use:

```
SELECT a.ProductNr, a.SalesPrice / 1.07 AS Net

FROM dbo.tblProducts AS a
```

as an alternate.

Saving a View

You must save views before you can execute them. Prior to saving, the system checks the view's SQL code for syntax errors because you cannot save a view that contains syntax errors.

You can use the Check SQL Syntax button or select Query, then Check SQL Syntax to run a syntax check at any time to make sure that your SQL commands do not contain any syntax errors.

When you save the view, the system creates and precompiles the view in SQL Server/MSDE. Every user with the appropriate permission can create views. Several users can create views with the same names, as users must add their user names to every view name. The Access window displays the view names followed by the user names in parentheses, except for views that are your own.

> **Note**   By default, Access does not provide an option for testing SQL commands ad hoc. Instead, you must always create views or stored procedures to execute SQL commands. In Chapter 14, "Command Objects," we introduce the form *frmSQL*, which you can use to execute SQL commands directly.

> **Tip**   If you are using the Windows Clipboard to copy the SQL text for an Access mdb query into a view's SQL area for the purpose of copying a query from an mdb to an Access project and thus to SQL Server/ MSDE, it is possible that the view's syntax check returns no errors, but you can still not save the view. This problem might be caused by the semicolon used to denote the end of the SQL text for queries in Access mdb. This is not a syntax error, but you cannot save the view unless you remove the semicolon first.

Executing a View

You can select Query, then View or click Execute or View to route a view to SQL Server/MSDE for execution. The result is displayed in a datasheet, which you are probably familiar with from working with Access mdb.

If you did not save the view, the program notifies you prior to executing the view. The view can be executed only if you routed it to SQL Server/MSDE by saving it.

Datasheet View

The results of executing a view are displayed in datasheet format, shown in Figure 7-3, which you are already familiar with from working with Access mdb. The datasheet provides the same options for viewing or editing data, with one important limitation: If you are creating a complex view that combines data from several tables, you might not be able to edit the data.

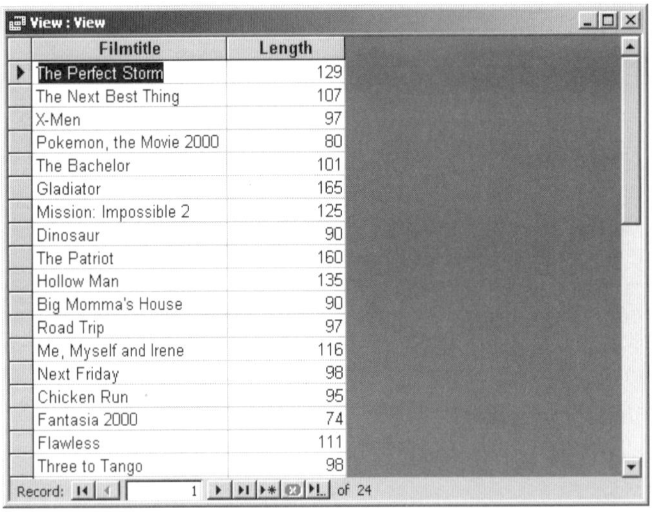

Filmtitle	Length
The Perfect Storm	129
The Next Best Thing	107
X-Men	97
Pokemon, the Movie 2000	80
The Bachelor	101
Gladiator	165
Mission: Impossible 2	125
Dinosaur	90
The Patriot	160
Hollow Man	135
Big Momma's House	90
Road Trip	97
Me, Myself and Irene	116
Next Friday	98
Chicken Run	95
Fantasia 2000	74
Flawless	111
Three to Tango	98

Record: 1 of 24

Figure 7-3   Datasheet view

> **Note**   If you are using a view consisting of multiple tables and define it as the origin for a form's data (see Chapter 10, "Forms"), you can specify the *Unique Table* form property to ensure that the system can process the fields of the unique table.

In contrast to the datasheet view for Access mdb databases, there is a limit on the number of data rows that can be imported in the SQL Server/MSDE datasheet view. By default, only 10,000 records are transmitted to Access from the server. To change this setting, select Tools, then Options to open the Options dialog box. Click the Advanced tab to change the Default Max Records entry accordingly. Keep in mind that increasing the number of records results in more data being transmitted to the client via the network, which means a workload increase for the server and the network. The limit on the maximum number of records makes sense, because larger SQL Server installations frequently include tables with several million records. If such a table were transmitted without restrictions, the transfer would be lengthy and consume a significant amount of the network's resources. Moreover, Access as the client would be overwhelmed by the volume of data because it is programmed to import all of the data to the client for display in datasheets and forms.

If you click Maximum Records Limit, the slider shown in Figure 7-4 opens above the button. Use this slider to specify how many records to download from the server.

Figure 7-4 Slider for downloading additional records (Access 2000)

If Cancel Query displays a red cross, then data from the server is currently being transferred to Access for display in the datasheet. Click Cancel Query to cancel the data transfer.

Criteria

In the grid area, you can use the *Criteria* or *Or* columns to define constraints on data selection. After you make entries in these columns, the view's SQL text displays the *WHERE* condition. Chapter 9, "Transact-SQL," provides a detailed description of all the options for *WHERE* conditions. In this section we briefly introduce their use in the query designer.

To specify criteria, you must take into account the data type of the field that you want to filter with criteria. Table 7-2 lists special features and displays in the query designer.

Table 7-2 Special Features for Entering Criteria

Data Type	Example of Displaying a Criterion in the Design View	Example of Displaying a Criterion in the SQL View	Description
bit	=1	=1	All values other than 0 return True, and 0 returns False. You cannot use the *True* or *False* syntax acceptable for Access mdb queries.
char	='text'	='text'	

continued

Table 7-2   Special Features for Entering Criteria   *(continued)*

Data Type	Example of Displaying a Criterion in the Design View	Example of Displaying a Criterion in the SQL View	Description
datetime	='01/01/2001 10:45:00 AM'	=CONVERT (DATETIME, '2001-01-01 10:45:00', 102)	The query designer transforms an entry such as, for example, 1/1/2001 10:45AM, for use with the SQL query, as illustrated on the left. Chapter 9, "Transact-SQL," contains detailed information about the *CONVERT* function. The constant 102 converts a date to the ANSI standard of *yyyy-mm-dd hh:mm:ss*, which applies regardless of the country setting selected for the server or client. Constant 100 is the default setting.
datetime	='01/01/2001'	=CONVERT (DATETIME, '2001-01-01 00:00:00', 102)	Works like *datetime* but affects only the date.
datetime	='10:45:00 AM'	=CONVERT (DATETIME, '1899-12-30 10:45:00 AM', 102)	Works like *datetime* but affects only the time of day.
decimal	=1,2345	=1.2345	The criterion can have up to 38 decimal places, including the decimal point.
float	=1,2345	=1.2345	The criterion can have up to 38 decimal places, including the decimal point.
image			You cannot use *image* columns as criteria.
int	=1	=1	

continued

Table 7-2   Special Features for Entering Criteria   *(continued)*

Data Type	Example of Displaying a Criterion in the Design View	Example of Displaying a Criterion in the SQL View	Description
money	=1,2345 = $123,45	=1.2345 = $123.45	Use $ to enter monetary values, which designates them as values of the type *money*. The $ is always placed in front of the number itself, regardless of the selected country setting. For the results display, the system formats the column according to the country setting.
nchar	= N'*text*'	= N'*text*'	Placing an *N* in front of the text constant itself initiates a Unicode text string.
ntext	LIKE N'*text*'	LIKE N'*text*'	Columns of the type *ntext* can be constrained only with *LIKE*. Placing an *N* in front of the text constant itself initiates a Unicode text string.
numeric	=1,2345	=1.2345	
nvarchar	= N'*text*'	= N'*text*'	Placing an *N* in front of the text constant itself initiates a Unicode text string.
real	1,2345	1.2345	
smalldatetime	='01/01/2001'	=CONVERT (DATETIME, '2001-01-01 00:00:00', 102)	Works like *datetime*.
smallint			Works like *int*.
smallmoney			Works like *money*.
text	LIKE '*text*'	LIKE '*text*'	Columns of the type *text* can be constrained only with *LIKE*.
timestamp			*timestamp* values are internal date stamps that are uniquely assigned to every record. You can work with them like *datetime* values.
tinyint			Works like *int*.
varchar	= '*text*'	= '*text*'	

When combining two operators of different data types, the operator with the higher rank takes precedence. The following list illustrates the sequence, starting with the highest ranked operator:

```
datetime > smalldatetime > float > real > decimal > money > smallmoney >
int > smallint > tinyint > bit > ntext > text > image > timestamp > nvar
char > nchar > varchar > char > varbinary > binary > uniqueidentifier
```

> **Note**   SQL Server and MSDE use different wildcards from Access mdbs. Instead of the asterisk (*) used by Access mdbs, SQL Server/MSDE uses a percent (%) symbol and an underscore (_) instead of a question mark (?). Refer to Chapter 9, "Transact-SQL," for more information about variables and the *LIKE* command.

Sometimes, the query designer simply drops criteria that you entered in the grid area. For example, if you enter a condition that does not make sense, such as 1=1 as the criterion for a column, the criterion disappears from the grid area. However, this does not mean that the condition disappeared entirely, because it is still integrated in the *WHERE* clause in the SQL area.

Entering or Editing Data with Views

If you enter or edit data in a view constrained by a *WHERE* clause, it is possible that your entries cause the record to no longer conform to the view's conditions. If you enter a record that does not meet the view's conditions, an error message appears, as shown in Figure 7-5.

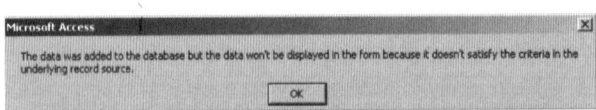

Figure 7-5   Error message caused by the *WHERE* clause

The system saves the record correctly, but you can no longer see the record in the view's datasheet view (or in a form based on the view). This behavior differs from that of queries for Access mdb, where the new record is displayed in the datasheet view or form, even if the record does not meet the query's condition.

Joins

In the query designer, you can create joins between tables, which is similar to creating joins in the Design mode for Access mdb queries. First, use the Add Table or Show Table dialog box to move all tables or views into the diagram area. Alternatively, you can use the mouse to drag the tables directly from the Access database window into the query designer.

Automatic Joins

The query designer automatically creates joins between two tables if relationships have been defined between the tables you moved into the diagram area. The relationships are represented by join lines, as you can see in Figure 7-6, which illustrates the foreign key relationship between *tblProductSales* and *tblProducts*.

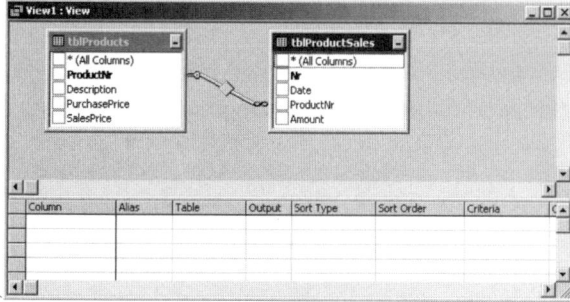

Figure 7-6   View with two tables

Whenever it is possible to infer the relationship between two tables from the foreign key relationships, the system uses key symbols on each side of the join line to represent a one-to-one relationship and key and infinity symbols on each side of the join line to represent a one-to-many relationship, as shown in Figure 7-6.

The system also creates an automatic join if columns from two tables have the same name and one of the columns is defined as the primary key. For example, if no foreign key relationship existed between the tables shown in Figure 7-6, the query designer would have drawn a join line anyway, because the *ProductNr* field occurs in both tables and it is the primary key in one of the tables.

New Join Line

If you want to join columns with no automatically defined relationship, follow these steps: Select the column you want to join in the first table window, and then hold down the mouse button and drag that column onto the column in the second table window.

The linked columns must have matching data types, or SQL Server/MSDE must be able to convert them. Otherwise, you will see an error message, such as the one shown in Figure 7-7, during execution. You cannot use *text*, *ntext*, or *image* columns to create joins.

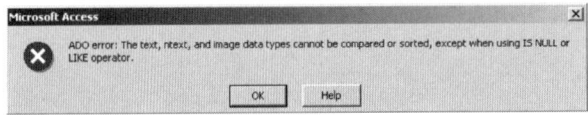

Figure 7-7   Conversion error message

> **Note**   The view's execution speed improves if the two linked columns are individually indexed or belong to a larger index. Lookup tables that are small in size, however, might not benefit from additional indexing.

Deleting a Join Line

Click on the join line to select it, and then delete it. You can press Delete, or select Remove from the shortcut menu (see Figure 7-8).

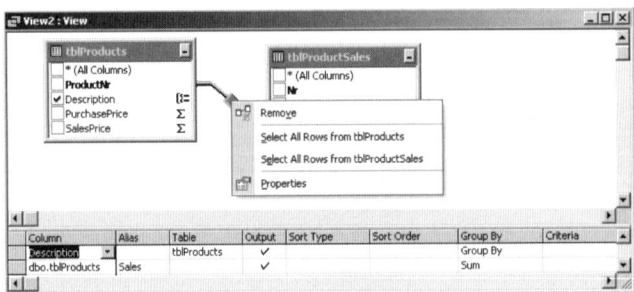

Figure 7-8   Design View Shortcut menu

Join Types

SQL Server and MSDE recognize the join types listed in Table 7-3.

Table 7-3   Join Types

Join Type	Description
INNER JOIN	With an *INNER JOIN*, the system returns those rows in the resultset with columns that have the same value on both sides of the join.
LEFT [OUTER] JOIN	With a *LEFT OUTER JOIN*, the resultset contains all of the left table's rows, even if there is no concordance in the table on the right. The *SELECT* command sequence determines which table is designated as the left table and which is the right table.
RIGHT [OUTER] JOIN	With a *RIGHT OUTER JOIN*, the system joins the data just like it does for a *LEFT JOIN*, except that left and right are transposed.
FULL [OUTER] JOIN	With a *FULL OUTER JOIN*, the system uses all rows from both tables, even if there is no concordance. You cannot select this variant with Access mdb queries.
CROSS JOIN	The resultset contains all of the data from the table on the left as well as the one on the right.

By default, the system creates an automatic or a manual join as an *INNER JOIN*. To change the join type, activate the join line shortcut menu (right-click the join line). The second menu option, Select All Rows From Table, creates a *LEFT OUTER JOIN*, and the third menu option generates a *RIGHT OUTER JOIN*. Selecting both options creates a *FULL OUTER JOIN*.

To open the Properties dialog box for a selected join line, as shown in Figure 7-9, you can either select the fourth shortcut menu item, select View, then Properties, or click Properties.

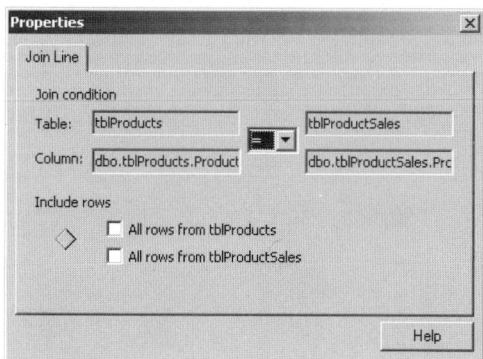

Figure 7-9   Join line Properties dialog box

Here you can use the Include Rows group to select the join type as previously described. In addition, you can use the combo box at the top of the dialog box to select the join operator. By default, the system uses the equal sign, meaning that rows are considered matches if the corresponding column values are identical. You can use join operators to select additional comparison conditions.

Reflexive Joins

A reflexive join joins a table with itself. With this function, the query designer works almost exactly like the query design view for Access mdb: If you enter a table in a view multiple times, the query designer automatically appends a sequential number, such as, for example, *tblMovieSchedule*, *tblMovieSchedule_1*, *tblMovieSchedule_2*, and so on. The query design view for Access 2000 only appends 1, 2, and so on, to the table names.

Groups

You might want to analyze your data in groups to determine, for example, attendance numbers by film title. Select Query, then Group, or click Group to activate this function. You might be familiar with this procedure from using Access mdb queries, shown in Figure 7-10.

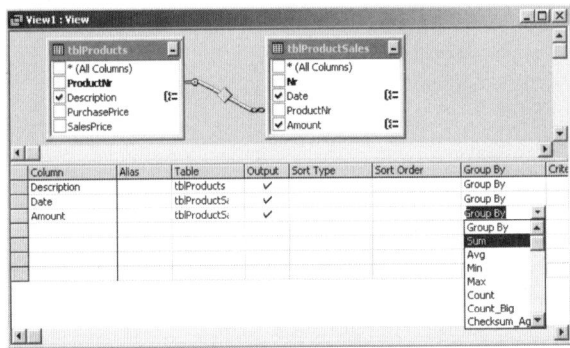

Figure 7-10   View with groups

Use the combo box in the *Group By* column to select the settings shown in Table 7-4 for views.

Table 7-4 Aggregate Functions for Grouped Columns

Group Type	SQL Function	Description	Access Mdb Equivalent
Group By		Defines a grouping criterion.	
Sum	*SUM*	Calculates the sum of all values in a column.	
Avg	*AVG*	Calculates the average for all values in a column while ignoring *Null* values.	
Min	*MIN*	Determines a column's smallest value.	
Max	*MAX*	Determines a column's largest value.	
Count	*COUNT*	Counts the resultset's rows.	
Count_Big	*COUNT_BIG*	Counts the resultset's rows and returns *bigint* data type value.	
Checksum_Agg	*CHECKSUM_AGG*	Returns the checksum of the values in a group. *Null* values are ignored.	
Expression		This function is used for deriving one column from another.	
Where		This setting defines constraints that are analyzed prior to grouping the data. The system implements the constraint as a *WHERE* clause.	*Condition*
Sum Distinct	*SUM(DISTINCT)*	This function corresponds to the *Sum* function, but the system only takes into account distinct values. Thus, a value that occurs multiple times in a column enters into the sum only once.	Not supported

continued

Table 7-4   Aggregate Functions for Grouped Columns   *(continued)*

Group Type	SQL Function	Description	Access Mdb Equivalent
Avg Distinct	*AVG(DISTINCT)*	This function corresponds to the *Average* function, but the system only takes into account distinct values. Thus, a value that occurs multiple times in a column enters into the average only once.	Not supported
Min Distinct	*MIN(DISTINCT)*	Corresponds to the *Minimum* function.	Not supported
Max Distinct	*MAX(DISTINCT)*	Corresponds to the *Maximum* function.	Not supported
Count Distinct	*COUNT (DISTINCT)*	This function corresponds to the *Count* function, but the system only takes into account distinct values. Thus, a value that occurs multiple times in a column enters into the count only once.	Not supported
Count_Big Distinct	*COUNT_BIG (DISTINCT)*	Works like *COUNT(DISTINCT)*, but returns *bigint* data type value.	
Checksum_Agg Distinct	*CHECKSUM_AGG (DISTINCT)*	Returns the checksum of unique values in a group. *Null* values are ignored.	
StDev	*STDEV*	Returns the standard deviation.	
StDevP	*STDEVP*	Returns the standard deviation for a sample.	
Var	*VAR*	Returns the variance.	
VarP	*VARP*	Returns the variance for a sample.	

Note   With Access mdb queries, the system automatically sorts by those columns that were defined as grouping criteria. SQL Server/ MSDE does not do this type of sorting in views. SQL Server behavior corresponds to the ANSI SQL standard.

Conditions for Groups

You can use two variants to define conditions for grouped views: one to constrain grouped data and the other to select data prior to grouping.

Figure 7-11 shows the view used earlier with the constraint to display only products for which the amount sold is at least 1000. SQL implements the constraint as a *HAVING* clause. Refer to Chapter 9, "Transact-SQL," for more information.

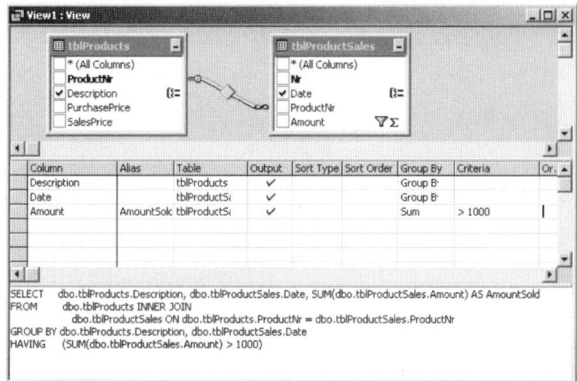

Figure 7-11   Grouped view with constraint

If you want to select data before grouping it, select *WHERE* from the *Group By* group and then enter a corresponding condition in the *criteria* column. For our example, we selected a time period, as shown in Figure 7-12.

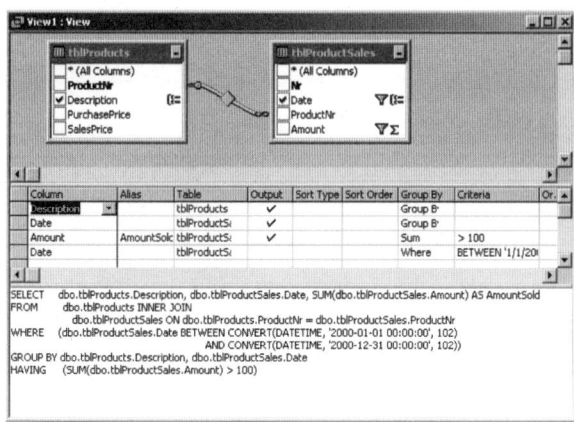

Figure 7-12   Constraint prior to grouping

Calculated Columns

You can enter calculated columns in a view just as you do with Access mdb queries, such as, for example **=[Price] * 1.16**.

With both views and stored procedures, you cannot use references to form fields (such as *Forms!Form!Control*). See Chapter 10, "Forms," for more information.

Chapter 9, "Transact-SQL," contains a detailed description of options for calculating columns, as well as a list of the operators and available functions. Note that with views or stored procedures you cannot use Access VBA functions as you can in Access mdb. In Access mdb, Access did not noticeably distinguish between the use of a SQL function or a VBA function for a query.

Differences in the Use of Calculated Columns in Access Mdb

When creating views and stored procedures, note one difference between the use of calculated columns with Access mdb and SQL Server/MSDE. Figure 7-13 displays an Access mdb query that calculates a sum for sales and purchase of the sold products. Another column calculates the difference between sales and purchase price with *Diff: [Sales] - [Purchase Price]*. The calculation of the difference refers to the column names defined for the column sums *Sales* and *Purchase Price*.

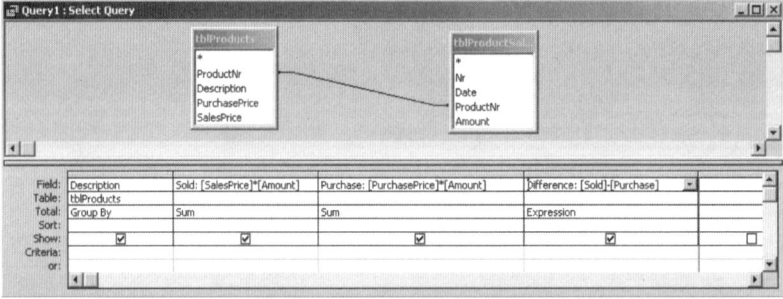

Figure 7-13 Query in Access mdb

We have entered the query as a new view, as shown in Figure 7-14. For this purpose, we used the Windows Clipboard to simply copy the Access mdb query's SQL text from the SQL view into the view's SQL area, omitting the final semicolon.

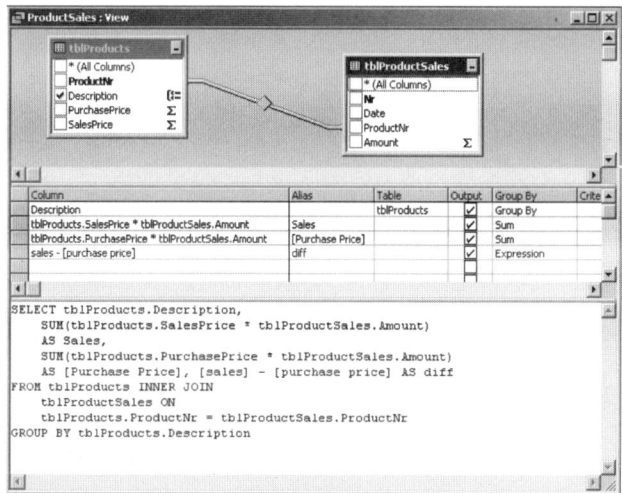

Figure 7-14   Access project view

The system analyzes the view as being syntactically correct and then saves it. During execution, the system returns an error message, shown in Figure 7-15, indicating that the column names *Sales* and *Purchase Price* are invalid.

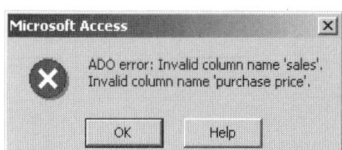

Figure 7-15   Error message during syntax check

In contrast to the SQL variant used by Access mdb, SQL Server/MSDE works correctly according to the ANSI standard. That is why the query must be converted as follows:

```
SELECT

tblProducts.Decription,

SUM(tblProducts.SalesPrice * tblProductSales.Amount) AS Sales,

SUM(tblProducts.PurchasePrice * tblProductSales.Amount) AS
PurchasePrice,

SUM(tblProducts.SalesPrice * tblProductSales.Amount)

- SUM(tblProducts.PurchasePrice * tblProductSales.Amount) AS Diff

FROM

dbo.tblProducts INNER JOIN dbo.tblProductSales ON

dbo.tblProducts.ProductNr = dbo.tblProductSales.ProductNr
```

```
GROUP BY

dbo.tblProducts.Description
```

Properties of a View

Select View, then Properties, or click Properties to open the Properties dialog box shown in Figure 7-16. The *TOP* field appears only if you did not specify a group for the view. In that case, the system shares the group *GROUP BY* extension.

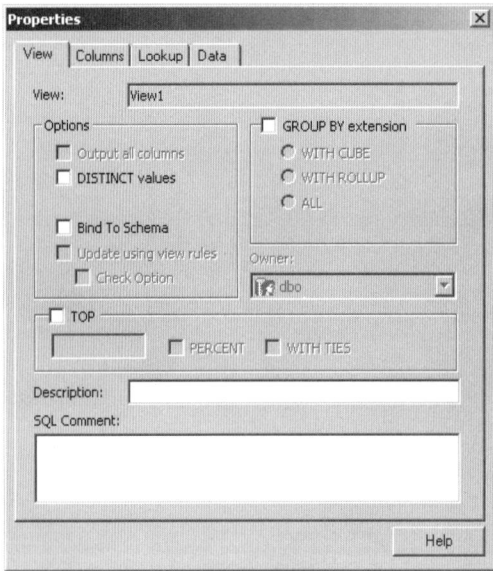

Figure 7-16   The View tab of the Properties dialog box of a view

Table 7-5 lists the different options you can select in the View tab of the Properties dialog box.

Table 7-5   View Options

Option	Description
TOP	Here you can enter a number n or a percentage $n\%$. The system then outputs the first n values or the first $n\%$ of values.
Output All Columns	Creates the view with *SELECT * FROM* to output all columns.
DISTINCT Values	The system returns unique rows only.
GROUP BY Extension	These are described in Chapter 9, "Transact-SQL."

The Columns, Lookup, and Data tabs provide you with further options.

Union Queries

You can use the *UNION* command to unite multiple *SELECT* resultsets into a single resultset. Chapter 9, "Transact-SQL," contains a detailed description of the *UNION* command.

If you use *UNION* in a view's SQL area, Access cannot display it in the grid and diagram areas. The same is true for Access mdb queries. When you save a view, Access displays an error message indicating that *UNION* is not supported. However, you can still save the view and execute it without problems. The error message indicates only that Access does not support displaying *UNION* in the query designer.

Subqueries

Subqueries are queries within a query. The view shown in Figure 7-17 illustrates using subqueries. Chapter 9, "Transact-SQL," contains a detailed description of the options available for using subqueries. If you have previously used subqueries with Access mdb queries, you can now use the same methods with views and stored procedures.

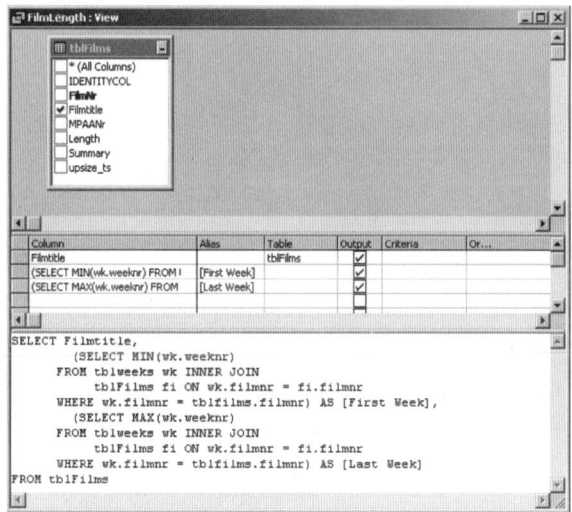

Figure 7-17   View with subqueries

Creating Views with SQL

The following code is the SQL command for creating a view. The query designer also uses this command internally.

```
CREATE VIEW view_name [ ( column [ ,...n ] ) ]

[ WITH ENCRYPTION ]

AS

select_statement

[ WITH CHECK OPTION ]
```

In an Access project, you cannot send the *CREATE VIEW* command to SQL Server/MSDE directly unless you program the system with an ADO command object (see Chapter 14, "Command Objects") or use a trick involving the SQL command *EXEC* in a stored procedure.

If you use the additional *WITH CHECK OPTION* option in a view with a *WHERE* clause and you want to insert or edit data, you can only insert or edit data that meets the *WHERE* clause conditions. For example, if you specified *number > 100* as the view's condition, the system rejects all data with numerical values equal to or less than 100. Unfortunately, you cannot use *WITH CHECK OPTION* directly from Access.

Also, the SQL command *DROP VIEW view_name* can be used only from ADO programs. This command deletes the view.

8

Stored Procedures

Stored procedures let you harness the full power of Microsoft SQL Server/ MSDE. Stored procedures consist of SQL commands that can be supplemented with program commands like branches, loops, and so on. The program control elements are no longer an integrated part of the standardized SQL language, but instead they are Microsoft-specific extensions. Microsoft calls this programming language Transact-SQL. This chapter and the next one cover stored procedures and Transact-SQL. In this chapter we focus primarily on the use of stored procedures and the most important program commands. Chapter 9, "Transact-SQL," introduces the many programming possibilities offered by Transact-SQL.

Stored procedures offer the following advantages:

- Network traffic is minimized by processing SQL commands and program logic directly on the server.

- The commands controlling the programming logic also enable you to program complex processes.

- Stored procedures are precompiled and saved on the server, whereas SQL queries sent by a client have to be interpreted and compiled.

- All the stored procedures are saved centrally on the server so that any changes made to a stored procedure are immediately available to all users. In addition, it is easier to maintain the programs on the clients this way.

- Stored procedures offer input and output parameters, can return multiple recordsets, and offer error handling.

- Permission to execute a procedure can be granted or revoked on a per-user basis. Typically, only the owner of a stored procedure has the right to execute it (see Chapter 20, "Security").

Creating Stored Procedures

A stored procedure can be created using the relevant designer from Access projects. In the Access 2000 Database window, select Stored Procedures and click New to open the Stored Procedure editor window shown in Figure 8-1.

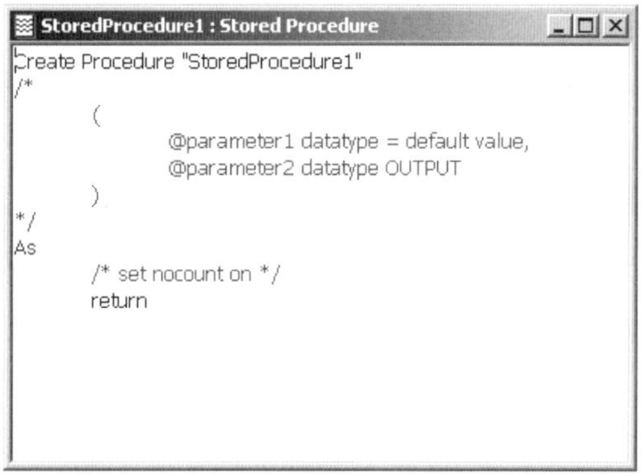

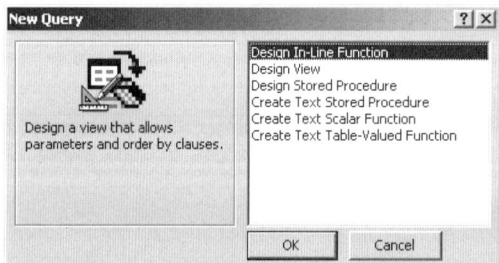

Figure 8-1   New stored procedure

In Microsoft Access 2002 you can specify whether you want to create your stored procedure as text, as shown in Figure 8-1, or in a *Design* view similar to a view. If you select Queries in the Database window in Access 2002 and then select New, the New Query dialog box (see Figure 8-2) is displayed so that you can choose the variant you prefer. If you select Design Stored Procedure, the *Design* view is displayed. If you select Create Text Stored Procedure, the text view shown in Figure 8-1 is used. It is assumed that you are familiar with the *Design* view and how to work with it from Chapter 7, "Views."

Figure 8-2   Selection dialog box in Access 2002

The Designer window provides the basic framework for stored procedures. Otherwise, the Designer is a simple text editor in which you can enter the text for the procedure. There are no formatting specifications for stored procedures. With very few exceptions, it makes no difference whether you enter the entire procedure in a single line or whether you include empty lines. In Microsoft Access 2000, the different sections of the stored procedures are represented in different colors, allowing you to distinguish the SQL commands, for example, from the rest of the text. Unfortunately, this is not the case in Access 2002.

The full syntax for creating a stored procedure is as follows:

```
CREATE PROC[EDURE] procedure_name [ ; number ]

 [ { @parameter data_type }

 [ VARYING ] [ = default ] [ OUTPUT ]

 ] [ ,...n ]


[ WITH

 { RECOMPILE | ENCRYPTION | RECOMPILE , ENCRYPTION } ]


[ FOR REPLICATION ]


AS sql_statement [ ...n ]
```

This chapter describes the different options for the commands. Also, the *RETURN* command that completes the option in Figure 8-1 is optional. It is, however, included by default in the template for procedures.

When you first save a procedure, the *CREATE PROCEDURE* command changes to *ALTER PROCEDURE* because the next time you save you alter an existing procedure.

When you change the name of an existing stored procedure, the procedure is saved under the changed name, but the procedure with the old name also remains.

> **Note**   Do not use any names that begin with *sp_* for your procedures. SQL Server/MSDE searches first in the *master* database for procedures with this prefix because it assumes that they are system stored procedures.

Members of the *sysadmin* fixed server role and the *db_owner* and *db_ddladmin* fixed server roles have permission to create stored procedures. Members of the *sysadmin fixed* server role and the *db_owner* fixed database role can give other users permission to create stored procedures. The permission to execute a stored procedure is given to the procedure owner, who can then assign permissions to other database users.

Stored procedures are created by SQL Server/MSDE on a user-specific basis (that is, every user with appropriate permissions can create stored procedures in the current database). Different users can also use the same procedure names. In the Access Database window, procedures for the current user are displayed with the table name only and stored procedures belonging to other users are displayed with the user name in parentheses.

> **Note**   Access 2002 supports creation of *SELECT* statements in stored procedures with a query builder accessed by selecting Edit, then Insert SQL. This allows the interactive combination of *SELECT* commands in the view that you used during view creation.

Options for Procedures

Table 8-1 provides an overview of the available options for stored procedures.

Table 8-1   Procedure Options

Option	Description
WITH RECOMPILE	The procedure is recompiled every time it is called (that is, it does not access the stored run schedule). This option can be applied if every execution differs greatly from the previous one due to variables or parameters.
WITH ENCRYPTION	The procedure is encrypted and saved (that is, the source code cannot be read). This encryption cannot be reversed.
WITH RECOMPILE, ENCRYPTION	Combines the two previous options.
FOR REPLICATION	Specifies that the procedure is only executed during replication.

Comments

A great advantage of stored procedures over views or queries in Access .mdb files is that you can add comments to the stored procedure listing. There are two options for writing comments. If you start the comment with two minus symbols (– –), then the rest of the line can be used as a comment line. Alternatively, you can insert a comment between (/* and */). In this case the comment can run several lines long, as shown in Figure 8-3.

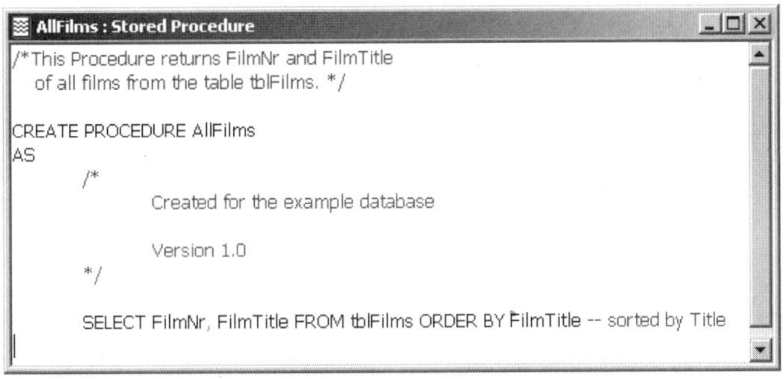
AllFilms : Stored Procedure
/*This Procedure returns FilmNr and FilmTitle
of all films from the table tblFilms. */
CREATE PROCEDURE AllFilms
AS
/*
Created for the example database
Version 1.0
*/
SELECT FilmNr, FilmTitle FROM tblFilms ORDER BY FilmTitle -- sorted by Title

Figure 8-3 Procedure with comments

Parameters and Variables

Stored procedures can be assigned parameters, which are read when the procedure is executed in much the same way as parameters for Access mdb queries.

Parameters

Unlike Access mdb queries, all parameters for stored procedures must be declared. In mdb queries, you simply needed to use a parameter to define it. For parameters' data types, you can use the SQL Server data types described in Chapter 5, "Tables in Access Projects."

Parameters are inserted after the name of the procedure and before the *AS* command, as shown in Figure 8-4. A parameter name starts with @. The data type is specified directly after the name. Where there is more than one parameter, they are separated by commas. All parameters can be enclosed together in parentheses.

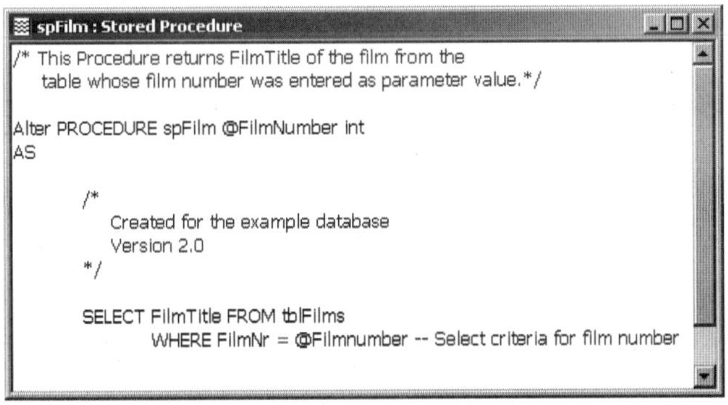
spFilm : Stored Procedure
/* This Procedure returns FilmTitle of the film from the
table whose film number was entered as parameter value.*/
Alter PROCEDURE spFilm @FilmNumber int
AS
/*
Created for the example database
Version 2.0
*/
SELECT FilmTitle FROM tblFilms
WHERE FilmNr = @Filmnumber -- Select criteria for film number

Figure 8-4 Stored procedure with *FilmNumber* parameter

Execute the stored procedure displayed in Figure 8-4. The system will display the Enter Parameter Value dialog box shown in Figure 8-5, in which the user must enter the parameter.

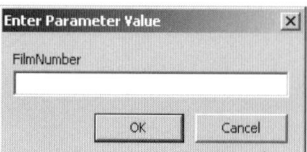

Figure 8-5   Enter Parameter Value dialog box

The system checks the type when you enter the parameter. In this example, the dialog box rejects all alphanumerical entries made for the parameter, because *@Filmnumber* is declared as *int*.

To pass a value to the parameter, you can also create a corresponding ADO program that executes the procedure using a *Command* object, as described in Chapter 14, "*Command* Objects." When using forms and reports, you can pass values to parameters using the *Input Parameters* property of the form or report (see Chapter 10, "Forms").

Presetting a Default Value

You can preset a default value for a parameter, so that if a value is not explicitly specified, SQL Server/MSDE uses the default value. Define a default value by entering an equal sign (=) after the parameter declaration as shown in line four in Figure 8-6.

```
spFilmTitle : Stored Procedure
/* This Procedure returns the FilmNr and FilmTitle of all films from the
   table tblFilms whose FilmTitle corresponds to the select criteria.*/

CREATE PROCEDURE spFilmTitle @FilmTitle varchar(100) = "%"
AS

      /*
         Created for the example database

         Version 1.0
      */

      SELECT FilmNr, FilmTitle FROM tblFilms
            WHERE FilmTitle LIKE @FilmTitle -- Select criteria for film title
```

Figure 8-6   Stored procedure *FilmTitle* with parameter with default value

Remember that the default value is always used if you are executing stored procedures from the Access user interface or if you are using it as the data origin for a form or a report. Access does not display a dialog box requiring the user to enter the parameter value unless additional parameters without a default value are also defined. In that case, a dialog box prompts the user to specify a value for all parameters, including those with default values.

Output Parameters

You can also define parameters for stored procedures that return a value to the calling program or procedure (that is, they report a value determined in the stored procedure). To define an output parameter, add the *OUTPUT* command to the parameter declaration, as shown in Figure 8-7.

```
FilmTitle2 : Stored Procedure                                          _ | □ | ×

/* This Procedure returns the FilmNr and FilmTitle of all films from the
   table tblFilms whose FilmTitle corresponds to the select criteria.*/

CREATE PROCEDURE FilmTitle2 @FilmTitle varchar(100) = "%", @Number int OUTPUT
AS

        /*
            Created for the example database

            Version 1.0
        */

        SELECT FilmNr, FilmTitle FROM tblFilms
            WHERE FilmTitle LIKE @FilmTitle          -- Select criteria for film title
        -- Determine number of films
        SELECT @Number = COUNT(*) FROM tblFIlms
            WHERE FilmTitle LIKE @FilmTitle          -- Select criteria for film title
```

Figure 8-7   Stored procedure with Number *OUTPUT* parameter

If you call the procedure displayed in Figure 8-7 from the Access user interface, a dialog box prompts the user for values for both parameters. Access also prompts for an entry value for *OUTPUT* parameters, but you cannot access the returned *OUTPUT* parameter values via the Access user interface.

OUTPUT parameters can actually only be used in programs with the aid of ADO *Command* objects (see Chapter 14, "*Command* Objects") or from other stored procedures.

The displayed form of assignment to a parameter variable within a *SELECT* command is described in greater detail later.

Return Values

With the help of the *RETURN [Integer-Value]* command, a stored procedure can provide a return value to the calling procedure or program, making it possible to report results or error values, for example.

The system stored procedures provided by Microsoft, for example, return the value 0 if they are executed without any errors and a value greater than 0 to report an error. You should use the resulting value for a function in a similar fashion.

To provide an example for the commands to be described later in this section, the following code uses the Transact-SQL command *IF*, which is similar to its counterpart of the same name in Microsoft Visual Basic:

```
/*

The procedure returns the FilmNr and Filmtitle of all films

in the table tblFilms whose Filmtitle corresponds to the select criteria;

The procedure returns 1 when no films were found.

*/


CREATE PROCEDURE Filmtitle3 @Filmtitle varchar(100) = "%"

AS

        /*

 Created for the example database


 Version 1.1

 */


        SELECT FilmNr, Filmtitle FROM tblFilms

            WHERE Filmtitle LIKE @Filmtitle -- Select criteria for
            Filmtitle

        -- Are films present?

        IF (SELECT COUNT(*) FROM tblFilms

            WHERE Filmtitle LIKE @Filmtitle) >= 1 -- Films found?

            RETURN 0

        ELSE

            RETURN 1
```

Return values cannot be evaluated in the Access user interface. You can only access the return value by calling the stored procedure from another stored procedure or from a program utilizing ADO or smilar components.

Variables

In a stored procedure, you can define and use your own variables. Variables are attached at the beginning of a stored procedure using *DECLARE @variable datatype [, ...].*

The subsequent procedure (see Figure 8-8) can be used, for example, to determine the average number of units of a sold item using the aggregation function *AVG* and assigning the value to the variable *@Average*. Make sure that the number is defined in the table as an integer value. When SQL Server/MSDE calculates the average using an integer, the result is also an integer (no decimal places). In the current example, this leads to an unusable result. For this reason, the value is converted into a floating-point number using the SQL Server function *CONVERT*, type *FLOAT*. You can find a complete list of all functions in Chapter 9, "Transact-SQL."

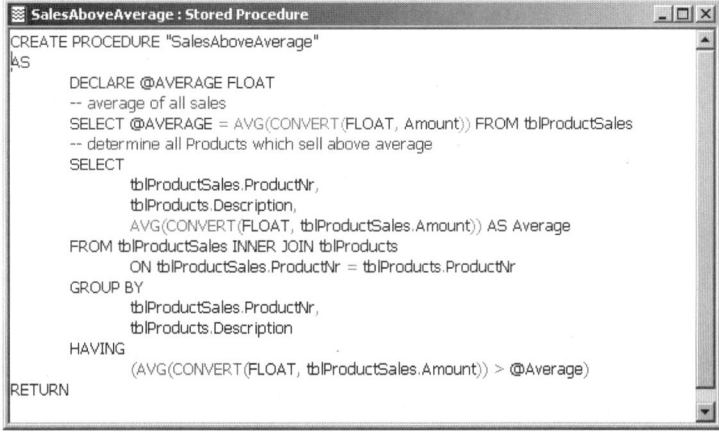

Figure 8-8   Using a variable

The calculated variable *@Average* is then used in the *WHERE* clause of the subsequent *SELECT* to determine all the items that sold better than the average.

> **Note**   For the stored procedures, you can apply the same standards for naming variables and parameters that apply within Visual Basic. See Appendix A, "Naming Conventions," which contains guidelines for naming variables in programs.

Assignment to Variables

You have several options for assigning a value to a variable, some of which are described here.

You can make a simple assignment to a variable with *SELECT @var = value* or *SET @var = value*.

You can also make the assignment to a variable within a *SELECT* command:

```
SELECT @var = field FROM table
```

For example, to assign the maximum duration of all films in table *tblFilms* to a variable:

```
DECLARE @MaxLength INT
```

```
SELECT @MaxLength = MAX(Length) FROM tblFilms
```

When using this kind of assignment, remember that the *SELECT* command can only return one value. If, for example, you write:

```
DECLARE @Length INT
```

```
SELECT @Length = Length FROM tblFilms
```

then the *SELECT* command returns more than one value from the example table. The duration of the last film will now be assigned to the *@Length* variable.

The following sections contain further examples of the practical application of variables.

Transact-SQL Program Commands

You can use the program commands listed in Table 8-2 to include branching, loops, and so on, in stored procedures.

Table 8-2   Program Commands

Command	Description
BEGIN ... END	Defines a block of commands (needed by *IF* and *WHILE*)
BREAK	Terminates a *WHILE* loop
CONTINUE	Starts the next *WHILE* loop
DECLARE	Declares variables
EXECUTE	Executes a stored procedure
GOTO	Branches within the program to named position
IF ... ELSE	Creates a branching
PRINT	Outputs a message text, but Access ignores the *PRINT* output

continued

Table 8-2   Program Commands *(continued)*

Command	Description
RETURN	Ends the stored procedure and can return a value as a result of the procedure
WAITFOR	When executing the stored procedure, waits until a certain time is reached or until a time interval has elapsed
WHILE	Defines a loop that runs until a termination condition is met

Executing Procedures

You can execute other stored procedures in a stored procedure using the *EXECUTE* command, as shown in this example:

```
EXEC [ UTE ]

 {

 [ @return_status = ]

 { procedure_name [ ;number ] | @procedure_name_var }

 }

 [ [ @parameter = ] { value | @variable [ OUTPUT ] | [ DEFAULT ] } ]

 [ ,...n ]

[ WITH RECOMPILE ]
```

The applications of *EXECUTE* can best be illustrated using examples. The simplest variant is executing stored procedures, for example: *EXECUTE AllFilms*.

The resultset for the called procedure is returned. If the procedure called with *EXECUTE* required parameters, these are passed together with the procedure name, for example: *EXECUTE Filmtitle 'D%'*, or with a predefined parameter name, such as *EXECUTE Filmtitle @Filmtitle = 'D%'*.

Remember that the predefined parameter's data type must agree exactly with the parameter in the called procedure. If this is not the case, then a runtime error is triggered for the *EXECUTE* command.

The name of the procedure to be called can also be passed with a variable, as shown here:

```
DECLARE @var VARCHAR(64)

SET @var = 'Filmtitle'

EXECUTE @var
```

Figure 8-9 displays an example of how the *EXECUTE* command can be used to determine the *RETURN* value for a procedure. The procedure *Filmtitle3* called in the example introduced earlier returns 0 if films are found that satisfy the passed parameter *@Filmtitle* and 1 if this is not the case. The commands *IF*, *BEGIN*, and *END* are described later.

```
/* Test Procedure for Exectue */

CREATE PROCEDURE ExecTest @Title VARCHAR(500)
AS
        DECLARE @Result INT

        -- Return value of the procedure FilmTitle3 assigned to variable @Result
        -- Procedure FilmTitle3 returns 0 when films were found
        EXECUTE @Result = FilmTitle3 @FilmTitle = @Title

        IF @Result = 1
        BEGIN
                -- When no films were found
                -- display error notice
                RAISERROR 55555 'No films found'
                -- Exit procedure
                RETURN
        END
        -- When films are present, execute procedure AllFilms
        EXECUTE AllFilms

        RETURN
```

Figure 8-9 *EXECUTE* example

The command *RAISERROR*, which triggers a user-defined run-time error, is included in the procedure. For further information, see the section in Chapter 9 entitled "The RAISERROR Command."

You can also use *EXECUTE* to execute stored procedures that return values using *OUTPUT* parameters. In the following example, the listing contains the procedure *NumberFilms*, which uses the *@Number* parameter to determine the number of films for the criterion passed in *@Filmtitle*.

```
/* The procedure returns the number of films in

 the OUTPUT-Parameter @Number whose Filmtitle corresponds

 to the select criteria */

CREATE PROCEDURE "NumberFilms" @Filmtitle VARCHAR(100) = "%", @Number
INT OUTPUT

AS

        -- Determine number of films

        SELECT @Number = COUNT(*) FROM tblFilms

             WHERE FilmTitle LIKE @FilmTitle -- Select criteria for
Filmtitle
```

In the following example, the procedure *NumberFilms* is called with *EXE-CUTE*. The procedure has two parameters, where the second parameter is defined as *OUTPUT*, as shown in Figure 8-10. Correspondingly, when called, a comma separates the two parameters.

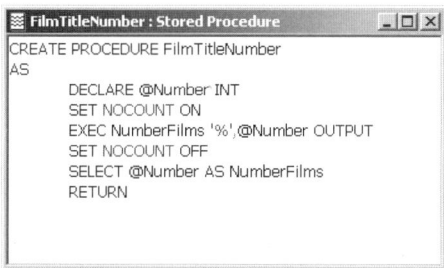

```
FilmTitleNumber : Stored Procedure                    _ □ ×
CREATE PROCEDURE FilmTitleNumber
AS
        DECLARE @Number INT
        SET NOCOUNT ON
        EXEC NumberFilms '%',@Number OUTPUT
        SET NOCOUNT OFF
        SELECT @Number AS NumberFilms
        RETURN
```

Figure 8-10   *EXECUTE* example with *OUTPUT* parameters

The *EXECUTE* command is extremely versatile, as it can also be used to execute SQL commands that are passed in character strings or variables, as shown here:

```
EXEC [ UTE ] ( { @string_variable | [ N ] 'tsql_string' } [ + ...n ] )
```

Remember that for this variant, the data passed to *EXECUTE* is placed in brackets.

In the first example, the *ExecString* procedure is able to pass a *WHERE* clause (for example, in the form of *FilmNr = 17*). The clause is combined by the *SELECT* command and executed by the *EXECUTE* command, as seen here:

```
CREATE PROCEDURE "ExecString"

(

        @Criteria VARCHAR(250)

)

AS

        -- compose SELECT command

        EXECUTE ('SELECT FilmNr, Filmtitle FROM tblFilms WHERE ' +
@Criteria)

RETURN
```

If you pass an incorrect clause, Access reports a run-time error because the *SELECT* query cannot be executed by *EXECUTE*. Remember that the error can only be identified on execution, not when the stored procedure is saved.

In the second example, the *SELECT* command that is assigned to a variable is executed. Remember that brackets must be placed around the name of the variables for *EXECUTE*.

```
CREATE PROCEDURE ExecString2

(

        @Criterium VARCHAR(250)

)

AS

        DECLARE @Query VARCHAR(300)


        -- compose SELECT command

        SET @query = 'SELECT FilmNr, Filmtitle FROM tblFilms WHERE ' +
@Criterium

        -- Execute

        EXECUTE (@Query)

RETURN
```

As an alternative to *EXEC()*, you can also use the system procedure *sp_executesql*. This procedure requires a parameter in the form of a character string. The advantage of *sp_executesql* is that the system generates a reusable execution schedule, increasing processing speed for multiple execution of similar queries.

Remember that when executing dynamic SQL commands with *EXEC()* or *sp_executesql*, these are not executed within the same security context as the stored procedure. In fact, they are executed according to the user security context. If the user does not have sufficient rights, then the corresponding dynamic commands cannot be executed.

Branching

Apart from a slightly different syntax, the *IF* command for branchings is the same as the Visual Basic *IF* command:

```
IF boolean_expression

{ sql_statement | statement_block }

[ ELSE

{ sql_statement | statement_block } ]
```

We have already provided a simple example of this command in the return values section, and Figure 8-11 provides another example.

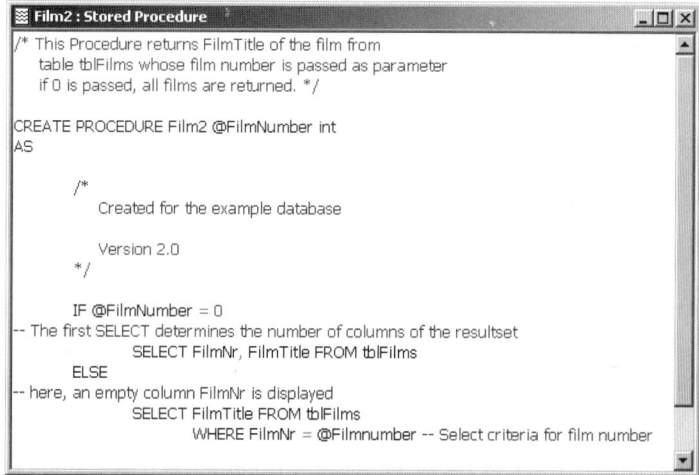

Figure 8-11   Branching

In the example, if parameter *@Filmnumber* receives the value 0, then all titles of the films in table *tblFilms* are returned. Otherwise, only the film title for which the film number was specified is returned.

SELECT Queries in Expressions

When the expression *boolean_expression* is used in an *IF* command, then subqueries can also be made, as shown in the following example:

```
CREATE PROCEDURE TurnAround @FilmNr INT

AS

IF (SELECT Length FROM tblFilms WHERE FilmNr = @FilmNr ) > 120

        SELECT 30
ELSE

        SELECT 45
RETURN
```

The subquery must be written in brackets and can only return one value. You can also include the operators *EXISTS* and *IN* in *IF* comparisons. *EXISTS* and *IN* are described in greater detail in Chapter 9, "Transact-SQL."

EXISTS checks whether a subquery returns records. In the following example, this is used to check whether a film existed for a criterion:

```
/* Test procedure for IF-EXISTS */


CREATE PROCEDURE "ExistsTest" @Title VARCHAR(500)
AS
        IF EXISTS (SELECT FilmNr FROM tblFilms WHERE Filmtitle LIKE
        @Title)
            -- When films are present, execute procedure AllFilms
            EXECUTE AlleFilme
        ELSE
            -- When no films were found
            -- show error notice
            RAISERROR 55555 'No Films Found'
        RETURN
```

You can use *IN* to check whether a value exists in the subquery result, as displayed in the following example:

```
/* Test procedure for IF-IN */


CREATE PROCEDURE INTest @Nr INT
AS
        IF @Nr IN( SELECT FilmNr FROM tblFilms)
            -- FilmNr is valid
            SELECT Filmtitle FROM tblFilms WHERE FilmNr = @Nr
        ELSE
            -- FilmNr not assigned
            RAISERROR 55555 'No Films Found.'
        RETURN
```

Blocks

To execute several commands after an *IF* or an *ELSE*, you can use

```
BEGIN

 one_or_more_statements

END
```

to define the commands as a block. The following example displays part of a stored procedure in which blocks are used:

```
IF (SELECT COUNT(*) FROM tblFilms WHERE Length > 180) > 0
BEGIN
        SELECT Filmtitle FROM tblFilms WHERE Length > 180
        RETURN 0
END
ELSE
BEGIN
        SELECT 'No Films are longer than 180 min.'
        RETURN 1
END
```

> **Note**   We recommend that you separate the contents of a block using spaces or tabs to make your stored procedure easier to read.

Jumps

The command *GOTO label* causes the program to go to the point marked with *label*, from which it then continues processing. Much as in Visual Basic, the following restriction applies: *GOTO* should only be used as an exception, because a program with *GOTO* commands is hard to read and can lead to *spaghetti code*.

Loops

The *WHILE* command allows you to program loops. The general form is:

```
WHILE boolean_expression
        { statement | statement_block }
```

An expression is included for *boolean_expression*, which returns a True or False value. The loop continues as long as the expression is true. If the loop is to include several commands, then the commands must be enclosed with *BEGIN ... END*.

You can use the *BREAK* command to interrupt a loop, causing the program to pick up again at the next command after the loop.

You can use *CONTINUE* to start the next loop run. All commands in the loop that come after *CONTINUE* will then no longer be executed in this loop run.

> **Tip** When programming loops, you should make sure that you do not create any endless loops. From Access, there is no way to stop the procedure from being executed. This means that Access is completely blocked unless you have executed the procedure asynchronously (see Chapter 15, "ADO Events"). To stop a procedure that is trapped in an endless loop, you must terminate the corresponding process on the SQL server. In Chapter 19, "SQL Server Tools," the section entitled "Enterprise Manager" describes how to view and cancel processes. If you are using MSDE, then you cannot use the Enterprise Manager. Chapter 23, "SQL-DMO Library," contains an Access form that can be used in conjunction with the SQL DMO library to display and cancel active processes.

The following example creates a character string from the film titles in table *tblFilms*. This character string contains the film titles, separated by semicolons.

```
CREATE PROCEDURE "AllFilmtitles"

AS

        DECLARE @strFilmtitle VARCHAR(4000)

        DECLARE @j INT

        DECLARE @intMin INT, @intMax INT

        -- Determine smallest and largest FilmNr

        SELECT @intMin = MIN(Filmnr), @intMAx= MAX(Filmnr) from
        tblFilms

        -- reserve Loop variable

        SET @j = @intMin

        -- Initialize string; this is necessary because
```

```
-- the variable has the value Null after the declaration.

-- When @s + 'String' is built, Null occurs again.

SET @strFilmtitle = ''

WHILE @j < @intMax

BEGIN

    -- Add the Filmtitle of the Film with the FilmNr @j to the
    string,

    -- end with semicolon

    SELECT @strFilmtitle = @strFilmtitle + Filmtitle + ';'
    FROM tblFilms

WHERE Filmnr = @j

    -- determine the next FilmNr larger than @j

    SELECT TOP 1 @j = Filmnr FROM tblFilms WHERE Filmnr > @j
    ORDER BY Filmnr

END

-- Add last film without semicolon

SELECT @strFilmtitle = @strFilmtitle + Filmtitle FROM tblFilms
WHERE Filmnr = @intMax

    -- resultset

    SELECT @strFilmtitle AS 'AllTitles'

    RETURN 0
```

The *WAITFOR* Command

You can use the *WAITFOR { DELAY 'waittime' | TIME 'time' }* command to instruct the stored procedure to wait for a certain amount of time or to start running again at a specific point in time. To specify a wait time of one hour, for example, you would use the following command:

```
WAITFOR DELAY '1:0:0'
```

If you used

```
WAITFOR TIME '11:00:00 PM'
```

the procedure would not start running again until the time specified.

Special Features

This section describes some of the special features used when programming stored procedures with Access projects.

Number of Returned Records

The number of records that a stored procedure returns is determined by the first executable command. *SELECT* commands filled by variables (*SELECT @variable = ...*) do not count.

Execute the following procedure, which first inserts a new record for a specific item number in table *tblProductSales* and then determines the total number of sold items with this item number:

```
CREATE PROCEDURE "NewProductSales"

(

        @ProductNr NVARCHAR(50),

        @Amount INT

)

AS

        -- Insert new record
        INSERT INTO tblProductSales

            (ProductNr, Amount, Date)

        VALUES

            (@ProductNr, @Amount, Getdate())


        -- Determine new amount of the sold product
        SELECT

            SUM(amount) AS AmountSum

        FROM

            tblProductSales

        WHERE

            ProductNr = @ProductNr


        RETURN
```

When you execute the stored procedure, you receive a message that the procedure does not contain any records. The first command, *INSERT*, is used to determine the number of records to be returned. The command returns no data lines, however, which is the reason for the message.

You can use the *SET NOCOUNT { ON | OFF }* command to determine whether the number of records returned by a command is to be evaluated. When a stored procedure inserts or updates data in tables and returns records back to a program utilizing ADO, you should use the *SET NOCOUNT OFF* and *SET NOCOUNT ON* commands around the code that manipulates the data. Otherwise, ADO will interpret the stored procedure results as containing multiple resultsets, some of them being empty.

If you add the *SET NOCOUNT ON* command to the foregoing procedure before the *INSERT*, then the next executable command will be used to determine the data line number, as shown here:

```
CREATE PROCEDURE "NewProductSales"

(

        @ProductNr NVARCHAR(50),

        @Amount INT

)

AS

SET NOCOUNT ON


        -- Insert new record

        INSERT INTO tblProductSales

            (ProductNr, Amount, Date)

        SET NOCOUNT OFF

...
```

Several *SELECT* statements in One Stored Procedure

If you are using several *SELECT* statements in your stored procedure that are being executed alternately rather than consecutively, then remember that the first *SELECT* determines the columns for output. To illustrate this problem, in Figure 8-12 we have changed the query so that two columns are output in the first *SELECT* (*FilmNr* and *Filmtitle*), whereas only one is displayed for the second *SELECT* (*Filmtitle*).

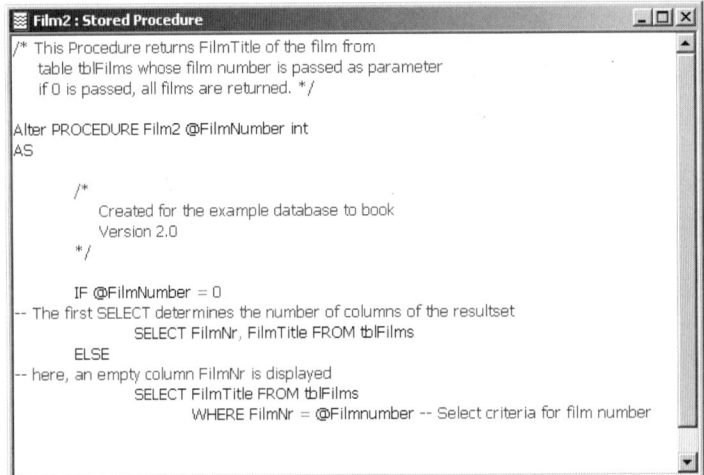

Figure 8-12   Different *SELECT* column specifications

Figure 8-13 contains the results for film number 11. Access displays two columns, although only the *Filmtitle* column contains a result.

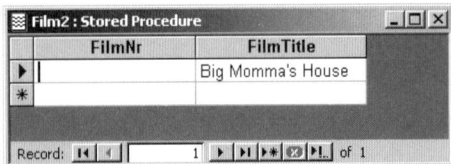

Figure 8-13   Result for *@Filmnumber = 11*

Multiple Resultsets

Stored procedures can return multiple resultsets that occur through execution of consecutive *SELECT* commands. The following procedure, for example, returns two resultsets because each *SELECT* creates its own resultset.

```
CREATE PROCEDURE TopSales

AS

        -- The five best sold products

        SELECT TOP 5

            B.Description,

            SUM(A.Amount) SumAmount

        FROM

            tblProductSales A INNER JOIN tblProducts B

            ON A.ProductNr = B.ProductNr
```

```
GROUP BY

    B.Description

ORDER BY

    SUM(A.Amount) DESC


-- The five most viewed films

SELECT TOP 5

    D.Filmtitle,

    SUM(A.NumberPersons) SumAmount

FROM

    tblBoxOffice A INNER JOIN tblMovieSchedule B ON
    A.ShowTimeNr = B.ShowTimeNr

    INNER JOIN tblWeeks C ON B.WeekNr = C.WeekNr

    INNer JOIN tblFilms D ON C.FilmNr = D.FilmNr

GROUP BY

    D.Filmtitle

ORDER BY

    SUM(A.NumberPersons) DESC


RETURN
```

From the Access user interface, you can only call the first resultset for a stored procedure. All subsequent resultsets are ignored, but they are executed by SQL Server/MSDE and are also transferred to the client.

Multiple resultsets can only be called with the ADO programming interface, as described in Chapter 13, "*Recordset* Objects."

Triggers

Triggers are a special variant of stored procedures that are linked to tables and executed when the event for which they are programmed occurs. There are three variants of triggers in SQL Server 7/MSDE: *INSERT*, *UPDATE*, and *DELETE*. SQL Server 2000/MSDE 2000 also introduces *INSTEAD OF* and *AFTER* triggers.

To create, change, or delete a trigger for a table, first select the corresponding table in the Database window. Right-click the table name and select Triggers from the shortcut menu.

Tables can include any number of triggers, which can be created using the Trigger Name combo box shown in Figure 8-14.

Figure 8-14   Creating a trigger

> **Note**   Remember that problems can occur if one trigger sets off another trigger in turn by updating another table. This can cause trigger call sequences with unforeseeable consequences. In SQL Server/ MSDE, you have the option to disallow nested triggers.

In the example shown in Figure 8-15, a trigger is to be created for table *tblMovieSchedule*. It will check whether the value for the *Day* field is in the correct area. (Remember that an easy check of this kind should normally be carried out using a check constraint.)

```
tblMovieSchedule_Trigger_CheckDay : Trigger

CREATE TRIGGER "tblMovieSchedule_Trigger_CheckDay"
On dbo.tblMovieSchedule
FOR INSERT, UPDATE
AS
        IF(SELECT COUNT(*) FROM inserted WHERE Day < 1 or Day > 12) > 0
                BEGIN
                        RAISERROR 55555 'Day value must be between 1 and 11'
                        ROLLBACK TRANSACTION
                END
```

Figure 8-15   New trigger

The trigger is programmed for events *INSERT* and *UPDATE*, so it is executed when records are inserted or changed.

If the value for *Day* is not in the correct value range, then an error message is issued using the *RAISERROR* command. For further information on this command and its parameters, see the section entitled "Error Handling" in Chapter 9, "Transact-SQL." Every insertion or change made to data includes an implicit transaction (that is, if the insertion or the change cannot be completed, then the original status of the table must be re-created). The *ROLLBACK TRANSACTION* command instructs SQL Server/MSDE to restore the original status. The information from the client and the server is also synchronized. For more information on transactions, see Chapter 26, "Transactions and Locking."

The Internal Tables: Inserted and Deleted

When programming triggers, you can use two tables, inserted and deleted, in which the data to be inserted or deleted is saved temporarily. These tables have the same structure as the table to which the triggers belong. These are tables, rather than simple variables, because more than one record can be inserted, changed, or deleted. Also, an update transaction is split into a deletion transaction and an insertion transaction.

The *UPDATE* Function

The special *UPDATE(Column)* function is provided for update triggers and can only be used in this type of trigger. You can use it to determine whether one or more columns specified as a parameter is to be changed during the update.

If you are converting an Access mdb database into an Access project and a SQL Server/MSDE database using the Upsizing Wizard described in Chapter 16, "Upsizing Wizard", triggers are created by the wizard to describe validity rules and cascading updates and deletes. You should look at this trigger and, if necessary, use it as a reference when developing your own triggers.

Trigger for Cascading Updates and Deletes

The following trigger was created by the Upsizing Wizard in Access 2000. It is used to cascade update a change in an item number in the *tblProducts* sample table to the corresponding record in table *tblProductSales*.

```
CREATE TRIGGER "tblProducts_UTrig" ON dbo.tblProducts

FOR UPDATE AS

SET NOCOUNT ON

/* * CASCADE UPDATES TO 'tblProductSales' */

IF UPDATE(ProductNr)

 BEGIN

 UPDATE tblProductSales

 SET tblProductSales.ProductNr = inserted.ProductNr

 FROM tblProductSales, deleted, inserted

 WHERE deleted.ProductNr = tblProductSales.ProductNr

 END
```

This example illustrates the use of internal tables inserted and deleted. Deleted contains the old item number and inserted always contains the new one.

Comments

Constraints are always evaluated before triggers. In other words, all constraints defined for the table are checked first before a trigger is run. The trigger is not executed if the insertion or the update encounters a constraint. It might be necessary to delete the constraint and re-create it as part of the trigger.

The system might issue the following message when deleting records: "The key column information is insufficient or incorrect. Too many lines are affected by the update." This could be due to a missing *SET NOCOUNT ON* at the beginning of the trigger. You should generally start all triggers with this command or use this command in the stored procedures that would invoke the trigger, otherwise Access (and ADO) receives an incorrect number of records, causing it to respond with the preceding error message.

Searching for Errors in Stored Procedures

Errors in stored procedures can lead to unforeseeable consequences in SQL Server and Access. Depending on the type and the gravity of the error, SQL Server will either continue or cancel execution of the stored procedure without informing Access what happened in SQL Server. Unfortunately, SQL Server often reacts to errors by terminating the corresponding database process, which can cause Access to freeze. Removing frozen database processes is described in Chapter 19, "SQL Server Tools," in the section entitled "Processes and Locks," and Chapter 23, "The SQL-DMO Library," in the section entitled "Processing Information."

The lack of support for Access 2000, Access 2002, and Microsoft SQL Server 7 when debugging stored procedures is extremely inconvenient. There is no option, for example, to run through a stored procedure step-by-step or to check the status and content of variables, and so forth. Only Microsoft SQL Server 2000 (but not MSDE 2000) provides more help in this area: The SQL Server program Microsoft Query Analyzer 2000, introduced in Chapter 19, "SQL Server Tools," allows you do to debug stored procedures.

It is not even possible to use the *poor man's* error search described in many books on SQL Server, using the *PRINT* command and additional resultsets to calculate intermediate results and status values. This is because the *PRINT* command is ignored in Access, which just returns the first resultset of a stored procedure.

The only debugging option that Microsoft provides for SQL Server 7 (not MSDE, however) is integrated with the Microsoft Visual Basic 6 development environment: Microsoft T-SQL Debugger. The T-SQL Debugger is a complex tool, with an intricate configuration on both server and client that allows you to execute stored procedures line by line.

The "Error Handling" section of Chapter 9, "Transact-SQL," describes the commands available for the finding and handling run-time errors in stored processes.

A Simple Debugging Solution

This section describes a simple debugging solution that you can use to write debug information to a table. A table named _Debug_ has been created for this purpose. The name was defined with the underscores to emphasize that this table is not one of the standard database tables. Figure 8-16 represents the table's structure.

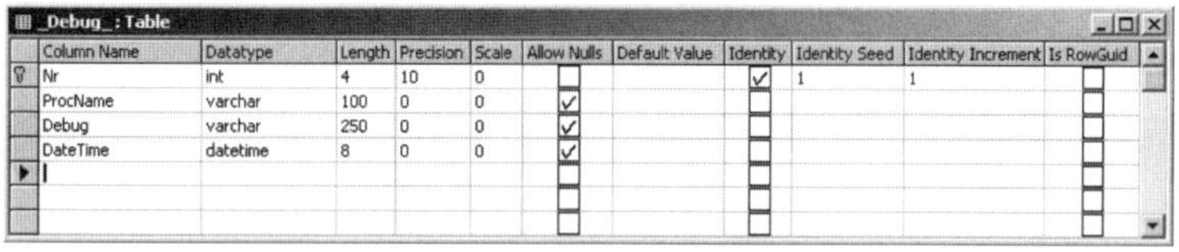

Figure 8-16   Structure of the debugging table

Every entry in this table receives a sequential number, the name of the stored procedure for which the entry was created, and text and date/time values.

The stored procedure _Debug_ is used to add a record to the __Debug__ table. When the procedure is called, two parameters must also be specified: _@debug_ as text and _@procid_ as an integer. _@procid_ is used to pass the internal procedure identification number of the calling procedure to the _Debug_ procedure. In _Debug_, the corresponding procedure name for this number is determined using the SQL Server function _object_name_.

```
CREATE PROCEDURE Debug

(

        @debug varchar(250),

        @procid int

)

AS

        SET NOCOUNT ON

        INSERT

            __debug__

        VALUES

        (

            object_name(@procid),

            @debug,

            getdate()

        )

RETURN
```

You can use the following short procedure to test the *Debug* procedure. Use *EXEC* to call the *Debug* procedure and pass the word *Test* for the first parameter. The system variable *@@procid* (with two @s) determines the internal identification number for the *DebugTest* procedure.

```
CREATE PROCEDURE DebugTest

AS

EXEC Debug 'Test', @@procid
```

After the procedure has been executed, the table *__Debug__* contains a new record with value *Test* in column *Debug* and procedure name *DebugTest* in column *Procname*.

User-Defined Functions

When Access programmers are asked what they miss most when programming Access projects with SQL Server/MSDE, the answer is usually the fact that there is no way for them to use their own Microsoft Visual Basic for Applications (VBA) functions in SQL queries, such as this:

```
SELECT FilmNr, FilmInfo(Filmtitle, MPAANr, Length) FROM tblFilms
```

The function *FilmInfo* in this example is a VBA function that assembles a formatted character string from the parameters passed.

There's good news and there's bad news: The good news is that SQL Server 2000/MSDE 2000 supports user-defined functions (UDFs). The bad news (from the point of view of most Access programmers) is that VBA functions are not supported. Instead, the UDFs have to be programmed in Transact-SQL.

UDFs are only supported directly by Access 2002; that is, it is possible to create and edit UDFs only with Access 2002. If you are using Access 2000, you can access SQL Server 2000/MSDE 2000 and use the functions in views and stored procedures. However, you cannot create these directly from an Access project. The description of UDFs that follows focuses on Access 2002.

Function Variants

There are three variants of UDFs:

■   Scalar functions return a single value. The return value can have any data type except for *text*, *ntext*, *image*, or *timestamp*. The return value can be determined with any Transact-SQL command in the function within a *BEGIN ... END* block.

■   Inline functions return a table. An inline function consists only of a *SELECT* statement.

■   Functions consist of several commands within a *BEGIN ... END* block
and return a table.

Scalar Functions

For the description of scalar functions, we use the SQL query that we used at
the beginning of this section as an example for UDFs:

```
SELECT FilmNr, FilmInfo(Filmtitle, MPAANr, Length) FROM tblFilms
```

We now create the function *FilmInfo*. In the Database window in Access
2002, select Queries and then select New. The New Query dialog box is displayed, as shown in Figure 8-17.

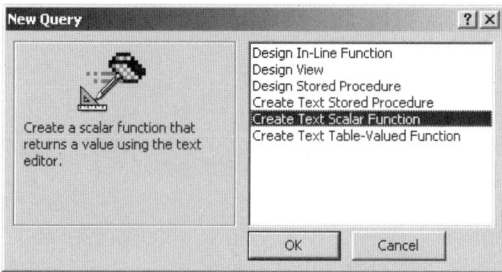

Figure 8-17   Creating a scalar function

In the dialog box, select Create Text Scalar Function. This option is not
shown in the dialog box if you are accessing a SQL Server 7/MSDE 1 database
with your project, and you cannot create functions here.

Access then opens a window, which includes the editor for entering a scalar function. The parameter definition of scalar functions is the same as for
stored procedures and is described in the section, "Parameters."

The *RETURNS* command describes the data type for the function's return
value, as shown in Figure 8-18.

```
Function1 : Function                                              _|□|x|
CREATE FUNCTION "Function1"
        (
        /*
        @parameter1 datatype = default value,
        @parameter2 datatype
        */
        )
RETURNS /* datatype */
AS
        BEGIN
                /* sql statement ... */
        RETURN /* value */
        END
```

Figure 8-18   Editor for a scalar function

Figure 8-19 shows the code for the sample function *FilmInfo*. A character string is assembled based on the film title and length.

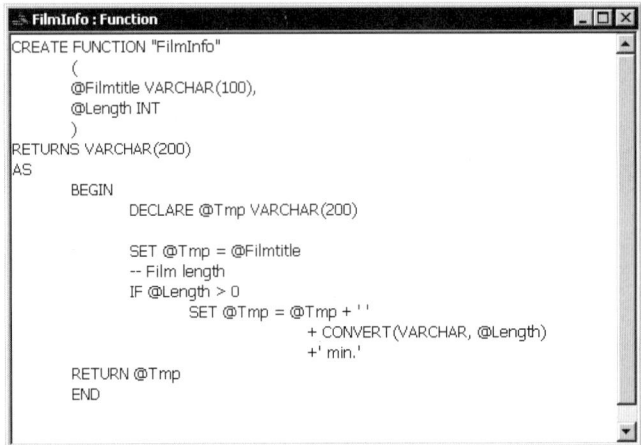

```
FilmInfo : Function
CREATE FUNCTION "FilmInfo"
        (
        @Filmtitle VARCHAR(100),
        @Length INT
        )
RETURNS VARCHAR(200)
AS
        BEGIN
                DECLARE @Tmp VARCHAR(200)

                SET @Tmp = @Filmtitle
                -- Film length
                IF @Length > 0
                        SET @Tmp = @Tmp + ' '
                                + CONVERT(VARCHAR, @Length)
                                +' min.'
                RETURN @Tmp
                END
```

Figure 8-19 *FilmInfo* example function

Please note that functions created on SQL Server/MSDE are user-specific, so every user with the relevant permission can create functions. When using functions in SQL queries, for example, the user name should come before the function name, as shown here:

```
SELECT FilmNr, dbo.FilmInfo(Filmtitle, Length) FROM tblFilms
```

The query returns the result displayed in Figure 8-20.

```
View3 : View
    FilmNr                  Expr1
►        1  The Perfect Storm 129 min.
         2  The Next Best Thing 107 min.
         3  X-Men 97 min.
         4  Pokemon, the Movie 2000 80 min.
         5  The Bachelor 101 min.
         6  Gladiator 165 min.
         7  Mission: Impossible 2 125 min.
         8  Dinosaur 90 min.
         9  The Patriot 160 min.
        10  Hollow Man 135 min.
        11  Big Momma's House 90 min.
        12  Road Trip 97 min.
        13  Me, Myself and Irene 116 min.
        14  Next Friday 98 min.
        15  Chicken Run 95 min.
        16  Fantasia 2000 74 min.
        17  Flawless 111 min.
Record: 14  ◄       1  ►  ►I ►* ⊠ ►I of 24
```

Figure 8-20 Query result with *FilmInfo*

In the following listing, we have rewritten the function *FilmInfo* as function *FilmInfo2*. Both functions return the same result, but *FilmInfo2* will pass *FilmNr* as a parameter and determine the film data using a *SELECT* query within the function.

```
CREATE FUNCTION dbo.FilmInfo2
        (
        @FilmNr INT
        )
RETURNS VARCHAR(200)
AS
        BEGIN
                DECLARE @Tmp VARCHAR(200)
                DECLARE @Filmtitle VARCHAR(100)
                DECLARE @Length INT

                SELECT
                    @Filmtitle = Filmtitle,
                    @Length = Length
                FROM
                    tblFilms
                WHERE
                    FilmNr = @FilmNr

                SET @Tmp = @Filmtitle
                -- Film Length
                IF @Length > 0
                    SET @Tmp = @Tmp + ' '
                            + CONVERT(VARCHAR, @Length)
                            + ' min.'
        RETURN @Tmp
        END
```

Functions That Return Tables

For functions that return tables as a result, SQL Server 2000/MSDE 2000 and Access 2002 offer two variants: inline and table functions.

Inline Functions

An inline function consists of a single *SELECT* query. To create an inline function, choose the Design In-Line Function entry in the New Query dialog box (see Figure 8-17). The Designer window is displayed.

Inline functions are created and used like views, but inline functions can contain parameters.

In the following example, shown in Figure 8-21, we create an inline function that lists all the films being shown in a specific calendar week. *=@Week* was thus specified as a criterion for the field *Week*.

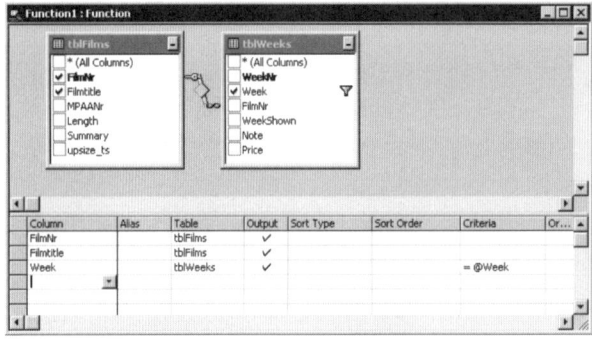

Figure 8-21   Design of an inline function

The SQL code for the inline function is as follows:

```
CREATE FUNCTION fnFilmsWeek

 ( @Week datetime )

RETURNS table

AS

RETURN (

    SELECT dbo.tblFilms.FilmNr,

      dbo.tblFilms.Filmtitle,

      dbo.tblWeeks.Week

    FROM dbo.tblFilms INNER JOIN

dbo.tblWeeks ON dbo.tblFilms.FilmNr = dbo.tblWeeks.FilmNr

    WHERE (dbo.tblWeeks.Week = @Week)

    )
```

With the query *select * from fnFilmsWeek('14.7.2000')* for example, you can determine all the films being shown in that particular week.

Table Functions

If you create a table function by selecting Create Text Table-Valued Function in the New Query dialog box (see Figure 8-17), the framework for defining your function is displayed, as shown in Figure 8-22.

```
Function1 : Function                                          _ □ ×
CREATE FUNCTION "Function1"
        (
        /*
        @parameter1 datatype = default value,
        @parameter2 datatype
        */
        )
RETURNS /* @table_variable TABLE (column1 datatype, column2 datatype) */
AS
        BEGIN
                /* INSERT INTO @table_variable
                                sql select statement  */
                /* alternative sql statement or statements */
        RETURN
        END
```

Figure 8-22   Framework for a table function

The table function and the inline function differ in two essential aspects: On the one hand, the *RETURNS* command is used to define the structure of the table returned by the function. On the other, any Transact-SQL statements can be used between the *BEGIN* and *END* commands of the function.

In Figure 8-23 the function *fnFilmsWeek2*, which we created as an inline function earlier, is implemented as a table function.

```
fnFilmsWeek2 : Function                                      _ □ ×
CREATE FUNCTION "fnFilmsWeek2"
        (
        @Week DATETIME
        )
RETURNS @FILMS TABLE (nr INT, Filmtitle VARCHAR(200), Week DATETIME)
AS
        BEGIN
                INSERT INTO @FILMS
                        SELECT
                                tblFilms.FilmNr, tblFilms.Filmtitle, tblWeeks.Week
                        FROM
                                tblFilms INNER JOIN tblWeeks
                                ON tblFilms.FilmNr = tblWeeks.FilmNr
                        WHERE
                                tblWeeks.Week = @Week
        RETURN
        END
```

Figure 8-23   *FnFilmsWeek2* table function

9

Transact-SQL

This chapter introduces the many options available for working with the SQL query language, along with the extensions and special features of Microsoft SQL Server/MSDE's SQL dialect.

The SQL standard was developed by the American National Standards Institute (ANSI) and the International Organization for Standardization (ISO). Today there are several standards whose names include the year in which they were released: SQL-89, SQL-92, and so on. The different standards vary in language functions and performance.

Database vendors have fully or partially implemented the SQL standards in their products. Unfortunately, they have not yet agreed on a unified standard. Almost all have added their own extensions to the SQL implementations, so there are some significant differences among the SQL variations of individual products.

Microsoft Access 2000 and Microsoft Access 2002 use Jet Engine 3.6—the database core for Access mdb databases—to support SQL-89 Level 1 with several extensions, as well as SQL-92 (albeit not completely) if you are using Jet Engine 4 with the ADO database interface.

SQL Server/MSDE supports SQL-92, which for the most part conforms to the ANSI/ISO standard.

The SQL language functions consist of two parts: The Data Definition Language (DDL) and the Data Manipulation Language (DML). With DDL, you can create, edit, and delete table structures and define indexes. The DML is used to query data or to edit and delete data. In Access, you usually only work with the DML, as tables and indexes are created with the tools available in Access.

Access mdb users rarely have to deal with SQL directly because the Access user interface makes it possible to create queries interactively, and it then generates the actual SQL command itself. In Access projects, you can interactively create SQL commands for views only with the View Designer. All other commands in stored procedures must be entered manually, directly in SQL.

> **Tip**   You can use the Access support functions for .mdb files when creating SQL commands for your Access projects, as well. Simply create an .mdb file in parallel with your Access project, and then use the file to define table links for the tables on SQL Server/MSDE (select File, then Get External Data, then Link Tables). If you then create new queries, you can select View, then SQL in Design mode to view the SQL commands that the query you created is based on. Copy the SQL text to the Windows Clipboard and then paste it into a stored procedure, for example, in the Access project. Note that character strings in Access mdb databases are delineated by double quotation marks, whereas SQL Server/MSDE uses single quotation marks.

Access mdb databases let you test SQL queries without first saving the query in the mdb database. By contrast, in Access projects, you must first save a query (with views as well as with stored procedures) before implementing it. You must do this in Access projects because saving the query transmits it to SQL Server/MSDE, which also checks the query to make sure the syntax is correct. If you want to perform ad hoc tests of your queries, you can use the *frmSQL* form, which is covered in Chapter 14, *"Command* Objects." You can also use the SQL Server Query Analyzer (see Chapter 19, "SQL Server Tools") if you are using SQL Server and not just MSDE.

Select Queries with *SELECT*

SELECT is the most important and most frequently used SQL command. It initiates select queries, which are queries that obtain data from tables and return a resultset.

The following is the complex *SELECT* command's general, if highly simplified, format:

```
SELECT select_list

[INTO new_table_]

FROM table_source

[WHERE search_condition]

[GROUP BY group_by_expression]

[HAVING search_condition]

[ORDER BY order_expression [ASC | DESC] ]
```

The following simple query returns all movies in the table *tblFilms*. The asterisk serves as the variable for all columns in the table.

```
SELECT * FROM tblFilms
```

Specify the column names to select specific columns, as shown here:

```
SELECT FilmNr, Filmtitle FROM tblFilms
```

> **Note**   To avoid unnecessary server and network load, select only those columns that you actually need.

If you use column names that contain spaces or special characters, you must enclose the names in angle brackets, as shown here, or apostrophes:

```
SELECT [Field name with spaces] FROM Table
```

The following is a better example that conforms to the ANSI SQL standard:

```
SELECT "Field name with spaces" FROM Table
```

Identity Column Output

You can use the default column name *IDENTITYCOL* to output the column that you defined as the table's *identity* column. For example, this command

```
SELECT IDENTITYCOL, Filmtitle FROM tblFilms
```

returns the *FilmNr* and the *Filmtitle* columns. The *FilmNr* column is defined as the identity column for the table *tblFilms*.

Use of Quotation Marks

The ANSI SQL standard allows only double quotation marks to identify database object names, whereas character strings are enclosed in single quotation marks. In Access mdb databases, angle brackets are used to enclose database object names, and double quotation marks are used to identify character strings.

If you copy queries from Access mdb databases, you must at least substitute single quotation marks for the double quotation marks that enclose character strings. If the character string already contains single quotation marks, you must replace them with two single quotation marks. For example, "Big Momma's House" would become 'Big Momma''s House.'

In SQL Server/MSDE, you can also use angle brackets for object names. However, if you adhere to the ANSI SQL programming standard, you should use double quotation marks, and make sure that the *QUOTED_IDENTIFIER* database option is *ON*. If the *QUOTED_IDENTIFIER* database option is *OFF*, you have to use angle brackets to delimit identifiers, and you may use double quotes to delimit character strings.

Aliases with *AS*

In the Access results display, the column names are used as the column headings. You can edit the column names with the *AS* command to specify new names, as shown here:

```
SELECT FilmNr AS Filmnumber, Filmtitle AS 'Film Title' FROM tblFilms
```

If the new column names contain spaces or special characters, be sure to enclose the column names in single quotation marks.

For aliases, you can also use the abbreviated version, as displayed here

```
SELECT FilmNr Filmnumber, Filmtitle 'Film Title' FROM tblFilms
```

without the *AS* command. You can also place an alias in front, like this:

```
SELECT Filmnumber = FilmNr, 'Film Title' = Filmtitle FROM tblFilms
```

You can use aliases for table names as well, such as, for example:

```
SELECT f.FilmNr, f.Filmtitle FROM tblFilms AS f
```

Tables from Other Users, Databases, or Servers

SQL Server/MSDE allows a user to create his or her own tables, provided that the user has the required permissions. This makes it possible for multiple users to choose the same table name. In those cases, SQL Server/MSDE differentiates between the tables by adding the user name as a prefix. By default, users can see only their own tables and those tables by the user *dbo*. With the appropriate permissions, a user can also access others' tables, even those in other databases located on the same or different servers. The general syntax is as follows:

```
SELECT * FROM server.database.user.table
```

Figure 9-1 illustrates the definition of a view that displays the *name* and *dbname* fields for the *syslogins* table from the *master* database.

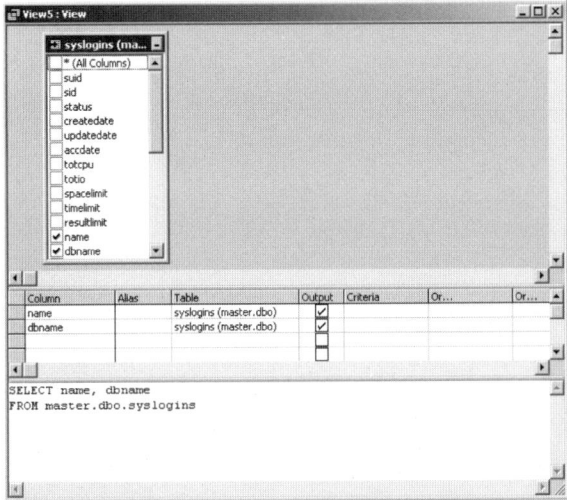

Figure 9-1   Access to the *master* database

SQL Server/MSDE lets you use tables and views from other servers. These other servers may be SQL Server/MSDE systems or systems that run other database products, such as Oracle or Microsoft Access. The servers must be accessible through the object linking and embedding database (OLE DB) provider or open database connectivity (ODBC) driver. Setting up access to another database server requires definition of a linked server or of linked tables through data sources. See Chapter 24, "External Data Sources," for more information on setting up linked servers.

The view shown in Figure 9-2 accesses the server PN-Notebook, where it reads the *tblFilms* table in the *ContosoSQL* database. PN-Notebook was set up as a linked server.

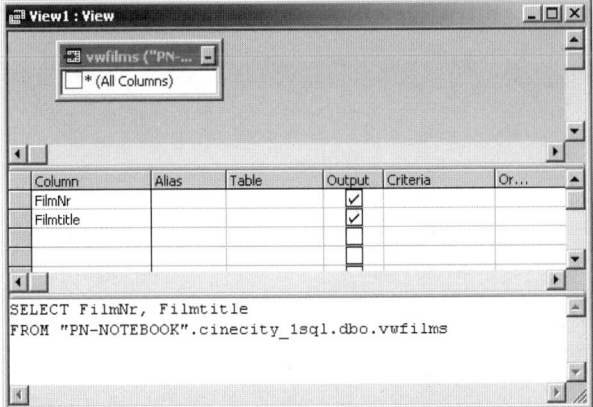

Figure 9-2   Access to a linked server PN-Notebook

Special Cases

The programming of stored procedures (see Chapter 8, "Stored Procedures") often involves special cases of the *SELECT* command. For example, the commands *SELECT 'Text'* or *SELECT 12+34/3* return a resultset based on a text column or a calculated value. If a query results in exactly one value, you can assign this value to a variable, such as *SELECT @Variable = Value* or *SELECT @Variable = Fieldname FROM Table*.

> **Note** SQL Server/MSDE allows the syntax *SELECT 'Text'* or *SELECT NumericalExpression*. With Access mdb queries, however, you must always specify a *FROM* table as well, even if *'Text'* or *NumericalExpression* are not relevant to the table.

Calculated Columns

Columns based on *SELECT* commands can also be calculated, which means they can be derived from other columns. The following query, for example, returns every film's length, plus 45 minutes:

```
SELECT Filmtitle, Length + 45 FROM tblFilms
```

If you do not use *AS* to specify a column name for a calculated field, SQL Server/MSDE uses the name *Expr<n>*, with *n* denoting the column number.

You can use the following query to determine a product's gross sales, plus value-added tax:

```
SELECT ProductNr, Description, SalesPrice * 1.16

AS Gross FROM tblProducts
```

Table 9-1 lists the operators you can use to perform column calculations.

Table 9-1   Operators

Operator	Description
+	Addition
<;$MI>	Subtraction
*	Multiplication
/	Division
%	Modulo

continued

Table 9-1 Operators *(continued)*

Operator	Description
&	Bit-wise And
|	Bit-wise Or
^	Bit-wise exclusive Or

Text Concatenation

The + operator is the only one available with SQL Server/MSDE for concatenating text, but you can use the + and & operators with Access mdb queries. For example, if you use the + operator to concatenate two columns, like this

```
SELECT Filmtitle + Summary AS Longtext FROM tblFilms
```

the text link result is *Null* whenever one of the two columns you want to link contains the value *Null*. This applies to Access mdb and SQL Server/MSDE.

With Access mdb queries, you can also use the join operator &, which interprets empty character strings as *Null* values and thus returns a result even if one of the two operands is *Null*. SQL Server/MSDE does not support the & operator for text concatenation.

To re-create the behavior of the & operator with SQL Server/MSDE, you should bracket the columns with the *ISNULL* function, as the following example illustrates:

```
SELECT ISNULL(Filmtitle,'') + ISNULL(Summary,'')

AS Longtext FROM tblFilms
```

In this example, *ISNULL* returns an empty character string whenever the *Filmtitle* or *Summary* column is *Null*.

Please refer to the section later in this chapter entitled "The ISNULL Function" for a description of this function. Be aware that this function differs from the function with the same name for Access mdb.

The section entitled "Comparisons with NULL" also covers the *NULL* function's special features.

Special Features of *text*, *ntext*, and *image* Fields

If you are using fields of the data type *text*, *ntext*, or *image* to sort or group a resultset, keep in mind that the system uses only the respective field's first 256 characters for sorting or grouping.

Differences Compared to Jet Databases

When calculating columns in Access mdb databases, you can utilize intermediate results from other columns, as the example in Figure 9-3 illustrates. Note the use of aggregate functions, which are described in detail in the section entitled "Aggregate Functions" later in this chapter.

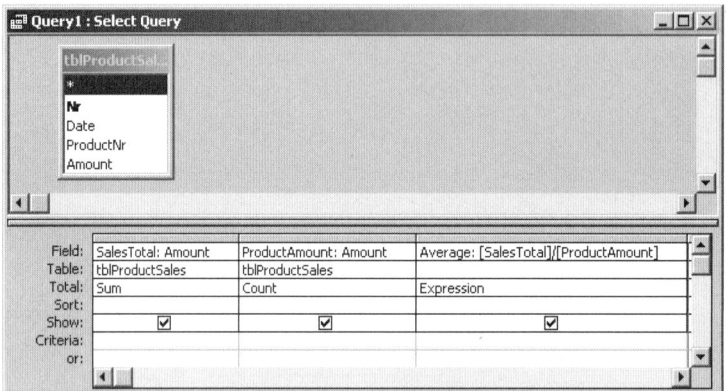

Figure 9-3   Access mdb query with calculated fields

The first two columns, named *SalesTotal* and *ProductAmount*, determine the total for the products sold and the number of records. The third column, *Average*, calculates the average. The defined column headings are used for the calculation.

```
SELECT

        Sum(tblProductSales.Amount) AS SalesTotal,

        Count(tblProductSales.Amount) AS ProductAmount,

        [SalesTotal]/[ProductAmount] AS Average

FROM tblProductSales;
```

You can use this query in Access mdb databases without problems. SQL Server/MSDE, on the other hand, cannot interpret the query. This means that the system returns an error message as soon as you create a corresponding view, as shown in Figure 9-4.

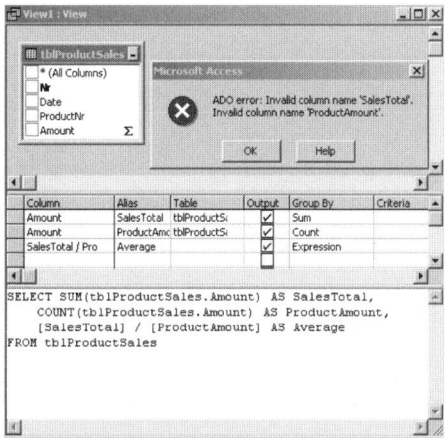

Figure 9-4   Query in the query designer

To transform the query, you can use this command sequence:

```
SELECT
        SUM(Amount) AS SalesTotal,
        COUNT(Amount) AS ProductAmount,
        SUM(CONVERT(float, Amount)) / COUNT(Amount) AS Average
FROM dbo.tblProductSales
```

This instructs the system to once again use the aggregate functions to perform column calculations. Note the *CONVERT* function, discussed in the section entitled "Data Type Conversion", which converts one of the two operands into a floating-point number, because both columns return integer values. Unlike Access mdb databases, which create a floating-point number as the return value, the division of two integers in SQL Server/MSDE returns an integer value.

SQL Functions

SQL Server/MSDE recognizes a large number of functions that you can use to calculate column values. Tables 9-2 through 9-10 give an overview of the functions you can use.

> **Note**   Access Microsoft Visual Basic for Applications (VBA) functions cannot be used in SQL queries (that is, in views, stored procedures, forms, reports, and when programming with VBA). This applies to the integrated VBA functions as well as those you create yourself. SQL Server/MSDE recognizes an equivalent function for most Access VBA functions. With Microsoft SQL Server 2000, you can also define user-defined functions (UDFs) on the server. Otherwise, you can determine Access VBA function results and pass these to a stored procedure using parameters.

Table 9-2   Date Functions

Function	Description
DATEADD(datepart, number, date)	Returns a new *datetime* value, which is obtained by adding an interval to the specified date
DATEDIFF(datepart, startdate, enddate)	Determines the number of date and time units between two specified date entries
DATENAME(datepart, date)	Returns the specified date unit of the specified date as a string
DATEPART(datepart, date)	Returns the specified part of the specified date as an integer
DAY(date)	Returns the day date unit of the specified date as an integer
GETDATE()	Returns the current system date and the current system time in the internal standard format for *datetime* values
MONTH(date)	Returns the month part of a specified date as an integer
YEAR(date)	Returns the year part of a specified date as an integer

Table 9-3   Configuration Functions

Function	Description
@@DATEFIRST	Returns the current value of the *SET DATEFIRST* parameter, which displays the specified first day of the week: 1 for Monday, 2 for Tuesday and so on up to 7 for Sunday.
@@DBTS	Returns the current value from the *timestamp* data type for the current database. This value only occurs once in the database.
@@LANGUAGE	Returns the name of the language currently being used.
@@LANGID	Returns the number of the language currently being used.
@@LOCK_TIMEOUT	Returns the current setting for the lock timeout for the current session in milliseconds.
@@MAX_CONNECTIONS	Displays the maximum number of user connections allowed on SQL Server at any one time. The result is not necessarily the number currently configured.
@@MAX_PRECISION	Returns the level of precision currently set on the server. The level is used by the *decimal* and *numeric* data types.
@@NESTLEVEL	Returns the nesting level of the current execution of a stored procedure.
@@OPTIONS	Returns information about current *SET* options.
@@REMSERVER	Returns the name of the remote database server.
@@SERVERNAME	Displays the name of the local server on which SQL Server is installed.
@@SERVICENAME	Returns the name of the registry key under which SQL Server is running.
@@SPID	Returns the server process ID of the current user process.
@@TEXTSIZE	Returns the current value of the *TEXTSIZE* option in the *SET* statement. This statement defines the maximum length in bytes of *text*, *ntext*, or *image* data returned by a *SELECT* statement.
@@VERSION	Returns the date, version number, and processor type of the current installation of SQL Server/MSDE.

Table 9-4 Mathematical Functions

Function	Description
ABS(numeric_expression)	Returns the absolute, positive value of the given numeric expression
ACOS(float_expression)	Returns the angle (in radians) whose cosine is the specified *float* expression (also called arc cosine)
ASIN(float_expression)	Returns the angle (in radians) whose sine is the specified *float* expression (also called arc sine)
ATAN(float_expression)	Returns the angle (in radians) whose tangent is the specified *float* expression (also called arc tangent)
ATN2(float_expression, float_expression)	Returns the angle (in radians) whose tangent is between the two specified *float* expressions (also called arc tangent)
CEILING(numeric_expression)	Returns the smallest integer greater than or equal to the specified numeric expression
COS(float_expression)	Returns the trigonometric cosine of a specified angle (in radians)
COT(float_expression)	Returns the trigonometric cotangent of a specified angle (in radians) in the respective *float* expression
DEGREES(numeric_expression)	Converts radians to degrees
EXP(float_expression)	Returns the base exponential value for a *float* expression
FLOOR(numeric_expression)	Returns the largest integer smaller than or equal to the specified numeric expression
LOG(float_expression)	Returns the natural logarithm of the given *float* expression
LOG10(float_expression)	Returns the base-10 logarithm of the given *float* expression
PI()	Returns the constant value of *PI*, 3.14…
POWER(numeric_expression, y)	Returns the value of the expression raised to the respective power
RADIANS(numeric_expression)	Returns the angle of a numeric expression specified in degrees
RAND([seed])	Returns a random *float* value between 0 and 1
ROUND(numeric_expression, length[, function])	Returns a numeric expression, rounded to the specified length or precision

continued

Table 9-4   Mathematical Functions   *(continued)*

Function	Description
SIGN(numeric_expression)	Returns the sign of the specified expression: positive (+1), null (0), or negative (−1)
SIN(float_expression)	Returns the trigonometric sine of the specified angle (in radians) in an approximate numeric expression
SQUARE(float_expression)	Returns the square number of the specified expression
SQRT(float_expression)	Returns the square root of the specified expression
TAN(float_expression)	Returns the tangent of the expression entered

Table 9-5   Metadata Functions

Function	Description
COL_LENGTH('table', 'column')	Returns the defined length, in bytes, of a column
COL_NAME(table_id, column_id)	Returns the name of the database column with the corresponding table and column identification number
COLUMNPROPERTY(id, 'column', 'property')	Returns information about a column or procedure parameter
DATABASEPROPERTY('database', 'property')	Returns the named database property for the specified database and property name
DB_ID('database_name')	Returns the database ID
DB_NAME(database_id)	Returns the name of the database
FILE_ID('file_name')	Returns the file ID for the specified logical file name in the current database
FILE_NAME(file_id)	Returns the logical file name for the specified file ID
FILEGROUP_ID('filegroup_name')	Returns the file group ID for the specified filegroup name
FILEGROUP_NAME(filegroup_id)	Returns the filegroup name for the specified filegroup ID
FILEGROUPPROPERTY ('filegroup_name', 'property')	Returns the property value for the specified filegroup and property name
FILEPROPERTY('file_name', 'property')	Returns the property value for the specified file name when a file name and property name are specified

continued

Table 9-5   Metadata Functions   *(continued)*

Function	Description
FULLTEXTCATALOGPROPERTY ('catalog_name', 'property')	Returns information about the properties of the full-text catalog
FULLTEXTSERVICEPROPERTY ('property')	Displays information about properties of the full-text service level
INDEX_COL('table', index_id, key_id)	Returns the name of an indexed column
INDEXPROPERTY(table_ID, 'index', 'property')	Returns the named index property value for the specified table ID number, the index name, and the property name
OBJECT_ID('object')	Returns the ID of the database object
OBJECT_NAME(object_id)	Returns the database object name
OBJECTPROPERTY(id, 'property')	Returns information about objects in the current database
@@PROCID	Returns the ID of the stored procedure for the current procedure
TYPEPROPERTY('type', 'property')	Returns information about a data type

Table 9-6   Rowset Functions

Function	Description
OPENDATASOURCE ('provider_name', 'init_string')	(Only SQL Server 2000) Defines the server name of a four-part object name without a connection server name, using an OLE DB provider connection definition.
OPENQUERY('linked_server', 'query')	Executes the specified pass-through query on the specified connection server. The server is an OLE DB data source. The *OPENQUERY* function can be referenced in the *FROM* clause of a query as if it were a table name. The *OPENQUERY* function can also serve as a destination table in an *INSERT, UPDATE,* or *DELETE* statement. The restrictions of the OLE DB provider apply. Although the query might return multiple resultsets, *OPENQUERY* returns only the first one.

continued

Table 9-6   Rowset Functions   *(continued)*

Function	Description
OPENROWSET('provider_name' { 'datasource' ; 'user_id'; 'password' | 'provider_string', {[catalog.][schema.]object | 'query'])	Contains all the necessary connection information for accessing remote data from an OLE DB data source. This method is an alternative to accessing tables on a connection server. It is a unique, direct method for connecting to and accessing remote data using OLE DB. The *OPENROWSET* function can be referenced in the *FROM* clause of a query as if it were a table name. The *OPENROW-SOURCE* function can also be referenced as a destination table in an *INSERT*, *UPDATE*, or *DELETE* statement. The restrictions of the OLE DB provider apply. Although the query might return multiple resultsets, *OPEN-ROWSET* only returns the first one.
OPENXML(idoc, 'rowpattern', | [flags]) [WITH (SchemaDeclaration | TableName)]	(Only SQL Server 2000) Returns an XML document in table form (as a rowset). The command can be used like *OPENROWSET*.

Table 9-7   Security Functions

Function	Description
HAS_DBACCESS('database_name')	Returns information about whether the user has access to the specified database
IS_MEMBER ({'group' | 'role' })	Shows whether the current user is a member of the specified Microsoft Windows NT/ Microsoft Windows 2000 group or SQL Server role
IS_SRVROLEMEMBER ('role' [, 'login'])	Shows whether the current user name is a member of the specified server role
SUSER_SID(['login'])	Returns the security ID (SID) for the user name of the user
SUSER_SNAME([server_user_sid])	Returns the user name from the SID of a user
USER_ID(['user'])	Returns the database ID of the user
USER	Allows a value, which is provided by the system, to be inserted for the database user name of the current user in a table when no default value is specified

Table 9-8   **Functions for System Statistics**

Function	Description
@@CONNECTIONS	Returns the number of connections or attempted connections since the last time SQL Server was started.
@@CPU_BUSY	Returns the elapsed time in milliseconds (based on the precision of the system timer) that the CPU was busy since the last time SQL Server was started
@@IDLE	Returns the time in milliseconds (based on the precision of the system timer) that SQL Server was idle since the last time it was started
@@IO_BUSY	Returns the time in milliseconds (based on the precision of the system timer) that SQL Server was required for input and output operations since the last time it was started
@@PACKET_ERRORS	Returns the number of network packet errors that occurred with SQL Server connections since the last time SQL Server was started
@@PACK_RECEIVED	Returns the number of packets received from the network since the last time SQL Server was started
@@PACK_SENT	Returns the number of packets sent to the network by SQL Server since the last time it was started
@@TIMETICKS	Returns the number of microseconds per time signal
@@TOTAL_ERRORS	Returns the number of disk read/write errors that occurred in SQL Server since it was last started
@@TOTAL_READ	Returns the number of disk read operations performed by SQL Server since it was last started
@@TOTAL_WRITE	Returns the number of disk write operations performed by SQL Server since it was last started

Table 9-9   **System Functions**

Function	Description
APP_NAME()	Returns the application name for the current session if a name was defined by the application.
CASE input_expression WHEN when_expression THEN result_expression [...n] [ELSE else_result_expression] END	The simple CASE function compares an expression with multiple simple expressions to determine the result.

continued

Table 9-9   **System Functions**   *(continued)*

Function	Description
CASE *WHEN Boolean_expression THEN* *result_expression* *[...n]* *[* *ELSE else_result_expression* *]* *END*	The searched *CASE* function evaluates multiple Boolean expressions to determine the result.
CAST(expression AS data_type)	Converts an expression explicitly from one data type to another.
CONVERT (data_type[(length)], *expression [, style])*	Converts an expression explicitly from one data type to another.
COALESCE(expression [,...n])	Returns the first non-*Null* expression from the arguments.
CURRENT_TIMESTAMP	Returns the current date and time. This function is the same as *GETDATE()*.
CURRENT_USER	Returns the current user. This function is the same as *USER_NAME()*.
DATALENGTH(expression)	Returns the number of bytes required to save the expression.
@@ERROR	Returns the error number of the last Transact-SQL statement to be executed.
FORMATMESSAGE(msg_number, *param_value[,...n])*	Creates a message from an existing message in *sysmessages*. The function of *FORMATMESSAGE* is similar to the *RAISERROR* statement. *RAISERROR* outputs the message directly, whereas *FORMATMESSAGE* returns the message for further processing.
GETANSINULL(['database'])	Returns the default nullability for the database for this session.
HOST_ID( )	Returns the workstation ID.
HOST_NAME( )	Returns the name of the workstation.
IDENT_CURRENT('table_name')	Returns the last identity value generated for a specified table in any session and any scope.
IDENT_INCR('table_or_view')	Returns the increment value (as *numeric(@@MAXPRECISION, 0)*) that was defined when creating an identity column in a table or view.
IDENT_SEED('table_or_view')	Returns the seed value (as *numeric(@@MAXPRECISION, 0)*) that was defined when creating an identity column in a table or view.

continued

Table 9-9   **System Functions**   *(continued)*

Function	Description
@@IDENTITY	Returns the last identity value to be inserted.
IDENTITY(data_type[, seed, increment]) AS column_name	Only used in a *SELECT* statement with an *INTO table* clause to insert an identity column into a new table.
	The *IDENTITY* function is similar to the *IDENTITY* property used with *CREATE TABLE* and *ALTER TABLE*. However, they are not identical.
ISDATE(expression)	Determines whether the entered expression is a valid date.
ISNULL(check_expression, replacement_value)	Replaces *NULL* with the specified value.
ISNUMERIC(expression)	Determines whether an expression is a valid numeric type.
NEWID()	Creates a new unique value of the type *uniqueidentifier.*
NULLIF(expression, expression)	Returns a *NULL* value if the two specified expressions are equivalent.
PARSENAME('object_name', object_piece)	Returns the specified part of an object name. The parts of an object that can be parsed are the object name, the owner name, the database name, and the server name.
PERMISSIONS([objectid [, 'column']])	Returns a value with a bitmap, which shows the statement, object, or column permissions for the current user.
@@ROWCOUNT	Returns the number of rows on which the last statement had an effect.
SERVERPROPERTY('propertyname')	Returns property information about the server instance.
SESSIONPROPERTY ('option')	Returns the SET options settings of a session.
SESSION_USER	This function allows a system-supported value to be inserted for the user name of the current session in a table if no default value has been specified. The function also permits the use of the user name in queries, error messages, and so on.
STATS_DATE(table_id, index_id)	Returns the date when the statistics of the specified index were last updated.

continued

Table 9-9   System Functions   *(continued)*

Function	Description
SYSTEM_USER	Allows a value, which is provided by the system, to be inserted for the current system user name in a table when no default value is specified.
@@TRANCOUNT	Returns the number of active transactions for the current connection.
USER_NAME([id])	Returns a database user name via a specific ID.

Table 9-10   Functions for String Editing

Function	Description
ASCII(character_expression)	Returns the ASCII value of the first character in a character expression
CHAR(integer_expression)	Converts an ASCII value to a character
CHARINDEX(expression1, expression2 [, start_location])	Returns the position of the first occurrence of the specified expression in a string
DIFFERENCE (character_expression, character_expression)	Returns the difference between the *SOUNDEX* values of two character expressions as an integer between 0 and 4
LEFT(character_expression, integer_expression)	Returns a portion of a string, starting at a specified number of characters from the left
LEN(string_expression)	Returns the number of characters in the given string expression (not the number of bytes), whereby following blanks are ignored
LOWER(character_expression)	Returns a string whose characters have been converted from uppercase to lowercase letters
LTRIM(character_expression)	Returns a string without leading spaces.
NCHAR(integer_expression)	Returns the Unicode character with the given integer code as defined by the Unicode standard
PATINDEX('%pattern%', expression)	Returns, for all the valid text and character data types, the position of the first occurrence of a pattern in a specified expression, or zero when the pattern is not found
QUOTENAME('character_string'[, 'quote_character'])	Returns a Unicode string with delimiters added so that the input string is converted to a valid, delimited SQL Server name

continued

Table 9-10 Functions for String Editing *(continued)*

Function	Description
REPLACE('string_expression1', 'string_expression2', 'string_expression3')	Replaces all occurrences of the second string expression in the first string expression with a third expression
REPLICATE(character_expression, integer_expression)	Repeats a character expression the specified number of times
REVERSE(character_expression)	Returns a reversed character expression
RIGHT(character_expression, integer_expression)	Returns a portion of a string, starting at a specified number of characters (specified by *integer_expression*) from the right
RTRIM(character_expression)	Returns a string without trailing spaces
SOUNDEX(character_expression)	Returns a four character *(SOUNDEX)* code consisting of four characters to evaluate the similarity between two strings
SPACE(integer_expression)	Returns a string consisting of repeated spaces
STR(float_expression[, length[, decimal]])	Converts numerical data to strings
STUFF(character_expression, start, length, character_expression)	Deletes a specified number of characters from a string starting at the specified position and inserts a different string in their place
SUBSTRING(expression, start, length)	Returns a portion of a character, binary, text, or image expression
UNICODE('ncharacter_expression')	Returns an integer for the first character in the specified expression according to the definition of the Unicode standard
UPPER(character_expression)	Returns a character expression, whereby lowercase letters are converted to uppercase letters

Some of the functions listed in the preceding tables are described in more detail using examples in the sections that follow.

The *ISNULL* Function

The *ISNULL(check_expression, replacement_value)* function allows you to replace Null values with other values. In the query

```
SELECT Filmtitle, ISNULL(Summary, 'No Entry') FROM tblfilms
```

the text *No Entry* is output for every instance where no additional text appears.

> **Note**   Note the different functionality of IsNull in Access mdb databases. The Jet Engine uses the function IsNull in the form IsNull(check_expression), which returns a *True* or *False* value.

The *CASE* Function

The *CASE* function is used to define columns independently of conditions. *CASE* is used in two variants: simple and searched. This is the simple variant:

```
CASE input_expression
 WHEN when_expression THEN result_expression
 [ ...n ]
 [
 ELSE else_result_expression
 ]
END
```

The searched variant is in the following format:

```
CASE
 WHEN boolean_expression THEN result_expression
 [ ...n ]
 [
 ELSE else_result_expression
 ]
END
```

The following sections show examples of both variants.

> **Note**   In Access mdb databases there is no equivalent of the *CASE* function. Nested *If* functions *Iif()* perform a similar function but are much less intuitive.

CASE: Simple Form

A value is analyzed using *CASE* in the simple form; that is, a corresponding branching is made in the *CASE* command depending on the value, as shown here:

```
CREATE PROCEDURE "WeekDay"

AS

    SELECT

        Filmtitle,

        CASE Day

            WHEN 1 THEN 'Mon'

            WHEN 2 THEN 'Tue'

            WHEN 3 THEN 'Wed'

            WHEN 4 THEN 'Thu'

            WHEN 5 THEN 'Fri'

            WHEN 6 THEN 'Sat'

            WHEN 7 THEN 'Sun'

            WHEN 8 THEN 'Fri/Sat'

            WHEN 9 THEN 'Sat/Sun'

            WHEN 10 THEN 'Thu/Sun-Wed'

            WHEN 11 THEN 'All Week'

            ELSE 'Not Defined'

        END AS Day,

        Time

    FROM tblMovieSchedule

        INNER JOIN tblWeeks ON tblMovieSchedule.WeekNr = tblWeeks.WeekNr

            INNER JOIN tblFilms ON tblWeeks.FilmNr = tblFilms.FilmNr


RETURN
```

Figure 9-5 displays the result of this procedure.

Figure 9-5   Result of the procedure

CASE: Searched Form

Boolean expressions are evaluated using the searched form. In the following example, all films are to be labeled with their running time duration. Films that run for longer than 180 minutes should be identified as *extended length,* films that play for between 90 and 180 minutes as *normal,* and shorter films as *short film,* as shown in the following procedure:

```
CREATE PROCEDURE [Filmlength]

AS

        SELECT

        Filmtitle,

        Length,

        CASE

            WHEN (Length > 180) THEN 'Extended Length'

            WHEN (Length <= 180 AND Length >=90) THEN 'Normal'

            WHEN (Length < 90 AND Length > 0) THEN 'Short Film'

            WHEN (Length = 0) THEN 'Not Determined'

            WHEN ISNULL(Length,0) = 0 THEN 'Not Indicated'

        END AS Addition

        FROM tblFilms

RETURN
```

The *COALESCE* Function

A list of expressions is transferred to the *COALESCE* function. It returns the value of the first expression that is different from *Null*.

```
COALESCE ( Statement [ ,...n ] )
```

Figure 9-6 shows a view in which the *COALESCE* function outputs the first *Note* column that actually contains a commentary. If no commentary exists, then the text "No notes present" is displayed.

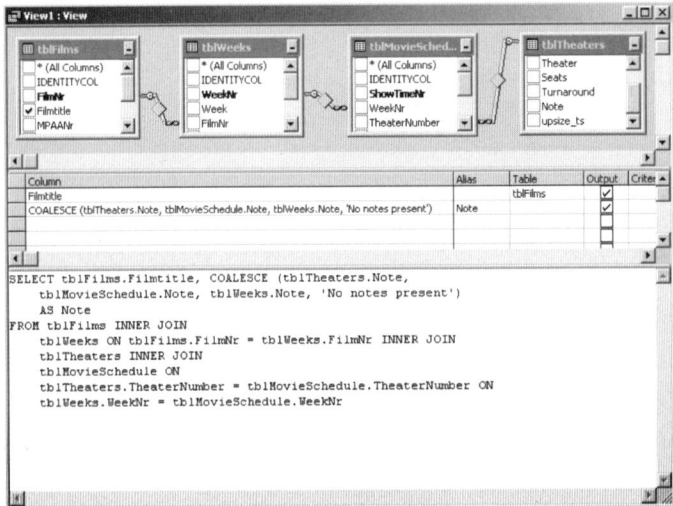

Figure 9-6   View with *COALESCE* function

The *COALESCE* function displayed in Figure 9-6 can also be written using *CASE* as follows:

```
...

CASE

  WHEN (dbo.tblTheaters.Note IS NOT NULL) THEN dbo.tblTheater.Note

  WHEN (dbo.tblMovieSchedule.Note IS NOT NULL) THEN
dbo.tblMovieSchedule.Note

  WHEN (dbo.tblWeeks.Note IS NOT NULL) THEN dbo.tblWeeks.Note

  ELSE 'No notes present'

...
```

The advantages of the *COALESCE* function compared with the displayed *CASE* statement is that the *COALESCE* function can be presented in the query designer. When you use *CASE*, the query designer displays a warning message indicating that it cannot show *CASE* constructions in the grid area.

Working with Text and Text Functions

In this section we present some of the text functions of SQL Server/MSDE that do not have any corresponding functions in Access mdb queries or that are named differently in the two applications.

The *SUBSTRING* Function

The SQL Server/MSDE *SUBSTRING* function is the same as the *Mid* function for Access mdb. *SUBSTRING(Expression, Start, Length)* returns a character string that contains the *Length* character from the *Start* of the *Expression*.

The *STUFF* Function

The *STUFF(Character_Expression1, Start, Length, Character_Expression2)* function makes it possible to cut the character number *Length,* for example, from the *Start* position of a *Character_Expression1* and replace it with the *Character_Expression2*.

In the following example, all film titles longer than 10 characters in length are truncated after the tenth character and the remaining characters are replaced by three periods. Note that the function returns *Null* if the film title is shorter than 15 characters, as shown in Figure 9-7. For this reason the *COALESCE* function has been used in the example, which uses the film titles if *STUFF* returns *Null*.

```
SELECT COALESCE( STUFF(Filmtitle, 15, LEN(Filmtitle), '...'),
Filmtitle)

 AS FilmtitleShort

FROM tblFilms
```

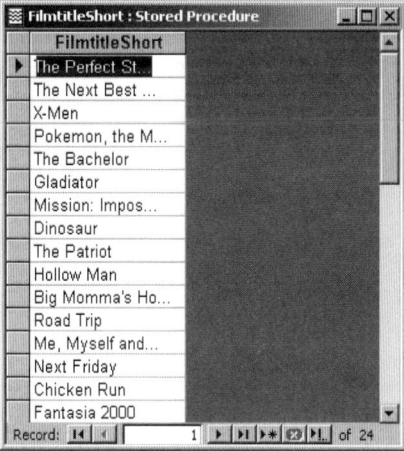

Figure 9-7   Shortened film titles

The *CHARINDEX* and *PATINDEX* Functions

The *CHARINDEX(Expression1, Expression2 [, Start_Location])* function corresponds to the VBA function *INSTR*. It shows at which position in *Expression1* *Expression2* occurs. If necessary, it is tested only from an optional *Start_Location*. The following query outputs a list of all positions for films with the word *Film* in their *Filmtitle*:

```
SELECT CHARINDEX( 'Film', Filmtitle ) FROM tblFilms
```

The function *PATINDEX ('%Pattern%' , Expression)* returns the location in the expression where *Pattern* first appears. *PATINDEX* is more powerful than *CHARINDEX* because the function allows the use of placeholder characters such as % and _ (representing the wildcards such as used with operator *LIKE*) for inputting the pattern. Using the function

```
SELECT PATINDEX( '%Film%', Filmtitle ) FROM tblFilms
```

you get a list of positions where the word *Film* occurs in the film title. Using the function

```
SELECT PATINDEX( '%m__er%', Surname ) FROM Addresses
```

you can identify the occurrences of *miler, mayer, mixer,* and so on, in the *Surname* column of a list of addresses.

The *REPLACE* Function

Using *REPLACE (String_ Expression1, String_ Expression2 , String_ Expression3)* you can replace all occurrences of *String_ Expression2* in *String_ Expression1* with *String_ Expression3*. The function returns the edited *String_ Expression1*. In the following query, for example, using the nested *REPLACE* functions replaces all umlauts (German extended characters) with their English keyboard equivalents:

```
SELECT REPLACE(REPLACE(REPLACE(Description, 'ä',
'ae'),'ü','ue'),'ö','oe') FROM tblProducts
```

The *REVERSE* Function

The *REVERSE(Character_Expression)* function returns the characters of the character strings in reverse order.

Working with the Date Function

Many applications handle date values. For calculation of dates, the relevant functions (see Table 9-3) should be used, as they take into consideration leap years, the different number of days in the different months, and much more. Further information and examples are given in the following sections.

Internal Date and Time Display

Using *datetime* values, date values and times from 1/1/1753 up to 12/31/9999 can be described. Internally, date values are represented as digits, where each date is assigned a unique value (1/1/1900 is equal to a 0 value), so, for example, 1/1/2005 is represented internally by 38,353.

For times, 24 hours is equal to a value of 1. The time 12:00 noon is represented by 0.5, 6:00 P.M. by 0.75, and so on. The value 38,353.25 corresponds to 1/1/2005, 6:00 A.M.

In Access, the date and time values are represented in much the same way, but there is one essential difference: Day 1 in Access is 12/31/1899. In addition, date values from 1/1/100 can be processed. However, Microsoft Office programs are not consistent: In Microsoft Excel, Day 1 is 1/1/1900 and dates prior to this cannot be coded.

The different internal representations of Access and SQL Server/MSDE can impact programming routines dependent on absolute date values. The example presented next illustrates this problem.

The following stored procedure first creates a table that is populated with date values from 12/29/1899 up to 1/2/1900. You might not have any applications with date values in this time period, but the values clearly show the differences between SQL Server/MSDE and Access.

```
CREATE PROCEDURE "TestDate"

AS

        -- Create table

        CREATE TABLE DateTest (Date DATETIME)


        -- Fill table

        INSERT INTO DateTest VALUES ('12/29/1899')

        INSERT INTO DateTest VALUES ('12/30/1899')

        INSERT INTO DateTest VALUES ('12/31/1899')

        INSERT INTO DateTest VALUES ('01/01/1900')

        INSERT INTO DateTest VALUES ('01/02/1900')

RETURN
```

The following program can be used to read the date values in the table. The date and the internal representations in SQL Server and Access are directly output in a Microsoft Visual Basic editor. The *CONVERT* function is used to convert the date in SQL Server to the internal number, as described in greater detail later. The ADO data access interface, presented in Part III, "Programming with ADO," is used for data access.

```
Sub DatesTest()

 Dim rec As ADODB.Recordset


 Set rec = New ADODB.Recordset


 rec.Open "SELECT Date, CONVERT(NUMERIC(8,2),Date) AS SerNumber _
 FROM DateTest", _
 CurrentProject.Connection, _
 adOpenStatic, _
 adLockReadOnly


 Debug.Print "Date", "SQL Server", "Access"
 Do Until rec.EOF
 Debug.Print rec!Date, rec!SerNumber, Format(rec!Date, "0")
 rec.MoveNext
 Loop
 rec.Close
 Set rec = Nothing


End Sub
```

The program produces the following output:

```
Date SQL Server Access
12/29/1899 -3 -1
00:00:00 -2 0
```

```
12/31/1899 -1 1
```

```
01/01/1900 0 2
```

```
01/02/1900 1 3
```

The *Date* column format is interesting here, as the display for 12/31/1899 is restricted by Access to time only. This is because the formatting routine for date values assumes that when the date part of a *datetime* variable is equal to 0, then probably only a time value is stored in the variable.

In general, the different internal representations of date and time values in SQL Server and Access pose no problem, as long as they do not attempt to compare the internal values.

The *DATEPART* Function

In the sample database table *tblWeeks*, the calendar weeks are listed in relation to the first day of the week in which a particular film is shown. The *Week* field is defined as *datetime*. The following query outputs the date of the first and last day as well as the weekday of each film's first showing for every week.

```
CREATE PROCEDURE Filmweek

AS

        SELECT

        Filmtitle,

        Week AS 'Week beginning',

        CASE DATEPART(dw,Week)

            WHEN 1 THEN 'Monday'

            WHEN 2 THEN 'Tuesday'

            WHEN 3 THEN 'Wednesday'

            WHEN 4 THEN 'Thursday'

            WHEN 5 THEN 'Friday'

            WHEN 6 THEN 'Saturday'

            WHEN 7 THEN 'Sunday'

        end,

        DATEADD(week,1,Week)-1 AS 'Week ending'

        FROM tblWeeks INNER JOIN tblFilms

            ON tblWeeks.Filmnr = tblFilms.Filmnr

RETURN
```

The *DATEPART* function returns a figure that is based on the date unit entered. Table 9-11 shows the possible date units.

Table 9-11   Date Units

Date Unit	Abbreviations	Description
Year	yy, yyyy	Year
Quarter	qq, q	Quarter
Month	mm, m	Month
Dayofyear	dy, y	Day of year
Day	dd, d	Day
Week	wk, ww	Week
Weekday	dw	Weekday (only for *DATEPART*)
Hour	hh	Hour
Minute	mi, n	Minute
Second	ss, s	Second
Millisecond	ms	Millisecond

Example: Determining the Calendar Week   The following example shows how the calendar week is determined according to European standards. European and American calculations of the calendar week differ, and SQL Server settings are based on American formats with default installation settings. The SQL Server *DATEPART* function is used in the procedure. The *CAST* function, which is also used in the example, is described in the next section.

```
'Determines the week according to european standards
CREATE PROCEDURE ISOweek

(@DATE datetime)
AS
BEGIN
 DECLARE @ISOweek INT
 SET @ISOweek = DATEPART(wk, @DATE) + 1 -
 DATEPART(wk, CAST( DATEPART( yy, @DATE ) AS CHAR(4) ) + '0104' )
-- Special case: 1st - 3rd Jan. can be counted as belonging to the
previous -- year
 IF ( @ISOweek = 0 )
 BEGIN
 DECLARE @Date2 datetime
```

```
SET @DATE2 = CAST( DATEPART( yy, @DATE ) - 1 AS CHAR(4) ) +
'12' + CAST( 24 + DATEPART( DAY, @DATE ) AS CHAR(2) )
-- Recursive call
EXEC @ISOWeek = ISOWeek @DATE2
SET @ISOWeek = @ISOWeek + 1
END
-- Special case: 29th - 31st Dec. can be counted as belonging to the
-- following year
IF ( ( DATEPART( mm, @DATE ) = 12 ) AND
( ( DATEPART( dd, @DATE ) - DATEPART( dw, @DATE) ) >= 28 ) )
SET @ISOweek=1
RETURN(@ISOweek)
END
```

Data Type Conversion

SQL Server/MSDE makes two data type conversion functions available, as described in the following sections.

Conversions Using *CAST*

The CAST function allows simple conversions of data types, and it takes the following standard form:

```
CAST( expression AS data_type )
```

Enter as *data_type* one of the data types given in Chapter 5, "Tables in Access Projects."

Conversions Using *CONVERT*

The conversion function *CONVERT* is capable of more conversions than *CAST*. In particular, the multiple possibilities for date and time conversions make *CONVERT* indispensable, using this format:

```
CONVERT( data_type [ ( length ) ] , expression [ , style ] )
```

The *expression* parameter is converted to the *data_type* entered. For data types with variable lengths, it is possible to agree on a corresponding *length*. The conversion can be further controlled using the optional *style* parameter. Possible *style* properties are listed in Table 9-12.

Table 9-12   Conversion Details

Constants (Year Two Places)	Constants (Year Four Places)	Standard	Output
–	0 or 100	Standard	mon dd yyyy hh:miA.M. (or P.M.)
1	101	USA	mm/dd/yy
2	102	ANSI	yy.mm.dd
3	103	British/French	dd/mm/yy
4	104	German	dd.mm.yy
5	105	Italian	dd-mm-yy
6	106		dd mon yy
7	107		mon dd, yy
8	108		hh:mi:ss
–	9 or 109	Standard with milliseconds	mon dd yyyy hh:mi:ss.mmmmAM (or PM)

Converting To Date Only

The SQL Server function *GETDATE()* returns a *DateTime* value that contains the current date and the time on the SQL Server machine. If you need a *DateTime* value that contains only the date, you can do the corresponding conversion using *convert(datetime,convert(char(10),GETDATE(),101))*.

> **Note**   SQL Server/MSDE does not have a *FORMAT()* function to format the expression's output. To format your results, use the text and conversion functions. In forms and reports you can also use the VBA formatting instructions recognized by Access mdb databases.

Overview of Data Type Conversions

Table 9-13 illustrates in which cases SQL Server is implicitly converted, when you must use *CONVERT* or *CAST* to convert, and for which data types a conversion is possible.

Table 9-13   Explicit and Implicit Data Type Conversions

	binary	varbinary	char	varchar	nchar	nvarchar	datetime	smalldatetime	decimal	float	real	int	smallint	tinyint	Money	smallmoney	bit	timestamp	uniqueidentifier	image	ntext	text
binary		i	i	i	i	i	i	i	i	n	n	i	i	i	i	i	i	i	i	i	n	n
varbinary	i		i	i	i	i	i	i	i	n	n	i	i	i	i	i	i	i	i	i	n	n
char	e	e		i	i	i	i	i	i	i	i	i	i	i	i	e	e	i	e	i	i	i
varchar	e	e	i		i	i	i	i	i	i	i	i	i	i	i	e	e	i	e	i	i	i
nchar	i	i	e	e		e	e	e	e	e	e	e	e	e	e	i	i	e	i	e	n	e
nvarchar	i	i	e	e	e		e	e	e	e	e	e	e	e	e	i	i	e	i	e	n	e
datetime	i	i	e	e	e	e		e	i	i	i	i	i	i	i	i	i	n	n	n	n	n
smalldatetime	i	i	e	e	e	e	e		i	i	i	i	i	i	i	i	i	i	e	n	n	n
decimal	e	e	e	e	e	e	e	e		e	e	e	e	e	e	e	e	e	n	n	n	n
float	e	e	e	e	e	e	e	e	e		e	e	e	e	e	e	e	n	n	n	n	n
real	e	e	e	e	e	e	e	e	e	e		e	e	e	e	e	e	n	n	n	n	n
int	e	e	e	e	e	e	e	e	e	e	e		e	e	e	e	e	n	n	n	n	n
smallint	e	e	e	e	e	e	e	e	e	e	e	e		e	e	e	e	n	n	n	n	n
tinyint	e	e	e	e	e	e	e	e	e	e	e	e	e		e	e	e	n	n	n	n	n
money	e	e	i	i	i	i	e	e	e	e	e	e	e	e		e	e	e	n	n	n	n
smallmoney	e	e	i	i	i	i	e	e	e	e	e	e	e	e	e		e	e	n	n	n	n
bit	e	e	e	e	e	e	e	e	e	e	e	e	e	e	e	e		e	n	n	n	n
timestamp	e	e	e	e	n	n	e	e	e	n	n	e	e	e	e	e	e		n	e	n	n
unique identifier	e	e	e	e	e	n	n	n	n	n	n	n	n	n	n	n	n		n	n	n
image	e	e	n	n	n	n	n	n	n	n	n	n	n	n	n	n	n	e	n		n	n
ntext	n	n	i	i	e	e	n	n	n	n	n	n	n	n	n	n	n	n	n	n		e
text	n	n	e	e	i	i	n	n	n	n	n	n	n	n	n	n	n	n	n	n	e	

i = implicit conversion ; e = explicit conversion necessary; n = no conversion allowed.

Sorting

The *ORDER BY* clause can be used to sort result values according to the columns you entered. The general form as part of a *SELECT* statement is as follows:

```
[ ORDER BY order_expression [ ASC | DESC ] ]
```

and makes ascending (*ASC*) or descending (*DESC*) sort orders possible, whereby *ASC* must not be explicitly entered, as it is the standard sort order type. If you wish to sort according to several fields simultaneously, enter the field names separated by commas.

Criteria with *WHERE*

You can use the *WHERE* clause to filter the required data. The options available are similar to those provided for Access queries with slightly different syntax. There are certain differences, especially for the specification of date and time, character strings, and placeholders, as described in the following sections.

Comparison Operators

You can use the comparison operators described in Table 9-14.

Table 9-14 Comparison Operators

Operator	Description
=	Equal to
!=	Not equal to
<>	Not equal to
<	Less than
<=	Less than or equal to
!<	Less than or equal to
>	Greater than
>=	Greater than or equal to
!>	Greater than or equal to
BETWEEN expr1 AND expr2	Between *expr1* and *expr2*
IS [NOT] NULL	Is (not) equal to *Null*
[NOT] LIKE	Comparison with wildcards (see Table 9-9)
expr [NOT] IN (val1, val2,...,valn)	Comparison with a value list

continued

Table 9-14   Comparison Operators   *(continued)*

Operator	Description
expr [NOT] IN (subquery)	Comparison with the resultset of a subquery (see the section entitled "Subqueries" later in this chapter)
ANY	Comparison with the resultset of a subquery (see "Subqueries" section)
SOME	Comparison with the resultset of a subquery (see "Subqueries" section)
ALL	Comparison with the resultset of a subquery (see "Subqueries" section)
[NOT] EXISTS	Comparison with the resultset of a subquery (see "Subqueries" section)

Comparisons with Character Strings

Remember that SQL Server/MSDE includes character strings with single quotation marks, as used in Chapter 8, "Stored Procedures." Double quotation marks are typically only used to indicate object names (for example, table names or column names). In this case, SQL Server/MSDE also allows brackets [and], although this does not conform to the ANSI SQL standard.

Uppercase and Lowercase Comparisons

By default, SQL Server/MSDE does not distinguish between uppercase and lowercase for comparisons in *WHERE* conditions (this can be configured on installation of SQL Server/MSDE; see Chapter 3, "Installation"). If uppercase and lowercase are to be considered for a comparison, convert the texts into binary data with *CONVERT(VARBINARY,text)*, as shown in the following example, or *CAST(text AS VARBINARY)*.

```
SELECT * FROM tblFilms
        WHERE CONVERT(VARBINARY, Filmtitle) = CONVERT(VARBINARY, N'Big
Momma"s House')
```

When comparing a character string (as in this example with *'Big Momma"s House'*), pay close attention to whether the field (in this case, *Filmtitle*) is created as *VARCHAR*, *CHAR/NVARCHAR*, or *NCHAR*. If it is an *NVARCHAR* or *NCHAR* field, then the character string must be written as *N'Big Momma"s House'*, so that the character string is also coded according to Unicode.

Comparisons with *LIKE*

For comparisons with the operator *LIKE*, SQL Server/MSDE uses other placeholder symbols (wildcards). Table 9-15 displays the differences compared with Access mdbs.

Table 9-15 Placeholders for *LIKE*

Description	Access Mdb/Jet	SQL Server/MSDE-ANSI-SQL
Any number of characters	*	%
Any character	?	_
A number	#	[0-9]
A single character within a specified range	For example, [f-o]	For example, [f-o]
A single character within a fixed quantity	For example, [aeiou]	For example, [aeiou]
All characters apart from the specified character	[!A]	[!A]
All characters apart from those in the specified range	For example, [!A-F]	For example, [^A-F]

Comparisons with Date and Time

Date and time values are normally specified in the formats common for the country concerned. In Germany, for example, this would be

```
SELECT * FROM tblWeeks WHERE Week < '10/15/2001'
```

Remember that date and time specifications, like character strings, must be enclosed within single quotation marks and not with the # symbol, as in Access mdb databases.

You can adjust the date format using the SQL command *SET DATEFOR-MAT option*. The values available for *option* are *mdy, dmy, ymd, ydm, myd*, and *dym*.

If your application is to be used internationally, your date specification must be interpreted independently of the date format. To ensure this, you must use the *CONVERT* function, as discussed earlier in the "Conversions Using CONVERT" section. For example, you could use this

```
SELECT * FROM tblWeeks

WHERE Week < CONVERT(datetime,'15.10.2001',104)
```

to obtain the correct result, regardless of the current language setting.

Comparisons with *NULL*

To check a column for *Null* values, you can use the commands *IS NULL* or *IS NOT NULL*. For example, to determine all films for which no duration is specified, you could use the following query:

```
SELECT * FROM tblFilms WHERE Length IS NULL
```

For further information on using *NULL*, see also the earlier section in this chapter, "The ISNULL Function".

> **Note**   When making *NULL* comparisons, always use the *IS NULL / IS NOT NULL* notation because the result for *= NULL* or *<> NULL* comparisons depends on whether the database configuration for *ANSI NULLS* is set. If the configuration for your database is *Yes*, then *= NULL* or *<> NULL* comparisons always return the value *Null*.

Aggregate Functions

You can use aggregate functions to perform calculations that refer to a result column (for example, determining the total of all values in a column, or finding the smallest value in a column). You can also use the *GROUP BY* command described in the next section, which causes the aggregate functions to be executed in the groups created by the command.

Table 9-16 provides an overview of the aggregate functions that you can use.

Table 9-16   Aggregate Functions

Function	Description
AVG([ALL | DISTINCT] expression)	Returns the average value of the values; *Null* values are ignored
*COUNT([[ALL | DISTINCT] expression] | *])*	Returns the number of values
MAX([ALL | DISTINCT] expression)	Returns the biggest value
MIN([ALL | DISTINCT] expression)	Returns the smallest value
SUM([ALL | DISTINCT] expression)	Returns the sum total of all values or all unique values (*DISTINCT*) in the specified expression; *Null* values are ignored

continued

Table 9-16 **Aggregate Functions** *(continued)*

Function	Description
STDEV(expression)	Returns the statistical standard deviation of all values in the specified expression
STDEVP(expression)	Returns the statistical standard deviation for a sample
VAR(expression)	Returns the statistical variance
VARP(expression)	Returns the statistical variance for a sample

Examples

With the following command

```
SELECT SUM(Amount) AS TotalSales FROM tblProductSales
```

you determine how many articles are sold in total. The following query

```
SELECT COUNT(*) AS 'Number of Weeks'
        FROM tblWeeks
        WHERE (FilmNr = 4)
```

determines for how many weeks film number 4 was shown.

Groups

You can use the *GROUP BY* command to group the result of a query by one or more columns. In the following example, the total of the sold articles is specified for each article number:

```
SELECT ProductNr, SUM(Amount) AS TotalSales
        FROM tblProductSales
GROUP BY ProductNr
```

In the next example, shown in Figure 9-8, a view is created that determines how moviegoer attendance is distributed across the individual days of the week. The *DATEPART* function is used with the date unit *weekday*, which determines the day of the week for a date. Groups are formed per day of the week.

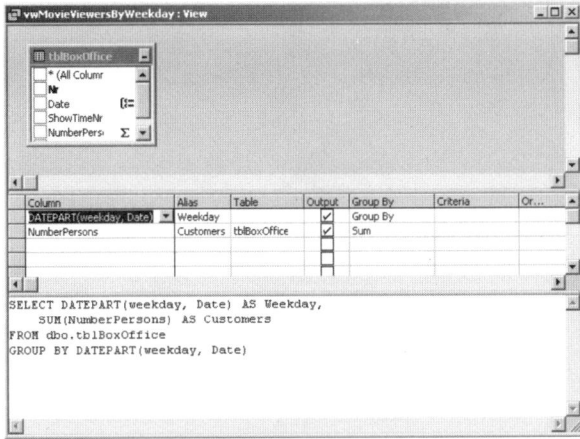

Figure 9-8   Query with *GROUP BY*

Figure 9-9 displays the result of the query. Remember that the result is not sorted because SQL Server/MSDE does not sort grouped data automatically, unlike Access database.

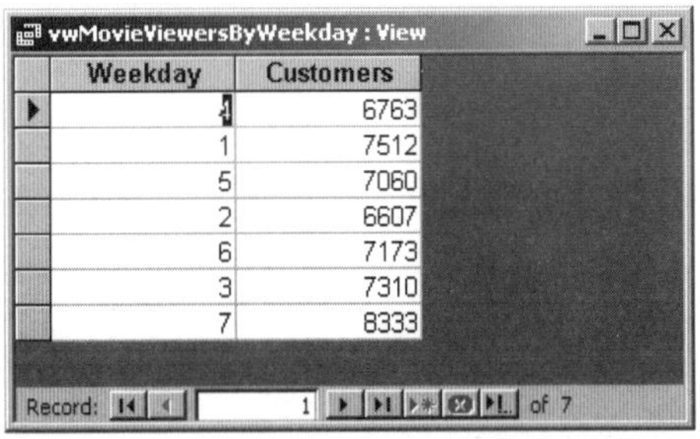

Figure 9-9   Result of the query

The *HAVING* Clause

You can use the *HAVING* SQL command to restrict grouped data. The *HAVING* clause is used much like a *WHERE* command, although it always refers only to the groups of a *GROUP BY* command.

The following view determines all films that have run for longer than four weeks. The condition is set using the *HAVING* clause, as seen in Figure 9-10.

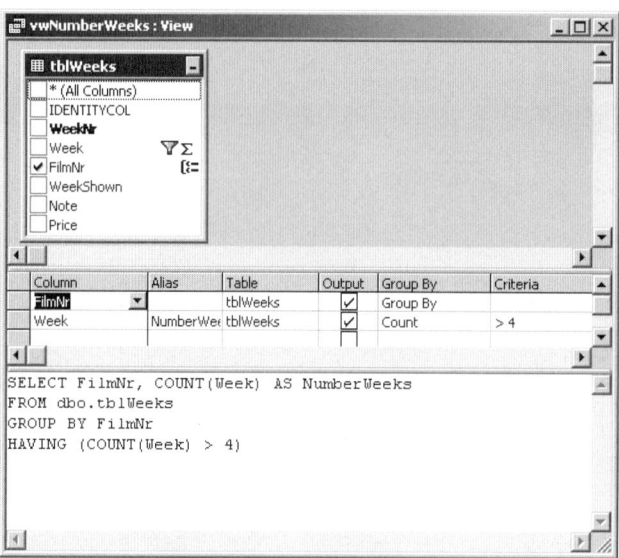

Figure 9-10 Query with *HAVING* clause

If you only want to evaluate all films with a film number greater than 5, you must add this as a *WHERE* condition, because the restriction must be put in place before the weeks are counted, as shown in Figure 9-11.

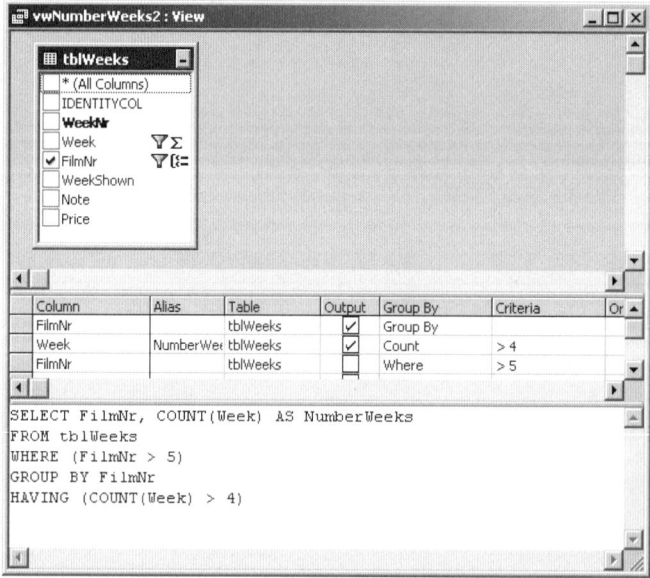

Figure 9-11 Query with *WHERE* and *HAVING* clauses

DISTINCT

You can use the *DISTINCT* command to remove duplicated records. The following query, for example, lists all articles that were sold in January 2000. Because articles in this time period were, of course, sold several times, the *DISTINCT* command is used to output each article number with its name only once.

```
SELECT DISTINCT
    TblProducts.ProductNr,
    tblProducts.Description
FROM dbo.tblProducts INNER JOIN dbo.tblProductSales
    ON dbo.tblProducts.ProductNr = dbo.tblProductSales.ProductNr
WHERE
    (dbo.tblProductSales.Date BETWEEN
    CONVERT(DATETIME, '2000-01-01 00:00:00', 102) AND
    CONVERT(DATETIME, '2000-01-31 00:00:00', 102))
```

In views, you can activate *DISTINCT* in the query properties by selecting View, then Properties, resulting in the Properties dialog box shown in Figure 9-12.

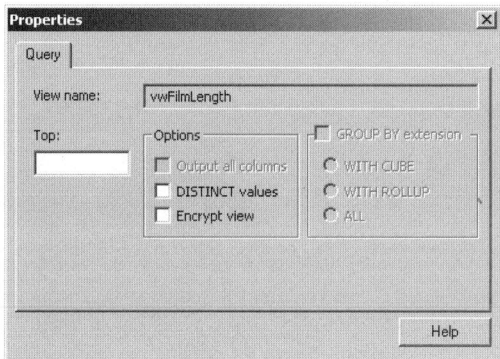

Figure 9-12   Properties of a view

SELECT TOP

You can use the *TOP* supplement to restrict the number of returned records for select queries. The full syntax is as follows:

```
SELECT TOP n [PERCENT] [WITH TIES]
```

where *n* is the number of returned lines or *PERCENT* is the percentage of the lines of the entire result. For example,

```
SELECT TOP 5 Filmtitle, Length FROM tblFilms ORDER BY Length DESC
```

returns the five films with the longest duration. If you specify

```
SELECT TOP 20 PERCENT
        SUM(SalesPrice * Amount) AS Gross, Description
        FROM tblProducts INNER JOIN tblProductSales
        ON tblProducts.ProductNr = tblProductSales.ProductNr
GROUP BY tblPoducts.Description
ORDER BY SUM(SalesPrice * Amount) DESC
```

then of all articles, the 20 percent with the best sales results are listed.

The *WITH TIES* supplement takes duplicated values into account when calculating the result. If, for example, the query were specified as

```
SELECT TOP 2
        Description, SUM(Amount) AS Amount
        FROM tblProducts INNER JOIN tblProdcutSales
        ON tblProducts.ProductNr = tblProdcutSales.ProductNr
GROUP BY tblProducts.Description
ORDER BY SUM(Amount) DESC
```

then the result would be as follows:

```
Popsicle          1371
Soft Ice Cream    1370
```

If you formulate the query with the *WITH TIES* supplement as

```
SELECT TOP 2 WITH TIES
        Description, SUM(Amount) AS Amount
        FROM tblProducts INNER JOIN tblProductSales
        ON tblProducts.ProductNr = tblProductSales.ProductNr
```

```
GROUP BY tblProducts.Decription
ORDER BY SUM(Amount) DESC
```

then the result would be as follows:

```
Popsicle             1371
Soft Ice Cream       1370
Lemonade             1370
```

> **Note**   In versions of SQL Server earlier than Micrsoft SQL Server 7, the number of lines that a select query returned was restricted by *SET ROWCOUNT*. The command is still supported for stored procedures, but should be replaced with *SELECT TOP*.

Links with *JOIN*

If you want to generate results columns for two or more tables simultaneously, you must link them. To create a join, use the *INNER JOIN, LEFT JOIN, RIGHT JOIN*, and other variants on the *JOIN* command. The different JOIN variants are described in Chapter 7, "Views."

You can, for example, use *INNER JOIN* to combine records from two tables as soon as corresponding values are determined for the *ON* condition in both tables. The following example determines all the film titles and the calendar weeks in which the films are shown:

```
SELECT
        tblFilms.Filmtitle,
        tblWeeks.Week
FROM
        tblFilms INNER JOIN tblWeeks
        ON tblFilms.FilmNr = tblWeeks.FilmNr
```

DISTINCTROW Command Is Not Supported

One of the major differences between SQL Server/MSDE and Access mdb in the area of *JOIN* comands is that SQL Server/MSDE does not support the *DISTINCTROW* command. *DISTINCTROW* is an Access SQL enhancement that allows you to edit resultsets from queries with joined tables. In the case of one-to-many relationships between the tables, for example, Access and the combination of Access 2002 with SQL Server 2000 support changes on both the "one" side and the "many" side. In Access 2000 and Access 2002 with SQL Server 7 and Access 2000 with SQL Server 2000 the data in views in which *JOIN*s occur can therefore not be edited.

If you use this kind of view as the basis for an Access form, then you can set the new property *Unique Table*, which allows you to process data in views with *JOIN* commands. For further information, see Chapter 10, "Forms."

UNION Queries

The *UNION* command is used to combine several query results into a single result, where the result can only be read. This is the complete syntax:

Select-statement1

UNION [ALL]

Select- statement2

[UNION [ALL]

Select- statement3]

[...]

All *SELECT* queries must generate the same number of columns, but the names of the columns are unimportant, because Access combines the columns. The column titles are always taken from the column name of the first *SELECT* query.

By default, Access eliminates duplicated records when executing the *UNION* command. If you are using the optional *ALL* parameter, then the duplicated records are retained. This option can considerably accelerate the execution of *UNION* queries, especially for large data stocks.

You can include only fields with data types *text*, *ntext*, or *image* in a *UNION* query if you are using *UNION ALL*.

Sorting *UNION* Queries

If you want the result of a *UNION* to be sorted, then add an *ORDER BY* statement to the last *SELECT* command. Only the sorting with *ORDER BY* of the last *SELECT* command is evaluated, even if sorting is also defined for the other *SELECT* commands. Remember that the column names of the *ORDER BY* for the last *SELECT* command refer to the column names of the first *SELECT* command.

Implicit Data Type Conversions

If the data types of a column of the *UNION* statement are not of the same type, as in the following example:

```
SELECT ProductNr, Description
FROM tblProducts
UNION
SELECT FilmNr, Filmtitle
FROM tblFilms
```

where the *ProductNr* has data type *nvarchar* and the *FilmNr* is an *int* value, then an implicit conversion is carried out. During implicit conversion, SQL Server/MSDE works according to the following hierarchy:

```
datetime > smalldatetime > float > real > decimal > money > smallmoney
> int > smallint > tinyint > bit > ntext > text > image > timestamp >
nvarchar > nchar > varchar > char > varbinary > binary >
uniqueidentifier
```

In this example, SQL Server/MSDE would attempt to convert the *Pro-ductNr* into an *int* value, because *int* is above *nvarchar* in the hierarchy. For explicit data type conversion, you can use the functions *CASE* and *CONVERT*, as described earlier.

Examples

Imagine that the data from table *tblBoxOffice* is archived once a year. To do this, the data is added to table *tblBoxOfficeArchive*, which contains all cash register data from the previous year. To evaluate all the cash register data, you can join the tables using the following:

```
SELECT * FROM tblBoxOffice
UNION
SELECT * FROM tblBoxOfficeArchive
```

If you use *UNION ALL* instead of *UNION*, then SQL Server/MSDE does not delete all duplicated records. This usually speeds up the query considerably.

Subqueries

A subquery is a query within a query. You can use subqueries to formulate a range of questions in SQL that are either difficult or impossible to represent using *WHERE* clauses and *JOIN* commands. The following sections provide some examples of how subqueries can be applied.

Subqueries for Columns

The stored procedure in the following example contains two subqueries that are used to determine values for columns:

```
CREATE PROCEDURE "FilmLength"

AS

 SELECT

        Filmtitle,

        'First Week'=(SELECT MIN(wo.Week)

               FROM tblWeeks wo

               WHERE wo.Filmnr = tblFilms.Filmnr),

        'Last Week'=(SELECT MAX(wo.Week)

               FROM tblWeeks wo

               WHERE wo.Filmnr = tblFilms.Filmnr)

 FROM tblFilms

 RETURN
```

Subqueries for Criteria

If you use a subquery within a *WHERE* clause, you have three different options. The first, *WHERE Statement [NOT] IN (Select Query)*, determines whether a specified expression is part of the resultset returned by the subquery. In the second, *WHERE Column1 {= | <> | < | <= | > | >=}|{{ANY | SOME | ALL}} (Select Query)*, an expression is compared with the result of a subquery. The third, *WHERE [NOT] EXISTS (Select Query)*, can be used to determine whether a subquery returns resultsets. The following sections illustrate these different variants.

Check for Inclusion

You can use the *IN* operator to check for inclusion in a resultset. For example, you want to determine all articles sold in January 2000. The subquery determines the article numbers of all articles that were sold in the specified period. The full SQL query is as follows:

```
SELECT_
ProductNr, _
Description

FROM_
tblProducts

WHERE
ProductNr IN

        (SELECT ProductNr

 FROM tblProductSales

 WHERE Date BETWEEN

 CONVERT(DATETIME, '2000-01-01 00:00:00', 102) AND

 CONVERT(DATETIME, '2000-01-31 00:00:00', 102))
```

Remember that the subquery used with *IN* can only generate one result column. Otherwise, Access issues an error message.

The displayed question can also be determined by the query designer with a join query. For example:

```
SELECT DISTINCT

 TblProducts.ProductNr, tblProducts.Description

FROM

 dbo.tblProducts INNER JOIN dbo.tblProductSales

ON dbo.tblProducts.ProductNr = dbo.tblProductSales.ProductNr

WHERE (dbo.tblProductSales.Date BETWEEN

 CONVERT(DATETIME, '2000-01-01 00:00:00', 102) AND

 CONVERT(DATETIME, '2000-01-31 00:00:00', 102))
```

Most Access users prefer to use the solution with the join query, but this is not always the easiest option. Let us now reverse the question posed in the query: Which articles from table *tblProducts* were not sold in January 2000?

When using the query with the subquery, you only need to add a single *NOT* command in front of *IN*, to obtain the correct query result: We determine all the article numbers that do not occur in the resultset of the subquery:

```
SELECT_

    ProductNr, _
    Description

FROM

    tblProducts
```

```
WHERE

        ProductNr NOT IN

        (SELECT ProductNr

            FROM tblProductSales

            WHERE Date BETWEEN

            CONVERT(DATETIME, '2000-01-01 00:00:00', 102) AND

            CONVERT(DATETIME, '2000-01-31 00:00:00', 102))
```

The result obtained from our example data is the one article not sold in January.

Comparisons with Results from Subqueries

Subqueries in the *WHERE* clause can also be used for comparisons with operators =, <, <=, >, and >=. For example, which films have a longer duration than the film "Gladiator"? Using a subquery that determines the length of the required film, you can filter out the films with longer durations. Remember that the subquery can only return a single value for comparison, not a range of values, as shown earlier for the *IN* operator:

```
SELECT

    tblFilms.Filmtitle, _
    tblFilms.Length

FROM

    tblFilms
WHERE

    tblFilms.Length > (SELECT Length FROM tblFilms WHERE
    Filmtitle ='Gladiator')

ORDER BY tblFilms.Length DESC
```

The second example shows that queries with subqueries can quickly become extremely complex and can also be combined with *JOIN*s. Which film has been seen by more viewers than "Gladiator"? The query compares the total number of film viewers for a film with the number of people who saw "Gladiator." Aagain, the subquery returns a single value that is used as a comparison criterion for all films in the table *tblFilms*:

```
SELECT

tblFilms.Filmtitle,

SUM(tblBoxOffice.NumberPersons) AS [Sum of NumberPersons]

FROM
```

```
tblFilms INNER JOIN tblWeeks

ON tblFilms.FilmNr = tblWeeks.FilmNr

INNER JOIN tblMovieSchedule

INNER JOIN tblBoxOffice

ON tblMovieSchedule.ShowTimeNr = tblBoxOffice.ShowTimeNr

ON tblWeeks.WeekNr = tblMovieSchedule.WeekNr

GROUP BY

tblFilms.Filmtitle

HAVING

(SUM(tblBoxOffice.NumberPersons)

>

(SELECT SUM(k.NumberPersons)

FROM (tblFilms AS f INNER JOIN tblWeeks AS w

ON f.FilmNr = w.FilmNr)

INNER JOIN (tblMovieSchedule AS t INNER JOIN tblBoxOffice AS k

ON t.ShowTimeNr = k.ShowTimeNr)

ON w.WeekNr = t.WeekNr

WHERE f.Filmtitle = 'Gladiator'))

ORDER BY

SUM(tblBoxOffice.NumberPersons) DESC
```

The operators =, <, <=, >, and >= can also be used if the subquery returns a data group. In this case, however, you must use the operators *ALL* and *ANY*. The following facts apply to the *ALL* operator:

- If the subquery has an empty column as a result, then the *ALL* test returns the value *True*.

- If the comparison with all data values that the subquery returns is true, then *ALL* also returns the value *True*.

- If the comparison with one of the data values of the subquery has the value not true, then *ALL* returns *False*.

- If none of the comparisons with the data values from the subquery return the value *False*, but one of the comparisons has the value *Null*, then the result of *ALL* is also *Null*.

The following facts apply to the *ANY* operator:

■ If the subquery has an empty column as a result, then the *ANY* test returns the value *False*.

■ If the comparison with at least one of the data values that the subquery returns is true, then *ANY* also returns the value *True*.

■ If the comparison with all data values of the subquery has the value *False*, then *ANY* returns the value *False*.

■ If none of the comparisons with the data values from the subquery return the value *True*, but one of the comparisons has the value *Null*, then the result of *ANY* is also *Null*.

Subqueries with *EXISTS*

You can use the *EXISTS* command to determine whether a subquery returns a result. Queries with *EXISTS* normally use correlated subqueries. In these subqueries, a value from the surrounding query is used in the subquery condition (that is, for every value in the query, the subquery is executed with the corresponding condition). For which films from table *tblFilms* are there no entries in table *tblWeeks*? In the SQL query, the *FilmNr* of *tblFilms* is used in the subquery condition:

```
SELECT

    tblFilms.Filmtitle

FROM

    tblFilms

WHERE

    NOT EXISTS (SELECT * FROM tblWeeks WHERE tblFilms.FilmNr =
    tblWeeks.FilmNr)

ORDER BY

    tblFilms.Filmtitle
```

Action Queries

Action queries are queries with which data can be added, changed, or deleted.

UPDATE Queries

The following is the basic syntax for update queries.

```
UPDATE Table_or_View

    SET Column1 = Statement1 [, Column2 = Statement2] [,...]

    [WHERE Conditions]
```

If you are using the *UPDATE* command to update columns in a table, you must ensure that the query can be edited.

You can use the following simple example to increase the sales price for all articles by a given percentage:

```
CREATE PROCEDURE "PriceIncrease" @Perc DECIMAL

AS

        SET NOCOUNT ON

        UPDATE tblProducts SET SalesProce = SalesPrice * @Perc

RETURN
```

Appending Queries with *INSERT*

You can use the *INSERT* command to enter new records in an existing table. There are different variants for using *INSERT*, as described in the following sections.

Appending with *INSERT*

The first variant of the *INSERT* command

```
INSERT Destination_Table [(Column1 [, Column2 [,...]])]

VALUES (Value1 [, Value2 [,...]])
```

allows you to enter values directly into a table, for example:

```
INSERT tblFilms (Filmtitle, MPAANr, Length)

VALUES ("Titanic", 12, 194)
```

creates a new record for the movie "Titanic."

Appending with *INSERT SELECT*

You can use *INSERT SELECT* to insert result records from a *SELECT* query in another table:

```
INSERT Destination_Table [(Column1 [, Column2 [,...]])] Select Query
```

If you do not specify any target columns, then the column names of the query result must be the same as those of the target table.

Appending with *INSERT EXECUTE*

The third variant is *INSERT EXECUTE*, which allows you to insert the resultset of a stored procedure into a table:

```
INSERT Destination_Table [(column1 [, column2 [,...]])] EXEC[UTE]
Procedure [[@Parameter=] {value}]
```

Deleting Data with *DELETE*

DELETE deletes records from a table:

```
DELETE

[FROM] Table_Name

[WHERE Conditions]
```

> **Note**   You can use Access mdb *Delete* queries to delete data from several tables simultaneously. SQL Server/MSDE and standard SQL queries do not support this functionality.

Delete Condition with Subquery

If you want to specify additional conditions for the deletion, then you can use subqueries for the *WHERE* clause. In the following stored procedure, for example, all Movie Schedule entries are deleted that correspond to entries in the table *tblWeeks* that occurred before a specified date:

```
CREATE PROCEDURE qdelShowtimeANSI

AS

DELETE FROM tblMovieSchedule

WHERE tblMovieSchedule.WeekNr in

        (select WeekNr FROM tblWeeks

        WHERE tblWeeks.Week <= '31/12/1999')
```

Delete Condition with Related Tables

Although *Delete* queries in Access mdb are often defined with related tables rather than subqueries, it makes sense to transfer this functionality to SQL Server/MSDE.

To enable the *DELETE* query to function with related tables, two consecutive *FROM* tables are needed. The first *FROM* displays in which table deletion is carried out, and the second *FROM* specifies the first table for the join:

```
CREATE PROCEDURE qdelShowTime

AS

DELETE

FROM tblMovieSchedule

FROM tblMovieSchedule INNER JOIN tblWeeks

          ON tblMovieSchedule.WeekNr = tblWeeks.WeekNr

WHERE tblWeeks.Week <= '31/12/1999'
```

The *DELETE* command with two *FROMs* is not standard SQL, but a specific variant of SQL Server. If you want to use a solution that conforms to ANSI SQL standards, then you must use subqueries, as described earlier.

Note   If you are transferring *Delete* queries with linked tables to an Access project using the Upsizing Wizard described in Chapter 16, "Upsizing Wizard," these are not created correctly because the process does not create two *FROMs*.

Resetting the Identity Value

Imagine that you are using a table in your Access application into which data is copied on a monthly basis. For example, every 1st day of the month, the data from the previous month is deleted, and the new data is inserted. The primary key of the table is an identity field in which a value is counted for every new record.

Normally, after deletion of all data in a table, the identity field is set further, starting with the value following the last assigned. If, for example, the system increments identity to 5000 and the table is then deleted, then the next value to be assigned is 5001. If you want to restart counting for the identity field at 1, use the *DBCC CHECKIDENT* command to reset the value.

The following stored procedure deletes the table whose name is passed as a parameter and then resets the identity value to 0, so that counting can restart at 1:

```
CREATE PROCEDURE "DeleteReseed" (@table nvarchar(64))
AS
        SET NOCOUNT ON
        -- Delete table
        EXEC ('DELETE ' + @table)
        -- Reset identity value to 0
        DBCC CHECKIDENT(@table,RESEED,0)
RETURN
```

Error Handling

During execution of stored procedures, run-time errors might occur (for example, during data insertion) if defined table restrictions or *NOT NULL* declarations for table fields are violated.

Error handling of SQL Server errors differs from error handling in VBA programs because when errors occur in a stored procedure, the system continues to process the rest of the procedure. In VBA, a run-time error always causes the program to terminate unless you have integrated suitable error handling. If you are familiar with VBA error handling, then you can configure error handling in stored procedures so that every procedure starts with *On Error Resume Next* and, when an error occurs, the next command will continue execution of the stored procedure.

There are very few errors that can terminate execution of a stored procedure. Most of these are fatal errors in SQL Server, such as insufficient memory or something similar. The system generally skips commands that trigger an error in a stored procedure and simply continues processing with the next command.

Error Classes

Every error has a level of severity, shown in Table 9-17, that specifies whether the error merely triggers a message, whether it was caused by the user (or by the user's stored procedure), or whether it is a critical system error. The SQL Server/MSDE system administrator should be informed of any errors occurring with severity levels between 17 and 24 because these errors usually require the entire system to be checked.

Table 9-17   **Levels of Severity**

Level of Severity	Description
1 to 10	For information messages
11 to 16	For errors that the user can solve
17	Insufficient resources
18	Medium-level internal error
19	SQL Server: Resource error
20	SQL Server: Fatal error in current process
21	SQL Server: Fatal error in database processes
22	SQL Server: Fatal error, table integrity questionable
23	SQL Server: Fatal error, database integrity questionable
24	Hardware error
25	Fatal error

The *@@ERROR* Function

After every command in a stored procedure, you can use the *@@ERROR* function to query whether an error has occurred. If the function returns a value not equal to 0, the preceding command triggered an error. *@@ERROR* always refers only to the immediately preceding command.

The *@@ERROR* function is used in the following procedure:

```
CREATE PROCEDURE PriceIncrease @Percentage REAL

AS

        SET NOCOUNT ON

        IF @Percentage IS NULL

                RETURN 0


        -- Price increase

        UPDATE tblProducts SET SalesPrice = SalesPrice * (1 +
@Percentage)

        IF @@ERROR > 0

        BEGIN

                SELECT 'Price increase could not be carried out!'

                RETURN 1
```

```
          END
          SET NOCOUNT OFF
          SELECT 'Price increase completed successfully!'
RETURN 0
```

When successful, this example procedure returns a value of 0. If unsuccessful, the returned value is 1. System stored procedures usually return a value of 0 indicating success, unless otherwise documented. The value returned with *RETURN* can only be read with an ADO program (see Chapter 14, "*Command Objects*"). For this reason, *SELECT* statements are also used to return a text that can be seen in the Access project user interface as the resultset of the procedure. Remember that the *SET NOCOUNT ON* and *SET NOCOUNT OFF* commands are needed so that Access can determine whether the procedure returns a resultset. If you do not use these commands, Access will not issue any resultsets and consequently no message texts.

If, when an error occurs (that is, when the value for the *@@ERROR* function is greater than 0), you want to issue a message informing the user of this value, then you cannot simply write this:

```
. . .

          -- Price increase

          UPDATE tblProducts SET SalesPrice = SalesPrice * (1 +
@Percentage)

          IF @@ERROR > 0

          BEGIN

               SELECT 'Price increase could not be carried out! (Error '
                         + CONVERT(VARCHAR, @@ERROR) + ')'

               RETURN 1

          END

. . .
```

If an error occurs during *UPDATE*, you will always receive the error message "Price increase could not be executed! (Error 0)," because the *@@ERROR* function always refers to the directly preceding command. In this example, to receive the actual error number, you must copy the *@@ERROR* value to a variable:

```
CREATE PROCEDURE PriceIncrease @Percentage REAL
AS
        DECLARE @ErrorValue INT

        SET NOCOUNT ON
        IF @Percentage IS NULL
            RETURN 1


        -- Price increase
        UPDATE tblProducts SET SalesPrice = SalesPrice * (1 +
@Percentage)
        SET @ErrorValue = @@ERROR
        IF @@ErrorValue > 0
        BEGIN
            SELECT 'Price increase could not be carried out! (Error '
                    + CONVERT(VARCHAR, @ErrorValue) + ')'


            RETURN 1
        END
        SET NOCOUNT OFF
        SELECT 'Price increase completed successfully!'
RETURN 0
```

> **Note**   If you are using transactions *(BEGIN TRANSACTION/COM-MIT TRANSACTION)* in a stored procedure (see Chapter 26, "Transactions and Locking"), then the *@@ERROR* function will only return a result that can be evaluated if you use the command *SET NOCOUNT ON* at the beginning of the transaction, and *SET NOCOUNT OFF* at the end.

The *RAISERROR* Command

You can use *RAISERROR* to trigger a user-defined error message for which you can configure the severity level. Severity levels 11 to 16 are the standard levels used in stored procedures. Remember that *RAISERROR* errors, which have a severity level of 0 to 10, are not forwarded to Access. The command takes the following standard form:

```
RAISERROR ({msg_id | msg_str}{, severity, state}
        [, argument [, ...n] )
        WITH option[,...n]]
```

The parameter *msg_id* specifies an error number. For further information on the predefined error numbers, see the next section "Error Messages." Alternatively, you can define your own error text with *msg_str*. This error then automatically receives error number 50,000.

The *severity* parameter defines the severity level of the error (see Table 9-17). You can specify any number between 1 and 127 as the *state*; this has no further significance for SQL Server. You can use *state* to provide additional information about an error.

Several *argument* parameters can be passed to the *RAISERROR* command. These are inserted in the placeholders within the error message. The *WITH* supplement allows you to transfer options; for example, *WITH LOG* is used to save the error to the Windows NT or Windows 2000 event log. For further information about these options, see the SQL Server online help.

The following code fragment shows *RAISERROR* being used with a user-defined message. The triggered error receives error number 50,000:

```
...

    -- Price increase

    UPDATE tblProducts SET SalesPrice = SalesPrice * (1 +
@Percentage)

    SET @ErrorValue = @@ERROR

    IF @@ErrorValue > 0

        RAISERROR ('Price increase could not be carried out!', 12,
1)

...
```

Error Messages

The predefined SQL Server/MSDE error messages are stored in the table *sysmessages* in the *master* database. The messages can be stored there in several languages. English error messages have the language setting *msglangid* =1033.

To display the error message in our Access project, we created the view shown in Figure 9-13.

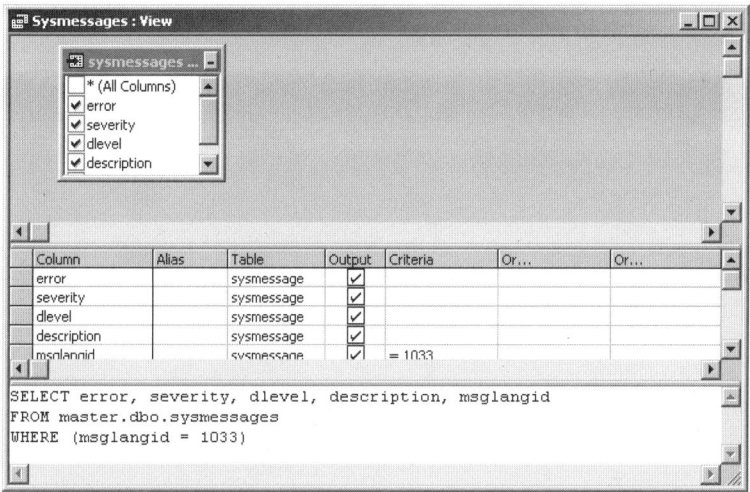

Figure 9-13   View for determining the error messages

You can use the *sp_addmessage* and *sp_dropmessage* system procedures to add or delete, respectively, user-defined error messages. For more information about these procedures, see Chapter 25, "System Stored Procedures," where all system stored procedures are listed alphabetically.

The *PRINT* Command

The Transact-SQL *PRINT* command issues a message in much the same way as the *Debug.Print* command in VBA. Unfortunately, *PRINT* cannot be used when working with Access projects, as the messages issued with *PRINT* do not reach Access (that is, they are not displayed and cannot be queried).

If you execute stored procedures using SQL Server Query Analyzer (see Chapter 19, "SQL Server Tools"), the system displays the *PRINT* messages.

Temporary Tables

SQL Server/MSDE allows you to create temporary tables in which subtotals or similar values can be stored. There are two types of temporary tables:

- Local temporary table IDs begin with #. These tables are accessible only via the connection that created them. From an Access project, every stored procedure works with its own connection. As a result, a temporary table created in a stored procedure is available only during execution of the procedure. The temporary table is deleted as soon as the procedure is completed.

- Global temporary table IDs begin with ##. These tables can be used regardless of connection, but are available only when the program that created them is connected to SQL Server/MSDE. A global temporary table could, for example, be created in your application by a stored procedure, and then be read by a different procedure. SQL Server/MSDE deletes the table when the application is terminated.

Temporary tables are created in the *tempdb* system database. Make sure that there is sufficient disk space for this database. In the standard configuration, *tempdb* is created on the hard disk drive on which SQL Server/MSDE software is installed.

The example in Figure 9-14 displays a procedure in which a temporary table is created, filled with three records, and then returned as the resultset.

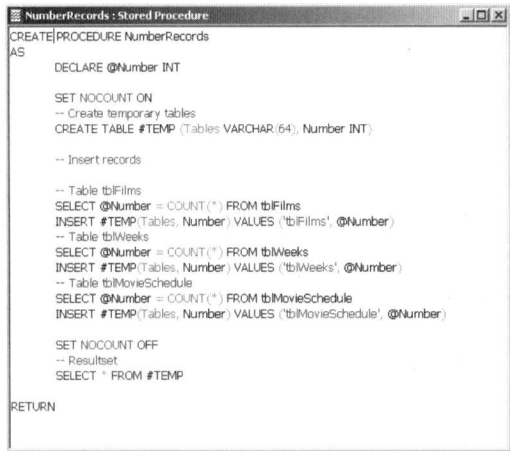

Figure 9-14   Example with temporary table

Programming a Cursor

The commands you have learned so far for programming stored procedures allow you to query resultsets and to use control structures, where necessary, to control the program flow using the procedure. You still need to learn how to view resultsets in the stored procedure record by record. You can do so using a cursor. If you are familiar with the DAO or ADO programming interfaces, then you will recognize similarities in recordsets and loops such as *DO WHILE NOT rs.EOF ... LOOP*.

Chapter 8, "Stored Procedures," in the section entitled "Loops," describes the procedure *AllFilms*, with which you can generate a list of all film titles, separated by semicolons. This example is used here in conjunction with a cursor:

```
CREATE PROCEDURE AllFilmtitlesWithCursor

AS

        DECLARE @strFilmtitle VARCHAR(4000)

        DECLARE @strTmp VARCHAR(500)


        DECLARE cursorFilms CURSOR FOR

            SELECT Filmtitle FROM tblFilms ORDER BY FilmTitle


        -- Initialize string;

        -- this is necessary because after the declaration the
variable

    -- has the value NULL.

        -- When @s + 'String' is built, NULL is again produced.

        SET @strFilmtitle = ''


        -- Open cursor

        OPEN cursorFilms

        -- Retrieve first record, save Filmtitle in @strTmp

        FETCH NEXT FROM cursorFilms INTO @strTmp

        -- As long as FETCH can retrieve a record

        WHILE @@FETCH_STATUS = 0
```

```
    BEGIN
        -- build Filmtitle string
        SET @strFilmtitle = @strFilmtitle + @strTmp + ';'
        -- Retrieve next record
        FETCH NEXT FROM cursorFilms INTO @strTmp
    END
    -- Close cursor
    CLOSE cursorFilms
    -- Free memory allocated for cursor
    DEALLOCATE cursorFilms


    -- Resultset
    SELECT @strFilmtitle AS 'AllTitles'


RETURN 0
```

Cursor Declaration

To work with a cursor, a corresponding cursor variable (*cursorFilms* in the current example) must be declared. The simplest syntax for the declaration is as follows:

```
DECLARE cursor_name [SCROLL] CURSOR
    FOR select_statement
```

The resultset for the *SELECT* command can be edited using the cursor. This means that records in the resultset can be changed and updated, or you can add new records if the *SELECT* command meets the relevant requirements (in other words, provided it does not contain *DISTINCT*, *GROUP BY*, and so forth).

If you use the *SCROLL* command, then the record pointer can be placed at any point in the resultset; otherwise the resultset can be run only from start to finish.

In the variant described here, cursors are global, so an opened cursor can be used by different stored procedures.

SQL Server/MSDE implements two variants of the cursor declaration: SQL-92-compliant or SQL Server-specific. Both variants have more commands than described here. For the full syntax, see the SQL Server online documentation.

The *OPEN* Command

A cursor must be opened before it is used. This is done with the *OPEN cursor_name* command.

The *FETCH* Command

To set the record pointer for the cursor and, if necessary, to copy the data from the current data line into the variables, use the *FETCH* command:

```
FETCH

[ [ NEXT | PRIOR | FIRST | LAST

| ABSOLUTE { n | @nvar }

| RELATIVE { n | @nvar }

]

FROM

]

{ cursor_name }

[ INTO @variable_name [ ,...n ] ]
```

You can use *NEXT* to fetch the next record, *PRIOR* to fetch the previous record, and *FIRST* and *LAST* to fetch the first and last records, respectively. *ABSOLUTE* and *RELATIVE* allow you to position the record pointer exactly over a line number.

You can use the *INTO* supplement to copy the columns of the current record for the cursor into variables. Remember that the sequence and the data type of the variables must agree with the columns of the cursor resultset.

System Function *@@FETCH_STATUS*

You can use the *@@FETCH_STATUS* system function to determine whether a *FETCH* command was successful. If the variable has the value 0, then the record was successfully accessed with *FETCH*. If –1 is returned, for example, then the end of the resultset has been reached. If the variable has the value –2, then the required record cannot be fetched because, for example, it might have already been deleted.

> **Note**   The use of cursors entails a significant drain on system resources and additional administration work for the server, especially if several users have opened the same cursor. Where possible, you should minimize the use of cursors so that server performance is not negatively influenced.

The *CLOSE* and *DEALLOCATE* Commands

You use the *CLOSE* command to close a cursor and the *DEALLOCATE* command to delete it from the server memory. As long as the cursor is not deallocated, it can be opened again using *OPEN*, either by the same stored procedure or by a different one.

Part II

Forms and Reports

When working with forms and reports in Access projects, there are a number of new features and changes regarding forms and reports in Access mdb databases to be aware of.

The majority of changes can be attributed to the fact that queries are run directly on the SQL server or MSDE server, so no links to a client form control can be used. The use of stored procedures as a data source for forms and for the combo box and list box controls is also explained.

10

Forms

This chapter describes the new functions and changes in the creation and use of forms in Access projects compared to Access mdbs. You will learn about restrictions and a number of new properties.

Forms in Access projects are essentially the same as the forms used in regular Microsoft Access databases, so this chapter focuses on the new functions and changes and does not cover all of the options available for working with forms in Access.

The choice to use Microsoft SQL Server/MSDE is often motivated by the presence of large amounts of data or numerous simultaneous users. In terms of programming, however, a lot of data and many users mean using different procedures than those required for Access mdbs, which are designed for single workstations or small networks. With SQL Server/MSDE you must avoid sending large amounts of data to a client over the network and you must make sure that editing data does not affect the work and pace of other users. Throughout the chapter, we point out techniques to help optimize your forms in Access projects.

Record Source

Regular Access mdb forms can be based on tables and queries. With forms for Access projects, you can select tables, views, and stored procedures as record sources, as shown in Figure 10-1.

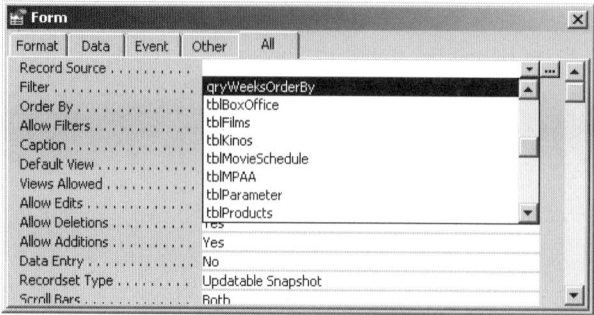

Figure 10-1   Record source selection

You can use wizards for support in creating a form, even though the wizards for diagrams and PivotTables are not available. Be sure to use the wizard only to select tables and views for the record source. If you want to use a stored procedure, you can select it as the record source only in the form's Design view. We discuss the use of stored procedures as the record source for forms later in this chapter.

Tables, views, and stored procedures are listed together and in alphabetical order in the *Record Source* combo box. The list does not specify whether a name refers to a table, view, or stored procedure, so we recommend that you name your objects so that their names reveal their sources. For example, you could use *tbl*, *vw*, or *sp* as a prefix in front of every name. Please refer to Appendix A, "Naming Conventions," for guidelines on naming objects.

Also, the combo box only lists objects for which you have access permissions, so if you have permission to access other users' objects, these are also listed. The names of these objects are preceded by the owner's name, such as, for example,*alex.vwSalesRevenue*.

There are several known errors related to using the form to access tables that you do not own, while you are using filters, for example (see the section later in this chapter entitled "Form Filters"). We recommend using the naming convention *Owner.Table* and placing the owner's name as a prefix in front of the table name, for example, *dbo.tblFilms*.

We also recommend that you use *Record Source* tables or views as part of complete *SELECT* queries only, instead of simply entering the table or view name. The *SELECT* command can sometimes prevent the occurrence of errors and side effects, especially in cases where the owner of the form is not the owner of the tables on which the form is based.

Microsoft Access 2002 introduced the new property *Record Source Qualifier*. You can use this property to specify the record source owner, so that you no longer need to explicitly enter the owner's name in the query.

> **Note**   The system displays the form's primary key field underlined in blue like a hyperlink if you use the wizard to create your new form on a computer on which the data access library ADO version 2.6 is installed. This version is included, for example, with Microsoft SQL Server 2000.

Stored Procedure as Record Source

There are a few restrictions you must keep in mind when using a stored procedure as the *Record Source*. For example, if you use the *DoCmd.OpenForm* command from a Microsoft Visual Basic for Applications (VBA) program to open a form that includes a *WHERE* clause (*WhereCondition*)

```
DoCmd.OpenForm "frmFilms", , ,"Filmtitle like 'D%'"
```

the system ignores the *WHERE* clause if the specified form's record source is a stored procedure. The system also doesn't apply a specified filter (parameter *FilterName*).

In the later section "Opening Forms with VBA," we introduce alternatives for working around these restrictions.

The Query Builder

As an alternative to making selections in the combo box, you can directly enter a SQL command as a *Record Source* as well. The query builder can assist you with creating the SQL command. To open the query builder, use the button with the ellipses to the right of the *Record Source* field.

The query builder opens whenever the *Record Source* field is empty or contains a SQL command. If you specify the name of a view as the record source, the query designer opens instead of the query builder. There are some differences between the query builder and the query designer, described next.

Note that if you specified a stored procedure as the record source, the button opens the designer for stored procedures.

The query builder works similar to the query designer for views. In addition, with the builder, you can use the columns *Sort Type* and *Sort Order* to define sort criteria.

In Figure 10-2, the table *tblProducts* was added to the query builder's diagram areas and the columns *ProductNr* and *Description* were designated for output.

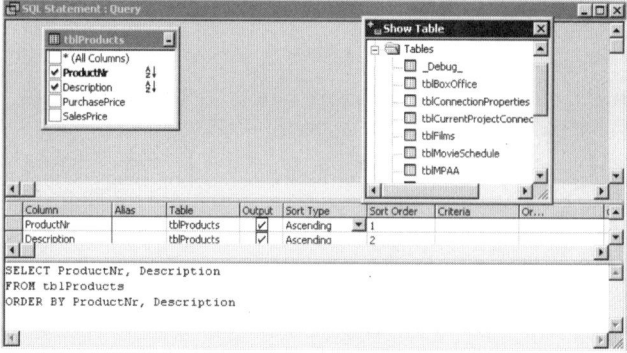

Figure 10-2   Query builder

Ascending was specified for both *Sort Type* columns. The entry in the *Sort Order* column defines the sort sequence for the columns in the *ORDER BY* clause. This function differs from the query design function for Access mdb queries, where the column's position in the query design determines the sort order.

Record Source with *EXEC*

If you want to use a stored procedure with a parameter as the record source for a form, and if the parameter's value is strictly defined so it does not change, you can use the *EXEC ProcedureName Parameter* command to specify the stored procedure as the form's record source, for example, *EXEC spFilms 1*. This command works just like defining the row source for combo boxes and list boxes.

If you enter a character string as the parameter, you must enclose it in single quotation marks, for example *EXEC spFilmtitle 'Gladiator'*.

> **Note**   With stored procedures and in the SQL Server Query Analyzer (see Chapter 19, "SQL Server Tools"), you can use *EXEC* as well as the command's long version, *EXECUTE*, to activate stored procedures. However, if you use this command with the *Record Source* property (for forms) or *Row Source* (for control elements), you can use *EXEC* only.

Record Source with ADO Recordset

You can also assign an ADO recordset directly to a form. See Chapter 13, "Recordset Objects," for a detailed description of ADO recordsets. For example, if you open a form, an assignment might look like this:

```
Dim mConn As ADODB.Connection

Dim mRec As New ADODB.Recordset


Private Sub Form_Load()

 Set mConn = CurrentProject.Connection

 mRec.Open "SELECT FilmNr, Filmtitle from tblFilms", _

 mConn, _

 adOpenStatic, _

 adLockOptimistic


 ' Assign to form

 Set Me.Recordset = mRec

End Sub
```

> **Note**   If a form is based on an ADO recordset, you can use aggregate functions such as *sum*, *count*, and so on, in the form. For example, if a form footer contains a text field with the string *=Sum([Field])*, the field returns the value *#Error* if you did not define a *Record Source*, but assigns an ADO recordset instead, as shown in the preceding listing.

Editing Data in Forms

In most cases, forms are used to edit data. This section describes the differences between Access project forms and mdb forms.

New Buttons

The form view, just like the datasheet view, comes with two new navigation buttons: Cancel Query and Maximum Record Limit. The functions of both buttons are described in Chapter 5, "Tables in Access Projects."

The form's properties provide you with the options Max Records and Max Rec Button. Use Max Records to specify the number of records to read and Max Rec Button to specify whether you want to display the Max Records button in the form view.

The *RecordsetType* Property

The form properties include *RecordsetType*, which you can use to define whether the changes made to the contents of the form's fields can be saved. This property can have one of two values: *Snapshot*, with which no changes are possible, and *Updatable Snapshot*, with which changes are possible under certain conditions; that is, you can make changes to the extent that doing so is permitted by the table, view, or stored procedure on which the form is based.

Joined Tables as Record Source

If a form refers only to one table's data, and if this table has a primary key, you can edit the data in the table. This applies to Access mdb as well as to adp projects.

When updating data in Access mdbs, the system conveniently provides you with forms. If a form is based on a query that joins several tables, depending on the query, you can edit the contents of the form's fields, even if the fields belong to different tables. We provide an illustrative example next. Figure 10-3 shows a query with two joined tables.

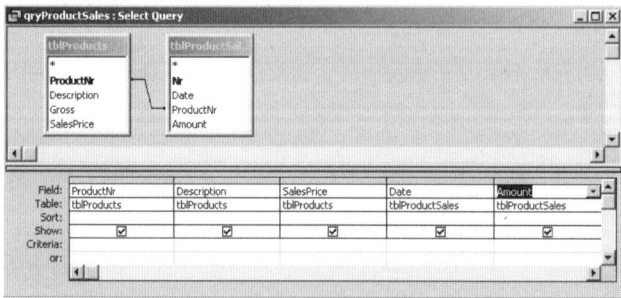

Figure 10-3 Query with joined tables

The query itself is as follows:

```
SELECT
    tblProducts.ProductNr,
    tblProducts.Description,
    tblProducts.SalesPrice,
    tblProductSales.Date,
    tblProductSales.Count
FROM tblProducts
    INNER JOIN tblProductSales
ON tblProducts.ProductNr = tblProductSales.ProductNr;
```

This query is the *Record Source* for the form shown in Figure 10-4.

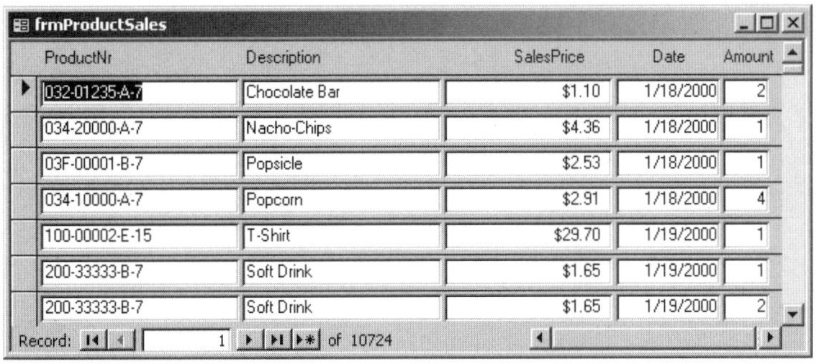

Figure 10-4 Sample form in tabular display format

Note For some cases in mdbs, Access uses the Access-specific SQL command *DISTINCTROW*, which ensures that data is unique and can be edited. SQL Server and MSDE do not support the *DISTINCTROW* command, and you must remove it from all SQL queries.

In our example form, you can edit the data in the *tblProducts* table, such as changing a product name, and the contents of the *tblProductSales* table, such as changing the quantity. There are very few databases that support editing both sides of a one-to-many relationship, which is one of the strengths of Access and Jet Engine.

Unfortunately, this also only works if you use Access 2002 and SQL Server 2000. For any other combination you have to consider the following limitation: In an Access project form, you can edit only one table's data. This means that the system only saves changes made to one table, even if data from multiple tables is displayed.

Figure 10-5 illustrates the new properties required in this context. We used the Windows Clipboard to copy the form shown in Figure 10-4 from an .mdb file to an .adp file. The .adp is connected to *ContosoSQL* database.

ProductNr	Description	SalesPrice	Date	Amount
032-01235-A-7	Chocolate Bar	$1.10	1/18/2000	2
034-20000-A-7	Nacho-Chips	$4.36	1/18/2000	1
03F-00001-B-7	Popsicle	$2.53	1/18/2000	1
034-10000-A-7	Popcorn	$2.91	1/18/2000	4
100-00002-E-15	T-Shirt	$29.70	1/19/2000	1
200-33333-B-7	Soft Drink	$1.65	1/19/2000	1
200-33333-B-7	Soft Drink	$1.65	1/19/2000	2
200-12346-B-7	Milk Shake	$2.20	1/19/2000	1
032-01235-A-7	Chocolate Bar	$1.10	1/19/2000	1
200-12345-B-7	Lemonade	$1.65	1/19/2000	4
03F-00003-B-7	Jelly Beans	$3.29	1/19/2000	2

Figure 10-5   Sample form in Access project

If you now open the form in the form view, you cannot edit the data. If you attempt to edit a field, the Access status bar displays the following message: "Form is read-only, because the 'UniqueTable' property was not selected."

The form includes only the table's first 10,000 records, even though the table contains 10,724 records. The form's Access mdb version included all of the records. You can use the *Max Records* property to specify the maximum number of records to transfer from the server to the Access project. The default setting for the maximum number of records is the value specified in the Advanced tab of the Options dialog box in the Default Max Records setting. Select Tools, then Options to open this dialog box. If you entered the value **0** under Max Records in the form properties, the system transfers all records.

The mdb application automatically sorts the data before displaying it. SQL Server/MSDE displays the data unsorted, which corresponds to the SQL standard. However, the unsorted display usually appears only if the system transmitted only a part of the total amount of data.

UniqueTable: A New Property

In the form's Design view, you can use the form properties to select one of the table names listed in the combo box for the property *UniqueTable*, shown in Figure 10-6. To fill in the combo box, Access analyzes the form's *Record Source*. Note that the *Record Source* analysis does not work if you are using a stored procedure that requires parameters. See the next section, "Defining the Unique Table with VBA," for more information. The section entitled "The *InputParameters* Property," later in this chapter contains additional information about stored procedures. Microsoft recommends that you define the *UniqueTable* property, even if the record source includes only one table.

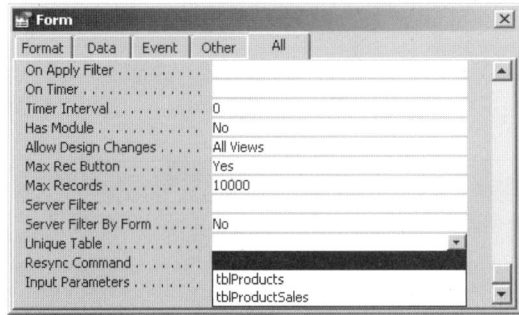

Figure 10-6   *UniqueTable* property

Our example *frmProductSales* is based on the following query:

```
SELECT      tblProducts.ProductNr,

      tblProducts.Description,

tblProducts.SalesPrice,

      tblProductSales.Date,

tblProductSales.Count

FROM tblProducts INNER JOIN tblProductSales ON

      tblProducts.ProductNr = tblProductSales.ProductNr

ORDER BY tblProducts.ProductNr
```

The Properties dialog box for the form *frmProductSales* displays the tables *tblProducts* and *tblProductSales* in the UniqueTable combo box. There is a one-to-many relationship between these two tables. Usually, the table on the "many" side is designated as the *UniqueTable*. In our example, that is *tblProductSales*.

If you use the table from the "one" side of the query's one-to-many relationship to define the *UniqueTable* property, you can edit the table fields, but the system does not update the display. Figure 10-7 provides an illustration of this peculiar feature. We defined the table *tblProducts* as the *UniqueTable*. For example, if we now edit the product name and save the change, the system displays the updated value only for the row that was edited.

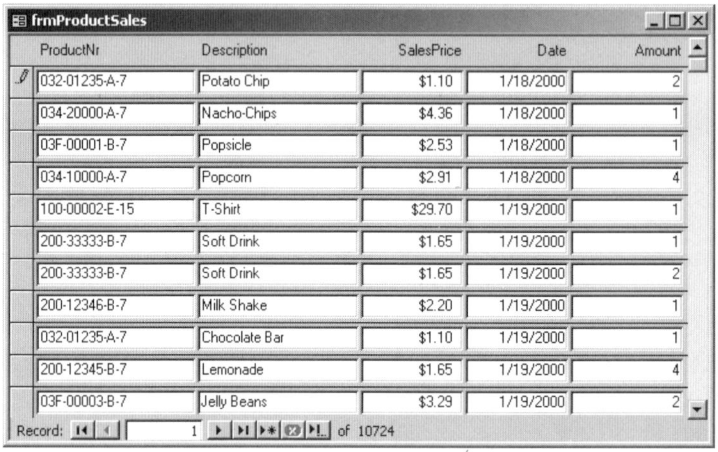

ProductNr	Description	SalesPrice	Date	Amount
032-01235-A-7	Potato Chip	$1.10	1/18/2000	2
034-20000-A-7	Nacho-Chips	$4.36	1/18/2000	1
03F-00001-B-7	Popsicle	$2.53	1/18/2000	1
034-10000-A-7	Popcorn	$2.91	1/18/2000	4
100-00002-E-15	T-Shirt	$29.70	1/19/2000	1
200-33333-B-7	Soft Drink	$1.65	1/19/2000	1
200-33333-B-7	Soft Drink	$1.65	1/19/2000	2
200-12346-B-7	Milk Shake	$2.20	1/19/2000	1
032-01235-A-7	Chocolate Bar	$1.10	1/19/2000	1
200-12345-B-7	Lemonade	$1.65	1/19/2000	4
03F-00003-B-7	Jelly Beans	$3.29	1/19/2000	2

Record: 1 of 10724

Figure 10-7   The product name in the first row was edited

The system corrects the display if you use the Access command *Records/ Refresh*. For example, if you attempt to edit the product name in the second row prior to updating the display, Access gets confused and returns a message indicating that another user already edited that record. This creates a type of infinite loop that prevents you from closing the form.

Note   If you delete a record, the system removes the record from the unique table only.

Defining the Unique Table with VBA

You can also use a VBA program to define the *UniqueTable* property. If you use a stored procedure with parameters as the record source, Access cannot determine the table selection combo box entries for the *UniqueTable* property. Unfortunately, you cannot enter the unique table's name in the Property field because the system only allows entries that also occur in the combo box.

You can correct this problem if you define the property in the VBA program for the form's *Form_Load* event, for example:

```
Private Sub Form_Load()

 Me.UniqueTable = "tblProducts"

End Sub
```

Refresh

If you are using stored procedures or complex queries as the record source, the form needs your help so it can update the display after you edited the data. Once again, Access project forms are more difficult to work with than Access mdb forms in this context, as you don't have to worry about these issues with Access mdb forms.

Here is an example to illustrate the problems of displays that don't update: We created a form based on the query shown in Figure 10-8. The goal is to add *Filmtitle* and *Length* to the data in the table *tblWeeks*, which contains *Week* and *FilmNr*.

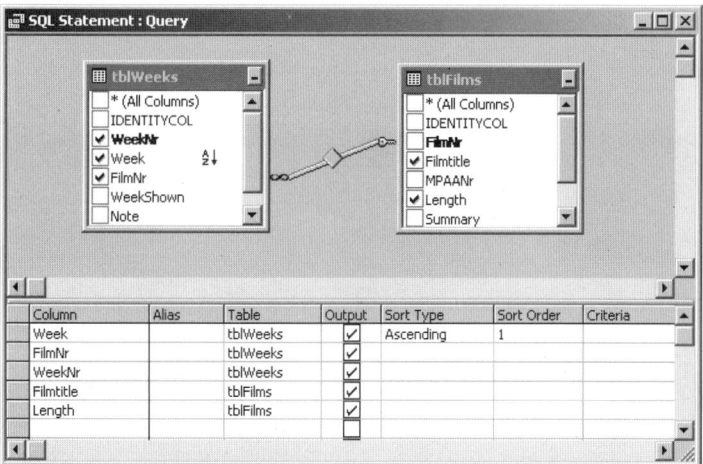

Figure 10-8   Query for the form

The table *tblWeeks* is defined as the *UniqueTable* for the form. This means that we can edit a film's assignment; that is, we can change which film to show during a specific calendar week.

The form's column for *tblWeeks.FilmNr* is set up as a combo box that lets you select a film. As Figure 10-9 illustrates, the entry in the first row is the movie "Frequency."

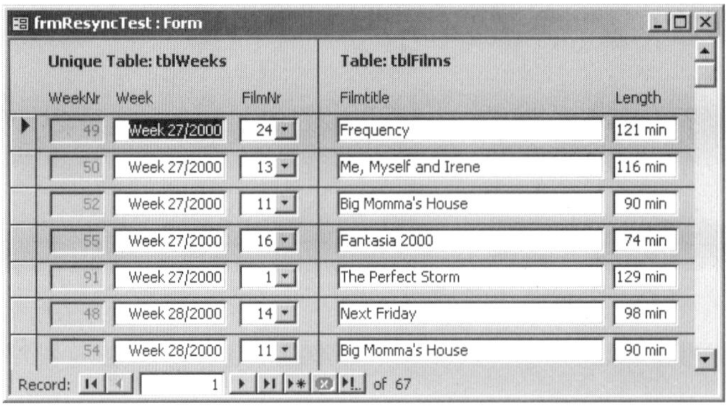

Figure 10-9 Film 24, "Frequency," in the first row

We now change the first record's film number to 1, "The Perfect Storm." As you can see in Figure 10-10, Access did change the film number, but did not update the display in the form on the right to reflect the latest status. There you still see the film title as it appeared before it was edited.

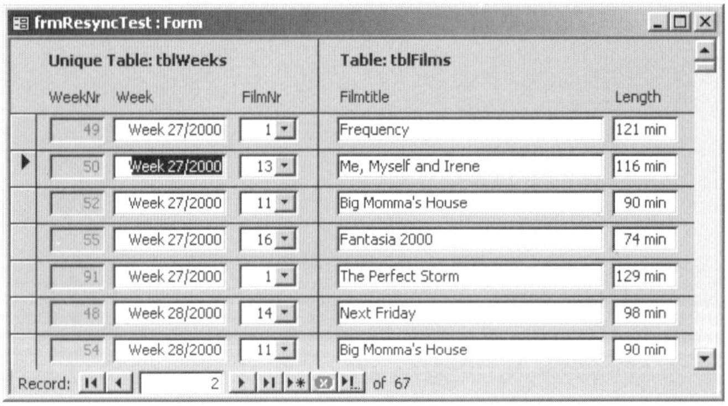

Figure 10-10 The film title for the first record was not updated

In contrast to Access mdb forms, you must intervene directly in Access project forms to refresh the Access display using the *ResyncCommand* in the form's properties, as shown in Figure 10-11.

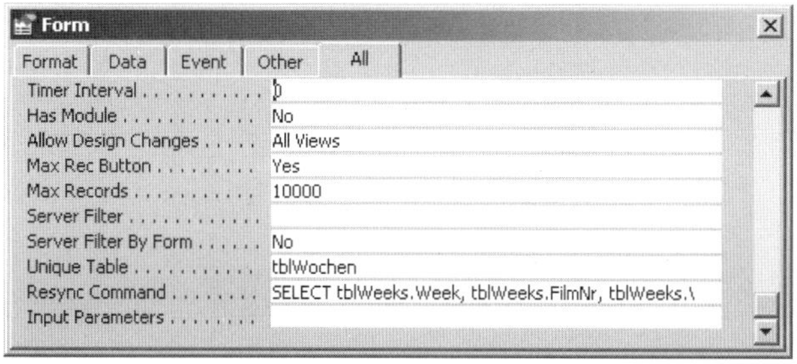

Figure 10-11   Form properties

For this property, enter a SQL query that includes all the columns used in the form. The query is extended with a *WHERE* condition that contains the unique table's key column. In our example, this is *WHERE tblWeeks.WeekNr = ?*. The question mark is a parameter that Access fills with the value of the key in the respective row. The following is the complete query for this example:

```
SELECT

tblWeeks.Week,

tblWeeks.FilmNr,

tblWeeks.WeekNr,

tblFilms.Filmtitle,

tblFilms.Length

FROM

tblWeeks INNER JOIN tblFilms

ON tblWeeks.FilmNr = tblFilms.FilmNr

WHERE

tblWeeks.WeekNr = ?
```

Unfortunately, no support is available for the *ResyncCommand* property as you create the query. Instead, you must enter the SQL code directly. Because the *ResyncCommand* must have the same structure as the query on which the form is based, it helps to copy the *Record Source* SQL code or the *SELECT* command from a stored procedure to the *ResyncCommand* field and then append the *WHERE* condition.

Be sure to remove any *ORDER BY* clauses from the SQL command for the *ResyncCommand* property. If an *ORDER BY* clause is present, Access does not return an error message, but also does not execute the resynchronization function. Access gets confused if you use erroneous *Resync* commands, such as, for example, specifying the wrong key column in the *WHERE* condition, which can cause crashes.

The *InputParameters* Property

If you specify a stored procedure with defined parameters as your record, Access prompts you to enter a value for each parameter in the Enter Parameter Value dialog box. The dialog box then displays the respective parameter's name without the initial @ character.

You can use the *InputParameters* property to instruct Access to display your own text in the query dialog boxes. In addition, you can refer to the control elements of other forms and display the parameter's value in those forms as well.

For subsequent examples, we are using the stored procedure in the following listing. A parameter named *@FilmNr* was defined for this stored procedure.

```
CREATE PROCEDURE Film @FilmNr INT

AS

        IF @FilmNr = 0
            SELECT
                FilmNr,
                Filmtitle
            FROM
                TblFilms
            ORDER BY
                Filmtitle
        ELSE
            SELECT
                FilmNr,
                Filmtitle
            FROM
                tblFilms
            WHERE
                FilmNr = @FilmNr
            ORDER BY
                Filmtitle
```

If you are using the stored procedure as a form's record source, the Enter Parameter Value dialog box, shown in Figure 10-12, appears when you open it. The parameter name is shown above the input line.

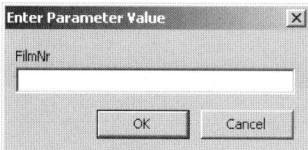

Figure 10-12   Use the Enter Parameter Value dialog box for a parameter query

You can use the *InputParameters* form property with the following syntax

```
@ParameterName DataType = [Text]
```

to edit the query text. For example, you could define

```
@FilmNr INT = [Film number or 0 for all films]
```

to prompt the user to enter the film number, as well as more detailed text, with the text enclosed in angle brackets. When you open the form, the Enter Parameter Value dialog box appears, as shown in Figure 10-13.

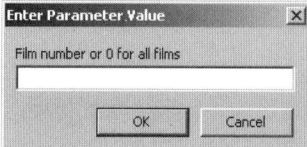

Figure 10-13   New query text

If multiple parameters have been defined for the stored procedure, you can use the *InputParameters* property to fill them by separating the individual parameter input definitions with commas.

Preallocating Input Parameters

You can also use the *InputParameters* property to preallocate parameters for queries or stored procedures. Enclose the value that you want to assign to a parameter in quotation marks. You always need to use quotation marks, as shown here, regardless of parameter type:

```
@Film VARCHAR = "Gladiator"
```

Referencing Forms and Reports

For form and report record sources, many Access mdb applications use queries that use *Forms!FormName!Control* to reference control elements in other forms. With Access project forms, you can no longer use these kinds of references in queries. Access projects do not execute queries locally on the client, but on the database server instead. The database server, however, cannot access the local client to determine a value in a form.

References Between Forms

If the query for a form's record source contains a reference to another form, you cannot simply use the solution for mdb forms with adp forms as well. Refer to the following example for an illustration.

Current Solution with Mdb Forms

Figure 10-14 shows an Access mdb form where you can double-click the movie theater combo box to open a dialog box that displays detailed data about the respective theater.

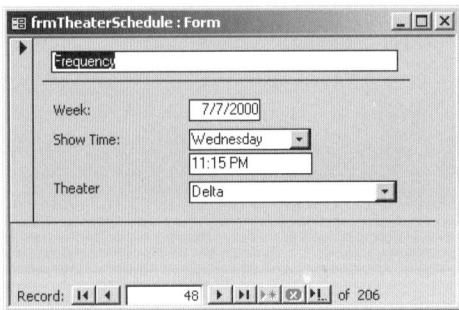

Figure 10-14   Test form

The following procedure was used for the double-click event in the combo box:

```
Private Sub cboTheater_DblClick(Cancel As Integer)

  DoCmd.OpenForm "frmTheater", WindowMode:=acDialog

End Sub
```

Figure 10-15 shows the *frmTheater* form that was opened using this procedure.

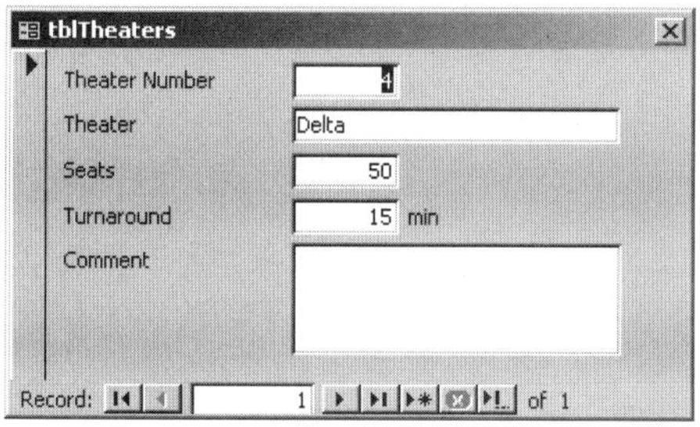

Figure 10-15   Detailed data about a theater

The form's *Record Source* was defined with the following:

```
SELECT * FROM tblTheaters

WHERE
((tblTheaters.TheaterNumber)=[forms]![frmTheaterSchedule]!
[cboTheater]);
```

This means that when you open the form, the current contents of the theater combo box for the form in Figure 10-14 are used for the *WHERE* clause.

Solution for Adp Forms

You can use the same functions with Access projects described earlier for Access mdb forms.

The form *frmTheaterSchedule* can be copied to our sample adp without changes. A stored procedure with parameters is programmed for the form *frmTheater*. This stored procedure serves as the form's record source:

```
CREATE PROCEDURE Theater @TheaterNumber INT

AS

        SELECT

        FROM tblTheaters

        WHERE tblTheaters.TheaterNumber = @TheaterNumber

RETURN
```

Figure 10-16 illustrates how to use the *InputParameters* property with a reference to the combo box, so that the system passes the current value from the *frmTheaterSchedule* form's theater combo box to the stored procedure when opening the form.

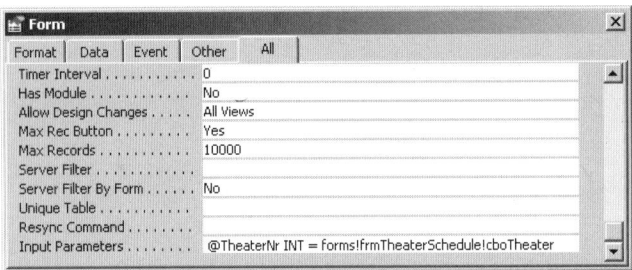

Figure 10-16   Input parameter with reference

Scenario Without Stored Procedure

You can also use the *InputParameters* property if the form's *Record Source* is not a stored procedure, but a *SELECT* query or view instead.

In the query, you must include a quotation mark for every parameter you want to fill with the *InputParameters* property. The system queries the parameters according to the question mark sequence, as shown in the following example. However, this is done in dialog boxes without text comments.

```
SELECT *

FROM tblTheaters

WHERE tblTheaters.TheaterNumber = ?
```

You can use the *InputParameters* property to define text for the parameter queries, such as, for example, *TheaterNr INT = [Enter a theater number]*. Note that here @ does not precede the parameter name.

The following sections explain how you can use parameters to reference control elements in forms.

References to Forms in Control Elements

Another frequently used method of referencing control elements in mdb forms is the use of references in combo boxes and list boxes.

The Mdb Solution

The sample form shown in Figure 10-17 displays a film's planned calendar weeks in a list box, which is dependent on the selection of the film in the combo box.

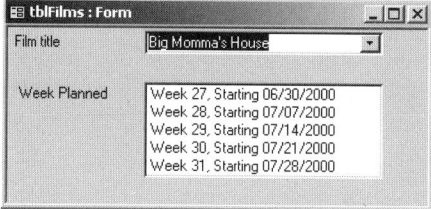

Figure 10-17   Form with linked control elements

Figure 10-18 displays a section of the properties for the list box. The figure has a two-column layout, with the first column suppressed.

Figure 10-18   Properties of the list box

The list box property Row Source was defined as follows:

```
SELECT

tblWeeks.WeekNr,

Format([Week],"""Week ""ww") & " Starting " & [Week] AS Week

FROM

tblWeeks

WHERE

((tblWeeks.FilmNr) = [Forms]![frmWeeks]![cboFilm])

ORDER BY

Format([Week],"""Week ""ww") & " Starting " & [Week];
```

Note that the *Format()* function formats the output in the list box. The *Format* function is a local VBA function that has no equivalent function in SQL Server/MSDE.

Whenever a film in the combo box that lists the film titles is changed, the following procedure is activated, re-executing the list box query:

```
Private Sub cboFilm_Click()

 lstWeek.Requery

End Sub
```

The Adp Solution

In an Access project, you cannot use the query for the record source of the *lstWeek* list box. First, it is not possible to use the reference *[Forms]![frmWeeks]![cboFilm]* and second, you cannot use the *Format()* function.

In Access projects, there is a solution that works with the assistance of a stored procedure. The stored procedure becomes the *Row Source* for the *lstWeek* list box. How can you transfer the contents of the form control element *cboFilm* so that the list box displays only the corresponding data for the film?

You can use the following undocumented trick: Create a stored procedure with a parameter that has the same name as the control element you want to refer to, but add the prefix @. In the example shown here, the parameter name is *@cboFilm* for the name of the combo box *cboFilm*:

```
CREATE PROCEDURE Weeks @cboFilm INT

AS

        SELECT

            tblWeeks.WeekNr,

            'Week ' + CONVERT(VARCHAR, DATEPART(ww, Week) )

            + ', Starting '

            + CONVERT(VARCHAR, Week, 101) AS Week

        FROM

            tblWeeks

        WHERE

            tblWeeks.FilmNr = @cboFilm

        ORDER BY

            'Week ' + CONVERT(VARCHAR, DATEPART(ww, Week) )

            + ', Starting '

            + CONVERT(VARCHAR, Week, 101)

        RETURN
```

The following event procedure is defined for the *cboFilm* combo box in the Access project as well as in the mdb database:

```
Private Sub cboFilm_Click()

 lstWeek.Requery

End Sub
```

When *lstWeek.Requery* is executed, the current content of the *cboFilm* combo box is passed as a parameter to the stored procedure *Weeks*.

In the listing for the stored procedure *Weeks*, the *Format()* function from the query in the mdb list box is replaced by the following:

```
...

'Week ' + CONVERT(VARCHAR, DATEPART(ww, Week) )

      + ', Starting '

      + CONVERT(VARCHAR, Week, 101) AS Week

...
```

The SQL Server function *DATEPART()* uses the *ww* statement to determine the calendar week for the specified date, in this case from the *Week* table column. The system uses the *CONVERT()* function to convert the calculated number into a character string so that the number can be linked to the character string *', Starting'*. In contrast to Access mdb queries, SQL Server/MSDE does not perform any implicit type conversions. The other *CONVERT()* function converts the *Week* date into a character string as well. The parameter *101* defines the date's formatting. See Chapter 9, "Transact-SQL," for a description of the *CONVERT()* function.

Adp Solution Alternative with *EXEC*

The solution introduced in the previous section does not work if the parameter name in the stored procedure does not match the control element's name. You can use the following alternate solution if you cannot match the names in the procedure and the form. For example, this can happen if you do not have permission to edit the stored procedure or if matching the names would cause an unreasonably large programming effort elsewhere.

As we described in the earlier section "Record Source with EXEC," you can use the *EXEC* command to execute stored procedures while also passing parameters.

Thus, we removed the *Row Source* property from the *lstWeek* list box, as shown in Figure 10-19.

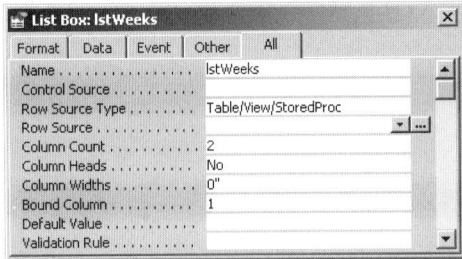

Figure 10-19 Properties of the *lstWeek* box

We then modified the event procedure for *On Click*, as you can see in the following listing:

```
Private Sub cboFilm_Click()

  lstWeek.RowSource = "EXEC Weeks " & cboFilm.Value

End Sub
```

> **Note** Note that if you use a character string as a parameter, you must enclose it in single quotation marks, for example: *listbox.RowSource = "EXEC Procedure '" & string & "'"*.

In contrast to the first solution, you do not need the *lstWeek.Requery* command here, because an assignment to the *RowSource* property automatically initiates execution of the passed command.

In addition, we programmed the following event procedure that is executed when loading the form. Here, the *cboFilm = cboFilm.ItemData(0)* command ensures that the first film on the list is displayed in the combo box. Normally, the combo box is empty and is filled in only if you open it and select a value from the list. The system then fills the list box *lstWeek* with the help of the *cboFilm_Click* command, which is used to execute the stored procedure.

```
Private Sub Form_Load()

  cboFilm = cboFilm.ItemData(0)

  cboFilm_Click

End Sub
```

Synchronized Subforms

Subforms are used to illustrate one-to-many relationships in forms. The main form and the subform are synchronized, which means that when you switch records in the main form, the subform displays the corresponding records for the "many" relationship. Figure 10-20 shows a form that displays product data. The subform displays the monthly sales figures for the respective product.

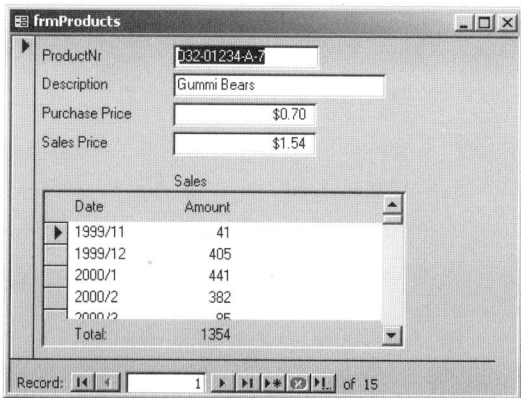

Figure 10-20 Form with subform

The subform's control element properties *Link Child Fields* and *Link Master Fields* define the relationship between the main form and the subform, as displayed in Figure 10-21.

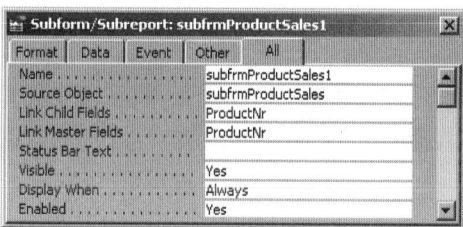

Figure 10-21 Properties of the subform control element

Note There is a bug in the Microsoft Access 2000 Subform Wizard, making it reject a link as invalid if you want to link the main form and subform queries with an *nvarchar* data type field. This means that you must manually enter the link field in the *Link Child Fields* and *Link Master Fields* properties for the subform object. This bug has been fixed in Access 2002.

Problems with Complex Queries

The synchronization of main form and subform causes problems in Access if a somewhat more complex query is defined as the record source in the subform. For example, the problem occurs if you use the query

```
SELECT * FROM tblProducts ORDER BY ProductNr
```

for the main form. The main form contains a subform with this query:

```
SELECT

ProductNr,

CONVERT(VARCHAR, DATEPART(yyyy, Date)) + '/' + CONVERT(VARCHAR,
DATEPART(mm, Date))

 AS Dat,

SUM(Amount) AS Amt

FROM

tblProductSales

GROUP BY

ProductNr,

CONVERT(VARCHAR, DATEPART(yyyy, Date)) + '/' + CONVERT(VARCHAR,
DATEPART(mm, Date))

ORDER BY

ProductNr,

CONVERT(VARCHAR, DATEPART(yyyy, Date)) + '/' + CONVERT(VARCHAR,
DATEPART(mm, Date))
```

When you open the main form, even though the SQL query is correct, the following error message appears: "Line 1: Syntax error near ')',." If you open the subform directly, the system correctly displays the data.

The simplest way to solve this problem is to create the query as a view and then access the view from the subform's record source object.

Synchronization with Stored Procedures

The synchronization of the main form with the subform does not work if the subform's record source is a stored procedure. You can use the three scenarios described next to synchronize subforms based on stored procedures.

Scenario 1: Stored Procedure with Parameter

With the first scenario, you can successfully synchronize the forms by defining a parameter for the stored procedure that is the subform's record source. This parameter must match the link field name.

In principle, this scenario is based on the same method that we previously introduced in the sections entitled "References Between Forms" and "References to Forms in Control Elements."

Usually, the *Link Child Fields* and *Link Master Fields* properties are used to create the relationship between the main form and the subform. In this scenario, however, it is sufficient to assign an appropriate name to the parameter for the stored procedure that is the subform's record source. In our example, we want to use the product number to synchronize the main form and the subform. That is why the name of the stored procedure's parameter is *@ProductNr*, as shown in the listing. It is interesting to note that you do not need to define the *Link Child Fields* and *Link Master Fields* properties for the subform's control element. This means that the synchronization process works even if these properties remain blank.

You can also use this procedure when the relationship between the main form and the subform was created with a control element, which means that the main form's control element name is entered under *Link Master Fields*. In this case, the stored procedure's parameter name must match the control element name.

In the subform's stored procedure, the system then summarizes the monthly sales figures for a specific product number. The data is grouped and sorted by year and month, both of which consist of a character string separated by a slash, as shown here:

```
CREATE PROCEDURE "spSales" @ProductNr VARCHAR(50)

AS

        SELECT

            ProductNr,

            CONVERT(VARCHAR, DATEPART(yyyy, Date))

            + '/'

            + CONVERT(VARCHAR, DATEPART(mm, Date)) AS Dat,
```

```
          SUM(Amount) AS Amt
FROM
     tblProductSales
WHERE
     ProductNr = @ProductNr
GROUP BY
     ProductNr,
     CONVERT(VARCHAR, DATEPART(yyyy, Date))
     + '/'
     + CONVERT(VARCHAR, DATEPART(mm, Date))
ORDER BY
     ProductNr,
     CONVERT(VARCHAR, DATEPART(yyyy, Date))
     + '/'
     + CONVERT(VARCHAR, DATEPART(mm, Date))
     RETURN
```

Scenario 2: Using an Input Parameter

If the stored procedure's parameter in the subform does not have the same name as the link field, you can still make sure that the corresponding function is available by defining the *InputParameters* property in the subform.

Let us assume that the stored procedure is defined as follows:

```
CREATE PROCEDURE "spSales" @PNr VARCHAR(50)

AS

...

     RETURN
```

In that case, for our example, you can use

```
@PNr = Forms!frmProducts!ProductNr
```

as the subform's input parameter.

Scenario 3: Using *EXEC*

The third scenario for synchronizing the main form and the subform uses the *EXEC* command. In this scenario, no *Record Source* is defined for the subform. Instead, this property is defined in the main form.

The following event procedure is entered for the main form's *On Current* event:

```
Private Sub Form_Current()

 subfrmProductSales.Form.RecordSource = "EXEC spSales '" &
Me!ProductNr & "'"

End Sub
```

Note that the product number is a character string in our example because product numbers can also contain letters. That is why the single quotation marks are essential.

If you use this solution scenario, you also do not need to define the *Link Child Fields* and *Link Master Fields* properties for the subform control element.

Form Filters

You can use the filter variants *Filter By Selection* and *Filter By Form* that you are familiar with from working with Access mdb forms for adp forms as well. Note that both filter variants work with local data, which means that prior to applying filters you must first import all data to the client. This can cause bottlenecks if there are large tables on the server, because all the data must first be transferred to the client. Also, the filter always edits only those records that were actually imported to the client, and the form property *Max Records* normally limits the number of records that can be imported (the default setting is 10,000).

Server Filters

Microsoft has introduced the properties *Server Filter By Form* and *Server Filter* that make it possible to filter all of the data while it is still on the server so that only the filtered data is transmitted to the client.

If you select Yes for the *Server Filter By Form* property, the system immediately prompts you for the filter conditions when you open the form. Figure 10-22 shows the form *frmMovieGoers* as an example.

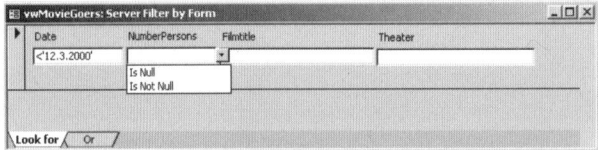

Figure 10-22   Form in *ServerFilterByForm* mode

After entering the conditions, click Apply Server Filter to instruct the server to extract the data and transfer it to the client. The filter conditions entered by the user are saved under the *Server Filter* property. You can also use this property to define default settings for the form.

Note that, due to a bug in Access 2000, the Filter By Form button is deactivated if the server filter is activated. Another bug prevents output of filter conditions for fields of the data type *money* or *smallmoney*.

Moreover, the system might generate error messages if you define a filter for a form that accesses a table you do not own. To avoid such error messages, the owner name must be added to the table name as a prefix. The general pattern is *Owner.Table*, of which *dbo.tblProducts* is an example.

> **Note**   You can use the *Server Filter By Form* property only if your form's record source is not a stored procedure.

General

The following sections describe differences between forms in conventional mdb databases and forms in Access projects.

Hot Keys

Access project forms do not support the following hot keys: Ctrl+Alt+Space, which pastes a field's default value; F9 to update a lookup field; and Shift+F9 to update a subform.

Chart Wizard

The Chart Wizard is available only in mdb databases, not in Access projects. Theoretically, it is possible to import diagram forms created with the wizard into an adp from an mdb, even though doing so requires a considerable amount of extra work. In part, this is due to the fact that the Chart Wizard generally uses the *TRANSFORM* command to collect data for crosstabs. SQL Server/ MSDE, however, does not support the *TRANSFORM* command. Moreover, the Chart Wizard uses the *FORMAT()* function to group data such as date values. This is another function that SQL Server/MSDE cannot execute.

If you want to display a chart in an Access project form, go to the form's Design view and use the *Insert/Object* command to place a Microsoft Graph 2000 object in the form, and then use the query designer to define the record source.

PivotTable Wizard (Access 2000)

Another wizard not available in Access projects is the PivotTable Wizard, which creates forms that analyze data with the Microsoft Excel *Pivot* function. You can try to use the PivotTable Wizard to create a form in an mdb and then import the form into the adp. Although it is possible to open the imported form, it is problematic to update data in the Pivot element. Once again, additional work is required to instruct Excel to collect the data over again.

PivotChart and PivotTable (Access 2002)

Access 2002 offers PivotChart and PivotTable with new functions that you can use to analyze your data and create charts. Both functions work smoothly in Access projects.

Event Sequence on Delete

The sequence of events during the delete process differs in mdb forms compared to adp forms. If you used VBA or macros to define event procedures for the delete events *On Delete*, *Before Del Confirm*, and *After Del Confirm*, you must check to make sure that the altered sequence does not affect your programming logic.

If you delete a record in an mdb form, the system initiates the events in the following order: *On Delete*, *Before Del Confirm*, *After Del Confirm*. In an Access project form, however, the events occur in a different order: *Before Del Confirm*, *After Del Confirm*, *On Delete*.

Domain Function with References to Forms

If you use domain functions in your forms, such as *DLookup()*, *DSum()*, and so on, you could enter references to forms in mdb forms, even though the syntax is rather inelegant. The following is an example:

```
=DLookup("[Filmtitle]";"tblFilms";"[FilmNr]=Forms!frmFilms!FilmNr")
```

The syntax is sloppy because the reference to the form appears within the character string for the *WHERE* clause. Although Access did analyze the expression correctly, unfortunately this is no longer the case in an Access project. You must now enter the expression so that it is syntactically correct, as shown here:

```
=DLookup("[Filmtitle]";"tblFilms";
"FilmNr=" & [Forms]![frmFilms]![FilmNr])
```

In other words, you must connect the character strings.

Hyperlinks

In Chapter 5, "Tables in Access Projects," you learned that there is no *Hyperlink* data type in SQL Server/MSDE tables. Basically, hyperlink fields are just regular text fields where the hyperlink information is coded. Therefore, in SQL Server/ MSDE tables, you can save hyperlink information in *char*, *varchar*, *nvarchar*, *ntext*, or *text* fields. The Upsizing Wizard described in Chapter 16, "Upsizing Wizard," creates *ntext* fields in the SQL Server/MSDE tables during the transfer of tables from an Access mdb text's *hyperlink* fields.

You can only use forms to execute the actual hyperlink functions, that is, further routing to the specified addresses, through the Internet as well as the intranet, to a file or a local database component. Be sure to set the *Is Hyperlink* property for a corresponding text field control element to Yes.

Opening Forms with VBA

There are two different procedures you can use to open forms from a Microsoft Visual Basic program: You can either use *DoCmd.OpenForm* or a form object. Generally, both procedures work with Access projects while providing the same options as Access mdb files. The one notable difference is that Access project forms (and reports) can be based on stored procedures as the record source.

You can assign a filter name or a *WHERE* clause as the parameter for the *DoCmd* object's *OpenForm* method. Both the filter name and the *WHERE* clause limit the records the system displays in the form (or report). Both parameters are ineffective if a form or report is based on a stored procedure.

What is the solution? A description of three scenarios that you can use to work around this limitation follows.

Scenario 1: Additional Parameter for the Stored Procedure

In the first scenario you can, for example, expand the stored procedure with an additional parameter. You can then use the *InputParameters* form property to assign a value to the stored procedure, as described earlier in this chapter in the "The InputParameter Property" section:

```
CREATE PROCEDURE ProductList @Description VARCHAR

AS

        SELECT * FROM tblProducts WHERE Description LIKE @Description
ORDER BY Description
```

The disadvantage of this solution is that you must specify for which field to define the condition.

Scenario 2: Assigning Any *WHERE* Clause

You can use the procedure's second scenario to permit any *WHERE* clause for a stored procedure. This procedure requires assembling the SQL query, with the assigned parameter *@Condition* containing the *WHERE* clause:

```
CREATE PROCEDURE ProductList2 @Condition VARCHAR(200)

AS

        DECLARE @TMP VARCHAR(250)


        SET @TMP = 'SELECT * FROM tblProducts'


        IF @Condition IS NOT NULL AND LTRIM(RTRIM(@Condition)) <> ''
            SET @TMP = @TMP + ' WHERE ' + @Condition


        SET @TMP = @TMP + ' ORDER BY Description'


        EXECUTE ( @TMP )
```

Use the *EXECUTE* command to execute the query in *@TMP*. This solution's disadvantage is that the SQL server cannot precompile the query, because the system does not assemble the query until it is run. This can negatively affect performance.

Scenario 3: Using the *Filter* Property

In the third scenario, you can use the form's *Filter* property to limit the data displayed in the form. In this scenario, however, the filter property implements the limits on the data on the client. This means that the SQL server sends all data retrieved by the stored procedure on which the form is based to the client. The filter does not select the data until the data arrives on the client.

Also, the server filter introduced in the earlier section entitled "Server Filters" cannot be used with stored procedures. This filter lets you place limits on the data on the server side.

The following program opens the form *frmProductList* and sets a filter. The system opens the form as an object:

```
Sub FilterTest()

DoCmd.OpenForm "frmProductList"


' Apply filter

Form_frmProductList.Filter = "Description like 'G%'"

' Activate filter

Form_frmProductList.FilterOn = True

End Sub
```

The following routine illustrates the solution with a form object:

```
Sub FilterTest2()

Dim frm As Form_frmProductList


Set frm = New Form_frmProductList

frm.Visible = True

' Apply filter

frm.Filter = "Description like 'G%'"

' Activate filter

frm.FilterOn = True

On Error Resume Next

Do While frm.Visible

DoEvents

Loop

Set frm = Nothing

End Sub
```

Note that for both of these routines, you must set the form property *Has Module* to Yes.

11

Reports

This chapter describes the options, restrictions, and extensions available for creating reports in Access projects. The procedures for designing and implementing reports generally correspond to those used by Access mdb, so you do not need to learn much new material. However, to minimize server and network traffic, you should make sure when creating reports in Access projects that the server only transmits data to the client you actually need to create the report.

Creating Reports

Reports can be based on tables, views, *SELECT* queries, or stored procedures. If you are using a wizard to create a new report, you can select only tables or views as data sources in Microsoft Access 2000. Reports based on a stored procedure can be created in Design view, because that is the only place where you can select a stored procedure as the *Record Source*.

In Microsoft Access 2002, you can also use wizards to select a stored procedure as the *Record Source*.

The next few sections describe innovations as well as errors and inconsistencies that occur when using reports in Access projects.

New Properties for Reports

Two new properties were added to reports in Access projects: *Server Filter* and *InputParameter*. We discussed these properties in Chapter 10, "Forms." These properties work similarly for reports. Note that you can continue to use the properties *Filter* and *Allow filter*, but these properties filter the data imported to the client, just as they do with forms. It makes more sense to select the data for the report earlier, on the SQL server.

Errors with Sorting Reports (Access 2000)

There is a strange feature related to the *ORDER BY* clause in a report's *Record Source*. If the *ORDER BY* clause includes the table name, for example, in the form

```
SELECT * FROM tblFilms ORDER BY tblFilms.Filmtitle
```

it is possible that calling the report can cause error messages such as the ones shown in Figure 11-1, even if the SQL query is syntactically correct and was correctly executed by itself.

Figure 11-1   Error message

If you redefine the report's *Record Source* like this

```
SELECT * FROM tblFilms ORDER BY Filmtitle
```

everything once again works as usual. This problem does not occur with forms and Microsoft Office 2000 Service Release 1 does not provide a solution, but this bug has been fixed in Access 2002.

Reports with Stored Procedures

Reports can be based on stored procedures. Note that in Access 2000, you can use only the Design view to select stored procedures as the *Record Source*. In Access 2002, you can also select stored procedures in the Report Wizards.

If you are using a stored procedure as the *Record Source*, Access tries to determine the data returned by the procedure. As part of this process, for example, the system analyzes the procedure to specify the field names that you can use to select as the *Control Source* for linked control elements.

In some cases, Access cannot determine the field names. See the following example, which uses temporary tables in the procedure. See the section entitled "Temporary Tables" in Chapter 9, "Transact-SQL," to review temporary tables. With such a procedure, the column names cannot be determined until the procedure is executed. Access, however, does not do this when analyzing the procedure.

```
CREATE PROCEDURE "ReportTest"

AS

        SET NOCOUNT ON
```

```
-- Create temporary table
CREATE TABLE #tmp (Description VARCHAR(100), Amount REAL)

-- Fill temporary table
INSERT INTO #tmp SELECT Description, SUM(Amount) AS Amount
          FROM tblProducts INNER JOIN tblProductSales
               ON (tblProducts.ProductNr
= tblProductSales.ProductNr)
          GROUP BY Description
          ORDER BY SUM(Amount) DESC

SET NOCOUNT OFF

-- Return temporary table
SELECT * FROM #tmp

RETURN
```

The example procedure returns two columns: *Description* and *Number*, as shown in Figure 11-2.

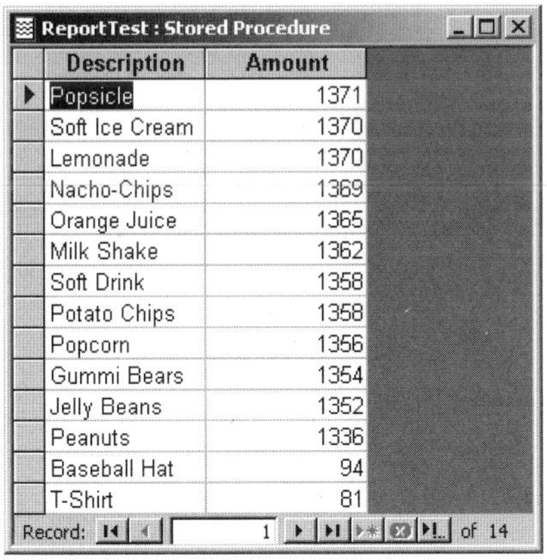

Description	Amount
Popsicle	1371
Soft Ice Cream	1370
Lemonade	1370
Nacho-Chips	1369
Orange Juice	1365
Milk Shake	1362
Soft Drink	1358
Potato Chips	1358
Popcorn	1356
Gummi Bears	1354
Jelly Beans	1352
Peanuts	1336
Baseball Hat	94
T-Shirt	81

Figure 11-2 The procedure's result

If you attempt to use the stored procedure as a report's *Record Source* with Access 2000, you will see the error message shown in Figure 11-3. Access 2002, however, does not display the error message.

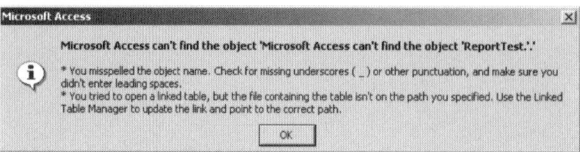

Figure 11-3   Error message

Still, you can go ahead and design the report anyway, as shown in Figure 11-4. If you want to use the columns *Description* and *Number* as the source for control elements, you must enter the desired field name directly in the control element's *Control Source* property. Unfortunately, in Access 2000, the same error message continues to appear.

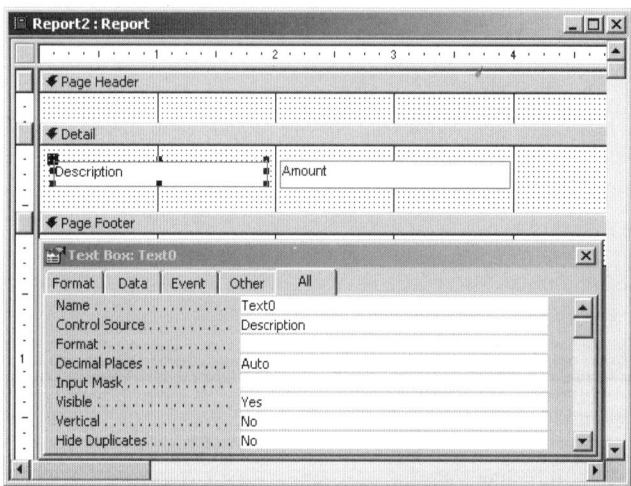

Figure 11-4   Report

Subreports

If you are placing subreports inside your report, they are usually joined to the report. This means that the subreport only displays data that refers to the main report's corresponding record. You can use the subreport's control element's properties *Link Master Fields* and *Link Child Fields* to define the relationship between the main report and the subreport. You can only create such a link if the main report's and subreport's *Record Source* is a query or a view, respectively.

If you defined a stored procedure as the main report's *Record Source*, you can manually create the relationship between main report and subreport yourself using the report properties. The wizard for defining the relationship does not work.

If the subreport's *Record Source* is a stored procedure, you can use the *Link Master Fields* or *Link Child Fields* properties to enter field names, but the entries have no effect. We described this problem in Chapter 10, "Forms," along with solution scenarios. Here we describe the most commonly used method for using subreports based on stored procedures.

Subreport with Stored Procedure with Parameter

To join a subreport based on a stored procedure with the main report, the stored procedure must contain a parameter with the same name as the main form field that you are using to define the relationship. Next we present a simple example for illustration purposes.

The goal is to generate a product list that lists the sales figures for all products. The main report is based on a simple query that returns all products sorted by product number, as shown in Figure 11-5.

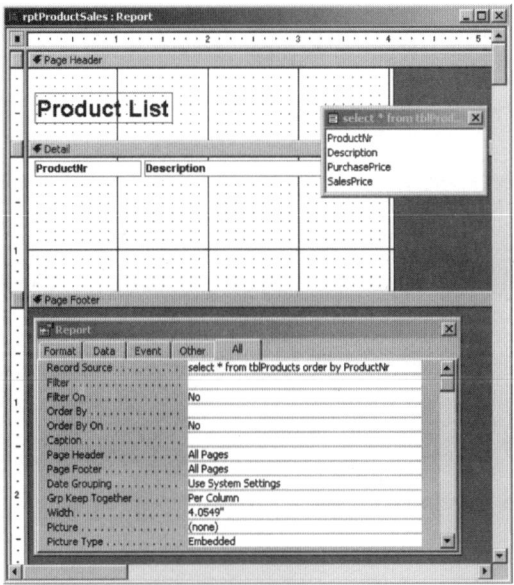

Figure 11-5   Report design

The main report is used to define a subreport, given in the following example, based on a stored procedure that groups and sorts the products sold by product number and date (see Figure 11-6):

```
CREATE PROCEDURE ProductSales

AS

SELECT ProductNr, Date, SUM(Amount)

        FROM tblProductSales

        GROUP BY ProductNr, Date

        ORDER BY ProductNr, Date

RETURN
```

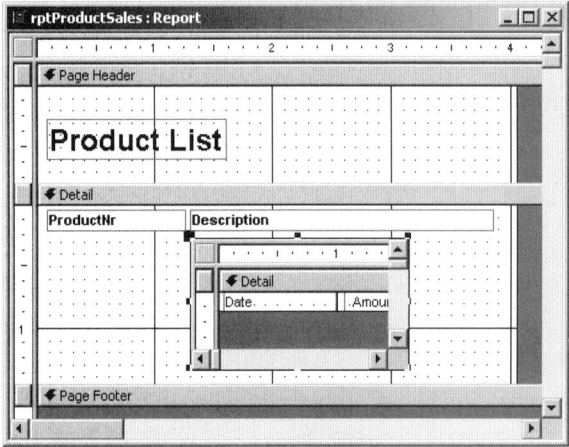

Figure 11-6   Report with subreport

Use the subreport control element's Properties dialog box to define the properties *Link Master Fields* and *Link Child Fields*, as shown in Figure 11-7.

![Subform/Subreport: rptsubProductSales1 properties dialog]
Format	Data	Event	Other	**All**

Name	rptsubProductSales1
Source Object	Report.rptsubProductSales1
Link Child Fields	
Link Master Fields	
Visible	Yes
Can Grow	Yes
Can Shrink	Yes
Left	1.2986"

Figure 11-7   Settings for the subreport's control element

As described in Chapter 10, "Forms," defining the two properties has no effect. For every main report's records, the subreport always prints all records returned by the stored procedure.

The only available solution is similar to the one introduced in Chapter 10, "Forms." Define a parameter for the stored procedure with the name of the field you want to use for linking the main report and the subreport. In our example, the parameter name is *@ProductNr*.

We have made changes to the procedure shown earlier. A parameter was added to extend the procedure so that a message text appears instead of a date if there are no sales for a product, as shown here:

```
CREATE PROCEDURE ProductSales @ProductNr VARCHAR(20)

AS

        SET NOCOUNT ON


        IF (SELECT COUNT(*) FROM tblProductSales WHERE ProductNr =
@ProductNr ) > 0


            SELECT CONVERT(VARCHAR,Date,101), SUM(Amount)

                FROM tblProductSales

            WHERE ProductNr = @ProductNr

                GROUP BY Date

                ORDER BY Date


        ELSE

            SELECT 'No sales in period.' AS Date,'' AS Amount

RETURN
```

Note that the *CONVERT* procedure formats the date at this point instead of doing it later in the report. You do not have to make any entries for the subreport's control element *Link Master Fields* and *Link Child Fields To* properties, as the stored procedure's correctly named parameter is sufficient.

See the section entitled "Synchronized Subforms" in Chapter 10, "Forms," for additional solution scenarios.

Joins with a Control Element

You can also use the main form to create a control element to join the main report and the subreport. In that case, the parameter of the stored procedure's subreport must have the same name as the main form's corresponding control element.

Opening Reports with *DoCmd.OpenReport*

In the section entitled "Opening Forms with VBA" in Chapter 10, "Forms," we pointed out that you cannot use the *DoCmd.OpenReport* method's parameters *Filtername* and *WhereCondition* if the form you want to open is based on a stored procedure.

Part III

Programming with ADO

ActiveX Data Objects (ADO) are required for all Microsoft Visual Basic for Applications (VBA) database access. There are currently several versions of ADO in use. Version 2.1 is supplied with Microsoft Office 2000 and Microsoft Access 2000, and version 2.5 comes with Microsoft Windows 2000 and Microsoft Office XP. The differences, at least with regard to their use in Access projects, are minimal. ADO 2.5 contains two new objects, *Record* and *Stream*. Both are designed for more complex programming tasks and nonrelational databases. These objects are not described further in this section. ADO 2.6 is supplied with Microsoft SQL Server 2000. ADO 2.7, better known as ADO.NET, is supplied with Visual Studio .NET. For more information on Microsoft ADO technology, visit *http://www.microsoft.com/data/* for updates, help files, or Software Development Kits (SDK).

The ADO object model consists of only a few objects and is easily maintained. The individual objects are the subject matter of the following chapters.

The *Connection* object contains information about the connection to the data source, and it is used to determine which data source is accessed with which OLE DB driver. Here, the user name, password, and other parameters for controlling the connection can be entered. Chapter 12, "*Connection* Objects," also describes error handling for ADO programs. ADO errors that occur when running ADO operations can be retrieved from the *Connection* object's *Errors* list.

Recordset objects have been designed for accessing records and are described in Chapter 13, "*Recordset* Objects." A record's individual fields are addressed through a *Recordset* object's *Fields* list. The records for a *Recordset* object are selected by means of SQL queries.

Using *Command* objects, queries can be run with or without parameters or action queries (*UPDATE, DELETE*, and so on). Chapter 14, "*Command* Objects," covers these objects in detail. The majority of ADO objects transmit events by which they indicate their current activity. You can intercept these events in your programs and respond accordingly.

Using ADO events, programs can further control the status of ADO connections, transactions, or recordsets without the necessity of checking the properties of these objects every step of the way. The ADO event model is explained in Chapter 15, "ADO Events."

12

Connection Objects

The top level of the ADO object model is the *connection* object, which describes the access to an OLE DB provider. The client establishes a connection to a server by using the user-entered data to search the network for the server and to log on. The connection can be used to exchange data in both directions. It is possible for a client to maintain multiple connections to a server that can be used to transmit data simultaneously and in parallel, if needed. Every connection requires resources on the client and the server, so normally the system tries to minimize the number of connections.

The *Connection* object describes the connection between the client and the server. Tables 12-1 through 12-3 list all of the properties, methods, and events related to the *Connection* object.

Table 12-1 Properties of the *Connection* Object

Property	Data Type	Description
Attributes	Long	Checks the object's behavior after using the methods *CommitTrans* or *RollbackTrans*.
Command-Timeout	*Long*	Specifies (in seconds) how long the system should wait to execute a query. The default is 30 seconds. If you enter the value **0**, the system waits without timing out. The time counter starts once your SQL query reaches the server and ends when the server returns the first record of the result.
		However, if the query does not reach the server due to network trouble or similar problems, the network card's settings determine when the system returns an error message. If the network load is very high, causing the transmission of the query to take a long time, the client waits without starting the *CommandTimeout* time counter.

continued

Table 12-1 **Properties of the *Connection* Object** *(continued)*

Property	Data Type	Description
Connection-String	*String*	Contains basic information used to establish the connection to a data source.
Connection-Timeout	*Long*	Specifies how long the system should try to establish a connection to the database. The default is 15 seconds. This value determines only how long the system can try to establish the connection after it has already established a network connection to the server. The network card software, not the value for *ConnectionTimeout*, determines how long the network card waits before returning an error because, for example, the network is down.
Cursor-Location	*Long*	Specifies the value that determines whether the system temporarily saves a query's resultset on the client or the server.
Default-Database	*String*	Specifies the property that determines which database name to use when accessing the SQL Server when no database name was explicitly entered.
Errors	*Collection*	Consists of error objects that contain the errors that occurred for the *Connection* object.
IsolationLevel	*Long*	Used for transaction monitoring.
Mode	*Long*	Determines the permissions for the modifying data for the connection.
Properties	*Collection*	Contains a list of all provider-specific properties.
Provider	*String*	Contains the name of the OLE DB provider.
State	*Long*	Describes the connection's current state: open (*adStateOpen*) or closed (*adStateClosed*). Returns the property *adStateConnecting* while the system is establishing the connection.
Version	*String*	Returns the ADO version.

Table 12-2 **Methods of the *Connection* Object**

Method/Function	Description
BeginTrans	Initiates a transaction
Cancel	Cancels an attempt to establish an asynchronous connection
Close	Closes the connection
CommitTrans	Commits a transaction

continued

Table 12-2   Methods of the *Connection* Object   *(continued)*

Method/Function	Description
Execute	Executes a query, SQL statement, stored procedure, or provider-specific text
Open	Opens a connection to a data source
OpenSchema	Retrieves structural information about a database
RollbackTrans	Aborts a transaction and restores the initial state

Table 12-3   Events of the *Connection* Object

Event	Description
BeginTransComplete	Initiated when the *BeginTrans* method is finished
CommitTransComplete	Initiated when the *CommitTrans* method is finished
ConnectComplete	Initiated when the attempt to connect to the database is completed successfully
Disconnect	Initiated after connection ends
ExecuteComplete	Initiated after the *Execute* method is finished
InfoMessage	Returns warning text messages for information purposes while connection is open
RollbackTransComplete	Initiated when a rollback is finished
WillConnect	Initiated immediately before connection starts
WillExecute	Initiated immediately before activating the *Execute* method or opening a recordset

See Chapter 14, "*Command* Objects," for information on programming with ADO Commands.

Connection Strings

A *Connection* object's most important property is the *ConnectionString*. The property contains a character string with the description of the connection, called the connection string. The connection string consists of several key–value pair parts that contain the OLE DB provider name, the server name, the database name, and user information.

Assembling the Connection String

The connection string's individual parts are separated by a semicolon and consist of a keyword followed by an equal sign and a value. Table 12-4 displays the most important keywords.

Table 12-4 The Most Important Keywords for Connection Strings

Keyword	Description
Provider=	The provider, used by the system to determine the OLE DB driver, is the most important part of the connection string. There are three ways to access Microsoft SQL Server/MSDE. The numbers at the end denote the version number.
	Provider=SQLOLEDB.1 uses the SQL Server OLE DB driver, *Provider=MSDataShape* uses the special driver for hierarchical result-sets, and *Provider=MSDASQL.1* uses the ODBC driver. By default, you should establish connections to SQL Server with SQLOLEDB.1 and use MSDataShape to run Access projects. If you use MSDataShape, you must specify a data provider.
Data Provider=	Some providers, such as MSDataShape, are really only special drivers for the preparation of data. The data provider then supplies you with the data. When using MSDataShape as the Provider setting, use *Data Provider= SQLOLEDB.1*.
Data Source=	Here you enter the name of the computer (the name NetBios, or IP of the SQL Server/MSDE) where the database is located. For connections to a database hosted on the same computer as the connection you can use *Data Source=(local)*.
Initial Catalog=	This keyword is used to specify the database you want to access.
Integrated Security=	If you specify this keyword, only use the value *SSPI*, which stands for Security Support Provider Interface, a library for security functions on Microsoft Windows NT and Microsoft Windows 2000. This value ensures that the system uses the Windows NT or Windows 2000 security functions.
User ID=	If you do not use the integrated Windows NT or Windows 2000 security functions, this keyword specifies the user ID.
Password=	If you do not use the integrated Windows NT or Windows 2000 security functions, this keyword specifies the password for the user ID.
Persist Security Info=	This parameter is important only if you do not use the integrated Windows NT or Windows 2000 security functions. It ensures that the client's password is not removed from the connection string after the connection has been established. *True* and *False* are the possible values for this parameter and you should use *False*.

If there are misspellings in the keywords, the system simply ignores the entry without returning an error message.

The following is the connection string for our sample database:

```
Provider=MSDataShape.1;Persist Security Info=False;Data
Source=(local);
Integrated Security=SSPI;Initial Catalog=ContosoSQL;Data
Provider=SQLOLEDB.1
```

Data Links

If you need connections to databases other than the current one for your applications, it can be labor-intensive to assemble the *ConnectionString*. For example, if you switch data sources while working, you must edit and reassemble the *ConnectionString* to select another data source. You can also use a data link file to save all information about a connection. The filename ends in the extension .udl.

You can also use data links to easily assemble connection strings that you can use in your program.

To create a new data link file, first select a folder in Windows Explorer. Right-click in the right part of the window, and then select Microsoft Data Link from the shortcut menu, or select File, then New, and then Microsoft Data Link. Next, name the new file. In the following example, the filename is CONTOSO.UDL.

> **Note**   You cannot select Microsoft Data Link through the File menu in Windows 2000. To get around this problem, you can create a text file with a .txt extension and then rename the file with a .udl extension. Additionally, you can edit the .udl file using a Notepad editor if you want to change the provider setting to MSDataShape.1.

Next, double-click the filename to open the Data Link Properties dialog box. Click the Provider tab and select a provider for the connection, as shown in Figure 12-1.

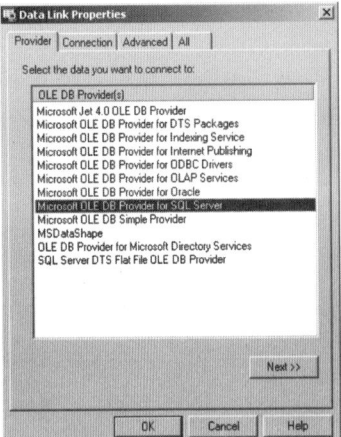

Figure 12-1 Provider selection

Use the Connection tab, shown in Figure 12-2, to specify the database name and path name as well as the user name and password. If you use a password, you can specify whether to save the password in the .udl file. If you do this, anyone who has access to the .udl file can also access the database with the specified user's access rights.

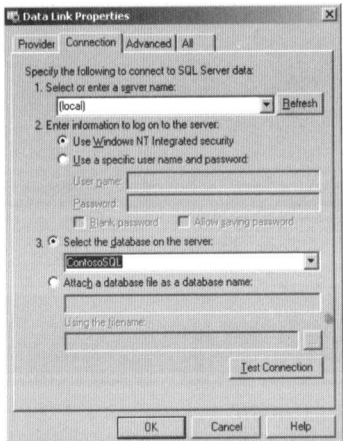

Figure 12-2 Connection settings

Use the Advanced tab, shown in Figure 12-3, to enter the mode for opening the database. In the All tab, displayed in Figure 12-4, you can select general and provider-specific settings.

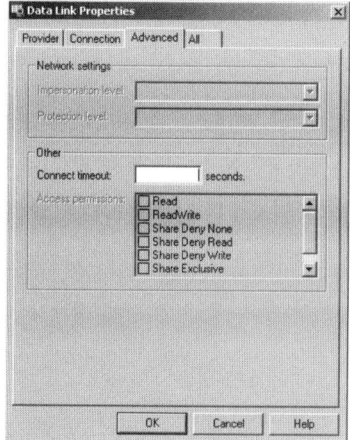

Figure 12-3   Advanced settings

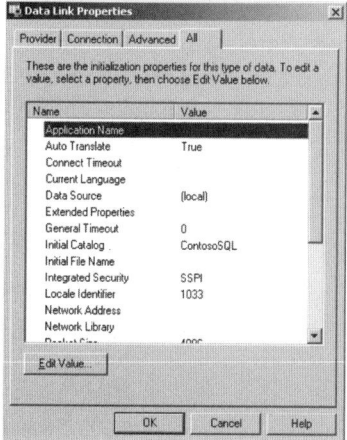

Figure 12-4   General and provider-specific parameters

The following small program illustrates how to open a connection with a data link file. A more detailed description of the *Open* command is provided later. The connection string consists of only the keyword *File Name*, followed by the data link filename.

```
Sub TestDatenlink()

 Dim cnn As ADODB.Connection

 Set cnn = New ADODB.Connection

 cnn.Open "File Name=C:\Contoso\Contoso.udl"

 Debug.Print cnn.ConnectionString

End Sub
```

Connections to Other Providers

In Access projects, you can establish connections to other providers if, for example, you want to access the data in mdb databases. The simplest way to establish such connections is to create a corresponding data link file, as described in the previous section.

The following command establishes a connection to the Access database CONTOSO.MDB:

```
...

Dim cnn As ADODB.Connection

Set cnn = New ADODB.Connection

cnn.Open "Provider=Microsoft.Jet.OLEDB.4.0; " & _

"Data Source=C:\Contoso\Contoso.mdb;User ID=Admin"

...
```

The MSDASQL provider establishes connections by using ODBC drivers. Use the following command to establish a connection to a Microsoft Excel file by using the general ODBC provider:

```
cnn.Open "Provider=MSDASQL;Driver={Microsoft Excel Driver" & _

"(*.xls)};DBQ=C:\Contoso\Contoso.xls"
```

Connection Objects in Access Projects

In Access projects, you usually work with the project's *Connection* object. A project is connected to a database server and a database (use the File, Connection command in the Data Link Properties dialog box to select the database and the database server). The *CurrentProject* object contains basic data about the current project.

CurrentProject is an Access object, not an ADO object. With respect to ADO programming, the object has two useful properties: *Connection* and *BaseConnectionString*.

The following code fragment illustrates the definition of a *Connection* object and the assignment of the project's *Connection* object:

```
...

Dim cnn As ADODB.Connection

Set cnn = CurrentProject.Connection

...
```

CurrentProject refers to the current database. The *Connection* property contains the reference to the corresponding *Connection* object. Here you do not need to create a new object. You can skip *New* when using the *Dim* command.

The *CurrentObject's BaseConnectionString* property contains the base connection string that Microsoft Access used to establish the connection to the SQL Server database. If you compare this to the *CurrentProject.Connection. ConnectionString*, you will notice that Access transforms the connection string because the system always uses the MSDataShape provider to establish an Access project connection. This results in a number of unusual features and restrictions that we point out through the remainder of this chapter.

Note that the *CurrentProject* object's *Connection* object is only a copy of the actual Access project *Connection* object. Using the *Close* method to close the connection does not affect the actual basic connection.

In Access project forms, you can edit, delete, or paste data only if the respective form is based on a recordset that established its connection to the database by using MSDataShape and SQLOLEDB. However, you can view data based on any recordsets in forms. Create a *Connection* object to connect to the database, then open a recordset for this connection and use the form property *Recordset* to assign the recordset to the form. Note that *Connection* and *Recordset* objects must be declared module-wide, that is, outside of all procedures.

The *Open* Method

The *Open* method lets you establish a new connection to any OLE DB provider, but you must pass a valid connection string to the method. The following is the general format for the *Open* method:

```
conn.Open ConnectionString, UserID, Password, Options
```

Three groups of information are used to assemble the *ConnectionString* parameter: the OLE DB provider name, default ADO information, and provider-specific information.

Note the *New* command in the dimensioning command, which is required to create a new *Connection* object before opening a connection:

```
Dim cnn As New ADODB.Connection

cnn.Open "Provider=SQLOLEDB.1;Data Source=(local);User ID=sa;" & _

    "Initial Catalog=ContosoSQL"
```

If you have to enter a user ID and a password to access the data with the OLE DB provider, you can use the *ConnectionString* parameter or you can enter the information explicitly using the *UserID* and *Password* parameters. If both methods are used simultaneously, the parameters take precedence.

Instead of using a connection string, you can directly define the *Connection* object properties, as illustrated by the following code. The sequence of the properties is important:

```
...

Dim cnn As ADODB.Connection

Set cnn = New ADODB.Connection

cnn.Provider = "MSDataShape"

cnn.Properties("Data Provider") = "SQLOLEDB.1"

cnn.Properties("Initial Catalog") = "ContosoSQL"

cnn.Properties("Persist Security Info") = False

cnn.Properties("Data Source") = "(local)"

cnn.Properties("Integrated Security") = "SSPI"

cnn.Open

...
```

You can establish multiple connections to different databases or to the same database. Note, however, that every connection uses up server resources, as well as client resources.

Other Properties and Methods

The following sections provide descriptions of additional *Connection* object properties and methods.

The *Execute* Method

The *Connection* object's *Execute* method lets you execute selection and action queries. If you execute the method using a selection query, the system returns a recordset (see Chapter 13, "*Recordset* Objects") that always presents the settings *adOpenForwardOnly* and *adLockReadOnly*.

This method is more interesting for executing action queries, which modify data. The following small program prompts the user for an action query name or a SQL text and then processes the query. The program returns the number of records that were edited as a result of the query:

```
Sub ConnectionExecute()
 Dim strQry As String
 Dim lngRecordsAffected As Long


 strQry = InputBox("View name or SQL-text")
 If strQry <> "" Then
 CurrentProject.Connection.Execute strQry, lngRecordsAffected
 MsgBox lngRecordsAffected & " records modified."
 End If
End Sub
```

Executing Stored Procedures

There are two ways you can use the *Connection* object to activate stored procedures. You can either use the *Execute* method already described, or you can use the name of stored procedures directly. Let's assume that your database contains a stored procedure named *PriceIncrease*. The following example illustrates how to activate the stored procedure.

The stored procedure is defined as follows:

```
CREATE PROCEDURE [PriceIncrease] @Proc Float
AS
 UPDATE tblProducts SET SalesPrice = SalesPrice * (1+@Proc)
RETURN
```

The following program raises all product prices by 10 percent:

```
Sub ConnectionExecuteSP()
 Dim cnn As ADODB.Connection


 Set cnn = CurrentProject.Connection
 ' 10% price increase
 cnn.Execute "exec PriceIncrease 0.1"
End Sub
```

Chapter 14, "*Command* Objects," contains a detailed description of available options for using the *Connection* object to activate stored procedures directly, because here the stored procedure's name actually describes a *Command* object.

The *ConnectionTimeout* and *CommandTimeout* Properties

These two properties specify (in seconds) how long the system should wait before returning an error message when the system is establishing a connection (*ConnectionTimeout*) or executing a query (*CommandTimeout*). The default value is 15 seconds for *ConnectionTimeout* and 30 seconds for *CommandTimeout*. If you enter **0** seconds as the wait time, the system waits indefinitely.

The *ConnectTimeout* value specifies only how long the system tries to establish the connection after it has already established a network connection to the server. The network card software controls how long the network card waits before returning an error due to the fact that, for example, the network is down or not working. You cannot use the *Connection* object to change the network card settings.

With *CommandTimeout*, the time counter starts once the SQL query reaches the server and ends when the server returns the first record of the result. However, if the query does not reach the server due to network or other problems, the network card's settings determine when the system returns an error message. If the network load is very high and causes the transmission of the query to take a long time, the client waits without starting the *CommandTimeout* time counter.

The *CursorLocation* Property

This property specifies where the system saves your queries so that your applications can access them. Possible settings are *adUseServer* and *adUseClient*. This property is the same as the *CursorLocation* property for recordsets, which is covered in detail in Chapter 13, "*Recordset* Objects."

The *Mode* Property

You can use the *Mode* property to specify certain permissions for the *Connection* object. You will not normally use this property because its effects are limited to Access and it is intended only for the purpose of setting certain states during application development. A user's database permissions specified in SQL Server/MSDE always take precedence. Even if at first glance it appears that you can, for example, use *adModeShareExclusive* on the client to lock out all other users, other users will still have access.

Table 12-5   *ConnectModeEnum* **Values**

Constant	Value	Description
adModeUnknown	0	This is the default setting. The system uses the permissions defined for the database for the connection.
adModeRead	1	The database connection is in read-only mode.
adModeWrite	2	You can use the connection only to write to the database. This constant can be used only in conjunction with *adModeRead*.
adModeReadWrite	3	Users can read and write to the database.
adModeShare-DenyRead	4	Other users cannot read from the database while you are connected.
adModeShare-DenyWrite	8	Other users cannot edit the data while you are connected.
adModeShare-Exclusive	12	Other users cannot establish connections to the database while you are connected.
adModeShare-DenyNone	16	Other users can read and edit the same records, but they cannot establish connections in *adModeShareDenyWrite* or *adModeShareExclusive* mode.

The Errors Collection

Error handling with ADO is a difficult topic because some error messages are meaningless, confusing, or just plain wrong. Even though ADO internal error handling improves with each new version, it still takes some experience to correctly interpret ADO error messages. In addition, messages such as "Several errors occurred" are frustrating.

ADO provides you with two ways to receive information about an error: You can either use the VBA's *Err* object or the *Connection* object's *Errors* collection.

The VBA *Err* object contains information about the error number, the description, and some other information about the error that occurred during the most recently executed VBA command. The *Errors* collection *Error* objects provide information in addition to that provided by the *Err* object. Moreover, the collection can contain several *Error* objects related to an ADO error, whereas the *Err* object always returns only the error information about the first object in the list.

If you are working with several *Connection* objects, each one has an *Errors* list. Table 12-6 details an *Error* object's properties.

Table 12-6 **Properties of the ADO _Error_ Object**

Property	Description
Description	Describes the error.
NativeError	Shows the error number returned by the _Provider_.
Number	Indicates the error number.
Source	Identifies the ADO object or the provider that caused the error.
SQLState	Returns a code consisting of five characters. The code is intended to conform to ANSI SQL conventions. Implementation, however, is provider-specific and does not always provide useful information.

The following procedure contains two deliberate errors. The code deals with these errors after the _ErrorHandler_ position:

```
Sub ADO_Error()
Dim cnn As ADODB.Connection
Dim rst As ADODB.Recordset

On Error GoTo ErrorHandler

Set cnn = CurrentProject.Connection
Set rst = New ADODB.Recordset
rst.Open "SELECT * FROM tblFilms", _
cnn,
adOpenStatic, _
adLockReadOnly

' The error occurs here,
' RollbackTrans without previous BeginTrans
' is not possible.
cnn.RollbackTrans
' Next error: Assignment in read only
' recordset is not possible.
rst!Filmtitle = "Test"

ExitSub:
```

```
    rst.Close

    Set rst = Nothing

    Exit Sub

ErrorHandler:

    Dim errADO As ADODB.Error

    Dim strErr As String

    strErr = "VBA-Error Information" & vbNewLine

    strErr = strErr & "Number: " & vbTab & vbTab & Err.Number & vbNewLine

    strErr = strErr & "Description: " & vbTab & Err.Description &
vbNewLine

    strErr = strErr & "LastDLLError: " & vbTab & Err.LastDllError &
vbNewLine

    strErr = strErr & vbNewLine

    If cnn.Errors.Count > 0 Then

    For Each errADO In cnn.Errors

    strErr = strErr & vbNewLine & "ADO-Error Information (ADO V." &
cnn.Version & ")" _
& vbNewLine

    strErr = strErr & "NativeError: " & vbTab & errADO.NativeError &
vbNewLine

    strErr = strErr & "Number: " & vbTab & vbTab & errADO.Number &
vbNewLine

    strErr = strErr & "Description: " & vbTab & errADO.Description &
vbNewLine

    strErr = strErr & "Source: " & vbTab & vbTab & errADO.Source &
vbNewLine

    strErr = strErr & "SQLState: " & vbTab & vbTab & errADO.SQLState &
vbNewLine

    strErr = strErr & "Source: " & vbTab & vbTab & errADO.Source &
vbNewLine

    Next

    End If

    MsgBox strErr, vbOKOnly + vbExclamation, "Error"

    Resume Next

End Sub
```

The first error in the sample procedure displays the message shown in Figure 12-5, telling you that the system returned two ADO error objects. Note that the *Source* information about the two errors differs.

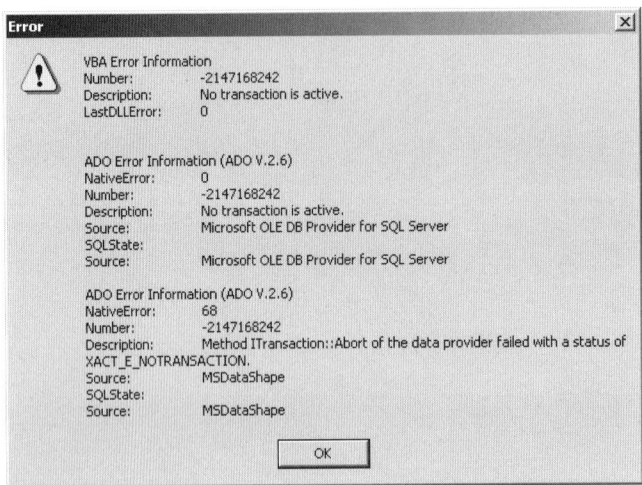

Figure 12-5   Error information

The second error in the example procedure initiates a VBA error only and the *Connection* object's *Errors* collection remains empty.

13

Recordset Objects

All database queries that return data usually transfer it to one or more ADO recordsets. In a database world, a recordset is always based on a table, a query, or a SQL command. A recordset is not considered to be a permanent object. Instead, the data is available only during the recordset object's lifespan.

The query on which the recordset is based consists of at least one field. A *Fields* list is used to access the fields. The data determined in a recordset can be processed record by record, row by row, and forward or backward. A record pointer marks the current data row. ADO provides you with a number of methods, described in Tables 13-1 through 13-3, to determine the current record's position.

Table 13-1 Recordset Properties

Property	Data Type	Description
AbsolutePage	Long	Returns the page where the recordset's current record is saved.
AbsolutePosition	*Long*	Returns the current record's relative record number in the recordset.
ActiveCommand	*Variant*	If you used the *Command* object (see Chapter 14, "*Command* Objects") to create the recordset, the property includes a reference to the object.
ActiveConnection	*String* or *Connection* object	Contains information about the connection the recordset uses to access the database.
BOF	*Boolean*	Stands for beginning of file. This is *True* if the record pointer is placed in front of the recordset's first record.

continued

Table 13-1 **Recordset Properties** *(continued)*

Property	Data Type	Description
Bookmark	*Variant*	Bookmarks (see the section entitled "Bookmarks" later in this chapter).
CacheSize	*Long*	Determines the number of records cached on the client.
CursorLocation	*Long*	Specifies whether to administer the result-set data on the client or on the server.
CursorType	*CursorType-Enum*	Defines how to administer the recordset data.
DataMember	*String*	Determines which ADO data source recordset to use.
DataSource	*Object*	Makes it possible to link the recordset to an ADO data source.
EditMode	*EditMode-Enum*	Returns the current recordset's edit mode status.
EOF	*Boolean*	Stands for end of file. This is *True* if the record pointer is placed behind the recordset's last record.
Fields	*Collection*	Returns a collection of *Field* objects that describe the recordset's columns.
Filter	*Variant*	Defines a filter condition.
Index	*String*	Specifies the index used for the recordset.
LockType	*LockType-Enum*	Defines the system's lock behavior.
MarshalOptions	*Long*	Determines batch update behavior for multilevel applications.
MaxRecords	*Long*	Specifies the maximum number of records the system retrieves from the server for the query result.
PageCount	*Long*	Returns the number of pages of the recordset.
PageSize	*Long*	Specifies the number of records per page.
Properties	*Collection*	Contains a collection of *Property* objects that describe the dynamic properties for the recordset.
RecordCount	*Long*	Returns the number of records in the recordset. Depending on the provider, the *RecordCount* is not current until you use *MoveLast* to jump to the last record; that is, not until the server has transmitted all records.

continued

Table 13-1   Recordset Properties   *(continued)*

Property	Data Type	Description
Sort	*String*	Defines a sort criterion.
Source	*String* or *Command* object	Returns the SQL string or the *Command* object on which the recordset is based.
State	*Long*	Returns the recordset's current status.
Status	*RecordStatusEnum*	Returns the current status of the update operation for the current record.
StayInSync	*Boolean*	For hierarchical recordsets, this property determines the behavior between the recordsets in the levels of the hierarchy.

Table 13-2   Recordset Methods

Method	Description
AddNew	Adds a new, empty record to the recordset.
Cancel	Cancels an asynchronous query.
CancelBatch	Cancels a batch process.
CancelUpdate	Cancels an edit or *AddNew* process.
Clone	Clones a recordset.
Close	Closes a recordset.
CompareBookmarks	Compares two of the current recordset's bookmarks.
Delete	Deletes the current recordset.
Find	Searches for the first record that meets the criteria.
GetRows	Gets records in an array.
GetString	Gets records in a string.
Move	Moves the number of specified rows, backward for negative values and forward for positive values.
MoveFirst	Moves the record pointer to the first record.
MoveLast	Moves the record pointer to the last record.
MoveNext	Moves the record pointer to the next record.
MovePrevious	Moves the record pointer to the previous record.
NextRecordset	Returns the next recordset's results for queries that return multiple resultsets.
Open	Opens a recordset.
Requery	Re-executes the query upon which the recordset is based.

continued

Table 13-2 Recordset Methods *(continued)*

Method	Description
Resync	Updates the recordset with current data from the database.
Save	Saves the contents of a recordset to a file.
Seek	Currently, only OLE DB provider for Jet 4.0 (for Microsoft Access databases) supports this method and only in certain cases.
Supports	Shows if a recordset has a specific capability.
Update	Writes a new or edited record. The program always performs an update if you edit a record and then move the record pointer to another record. Use the CancelUpdate method to cancel changes you made to a record.
UpdateBatch	Writes all of the batch operation's records to the database.

Table 13-3 Recordset Events

Event	Description
EndOfRecordset	Triggered when you attempt to move past the last row of the recordset
FetchComplete	Triggered when all of an asynchronous query's result data is present
FetchProgress	Triggered periodically when an asynchronous query's result data is partly returned
FieldChangeComplete	Triggered when a field's value is modified
MoveComplete	Triggered when the record pointer is moved to another record
RecordChangeComplete	Triggered when a record is modified
RecordsetChangeComplete	Triggered when the recordset object is modified
WillChangeField	Triggered before a field's content is modified
WillChangeRecord	Triggered before a record is modified
WillChangeRecordset	Triggered before a recordset object changes
WillMove	Triggered before the recordset pointer is moved

See Chapter 15, "ADO Events," for information on programming recordset events.

Understanding Recordsets

The *Recordset* object is the most commonly used ADO object. It allows you to access a query's resultset. A *Recordset* object is based on a *Connection* object, or at least one connection string. First, we introduce the different recordset types supported by ADO.

The term *cursor* is used in the database environment to describe what points to a record. In the literature, cursor is often used in the sense of a data set. There can be significant differences in how the system administers the records to which a cursor points. ADO uses four cursor types, which are described in the following sections.

Forward-Only Cursor

The forward-only cursor is the simplest cursor type. The records in a recordset based on such a cursor can be processed only from the top to the bottom.

This cursor's advantages are its simplicity, its speed, and its minimal database server capacity requirements. Because the cursor requires very little administrative information, the resulting client and server loads are quite small.

In developer jargon, this cursor type is also known as a firehose cursor, which evokes an image of the data traveling at very high speed through the hose that connects the server and the client.

For server-based connections created with the SQLOLEDB provider, you can use only a firehose cursor for every connection. Such a connection to the server cannot be disconnected until the system has read all of the cursor data. If you create a new firehose cursor based on the same connection and the connection is still blocked by a firehose cursor with data that has not yet been read completely, ADO automatically creates a new connection. If several users simultaneously open multiple connections, server performance might suffer.

> **Note**   You can use the Profiler, a Microsoft SQL Server tool, to determine the number of existing connections and much more. The profiler also enables you to log and analyze all actions that occur between the client and server. See Chapter 19, "SQL Server Tools," for a description of the program.

Static Cursor

The basic structure of the static cursor is the same as that of the forward-only cursor, but you can use the static cursor to scroll through a recordset in both directions.

As with the forward-only cursor, the static cursor does not let you view the changes that other users make to the data. New records created by other users are not included in the recordset, as it contains only the data that was in the recordset at the time the query was executed. Also, the cursor does not contain any information about the records that were deleted in the meantime, so you might be able to view data in the recordset that has actually already been deleted from the database.

Generally, static cursors are used in read-only mode. Access, however, represents an exception to this rule: Due to the use of the MSDataShape provider for *CurrentProject*, the system allows only those static cursors that are not write-protected.

Keyset Cursor

Unlike the two cursors previously described, a keyset cursor does not cache partial query results. Instead, it administers key values only, usually the primary key values, and caches the key values as well. Then, when you access a record, the system retrieves the actual data from the database at that point in time. Because the data is not transmitted until it is needed, you can see any changes other users made to the data. However, you cannot see any of the records that might meet your query condition that were added by other users until after you re-execute the query.

Dynamic Cursor

In principle, a dynamic cursor works like a keyset cursor, except that new records entered by the user are included in the recordset as long as they match the query condition.

CursorLocation: Client or Server?

Use the *CursorLocation* property to specify whether ADO caches the resultset on the client or on the server. With a client-based cursor, all the records are transmitted to the client when you open the recordset. With a server-based cursor, however, opening the recordset creates a list showing which records are part of the resultset. The records are transmitted to the client only at the client's request.

You should choose a cursor type for your application based on several factors. How much data does the resultset include? If you attempt to import one million records to the client, the process will be time-consuming, strain the network's capacity, and require tremendous resources on the client, assuming the client is even able to handle the load. If, on the other hand, you use this query to administer the recordset on the server, the task will take up a large portion of the server's resources. If multiple users send such queries to the server, it will experience capacity bottlenecks.

The *Recordset* object has a *MaxRecords* property that you can use to specify the maximum number of records in a recordset. This property, for example, enables you to prevent a client-based recordset from consuming too many resources.

Some recordset methods and properties work only with client-based recordsets, whereas others require server-based recordsets.

Advantages and Disadvantages of Client-Based Cursors

Client-based cursors provide more function, work faster, and require fewer server resources. However, in comparison with server-based cursors, they require more client resources. Disconnected recordsets have to use a client-side recordset and have a capability to release the server-side resources.

Advantages and Disadvantages of Server-Based Cursors

Server-based cursors do not require a lot of available memory on the client. In addition, they support all cursor types and pessimistic locks. However, they do require a lot of available memory on the server. They also result in heavy server loads, especially for numerous connections with server-based cursors.

Parameter Combinations

One of the peculiar features of working with ADO is that the program does not always implement user-defined parameter combinations for *CursorLocation*, *CursorType*, *LockType*, and *Options* as specified. Depending on the OLE DB provider being used, it is possible that the system does not support your desired parameter combination. In that case, ADO independently implements the parameters so that the OLE DB provider can process them intelligently. This action, however, could cause the recordset to behave in a manner inconsistent with the intentions defined by the parameters.

> **Note** All client-based cursors are static. Only server-based cursors can also be keyset, dynamic, or forward-only cursors.

Special Features of the *CurrentProject* Object

One of the *CurrentProject* object's special features is its connection to the database, which is created with the assistance of the MSDataShape provider. MSDataShape connections always use the *CursorLocation = adUseClient*, and the *CursorType = adOpenStatic*, and the *LockType* setting must not be *adLockPessimistic*. We have tested all possible parameter variants (for *CurrentProject*) for the SQL Server OLE DB provider. Refer to the table *tblRecordsetOpenTest*, located in the sample database for this chapter, for the results. The name of the corresponding program to fill this table is *RecordsetOpenTest()*. You can use the report *rptRecordsetOpenTest* to format the table contents for output.

Opening a Recordset

The *Open* method is used to open a recordset. The method is defined as follows:

```
recordset.Open [Source] [,ActiveConnection] [,CursorType] [,LockType]
[,Options]
```

You can use the name of a table, a query, or a SQL table as the *Source*. The *ActiveConnection* parameter specifies which connection to use for filling the recordset. Enter *CurrentProject.Connection* to access the database connected to the project.

Use the *CursorType* parameter to define the recordset type. A cursor is a data structure that stores a query's results. The cursor type determines a corresponding recordset object's functions. The default value for *CursorType* is *adOpenForwardOnly*.

Table 13-4 lists the four valid *CursorType* constants, described earlier, that you can enter when opening a recordset.

Table 13-4   *CursorType* Constants

Constant	Cursor Type
adOpenForwardOnly	Forward-only cursor
adOpenStatic	Static cursor
adOpenKeyset	Keyset cursor
adOpenDynamic	Dynamic cursor
adOpenUnspecified	Cursor not specified

The *CursorLocation* parameter is crucial to how the recordset methods and properties covered in this chapter work. The parameter can have one of two values: *adUseServer* or *adUseClient*. By default, the system uses *adUseServer* to open recordsets.

If the ADO methods and parameters do not work as expected with this value, it makes sense to check if the functions can be executed for more than one specific *CursorLocation*. For example, the batch processing functions described later work only with the *adUseClient* setting.

If you select *adUseServer* for the *CursorLocation*, you can specify the cache size on the client. The recordset object property *CacheSize* determines the number of records in the cache, and its default value is 1. If you request a record not currently in the cache, ADO reads the subsequent records into the cache. If records currently in the cache are modified in the database on the server, the data in the cache is not updated.

If two users simultaneously attempt to edit data in a table, it is possible for both to edit the same record at the same time. To prevent the users from overwriting each other's data, you can use *locks* to organize how users access data. That is why you need to specify the *LockType* parameter, using the options in Table 13-5, only if you want to edit the recordset's data, even if there is only one user accessing the data. Chapter 26, "Transactions and Locking," contains a detailed description of the different *Locking* constants. In this chapter, we always use the *adLockOptimistic* constant.

Table 13-5 *LockType* **Options**

Option	Description
adLockReadOnly	This is the default value. You cannot edit the recordset data.
adLockOptimistic	Specifies that the recordset data may be edited. This option uses the optimistic lock method.
adLockBatchOptimistic	See the section entitled "Batch Processing" later in this chapter for a description of this option. You can use batch updates to update multiple records in one operation.
adLockPessimistic	Specifies that the recordset data may be edited. This option uses the pessimistic lock method.
adLockUnspecified	Does not specify a type of lock.

CurrentProject has a special feature: Recordsets that are opened based on *CurrentProject*'s *Connection* object always use the optimistic lock method. If you want to switch to the pessimistic lock method, you can assign it, but Access will use the optimistic lock option *adBatchOptimistic* without generating any further messages.

You can use the *Options* parameter to better define the content of the *Source* parameter and thus assist ADO with the analysis, as described in Table 13-6. If you define the parameter, ADO does not need to analyze *Source* to define the analysis routines.

Table 13-6 *Options* **Constants**

Option	Description
adCmdUnknown	Specifies that ADO must determine how to evaluate the argument *Source* (default value).
adCmdText	Specifies that *Source* contains a character string with the corresponding SQL query.
adCmdTable	Specifies that *Source* contains the name of a table. ADO creates its own SQL query, which returns all lines with all columns of the table. Internally, ADO extends the table name with *"SELECT * FROM"*.
adCmdTableDirect	Specifies that *Source* contains the name of a table. The program directly returns all rows and columns.
adCmdStoredProc	Specifies that *Source* contains the name of a stored procedure; in Access this is the name of a query. The call is implemented as *{? = CALL proc(?)}*.
adCmdFile	Specifies that you can save a recordset's data to a file (see the section entitled "Saving Recordsets" later in this chapter). You can use the option adCmdFile to read a saved file.

The following program fragments illustrate some of the different variants you can use to open a recordset.

First, you open the table with default settings, that is, with *adOpenForwardOnly* as the *CursorType* and *adLockReadOnly* as the *LockType*, as shown in this example. This means that you can read the recordset data only from top to bottom.

```
Dim rst As ADODB.Recordset

Dim cnn As ADODB.Connection

Set cnn = CurrentProject.Connection

Set rst = New ADODB.Recordset

rst.Connection = cnn

rst.Open "tblFilms"
```

In the following example, all entries are specified as parameters of the *Open* method:

```
Dim rst As ADODB.Recordset

Set rst = New ADODB.Recordset

rst.Open "tblFilms", CurrentProject.Connection, adOpenStatic, adLockOptimistic
```

You can also use the defined parameters for the parameter list, as shown next. The advantage of doing so is that you do not need to observe the parameter sequence.

```
Dim rst As ADODB.Recordset

Set rst = New ADODB.Recordset

rst.Open _

CursorType:=adOpenStatic, _

LockType:=adLockOptimistic, _

Source:="tblFilms", _

ActiveConnection:=CurrentProject.Connection
```

You can also use the *Open* command as follows:

```
Dim rst As ADODB.Recordset

Set rst = New ADODB.Recordset

rst.Source = "tblFilms"

rst.ActiveConnection = CurrentProject.Connection

rst.CursorType = adOpenStatic

rst.LockType = adLockOptimistic

rst.Open
```

The following lines of code instruct the program to load the data in the table *tblFilms* sorted by film title:

```
Dim rst As ADODB.Recordset

Set rst = New ADODB.Recordset

rst.Open "SELECT * FROM tblFilms ORDER BY tblFilms.Filmtitle", _

 CurrentProject.Connection, adOpenStatic, adLockOptimistic
```

If you want to open a recordset based on a parameter-free stored procedure, you must pass the *Options* parameter with the value *acCmdStoredProc*, for example:

```
Dim rst As ADODB.Recordset
Set rst = New ADODB.Recordset
  rst.Open "AllFilms", _
  CurrentProject.Connection, _
  adOpenStatic, _
  adLockOptimistic, _
  acCmdStoredProc
```

Working with Recordsets

The following sections introduce *Recordset* object methods and properties that you can use in your programs, featuring examples in which recordset data is accessed with the *Fields* list (see the section entitled "The Fields List" later in this chapter). Several syntax variants are available to access the data.

For example, if you use the command

```
rst.Open "SELECT FilmNr, Filmtitle FROM tblFilms", _
CurrentProject.Connection, adOpenStatic, adLockOptimistic
```

to open the recordset, you can use *rst.Fields("Filmtitle").Value* to access the current record's *Filmtitle* field. Alternatively, you can use the shorter variant *rst.Fields("Filmtitle")* because *Value* is the default property. You can also use *rst("Filmtitle")* or an even shorter variant, *rst!Filmtitle*.

However, if you use this syntax, you must enclose the field name itself in angle brackets if the field contains spaces, such as, for example, *rst![Fieldname with Spaces]*.

Which Functions Does My Recordset Support?

You can use *Supports* to determine which functions your recordset supports. For example, you can use

```
...
If rst.Supports(adUpdate) Then
...
```

to find out if you can edit the data in a recordset. Table 13-7 lists the most important parameters for the *Supports* property.

Table 13-7   ***Supports* Constants**

Parameter	Description
adAddNew	Specifies that you can add new data
adApproxPosition	Specifies that you can use the properties *AbsolutePosition* and *AbsolutePage*
adBookmark	Specifies that you can use the *Bookmark* property to access certain records
adDelete	Specifies that you can delete records
adFind	Indicates that the *Find* method is being supported
adHoldRecords	Specifies that you can move the current record pointer without saving any changes you made to the current record
adIndex	Indicates whether or not you can use the *Index* property
adMovePrevious	Specifies that you can navigate backwards through the recordset
adNotify	Specifies whether or not the recordset can trigger events
adResync	Specifies that you can use the *Resync* method to synchronize the recordset with the data on which it is based
adSeek	Specifies that you can use the *Seek* method
adUpdate	Determines that you can edit data
adUpdateBatch	Specifies that you can edit batch data (see the section entitled "Batch Processing" later in the chapter)

Positioning the Record Pointer

You can use the different *Move* methods to determine the current record's position. The *Move NumRecords [,Start]* method moves the record pointer forward (with a positive value for *NumRecords*) or backward (with a negative value for *NumRecords*). You can use the optional *Start* parameter to define a bookmark that executes the *Move* operation. You can also pass one of the following constants to *Start*: *adBookmarkCurrent* for the current record, *adBookmarkFirst* for the first record, or *adBookmarkLast* for the last record.

MoveFirst moves the record pointer to the first record and *MoveLast* moves it to the last record. *MoveNext* and *MovePrevious* move the record pointer to the next record or the previous record, respectively, as shown here:

```
Sub LoopThruRecordset()
 Dim cnn As ADODB.Connection
 Dim rst As ADODB.Recordset


 Set cnn = CurrentProject.Connection
 Set rst = New ADODB.Recordset
 rst.Open "tblFilms", cnn, adOpenStatic, adLockReadOnly


 ' Loop
 Do While Not rst.EOF
    Debug.Print rst!Filmtitle
    rst.MoveNext
 Loop
 rst.Close
 set rst = Nothing
End Sub
```

At the beginning and the end of a recordset, you must pay attention to the behavior of the *BOF* and *EOF* properties and to the current record's position.

If the current record is the recordset's last record, and if you use *MoveNext* to move the position pointer, the value of the *EOF* property is *True*. There is then no current record, as the position pointer contains an invalid value. If you attempt to access the record, the system returns run-time error 3021 and the message "Either BOF or EOF is True, or the current record has been deleted. The requested operation requires a current record." The system returns the same error message if you try to use *MoveNext* to move beyond the end; that is, if *EOF* is *True*, every movement of the position pointer returns an error. Error routines can be used to capture errors such as 3021. The same applies to the beginning of the recordset and the *BOF* property.

If *BOF* or *EOF* is *True*, the record pointer does not point to a valid record. The system returns an error if you try to assign data to or read data from the invalid record.

You can use the command sequence

```
...
If rst.BOF And rst.EOF Then

 ' Empty Recordset

 ...

End If

...
```

to check if a recordset contains data. If both the *BOF* and *EOF* properties are *True*, the recordset is consequently empty.

The *RecordCount* Property

You can use the *RecordCount* property to determine the number of records in a recordset, at least in theory. Unfortunately, things are a bit different in practice. The property's behavior depends on the selected cursor or its location.

If you open your recordset based on the *CurrentProject.Connection* connection, the cursor is static and located on the client. In that case, all data is transmitted from the server to the client through the network, which is why the client knows how many records were transmitted.

With server-based cursors or keyset cursors, the client does not know how many records were transmitted. If you pass the command to the recordset, the system points the record pointer to the last record. That is how *RecordCount* also returns the correct value. Note that *MoveLast* transmits all records to the client.

RecordCount always returns the value –1 for all recordsets with *adLock-ForwardOnly*.

The *AbsolutePosition* Property

The *AbsolutePosition* property returns the current record number for the recordset data, a value between 1 and the total number of records. If *BOF* or *EOF* is *True*, the system returns the constant *adPosBOF* or *adPosEOF*.

Bookmarks

Programs often require that you remember the position of certain records so that you can locate them later. ADO administers bookmarks, which are unique marks for every recordset. You can save these marks in variables of their own, so that they can serve as originating addresses later on.

Bookmarks are not comparable to dBase or other product record numbers, because they apply only for the recordset's lifespan. The *Variant* type is assigned to an ADO bookmark.

Not all recordsets let you set bookmarks. You can use the *Supports (adBookmark)* recordset's function to access the bookmark support functions.

The following program fragment assigns the current recordset's bookmarks to a variable. At the end, the program fragment assigns the current record position to the record to which the saved bookmark belongs:

```
Dim varBookmark As Variant

...

' save the bookmark

varBookmark = rst.Bookmark

...

rst.MoveFirst

...

' jump to saved bookmark

rst.Bookmark = varBookmark
```

Comparing Bookmarks

You can use the *CompareBookmarks(bookmark1, bookmark2)* method of the recordset object to easily compare bookmarks. The method returns a value that defines the relative relationship between the two bookmarks in the recordset. Table 13-8 lists the possible values.

Table 13-8   *CompareBookmarks* Constants

Constant	Description
adCompareEqual	Specifies that the bookmarks are equal
adCompareGreaterThan	Specifies that the first bookmark is located behind the second
adCompareLessThan	Specifies that the first bookmark is located in front of the second
adCompareNotComparable	Specifies that the bookmarks are not comparable
adCompareNotEqual	Specifies that the bookmarks are not equal and not sorted

In this context, it is important that bookmarks belong to the same recordset, as shown in the following example, because you cannot compare bookmarks from different recordsets. Every bookmark is based on recordset-specific data.

```
Sub TestCompareBookmarks()

 Dim rst As ADODB.Recordset

 Dim bm1 As Variant

 Dim bm2 As Variant

 Dim i As Integer


 ' Open recordset

 Set rst = New ADODB.Recordset

 rst.Open "select * from tblFilms order by Filmtitle", _

 CurrentProject.Connection

 ' Generate a random number between 0 and number of records

 i = Fix(Rnd * rst.RecordCount)

 ' Go to record i

 rst.Move i, adBookmarkFirst

 ' Save first bookmark

 bm1 = rst.Bookmark

 ' Generate a random number between 0 and number of records

 i = Fix(Rnd * rst.RecordCount)

 ' Go to record i

 rst.Move i, adBookmarkFirst

 ' Save second bookmark

 bm2 = rst.Bookmark


 ' Compare bookmarks

 Select Case rst.CompareBookmarks(bm1, bm2)

   Case adCompareGreaterThan

     Debug.Print " adCompareGreaterThan "
```

```
    Case adCompareLessThan
      Debug.Print " adCompareLessThan "
    Case adCompareEqual
      Debug.Print " adCompareEqual "
    Case adCompareNotComparable
      Debug.Print " adCompareNotComparable "
    Case adCompareNotEqual
      Debug.Print " adCompareNotEqual "
  End Select
  Set rst = Nothing
End Sub
```

The section later in this chapter entitled "Using Bookmarks to Set Filters" describes how to use bookmarks for the *Filter* method.

Searching Records

The following scenarios are available for searching recordsets:

- Using a SQL query with a *WHERE* clause to constrain the recordset
- Searching with the *Find* method
- Setting *Filter* conditions

In general, you should always use the first scenario for working with recordsets. It is always faster and easier to select Access records based on a query or a SQL character string.

However, there are exceptions: For example, to minimize network traffic, it can be useful to open a recordset with a static cursor and import all data to the client, then search and filter the data in the recordset. This section does not address the option of using a SQL command to constrain a query's resultset. Instead, we introduce the methods for searching and filtering data within a recordset.

Searching with the *Find* Method

The *Find* method searches the recordset for data while analyzing the character string entered as the criterion. The syntax for the criterion is a simpler, derivative form of the SQL *WHERE* clause syntax:

```
recordset.Find Criteria [, SkipRecords][, SearchDirection][, Start]
```

where *Criteria* denotes a character string with the condition. You must use the *Column name, Comparative operation* format to specify the condition. You cannot use *AND* or *OR* to join multiple conditions. You can also use *LIKE* as a comparative operator, with some restrictions: *, %, and _ are possible placeholder characters. However, they all have the same meaning, as they are all variable for any number of characters. You can use the characters only at the end of a character string, as illustrated in the next example, but not in the form *Filmtitle LIKE 'T*tor'*.

The optional *SkipRecords* parameter lets you skip a number of records before starting the search itself. You can use *SearchDirection* to specify the direction of the search with *adSearchForward* or *adSearchBackward*. Use *Start* to specify a bookmark from which to start the search. In the process, you can also specify one of three constants: *adBookmarkCurrent* (current record; this is the default value), *adBookmarkFirst* (first record), or *adBookmarkLast* (last record).

Not all recordsets support the *Find* method. Use *Supports(adFind)* to see if you can use *Find*. The following program example illustrates the method's use:

```
Sub FindMethod()


 Dim rst As ADODB.Recordset

 Dim strCriteria As String

 Dim mark as Variant


 Set rst = New ADODB.Recordset

 rst.Open "SELECT * FROM tblFilms ORDER BY Filmtitle", _

 CurrentProject.Connection, _

 adOpenStatic, _

 adLockReadOnly


 If rst.Supports(adFind) Then

  strCriteria = "Filmtitle LIKE 'A*'"

  rst.Find strCriteria

  Do While Not rst.EOF

   Debug.Print rst("Filmtitle")
```

```
    mark = rst.Bookmark
    rst.Find strCriteria, 1, adSearchForward, mark
    ' try: rst.Find strCriteria, 1, adSearchForward, adBookmarkCurrent
  Loop
 End If
 rst.Close
 Set rst = Nothing
End Sub
```

Setting Filter Conditions

You can use filter conditions to constrain a recordset's data. Compared to SQL *WHERE* clauses, the filter condition syntax is very limited. Moreover, ADO's analysis logic (parser) contains a few bugs. Single quotes, for example, are processed incorrectly. The only solution is to try different things!

The following program illustrates the use of the *Filter* property:

```
Sub RecordsetWithFilter_ADO()


 Dim rst As ADODB.Recordset


 Set rst = New ADODB.Recordset
 rst.Open "SELECT * FROM tblFilms", CurrentProject.Connection
 rst.Filter = "Filmtitle like 'A%'"


 ' Continue until end of the recordset
 Do While Not rst.EOF
  Debug.Print rst!Filmtitle
  rst.MoveNext
 Loop
 rst.Close
 Set rst = Nothing
End Sub
```

Filter Constants

To set the *Filter* property, you can either use a string with a filter condition, one of the constants listed in Table 13-9, or a bookmark field.

Table 13-9   *Filter* Constants

Option	Description
adFilterNone	Removes the current filter.
adFilterPendingsRecords	Filters out all records during batch processing (see the section entitled "Batch Processing" later in this chapter) that were edited, but have not yet been transferred to the database.
adFilterAffectedRecords	Only displays those records affected by the most recent *Delete-*, *Resync-*, *UpdateBatch-*, or *CancelBatch-* call (see the section entitled "Batch Processing").
adFilterFetchedRecords	Displays only those records saved in the local ADO cache. The *CacheSize* property specifies the number of records in the cache. With a server-based cursor, the system only filters the records currently in the cache. With a client-based cursor, which does not actually have a client cache, the system only filters the *CacheSize* number of records.
adFilterConflictingRecords	Displays only those records that could not be saved during the most recent batch process (see the section entitled "Batch Processing").

Using Bookmarks to Set Filters

There is an interesting way to use bookmarks in conjunction with the *Filter* property. You can assign a field with bookmarks to the property. The recordset then contains exactly those records with bookmarks that were saved in the array.

In the following example, the bookmarks of the first, last, and second to last record are passed to the *aBookmarks* array:

```
Sub FilterWithBookmark()


Dim rst As ADODB.Recordset
' Array for 3 bookmarks
Dim aBookmarks(2) As Variant
```

```
Set rst = New ADODB.Recordset
With rst
   .Open "select * from tblFilms", _
   CurrentProject.Connection, _
   adOpenStatic, adLockOptimistic

   If Not .Supports(adBookmark) Then Exit Sub

   ' Remember first, last und next to last record
   .MoveFirst
   Debug.Print !Filmtitle
   aBookmarks(0) = .Bookmark
   .MoveLast
   Debug.Print !Filmtitle
   aBookmarks(1) = .Bookmark
   .MovePrevious
   Debug.Print !Filmtitle
   aBookmarks(2) = .Bookmark
   ' Set filter
   .Filter = aBookmarks
End With

Do While Not rst.EOF
   Debug.Print rst!Filmtitle
   rst.MoveNext
Loop
rst.Close
set rst = Nothing
End Sub
```

Sorting Recordsets

Two different procedures are available for sorting recordsets: sorting with an *ORDER BY* clause in the SQL query or sorting with the *Sort* property. In the first case, the system transfers the sorted data from the database to the recordset; in the second case, the system only sorts the data in the recordset. The second scenario can be useful with a client-based cursor, because it requires no server or network resources.

You can use the same syntax that you use for *ORDER BY* for the *Sort* property as well. For example:

```
rst.Sort = "Filmtitle DESC"
```

To undo the sort process defined with *Sort*, assign an empty "" string to *Sort*.

Editing Data

To edit the data in a recordset or to add new records, several conditions must be met. On one hand, the recordset on which the query is based must return a modifiable resultset; that is, it cannot contain an aggregate function such as *Max()* or *Sum()*. On the other hand, you must open the recordset with the lock method *adLockOptimistic* (or *adLockBatchOptimistic*; see the section later in this chapter entitled "Batch Processing"). If you are not using the *CurrentObject.Connection* connection object, and if you are creating a connection object with the SQLOLEDB provider instead, you can also use the *adLockPessimistic* option. See Chapter 26, "Transactions and Locking," for a description of the locking mechanisms.

If you want to edit the data in the recordset, *Supports(adEdit)* must return the value *True*. You can add new records if *Supports(adAddNew)* is *True*.

The *Fields* Collection

You can use the *Fields* collection to access a recordset's result data. For example, if you used the SQL query *SELECT FilmNr, Filmtitle FROM tblFilms* to open your recordset, the recordset's *Fields* collection contains two *Field* objects for the columns *FilmNr* and *Filmtitle*. The following program illustrates this process:

```
Sub FieldsCollection()

Dim rst As ADODB.Recordset

Dim fld As ADODB.Field
```

```
Set rst = New ADODB.Recordset
rst.Open "SELECT FilmNr, Filmtitle FROM tblFilms", _
 CurrentProject.Connection
' Field names
For Each fld In rst.Fields
 Debug.Print fld.Name
Next
Debug.Print

' Field values
Do While Not rst.EOF
   For Each fld In rst.Fields
    Debug.Print fld.Value
   Next
   Debug.Print
   rst.MoveNext
 Loop
 rst.Close
 Set rst = Nothing
End Sub
```

Use the *Count* property in the *Fields* collection, described in Table 13-10, to define the number of *Field* objects in the collection.

Table 13-10   Properties of the *Fields* Collection

Property	Description
Count	Returns the number of *Field* objects in the collection
Item	Enables access to a *Field* object

Table 13-11 describes the methods available for the *Fields* collection. Note that ADO version 2.5 has introduced two new objects, *Record* and *Stream*. Some of the methods listed in this table are only available for version 2.5 and later, and they work only with *Record* objects.

Table 13-11   Methods for the *Fields* Collection

Method	ADO Version	Description
Append		Appends a new *Field* object to the collection. See the section entitled "Recordsets Without a Database Connection" later in this chapter for an example.
CancelUpdate	2.5 and later	Works with record objects only and therefore is not described here in detail.
Delete		Removes a *Field* object from the collection. See the section later in this chapter entitled "Recordsets Without a Database Connection."
Refresh		Refreshes the collection.
Resync	2.5 and later	Works with record objects only and therefore is not described here in detail.
Update	2.5 and later	Works with record objects only and therefore is not described here in detail.

Table 13-12 lists the properties of a *Field* object, and Table 13-13 lists the methods for these objects.

Table 13-12   Properties for *Field* Object

Property	Data Type	Description
ActualSize	Long	Returns the field's actual size in bytes. This property is primarily used to determine the actual size of text fields with variable lengths. Note that you need to count two bytes for *Unicode* fields, which means you need to divide *ActualSize* in half to determine the number of characters.
Attributes	*Long*	Returns the field's attributes.
DataFormat	*Object*	Enables you to format the contents of *Value*.
DefinedSize	*Long*	Returns the field's defined size, which is the number of characters for text fields. For *Unicode* fields, the property also returns the number of characters and not the size in bytes, as with *ActualSize*.
Name	*String*	Returns the field name.
NumericScale	*Byte*	Determines the number of decimal places.
OriginalValue	*Variant*	Contains the field's original value.

continued

Table 13-12   **Properties for *Field* Object**   *(continued)*

Property	Data Type	Description
Precision	*Byte*	Returns the maximum number of places that can be saved in a numeric field, including the number of places to the right of the decimal point.
Properties	Collection of property objects	Enables you to access provider-specific properties.
Status	*Enum value*	Returns *FieldStatusEnum* value, default is *adFieldOK*. Mainly used with *Record* Object and recordsets without a database.
Type	*Byte*	Returns a constant that describes the field's data type. The constants are named in *DataTypeEnum*.
UnderlyingValue	*Variant*	Enables you to query the field's current value in the database (which can differ from the value in the recordset if another user edited the database value in the meantime).
Value	*Variant*	Returns the field's content.

Table 13-13   **Methods for *Field* Objects**

Method	Description
AppendChunk	Appends data to a field of the database type *image* (*adLongVarBinary*), *text* (*adLongVarChar*), or *ntext* (*adLongVarWChar*)
GetChunk	Reads data from a field of the database field types listed earlier

The Fields List

If you open a recordset based on a SQL query with a *JOIN*, note the following special feature of the SQLOLEDB provider (and, in the case of Access, the MSDataShape provider as well). For example, if you open a recordset with the following query

```
SELECT tblFilms.FilmNr, tblWeeks.FilmNr

 FROM tblFilms LEFT OUTER JOIN tblWeeks

 ON tblFilms.FilmNr = tblWeeks.FilmNr
```

the system returns a *Fields* list with two *Field* objects both named *FilmNr*. If, for example, you then use *rst!FilmNr* to access the content of the *FilmNr* field, does the system return the content of the *FilmNr* field from the table *tblFilms* or *tblWeeks?* You could now argue that this does not appear to be an important issue in this example, as *FilmNr* is the *JOIN* condition. However, what happens if you now navigate through the recordset to determine for which film number there is no record in the table *tblWeeks*; that is to say, for which film number *tblWeeks.FilmNr* has the value *Null?*

The only solution to this problem is to uniquely name the fields in the SQL query, which means you must use *AS* to assign a name to every field, as shown here:

```
SELECT tblFilms.FilmNr AS FilmNr, tblWeeks.FilmNr AS FilmNrWeeks

 FROM tblFilms LEFT OUTER JOIN tblWeeks

 ON tblFilms.FilmNr = tblWeeks.FilmNr
```

Incidentally, if you use the view designer to assemble views, the system automatically assigns unique names during the creation of views. With stored procedures you receive erroneous output if you do not use unique names in the query.

Modifying Data

You can modify the current record's data by assigning new values to its fields. ADO internally creates a buffer for the new data when you first assign a value to a field.

To save the data, you can either call the *Update* method or you can designate another record as the current one by using, for example, one of the *Move* methods.

You can use *CancelUpdate* to cancel changes you made to a record that have not yet been saved.

The following program enables you to edit the title of a film accessed with the help of the film number:

```
Sub ModifyFilmtitle()


Dim cnn As ADODB.Connection

Dim rst As ADODB.Recordset

Dim lng As Long

Dim strTmp As String


Set cnn = CurrentProject.Connection
```

```
Set rst = New ADODB.Recordset

rst.Open "select * from tblFilms", _
   cnn, adOpenStatic, adLockOptimistic
With rst
  If .Supports(adUpdate) Then

    lng = InputBox("Modify Filmtitle for which FilmNr?")
      .Find "FilmNr=" & lng, Start:=adBookmarkFirst

     If Not rst.EOF Then

        !Filmtitle = InputBox( _
        Prompt:="Filmtitle:", _
        Default:=!Filmtitle, _
        Title:="Modify Filmtitle")

        If !Filmtitle <> "" Then
         .Update
        Else
         .CancelUpdate
        End If
      Else
        MsgBox "No film with this filmnumber!"
      End If
    End If
   .Close
  End With
  Set rst = Nothing
End Sub
```

Modifications with the SQL Command *UPDATE*

If ADO data is being updated in the database (that is, whenever you use *Update* for the recordset or switch to another record), ADO creates a SQL *UPDATE* instruction internally to modify the data in the database. You can view this process in the SQL Server's profiler (see Chapter 19, "SQL Server Tools").

This leads to the realization that it might be useful to directly execute *UPDATE* commands from your programs by using, for example, the *Connection* object's *Execute* method or by using the *Command* objects introduced in Chapter 14, "*Command* Objects."

The *OriginalValue* Property

If you modified field contents but did not yet save the record, you can use the *Field's OriginalValue* property to access the original field values.

The *UnderlyingValue* Property

The *UnderlyingValue* property lets you read a field's current value from the database, as shown in the next example. This procedure is useful when you want to determine if another user has modified a record in the meantime. This property is not available for every provider and cursor type.

```
Sub TestUnderlyingValue()

Dim rst As ADODB.Recordset

Dim fld As ADODB.Field

Dim cnn As ADODB.Connection

Dim strTmp As String


Set cnn = New ADODB.Connection

cnn.Open "Data Source=SERVER;Initial Catalog=ContosoSQL;" & _

  "Provider=SQLOLEDB.1;Integrated Security=SSPI"

Set rst = New ADODB.Recordset

rst.Open "SELECT filmnr,Filmtitle FROM tblFilms WHERE FilmNr=1", _

  cnn, adOpenStatic, adLockOptimistic

' First record

For Each fld In rst.Fields

  Debug.Print fld.Name; "="; fld.Value

Next
```

```
strTmp = rst!Filmtitle
'Simulation of a change by another user
cnn.Execute "UPDATE tblFilms SET Filmtitle='" & StrReverse(strTmp) & _
   "' WHERE FilmNr=1"
' Read first record
For Each fld In rst.Fields
   Debug.Print fld.Name & ":" & fld.Value & ":" & fld.UnderlyingValue
Next
' Undo simulation changes
cnn.Execute "UPDATE tblFilms SET Filmtitle='" & strTmp & _
   "' WHERE Filmnr=1"
Set rst = Nothing
Set cnn = Nothing
End Sub
```

Adding New Records

Use the *AddNew* method shown in the next example to add a new, empty record to the recordset, when empty means that all fields have the value *Null*.

You can then assign values to the fields. After an *Update* procedure, the data is written to the table on which the fields are based. ADO, however, performs an automatic update whenever you switch to another record or whenever you activate *AddNew*.

```
Sub AddRecord()


Dim rst As ADODB.Recordset


Set rst = New ADODB.Recordset
rst.Open "tblFilms", CurrentProject.Connection, _
      adOpenStatic, adLockOptimistic
```

```
With rst

    If .Supports(adAddNew) Then

      .AddNew

      !Filmtitle = "Gladiator"


      If MsgBox("Save modifications?", vbYesNo) = vbYes Then

        .Update

      Else

        .CancelUpdate

      End If

    End If

End With

rst.Close

Set rst = Nothing

End Sub
```

Querying Defined Auto Values

In the preceding example, saving the new record automatically creates a new *FilmNr* because *FilmNr* is defined as the auto value. If you need the newly created number in your program, you can use *rst!FilmNr* to directly access the auto value after performing the *Update* procedure.

The SQL character string *SELECT @@IDENTITY* provides a general method to determine the most recently created auto value independent of the table for which it was generated. If you modify the preceding program as shown next, the system displays the new film number twice:

```
...

If MsgBox("Save modificatons?", vbYesNo) = vbYes Then

    .Update

    ' New filmnumber: Variant 1

    MsgBox "New filmnumber " & !FilmNr

    ' New filmnumber: Variant 2

    Dim rst2 As ADODB.Recordset

    Set rst2 = New ADODB.Recordset
```

```
        rst2.Open "SELECT @@IDENTITY as ID", CurrentProject.Connection

        MsgBox "New filmnumber " & rst2!ID

        rst2.Close

        Set rst2 = Nothing

    Else

        .CancelUpdate

    End If

    ...
```

Deleting Records

You can use the *Delete* method to delete the current record. After this procedure, the position pointer still points to the same record that has now been deleted.

The *Delete* procedure is irrevocable, so you cannot restore a record deleted with the program. Working with transactions constitutes one exception to this rule: As long as transactions are not finalized, you can restore any data deleted within the transaction. For more information on transactions, see Chapter 26, "Transactions and Locking."

The *GetRows* Method

You can use the *GetRows()* recordset method to transfer all or some of a recordset's resultset to a two-dimensional field. In the process, the system uses the *GetRows()* parameter to pass the number of rows to be included in the array. If the number exceeds the number of records in the recordset, the array dimensions are modified accordingly. Use *UBound(var,2) + 1* to specify the number of rows that are actually transmitted. You must pass the number of dimensions as a second parameter to the array so that the *UBound()* function returns the correct number of rows in the two-dimensional array. In the following example, the *conDimension* constant executes this process.

The following is the general definition for *GetRows()*:

```
varArr = rec.GetRows([Rows][, Start][, Fields])
```

Rows determines the number of records to read. If you do not specify a value, the system uses *adGetRowsRest* by default. For *Start*, you can enter a bookmark from which to begin reading the records. You can use *Fields* to pass an array from variants that contains the field names to read, such as

```
varArr = rec.GetRows(Fields:=Array("FilmNr","Filmtitle"))
```

which instructs the system to read only the columns *FilmNr* and *Filmtitle*.

The following example illustrates the usage of *GetRows*:

```
Sub FillArray()
 Const conDimension = 2


 Dim rec As ADODB.Recordset
 Dim varArr As Variant


 Set rec = New ADODB.Recordset
 rec.Open "SELECT FilmNr, Filmtitle FROM tblFilms", _
 CurrentProject.Connection
 ' Request the resultset
 varArr = rec.GetRows(rec.RecordCount)


 MsgBox Str(UBound(varArr, conDimension) + 1) & " rows read."
 rec.Close
 Set rec = Nothing
End Sub
```

With respect to transmitting data, *text, ntext,* and *image* fields in particular can contain large amounts of data that are then saved to the application runtime memory with *GetRows( )*.

If the *GetRows( )* method attempts to access a record that was deleted in the meantime, *GetRows( )* aborts the process, which means that not all of the requested records were transmitted. Thus, you should check if all of the data has actually been passed to the array, as shown in the following example:

```
If UBound(varArr, conDimension) + 1 <> rec.RecordCount Then

        ' some records are missing

End If
```

The *GetString* Method

Whereas the *GetRows* method just described returns an array, *GetString* fills a character string, as shown in the following example. Here you can define how to separate the string's individual fields and records and how to handle null values. *GetString* recognizes the optional parameters listed in Table 13-14.

```
var = rst.GetString([StringFormat][, NumRows][, ColumnDelimeter][,
RowDelimeter][, NullExpr])
```

> **Note** Note the misspelled terms *ColumnDelimeter* and *RowDelimeter*. The correct English terms are *ColumnDelimiter* and *RowDelimiter*. When using named parameters with *GetString* method you will have to use the misspelled parameter names.

Table 13-14 *GetString* **Parameters**

Parameter	Description
StringFormat	Lets you select only the constant *adClipFormat*.
NumRows	Specifies the number of rows to be included in the result string.
ColumnDelimeter	Expects a character string that is used to separate a record's individual columns. By default, tabs are used to separate columns.
RowDelimeter	Expects a character string that is used to separate individual records. By default, a new line is used for each record.
NullExpr	Accepts a string that the system returns whenever a field value is *Null*.

The following example illustates usage of *GetString* with custom row and column delimiters:

```
Sub GetString()

    Dim rec As ADODB.Recordset
    Dim strData As String
```

```
Set rec = New ADODB.Recordset
rec.Open "SELECT FilmNr, Filmtitle, Length FROM tblFilms", _
CurrentProject.Connection, adOpenForwardOnly, adLockReadOnly

' Request the resultset
strData = rec.GetString(ColumnDelimeter:="=", RowDelimeter:=" / ")

' Msgbox shows not the complete string, if length is too long
MsgBox strData
rec.Close
Set rec = Nothing
End Sub
```

The *Clone* Method

The *Clone( )* method creates an identical copy of a recordset, which is useful, for example, if you need to simultaneously process two of the recordset's records. The initial recordset must support bookmarks. The bookmarks of the original and cloned recordsets are interchangeable, which means that an assignment such as *recClone.Bookmark = rec.Bookmark* is permissible. To compare bookmarks, you can use the *CompareBookmarks* method (see the earlier section entitled "Comparing Bookmarks").

The *Requery* and *Resync* Methods

The *Requery* method executes the query on which the recordset is based to update the recordset data. For example, if other database users in the network have deleted or added records, the changes are copied to your recordset.

You can use the *Resync* method for client-based recordsets, but only for those for which *Supports(adUpdate)* is *True*. In the process, the existing records in the recordset are leveled, but the system does not re-execute the query. Thus, new records added by other users are not added to the recordset. The system only adds the changes made by other users to the recordset. If records are deleted from the database in the meantime, corresponding errors are noted in the recordset object's *Errors* list and a run-time error is triggered.

The following is the *Resync* instruction's general format:

```
Recordset.Resync [AffectRecords][[,] ResyncValues]
```

Table 13-15 and Table 13-16 list the possible constants for these two optional parameters.

Table 13-15 *AffectRecords* **Constants**

Constant	Description
adAffectAll	Synchronizes all records. This is the default setting.
adAffectAllChapters	Synchronizes only the so-called chapter records that are used in hierarchical recordsets.
adAffectCurrent	Synchronizes only the current record.
adAffectGroup	Synchronizes only those records selected by the current filter settings.

Table 13-16 *ResyncValues* **Constants**

Constant	Description
adResyncAllValues	Causes existing recordset data to be overwritten and unfinished update procedures to be canceled. This is the default setting.
adResyncUnderlyingValues	Causes the system to update only the recordset data in the record's *UnderlyingValue* (*Field* object) property.

The following program lets you test the *Resync* method. If the procedure stops at the *Stop* command, you can manually delete a record in the table *tbl-Films*. If you then continue to execute the program, you should see the error message.

```
Sub ResyncTest()

Dim rst As ADODB.Recordset

Dim fld As ADODB.Field

Dim cnn As New ADODB.Connection

Dim strTmp As String


On Error GoTo ErrorHandler
```

```
Set cnn = CurrentProject.Connection
Set rst = New ADODB.Recordset
rst.Open "SELECT filmnr, Filmtitle FROM tblFilms", _
        cnn, adOpenStatic, adLockBatchOptimistic
' When program has stopped, delete a film
Stop


rst.Resync


Set rst = Nothing
Exit Sub


ErrorHandler:
MsgBox Err.Number & " - " & Err.Description
Dim e As ADODB.Error
For Each e In cnn.Errors
Debug.Print e.Number & " - " & e.Description
Next
Resume Next
End Sub
```

The error caused by deleted records during *Resync* has the number –2147217885, with the following text: "Key value for this row was changed or deleted at the data store. The local row is now deleted."

State Properties

You can use the *State*, *Status*, and *EditMode* properties to receive information about the state of a recordset or the current record.

The *State* Property

You can use the *State* property to obtain information about the current record-set. The property returns one of the constants described in Table 13-17.

Table 13-17   *State* Property Constants

Constant	Description
adStateClosed	Specifies that the recordset is closed
adStateConnecting	Specifies that the recordset object is currently establishing a connection
adStateExecuting	Specifies that the recordset object is currently executing a query
adStateFetching	Specifies that the recordset object is currently fetching the query result
adStateOpen	Specifies that the recordset is open

The *Status* Property

The *Status* property provides you with information about the state of the current record or recordset. *Status* returns one of the constants listed in Table 13-18.

Table 13-18   *Status* Property Constants

Constant	Description
adRecCanceled	Specifies that the record was not saved because the operation was canceled
adRecCantRelease	Specifies that the record was not saved because of existing locks
adRecConcurrencyViolation	Specifies that the record was not saved because of optimistic locks
adRecDBDeleted	Specifies that a record was deleted from the database
adRecDeleted	Specifies that a record was deleted
adRecIntegrityViolation	Specifies that the record was not saved because referential integrity rules were violated
adRecInvalid	Specifies that the record's bookmark is no longer valid; changes cannot or could not be saved
adRecMaxChangesExceed	Specifies that the record was not saved because of too many unsaved changes
adRecModified	Specifies that an existing record was edited, but has not yet been saved

continued

Table 13-18 ***Status* Property Constants**   *(continued)*

Constant	Description
adRecMultipleChanges	Specifies that the record was not saved because doing so would have affected multiple records
adRecNew	Specifies that the new record has not yet been saved
adRecObjectOpen	Specifies that the record was not saved because of a conflict with an open memory object
adRecOK	Specifies that the record has not been edited or has not yet been successfully saved
adRecOutOfMemory	Specifies that the record was not saved because the computer had insufficient memory
adRecPendingChanges	Specifies that the record was not saved because it refers to another record that has not yet been inserted
adRecPermissionDenied	Specifies that the record was not saved because the user did not have the required permissions
adRecSchemaViolation	Specifies that the record was not saved because of a conflict with the table structure
adRecUnmodified	Specifies that the record was not modified

The *EditMode* Property

You can use the EditMode property to receive information about the current edit status. Table 13-19 lists the possible values for this property.

Table 13-19. ***EditMode* Property Constants**

Constant	Description
adEditAdd	Specifies that the new record was added, but has not yet been saved
adEditDelete	Specifies that the current record was deleted and that the record pointer is still pointing to this record
adEditInProgress	Specifies that the current record is being edited, but has not yet been saved
adEditNone	Specifies that no records are being edited

Batch Processing

ADO gives you the option to edit records in batches. This involves saving the changes locally on the client first, and then transferring them to the database as a block. Note that batch operations work only if your recordset's *CursorLocation* is set to *adUseClient*.

To open a recordset for batch processing, you must enter the value *adLockBatchOptimistic* as the constant for the *LockType* parameter. You can use the method to write the change you made to the recordset records to the database. Use *CancelBatch* to cancel the changes.

The following example raises the retail prices for all products by 10 percent:

```
Sub Batch()

 Dim rst As ADODB.Recordset

 Set rst = New ADODB.Recordset

 rst.Open "select * from tblProducts", _

       CurrentProject.Connection, adOpenStatic, adLockBatchOptimistic

 With rst

         If .Supports(adUpdateBatch) Then

         ' 10% price increase

         Do While Not .EOF

           !SalesPrice = !SalesPrice * 1.1

           .MoveNext

         Loop

         End If

     If MsgBox("Save modifications?", vbYesNo) = vbYes Then

           .UpdateBatch

         Else

           .CancelBatch

         End If

     .Close

 End With

 Set rst = Nothing

End Sub
```

Recordsets Without a Database Connection

You can create ADO recordsets that exist without a connection to a database and are saved only to memory. The following example illustrates this option:

```
Sub RecordsetWithoutDatabaseConnection()
 Dim rec As Recordset

 Set rec = New ADODB.Recordset
 With rec
        ' Create two fields
        .Fields.Append "Filmtitle", adVarChar, 255
        .Fields.Append "Sum", adCurrency
        .Open
        .AddNew
        !Filmtitle = "Gladiator"
        !Sum = 10000
        .Update
        .AddNew
        !Filmtitle = "Terminator"
        !Sum= 20000
        .Update

        .Sort = "Sum DESC"
     .MoveFirst

        Do While Not .EOF
           Debug.Print !Filmtitle, !Sum
           .MoveNext
        Loop
 End With
End Sub
```

Recordsets without a database connection are quite efficient if, for example, you want to quickly sort data in memory or search data according to specific criteria. Recordsets without a database connection are useful alternatives to simple arrays, because their numerous methods and properties let you perform many tasks without programming the required functions yourself.

Working with Multiple Recordsets

SQL Server can process SQL queries and stored procedures that return multiple resultsets. The Access user interface always displays the first resultset only in response to executing the following stored procedure, for example:

```
CREATE PROCEDURE MultipleResultsets

AS

/* This SP returns two resultsets;

 the second resultset could only retrieved with ADO */

        SELECT * FROM tblFilms

        SELECT * FROM tblProducts

RETURN
```

The following procedure uses the *Recordset* object's *NextRecordset* method to call the second resultset:

```
Sub MultipleRecordsets()

 Dim cnn As ADODB.Connection

 Dim rst As ADODB.Recordset

 Dim fld As ADODB.Field


 Set cnn = CurrentProject.Connection

 Set rst = New ADODB.Recordset


 rst.Open "MultipleResultsets", cnn


 Do While Not rst Is Nothing

        With rst

             Do While Not .EOF
```

```
            For Each fld In rst.Fields
                Debug.Print fld.Value
            Next
            Debug.Print
            .MoveNext
        Loop
    End With
    Set rst = rst.NextRecordset
 Loop
End Sub
```

When you open the recordset, you can also directly enter a SQL character string instead of a stored procedure, such as, for example *SELECT * FROM tbl-Films; SELECT * FROM tblProducts*. The semicolon between the two *SELECT*s is not required, but adding it enhances the legibility of the character string.

> **Note**   The *NextRecordset* method does not work properly if you use *Dim rst As New ADODB.Recordset* to create the recordset.

Once you call the *NextRecordset* method, you can only access the current recordset's data and you can no longer access the data of the previous recordset.

Saving Recordsets

You can use the *Save* method to save a recordset's data to a file. Two data formats are available: Advanced Data Tablegram (ADTG) or XML.

The following two routines save a recordset and load a saved recordset in XML file format. Note the *adCmdFile* option while opening the recordset in the second routine:

```
Sub SaveXML(strSQL As String, strFileName As String)

 Dim rec As ADODB.Recordset


 Set rec = ADODB.Recordset
```

```vba
    Set rec = New ADODB.Recordset
    rec.Open strSQL, CurrentProject.Connection
    ' Save as XML
    rec.Save strFileName, adPersistXML
    rec.Close
    Set rec = Nothing
End Sub


Sub LoadXML(strFileName As String)

  Dim rec As ADODB.Recordset
  Dim f As ADODB.Field

  Set rec = New ADODB.Recordset
  rec.Open strDateiname, _
        CursorType:=adOpenStatic, _
        LockType:=adLockOptimistic, _
        Options:=adCmdFile

  Do While Not rec.EOF
        For Each f In rec.Fields
            Debug.Print f.Name & "=" & f.Value & " / "
        Next
        rec.MoveNext
        Debug.Print
  Loop
  Set rec = Nothing
End Sub
```

14

Command Objects

You can use *Command* objects to execute select queries, action queries, or data definition queries. If the select queries executed with *Command* objects report values, then these are transferred to a recordset. You can use *Command* objects to execute stored procedures with parameters and to request return values from stored procedure parameter values. Using parameters, it is also possible to simplify the composition of complicated *WHERE* clauses.

Command objects accelerate execution of requests because ADO requires the provider to compile the *Command* before executing it. If a query is carried out multiple times, but the values of parameters in the *WHERE* clause are different, then the server can access an existing run schedule from the second execution forward. This reduces the server load and therefore speeds up execution of the query.

You can also execute stored procedures using the *Execute* method of a *Connection* object, as described in Chapter 11, "Reports."

Table 14-1 and Table 14-2 provide you with an overview of the properties and methods, respectively, of the *Command* object.

Table 14-1 *Command* **Object Properties**

Property	Description
ActiveConnection	Specifies the current connection
CommandText	Contains the name of a table, query, or SQL text
CommandTimeout	Determines the number of seconds before the query is terminated
CommandType	Determines the type of query (see Table 14-3)
Name	Contains the name of the *Command* object
NamedParameters	Indicates whether parameter names should be passed to the provider (otherwise the parameter order is used)

continued

Table 14-1 *Command* **Object Properties** *(continued)*

Property	Description
Parameters	Provides a list of *Parameter* objects
Prepared	Ensures that the query is stored temporarily in prepared format, allowing optimized execution when it is called repeatedly
Properties	Contains a collection with all properties for the *Command* object
State	Returns the status

Table 14-2 *Command* **Object Methods**

Method	Description
Cancel	Terminates execution of an asynchronous query
CreateParameter	Creates a new parameter for a query
Execute	Executes a query

Using *Command* Objects

The following example represents the use of a *Command* object for the execution of SQL queries that can be entered by the user:

```
Sub ExecuteSQL ()

  Dim cmd As ADODB.Command

  Dim strQry As String

  Dim lngRecordsAffected As Long


  On Error GoTo Errorhandler


  Set cmd = New ADODB.Command

  cmd.ActiveConnection = CurrentProject.Connection

  Do

    strQry = InputBox("Name of Query or SQL-text" , Default:=strQry)

    If strQry <> "" Then

      cmd.CommandText = strQry

      cmd.Execute lngRecordsAffected
```

```
        MsgBox lngRecordsAffected & " records modified."
    End If
  Loop Until strQry = ""
exitsub:
  Set cmd = Nothing
  Exit Sub
Errorhandler:
  Dim strTmp As String
  strTmp = "VBA:" & vbTab & Err.Number & " - " & Err.Description & _
    vbNewLine
  Dim e As ADODB.Error
  For Each e In CurrentProject.Connection.Errors
    strTmp = strTmp & "ADO:" & vbTab & e.Number & " - " & e.Description
& _
        "(" & e.Source & ")" & vbNewLine
  Next
  strTmp = strTmp & vbNewLine & "<OK> to continue, <Cancel> to stop"
  If MsgBox(strTmp, vbOKCancel, "Error") = vbOK Then
    Resume Next
  Else
    Resume exitsub
  End If
End Sub
```

The *ActiveConnection* Property

A *Command* object refers to an active connection. For this reason, a valid *Connection* object must first be assigned to the *ActiveConnection* property. If this assignment is not made, then an error is issued either before or during execution of the *Execute* method, alerting you to the missing connection.

In the preceding example, the connection of the current Access project *CurrentProject.Connection* was assigned to the *Command* object.

The *CommandText* Property

The *CommandText* property is used to define a SQL query or the name of a stored procedure. If the character string provided is not a valid table name or stored procedure or it is not an error-free SQL command, the system issues a run-time error.

The *CommandType* Property

You can use the *CommandType* property to support ADO. When you set the property, ADO does not have to determine what type of query the *Command-Text* you specified refers to. In the standard system, the default value for *CommandType* is *adCmdUnknown* (that is, the type of query is unknown). Other values are shown in Table 14-3.

Table 14-3   Options: Constants

Option	Description
adAsyncExecute	The query is executed asynchronously. Chapter 15, "ADO Events," describes how this option is used.
adAsyncFetch	Allows a query resultset to be called asynchronously (that is, in the client, the system does not wait until all the result data has been transferred; it merely takes the first data). See the example in Chapter 15, "ADO Events."
adAsyncFetchNonBlocking	Allows a query resultset to be released asynchronously (that is, in the client, the system does not wait until data arrives). See the example in Chapter 15, "ADO Events."
adCmdFile	This is not for *Command* objects, but for recordsets (see Chapter 12, "*Connection* Objects").
adCmdStoredProc	*CommandText* contains the name of a stored procedure; in Microsoft Access this is the name of a query. The call is reformatted as *{? = CALL proc(?)}*.
adCmdTable	*CommandText* contains the name of a table. ADO creates its own SQL query, which returns all lines with all columns of the table. Internally, ADO extends the table name with *"SELECT * FROM"*.
adCmdTableDirect	This is not for *Command* objects, but for recordsets (see Chapter 12, "*Connection* Objects").
adCmdText	*CommandText* contains a character string with the corresponding SQL query.

continued

Table 14-3   Options: Constants   *(continued)*

Option	Description
adCmdUnknown	This is the default value. ADO must determine how to evaluate the argument *CommandText*.
adExecuteNoRecords	Indicates that no records are returned. This option can only be used in conjunction with *adCmdText* or *adCmdStoredProc*.

The *CommandTimeout* Property

The *CommandTimeout* property is used to define how long your program waits for the query result before issuing a run-time error. The period is measured from the point at which the server starts processing until the moment at which the first data arrives at the client. *CommandTimeout* does not take into account the time required by the network to transfer the data. If, for example, the query does not reach the server due to network problems, this does not affect *CommandTimeout* at all, unfortunately. In this situation, the configuration of the network card determines whether or not an error message is issued.

The *Execute* Method

Execute is used to execute the queries. There are two variant approaches to applying *Execute*, depending on whether or not the query returns data. For action queries, use the following:

```
cmd.Execute [RecordsAffected][, Parameters][, Options]
```

If the server returns records in response to the query, work with the following:

```
Set Recordset = cmd.Execute( [RecordsAffected][, Parameters][,
Options] )
```

All three method parameters are optional. The recordset returned by *Execute* has the settings *acOpenForwardOnly* and *acLockReadonly*, meaning that data cannot be changed. If you want to use *Command* objects to access recordsets that can be changed, use the method described in the next section, "Changeable Recordsets with *Command* Objects."

Transfer of parameters using the *Parameters* list is described later. The *Options* parameter can take the values described in Table 14-3.

> **Note**   If you use the *SET NOCOUNT ON* command at the beginning of a stored procedure, then –1 is reported in *RecordsAffected* if the procedure was executed successfully, and 0 is reported if an error occurred.

Changeable Recordsets with *Command* Objects

If you want to open a recordset that can be edited and that is based on a *Command* object, you must use the procedure described in the following listing. When the recordset is opened, the *Command* object is transferred as a *Source* parameter. The sample procedure also uses the *Parameters* collection (described later in this chapter in "Queries With Parameters") because the stored procedure requires a film number as the transfer value.

```
Sub RecordsetWithCommand()
  Dim rst As ADODB.Recordset
  Dim cmd As ADODB.Command


  Set cmd = New ADODB.Command
  Set rst = New ADODB.Recordset


  ' Command-Object
  cmd.ActiveConnection = CurrentProject.Connection
  cmd.CommandText = "FilmInfo"
  cmd.CommandType = adCmdStoredProc
  ' Parameter
  cmd.Parameters.Append cmd.CreateParameter(Name:="FilmNr", _
           Type:=adInteger, _
           Direction:=adParamInput, _
           Value:=1)
  ' Open recordset
  rst.Open cmd, _
    CursorType:=adOpenStatic, _
    LockType:=adLockOptimistic, _
    Options:=adCmdStoredProc
  ' Modification
  rst!Filmtitle = StrReverse(rst!Filmtitle)
  rst.Update
```

```
    rst.Close

    Set rst = Nothing

    Set cmd = Nothing

End Sub
```

The *Prepared* Property

The *Prepared* property of the *Command* object was originally intended to reduce preparatory compilation of queries on the server when several similar queries are executed in succession. This creates a temporary stored procedure on the server that is then used for the repeated queries.

Since then, Microsoft SQL Server/MSDE has developed sufficiently to render this property redundant, as it creates its own internal temporary stored procedure when a query is executed. SQL Server/MSDE then reuses this precompiled procedure when a similar query needs to be processed on the server. Because ADO and the SQLOLEDB provider also have this feature, the *Prepared* property is irrelevant and does not improve performance. You should always set the *Prepared* property to *False* (the default value for this property) because ADO can occasionally become confused and slowed if *Prepared* is set to *True*.

Queries with Parameters

Parameters are used when a stored procedure is called to transfer values for the parameters assigned to that procedure. You can also use parameters to recall queries with varying values.

For a query with parameters, you must create a *Command* object and set the parameters. The *Command* object has a *Parameters* collection in which the individual parameters are described. Table 14-4 and Table 14-5 list the properties and method, respectively, for a *Parameter* object.

Table 14-4 *Parameter* **Object Properties**

Property	Description
Attributes	Can take one of the values or the total value of *adParamSigned*, *adParamNullable*, and *adParamLong*.
Direction	Displays whether or not the parameter for input/output is to be used. The default value is *adParamInput*. Other possible values are *adParamOutput*, *adParamInputOutput*, *adParamReturnValue*, and *adParamUnknown*.

continued

Table 14-4 *Parameter* **Object Properties**   *(continued)*

Property	Description
Name	Displays or sets the name of the *Parameter* object.
NumericScale	Specifies the number of decimal places for numeric parameters.
Precision	Determines the maximum number of digits for a numeric value.
Properties	Contains a collection with all properties.
Size	Determines the size of a parameter.
Type	Defines the data type of a parameter.
Value	Contains the value of the parameter.

Table 14-5 *Parameter* **Object Method**

Method	Description
AppendChunk	Allows you to append data to parameters in the formats *text*, *ntext*, or *image*

Transferring Parameters

There are options for transferring parameters using the following SQL query. The query determines the total number of sold articles using the entries in the *tblProductSales* table for a particular period (in this case the year 2000). We created the query using the View Designer, which was also used to insert the statement for date formatting using *CONVERT*. The conversion was inserted so that the date appears in the correct format.

```
SELECT tblProducts.ProductNr, tblProducts.Description,
   SUM(tblProductSales.Amount) AS TotalSales
FROM dbo.tblProducts INNER JOIN
   dbo.tblProductSales ON
   dbo.tblProducts.ProductNr = dbo.tblProductSales.ProductNr
WHERE (dbo.tblProductSales.Date BETWEEN
   CONVERT(DATETIME, '2000-01-01 00:00:00', 102) AND
   CONVERT(DATETIME, '2000-012-01 00:00:00', 102))
GROUP BY dbo.tblProducts.ProductNr, dbo.tblProducts.Description
```

Let us assume that this query is now executed several times in succession for different periods specified by the user. How can the data for the period in the Microsoft Visual Basic for Applications (VBA) program be transferred to the query?

This example program contains sample solutions for the five scenarios described in the following sections:

```
Sub ParameterVariations()
  Dim rst As ADODB.Recordset
  Dim cmd As ADODB.Command
  Dim strSQL As String
  Dim strDate As String

  Const conSQL1 = "SELECT tblProducts.ProductNr, " & _
          "tblProducts.Description, " & _
          "SUM(tblProductSales.Amount) As TotalSales " & _
          "FROM tblProducts INNER JOIN " & _
          " tblProductSales ON " & _
          " tblProducts.ProductNr = tblProductSales.ProductNr " & _
          "WHERE (tblProductSales.Datum BETWEEN "
  Const conSQL2 = ") GROUP BY tblProducts.ProductNr, " & _
          "tblProducts.Description"
  Select Case InputBox("Scenario 1,2,3,4,5?")

  Case 1
    '***** Scenario 1: Building a string
    ' Request time period and build string
    strDate = InputBox("From:")
    strSQL = conSQL1 & "'" & strDate & "' AND '"
    strDate = InputBox("To:")
    strSQL = strSQL & strDate & "' " & conSQL2

    Set rst = New ADODB.Recordset
    rst.Open strSQL, CurrentProject.Connection
    ShowRecordset rst
    Set rst = Nothing
```

```
Case 2
  '***** Scenario 2: Passing as an array
  strSQL = conSQL1 & " ? AND ? " & conSQL2
  Set cmd = New ADODB.Command
  cmd.ActiveConnection = CurrentProject.Connection
  cmd.CommandText = strSQL
  cmd.CommandType = adCmdText
  Dim strFrom As String
  Dim strTo As String
  strFrom = InputBox("From:")
  strTo = InputBox("To:")
  Set rst = cmd.Execute(Parameters:=Array(strFrom, strTo))
  ShowRecordset rst
  Set rst = Nothing

Case 3
  '***** Scenario 3: Creating parameter objects
  strSQL = conSQL1 & " ? AND ? " & conSQL2
  Set cmd = New ADODB.Command
  cmd.ActiveConnection = CurrentProject.Connection
  cmd.CommandText = strSQL
  cmd.CommandType = adCmdText

  Dim par As New ADODB.Parameter
  Set par = cmd.CreateParameter("From", adDate)
  cmd.Parameters.Append par
  Set par = cmd.CreateParameter("To", adDate)
  cmd.Parameters.Append par

  cmd.Parameters("From") = InputBox("From:")
  cmd.Parameters("To") = InputBox("To:")
  Set rst = cmd.Execute
  ShowRecordset rst
  Set rst = Nothing
```

```
Case 4
  '***** Scenario 4: Using the Refresh method
  strSQL = conSQL1 & " ? AND ? " & conSQL2
  Set cmd = New ADODB.Command
  cmd.ActiveConnection = CurrentProject.Connection
  cmd.CommandText = strSQL
  cmd.CommandType = adCmdText
  cmd.Parameters.Refresh
  For Each par In cmd.Parameters
    par.Value = InputBox(par.Name)
  Next
  Set rst = cmd.Execute
  ShowRecordset rst
  Set rst = Nothing

Case 5
  '***** Scenario 5: Using a Stored Procedure
  strSQL = "spProductsSold"
  Set cmd = New ADODB.Command
  ' Parameters.Refresh only functions for
  ' DataShape-Provider with ADO Version 2.6 or later
  If CurrentProject.Connection.Version < "2.6" Then
    Dim cnn As ADODB.Connection
    Set cnn = New ADODB.Connection
    cnn.ConnectionString = CurrentProject.BaseConnectionString
    cnn.Open
    cmd.ActiveConnection = cnn
  Else
    cmd.ActiveConnection = CurrentProject.Connection
  End If
```

```
        cmd.CommandText = strSQL
        cmd.CommandType = adCmdStoredProc
        cmd.Parameters.Refresh
        For Each par In cmd.Parameters
          ' Only for input parameters
          If par.Direction = adParamInput Then
            par.Value = InputBox(par.Name)
          End If
        Next
        Set rst = cmd.Execute
        ShowRecordset rst
        Set rst = Nothing
        If Not cnn Is Nothing Then
          cnn.Close
          Set cnn = Nothing
        End If
    End Select
End Sub


Sub ShowRecordset(rst As ADODB.Recordset)
    Do Until rst.EOF
      Dim fld As ADODB.Field
      For Each fld In rst.Fields
        Debug.Print fld.Name & " " & fld.Value
      Next
      Debug.Print
      rst.MoveNext
    Loop
    rst.Close
End Sub
```

Scenario 1: Constructing a Character String

The first scenario for the transfer of parameters for the period specified is the construction of a character string. The following section from the program shows how the string *strSQL* is combined. Remember that date values must be enclosed by single quotation marks:

```
...

' Request time period and build string

strDate = InputBox("From:")

strSQL = conSQL1 & "'" & strDate & "' AND '"

strDate = InputBox("To:")

strSQL = strSQL & strDate & "' " & conSQL2

...
```

The advantage of composite SQL character strings is that you do not necessarily need a *Command* object to execute select queries. You can simply transfer the SQL query directly when the recordset is opened.

> **Note** When combining character strings, problems arise with character strings that also contain single quotation marks.

Scenario 2: Transferring as Array

If you enhance the SQL character string as displayed in the following code segment, using placeholders *?*

```
...

strSQL = conSQL1 & " ? AND ? " & conSQL2

...
```

this creates two parameters. The SQL character string is assigned to property *CommandText* or a *Command* object. When the *Execute* command of the *Command* object is called, values must be transferred for the parameters using an array (from *Variants*). For example:

```
...

Set rst = cmd.Execute(Parameters:=Array('1.1.2000', '1.2.2000'))

...
```

or as in the preceding example:

...

```
Set rst = cmd.Execute(Parameters:=Array(strForm, strTo))
```

...

In this case, it is advisable to set value *adCmdText* for property *CommandType* of *Command* object to inform ADO that *CommandText* contains a SQL query. The advantage of this approach is that the SQL text does not have to be re-created (as in the first scenario). Different values for the transfer are merely written in the array.

The number of *Variant* values in the array must agree with the number of ? parameters in the SQL query or the system issues a run-time error.

> **Note**   When transferring parameters to a stored procedure (*CommandType = adStoredProc*), remember that a stored procedure always displays the parameter *RETURN_VALUE* that is transferred first.

Scenario 3: Creating *Parameter* Objects

In this scenario, as in the second scenario, the parameters are replaced in the SQL query by question marks. For the transfer of parameters, two new *Parameter* objects are created with the *CreateParameter* method and appended to the *Parameters* collection of the *Command* object.

The general form of the *CreateParameter* method of the *Command* object is:

```
Set Parameter = cmd.CreateParameter ([Name][, Type][, Direction][,
Size][, Value])
```

You use *Name* to name the parameter. The *Type* determines the data type of the parameter. *Direction* is only useful for calling stored procedures, as described in the section entitled "Scenario 5: Using a Stored Procedure." You can use *Size* to define the field size (depending on data type) of the parameter.

You can use *Value* to define a standard value for the parameter. After every *Execute*, the parameter is reset to this value:

...

```
Dim par As New ADODB.Parameter

Set par = cmd.CreateParameter("From", adDBTimeStamp)
```

```
cmd.Parameters.Append par

Set par = cmd.CreateParameter("To", adDBTimeStamp)

cmd.Parameters.Append par


cmd.Parameters("From") = InputBox("From:")

cmd.Parameters("To") = InputBox("To:")
```
. . .

The next section provides examples of some of the various syntax conventions for setting parameters. This is the complete syntax:

```
cmd.Parameters("ParName").Value = ParValue
```

where *ParValue* can be a number, a string, or another type. Because *Value* is the standard property, you do not need *.Value*:

```
cmd.Parameters("ParName") = ParValue
```

Access also accepts the *cmd("ParName") = ParValue* syntax. You can also count the parameters and use the *cmd.Parameters(0) = ParValue* syntax.

Settings for the *Type* Property of Parameters   Table 14-6 displays ADO constants and their assignments to SQL Server/MSDE data types for configuring the *Type* property of parameters.

Table 14-6   SQL Server/MSDE and ADO Parameter Data Types

SQL Server/MSDE Data Type	ADO Parameter Data Type	Precision	Size
(RETURN_VALUE)	adInteger	10	0
varchar	*adVarChar*		User-defined
char	*adVarChar*		User-defined
int	*adInteger*	10	0
smallint	*adSmallInt*	5	0
tinyint	*adUnsignedTinyInt*	3	0
datetime	*adDBTimeStamp*		0
smalldatetime	*adDBTimeStamp*		
bit	*adBoolean*		
text	*adVarChar*		2,147,483,647
image	*adVarBinary*		2,147,483,647

continued

Table 14-6   SQL Server/MSDE and ADO Parameter Data Types   *(continued)*

SQL Server/MSDE Data Type	ADO Parameter Data Type	Precision	Size
binary	*adVarBinary*		1
varbinary	*adVarBinary*		1
decimal	*adNumeric*	18	0
smallmoney	*adCurrency*	10	0
money	*adCurrency*	19	0
numeric	*adNumeric*	18	0
real	*adSingle*	7	0
float	*adDouble*	15	0
nchar	*adVarWChar*		1
ntext	*adVarWChar*		1,073,741,823
nvarchar	*adVarWChar*		1

Scenario 4: Using the Refresh Method

In the third scenario, *Parameter* objects were created with *CreateParameter*. To do this, you need to know the number of parameters (and therefore the number of question marks in the SQL text) to generate a corresponding number of *Parameter* objects. Using the *Refresh* method from the *Parameter* collection, you can assign the task of determining the number of parameters to SQL Server/MSDE. *Refresh* transfers the SQL query to the server where it is evaluated. On the basis of the server response, a corresponding number of *Parameter* objects are then created in the *Parameters* collection, as shown here:

```
...
cmd.Parameters.Refresh

For Each par In cmd.Parameters

  par.Value = InputBox(par.Name)

Next

...
```

The disadvantage of this procedure is the increased workload for the server, as the SQL query is transferred twice: once for evaluation and once for execution.

The *Name* property of the *Parameter* objects generated in this way receives the content *Param1*, *Param2*, and so forth.

> **Note**   You can use the following two parameters to access the parameters created with Refresh in this example:
> *cmd.Parameter(0)*
> *cmd.Parameter(1)*
> Or in an even shorter form:
> *cmd(0)*
> *cmd(1)*

Scenario 5: Using a Stored Procedure

If you do not want to call a SQL query with placeholders, but instead you want to use a stored procedure for which transfer parameters have been defined, you can use the *Refresh* method to determine the names, data types, and so on, of the procedure parameters.

> **Note**   The *Refresh* method only works for stored procedures as of ADO version 2.6 for the connection *CurrentProject.Connection*, which is based on the MSDataShape provider. If you want to use *Refresh*, you need connections with the SQLOLEDB provider.

The following listing displays the stored procedure used in the example with parameters *@From* and *@To*:

```
CREATE PROCEDURE spProductsSold (@From DATETIME, @To DATETIME)
AS
  SELECT tblProducts.ProductNr, tblProducts.Description,
    SUM(tblProductSales.Amount) AS TotalSales
  FROM tblProducts INNER JOIN
    tblProductSales ON
    tblProducts.ProductNr = tblProductSales.ProductNr
  WHERE (tblProductSales.Datum BETWEEN
    @From AND @To )
  GROUP BY tblProducts.ProductNr, tblProducts.Description
RETURN
```

Remember that you must set the *CommandType* of the *Command* object to *adCmdStoredProc* for the stored procedure before calling *cmd.Parameter. Refresh*, otherwise the system will issue a run-time error.

```
. . .
cmd.CommandText = "spProductsSold"

cmd.CommandType = adCmdStoredProc

cmd.Parameters.Refresh

For Each par In cmd.Parameters

  ' Only for input parameters

  If par.Direction = adParamInput Then

    par.Value = InputBox(par.Name)

  End If

Next
. . .
```

Return Value and Output Parameter   In stored procedures, parameters can be defined for both input and output (that is, parameters that you enter for the procedure as well as parameters that the procedure can use to return values). Also, every stored procedure has the parameter *RETURN_VALUE*, with which the return value of the procedure can be queried. The return value is always the first parameter in the collection (that is, *cmd.Parameters(0)* or the shorter form, *cmd(0)*).

You can use the *Direction* property of the parameter object to determine whether or not a parameter is defined for input, output, or both. Table 14-7 displays the possible values. In the preceding listing, you can see that only input parameters are queried by the user.

> **Note**   Every parameter set as *OUTPUT* in a stored procedure receives the value *adParamInputOutput* after *cmd.Parameters. Refresh* for the *Direction* property. We were unable to determine whether this was an ADO error or intentional on the part of the programmer.

Table 14-7   *Direction* **Constants**

Constant	Description
adParamInput	Defines the parameter for the input. This is the default value.
adParamInputOutput	Defines that the parameter is to be used for both input and output.
adParamOutput	Specifies an output parameter.
adParamReturnValue	Specifies a return value.
adParamUnknown	Specifies that the parameter direction is unknown.

Filling List Boxes and Combo Boxes with Value Lists

This section describes how you can use ADO to fill list boxes and combo boxes in forms. The scenario described here works with an auxiliary function that returns a character string that can be used as a value list in a list box or a combo box. For the list box or combo box, you must specify *Value List* as the origin type.

For a value list, all entries that are to appear in the list box or combo box are written to the row source property, separated with semicolons (for example, *One;Two;Three;Four*). A list box or combo box can also be defined in several columns. In our example, a two-column definition, *One/Two* and *Three/Four* would each form a line. Remember that the character string for the row source of a list box or combo box can have a maximum of 2047 characters.

The following function returns a character string in which the resultset determined by a stored procedure is stored for transfer to a value list. The name of the stored procedure and, if necessary, the required parameters, are transferred when the function is called. To permit the function to be used for any number of stored procedures with or without parameters, parameter transfer is executed with *ParamArrays*:

```
Public Function GetList(strSP As String, _

        ParamArray varP() As Variant) _

    As String


Dim rst As ADODB.Recordset

Dim cmd As ADODB.Command

Dim prm As ADODB.Parameter
```

```
Dim v As Variant
Dim strTmp As String


On Error GoTo err_


Set cmd = New ADODB.Command
With cmd
    .ActiveConnection = CurrentProject.Connection


    ' Assign text and type
    .CommandText = strSP
    .CommandType = adCmdStoredProc


    ' For each entry in ParamArray
    For Each v In varP
        ' Create new parameter, add to collection
        Set prm = .CreateParameter("", adVarChar, adParamInput, 100, v)
        .Parameters.Append prm
    Next
    ' Execute the SP
    Set rst = .Execute
    ' With the resultset
    If Not (rst.EOF And rst.BOF) Then
        ' Read as string
        strTmp = rst.GetString(adClipString, -1, ";", ";", "")
        ' Cut if longer than 2047 chars
        GetList = Left(strTmp, 2047)
    Else
        GetList = ""
    End If
End With
```

```
exit_:

  Set cmd = Nothing

  Exit Function


err_:

  ' Error handling

  Select Case Err.Number

    Case -2147217904

      MsgBox "Not enough parameters!"

    Case -2147217900

      MsgBox "Too many parameters!"

    Case Else

      MsgBox Err.Description & " (" & Err.Number & ")"

  End Select

  GetList = ""

  Resume exit_

End Function
```

The *GetList()* function is called, for example, when you load a form to fill a list box or combo box in the form with values. The following example is a list box, List0, that has been created in a form. In this case, the following event procedure could be used for the event *On Load*:

```
Private Sub Form_Load()

  ' Two columns

  List0.ColumnCount = 2

  List0.RowSource = GetList("AllFilms", 2)

End Sub
```

Executing Queries with the Example Form *frmSQL*

Using the example form *frmSQL*, shown in Figure 14-1, you can execute parameter queries directly and test the different configuration options for *Command* objects. If errors arise due to the SQL query you enter and the configurations you make, these are displayed in the lower section of the form.

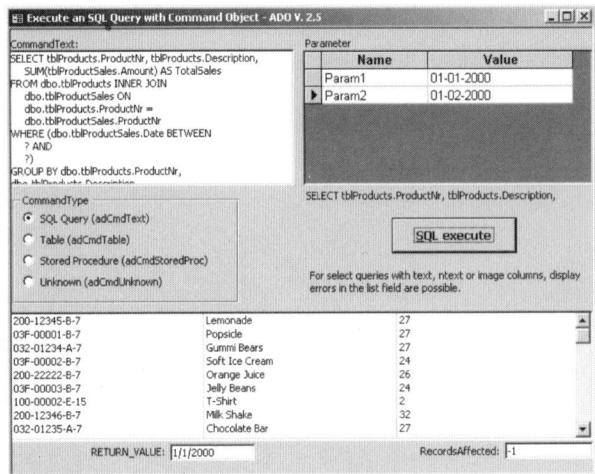

Figure 14-1   Example form *frmSQL*

The listing for the example form uses the method *mcmd.Parameters. Refresh* to have SQL Server analyze the parameters of the query entered. The name and value of the parameters are stored temporarily in table *tblParameter*. The subform *subfrmParameter* enables you to enter values into table *tblParameter*. When executing the query with the SQL Execute button, the values entered in *tblParameter* are transferred to the *Parameter* objects.

```
Option Compare Database

Option Explicit


Dim mcnn As ADODB.Connection

Dim mrst As ADODB.Recordset

Dim mcmd As ADODB.Command

Dim maRows As Variant


Private Sub cmdParameter_Click()

  Dim rst As ADODB.Recordset

  Dim par As ADODB.Parameter


  On Error GoTo ErrorHandler
```

```
If txtSQL <> "" Then
  ' Show result list box
  lstResult.Visible = True
  ' Empty parameter table
  EmptyParameterTable
  ' Retrieve query text from field
  mcmd.CommandText = txtSQL
  ' Set type of query
  mcmd.CommandType = fraCommandType
  ' Determine Parameters
  mcmd.Parameters.Refresh
  ' When parameters present, save in table
  If mcmd.Parameters.Count > 0 Then
    Set rst = New ADODB.Recordset
    rst.Open "tblParameter", mcnn, adOpenStatic, adLockOptimistic
    For Each par In mcmd.Parameters
      ' Query parameter values
      ' Ignore output parameter and return value

      If par.Direction = adParamInput Then
        rst.AddNew
        rst!name = par.name
        rst!Value = par.Value
        rst.Update
      End If
    Next
  End If
  ' Refresh list box
  subfrmParameter.Requery
  ' Refresh caption
```

```
            lblSQLText.Caption = mcmd.CommandText
        End If
    Exitsub:
        Exit Sub


    ErrorHandler:
        ErrorHandler
        Resume Exitsub
    End Sub


    Private Sub cmdSQL_Click()
        Dim lngRecordsAffected As Long


        On Error GoTo ErrorHandler


        ' Retrieve parameters from table
        If mcmd.Parameters.Count > 0 Then
            Dim par As ADODB.Parameter
            Dim rst As ADODB.Recordset


            Set rst = New ADODB.Recordset
            rst.Open "tblParameter", mcnn
            Do Until rst.EOF
                mcmd.Parameters(Trim(rst!name)).Value = rst!Value
                rst.MoveNext
            Loop
            rst.Close
            Set rst = Nothing
        End If
```

```
' Execute query
Set mrst = mcmd.Execute(RecordsAffected:=lngRecordsAffected)


' Output Affected Records
txtRecordsAffected = lngRecordsAffected
' Query output parameter, if present
On Error Resume Next
For Each par In mcmd.Parameters
    If (par.Direction = adParamInputOutput) Or (par.Direction = adPar
amOutput) Then
        MsgBox par.name & " = " & par.Value
    End If
Next
' Query return value, if present
txtReturnValue = mcmd.Parameters(0).Value
If err.Number > 0 Then
    txtReturnValue = "Not Present"
End If
On Error GoTo ErrorHandler
' Retrieve data and show in list box
If (mrst.State = adStateOpen) Then
    If Not (mrst.BOF And mrst.EOF) Then
        maRows = mrst.GetRows
        ' Determine number of columns
        lstResult.ColumnCount = UBound(maRows, 1) + 1
        mrst.Close
        GoTo refresh_box
    End If
End If
' Empty list box
```

```
    ReDim maRows(1, 1) As Variant
    lstResult.ColumnCount = 1
refresh_box:
    ' refresh list box
    lstResult.Requery
Exitsub:
    Exit Sub


ErrorHandler:
    ErrorHandler
    Resume Exitsub
End Sub


Private Sub Form_Load()
    Set mcmd = New ADODB.Command
    Set mrst = New ADODB.Recordset
    Set mcnn = New ADODB.Connection
    ' Important: the method mcmd.Parameters.Refresh for stored
    ' procedures with the MSDataShape provider
    ' only operates with ADO version 2.6 and later;
    ' therefore, new connection without MSDataShape;
    ' Connection data without MSDataShape for current project
    ' are in CurrentProject.BaseConnectionString
    If CurrentProject.Connection.Version < "2.6" Then
      Set mcnn = New ADODB.Connection
      mcnn.ConnectionString = CurrentProject.BaseConnectionString
      mcnn.Open
    Else
      Set mcnn = CurrentProject.Connection
    End If
```

```
    Me.Caption = Me.Caption & " - ADO V. " & mcnn.Version


    mcmd.ActiveConnection = mcnn
    fraCommandType = 8
    EmptyParameterTable
    subfrmParameter.Requery
End Sub


' User defined fill function for list box
Function ShowRecords(ctlField As Control, _
            varID As Variant, _
            varRow As Variant, _
            varColumn As Variant, _
            varCode As Variant _
            ) As Variant
    Select Case varCode
        Case acLBInitialize:
            lstResult.Visible = True


            ShowRecords = True
        Case acLBOpen:
            ' Generate internal IDs
            ShowRecords = Timer
        Case acLBGetRowCount:
            ' Number of rows
            ShowRecords = UBound(maRows, 2) + 1
        Case acLBGetColumnCount:
            ' Number of columns
            ShowRecords = UBound(maRows, 1) + 1
        Case acLBGetColumnWidth:
```

```
         ' Standard width
         ShowRecords = -1
      Case acLBGetValue:
         ' Retrieve values
         ShowRecords = maRows(varColumn, varRow)
   End Select
End Function


Private Sub fraCommandType_Click()
   cmdParameter_Click
End Sub


Private Sub txtSQL_Exit(Cancel As Integer)
   cmdParameter_Click
End Sub


Sub ErrorHandler()
   Dim errADO As ADODB.Error
   Dim strErr As String


   strErr = "VBA Error Information" & vbNewLine & vbNewLine
   strErr = strErr & "Number: " & err.Number & vbNewLine
   strErr = strErr & "Description: " & err.Description & vbNewLine
   strErr = strErr & vbNewLine
   If mcnn.Errors.Count > 0 Then
      For Each errADO In mcnn.Errors
        strErr = strErr & vbNewLine & "ADO Error Information (ADO V." & _
                 mcnn.Version & ")" & _
                 vbNewLine & vbNewLine
```

```
        strErr = strErr & "NativeError: " & errADO.NativeError &
vbNewLine

        strErr = strErr & "Number: " & errADO.Number & vbNewLine

        strErr = strErr & "Description: " & errADO.Description &
vbNewLine

        strErr = strErr & "Source: " & errADO.Source & vbNewLine

        strErr = strErr & "SQLState: " & errADO.SQLState & vbNewLine

        strErr = strErr & "Source: " & errADO.Source & vbNewLine

    Next

  End If

  ' Output list box

  lstResult.Visible = False

  ' Show and fill error text box

  txtError.Visible = True

  txtError = strErr

End Sub


Sub EmptyParameterTable()

  mcnn.Execute "delete from tblParameter"


End Sub
```

Dynamic SQL Queries

In the *Parameter* queries previously described, values from *WHERE* clauses and
so on are transferred as parameters to stored procedures. In some cases it
makes sense to use a parameter to control the query, part of the query, or even
the stored procedure.

Imagine that you are using the following simple stored procedure:

```
CREATE PROCEDURE Parameter @Column VARCHAR(100) AS

  SELECT @Column FROM tblFilm

RETURN
```

You want to use the parameter to control which field in the table is to be output. If you specify *Filmtitle* for *@Column*, then the stored procedure should output the movie title. Unfortunately, the procedure just described does not function as planned, because if, for example, you enter *Filmtitle* as the parameter, then SQL Server/MSDE forms *SELECT 'Filmtitle' FROM tblFilms*. This means that the word *Filmtitle* is output for every record in table *tblFilms*.

You can use the *EXEC* command to instruct SQL Server/MSDE to interpret the parameter as part of the SQL statement, as shown in the following example. The character string that *EXEC* transfers is re-evaluated and compiled by SQL Server.

```
CREATE PROCEDURE Parameter @Column VARCHAR(100) AS

  EXEC ('SELECT ' + @Column + ' FROM tblFilms')

RETURN
```

> **Note**   The linking of text sections for the *EXEC* statement only functions correctly if you set a fixed length for the character string for parameter *@Column*, as in the example: *varchar(100)*, rather than just *varchar*.

15

ADO Events

When ADO *Connection* and *Recordset* objects are working, they both send out events you can capture. If you use the *WithEvents* supplement to declare the respective objects, you can capture and process the events in your programs.

You can use event procedures to handle the events initiated by *Connection* and *Recordset* objects. This is similar to working with forms and reports, where your actions, such as mouse clicks or keyboard entries, initiate events that are handled by event procedures; for example, *Form_Load*, *Control_Click*, and so forth.

You can handle events only in class modules (that is, form and report class modules) or in independent class modules.

Events

Table 15-1 and Table 15-2 list the possible events for *Connection* objects and *Recordset* objects.

Table 15-1   *Connection* Object Events

Event	Description
BeginTransComplete	Initiated after a *BeginTrans* operation
CommitTransComplete	Initiated after a *CommitTrans* operation
ConnectComplete	Initiated after the connection starts
Disconnect	Initiated after the connection ends
ExecuteComplete	Initiated after the command's execution is complete
InfoMessage	Initiated whenever additional information is available about the current operation

continued

Table 15-1 *Connection* **Object Events** *(continued)*

Event	Description
RollbackTransComplete	Initiated after a *RollbackTrans* operation
WillConnect	Initiated before the connection starts
WillExecute	Initiated shortly before a command is executed through this connection

Table 15-2 *Recordset* **Object Events**

Event	Description
FetchProgress	Raised periodically during asynchronous operations while the system fetches records from the server and places them in the recordset. This event provides information about the number of records already on the client.
FetchComplete	Raised during an asynchronous operation after the system has fetched all records and placed them in the recordset.
WillChangeField	Raised shortly before the content of a record field changes. Such changes can be caused by, for example, assignment to the field's *Value* property.
FieldChangeComplete	Raised when the field content change is complete.
WillMove	Raised shortly before the record pointer is moved.
MoveComplete	Raised after the record pointer move is complete.
EndOfRecordset	Raised when there is an attempt to move past the end of the recordset.
WillChangeRecord	Raised shortly before a record is changed with *Update, UpdateBatch, AddNew, Delete, Cancel,* or *CancelBatch.*
RecordChangeComplete	Raised shortly after a record has been changed with *Update, UpdateBatch, AddNew, Delete, Cancel,* or *CancelBatch.*
WillChangeRecordset	Raised shortly before the *Requery, Resync, Close, Open,* or *Filter* command is used for a recordset.
RecordsetChangeComplete	Raised after the *Requery, Resync, Close, Open,* or *Filter* command has been used for a recordset.

An Example with Event Handling

The form shown in Figure 15-1 is a simple example that illustrates event handling. The form displays data from the table *tblFilms*. There is one check box each located in front of the control elements for *FilmNr, Filmtitle,* and *Length*.

A selected check box means that the content of the field on which the control element is based was modified in the recordset. The event handling routine *FieldChangeComplete* sets the check marks.

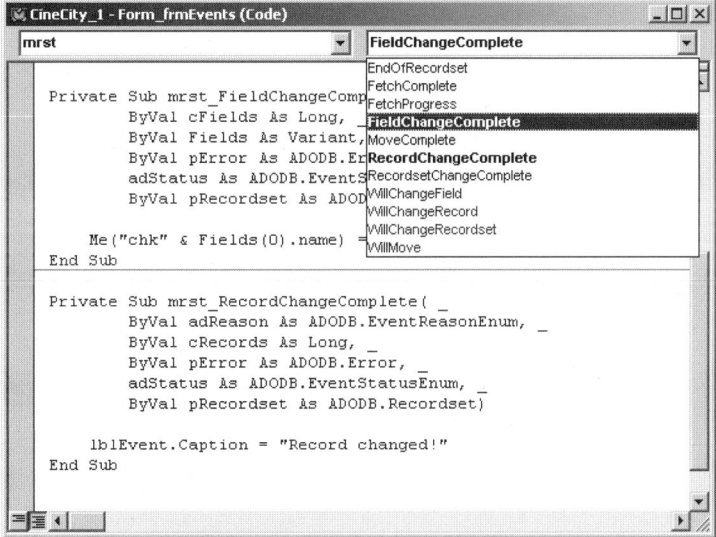

Figure 15-1   Example form for events

You must define an additional recordset variable to capture the events of the recordset on which the form is based. Use the *WithEvents* keyword to declare the object. *WithEvents* specifies that the declared object can send events.

Once you use *WithEvents* for the declaration, you can select the variable in the Microsoft Visual Basic editor's Object combo box in the upper left, as shown in Figure 15-2. The selection of events you can capture is shown on the right.

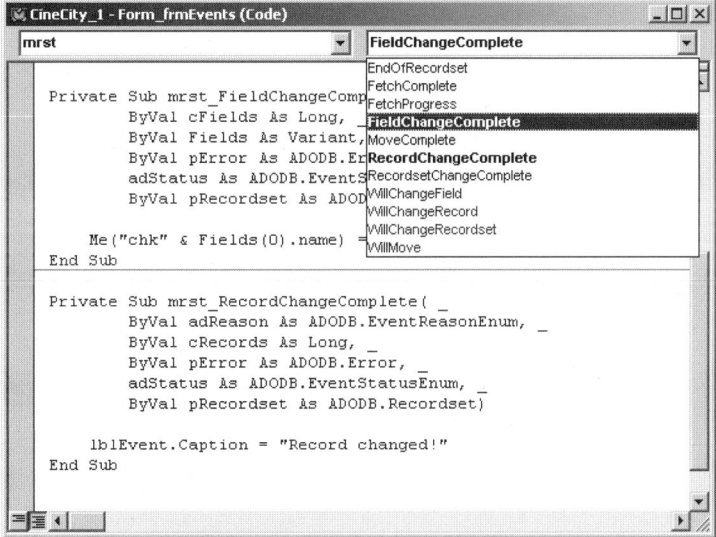

Figure 15-2   Selection of events

Make sure that the recordset on which the form is based is assigned to the *mrst* variable in the *Form_Load* procedure, as shown here:

```
Option Compare Database
Option Explicit


Dim WithEvents mrst As ADODB.Recordset


Private Sub Form_Current()
  lblEvent.Caption = ""
  chkFilmNr = False
  chkFilmtitle = False
  chkLength = False
End Sub


Private Sub Form_Load()
  Set mrst = Me.Recordset
End Sub


Private Sub mrst_FieldChangeComplete( _
    ByVal cFields As Long, _
    ByVal Fields As Variant, _
    ByVal pError As ADODB.Error, _
    adStatus As ADODB.EventStatusEnum, _
    ByVal pRecordset As ADODB.Recordset)

  Me("chk" & Fields(0).Name) = True
End Sub


Private Sub mrst_RecordChangeComplete( _
    ByVal adReason As ADODB.EventReasonEnum, _
```

```
        ByVal cRecords As Long, _

        ByVal pError As ADODB.Error, _

        adStatus As ADODB.EventStatusEnum, _

        ByVal pRecordset As ADODB.Recordset)


    lblEvent.Caption = "Record modified!"
End Sub
```

Asynchronous Queries

An *asynchronous query* is a query during which the calling program does not wait for the server results. Instead, the program continues to run. In descriptions in previous chapters, the client program waited until the data was available in the recordset, for example, when it wanted to open a recordset. The program was locked until after the server delivered the data. The same thing happened during the execution of action queries with command objects: The client program waited until the query was processed.

In Chapter 14, "*Command* Objects," we briefly described several options for executing asynchronous queries. This section describes the use of asynchronous queries in more detail. Why in this chapter about events? The answer is simple: With asynchronous queries, you need events that tell you, for example, when a query was completed and when the results are available.

ADO has two scenarios for asynchronous processing. In the first scenario, the query is started asynchronously during execution of the *Command* object. This means that ADO passes the query to Microsoft SQL Server and returns an event when the query is complete. The second scenario lets you fill a recordset asynchronously. In the process, the system only transmits the resultset from the server to the client. After the first data has arrived on the client, the client can continue working without waiting for the remaining data.

Asynchronous Execution

To execute asynchronous queries, you must use the *Options* parameter to pass the *adAsyncExecute* constant to the *Command* object's *Execute* method.

We have modified the example form in Chapter 14, "*Command* Objects," to adapt it for asynchronous queries, as seen in Figure 15-3. The form can then execute queries asynchronously. A check box and a time display are included for that purpose. The time display measures the time (in milliseconds) needed to process a query.

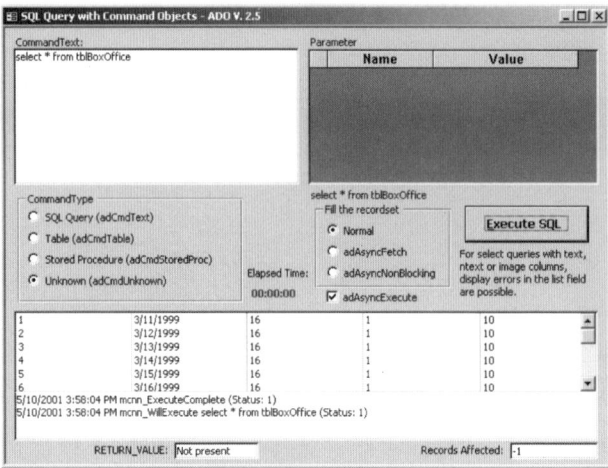

Figure 15-3   Form *frmSQLAsynchron*

If you start a query asynchronously, you can continue working in the form while the query is being executed. The timer measures and displays the elapsed time. If you do not start a query asynchronously, the timer does not measure the elapsed time and returns an erroneous display at the end.

To better understand the following listings, start reading the listing with the routine *cmdSQL_Click()*. The system processes this routine when you click Execute SQL. The timer to measure the elapsed time is also started in this routine.

If the query completes successfully, the system raises the *ExecuteComplete* event for the *Connection* object. The corresponding event handling routine is *mcnn_ExecuteComplete*, which initiates output of the resultset in the list box and the display of return parameter values.

```
Option Compare Database

Option Explicit


Dim WithEvents mcnn As ADODB.Connection

Dim WithEvents mrst As ADODB.Recordset

Dim mcmd As ADODB.Command

' For list box

Dim maRows As Variant

' For timer

Dim mvElapsedMS As Variant
```

```vbnet
Private Sub cmdParameter_Click()
  Dim rst As ADODB.Recordset
  Dim par As ADODB.Parameter


  On Error GoTo ErrorHandler


  If txtSQL <> "" Then
    ' Show result list box
    lstResult.Visible = True
    ' Empty parameter table
    EmptyParameterTable
    ' Get query text
    mcmd.CommandText = txtSQL
    ' Assign command type
    mcmd.CommandType = fraCommandType
    ' Retrieve parameters
    mcmd.Parameters.Refresh
    ' Save parameter to table
    If mcmd.Parameters.Count > 0 Then
      Set rst = New ADODB.Recordset
      rst.Open "tblParameter", mcnn, adOpenStatic, adLockOptimistic
      For Each par In mcmd.Parameters
        ' Parameter values
        ' Ignore Output-Parameters like RETURN_VALUE
        If par.Direction = adParamInput Then
          rst.AddNew
          rst!Name = par.Name
          rst!Value = par.Value
          rst.Update
        End If
```

```vba
        Next
      End If
      subfrmParameter.Requery
      lblSQLText.Caption = mcmd.CommandText
    End If
Exitsub:
  Exit Sub


ErrorHandler:
  ErrorHandler
  Resume Exitsub
End Sub


Private Sub cmdSQL_Click()
  Dim lngRecordsAffected As Long
  Dim lngOption As Long


  On Error GoTo ErrorHandler


  txtEvents = ""


  ' Retrieve parameters from table
  If mcmd.Parameters.Count > 0 Then
    Dim par As ADODB.Parameter
    Dim rst As ADODB.Recordset

    Set rst = New ADODB.Recordset
    rst.Open "tblParameter", mcnn
    Do Until rst.EOF
      mcmd.Parameters(Trim(rst!Name)).Value = rst!Value
```

```
        rst.MoveNext
      Loop
      rst.Close
      Set rst = Nothing
    End If
    ' Execute query
    mvElapsedMS = 0
    TimerInterval = 1
    lblTime.Caption = ""
    DoCmd.Hourglass True
    If chkAsyncExecute Then
      lngOption = adAsyncExecute
    End If
    Set mrst = mcmd.Execute(RecordsAffected:=lngRecordsAffected, _
      Options:=lngOption)
Exitsub:
    Exit Sub


ErrorHandler:
    DoCmd.Hourglass False
    ErrorHandler
    Resume Exitsub
End Sub


Private Sub Form_Load()
    Set mcmd = New ADODB.Command
    Set mrst = New ADODB.Recordset
    Set mcnn = New ADODB.Connection
    ' Important: the method mcmd.Parameters.Refresh for stored
    ' procedures with the MSDataShape provider
```

```
' only operates with ADO version 2.6 and later;
' therefore, new connection without MSDataShape;
' Connection data without MSDataShape for current project
' are in CurrentProject.BaseConnectionString
If CurrentProject.Connection.Version < "2.6" Then
  Set mcnn = New ADODB.Connection
  mcnn.ConnectionString = CurrentProject.BaseConnectionString
  mcnn.Open
Else
  Set mcnn = CurrentProject.Connection
End If
Me.Caption = Me.Caption & " - ADO V. " & mcnn.Version


mcmd.ActiveConnection = mcnn
' Initialize
fraCommandType = 8
chkAsyncExecute = True
txtEvents = ""
EmptyParameterTable
subfrmParameter.Requery
End Sub


' User defined fill function for list box
Function ShowRecordsAsync(ctlField As Control, _
        varID As Variant, _
        varRow As Variant, _
        varColumn As Variant, _
        varCode As Variant _
        ) As Variant
On Error Resume Next
```

```
    Select Case varCode
      Case acLBInitialize:
        lstResult.Visible = True
        ShowRecordsAsync = True
      Case acLBOpen:
        ' Generate unique internal IDs
        ShowRecordsAsync = Timer
      Case acLBGetRowCount:
        ' Number of rows
        ShowRecordsAsync = UBound(maRows, 2) + 1
      Case acLBGetColumnCount:
        ' Number of columns
        ShowRecordsAsync = UBound(maRows, 1) + 1
      Case acLBGetColumnWidth:
        ' Standard width
        ShowRecordsAsync = -1
      Case acLBGetValue:
        ' Retrieve values
        ShowRecordsAsync = maRows(varColumn, varRow)
    End Select
End Function


Private Sub Form_Timer()
  mvElapsedMS = mvElapsedMS + Me.TimerInterval
  ShowElapsedTime mvElapsedMS


End Sub


Sub ShowElapsedTime(ElapsedMS As Variant)
  Dim Hours, Minutes, Seconds, MS
```

```
    Hours = Format((ElapsedMS \ 360000), "00")
    Minutes = Format(((ElapsedMS \ 6000) Mod 60), "00")
    Seconds = Format((ElapsedMS \ 100) Mod 60, "00")
    MS = Format((ElapsedMS) Mod 100, "00")

    lblTime.Caption = Hours & ":" & Minutes & ":" & Seconds & ":" & MS
End Sub


Private Sub fraCommandType_Click()
  cmdParameter_Click
End Sub


Private Sub mcnn_ExecuteComplete( _
        ByVal RecordsAffected As Long, _
        ByVal pError As ADODB.Error, _
        adStatus As ADODB.EventStatusEnum, _
        ByVal pCommand As ADODB.Command, _
        ByVal pRecordset As ADODB.Recordset, _
        ByVal pConnection As ADODB.Connection)


    Dim par As ADODB.Parameter


    DoCmd.Hourglass False
    ShowEvents "mcnn_ExecuteComplete", "(Status: " & adStatus & ")"


    On Error Resume Next
    TimerInterval = 0
    ShowElapsedTime mvElapsedMS
    mvElapsedMS = 0
    ' Show "Records Affected"
```

```
    txtRecordsAffected = RecordsAffected
    ' Query parameter, if present
    For Each par In mcmd.Parameters
      If (par.Direction = adParamInputOutput) Or _
            (par.Direction = adParamOutput) Then
        MsgBox par.Name & " = " & par.Value
      End If
    Next
    ' First parameter is return value
    txtReturnValue = mcmd.Parameters(0).Value
    If Err.Number > 0 Then
      txtReturnValue = "Not present"
    End If


    On Error GoTo ErrorHandler
    If (mrst.State = adStateOpen) Then
      If Not (mrst.BOF And mrst.EOF) Then
        maRows = mrst.GetRows
        lstResult.ColumnCount = UBound(maRows, 1) + 1
        mrst.Close
        GoTo goon
      End If
    End If
    ' List field empty
    ReDim maRows(1, 1) As Variant
    lstResult.ColumnCount = 1
goon:
    lstResult.Requery
Exitsub:
    Exit Sub
```

```
ErrorHandler:
  DoCmd.Hourglass False
  ErrorHandler
  Resume Exitsub
End Sub


Private Sub mcnn_InfoMessage( _
      ByVal pError As ADODB.Error, _
      adStatus As ADODB.EventStatusEnum, _
      ByVal pConnection As ADODB.Connection)


  ShowEvents "mcnn_InfoMessage", pError.Number, _
      pError.Description, "(Status: " & adStatus & ")"
End Sub


Private Sub mcnn_WillConnect( _
      ConnectionString As String, _
      UserID As String, _
      Password As String, _
      Options As Long, _
      adStatus As ADODB.EventStatusEnum, _
      ByVal pConnection As ADODB.Connection)


  ShowEvents "mcnn_WillConnect", ConnectionString, "(Status: " & _
      adStatus & ")"
End Sub


Private Sub mcnn_WillExecute( _
      Source As String, _
      CursorType As ADODB.CursorTypeEnum, _
```

```
              LockType As ADODB.LockTypeEnum, _
              Options As Long, _
              adStatus As ADODB.EventStatusEnum, _
              ByVal pCommand As ADODB.Command, _
              ByVal pRecordset As ADODB.Recordset, _
              ByVal pConnection As ADODB.Connection)


    ShowEvents "mcnn_WillExecute", Source, "(Status: " & adStatus & ")"
End Sub


Private Sub txtSQL_Exit(Cancel As Integer)
    cmdParameter_Click
End Sub


Sub EmptyParameterTable()
    CurrentProject.Connection.Execute "delete from tblParameter"
End Sub


Sub ShowEvents(ParamArray pa() As Variant)
    Dim v As Variant
    Dim strTmp As String


    strTmp = Time
    For Each v In pa
      strTmp = strTmp & " " & v
    Next
    strTmp = strTmp & vbNewLine
    txtEvents = strTmp & txtEvents
    DoEvents
End Sub
```

```vba
Sub ErrorHandler()
  Dim errADO As ADODB.Error
  Dim strErr As String


  strErr = "VBA-error information" & vbNewLine & vbNewLine
  strErr = strErr & "Number: " & Err.Number & vbNewLine
  strErr = strErr & "Description: " & Err.Description & vbNewLine
  strErr = strErr & vbNewLine
  If mcnn.Errors.Count > 0 Then
    For Each errADO In mcnn.Errors
      strErr = strErr & vbNewLine & "ADO-error information (ADO V." & _
             mcnn.Version & ")" & _
             vbNewLine & vbNewLine
      strErr = strErr & "NativeError: " & errADO.NativeError & _
             vbNewLine
      strErr = strErr & "Number: " & errADO.Number & vbNewLine
      strErr = strErr & "Description: " & errADO.Description & _
             vbNewLine
      strErr = strErr & "Source: " & errADO.Source & vbNewLine
      strErr = strErr & "SQLState: " & errADO.SQLState & vbNewLine
      strErr = strErr & "Source: " & errADO.Source & vbNewLine
    Next
  End If
  lstResult.Visible = False
  txtError.Visible = True
  txtError = strErr
End Sub
```

Fetching Records Asynchronously

Asynchronous transmission of data to the client minimizes wait times for the user. As soon as the first data is available, the user can continue working while ADO completes the recordset in the background. Microsoft Access uses this option to make data available for forms. You can view the first records while additional records are still being fetched.

You can use the *FetchComplete* and *FetchProgress* recordset events to control how much data the server transmits to the client.

The *State* Property

Use the *Command* object's *State* property to determine the current status of an asynchronous query. Its constants are described in Table 15-3. The object's *State* property can have a combination of values, for instance *adStateOpen* and *adStateExecuting* when a statement is being executed.

Table 15-3   Constants for the *Command* Object's *State* Property

Constant	Description
adStateClosed	Returned during asynchronous queries as soon as the first data arrives at the client
adStateConnecting	Indicates that the object is connecting
adStateExecuting	Returned during asynchronous queries while the system executes the query
adStateFetching	Indicates that the rows of the object are being retrieved
adStateOpen	Indicates that the object is open

Part IV

Upsizing

Many Access projects are initiated because existing Microsoft Access applications, due to the volume of data or the number of simultaneous network users, have reached capacity.

Access provides the Upsizing Wizard to convert Access mdb applications into Access projects. This wizard helps with the conversion, as it can transfer the data from an mdb database to a SQL Server/MSDE database. In upsizing, attempts are made to also transfer all queries, forms, reports, macros, and modules to an Access project. In most cases, manual work is required following upsizing because many Access mdb application structures cannot be transferred to Access projects.

All Microsoft Visual Basic for Applications (VBA) programs also have to be revised manually because only ActiveX Data Objects (ADO) is supported in Access projects, not Data Access Objects (DAO). Generally, converting programs from DAO to ADO is simple because many structures are similar, but sometimes the underlying logic also has to be revised.

16

Upsizing Wizard

Microsoft Access supports conversion of .mdb files into Access projects using the Upsizing Wizard. The wizard attempts to convert as many objects in an .mdb file as possible, although some structures cannot be transferred. It divides the .mdb file into an .adp file for access project and a database in Microsoft SQL Server/MSDE. You have an option of creating a new adp project, keeping an existing mdb project with linked tables, or keeping your project intact. In the next step, you must then enhance the unconverted queries, where required, and check forms, reports, and modules. This chapter describes common problems that you might encounter during upsizing. It also details the Access commands and program constructions that cannot be converted by the Upsizing Wizard.

The Upsizing Wizard

To use the Upsizing Wizard, open the mdb database that you want to convert and then call the Wizard from the Tools menus by selecting Database Utilities, then Upsizing Wizard. In the first dialog box, select whether you want to create a new SQL Server database or use an existing database.

Creating a New Database

In the next step, select the SQL server to which the database is to be saved. If you are using MSDE, this will probably be your own computer. SQL Server and MSDE have their own security system, described in detail in Chapter 20, "Security." This system regulates access to SQL Server/MSDE and the rights for users and user groups to the databases. If SQL Server or MSDE are installed on a Microsoft Windows NT or Microsoft Windows 2000 system, the Windows security information can be used. This is known as a *trusted connection.* In this case you do not need to fill in the Login ID and Password text boxes (see *Figure 16-1*).

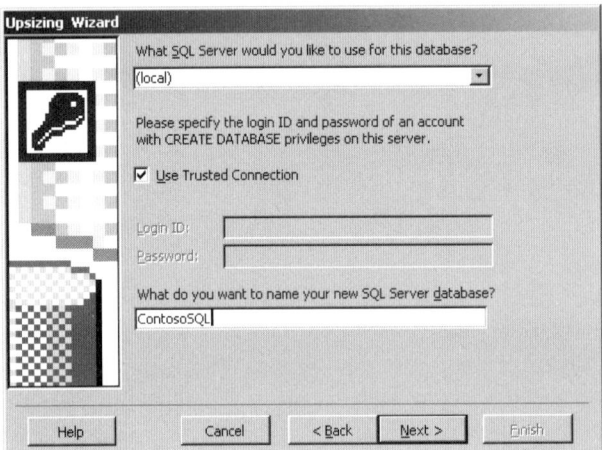

Figure 16-1   Information on SQL Server and permissions

Otherwise, user *sa* (representing the system administrator) is always provided for SQL Server/MSDE installed in a Mixed Mode. This user possesses all rights and permissions in SQL Server and should always be password-protected. Choose this user if you do not have a specific user ID and password and your server has not been configured in Windows Authentication Mode.

Using an Existing Database

If you want to use an existing database on the corresponding SQL server, then you must set up an open database connectivity (ODBC) connection for this database. Access opens the Select Data Source dialog box (see Figure 16-2) for this purpose, in which you enter the ODBC connection information. If an ODBC connection definition already exists for the SQL server and the required database, then you can select it.

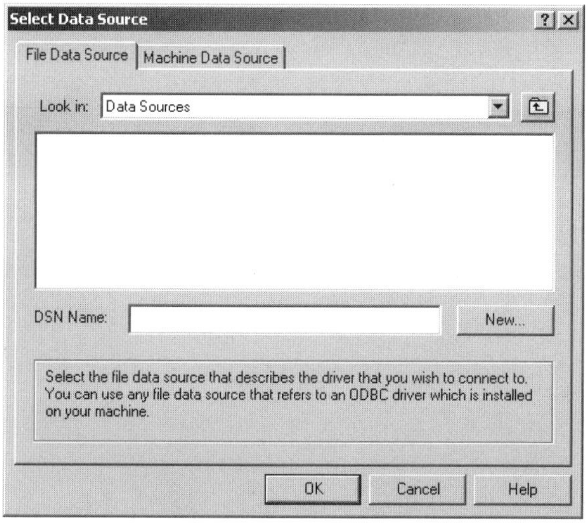

Figure 16-2   Select Data Source dialog box

ODBC data source definitions can be created as file and machine data sources. The ODBC connection information is stored in a file (usually in the folder \Program Files\Common Files\ODBC\Data Sources) as the file data source. Alternatively, user-specific computer data source information is stored in the Windows registry. For further information, see the online help for ODBC.

Figure 16-3 provides an example of how to set up a file data source. Activate the relevant dialog boxes with the New button. In the first dialog box, you determine the ODBC driver, in this case SQL Server driver.

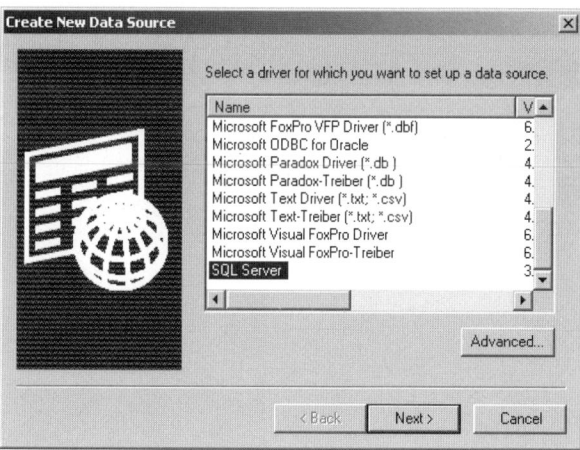

Figure 16-3   Selecting the driver

In the Create A New Data Source To SQL Server dialog box, shown in Figure 16-4, you specify the name of the data source. You then select the appropriate SQL server on which the database is created.

Figure 16-4   Selecting the SQL server

In the next part of the ODBC Wizard, you specify whether you are accessing the SQL server with Windows security settings or SQL Server security settings.

The next step allows you to change the default database if the database you want to access is not the default database assigned to your SQL Server user ID, as shown in Figure 16-5.

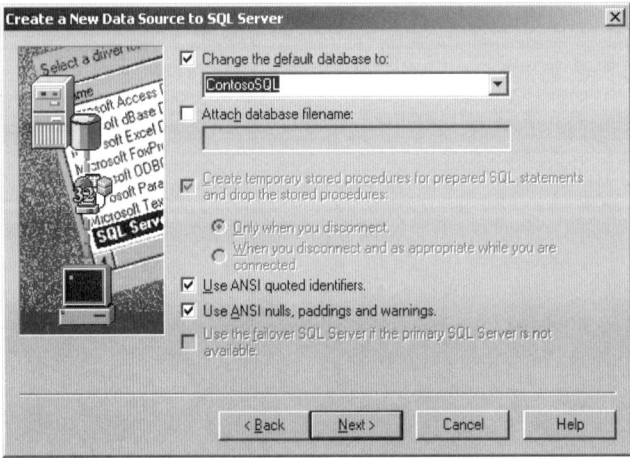

Figure 16-5   Selecting the default database

The last part of the ODBC Wizard then appears in which you can make additional settings for the connection. You can usually accept the default settings.

You have now finished defining the data source. The name of the data source appears in the Select Data Source dialog box displayed in Figure 16-2 and can be selected from there.

Additional Wizard Tasks

In the next Upsizing Wizard page, shown in Figure 16-6, select which of the mdb database tables are to be exported to SQL Server/MSDE.

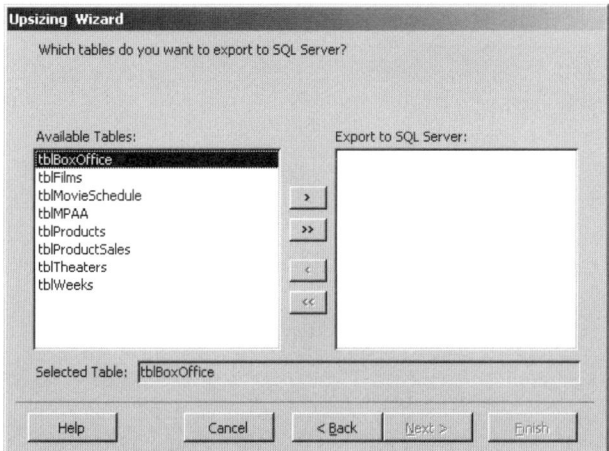

Figure 16-6   Tables to be exported

In the subsequent step (see Figure 16-7) you can select which table attributes you would also like to export. If you select Indexes, the wizard attempts to create SQL Server indexes that reflect the existing Access indexes. If the Validation Rules check box is activated, the Microsoft Access 2002 Wizard provides a choice of conversion of the rules to DRI constraints or triggers. With Microsoft Access 2000, the validation rules are converted into triggers, which are table-assigned procedures executed when data is inserted, updated, or deleted in the table. A trigger is written in Transact-SQL. This language and the use of triggers are described in Chapter 8, "Stored Procedures." If a table and its fields have several validation rules, these are usually combined into a single trigger.

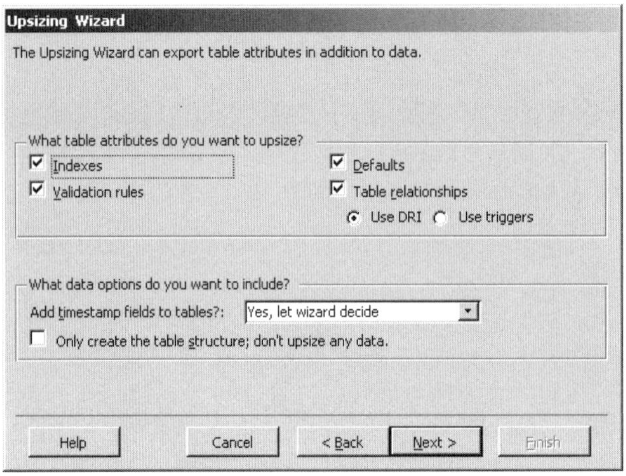

Figure 16-7   Defining table attributes to be exported

The system also attempts to reflect the Access table standard values in SQL Server/MSDE.

Table relationships in Access are represented with triggers or declarative referential integrity (DRI) in SQL Server. DRI works in the same way as referential integrity in Access: Primary key restrictions are defined for base tables and foreign key restrictions are defined for foreign tables. With Access 2002 and Microsoft SQL Server 2000 the definitions for cascading updates and deletes are transferred.

You should use the Use Triggers option with all other Access/SQL Server combinations, because this best converts the behavior of mdb databases to SQL Server.

> **Note**   Only SQL Server 2000/MSDE 2000 recognize cascading updates and deletes; Access 2000, however, cannot use these new options.

The Upsizing Wizard normally inserts timestamp fields into its tables. These fields are helpful if several users access a table simultaneously, because they make it possible to determine quickly when the corresponding record was last modified. If you select the option that allows the wizard to decide whether a timestamp field is added to a table or not, timestamps are added to all tables in which data fields contain single, double, memo, or OLE object types.

In the bottom section of the dialog box you can specify that you want to export the structure of the tables but not the contents. This is useful primarily if you want to quickly detect any problems that might arise when exporting your database, without having to transfer large quantities of data.

> **Note**   Large quantities of data can cause the wizard to terminate if certain processes take too long. In this case, you must change a registry entry or use more basic methods to transfer the table contents. The registry entry to modify is HKEY_LOCAL_MACHINE\Software\ Microsoft\Jet\4.0\Engines\ODBC\QueryTimeout. Set this value to **0** for unlimited query execution time. You could also use the DTS Import/ Export Wizards (see Chapter 22, "Data Transformation Services") in SQL Server/MSDE. In the case of new tables created in SQL Server/ MSDE, you must create links in your .mdb file and then use append queries to transfer the data from the .mdb file to the SQL Server/MSDE database.

The next step provides you with three different upsizing options, as shown in Figure 16-8. If you select the first option, the wizard creates an Access project. Both an .adp file and a database are created on the server. The database contains the tables, views, and stored procedures that the Upsizing Wizard created from the original Access queries.

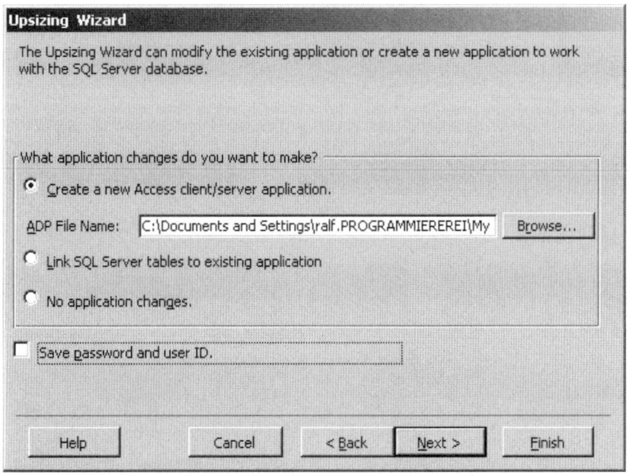

Figure 16-8   Selecting the type of exporting

The second option also creates a database with the tables of the .mdb file, which are also linked to the .mdb file. The .mdb file now contains the original tables (with _local added) as well as the tables exported to the server that are linked with ODBC to the tables in the SQL Server/MSDE database.

If you select the last option, your .mdb file remains as it is and only the database is created in SQL Server/MSDE.

The Access 2000 Upsizing Wizard reverses the options above; the first one leaves the mdb project intact, the second links the SQL Server/MSDE tables, and the third creates the adp application.

If you select the Save Password And User ID option, these values are both stored in the mdb or .adp file. This means that anyone who opens the .mdb or .adp file has access to the database on SQL Server/MSDE.

When the wizard has completed processing and converting the database, it issues a confirmation in the form of a snapshot report that is stored in the same file as the original database, as shown in Figure 16-9. This report contains any problems encountered by the wizard during the upsizing process. It records which data types were converted, for which queries upsizing was carried out, and for which queries it was unsuccessful. You can also save the upsizing result report as a snapshot to check it later.

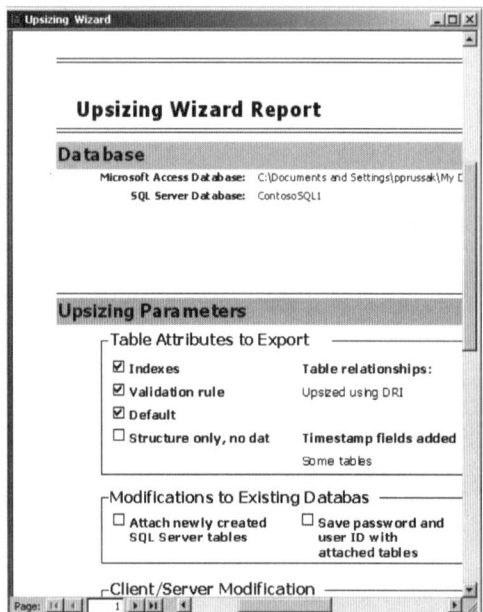

Figure 16-9   The database upsizing report

Converting Tables

During table conversion, some of the settings and properties of the tables and their fields might not be converted or might be altered in some way. This is described in greater detail in the following sections.

> **Note**   If a table name contains an apostrophe or a single quotation mark, the table will not be converted.

Converting Data Types

Table 16-1 contains Access data types and their conversion counterparts as SQL Server data types. Contrary to the information in the report, some data types are converted into larger data types. Instead of the SQL Server data types *varchar* and *text*, the data types *nvarchar* and *ntext* are used, which both support representation of contents in Unicode (the *n* stands for *national*). The Unicode representation is only practical if you are managing text in a foreign language such as Cyrillic, Chinese, and so forth, because Unicode can also display these, although every character takes up a 2-byte coding. If you are only using English, German, or another language that can be represented with ANSI characters, using Unicode is a waste of memory because all texts take up twice as much space with the 2-byte Unicode coding.

Table 16-1   Data Type Conversion

Access Mdb Data Type	SQL Server Data Type
Currency	money
Date/time	datetime
Hyperlinks	ntext
Memo	ntext
Number: byte	smallint
Number: decimal	float
Number: double	float
Number: integer	smallint
Number: long integer	int
Number: single	real
OLE object	image
Text	nvarchar
Yes/No	bit

Because SQL Server/MSDE does not support hyperlinks, these are converted into *ntext* fields, meaning that they lose their hypertext functionality. If one of your tables contained hyperlinks, the system issues a corresponding message in the error category at the beginning of the report.

Validation Rules and Messages

If your Access mdb tables contain validation rules and messages, then these are converted into constraints (Access 2002) or triggers (Access 2002 and Access 2000).

The following listing displays an insert trigger, that checks fields *SalesPrice* and *PurchasePrice* for the correct entries. Transact-SQL is used to program triggers for validation rules and messages. For more information on triggers, see Chapter 8, "Stored Procedures."

```
CREATE TRIGGER "tblProducts_ITrig" ON dbo.tblProducts FOR INSERT AS

SET NOCOUNT ON


/* * VALIDATION RULE FOR FIELD 'SalesPrice' */

IF (SELECT Count(*) FROM inserted WHERE NOT (SalesPrice > Purchase
Price) > 0

  BEGIN

    RAISERROR 44444 'SalesPrice must be greater than PurchasePrice'

    ROLLBACK TRANSACTION

  END
```

Labeling and Formatting Statements

The *Format, Input Mask,* and *Caption* properties of table fields are not supported. *Format* and *Input Mask* properties have no equivalent for SQL Server/MSDE, and the *Caption* property is replaced by the actual field name.

Lookup Fields

Lookup fields are used in Access mdb databases to look up a given value stored in a different linked table and display it for a value in the current table. SQL Server/MSDE versions earlier than SQL Server 2000 do not provide the option to define lookup tables. For this reason, lookup tables are converted by transferring the actual values stored in the table.

The *Required* Property

The *Required* property is converted so that the Allow Nulls option is activated in SQL Server/MSDE if the property *Required* is not set.

The *Allow Zero Length* Property

If you have set the *Allow Zero Length* property to No, then no character string with length 0 ("") can be entered there because this setting is not supported. If you need to set this kind of restriction in SQL Server/MSDE, you must define a suitable constraint (see Chapter 5, "Tables in Access Projects") or a trigger (see Chapter 8, "Stored Procedures").

Porting Relationships

As mentioned earlier, the Upsizing Wizard can convert relationships between tables in two different variants: with DRI or with triggers.

Declared Referential Integrity (DRI)

If you select DRI for the upsizing process (see Figure 16-7), the relationships between the tables are reflected using constraints.

If you use the Upsizing Wizard to create an Access project (see Figure 16-8, first option), you will not be able to see the relationships created by DRI when you open the project. These relationships are only visible when you create a new database diagram (see Chapter 6, "Database Diagrams") and add the relevant tables.

Triggers

If you choose conversion with triggers to retain the cascading update and deletion, for example, the Upsizing Wizard adds triggers to the relevant tables. Triggers can be defined for every table and can be activated on insertion, changing, and deletion of data. Chapter 8, "Stored Procedures," explains how to create and maintain triggers using Transact-SQL.

The following listing displays a deletion trigger, which is activated when an article is deleted in the table *tblProducts* to delete all records with the same article number in the table *tblProductSales*.

```
CREATE TRIGGER "tblProducts_DTrig" ON tblProducts FOR DELETE AS

SET NOCOUNT ON

/* CASCADING DELETE ON 'tblProductSales' */

DELETE tblProductSales FROM deleted, tblProductSales WHERE
deleted.ProductNr = tblProductSales.ProductNr
```

Relationship Visibility

Table 16-2 lists the relationships that are visible in Access. The selected variant governs which relationships can be viewed or changed.

Table 16-2   Relationship Variants

Exporting	DRI	Triggers
Access project (client/server)	Relationships are visible if a new database diagram is created with the relevant tables. New relationships in the database diagram are stored on the SQL server.	Relationships are not visible; the triggers can be edited.
Attached tables	Relationships in the relationship window of the .mdb file are visible. When new relationships are added, these are only created locally in the mdb.	Relationships are not visible and it is not possible to change triggers.
Without change	Relationships not visible because tables not visible.	Relationships not visible and no change to triggers possible because the tables are not visible.

Upsizing Queries

When you view the report created by the Upsizing Wizard, you will see that upsizing was either not possible or not even attempted for some queries. The report displays the SQL code that the wizard used when attempting to convert the query. Under the name specified, however, there is no view or stored procedure in the database. The following section describes typical problems that might occur during upsizing, along with explanations and tips for dealing with them.

The next section assumes that you have instructed the Upsizing Wizard to create an Access project. The problems and shortcomings described refer to both the SQL Server/MSDE database and the Access project.

Views and Stored Procedures with the Name *ut_…*

Views and stored procedures created by the Upsizing Wizard with names beginning with *ut_* are queries that are used for controls in forms or reports.

Sorting

Because it is not possible to sort in views with versions earlier than SQL Server 2000, queries with sort statements are replaced with a view and a stored procedure, as illustrated by the following example:

```
CREATE VIEW qryFilmsSortedByLengthView

AS

SELECT Length, COUNT(FilmNr)

FROM tblFilms

GROUP BY Length

GO

CREATE PROCEDURE qryFilmsSortedByLength

AS

SELECT * FROM "qryFilmsSortedByLengthView"

ORDER BY "qryFilmsSortedByLengthView".Length
```

This completes the actual query of the view, and the sorting is carried out by the stored procedure. SQL Server 2000/MSDE 2000 also allows the specification of sorted views that you can create directly with Access 2002.

> **Note**   SQL Server/MSDE uses double quotation marks to enclose names of tables and columns (for example, if spaces appear in the name). In Access .mdb files, the double quotation marks are used to restrict character strings. SQL Server/MSDE uses single quotation marks for this.

Some Query Properties Are Not Converted

Several query properties, listed in Table 16-3, are not converted.

Table 16-3   Conversion of Query Properties

Access Property	Conversion
Description	Not converted.
Output All Fields	SELECT *
Top Values	TOP x, TOP x%

continued

Table 16-3   Conversion of Query Properties   *(continued)*

Access Property	Conversion
Unique Values	*DISTINCT* command is not converted. For further information, see the section later in this chapter entitled "*DISTINCT* Is Not Converted."
Unique Records	Not converted; *DISTINCTROW* command is deleted.
Run Permissions	Not converted; *WITH OWNERACCESS OPTION* command is deleted.
Source Database	Not converted.
Source Connect String	Not converted.
Record Locks	Not converted.
Recordset Type	Not converted.
ODBC Timeout	Not converted.
Filter	Not converted.
Order By	Not converted.
Max Records	Not converted.
Subdatasheet Name	Not converted.
Link Child Fields	Not converted.
Link Master Fields	Not converted.
Subdatasheet Height	Not converted.
Subdatasheet Expanded	Not converted.

Nested Queries

Nested queries (queries that call other queries) are only converted if the queries used by another query fulfill the following conditions:

- They do not use parameters.
- They are not sorted (do not use *ORDER BY*).
- They do not contain commands that cause the Upsizing Wizard to convert them as stored procedures.

Problems When Upsizing Queries

This section describes frequent problems that occur when converting queries.

DISTINCT Is Not Converted

A source of many errors is the nonconversion of the SQL command *DISTINCT*, which ensures the unique nature of the records in the resultset. The Upsizing Wizard deletes the command from the queries but then writes in the upsizing report that the query was successfully converted.

This incorrect conversion can cause subsequent errors that, for example, can prevent proper functioning of groupings in reports. The only way to guard against this is to check all queries after conversion. For example, the following query issues the calendar week, the movie title, the internal week number, and the current week for every film:

```
SELECT DISTINCT tblWeeks.Week, tblFilms.Filmtitle,

tblWeeks.WeekNr, tblWeeks.WeekShown

FROM (tblFilms INNER JOIN

tblWeeks ON tblFilms.FilmNr = tblWeeks.FilmNr) INNER JOIN

tblMovieSchedule ON

tblWeeks.WeekNr = tblMovieSchedule.WeekNr

WHERE (((tblMovieSchedule.TerminNr) Is Not Null));
```

After upsizing to SQL Server/MSDE, the following view is issued:

```
SELECT tblWeeks.Week, tblFilms.Filmtitle,

  tblWeeks.WeekNr, tblWeeks.WeekShown

FROM dbo.tblFilms INNER JOIN

  dbo.tblWeeks ON

  dbo.tblFilms.FilmNr = dbo.tblWeeks.FilmNr INNER JOIN

  dbo.tblMovieSchedule ON

  dbo.tblWeeks.WeekNr = dbo.tblMovieSchedule.WeekNr

WHERE (dbo.tblMovieSchedule.TerminNr IS NOT NULL)
```

Because several dates generally occur in a calendar week, many duplicated data lines now appear in the resultset for the view.

Crosstabs

Crosstabs cannot be transferred to views or stored procedures. As an alternative, you can use pivot controls in forms and reports or create pivot tables with Microsoft Excel.

In Access 2002, the new pivot diagrams and tables provide high-performance options for replacing crosstabs.

Update Queries

Update queries often seem to cause problems for the Upsizing Wizard, although the SQL code for the query is not unusual. You usually just need to create a new stored procedure and copy the SQL code in the old update query from the .mdb file to the Access project using the Windows Clipboard.

Data Definition Language Queries 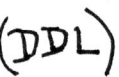 (DDL)

The Upsizing Wizard cannot convert Data Definition Language (DDL) queries. In most cases, you just need to copy the SQL code for the corresponding query from the .mdb file to a stored procedure.

References to Custom Column Names

The Upsizing Wizard cannot deal with column names defined in the Access query to which other columns in the same query refer. This problem is easy to solve by replacing the relevant column name with the actual operation. In our example, the fourth line is calculated with the previously defined column name. SQL Server/MSDE cannot process this. So you would replace this:

```
SELECT tblProducts.Description,

        SUM(tblProductSales.Amount) AS SumSales,

        Count(tblProductSales.Nr) AS Sales,

        [SumSales]/[Sales] AS Average

FROM tblProducts INNER JOIN tblProductSales ON tblProducts.ProductNr =
        tblProductSales.ProductNr

GROUP BY tblProducts.Description
```

with this:

```
SELECT tblProducts.Description,

SUM(tblProductSales.Amount) AS SumSales,

COUNT(tblProductSales.Nr) AS Sales,

SUM(tblProductSales.Amount) / COUNT(tblProductSales.Nr) AS Average

FROM tblProducts INNER JOIN tblProductSales ON

tblProducts.ProductNr = tblProductSales.ProductNr

GROUP BY tblProducts.Description
```

Integer Divided by Integer Equals Another Integer

The calculation used in the previous example *SUM(tblProductSales.Amount)/ COUNT(tblProductSales.Nr)* does not return the required result, because a whole number is being divided by another whole number and the result is another whole number (that is, the decimal places are cut off). Use the *CONVERT* function to obtain the correct result. See the section in Chapter 9, "Transact-SQL," entitled "Converting with *CONVERT*," as shown here:

```
CONVERT(FLOAT, SUM(tblProductSales.Amount)) /
COUNT(tblProductSales.Nr)
```

Alternatively, you can use *CAST*, as seen here:

```
CAST(SUM(tblProductSales.Amount AS FLOAT) / COUNT(tblProductSales.Nr)
```

It is sufficient if the dividend or the divisor is converted into a floating-point number.

If you are calculating the average with the aggregate function *AVG*, rather than with the preceding formula, you must also ensure that the correct data types are being used:

```
SELECT tblProducts.Description,

SUM(tblProductSales.Amount) AS SumSales,

COUNT(tblProductSales.Nr) AS Sales,

AVG(CAST(tblProductSales.Amount AS FLOAT) AS Average

FROM tblProducts INNER JOIN tblProductSales ON

tblProducts.ProductNr = tblProductSales.ProductNr

GROUP BY tblProducts.Description
```

Not All Access Functions Are Supported by SQL Server/MSDE

If you have used Access functions in a query, it is possible that they will not be converted because SQL Server/MSDE does not support the function. Table 16-4 contains the Access functions and their SQL Server/MSDE counterparts. For a full description of all SQL Server/MSDE functions, see the section in Chapter 9, "Transact-SQL," entitled "SQL Functions" or the online help.

Table 16-4   Access Functions and SQL Server Counterparts

Access Functions	SQL Server Functions
Asc(x)	ASCII(x)
Ccur(x)	CONVERT(money,x)
Cdbl(x)	CONVERT(float,x)
Chr(x)	CHAR(x)
Cint(x)	CONVERT(smallint,x)
Clng(x)	CONVERT(int,x)
Csng(x)	CONVERT(real,x)
Cstr(x)	CONVERT(varchar,x)
CvDate(x)	CONVERT(datetime,x)
Date(x)	CONVERT(datetime, convert(varchar,getdate(x)))

continued

Table 16-4 Access Functions and SQL Server Counterparts *(continued)*

Access Functions	SQL Server Functions
DateAdd("<Access datepart>", x, y)	*DATEADD(<SQL Server datepart>, x, y)*
DateDiff("<Access datepart>", x, y)	*DATEDIFF(<SQL Server datepart>, x, y)*
DatePart("<Access datepart>", x, y)	*DATEPART(<SQL Server datepart>, x, y)*
Day(x)	*DATEPART(dd, x)*
Hour(x)	*DATEPART(hh, x)*
Int(x)	*FLOOR(x)* or *CEILING(x)*
Lcase(x)	*LOWER(x)*
Len(x)	*LEN(x)*
Ltrim(x)	*LTRIM(x)*
Mid(x)	*SUBSTRING(x)*
Minute(x)	*DATEPART(mi, x)*
Month(x)	*DATEPART(mm, x)*
Now(x)	*GETDATE(x)*
Right(x)	*RIGHT(x)*
Rtrim(x)	*RTRIM(x)*
Second(x)	*DATEPART(ss,x)*
Sgn(x)	*SIGN(x)*
Space(x)	*SPACE(x)*
Str(x)	*STR(x)*
Ucase(x)	*UPPER(x)*
Weekday(x)	*DATEPART(dw,x)*
Year(x)	*DATEPART(yy,x)*

Remember that you can still apply the Access functions in Microsoft Visual Basic programs; they are just no longer permitted in queries. Because queries are now processed on the server in the form of views and stored procedures, you can also use only functions that are known to the server.

> **Note** SQL Server 2000 allows you to define user-defined functions (UDFs). You can use UDFs to enhance SQL Server/MSDE with new functionality (see the section in Chapter 8, "Stored Procedures," entitled "User-Defined Functions"). In Access 2002 you can create and edit UDFs directly.

Problems Converting Characters and Operators

In some cases the Upsizing Wizard cannot convert characters and operators correctly. Table 16-5 displays the SQL Server counterparts for certain Access characters or operators that cannot usually be converted.

Table 16-5   SQL Server Counterparts for Characters and Operators

Description	Access	SQL Server
Concatenation operator	&	+
Date separator	#	'
Mod operator	mod	%
String separator	' or "	'
Wildcard for a character	?	_
Wildcard for several characters	*	%

Remember that the Access concatenation operator & is different from the SQL Server concatenation operator when handling null values. In Access, concatenations with null values are treated as empty strings.

Queries with Parameters

Queries that use parameters are often converted incorrectly with the Upsizing Wizard. In a functioning stored procedure with parameters (as in the following example), the parameter that is marked with @ is declared after the procedure name. The Upsizing Wizard often forgets the @ in front of the parameter, or it does not declare the parameter at all. Both errors prevent conversion. A procedure converted incorrectly in this way displays the following listing, which requires only the addition of @:

```
CREATE PROCEDURE qdelArchiveBoxOffice ArchiveDate DATETIME

AS

DELETE

FROM tblBoxOffice

WHERE tblBoxOffice.Date < @ArchiveDate
```

DELETE Queries with Joins

DELETE queries that contain linked tables (joins) are not converted correctly by the Upsizing Wizard because the syntax is different for SQL Server/MSDE. The following query from the example mdb database cannot be converted by the Upsizing Wizard:

```
DELETE tblMovieSchedule.*

FROM tblWeeks INNER JOIN tblMovieSchedule

      ON tblWeeks.WeekNr = tblMovieSchedule.WeekNr

WHERE (((tblWeeks.Week)<=#12/31/1999#));
```

For the *DELETE* query to function, it requires two consecutive *FROM* tables. The first *FROM* displays in which table deletion is carried out, and the second *FROM* specifies the first table for the join:

```
CREATE PROCEDURE qdelMovieSchedule

AS

DELETE FROM tblMovieSchedule

FROM tblMovieSchedule INNER JOIN tblWeeks

      ON tblMovieSchedule.WeekNr = tblWeeks.WeekNr

WHERE tblWeeks.Week <= '31.12.1999'
```

The *DELETE* command with two *FROMs* is not standard SQL, but a specific variant for SQL Server. If you want to use a standard ANSI SQL solution, you must use subqueries:

```
CREATE PROCEDURE qdelTMovieScheduleANSI

AS

DELETE FROM tblMovieSchedule

WHERE tblMovieSchedule.WeekNr in

      (SELECT WeekNr FROM tblWeeks

      WHERE tblWeeks.Week <= '31.12.1999')
```

Format Function Cannot Be Converted

In Access mdb queries, the *Format* function of Microsoft Visual Basic for Applications (VBA) can be used to extract only the month or the year from a date, for example. It was used in the following query to calculate total sales income for certain items per month. SQL Server/MSDE does not support the *Format* function, so it can only be used in Access projects in VBA programs.

```
SELECT tblProducts.Description, Format([Date],"yyyy\/mm") AS Month,
      Sum([Amount]*[SalesPrice]) AS SalesSum

FROM tblProducts INNER JOIN tblProductSales

      ON tblProducts.ProductNr = tblProductSales.ProductNr

GROUP BY tblProducts.Description, Format([Date],"yyyy\/mm");
```

The Upsizing Wizard cannot convert this query, which is not surprising when you look at the manually converted query:

```
CREATE PROCEDURE qrySales

AS

SELECT tblProducts.Description,
        CONVERT(VARCHAR,DATEPART(yy,[Date]))
    + '/' +
        CASE WHEN LEN(CONVERT(CHAR,DATEPART(mm,[Date])))=1 THEN
            '0' + convert(char,datepart(mm,[Date]))
        ELSE
            CONVERT(CHAR,DATEPART(mm,[Date]))
        END AS Month,
    Sum([Amount]*[SalesPrice]) AS SalesSum
FROM tblProducts INNER JOIN tblProductSales
        ON tblProducts.ProductNr = tblProductSales.ProductNr
GROUP BY tblProducts.Description,
        CONVERT(VARCHAR,DATEPART(yy,[Date]))
    + '/' +
        CASE WHEN LEN(CONVERT(CHAR,DATEPART(mm,[Date])))=1 THEN
            '0' + CONVERT(CHAR,DATEPART(mm,[Date]))
        ELSE
            CONVERT(CHAR,DATEPART(mm,[Date]))
        END
ORDER BY tblProducts.Description,
        CONVERT(VARCHAR,DATEPART(yy,[Date]))
    + '/' +
        CASE WHEN LEN(CONVERT(CHAR,DATEPART(mm,[Date])))=1 THEN
            '0' + CONVERT(CHAR,DATEPART(mm,[Date]))
        ELSE
            CONVERT(CHAR,DATEPART(mm,[Date]))
        END
```

The simple *Format([Date],"yyyy\/mm")* function becomes *CONVERT(VAR-CHAR, DATEPART(yy,[Date])) +'/'+ CONVERT(VARCHAR,DATEPART (mm,[Date]))*. *DATEPART* is used to extract the year (yy) and/or the month (mm) from the date and then convert it into a character string. The three character strings (made up of year number, a hyphen, and the month) are then combined.

When sorting the date, there is a problem with the months being assigned incorrectly because the numbers for the months are composed of both one digit and two digits, so they are sorted as follows: 1, 11, 12, 2, and so on. To change this, you must ensure that the months are all represented with two digits. This can be solved with a *CASE* statement, as shown here:

```
CASE WHEN LEN(CONVERT(CHAR,DATEPART(mm,[Date])))=1 THEN

        '0' + CONVERT(CHAR,DATEPART(mm,[Date]))

ELSE

        CONVERT(CHAR,DATEPART(mm,[Date]))

END
```

Dividing this procedure into a view and a stored procedure would make it much easier to view. The view is based on the SQL command in the following listing. Because neither the View Designer in Access 2000 or Access 2002 nor the View Designer in Microsoft SQL Server Enterprise Manager 7 or Microsoft SQL Server Enterprise Manager 2000 can represent *CASE* constructs directly, a slight workaround is needed to create the view. If you are working with Access, open the View Designer and activate the SQL view by selecting View, then Show Panes, and then SQL, and create the SQL code directly in that view. When you save, the system issues a warning message because of the *CASE* command, but the view is saved anyway and can be executed. In the following example, the view is called *vwSales*:

```
SELECT tblProducts.Description,

        CONVERT(VARCHAR, DATEPART(yy, [Date]))

        + '/' +

        CASE WHEN LEN(CONVERT(CHAR, DATEPART(mm, [Date]))) = 1 THEN

            '0' + CONVERT(char, datepart(mm, [Date]))

        ELSE

            CONVERT(CHAR, DATEPART(mm, [Date]))

        END AS Month,

        [Amount] * [SalesPrice] AS Brutto
```

```
FROM tblProducts INNER JOIN tblProductSales

      ON tblProducts.ProductNr = tblProductSales.ProductNr
```

In the stored procedure, the view *vwSales* is accessed:

```
CREATE PROCEDURE qrySales

AS

      SELECT Description,

         Month,

            Sum(Brutto) AS SalesSum

      FROM vwSales

      GROUP BY Description, Month

      ORDER BY Description, Month

RETURN
```

Cross-References to Forms

To transfer values from a form control to a query, cross-references are often defined in Access from the control to the query as follows: *Forms!Form name!Control name* or *Forms("Form name").Controls("Control name")*. This type of cross-reference is no longer possible in views or stored procedures because the view or stored procedure is executed on the server, which has no access to forms and controls on the client.

Chapter 10, "Forms," describes a method for stored procedures that allows you to achieve the same functionality. A stored procedure is created from the query. This stored procedure contains a parameter with the same name as the control in the corresponding form.

Converting Forms and Reports

When converting forms and reports, the special considerations described in the following sections must be taken into account.

Record Source

When transferring forms to an adp project, the *Record Source* property is processed by forms or reports as shown in Table 16-6.

Table 16-6 **Converting *Record Source***

Defined *Record Source*	Conversion
Select query (*SELECT*) without sort criterion	View
Select query (*SELECT*) with sort criterion	Stored procedure
Stored select query without sort criterion	View
Stored select query with sort criterion	Stored procedure
Query with parameters	Stored procedure
Table name	Table name

The form or report property *Sort by* is not converted. You should enhance the *Record Source* property with a sort criterion. The *Filter* property is also ignored during transfer. Remember that forms in Access projects have new filter options (see the section in Chapter 10, "Forms," entitled "Form Filters").

Form Controls

The list box and combo box controls can be used to display data from a table or query. The corresponding table or query is defined in the *Row Source* property for the field.

Usually, the property is converted by the Upsizing Wizard creating a view or stored procedure with a name that starts with *ut_qry*. If the Upsizing Wizard cannot convert the row source (for example, because it contains parameters, links to form fields, or sometimes column names in the *[tablename].[fieldname]* format), then the corresponding view or stored procedure is not created. In the *Row Source* for the list box or combo box, however, the actual corresponding name *ut_qry...* is entered. When the converted form is called, you receive the corresponding error message for the control, informing you that this view or stored procedure cannot be found.

We found it extremely laborious to check for every single combo box and list box, whether the view or stored procedure specified as the record source for the corresponding field actually existed. The Upsizing Wizard result report contains no indication of unconverted queries for *Row Source* properties, so you must look up the actual query in the original mdb database to re-create it in the Access project.

Forms or Reports with Diagrams

For diagrams in forms and reports, the *Record Source* is not migrated correctly because the Access SQL command *TRANSFORM* is used in forms for data source. This is an Access-specific enhancement.

Converting VBA Programs

Access projects only support the ActiveX Data Objects (ADO) database programming interface. In Access 2000 and Access 2002 mdb databases you can use ADO and Data Access Objects (DAO). In Access releases earlier than Access 2000, only DAO was available for Visual Basic programming. In Access 2000 and Access 2002 mdb databases, both database interfaces work in parallel: DAO is used internally for all queries, forms, and reports; and ADO is generally intended for user programming.

In our Access 2000 and Access 2002 mdb applications, we were unable to use ADO alone because we almost always had to use DAO for programming complex forms and reports, for example. In our seminars we often recommend that users program with DAO to avoid having to learn two different database programming interfaces. On the other hand, the future belongs to ADO!

In Access projects, ADO is used throughout, avoiding the confusion between ADO and DAO created in mdb databases. This means, however, that all program sections that use DAO must be reprogrammed. In many cases this does not pose many problems and can be carried out by simply replacing the relevant commands. There are, however, many constructions that cannot be converted or are resolved in Access projects using different techniques.

Chapter 17, "From DAO to ADO," deals with conversions from DAO to ADO. If you have already programmed your Access 2000 or Access 2002 mdb database with ADO, then there should be few problems in converting the programs. Unfortunately, however, if you have used the ADO Extensions for Data Definition and Security (ADOX) library, be aware that the OLE DB provider for SQL Server only supports a small portion of the ADOX functionality, thus making it impractical to use ADOX.

17

From DAO to ADO

If you need to convert Data Access Objects (DAO) programs to Microsoft ActiveX Data Objects (ADO), or if you are familiar with DAO, you might find the descriptions and listings presented in this chapter helpful. They compare DAO commands and ADO commands.

Many DAO commands do not have corresponding commands in ADO. In some cases, DAO commands are no longer needed or no longer functional due to the new structures of Access projects. Specifically, you cannot convert any commands for creating tables and queries, as ADO does not have corresponding commands for these functions. With mdb databases based on Jet Engine, you can also use the routines in the Microsoft ADO Extensions for Data Definition and Security (ADOX) library to create tables and queries. However, ADOX has primarily read-only support with the Microsoft SQL Server OLE DB provider, and many of the methods are not supported. The same applies to the DAO replication commands, which are available for Jet Engine ADO programming in the Microsoft Jet and Replication Objects (JRO) library. This library also cannot be used with SQL Server/MSDE. SQL Server/MSDE exposes most of the functionality of ADOX and JRO directly through systems stored procedures and the SQL Distributed Management Objects (SQL-DMO) library, covered in Chapter 25, "System Stored Procedures," and Chapter 23, "The SQL-DMO Library," respectively.

Basics

The DAO object model is more complex than the ADO model. In addition to data access, DAO also enables users to administer, for example, users, user groups, and many other structures supported by Jet Engine. ADO, on the other hand, is purely a data access interface that provides only those objects directly required for accessing data. To administer users, user groups, and much more, you must either use the corresponding Transact-SQL commands or other programming interfaces, such as SQL-DMO. Table 17-1 compares the objects for the two data access interfaces.

Table 17-1   Comparison of the Most Important DAO and ADO Objects

DAO Object	ADO Object
Container	—
Database	*Connection*
DBEngine	—
Document	—
Group	—
QueryDef	*Command* (for executing queries only)
Recordset	*Recordset*
Relation	—
TableDef	—
User	—
Workspace	—
—	*Record*
—	*Stream*

Opening a Database

In DAO, you must use a *Database* object to access a database. ADO uses a *Connection* object to access a database.

In DAO, you can use the *CurrentDB* function to determine the currently loaded database. ADO, on the other hand, provides you with the Access project's current connection to the SQL Server/MSDE database with *CurrentProject.Connection.*

In DAO, write the following commands:

```
Dim db As DAO.Database

Set db = CurrentDB
```

In ADO, use the following format:

```
Dim cnn As ADODB.Connection

Set cnn = CurrentProject.Connection
```

Note that in ADO, you must generally use *New* to create a new *Connection* object, for example:

```
Set cnn = New ADODB.Connection
```

The only exception is the assignment, by reference, of *Current-Project.Connection*, as this means that the *CurrentProject* object's *Connection* object already exists. In other cases, you may not use *New* keyword when an object is automatically created by calling a method of another object.

Accessing the Data by Recordset

DAO and ADO use recordsets to access the data itself. In DAO, use the following commands:

```
Dim db As DAO.Database

Dim rec As DAO.Recordset


Set db = CurrentDB

Set rec = db.OpenRecordset("SELECT * FROM tblFilms", dbOpenDynaset)
```

The following is the ADO variant:

```
Dim cnn As ADODB.Connection

Dim rs As ADODB.Recordset


Set cnn = CurrentProject.Connection

Set rs = New ADODB.Recordset

rs.Open "SELECT * FROM tblFilms", _

        ActiveConnection:=cnn, _

        CursorType:=adOpenStatic, _

        LockType:=adLockOptimistic
```

Table 17-2 compares the parameters that you can specify for opening a recordset.

Table 17-2   Comparison of Recordset Types

DAO	ADO
dbOpenDynaset	CursorType = *adOpenStatic*, LockType = *adLockOptimistic*
	CursorType = *adOpenDynamic*, LockType = *adLockOptimistic*
dbOpenForward-Only	CursorType = *adOpenForwardOnly*, LockType = *adLockReadonly*
dbOpenSnapshot	CursorType = *adOpenStatic*, LockType = *adLockReadonly*
dbOpenTable	CursorType = *adOpenStatic*, LockType = *adLockOptimistic*, Options = *adCmdTableDirect* CursorType = *adOpenDynamic*, LockType = *adLockOptimistic*, Options = *adCmdTableDirect*
—	CursorType = *adOpenKeyset*

Moving the Record Pointer

DAO and ADO use the methods *MoveNext*, *MovePrevious*, *MoveFirst*, and *MoveLast* to move the record pointer through the recordset.

In both DAO and ADO, you can use the *EOF* and *BOF* functions to determine if you have reached the end or the beginning of the recordset.

Adding, Editing, and Deleting Data

This section introduces the commands for adding, editing, and deleting records. The commands differ only slightly for DAO compared with ADO.

Adding Records

DAO and ADO use the *AddNew* method to add a new record. In ADO, the newly added record automatically becomes the current record. In DAO, the record pointer continues to point to the record it pointed to before the new record was added. Both data access interfaces use the *Update* method to save the new record.

The following listing illustrates the DAO variant:

```
...
' DAO
Dim rec As DAO.Recordset
Set rec = CurrentDB.OpenRecordset("SELECT * FROM tlbFilms",
dbOpenDynaset)
' Add new record
rec.Addnew
rec!Filmtitle = "Erin Brockovich"
rec!Length = 131
rec.Update
rec.Close
...
```

The ADO code is almost exactly the same, as shown here:

```
...
' ADO
Dim rec As ADODB.Recordset

Set rec = New ADODB.Recordset
rec.Open "SELECT * FROM tblFilms", CurrentProject.Connection, _
        adOpenStatic, adLockOptimistic
' Add new record
rec.Addnew
rec!Filmtitle = "Erin Brockovich"
rec!Length = 131
rec.Update
rec.Close

...
```

Editing Records

There are small differences between DAO and ADO with respect to editing records. You must use the *Edit* method to edit a current record's content with DAO. In ADO, you can modify the content directly.

In DAO, you must call the *Update* method to save the changes. You can also use *Update* in ADO, but ADO automatically saves the changes once you move the record pointer to a different record. Use the *CancelUpdate* method to cancel the changes you made without saving them.

```
...

' DAO


Dim rec As DAO.Recordset


Set rec = CurrentDB.OpenRecordset("SELECT * FROM tblFilms",
dbOpenDynaset)


' Modify first record

rec.MoveFirst

rec.Edit

rec!Summary = "abcdefghijklmnopqrstuvwxyz"


If MsgBox("Save record?", vbYesNo) = vbYes Then

        rec.Update

End If

' Go to next record

rec.MoveNext

...



...

' ADO
```

```
Dim Rec As ADODB.Recordset

Set Rec = New ADODB.Recordset
rec.Open "SELECT * FROM tblFilms", CurrentProject.Connection, _
        adOpenStatic, adLockOptimistic

' Modify first record
rec.MoveFirst
rec!Summary = " abcdefghijklmnopqrstuvwxyz "
If MsgBox("Save record?", vbYesNo) = vbYes Then
        rec.Update
Else
        rec.CancelUpdate
End If
' Go to next record
rec.MoveNext

...
```

Deleting Data

Use the *Delete* method in both DAO and ADO to delete the current record.

Finding Data

DAO uses the methods *FindFirst, FindLast, FindNext,* and *FindPrevious* to find records in a recordset. In ADO, you can use the *Find* method, which is controlled by a parameter so that it has the same functions as the four DAO methods. Table 17-3 compares the methods.

Table 17-3   Comparison of Search Methods

DAO	ADO
recDAO.FindFirst Criterion	recADO.MoveFirst recADO.Find Criterion, 0, adSearchForward
recDAO.FindLast Criterion	*recADO.MoveLast* *recADO.Find Criterion, 0, adSearchBackward*
recDAO.FindNext Criterion	*recADO.Find Criterion, 1, adSearchForward*
recDAO.FindPrevious Criterion	*recADO.Find Criterion, 1, adSearchBackward*

The ADO *Find* method's second parameter, *SkipRows*, specifies how many records to skip before applying the search criterion.

You cannot use the ADO *Seek* method for finding records with an index if you are using the SQLOLEDB provider. If you are using *Seek* in your DAO programs, you must use *Find* to convert this method for Access projects.

Filtering Data

DAO and ADO both use the *Filter* property to constrain a recordset's data according to a criterion. However, the two data access interfaces differ in how they use the *Filter* property.

If you use the *Filter* property to filter a DAO recordset, you need a second recordset to access the filtered data:

```
. . .
Dim rec As DAO.Recordset
Dim recFilter As DAO.Recordset


Set rec = CurrentDB.OpenRecordset("SELECT * FROM tblFilms",
dbOpenDynaset)
' Select all movies with showtime greater than two hours
rec.Filter = "Length > 120"
' Create new filtered recordset
Set recFilter = rec.OpenRecordset(dOpenDynaset)
Do Until recFilter.EOF
        Debug.Print recFilter!Filmtitle
        recFilter.MoveNext
Loop
recFilter.Close
rec.Close
. . .
```

In an ADO recordset, the *Filter* property applies to the recordset itself, which means that a second recordset is not needed:

```
. . .
Dim rec As ADODB.Recordset
```

```
Set rec = New ADODB.Recordset

rec.Open "SELECT * FROM tblFilms", CurrentProject.Connection,
adOpenStatic, adLockOptimistic

' Select all movies with showtime greater than two hours

rec.Filter = "Length > 120"

Do Until rec.EOF

        Debug.Print rec!Filmtitle

        rec.MoveNext

Loop

rec.Close

...
```

Sorting Data

You can use the *Sort* property to sort a recordset's data in DAO and ADO later on. *Sort* is used like the *Filter* property described earlier, which means there are differences between how the property is used in DAO and ADO.

Bookmarks

DAO and ADO both support the definition of bookmarks. The use of bookmarks for a specific recordset depends on the options you want to use to open the recordset. In DAO, use the *Bookmarkable* property to find out if the recordset supports bookmarks. In ADO, use the *Supports(adBookmark)* function.

DAO and ADO use the same syntax for working with bookmarks. DAO bookmarks are saved as *String* variables, whereas ADO bookmarks request variables of the type *Variant*:

```
...

Dim vBookmark As Variant


' Remember the current record

vBookmark = rec.Bookmark

...

' Go to remembered record

rec.Bookmark = vBookmark

...
```

Executing Queries

DAO and ADO differ significantly in how they handle queries. You can create and execute queries with DAO *QueryDef* objects, but the ADO *Command* objects can be used only to execute queries. In most cases, *QueryDef* or *Command* objects are used to execute action queries or queries with parameters.

Administering Queries

A DAO *QueryDef* object describes a query in an mdb database. The *QueryDefs* collection displays the *QueryDef* objects for all queries. DAO lets you add new objects to the *QueryDefs* list; that is, it lets you create new queries in the mdb database.

With ADO, the purpose of *Command* objects is the execution of queries only. In an mdb database or an Access project, the collections *AllQueries* and *AllStoredProcedures* and the Access *CurrentData* object's *AllViews* collection are used to administer queries. The collections consist of *AccessObject* objects and you cannot create any new objects from a Microsoft Visual Basic for Applications (VBA) program.

Simple *SELECT* Queries

This section describes how to execute simple *SELECT* queries that return a resultset in a recordset. To execute the predefined query *Query1* with DAO, write the following code, which uses the variable *rec* to return a recordset with data:

```
...
' DAO

Dim db As DAO.Database
Dim qry As DAO.QueryDef
Dim rec As DAO.Recordset

Set db = CurrentDB
Set qry = db.QueryDefs("Query1")
Set rec = qry.OpenRecordset(dbOpenDynaset)

...
```

In ADO, the call is coded as shown in the following example. The code lets you specify a *SELECT* query or call a view or stored procedure as *CommandText* for the *Command* object. You can only read the resulting recordset, and in contrast with DAO, you cannot edit the data.

```
...
' ADO

Dim cnn As ADODB.Connection
Dim cmd As ADODB.Command
Dim rec As ADODB.Recordset

Set cnn = CurrentProject.Connection
Set cmd = New ADODB.Command
Set cmd.ActiveConnection = cnn
cmd.CommandText = "Query1"
Set rec = cmd.Execute
...
```

Queries with Parameters

Use the *Parameters* collection for *QueryDef* or *Command* objects to execute DAO queries with parameters or stored procedures with parameters in ADO:

```
...
' DAO

Dim db As DAO.Database
Dim qry As DAO.QueryDef
Dim rec As DAO.Recordset
Dim par As DAO.Parameter

Set db = CurrentDb
Set qry = db.QueryDefs("Query1")
```

```
For Each par In qry.Parameters

  par.Value = InputBox(par.Name)

Next


Set rec = qry.OpenRecordset(dbOpenForwardOnly)

Do Until rec.EOF

  Debug.Print rec(0).Value

  rec.MoveNext

Loop

...
```

To program the same function in ADO, proceed as shown in the next listing. Note that ADO recognizes input and output parameters.

```
...

' ADO


Dim cnn As ADODB.Connection

Dim cmd As ADODB.Command

Dim rec As ADODB.Recordset

Dim par As ADODB.Parameter


Set cnn = CurrentProject.Connection

Set cmd = New ADODB.Command

Set cmd.ActiveConnection = cnn


cmd.CommandType = adCmdStoredProc

cmd.CommandText = "Films"


' Refresh works only with ADO 2.6 and up, see chapter 14

cmd.Parameters.Refresh
```

```
For Each par In cmd.Parameters
  If par.Direction = adParamInput Or _
          par.Direction = adParamInputOutput Then
    par.Value = InputBox(par.Name)
  End If
Next

Set rst = cmd.Execute
Do Until rec.EOF
  Debug.Print rec(0).Value, rec(1).Value
  rec.MoveNext
Loop
...
```

Action Queries

In most cases, *QueryDef* and *Command* objects are used to execute action queries that do not return any resultsets. For example, the following program executes the update query *IncreasePrice*:

```
...
' DAO

Dim db As DAO.Database
Dim qry As DAO.QueryDef

Set db = CurrentDb
Set qry = db.QueryDefs("IncreasePrice")

qry.Execute
...
```

Alternatively, you can use the *Database* object's *Execute* method to write

```
db.Execute "IncreasePrice"
```

more briefly. Use the following format with ADO:

```
...
Dim cnn As ADODB.Connection
Dim cmd As ADODB.Command

Set cnn = CurrentProject.Connection
Set cmd = New ADODB.Command
Set cmd.ActiveConnection = cnn

cmd.CommandType = adCmdStoredProc
cmd.CommandText = "IncreasePrice"

cmd.Execute
...
```

Using the *Connection* object's *Execute* method is another possible variant:

```
...
Dim cnn As ADODB.Connection
Dim cmd As ADODB.Command

Set cnn = CurrentProject.Connection
cnn.Execute "IncreasePrice"
```

DAO in Access Projects

There is a trick that lets you use existing DAO code in Access projects as well. The trick involves using a DAO *Database* object that establishes an open database connectivity (ODBC) connection to the SQL Server/MSDE database to which the project is connected. It is our experience that a majority of existing DAO programs can be executed using this trick. We have been using it for a number of projects during a transition period to quickly access working applications while converting database applications to Access projects.

The *DAODatabase* function shown in the following listing returns a *DAO.Database* object. The *Database* object does not refer to an Access mdb database. Instead, it uses an ODBC connection string derived from the *Current-*

Project.Connection property's connection string data to refer to the SQL Server/ MSDE database to which the current project is connected.

```
Public Function DAODatabase() As DAO.Database

  Dim cnn As ADODB.Connection

  Dim dbDAO As DAO.Database

  Dim strConnect As String


  Set cnn = CurrentProject.Connection


  ' Connection based on MSDataShape- or SQLOLEDB-Provider?

  If InStr(cnn.Provider, "MSDataShape") > 0 Or _

      InStr(cnn.Provider, "SQLOLEDB") > 0 Then

    ' Build the connection string

    strConnect = "ODBC;driver=SQL Server;server=" & _

        cnn.Properties("Data Source") & ";"

    ' Database name

    strConnect = strConnect & "database=" & _

        cnn.Properties("Initial Catalog") & ";"

    ' SQL Server- or Windows security?

    If cnn.Properties("Integrated Security") = "SSPI" Then

      strConnect = strConnect & "Trusted_Connection=Yes;"

    Else

      strConnect = strConnect & "UID=" & cnn.Properties("User ID") & _
        ";"

      strConnect = strConnect & "PWD=" & cnn.Properties("Password") & _
        ";"

    End If

  Else

    MsgBox "DAO-Database not opened!"

    Set DAODatabase = Nothing

    Exit Function

  End If
```

```
' Open new database
Set dbDAO = DBEngine.OpenDatabase("", False, False, strConnect)


Set DAODatabase = dbDAO
End Function
```

You can use the following procedure to test the *DAODatabase* function:

```
Sub DAO_Test()
   Dim db As DAO.Database
   Dim rec As DAO.Recordset


   Set db = DAODatabase()
   Set rec = db.OpenRecordset("select * from tblFilms",
      dbOpenForwardOnly)
   Do Until rec.EOF
      Debug.Print rec!Filmtitle
      rec.MoveNext
   Loop
   Set db = Nothing
End Sub
```

Part V

SQL Server/MSDE Administration

The purpose of the chapters in this part of the book is to explain the numerous tools and programming interfaces for administering Microsoft SQL Server and Microsoft Data Engine (MSDE). All administrative activities can be performed with specific programs, Transact-SQL commands, and system procedures, as well as with the SQL Distributed Management Objects (SQL-DMO) programming interface.

First, there is an introduction to the administrative features provided by an Access project for SQL Server and MSDE. Next, we present a description of SQL Server tools such as Enterprise Manager, Query Analyzer, Profiler, and so on.

We provide a review of the security features of SQL Server/MSDE, for example, creating users and user groups (roles) and defining access permissions.

Performing regular data backups and restoring backups are also part of SQL Server/ MSDE operations.

Information is provided on Data Transformation Services (DTS), which facilitate the transfer of data between various data sources. Integrating external data sources with SQL Server/MSDE is also explained.

We also explain direct programming of SQL Server functions with the SQL-DMO library. You are also provided with a list of all system stored procedures with which you can call the administrative functions of SQL Server/MSDE.

18

Database Administration

Most of the Access project database administration functions introduced in this chapter can be used only if Microsoft SQL Server/MSDE and the databases you want to administer have been set up on the same computer on which Microsoft Access is running.

In our experience, the internal Access project administration functions are used only rarely because SQL Server/MSDE is almost always installed on a server that users and administrators access only through the network. This means the Access project administration functions, which are only a small subset of the tools available with SQL Server Enterprise manager, are unusable, however.

If you are running Microsoft Data Engine (MSDE) only and thus do not have access to the SQL Server administration tools that we introduce in the following chapters, you must install Access on the network server and then install the database there, use stored procedures to call the SQL Server/MSDE administration procedures, or develop programs based on the SQL Distributed Management Objects (SQL-DMO) library. You can also purchase the SQL Server administration tools for MSDE to complete your package.

> **Note** The administration functions assume that you have the necessary SQL Server/MSDE permissions. The individual functions list the respective permission level required to use that function.

Creating Databases

To create a new database, you must choose the method that involves creating a new Access project, as described in Chapter 4, "Databases." Select File, then New to open the corresponding dialog box and select Project (New Database). Once you have named the new project, the Microsoft SQL Server Database Wizard guides you through the steps to create a new database.

At the beginning of Chapter 16, "Upsizing Wizard" we briefly explained how to use wizards to create databases. The wizard provides almost no setting and configuration options for the new database. If you create a new database with the SQL Server Enterprise Manager, you can use numerous configuration options, as described in Chapter 19, "SQL Server Tools."

Alternatively, you can use SQL to create a new database, as the next section illustrates.

To create databases, you must be a member of the *sysadmin* or *dbcreator* server role (see Chapter 20, "Security").

> **Note**   You cannot use the Microsoft Access 2000 Microsoft SQL Server Database Wizard if you want to create a database on Microsoft SQL Server 2000 without the Microsoft Office Service Pack 1 and Access 2000 and SQL Server 2000 Readiness Update. If you try to use the wizard, the system returns the error message, "Overflow."

During the creation of a database, SQL Server/MSDE copies the system database *model*. All of the existing objects in the *model* database are then available in the new database. You can use your own objects to expand the *model* database. For example, you might need specific tables, views, or procedures.

Creating Databases with SQL

You can use the SQL command *CREATE DATABASE* to create a database. The command's full syntax is shown here:

```
CREATE DATABASE Databasename
[ ON
  [ < File > [ ,...n ] ]
  [ , < Filegroup > [ ,...n ] ]
]
[ LOG ON { < File > [ ,...n ] } ]
```

```
[ FOR LOAD | FOR ATTACH ]
```

For the < File >, you can write:

```
< File > ::=
[ PRIMARY ]
( [ NAME = Logical_Filename , ]
  FILENAME = 'Filename'
  [ , SIZE = size ]
  [ , MAXSIZE = { Max Size | UNLIMITED } ]
  [ , FILEGROWTH = Increment ] ) [ ,...n ]
```

The optional parameter *<Filegroup >* is defined as follows:

```
< Filegroup > ::=

FILEGROUP Filegroupname < File > [ ,...n ]
```

You can designate the files in a database as file groups, to run backups by groups, for example. With smaller installations, you are usually working with only one file group, *PRIMARY*.

In the simplest case, just enter a database name to create a database, for example, *CREATE DATABASE Marketing*. This means that the system uses default values for all settings. Write the following command if you do not want to save the database to your default folder (for example, C:\Program Files\Microsoft SQL Server\MSSQL\Data or C:\MSSQL7\Data), but to another user-specified folder instead:

```
CREATE DATABASE Marketing

ON

  (Name=Marketing,FILENAME='D:\MarketingData.mdf', SIZE=2,
FILEGROWTH=10%)

LOG ON

  (Name=Marketing_Log, FILENAME='D:\MarketingLog.ldf',size=1,
FILEGROWTH=1)
```

For a database, you can also specify multiple master data files (.mdf) or log data files (.ldf) with different path names.

To execute this command from Access, you must either create a stored procedure or use the Access form *frmSQL* introduced in Chapter 10, "Forms." As an alternative, you can use the OSQL utility that is included with SQL Server and with MSDE. See Chapter 19, "SQL Server Tools," for a description of OSQL.

Determining the Properties and Settings for a Database

As a preview of *Chapter 19, "SQL Server Tools,"* this section explains how to view the settings for a database with the SQL Server Enterprise Manager. Figure 18-1 displays the Database Properties dialog box for the newly created *Marketing* database. The General tab contains the basic data for the database's files.

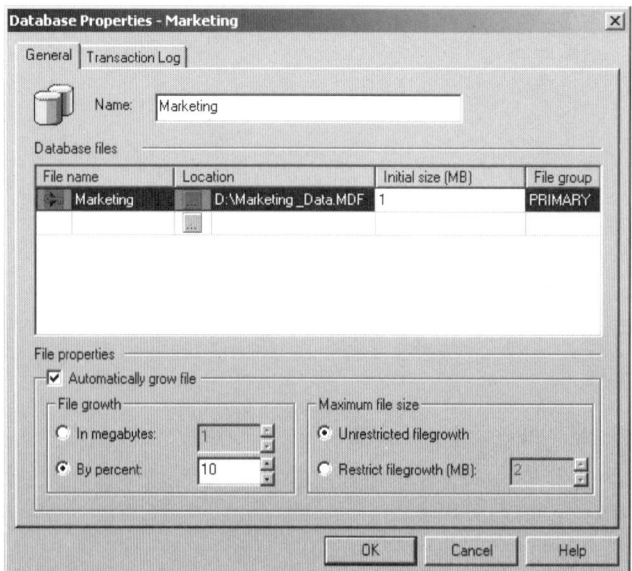

Figure 18-1   The Database Properties dialog box in SQL Server Enterprise Manager

If you are running only MSDE without SQL Server, you can determine the database settings only with the assistance of the corresponding system procedures or the SQL-DMO library objects (see Chapter 23, "SQL-DMO Library").

The example project in this chapter includes the form *frmDatabases*, which uses the system procedures *sp_databases* and *sp_helpdb* to determine the information shown in Figure 18-2 (see Chapter 25, "System Stored Procedures").

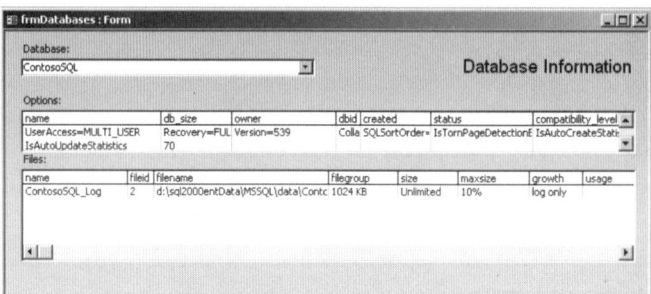

Figure 18-2   Form with database information

The next listing shows the program for the form. The combo box and the list boxes in the form have been defined so that the *Row Source Type* property is the value list and a character string is assigned to the *Row Source*. The character string lists the data for display separated by semicolons. Note that the system procedure *sp_helpdb* returns two resultsets in this listing:

```
Option Compare Database
Option Explicit


Private Sub Form_Load()
  Dim cmd As ADODB.Command
  Dim rec As ADODB.Recordset
  Dim strTmp As String


  Set cmd = New ADODB.Command
  cmd.ActiveConnection = CurrentProject.Connection
  cmd.CommandText = "sp_databases"
  cmd.CommandType = adCmdStoredProc
  Set rst = cmd.Execute
  ' Concatenate all database names
  Do Until rec.EOF
    strTmp = strTmp & rec("DATABASE_NAME") & ";"
    rec.MoveNext
  Loop
  Set cmd = Nothing
  ' Assign combo box as value list
  cboDatabases.RowSource = strTmp
  ' Select first entry
  cboDatabases.value = cboDatabases.ItemData(0)
  ' Refresh all combo boxes
  cboDatabases_Click
End Sub
```

```
Private Sub cboDatabases_Click()
  Dim cmd As ADODB.Command
  Dim rec As ADODB.Recordset
  Dim fld As ADODB.Field
  Dim strTmp As String
  Dim intCol As Integer

  Set cmd = New ADODB.Command
  cmd.ActiveConnection = CurrentProject.Connection
  cmd.CommandText = "sp_helpdb " & Trim(cboDatabases.value)
  ' Called with adCmdText, not adCmdStoredProc,
  ' to avoid using parameter objects
  cmd.CommandType = adCmdText
  Set rst = cmd.Execute

  ' Retrieve field names and build strTmp
  intCol = 0
  For Each fld In rec.Fields
    strTmp = strTmp & fld.name & ";"
    intCol = intCol + 1
  Next
  ' Append field values to strTmp
  Do Until rec.EOF
    For Each fld In rec.Fields
      strTmp = strTmp & Trim(Replace(fld.value, ";", ",")) & ";"
    Next
    rec.MoveNext
  Loop
  ' Assign to list box as value list
  lstOptions.ColumnCount = intCol
  lstOptions.RowSource = strTmp
```

```
    strTmp = ""
    ' Retrieve next recordset
    Set rec = rec.NextRecordset
    ' Field names
    For Each fld In rec.Fields
        strTmp = strTmp & fld.name & ";"
    Next
    ' Values
    intCol = 0
    Do Until rec.EOF
        For Each fld In rec.Fields
            strTmp = strTmp & Trim(Replace(fld.value, ";", ",")) & ";"
            intCol = intCol + 1
        Next
        rec.MoveNext
    Loop
    ' Assign to list box as value list
    lstFiles.ColumnCount = intCol
    lstFiles.RowSource = strTmp
    Set cmd = Nothing
End Sub
```

Deleting Databases

In Access projects, you can select Tools, then Database Utilities, and then Drop SQL Database to delete a database from the local SQL Server/MSDE. Note that this deletes the database to which the currently opened Access project is connected.

If you are using the SQL Server Enterprise Manager, you can delete databases there, as described in Chapter 19, "SQL Server Tools." To delete databases, you must be a member of the *sysadmin* or *dbcreator* server role (see Chapter 20, "Security").

Deleting Databases with SQL

Use the following command to delete a database with SQL:

```
DROP DATABASE Databasename
```

You cannot drop the system databases *master*, *model*, *msdb*, and *tempdb*.

Additional Administration Functions

We have devoted separate chapters to detailed descriptions of additional administration functions.

Data Backup Functions

See Chapter 21, "Data Backup Functions," for a detailed description of available backup and restoration options.

Database Security

Refer to Chapter 20, "Security," for more information about setting up users and assigning permissions.

19

SQL Server Tools

In this chapter, we introduce you to the most important Microsoft SQL Server tools. These programs are not included with Microsoft Data Engine (MSDE). However, you can purchase them for MSDE later on.

We also point out that all the programs and functions included in this chapter are described as if a system administrator were using them. If you have only limited access rights to the server, you cannot activate all of the functions.

Enterprise Manager

SQL Server Enterprise Manager is the main administrative utility for SQL Server. With its assistance, you can administer local and remote installations of SQL Server or MSDE. Select Start, then Programs, then Microsoft SQL Server, and then Enterprise Manager to start Enterprise Manager.

Enterprise Manager starts up with a window similar to the one shown in Figure 19-1. Microsoft has based its Enterprise Manager on the Microsoft Management Console (MMC), which is used as a uniform interface for many Micrsosoft BackOffice programs.

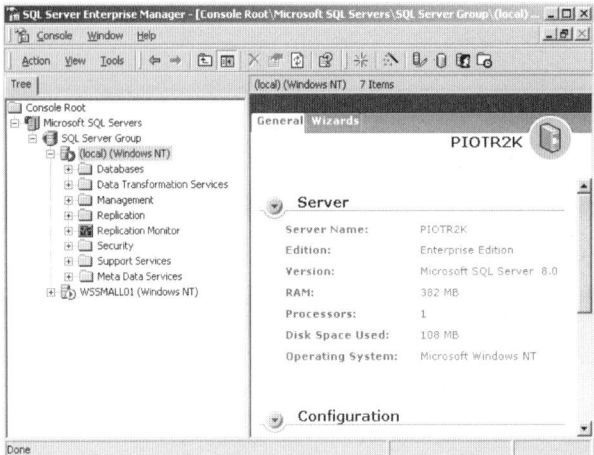

Figure 19-1   SQL Server Enterprise Manager

The left pane of the window displays a list of the different MMC snap-ins installed, within the instance of the console, in the form of a directory tree, starting with the console root directory. In this example, only Microsoft SQL Enterprise Manager has been set up, and a single server has been connected to the snap-in.

In the right pane of the window, you can see the taskpad, which makes it easy for you to use the different functions. If you cannot see the taskpad, select View, then Taskpad to activate it.

All Enterprise Manager functions can be activated from the menu, the respective shortcut menu for an object (activated by right-clicking), and the taskpad. Throughout the remainder of this chapter, we use the taskpad and describe only the menu commands.

Enterprise Manager can administer several instances of SQL Server/MSDE simultaneously. For a better overview, you can subdivide the servers into groups. By default, Enterprise Manager displays the SQL Server Group (you can rename the group with Enterprise Manager). You can assign subgroups to every group. The administration of servers in groups makes sense only for larger installations if, for example, all of a network's SQL Servers/MSDE instances are administered at a central location.

As you can see in Figure 19-1, in the next level, the system displays Databases, Data Transformation Services, Management, Replication, Security, and Support Services for every SQL Server/MSDE installation. If Replication is active on a given server, the Replication Monitor branch is also displayed within the tree.

Databases

All databases (theoretically up to 32,767) created on the respective SQL Server/ MSDE can be listed in the Enterprise Manager window (you can hide system databases by editing SQL Server Registration Properties). By default, the system creates the databases listed in Table 19-1.

Table 19-1   Predefined Databases

Database	Explanation
master	This is a database with system tables containing the information needed to run SQL Server as well as numerous system procedures.
model	This is a model database used as a template for creating new databases.
msdb	This is used by Microsoft SQL Server Agent. It contains information about data backup procedures, replication, and so forth.
Northwind	This is a sample database that is not required to operate SQL Server.
pubs	This is a sample database that is not required to operate SQL Server.
tempdb	This is a database for temporary objects and data created during operation.

Creating Databases

To create a new database, select the Databases level in the left pane of the Enterprise Manager window. Select Action, then New Database to open the Database Properties dialog box, shown in Figure 19-2, for creating a database, along with the associated transaction log. First, in the General tab, enter the name of the new database.

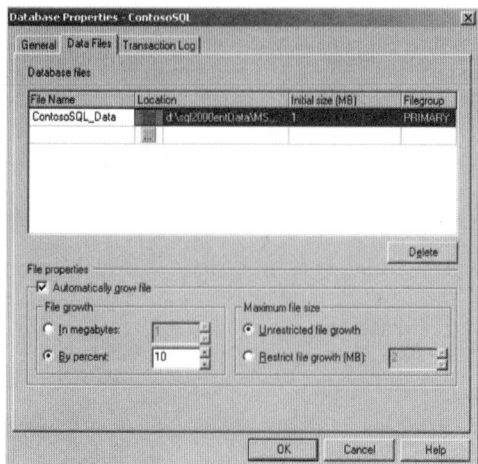

Figure 19-2   Creating a new database

The Data Files tab uses this name to create a filename that the system saves in the default database folder. You can change the Location and the File Name values anyway you wish.

If you select the Automatically Grow File check box, you can select an initial size of just a few megabytes. The system then expands the file according to the selected file expansion. Usually, there are no limits on maximum file size.

A database can be distributed across several database files, which can also be located on different drives.

You can use the Transaction Log tab to select the same settings for the transaction log.

> **Note** Whenever possible, you should create the data and the transaction log on different hard drives. This separation can prevent data loss in case of a drive failure. If the data drive fails, you can use the backup files and the transaction log to re-create the most recent database state prior to the failure. If the drive with the transaction log fails, you should not lose any data other than the most recent transactions not yet written to the database.

Database Properties

If you select a database in Enterprise Manager, the system displays information about the database in the right pane of the window, provided that you activated the taskpad by selecting View, then Taskpad. The taskpad offers three view options, as shown in Figure 19-3: General, Table Info, and Wizards.

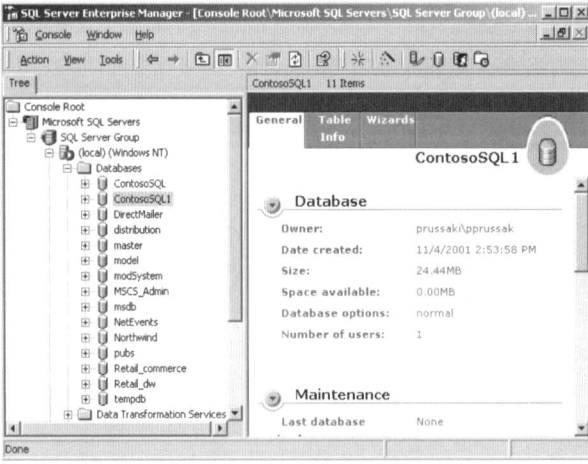

Figure 19-3 Information about the selected database

The General view displays the database's definitions and information like total size of database and transaction log.

The Table Info view displays how many records are stored in all of the tables and how much disk space they take up. For indexes, the system displays the type of index and the amount of disk space used.

Using the Wizards view, you can start wizards for configuration, backing up databases, restoring databases, and much more.

Deleting Databases

To delete a database, select it in Enterprise Manager in the left pane of the window, then right-click and select Delete from the shortcut menu.

Data Transformation Services

You can use Data Transformation Services (DTS) to exchange data between SQL Server/MSDE and other data sources. DTS lets you select the data to be imported or exported. It is also possible to exchange objects, such as views, stored procedures, and so forth, between SQL Server/MSDE systems, as well as other databases through OLE DB provider. In addition, you can also program scripts (in VBScript or JScript) that can manipulate the data during the transfer process.

DTS permits the coordination of *packages* that you can use to implement complex data transmission scenarios (see Chapter 22, "Data Transformation Services").

Administration

The Management tools include the SQL Server Agent and its subordinate items Alerts, Operators, and Jobs, as shown in Figure 19-4. Please see the section later in this chapter entitled "Alerts, Operators, and Jobs," for more information. Table 19-2 details the Management tool functions.

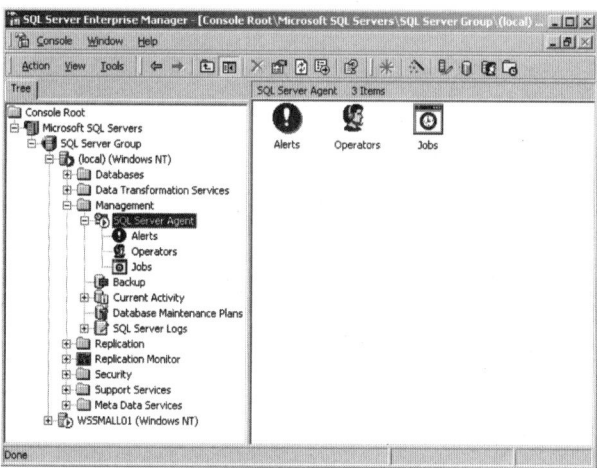

Figure 19-4   Management tools

Table 19-2 **Management Functions**

Function	Description
Backup	This is described in Chapter 21, "Data Backup Functions."
Current Activity	You can check, for example, which users or applications are on the system, what processes are running, what processes are causing database deadlocks, and much more.
Database Maintenance Plans	These are described in the section later in this chapter entitled "Database Maintenance."
SQL Server Logs	This function displays the logs associated with the SQL server.
Web Publishing	Avaliable in SQL Server 7/MSDE only. This is described in Chapter 27, "Web Publishing with SQL Server."

Security

Security functions are described in Chapter 20, "Security." Security functions include setting up server logon names and database user names, definition and assignment of server and database roles, and assignment of access rights.

Security also includes linked servers and remote servers, with remote servers listed only for reasons of compatibility with Microsoft SQL Server 6. With Microsoft SQL Server 7 or SQL Server 2000, remote servers are replaced by linked servers.

The definition of a linked server permits access to another database server to use the data stored there (provided you have the necessary access rights) and possibly to execute procedures stored on the other database server. A linked server can be any object linking and embedding database (OLE DB) or open database connectivity (ODBC) data source, which means that it can also be an Access mdb database, for example, which is accessed with the help of the Jet OLE DB provider. The definition and use of linked servers is explained in Chapter 24, "External Data Sources."

Support Services

Two support services are available by default. The Distributed Transaction Coordinator (DTC) is used to monitor and execute distributed transactions, which are database operations that simultaneously edit tables located on different servers. DTC is a SQL Server-specific service that is started with the SQL Server Service Manager.

If you create the SQL Mail support service, SQL Server/MSDE can send e-mail messages for purposes such as notifying the administrator about certain server states. To use SQL Mail, you must have a valid messaging application programming interface (MAPI) profile, as shown in Figure 19-5; for example, Microsoft Outlook needs to be configured accordingly on the SQL Server/MSDE computer.

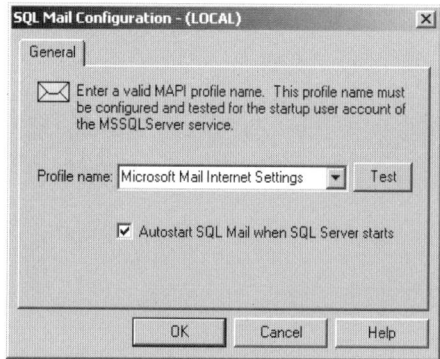

Figure 19-5   SQL Mail settings

Managing the Server

In the right pane of the Enterprise Manager window, shown in Figure 19-1, use the taskpad to select Wizards, or select Manage Servers if you are using SQL Server 7. The system then displays the taskpad shown in Figure 19-6. The taskpad provides you with access to the functions described in Table 19-3. SQL Server 7 Enterprise Manager offers only 10 wizards from the taskpad, but other wizards are still available from the Tools menu.

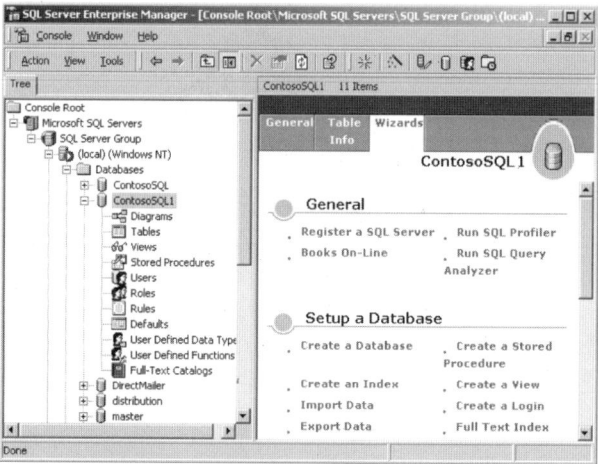

Figure 19-6   Managing SQL Server

Table 19-3 Administrative Wizards and Utilities

Administration Function	Description
Register A SQL Server	Registers a SQL Server/MSDE in Enterprise Manager. The server is assigned to a server group.
Books On-Line	Activates the online documentation.
Run SQL Profiler	Launches the SQL Profiler application, allowing the system administrator to monitor and capture events in a single instance of SQL Server.
Run SQL Query Analyzer	Launches the SQL Query Analyzer application, allowing the administrator or programmer to execute, debug, and analyze performance of queries or stored procedures in SQL Server.
Configure Clients (SQL Server 7 only)	Specifies the settings for the client's network access to the server. Launches the SQL Server Network Utility tool, otherwise available from the SQL Server program group.
Create A Database	Activates the Database Creation Wizard, prompting you to provide basic information about a new database.
Create An Index	Uses the Create Index Wizard to assist in the creation of indexes for tables within a database.
Import Data	Activates the DTS Import/Export Wizard and makes the originating server the target of the import.
Export Data	Activates DTS Import/Export Wizard and makes the originating server the source for the export.
Create A Stored Procedure	Launches the Create Stored Procedure Wizard, allowing automated creation (and limited editing) of stored procedures for inserts, updates, and deletes against user-selected fields within the wizard.
Create A View	Launches the Create View Wizard, providing a simple way of choosing tables and fields that participate in a view.
Create A Login	Activates the Login Name Creation Wizard, providing support during the process of creating new users for SQL Server/MSDE.
Full Text Index	Launches the Full-Text Indexing Wizard, aiding in the creation of full-text catalogs in a database.
Backup A Database	Lets you create data backups with the assistance of the Backup Wizard.

continued

Table 19-3 Administrative Wizards and Utilities *(continued)*

Administration Function	Description
Create An Alert	Activates the Alert Creation Wizard. You can use alerts to notify administrators or users of certain server states.
Create A Job	Automates repeating administration tasks. Enterprise Manager also provides a wizard for this purpose.
Copy Database	Launches the Copy Database Wizard, simplifying copying of databases between servers and dependent objects.
Index Tuning	Launches the Index Tuning Wizard, which analyzes data gathered by SQL Profiler to make recommendations regarding use of indexes in the database.
Make A Master Server	Activates the Make MSX Wizard, which proceeds through the steps of making a server the master of multiserver jobs.
Make A Target Server	Launches the Make TSX Wizard, which sets the server as a target server by enlisting it within the MSX.
Create A Maintenance Plan	Runs the Database Maintenance Plan Wizard to set up regularly scheduled jobs for the server. Ensures data integrity, updates statistics, performs backups, and ships logs to another server through regular maintenance.
Publish To The Web (SQL Server 7 only)	Lets you publish database contents on the Internet or an intranet. These database contents are saved as Hypertext Markup Language (HTML) files either once, automatically at periodic intervals, or when a database's contents change.
Configure Publishing And Distribution	Sets up a server to be the replication distributor with the Configure Publishing And Distribution Wizard.
Create Publication	Launches the Create Publication Wizard to set up database elements for sharing through replication with subscribers.
Disable Publishing And Distribution	Allows you to disable Distributions and Publications on the server.
Create A Pull Subscription	Activates the Pull Subscription Wizard, which helps you set up a database as a Subscriber within the Replication.
Create A Push Subscription	Launches the Create Publication Wizard, setting up a push subscription for a database.

SQL Server Properties

If you select SQL Server/MSDE in Enterprise Manager by clicking the corresponding name, you can select Tools, then SQL Server Configuration Properties to open the SQL Server Properties (Configure) dialog box shown in Figure 19-7.

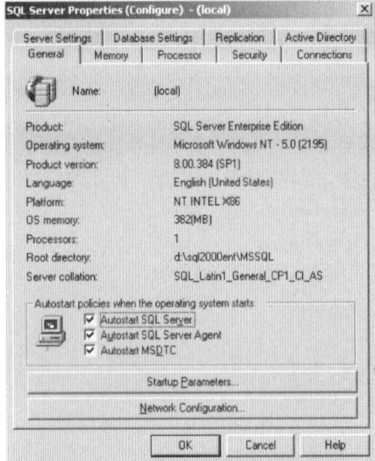

Figure 19-7   SQL Server settings

You can use the different tabs in this dialog box to edit the server's basic settings. The Server Settings tab, displayed in Figure 19-8, is of interest when you access SQL Server/MSDE with Access projects. You can choose the default language here, which defines the language in which server error messages are displayed.

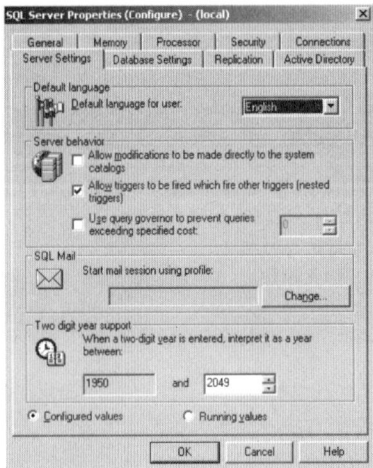

Figure 19-8   SQL Server Server Settings tab

Please also note the Two Digit Year Support settings. The default values entered here (1950 through 2049) differ from those used by Microsoft Office. Microsoft Office interprets two-digit entries as years between 1930 and 2029. If you enter the two-digit number 35 in Office to specify a year, Office interprets this number as 1935, whereas SQL Server/MSDE processes this number as 2035.

Database Maintenance

To optimize the performance of SQL Server/MSDE, you should perform regular maintenance on the databases. SQL Server Enterprise Manager provides you with a Database Maintenance Plan Wizard, which you can use to create maintenance plans that can be executed manually or automatically at periodic intervals.

> **Note**   All database maintenance information (job) is saved in the *msdb* database in SQL Server/MSDE. There you can also find procedures that permit the definition of maintenance plans.

It is very difficult to create database maintenance plans without Enterprise Manager and the Database Maintenance Plan Wizard. Only SQL Server 2000 adds easy-to-use procedures (in the *msdb* database) for this purpose. If you have MSDE only, you need to use the SQL maintenance commands that we introduce in the section later in this chapter entitled "Maintenance with SQL."

The Database Maintenance Plan Wizard

To create a new database maintenance plan, select Management, then Database Maintenance Plans in the Enterprise Manager window's left pane, as shown in Figure 19-9, or select the wizard through the main taskpad, or from the Tools menu.

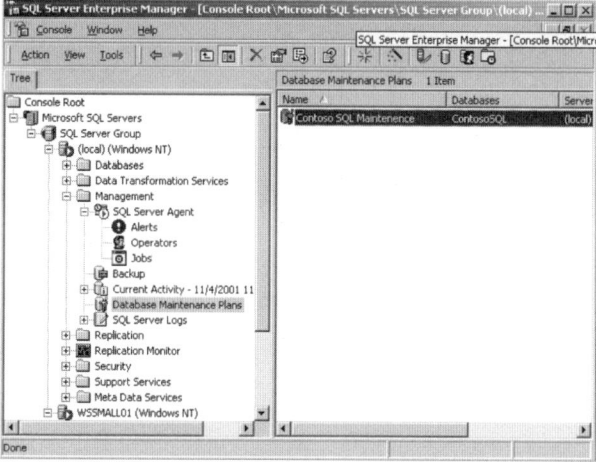

Figure 19-9   Database maintenance plans

Next, select Action, then New Maintenance Plan to activate the Database Maintenance Plan Wizard. The first wizard screen provides you with some information about the wizard. Use the second wizard screen, Select Databases (see Figure 19-10), to select the databases that you want to perform maintenance work on.

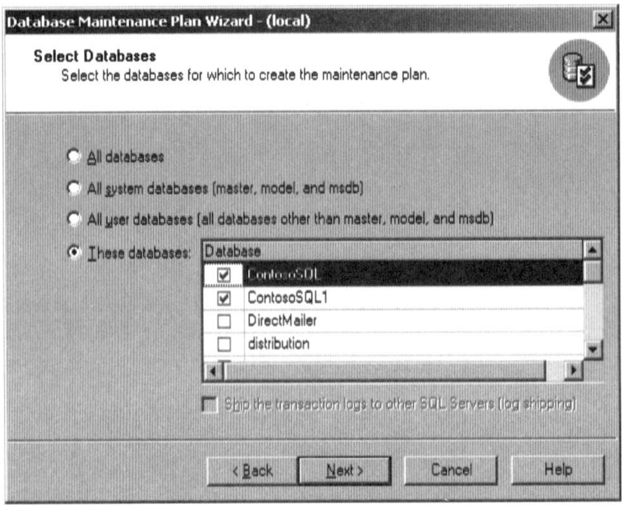

Figure 19-10 Database selection

Use the Update Data Optimization Information wizard screen, shown in Figure 19-11, to specify the optimization options for the selected databases. The optimization processes can take some time for larger databases, and the server load during this time is relatively high.

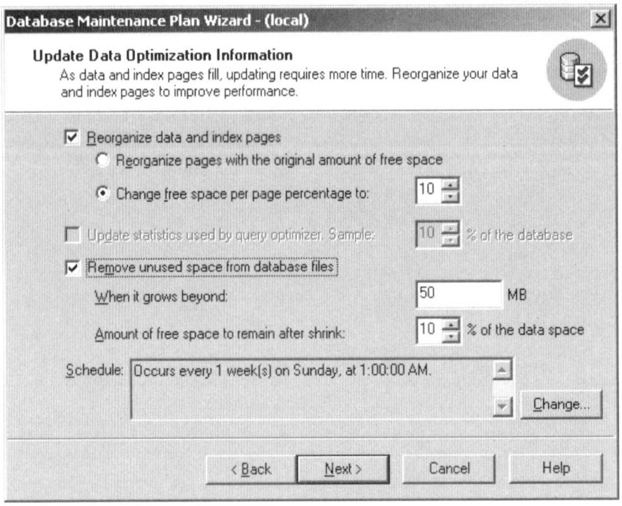

Figure 19-11 Data optimization parameters

You can work out a data optimization schedule for implementing time-controlled optimization tasks, meaning you can schedule optimization work for times when there are no users working with the respective databases.

> **Note**   Keep in mind that you must start the SQL Server Agent service on the SQL Server/MSDE computer to use time-controlled procedures.

Use the next wizard screen, Database Integrity Check, to specify which checking procedures to execute for the selected databases, as displayed in Figure 19-12. If you select the Attempt To Repair Any Minor Problems check box, SQL Server/MSDE will try to fix minor problems on its own.

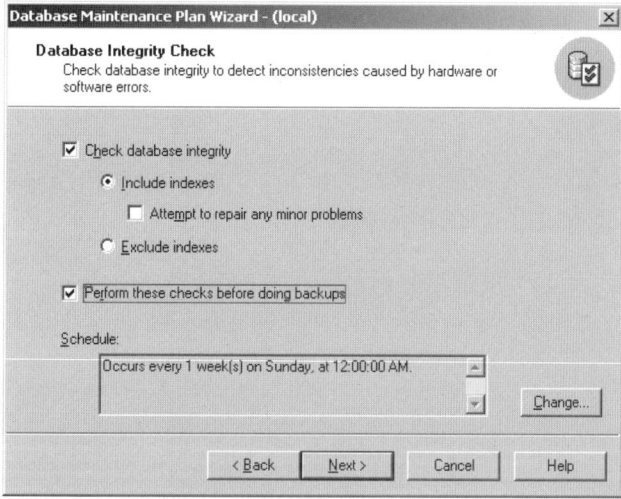

Figure 19-12   Database integrity check

A database maintenance plan can also include data backup strategies that can be controlled with the help of a planned schedule. The Specify The Database Backup Plan wizard screen is shown in Figure 19-13. Refer to Chapter 21, "Data Backup Functions," for detailed information about SQL Server/MSDE backup functions.

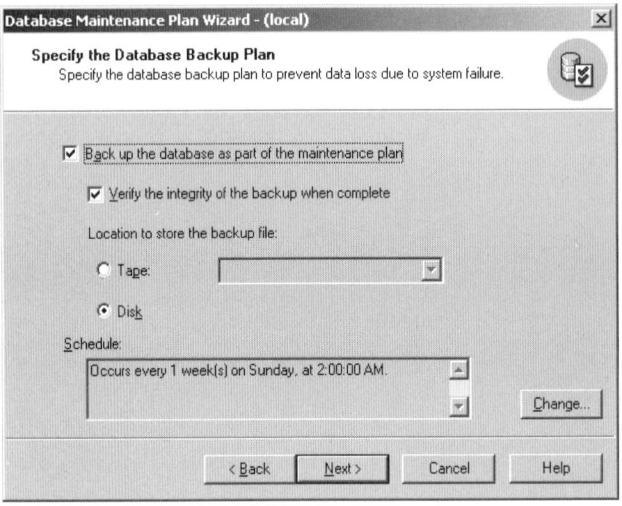

Figure 19-13   Backing up as part of the maintenance plan

You can use the Specify Backup Disk Directory wizard screen, shown in Figure 19-14, for additional backup entries. Notice the option to delete old backup files after a designated time period.

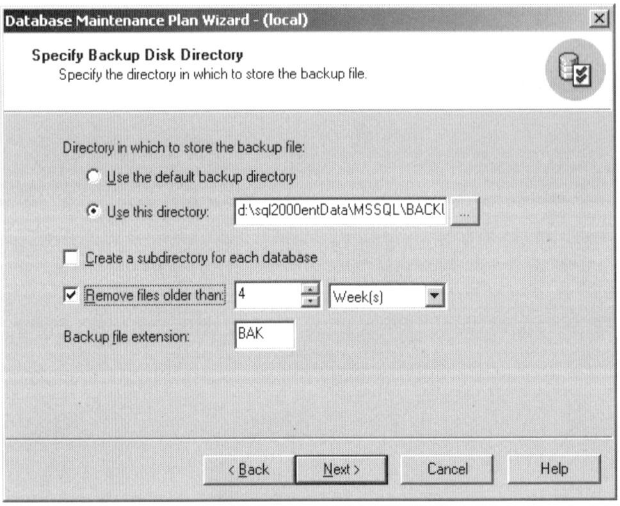

Figure 19-14   Defining the backup destination

In addition to backing up the entire database, the next wizard screen gives you the option to back up only the transaction log, as shown in Figure 19-15. This procedure can also be controlled with a planned schedule.

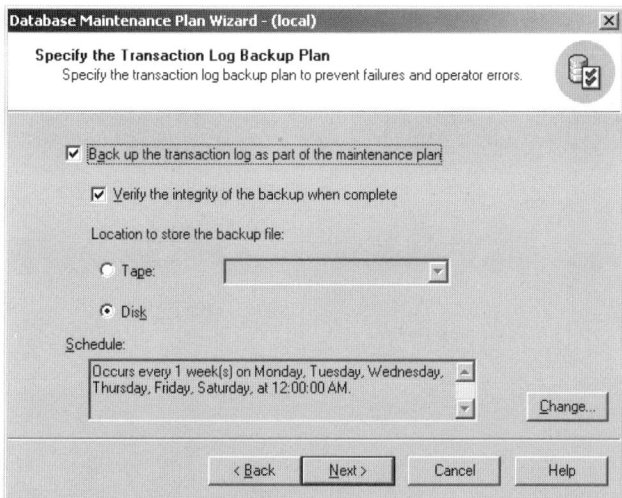

Figure 19-15   Transaction log backup

The next wizard screen, shown in Figure 19-16, lets you specify transaction log settings that match those in Figure 19-15. All SQL Server/MSDE messages returned during the implementation of the database maintenance plan can be logged in report files, which provide you with maintenance work documentation.

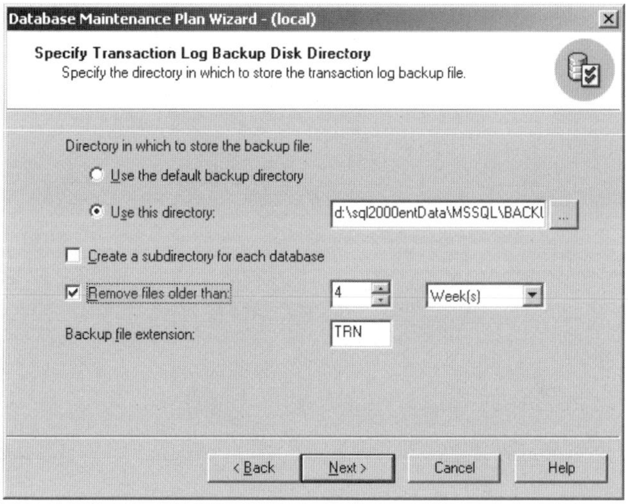

Figure 19-16   Saving result reports

In addition, SQL Server/MSDE creates a maintenance chronology that backs up the database maintenance plan's implementation data. You can set the options for this feature in the Maintenance Plan History wizard screen displayed in Figure 19-17.

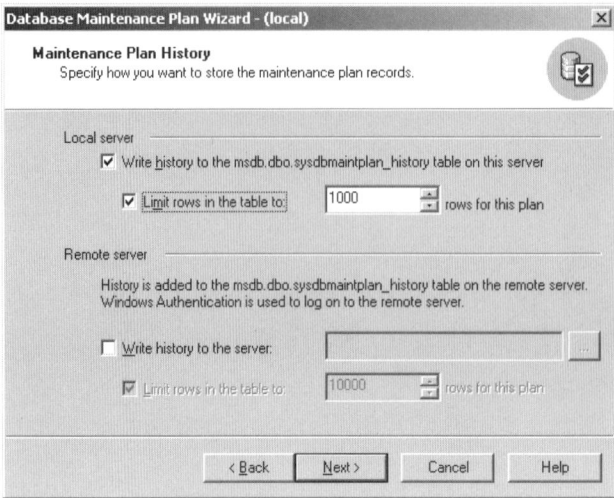

Figure 19-17   Recording a maintenance history

Use the Completing The Database Maintenance Plan Wizard screen, displayed in Figure 19-18, to specify a name for the database maintenance plan.

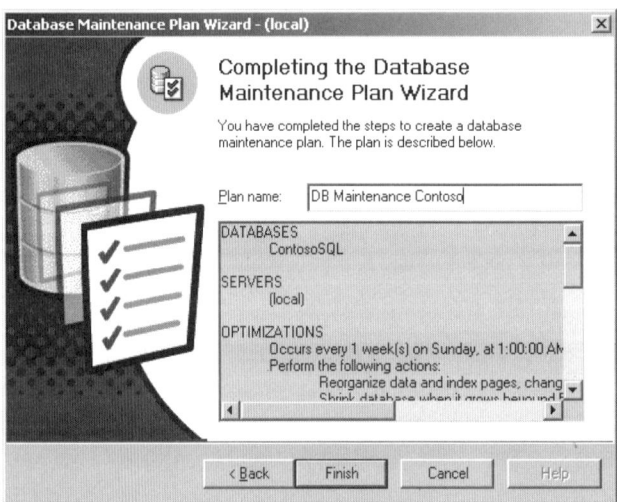

Figure 19-18   Naming the maintenance plan

The system uses this name to save the plan in SQL Server Enterprise Manager under Management\Database Maintenance Plans. That is where you can edit and work with the plan later on. Individual elements of the plan may also be saved as SQL Server Agent Jobs.

Maintenance with SQL

Individual maintenance activities that can be compiled in a database mainte-nance plan can also be accessed individually directly with SQL. Chapter 21, "Data Backup Functions," describes how to create database backup plans and restore the data using the SQL commands *BACKUP* and *RESTORE*.

In this section, we introduce you to the SQL Server/MSDE-specific *DBCC* command. This command can provide you with a lot of information about a database and execute a series of actions, such as integrity checks. Table 19-4 lists a few of the functions available with *DBCC*.

Table 19-4   Selected DBCC Commands

Command	Description
DBCC CHECKCATALOG	Checks consistency within and across system tables for the specified database
DBCC CHECKDB	Checks the integrity of the specified database and corrects minor errors, if needed
DBCC SHRINKDATABASE	Shrinks the database files (data and log) for the specified database, if possible
DBCC UPDATEUSAGE	Updates the internal statistics of table indexes for the specified database

We discuss here the *DBCC CHECKDB* command in more detail, with an integrity check as the example. This is the complete syntax:

```
DBCC CHECKDB
        ( 'database_name'
            [ , NOINDEX
            | { REPAIR_ALLOW_DATA_LOSS
            | REPAIR_FAST
            | REPAIR_REBUILD }
        ] )
        [ WITH {
            [ ALL_ERRORMSGS ]
            [ , [ NO_INFOMSGS ] ]
            [ , [ TABLOCK ] ]
            [ , [ ESTIMATEONLY ] ]
            [ , [ PHYSICAL_ONLY ] ]
            }
        ]
```

If you specify one of the three *REPAIR* constants for this command, the system attempts to fix possible incongruities in the database. *REPAIR_REBUILD* conducts a full search and completes all repairs, including rebuilding the indexes. *REPAIR_FAST* is the fast option and does not rebuild the indexes. *REPAIR_ALLOW_DATA_LOSS* restructures the database to restore integrity, but at the expense of possible data loss.

The additional options with *WITH* refer to the command's output. If you do not enter any additional options, the system outputs the first 200 messages. If you want to see all messages, you must use *DBCC CHECK* with the option *ALL_ERRORMSGS*.

Figure 19-19 illustrates the command's execution in the Query Analyzer for the *ContosoSQL* database. The bottom window displays the result messages.

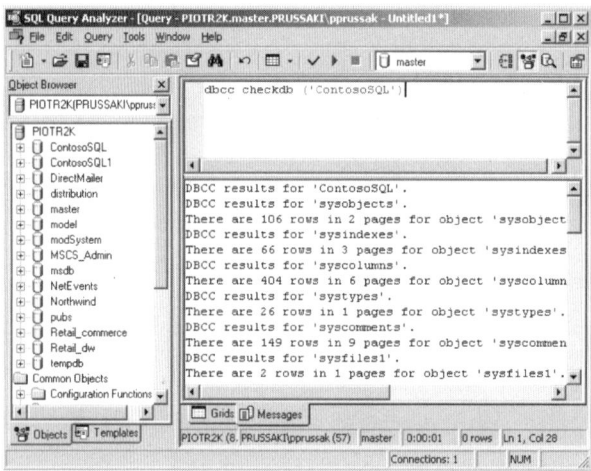

Figure 19-19 Integrity check with *DBCC CHECKDB*

The activation of maintenance functions from an Access .adp file has some limitations: Neither the activation of a stored procedure nor the implementation with ADO can display the text output shown in Figure 19-19. This means that you can execute the command, but you will not see any information about potential problems.

The solution is the DOS program OSQL, which lets you execute SQL scripts directly from the DOS interface. OSQL returns the text messages. This program is included with SQL Server as well MSDE.

For example, if you create a text file named CHECKDB.SQL that includes the *DBCC CHECKDB* command, you can execute it with the following command:

```
OSQL -S SERVER -U sa -i checkdb.sql -o result.txt
```

You can then view the *DBCC CHECKDB* command's messages in the file RESULT.TXT. For further information on OSQL, refer to the section later in this chapter entitled "The OSQL Program."

Alerts, Operators, and Jobs

You can use the SQL Server Agent to simplify and automate server-related management tasks by defining alerts, operators, and jobs for the agent. This section describes their significance and use.

> **Note**   You must start the SQL Server/MSDE SQL Server Agent service to use alerts, operators, and jobs. Use the SQL Server Service Manager to start the service.

Defining Operators

You can define operators for SQL Server/MSDE. You can choose any name for operators, and they can receive information about errors, the system state, or specific events on the server by e-mail, pager, or *NET SEND*.

Use the New Operator Properties dialog box, shown in Figure 19-20, to define an operator. To open this dialog box, select Management, then SQL Server Agent, then Operators in the left pane of the SQL Server Enterprise Manager window for the server, and then select Action, then New Operator from the menu.

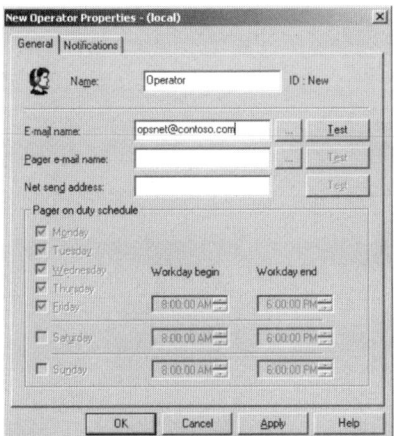

Figure 19-20   Setting up an operator

Use the Notifications tab, displayed in Figure 19-21, to specify which notification version to use for which events. The events that generate notifications are labeled as warnings in SQL Server/MSDE.

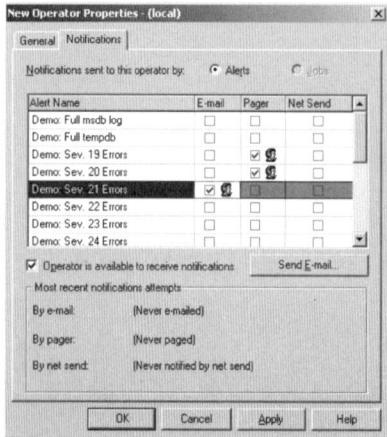

Figure 19-21 Notifying an operator

Defining Alerts

Events must be specified so that the operator(s) can be notified about them. This is accomplished by defining alerts.

In the left pane of the Enterprise Manager window, select Management, then SQL Server Agent, then Alerts to display the defined alerts. SQL Server/MSDE includes default alerts that you can use as examples for your own. To define a new alert, select Action, then New Alert from the menu. This activates the New Alert Properties dialog box, shown in Figure 19-22.

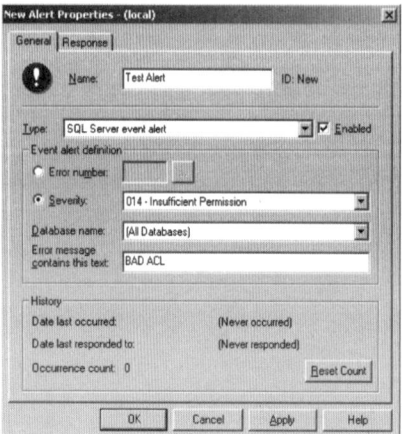

Figure 19-22 Defining an alert

Specify a name for the alert. Define the alert type as a SQL Server event or a SQL Server performance condition alert. For SQL Server events, the alert can react either to a certain error number or the seriousness of an error. For SQL Server performance status warnings, different performance ID code numbers are available.

Use the Response tab, shown in Figure 19-23, to define which operators to inform about the alert's occurrence and how to inform them.

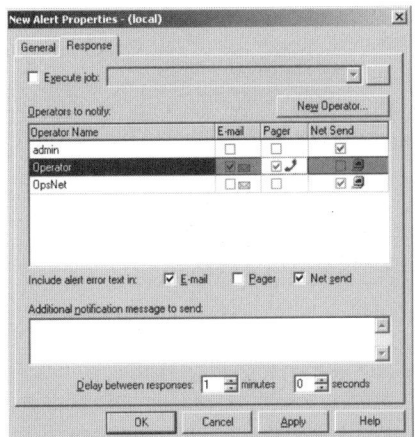

Figure 19-23 Specifying the response to an event

Creating Jobs

You can use jobs to automate recurring activities. To define a new job, select Management, then SQL Server Agent, then Jobs in the left pane of the Enterprise Manager window, and then select Action, then New Job from the menu. This displays the New Job Properties dialog box illustrated in Figure 19-24.

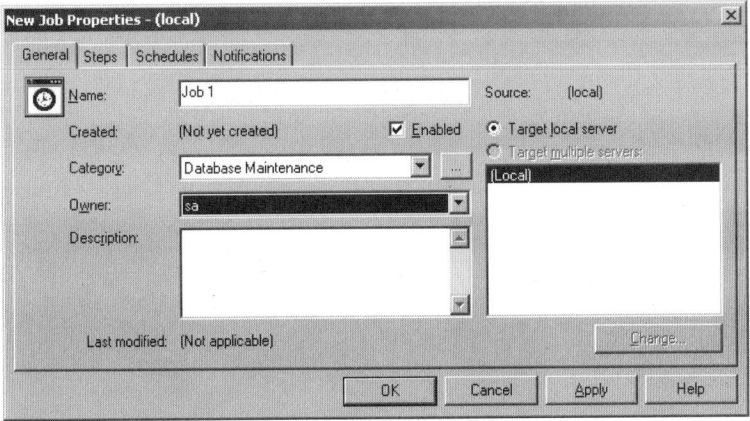

Figure 19-24 A job's general data

Use the General tab to define the job's basic data. Use the Steps tab, shown in Figure 19-25, to define the different actions that must be taken consecutively to carry out the job.

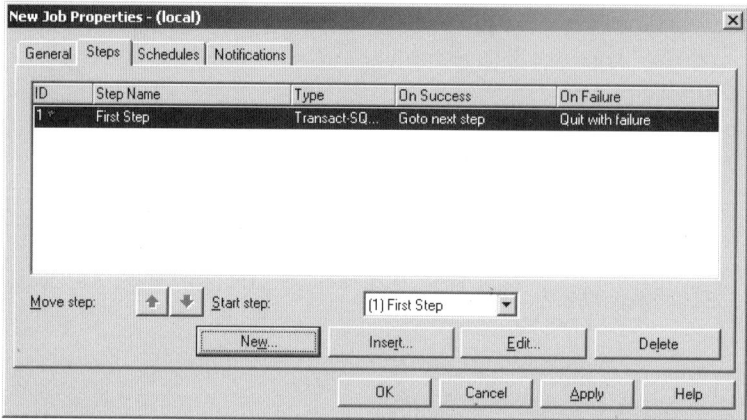

Figure 19-25 Specifying the steps for a job

Click New or Insert to open the New Job Step dialog box, shown in Figure 19-26, where you can define a step.

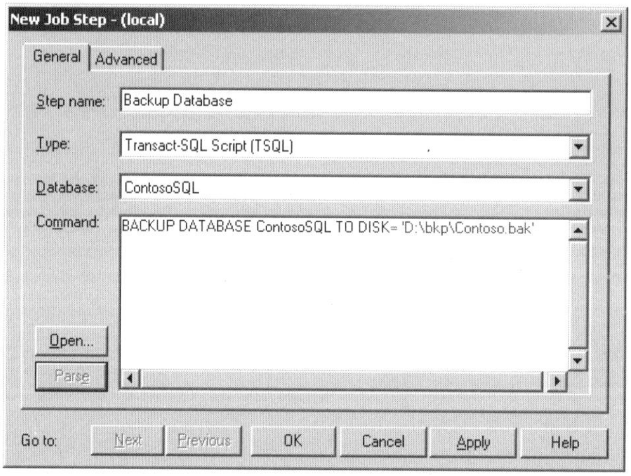

Figure 19-26 Defining a step for a job

Once you have defined the steps, you can create a job schedule that specifies when you want the job to be executed using the Schedules tab, shown in Figure 19-27. Alternatively, you can also start a job manually.

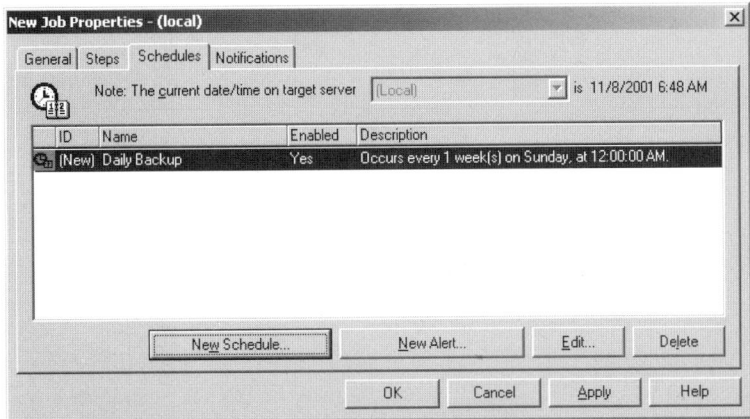

Figure 19-27   Optional definition of a schedule

Finally, in the Notifications tab, you can specify whether the system should inform certain operators about the course of the job (see Figure 19-28).

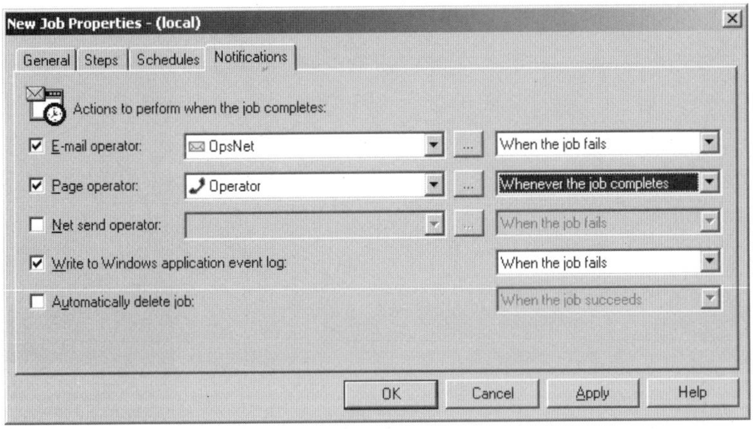

Figure 19-28   Setting up an operator

If you have not set up a job schedule, you can start the job manually. To do so, select the job from the Enterprise Manager, and then select Action, then Start Job from the menu.

Setting Up Operators, Alerts, and Jobs with SQL

You can also utilize SQL to set up operators, alerts, and jobs using system procedures. All of the procedures described here are saved in the database *msdb*. If you are using procedures from the context of your own database, you should insert **msdb** in front of the respective procedure name. The following example illustrates this for a procedure that displays all defined operators:

```
CREATE PROCEDURE Operators

AS

    EXEC msdb.dbo.sp_help_operator

RETURN
```

The following procedures are available for setting up and administering operators: *sp_add_operator*, *sp_update_operator*, *sp_delete_operator*, and *sp_help_operator*.

You can create, edit, and delete alerts with these procedures: *sp_add_notification*, *sp_update_notification*, *sp_delete_notification*, and *sp_help_notification*.

SQL Server/MSDE provides the following procedures for jobs: *sp_add_job*, *sp_add_jobschedule*, *sp_add_jobstep*, *sp_update_job*, *sp_delete_job*, *sp_help_job*, and *sp_help_jobstep*. Use *sp_start_job* or *sp_stop_job* to start and end jobs.

Processes and Locks

Select Management, then Current Activity in the left pane of the Enterprise Manager window to display a list of all internal SQL Server processes and the locks for database objects.

Process Info

Select Management, then Current Activity, then Process Info, as shown in Figure 19-29, to see a list of the current processes.

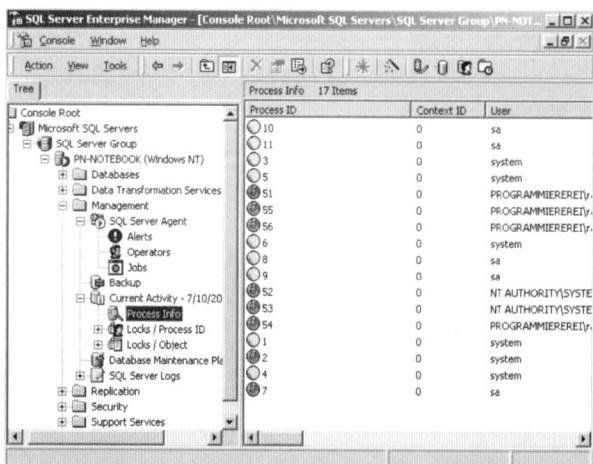

Figure 19-29   Current processes

Double-click a process to display its details. Figure 19-30 illustrates an example.

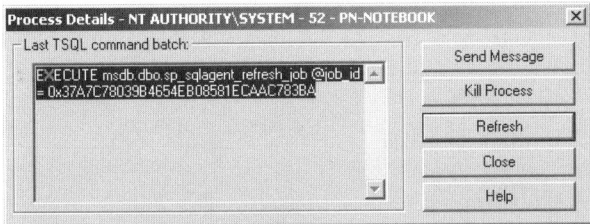

Figure 19-30   Process details

In Chapter 8, "Stored Procedures," we discussed the problems associated with endless loops. Such a procedure can be stopped only by aborting the procedure's process. Look for this process by examining all processes for the respective user to see if you can find the one with the stored procedure, and then terminate that process.

Locks

You can use locks to control the activities of different users. This means that once a user edits data or objects, other users cannot prevent or interfere with the activity. For example, if a user edits a table's structure, other users cannot read or write to the table. For more information on locks, see Chapter 26, "Transactions and Locking."

Query Analyzer

You can use the SQL Server Query Analyzer to execute and analyze SQL queries. To start the Query Analyzer, select Tools, then SQL Server Query Analyzer from the Enterprise Manager, or select Start, then Programs, then Microsoft SQL Server, and then Query Analyzer.

The system first establishes a connection to a server, and a Connect To SQL Server dialog box prompts the user to enter the server name, user name, and password, if necessary. The Query Analyzer then appears with a window similar to the one shown in Figure 19-31. You can select the database to which the SQL commands are to be applied in the top right pane of the window. As shown in the figure, we selected the *ContosoSQL* database for this example.

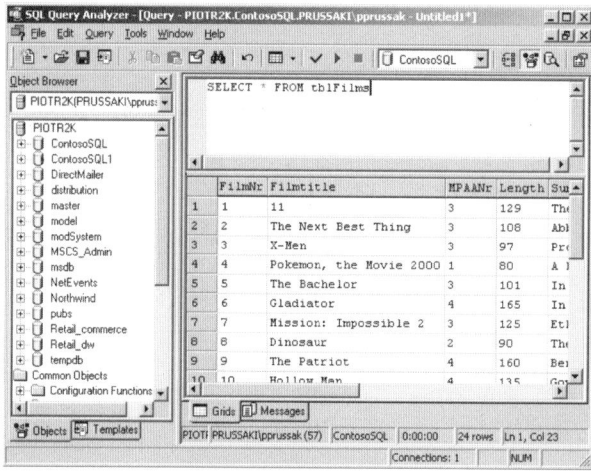

Figure 19-31 Query Analyzer

Using the Query Analyzer

Enter the text for your SQL query in the window at the top. Alternatively, you can load a text file with a SQL script or paste text from the Clipboard.

Select Query, then Execute, or press F5, or click Execute Query and SQL Server processes your query. The result and execution-related messages appear in the bottom window. Table 19-5 displays the Query Analyzer buttons and provides a description of each.

Table 19-5   Query Analyzer Buttons

Button	Description
New Query	Opens a new query window
Load SQL Script	Loads a SQL script text file
Save Query/Result	Saves the query or the query result to a file, depending on the window in which the cursor is located
Insert Template	Inserts code from the template (.tql); SQL 2000 only
Cut	Cuts the selected items and puts them on the Windows Clipboard
Copy	Copies items to the Windows Clipboard
Paste	Pastes items from the Windows Clipboard
Clear Window	Deletes contents of the query pane
Find	Searches for specified text in the query window
Undo	Performs Undo on the last action in the right hand pane (editing of text only)

continued

Table 19-5   Query Analyzer Buttons   *(continued)*

Button	Description
Show Execution Plan/ Results In Text	Displays the query result in the results window in text format and displays the execution plan
Results In Grid	Displays the query result in grid format
Results In File	Saves results to an .rpt file
Show Execution Plan/ Results In File	Saves results of a query to a file and displays the query's execution plan in the results window (that is, the individual steps the server must process to execute the query)
Parse Query	Checks to make sure that the query's syntax is correct
Execute Query	Transmits the SQL run command to the server
Cancel Query Execution	Terminates queries that take a long time to process
Display Estimated Execution Plan	Displays the execution plan likely to be used for executing the query
Object Browser	Toggles visibility of the navigation window on the left
Current Connection Properties	Permits the selection of different options for executing queries
Show/Hide Results Pane	Shows or hides the bottom window

Multiple Resultsets

The Query Analyzer lets you enter multiple consecutive SQL commands. If the SQL commands lead to multiple resultsets, as in our example in Figure 19-32, the resultsets are displayed one after another or in different tabs (SQL Server 7) in the result window when result grids are enabled by selecting Query, then Results In Grid.

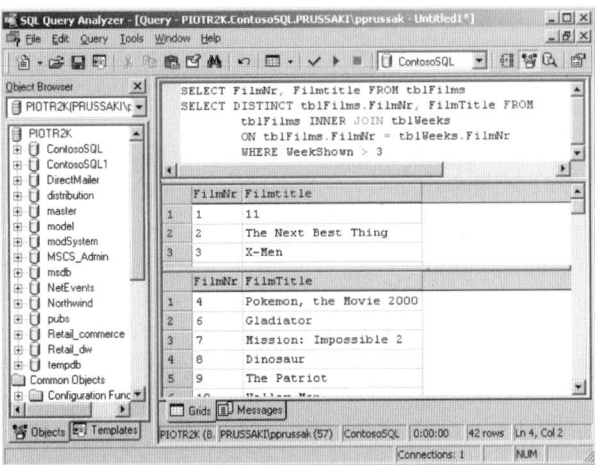

Figure 19-32   Result with multiple resultsets

The Pseudo-Command *GO*

Many scripts use the pseudo-command *GO* to separate the individual SQL commands from each other. *GO* is not a SQL command, but an instruction for the Query Analyzer to follow the instructions until it reaches *GO* and then continue with the next command. Many SQL commands cannot be used sequentially to write a script without the *GO* separator, as writing scripts without *GO* would result in error messages.

The following script was generated by SQL Server (also see Chapter 23, "The SQL-DMO Library"). If you try to run this script without the *GO* commands, the system returns error messages.

```
SET QUOTED_IDENTIFIER ON

GO

SET ANSI_NULLS ON

GO

CREATE PROCEDURE qryMovies

AS

SELECT DISTINCT

        tblWeeks.Week, tblTheaters.Theater, tblFilms.Filmtitle,

        tblMovieSchedule.Day AS Weekday, tblMovieSchedule.Time,

        tblWeeks.WeekShown, tblFilms.Length

FROM

        (tblFilms INNER JOIN tblWeeks ON tblFilms.FilmNr =
        tblWeeks.FilmNr)

INNER JOIN

        (tblTheaters INNER JOIN tblMovieSchedule ON
        tblTheaters.TheaterNr = tblMovieSchedule.TheaterNr)

        ON tblWeeks.WeekNr = tblMovieSchedule.WeekNr

ORDER BY

        tblWeeks.Week, tblTheaters.Theater, tblFilms.Filmtitle,

        tblMovieSchedule.Day, tblMovieSchedule.Time

RETURN

GO

SET QUOTED_IDENTIFIER OFF

GO

SET ANSI_NULLS ON

GO
```

Execution Plan

You can analyze execution plans to optimize your queries. An execution plan subdivides the server query into its individual partial tasks. The system determines what proportion (in percent) of the overall execution a partial task constitutes. The Query Analyzer refers to this topic in terms of query costs.

Figure 19-33 displays the execution plan for the following query, which looks for all films that have been part of the program for more than three weeks:

```
SELECT DISTINCT

tblFilms.FilmNr,

Filmtitle

FROM tblFilms INNER JOIN tblWeeks

        ON tblFilms.FilmNr = tblWeeks.FilmNr

WHERE WeekShown > 3
```

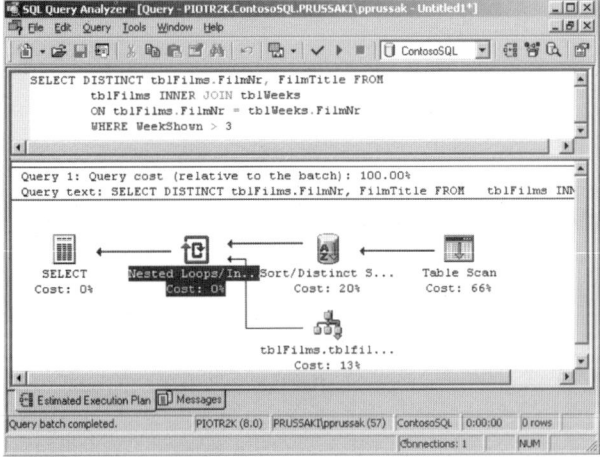

Figure 19-33   Execution plan

Prior to execution, you can display an estimate of the execution plan, or you can display the actual execution plan after the query is complete. It makes sense to ask for an estimate of the execution plan for very extensive queries, those that take a long time to complete, or for queries that edit, paste, or delete data.

Select Query, then Display Estimated Execution Plan to display the estimate. Select Query, then Display Execution Plan if you want to see the actual execution plan after the query has been executed.

If you move your pointing device over the execution plan icons, the system opens a window with additional detailed information about the respective execution step, as displayed in Figure 19-34.

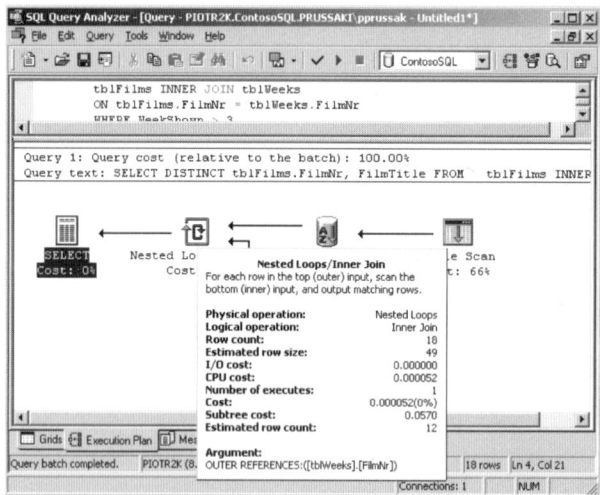

Figure 19-34   Execution details

Index Analysis (SQL Server 2000)

The indexes defined in the tables used for the query play an important role in executing the query as quickly as possible. Thus, the Query Analyzer provides you with an index analysis function to optimize queries.

SQL Query Analyzer 2000 provides the Index Tuning Wizard to optimize your indexes. This wizard is described in the section later in this chapter entitled "Profiler."

Index Analysis (SQL Server 7)

The index analysis identifies the tables and fields for which an additional index would result in increased performance.

For this example, we activated the index analysis command, by selecting Query, then Perform Index Analysis, for a complex query involving multiple tables. The Query Analyzer Index Analysis dialog box, shown in Figure 19-35, opens to display the result.

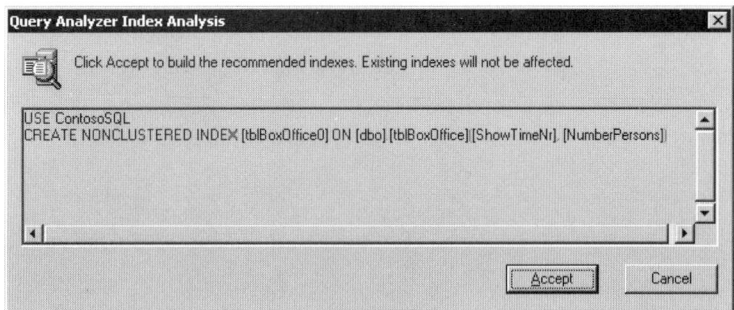

Figure 19-35   An index analysis result

If you click Accept, the system immediately creates the new index. When creating new indexes, note that although a new index can be advantageous for the analyzed query, your other applications might slow down, as SQL Server/MSDE must update an additional index. An additional index also takes up disk space.

> **Note**   The section later in this chapter entitled "Profiler" introduces the Index Tuning Wizard. This wizard tries to optimize the database indexes by using logged information about database usage.

The OSQL Program

The OSQL program is included with SQL Server and MSDE. It lets you execute database commands from DOS. OSQL is used, for example, to execute SQL scripts within batch files.

> **Note**   SQL Server 7 and SQL Server 2000 also include the ISQL program. ISQL is OSQL's predecessor and it supports SQL Server 6.5 functions only. We recommend using OSQL exclusively. Both programs are identical to operate.

Figure 19-36 illustrates the OSQL help function that opens when you activate the program with the -? suffix.

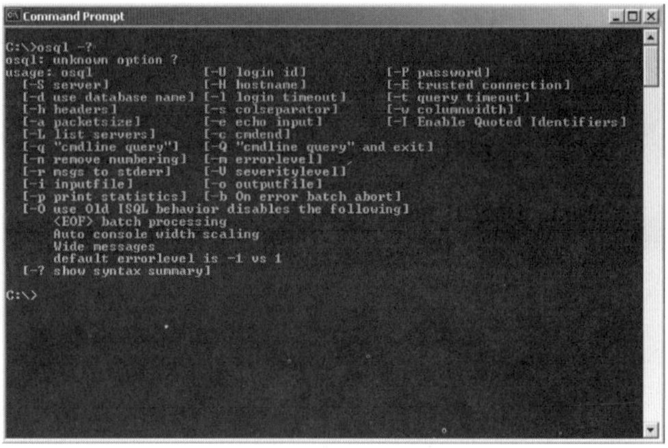

Figure 19-36 OSQL help function

To provide a quick example, we have started OSQL for direct command input (see Figure 19-37). In the first line, you can see the program's activation information, including the server name and the agreement for access with integrated Windows security.

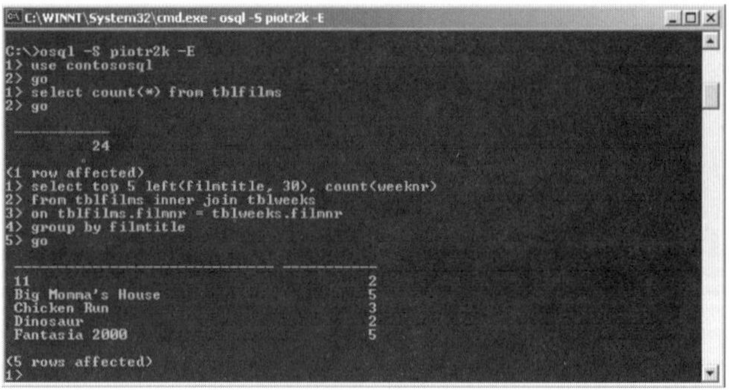

Figure 19-37 OSQL command examples

After startup, OSQL displays the 1> prompt and awaits your entries. We have entered the command for changing databases. After you press Enter, the program begins the next line with 2>. You can enter every command in as many lines as you like. Use the *GO* command to start execution.

OSQL can also execute commands that are saved in a text file. Use the following command:

```
OSQL -S Server -U loginid -P password -i inputfile
```

OSQL also recognizes pseudo-commands other than *GO*. *RESET* deletes all the instructions you entered. The pseudo-command *ED* activates the DOS editor. You can use *!!* to execute an operating system command and you can exit OSQL with *QUIT* or *EXIT*.

Profiler

The SQL Server Profiler allows you to track the data traffic between clients and the server. Figure 19-38 shows a typical example.

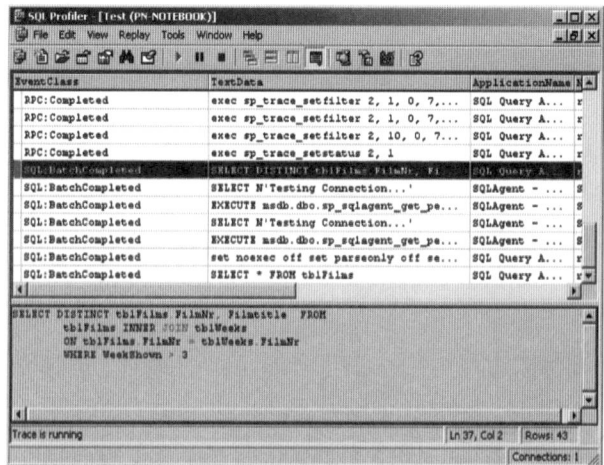

Figure 19-38   SQL Server Profiler

When you start the Profiler, the system opens an empty window. You can select File, then New, then Trace to open the Trace Properties dialog box shown in Figure 19-39. Use this dialog box to specify which server's traffic you want to log. The system creates a new process-tracking specification under the name Test in the Trace Name field.

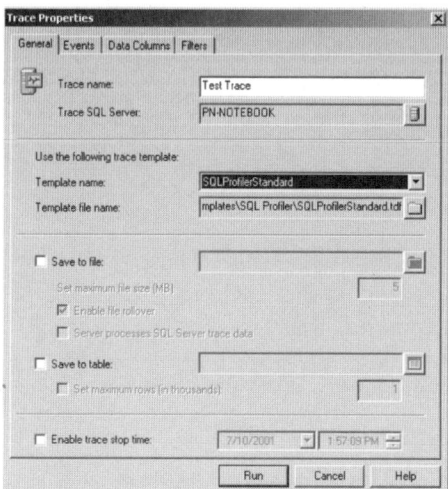

Figure 19-39   Defining a trace

If you want to use a previously created trace, select File, then Open, and then Trace File.

Defining a New Trace

Select a name and type for the trace and specify the server on which you want to execute it. By default, the system displays the trace results on the screen. However, you can also save the results to a file or table on the server.

Use the Events tab, shown in Figure 19-40, to define the events you want to log. The results are divided into different classes. Double-click a result or a result class to select the result or all of the results in a class.

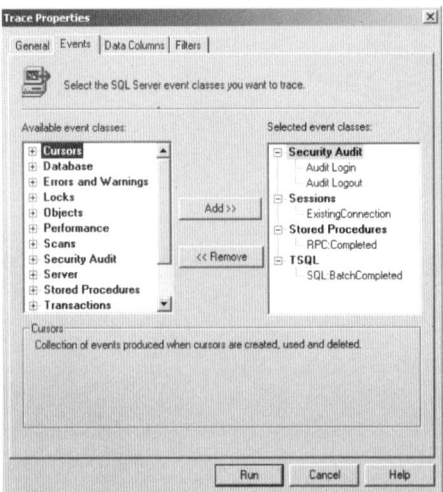

Figure 19-40   Defining which events to trace

Use the Data Columns tab, shown in Figure 19-41, to specify which event-related data to display on the screen.

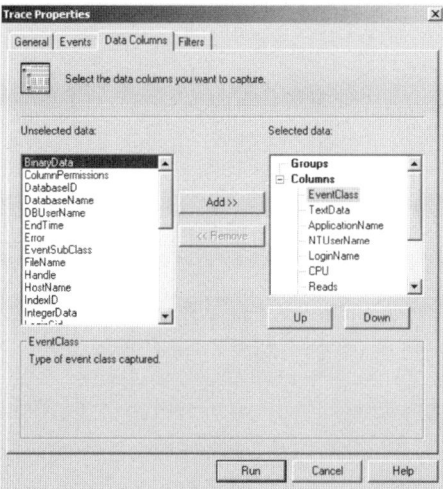

Figure 19-41   Selecting data columns for display

Only select results to log and data columns for display that you need for an error search or to optimize your applications. The logging or display of unnecessary information only creates an additional load on SQL Server. Such information can also take up a lot of storage space if you are using the trace function for an extended period of time on a SQL server with many users who are working simultaneously on extensive projects.

The Filters tab, displayed in Figure 19-42, lets you specify certain events to exclude from the trace. By default, the system does not log any events initiated by the SQL Server Profiler itself.

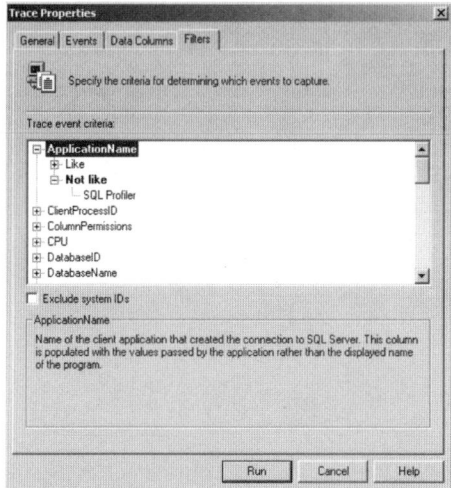

Figure 19-42   Excluding events from being traced

The Index Tuning Wizard

Correctly indexed tables are crucial for SQL Server's performance, because all SQL selection queries are processed faster if the system can refer to indexes.

When you created the tables, you most likely indexed those columns that you expected to be useful as search or sort criteria. Tuning the indexes during actual operation can increase performance if the indexes are matched to the queries that were actually executed.

You can use the Index Tuning Wizard to analyze your indexes based on the Profiler's trace results.

First, select File, then New, and then Trace from the Profiler to start the trace function, which logs the queries and their duration. In the General tab of the Trace Properties dialog box (see Figure 19-43), enter **SQLProfilerTSQL_Duration** in the Template File Name field, which includes a predefined trace definition, or select the appropriate settings to create your own definition.

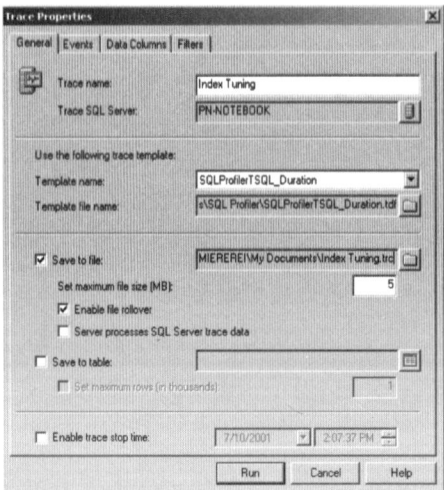

Figure 19-43   Selecting the trace definition

During regular operations, the trace function should be running as long as possible to ensure that the resulting profile is as informative as possible. The trace data should be written directly to a workload file (see Figure 19-39). Once the trace is complete, the system provides you with that workload file, which forms the basis for the functioning of the Index Tuning Wizard. You can also write the workload data to a table on the SQL server.

You can start the Index Tuning Wizard by selecting Tools, then Index Tuning Wizard in the Profiler or by selecting Tools, then Wizards, then Management, and then Index Tuning Wizard in Enterprise Manager.

In the Select Server And Database screen, shown in Figure 19-44, the wizard queries the server and database you want to analyze. In addition, you can specify if you want to retain the existing indexes. If you do not select this option, the system resets all indexes, meaning that it removes all of your index definitions.

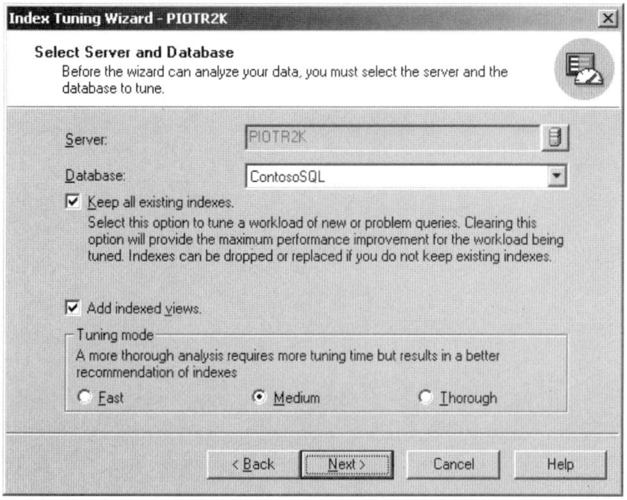

Figure 19-44   Selecting the database to analyze

You should generally always select the Thorough option in the Tuning Mode window, even if that means that tuning will take significantly more time.

Use the Specify Workload wizard screen (see Figure 19-45) to specify if you have a workload file that was logged by the Profiler. If you select the My Workload File option, the Select Tables To Tune wizard screen, shown in Figure 19-46, is displayed. This is where you specify the file or table. If you instead select the SQL Server Trace Table option, the wizard closes because you must first create the workload file. In this case, click Advanced Options to define defaults for the optimizer, for example the number of queries to be used in the workload file for tuning, and then define the tables to tune.

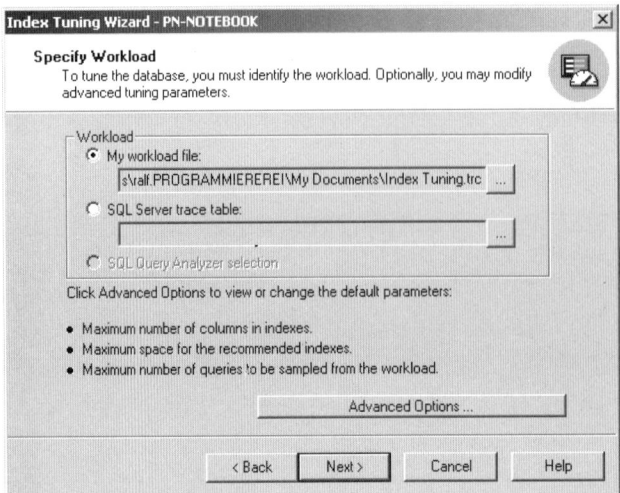

Figure 19-45 Select the analysis source

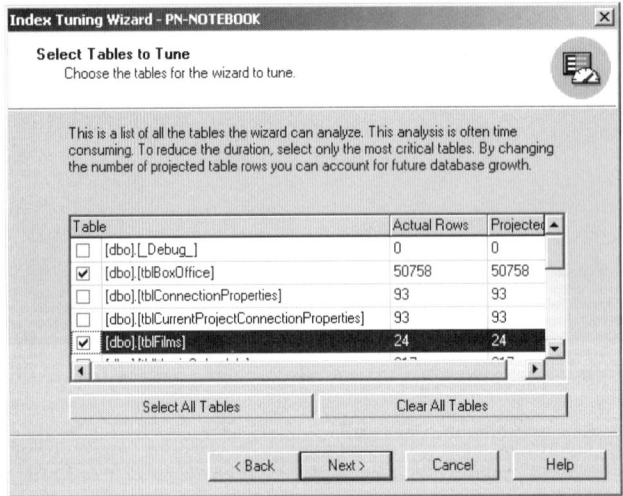

Figure 19-46 Select the tables to tune

The tuning process then runs. The computer on which tuning is carried out is subjected to heavy loads, so in the case of extensive workload files, this process can take some time.

When tuning is complete, the Index Recommendations wizard screen is displayed, as shown in Figure 19-47, listing the tables for which indexes are recommended.

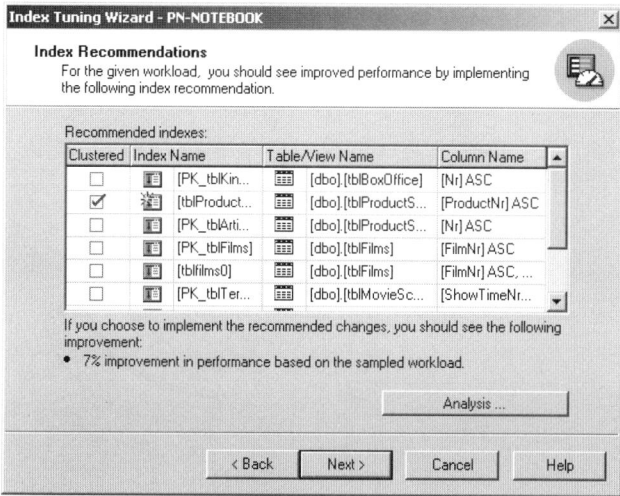

Figure 19-47   Recommended indexes

If you click Analysis, you will see an Index Tuning Wizard dialog box in which different tuning analyses and reports can be displayed.

The next dialog box, Completing The Index Tuning Wizard, asks whether you want to create the recommended indexes. You can specify a time for this operation if you wish. Alternatively, you can have the change recommendations written to a script file, which you can review later.

20

Security

How can you protect your data and your programs so that unauthorized users cannot read and alter data and programs? In Access projects, Microsoft SQL Server/MSDE secures the data, while forms, reports, modules, and so forth, can be protected in the .adp file.

Security for .Adp Files

To protect forms, reports, and so forth in Access projects, you must create an .ade file from the .adp file. The .ade file saves all objects without source code; in other words, the .ade file only saves the precompiled Access-internal displays of all objects.

Select Tools, then Database Utilities, then Make .ade File to create an .ade file. Be sure to retain the original .adp file because you cannot edit an .ade file and you cannot open forms and so on in the Design view. Note that with Microsoft Access 2002 you can create an .ade file only if the .adp file was saved in Access 2002 file format.

In contrast to .mdb or .mde files, it is not possible to specify a database password for .adp or .ade files. Only SQL Server/MSDE prompts you for a password. That is why you can always open an .adp or .ade file even though you cannot see the data unless you have completed the SQL Server/MSDE authentication process.

> **Note** If you use the SQL Server security functions to establish the database connection and then save the password, anyone who opens the .adp file has access to the data.

Securing VBA Modules

You can also protect an .adp file's Microsoft Visual Basic for Application (VBA) modules only; that is, you can lock the function that displays the modules. You cannot view or edit VBA modules unless you enter a password.

To secure VBA modules, select Tools, then Properties in the VBA editor and select the Lock Project For Viewing option in the Protection tab to specify a password.

Security with SQL Server/MSDE

The SQL Server/MSDE security system protects all tables, views, stored procedures, and other elements. SQL Server/MSDE has a two-tier security system that can grant or revoke very specific access rights.

As a user who grants permissions, you must have the permissions required to do so. A system administrator usually performs these tasks for larger SQL Server/MSDE installations, and regular users cannot edit the security settings.

You can fully use the options described next only if you have administrator privileges, such as, for example, the SQL Server/MSDE login name *sa* or membership in the system administrator server role.

Changes in Access 2002

In Access 2002 you can no longer administer users, access rights, and so forth, directly from an Access project. Instead, you must use the SQL Server Enterprise Manager or the corresponding SQL commands and system procedures. However, performing administration tasks from an Access project was quite helpful, especially for MSDE.

Understanding the Security System

The SQL Server/MSDE two-tier security system differentiates between SQL Server/MSDE access and access to the server's individual databases.

The first level, user authentication, checks to determine if the user is authorized to use SQL Server/MSDE. You can link this user authentication process with the one used by Microsoft Windows NT, Microsoft Windows 2000, or Microsoft Windows XP. The second level grants specific database access rights to a user.

SQL Server/MSDE distinguishes between the two levels *logins* and *user*. Logins enables access to the server. To simplify user administration tasks, you can classify logins or user as groups and then assign access rights and other rights to the groups. SQL Server/MSDE designates the groups as *roles*. You can use logins for server roles and user for database roles.

SQL Server Login

Server login is the first step for every user. There are two methods to identify the user: SQL Server or Windows NT authentication.

Windows Authentication

If you are using SQL Server/MSDE under Windows NT, SQL Server/MSDE can accept the Windows NT user authentication. This means that all users must log on to the Windows NT, Windows 2000, or Windows XP computer to access SQL Server/MSDE. For example, if the SQL Server/MSDE computer is integrated with a domain, the domain controller can authenticate users.

The advantage of Windows authentication is that Windows NT, Windows 2000, and Windows XP user groups can receive a server login name as well. This means that every member of a Windows NT, Windows 2000, or Windows XP user group can access SQL Server/MSDE as long as the group has been granted the relevant permission.

Microsoft also refers to Windows authentication as *integrated security* or *trusted connection.*

All members of the Windows NT, Windows 2000, and Microsoft Windows XP Administrators user groups are also automatically administrators for SQL Server/MSDE.

SQL Server Authentication

If SQL Server/MSDE is installed under Microsoft Windows 95, Microsoft Windows 98, or Microsoft Windows Me, you can use only SQL Server authentication. The system saves the user name and password in SQL Server/MSDE. If SQL Server/MSDE is installed under Windows NT, Windows 2000, or Windows XP, SQL Server authentication is possible as well. One disadvantage of SQL Server authentication is that you must enter every individual user account in SQL Server/MSDE.

Defining Users

Once installation is complete, the user *sa* (for system administrator) is created on every SQL Server/MSDE by default. This user has unlimited access to all functions. We recommend that you specify a password for *sa* and then refrain from using this user name. Instead, set up corresponding user names to perform administrative functions.

In Access 2000, select Tools, then Security, and then Database Security to open the dialog box shown in Figure 20-1. The SQL Server Security dialog box is not available in Access 2002.

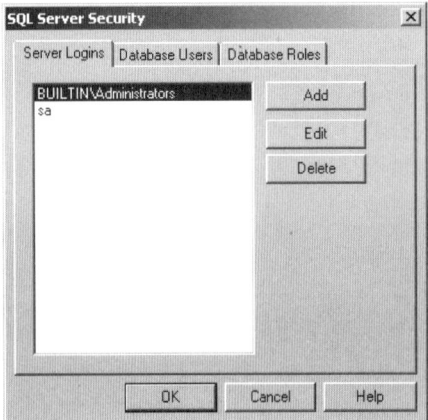

Figure 20-1 Server logins

Server Logins

The purpose of the Server Logins tab is to administer the users (logins) who have access to SQL Server/MSDE. After you reinstall SQL Server/MSDE, the only user is *sa*.

If SQL Server/MSDE is running under Windows NT, Windows 2000, or Windows XP, the list box displays the Windows group Administrators as BUILTIN/Administrators in addition to *sa*.

> **Note** All members of the Windows NT, Windows 2000, and Windows XP Administrators user groups are automatically also SQL Server administrators (members of the *sysadmin* server role).

Be sure to assign a password for *sa* immediately because by default no password is defined after SQL Server/MSDE has been installed. In general, *sa* should not be used as a user name, except during installation and configuration.

Server Roles

You can assign one or more server roles to every server login name. A server role specifies which tasks a user can perform on the server. Table 20-1 provides an overview of the different server roles. These roles are predefined and you cannot define your own. By default, no server roles are assigned to a new user.

Table 20-1   Server Roles

Server Role	Description
System Administrators	Can use all server functions
Security Administrators	Can Administer server login names and so on
Server Administrators	Can configure servers
Setup Administrators	Can manage startup procedures and connections to other servers
Process Administrators	Can administer server-internal processes
Disk Administrators	Can manage data files and drives
Database Creators	Can create and edit databases and can restore data from backups

Database Users

A server login is not sufficient to access the SQL Server/MSDE databases. A server login name must first be assigned to the database user in the Database Users tab, shown in Figure 20-2, before he or she can work with databases as well. Multiple server login names can be assigned to the same database user.

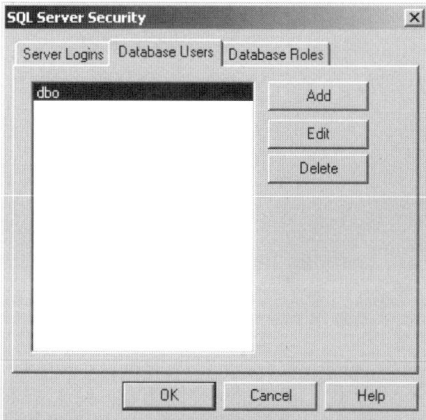

Figure 20-2   Database users

If you create a new server login name and grant it database access rights as detailed here, SQL Server/MSDE automatically creates a corresponding user name.

The database user *dbo* (for database owner) is predefined for *sa* or for the system Administrators group.

Note   In an Access project, the different object names in the Tables, Views (2000), Stored Procedures (2000), and Queries (2000) tabs in the database window are expanded by adding the name (enclosed in parentheses) of the database user who created the respective object. Your own objects are the only ones displayed without additional database user information.

If you want to use objects created by other database users, you must place the table user name in front of the object name for *SELECT* queries or form and report row sources, for example, *SELECT * FROM Kate.tblDates.*

If you create new tables, views, or stored procedures and program an Access project application as the database user *dbo*, another database user can use your application only if you consistently place *dbo* in front of all *SELECT* queries.

Access 2002 introduced the new *Record Source Qualifier* property for forms and reports. You can use this property to specify the row source owner, so that you do not need to explicitly enter the owner's name in the query. In addition, you can select View, then Server Properties to direct the Access project so that all operations are performed under the database user name *sa* (use the Enable System Administrator (SA) User Name option).

Database Roles

You can assign certain permissions to a database role. The option to assign database users to one or more roles facilitates administrative tasks. The database roles shown in Figure 20-3 are predefined. All users are automatically members of the *public* role.

Figure 20-3   Database roles

Adding a New User

Next, we work through an example to illustrate the process of adding a new user. To open the dialog box shown in Figure 20-4, in the SQL Server Security dialog box, click the Server Logins tab and then click Add. This dialog is also available from within the Security/Logins branch of the SQL Server tree within the SQL Server Enterprise Manager.

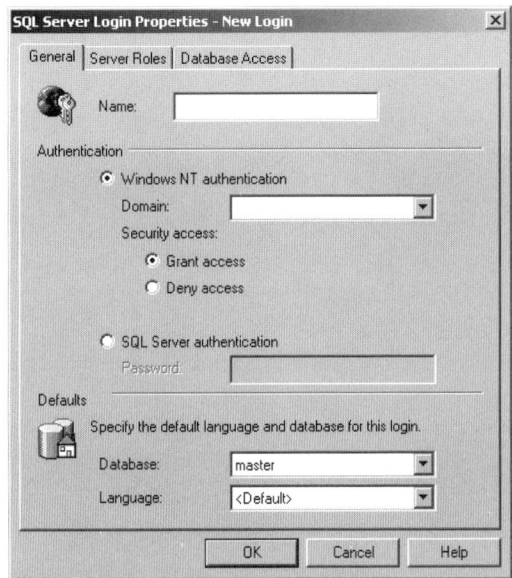

Figure 20-4   General user settings

The General Tab

Enter a user name in the Name field. If SQL Server/MSDE is running under Windows NT, Windows 2000, or Windows XP, you can enter the name of a Windows user to use a trusted connection. You must place the Windows domain name in front of the Windows user name, for example, **_DOMAIN\Username_**. You can also define an entire Windows user group as a user. Replace the user name with the user group name. Be sure to place the domain name in front of the user group name as well.

> **Note**   If you access Microsoft SQL Server 2000 within a domain, you can use an additional button to the right of the Name field. Clicking this button displays a dialog box to select Windows NT, Windows 2000, and Windows XP users and user groups.

The Windows NT Authentication option is enabled only if SQL Server/ MSDE is installed under Windows NT, Windows 2000, or Windows XP.

In the Defaults section of the dialog box, you can define a database and a language for every user. The entry in the Language field determines which language the system uses to display system and error messages.

Server Roles

Use the Server Roles tab, shown in Figure 20-5, to define any special permissions you want to grant the new user. See Table 20-1 for a description of the server roles.

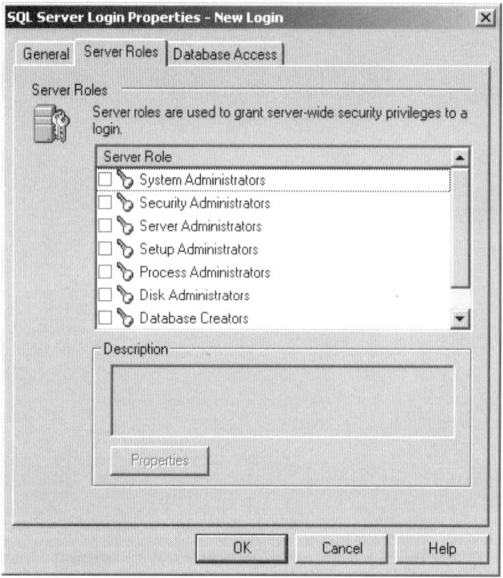

Figure 20-5 Server roles

Database Access

You can use the Database Access tab, displayed in Figure 20-6, to specify the databases that the user is allowed to access.

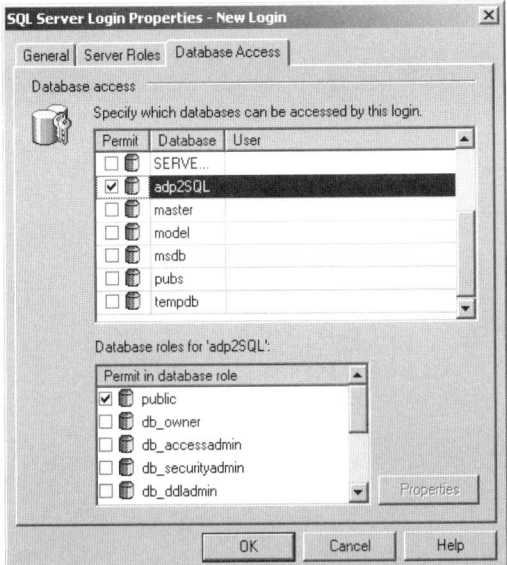

Figure 20-6   Database access

Granting permission to the user generates DB user names in the corresponding databases (the column entitled User in the top list should actually be named DB User Name to make life less confusing).

When you select a database from the Database Access tab, SQL Server/ MSDE automatically creates a database user name (user) from the server login name (login).

You can choose different database roles for the DB user name for the selected database, and you can define your own database roles for your databases. Table 20-2 lists the available database roles.

Table 20-2   Database Roles

Database Role	Description
public	All database users are members of this database role.
db_owner	Can perform all database administration functions, which means that the owner has all rights to the database objects.
db_accessadmin	Can administer the user login names of the database.
db_datareader	Can read data from tables.

continued

Table 20-2   Database Roles *(continued)*

Database Role	Description
db_datawriter	Can add, edit, or delete data.
db_ddladmin	Can execute data definition commands, which include creating or deleting tables, views, stored procedures, and so on.
db_securityadmin	Can grant permissions for users and roles.
db_backupoperator	Can perform data backups.
db_denydatareader	Cannot read data from any user tables.
db_denydatawriter	Cannot add, edit, or delete data to any user table.

Special Case: Execution Rights for Stored Procedures

You might have noticed that that the preceding description of database roles does not include permission to execute stored procedures for any role. In fact, only the owner (*db_owner*) has all of the rights to these database objects and thus can execute stored procedures. Users who are members of the *db_ddladmin* database role can create or edit stored procedures (their own and those of others), but they can execute only those stored procedures they created themselves.

Execution rights for stored procedures must be explicitly granted for database roles or DB user names, as described in the section later in this chapter entitled "Permissions for Database Users." If you create a new stored procedure, other database users cannot execute it. During the course of our projects we constantly ran into problems related to the denial of run permissions when revising stored procedures or introducing new ones. The section entitled "Execute for All Users" later in this chapter describes stored procedures you can use to grant users permission to execute all of the stored procedures in the database.

Permissions

You can select detailed permissions for database users and database roles.

Permissions for Database Users

Use the Database User tab (see Figure 20-2) to select the permissions for a database user. Select a user, then click Edit. This activates the Database User Properties dialog box with the General tab active, as shown in Figure 20-7.

Figure 20-7   Properties of a database user

This dialog box shows the user's assignments to database roles. Click Permissions to define specific rights for the user. This opens the Database User Properties dialog box with the Permissions tab active, as shown in Figure 20-8.

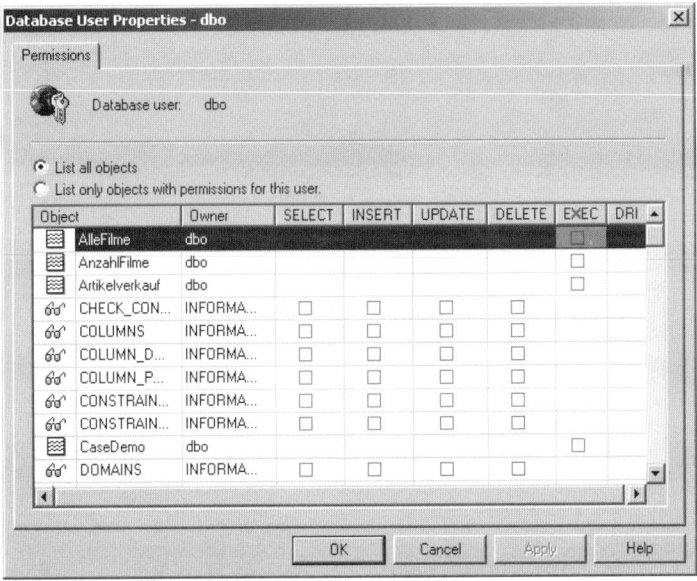

Figure 20-8   Specific permissions for a user

For tables and views, SQL Server/MSDE distinguishes between viewing (*SELECT*), inserting (*INSERT*), updating (*UPDATE*), and deleting (*DELETE*). There is also the permission to execute (*EXEC*) for stored procedures. In addition, you can define if the user can edit the declarative referential integrity (*DRI*) definitions.

Click Properties in the General tab of the Database User Properties dialog box shown in Figure 20-7 to receive information about the selected database role. The next section explains the options available to grant permissions for database roles.

Permissions for Database Roles

Use the Database Roles tab in the SQL Server Security dialog box to edit permissions for database roles, delete roles, and add new database roles. This function applies only to the *public* role and to user-defined database roles.

Figure 20-9 shows the Database Role Properties dialog box for editing the predefined database role *public*. By default, every database user is a member of this role. Click Permissions to open a dialog box to edit the permissions, which corresponds to the one shown in Figure 20-8.

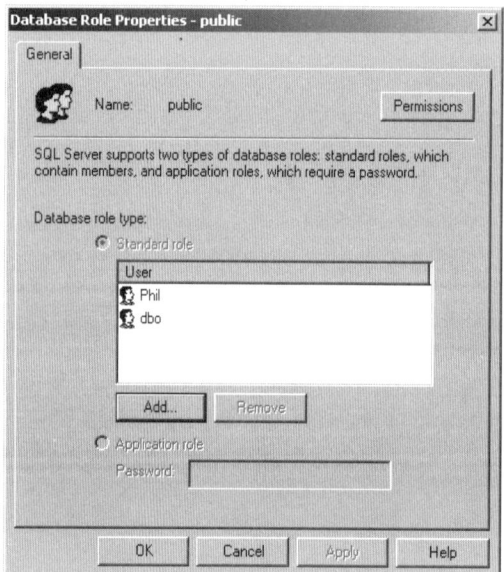

Figure 20-9   Properties of a database role

As a rule, you should not grant the database role *public* any additional rights. Instead, you should define new, corresponding database roles to which you can then assign defined users.

Creating New Database Roles

There are two steps you must follow to create a new database role. First, in the Database Roles tab (Figure 20-3), click Add. The dialog box shown in Figure 20-10 opens.

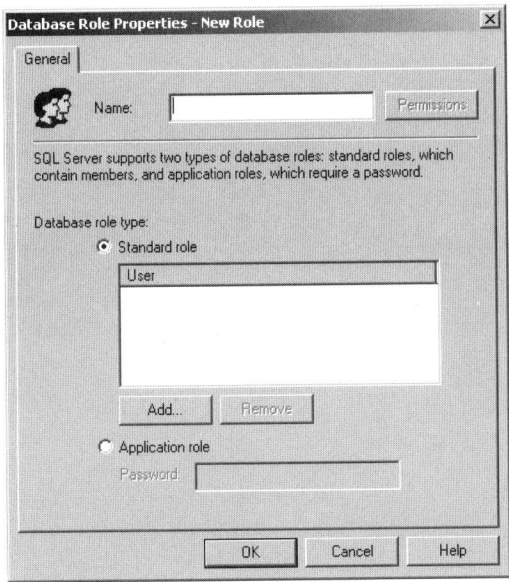

Figure 20-10   New database role

Enter a name for the new database role in the Name field. Now specify whether the new database role is a standard role or an application role. For a standard role, use the appropriate button to add Database user names. An application role lets you allocate permissions to a specific application.

Click OK in the dialog box and open it once more to assign permissions to the new database role. Once you have completed this second step, the system enables the Permissions button and the corresponding dialog box for defining rights, then opens.

User Administration with SQL Server Enterprise Manager

The SQL Server Enterprise Manager included with SQL Server uses the same user administration dialog boxes as Access 2000 (see Figure 20-11).

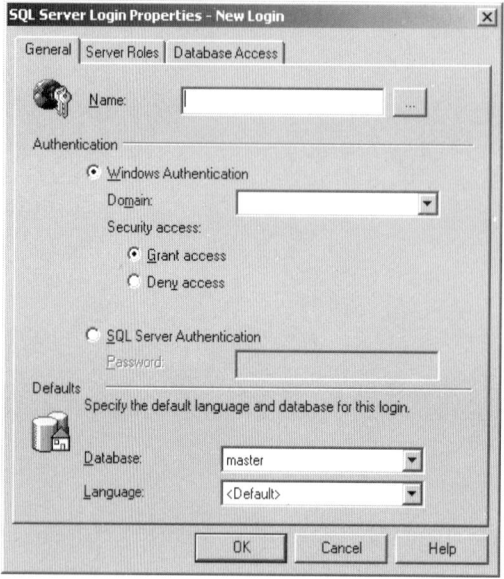

Figure 20-11 SQL Server Login Properties – New User dialog box

The Logins section under Security in the Enterprise Manager window's left pane lists the server logins, as shown in Figure 20-12. The Server Roles option is also located under Security.

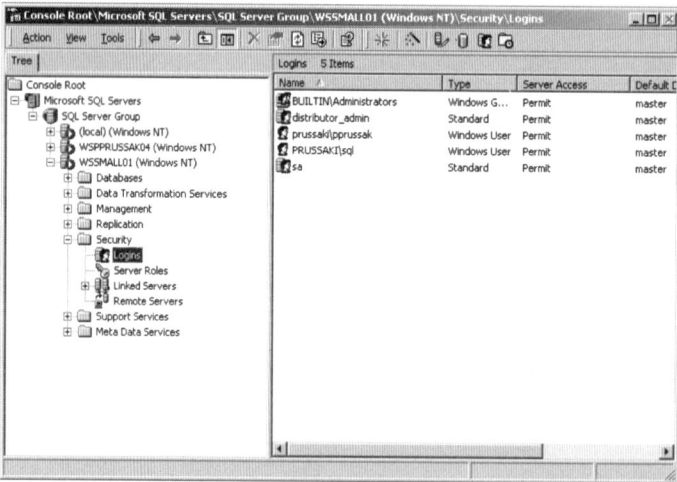

Figure 20-12 The Logins section of the Enterprise Manager

The Databases subtree provides two sections for every database: DB User Names and Roles.

SQL Commands for Granting Permissions

Given the required permissions, you can use SQL commands to grant or revoke rights. Note that SQL does not recognize any commands that return the permissions of a user or a role. However, you can use another method, such as the system stored procedure *sp_helpprotect*, described in the "System Stored Procedures for Users and Roles" section of this chapter.

Granting Rights with *GRANT*

You can use the *GRANT* command to authorize permissions for objects and statements. The general syntax to grant permissions for objects is as follows:

```
GRANT
    { ALL [ PRIVILEGES ] | permission [ ,...n ] }
    {
        [ ( column [ ,...n ] ) ] ON { table | view }
        | ON { table | view } [ ( column [ ,...n ] ) ]
        | ON { stored_procedure | extended_procedure }
        | ON { user_defined_function }
    }
TO security_account [ ,...n ]
[ WITH GRANT OPTION ]
[ AS { group | role } ]
```

You can enter a user or a group as *security_account*. See Table 20-3 for a list of available permission constants. The *GRANT* command makes it possible to grant permissions for a table's individual columns.

> **Note** You can grant or revoke permissions for user-defined functions (*User_definied_function*) for SQL Server 2000 only, because earlier versions do not support the creation of user-defined functions.

Table 20-3 **SQL Permission Constants**

Constant	Description
SELECT	Grants permission to read records
DELETE	Grants permission to delete records
INSERT	Grants permission to insert records
UPDATE	Grants permission to update records

continued

Table 20-3   SQL Permission Constants *(continued)*

Constant	Description
EXECUTE	Grants permission to execute stored procedures
REFERENCES	Grants permission to access the key columns of tables that have a foreign key relationship for which the user does not have *SELECT* permission

Execute for All Users

This section introduces two stored procedures you can use to grant one database user or all database users permission to execute all of the stored procedures in the database.

Use the *GrantExecuteAllProcedures* procedure to grant a user permission to execute all stored procedures. This procedure expects a valid user name as a parameter, and it uses a cursor to move through the system table *sysobjects*. This table contains information about all database objects. The cursor returns the names of the stored procedures preceded by the user names. The user name is important because different users could have created the procedures. You must have the required permissions to execute the procedure, shown here:

```
CREATE PROCEDURE GrantExecuteAllProcedures @username VARCHAR(100)

AS

    -- This procedure grants execution rights

    -- for all stored procedures to @username


    -- Retrieve all stored procedures (username.storedproc)

DECLARE sysobj CURSOR FOR

    SELECT sysusers.name + '.' + sysobjects.name FROM sysobjects

        INNER JOIN sysusers ON sysobjects.uid = sysusers.uid

        WHERE sysobjects.xtype = 'P'

    -- Temporary string for sp

DECLARE @name VARCHAR(100)

    -- Open cursor

OPEN sysobj

    -- Retrieve first record

FETCH sysobj INTO @name

    -- While there are records

WHILE (@@FETCH_STATUS=0) BEGIN

        -- Build command and execute with EXEC
```

```
        EXEC ('GRANT EXECUTE ON ' + @name +' TO ' + @username)

        -- Retrieve next record

        FETCH sysobj INTO @name

    END

    -- Close cursor

    CLOSE sysobj

    DEALLOCATE sysobj

RETURN
```

The second procedure, *GrantExecuteAllUsersAllProcedures*, executes the procedure just described (*GrantExecuteAllProcedures*) for all users of the current database:

```
CREATE PROCEDURE "GrantExecuteAllUsersAllProcedures"

AS

    -- Cursor for all database users

    DECLARE usr CURSOR FOR

        SELECT name FROM sysusers

            WHERE hasdbaccess = 1

    DECLARE @usrname VARCHAR(100)


    -- Open cursor

    OPEN usr

    -- Retrieve first user name

    FETCH usr INTO @usrname

    -- While more users

    WHILE (@@FETCH_STATUS=0) BEGIN

        -- Execute stored procedure to grant execution rights

        EXEC GrantExecuteAllProcedures @usrname

        -- Retrieve next user

        FETCH usr INTO @usrname

    END

    CLOSE usr

    DEALLOCATE usr

RETURN
```

Revoking Rights with *REVOKE*

Use the *REVOKE* command to revoke the permissions of a user or group:

```
REVOKE [ GRANT OPTION FOR ]
    { ALL [ PRIVILEGES ] | permission [ ,...n ] }
    {
        [ ( column [ ,...n ] ) ] ON { table | view }
        | ON { table | view } [ ( column [ ,...n ] ) ]
        | ON { stored_procedure | extended_procedure }
        | ON { user_defined_function }
    }
{ TO | FROM }
    security_account [ ,...n ]
[ CASCADE ]
[ AS { group | role }
```

Granting or Revoking Command Execution Rights

You can also use *GRANT* and *REVOKE* to grant or revoke rights to execute certain commands and actions for the current database. The general format for *GRANT* is shown here:

```
GRANT { ALL | statement [ ,...n ] }
TO security_account [ ,...n ]
```

The corresponding format for *REVOKE* is as follows:

```
REVOKE { ALL | statement [ ,...n ] }
FROM security_account [ ,...n ]
```

Table 20-4 lists the constants that can be used as *statement* along with their descriptions.

Table 20-4   Constants for Execution Permission statement

Constant	Description
BACKUP DATABASE	Permits backup of the current database
BACKUP LOG	Permits backup of the current database's log file
CREATE DATABASE	Permits the creation of databases
CREATE DEFAULT	Permits the creation of default values
CREATE FUNCTION	Permits the creation of user-defined functions (SQL Server 2000 only)
CREATE PROCEDURE	Permits the creation of stored procedures
CREATE RULE	Permits the creation of rules
CREATE TABLE	Permits the creation of tables
CREATE VIEW	Permits the creation of views

System Stored Procedures for Users and Roles

SQL Server/MSDE provides numerous system stored procedures you can use to create, delete, and edit server login names, database user names, server roles, database roles, and so on.

You can use these system stored procedures in your stored procedures, forms, reports, and VBA programs. Table 20-5 and Table 20-6 list the most important system stored procedures. After the tables we introduce a form that provides information about server login names, server roles, database user names, database roles, and so on.

> **Note**   The naming syntax for system stored procedures and their parameters always suppresses the second of two identical successive letters. For example, *loginname* with a double *n* becomes *loginame* with a single *n*.

Table 20-5   **System Stored Procedures for Logins and Server Roles**

System Stored Procedure	Description
sp_addlogin	Sets up a new server login name for SQL Server authentication
sp_addsrvrolemember	Assigns a login name to a server role
sp_helplogins	Returns information about server login names
sp_denylogin	Specifies a Windows NT, Windows 2000, or Windows XP user or user group that is denied permission to log in at the server
sp_dropsrvrolemember	Drops the assignment of a login name to a server role
sp_grantlogin	Creates a Windows NT, Windows 2000, or Windows XP user or user group as a new server login name for known connections
sp_helpsrvrole	Returns information about one or all pre-defined server roles.
sp_helpsrvrolemember	Returns information about the members of one or all predefined server roles
sp_revokelogin	Revokes a server login name
sp_srvrolepermission	Returns the permissions applicable to one or all server roles

Table 20-6 System Stored Procedures for Database Users and Roles

System Procedure	Description
sp_addrolemember	Adds a new user to a database role
sp_droprolemember	Drops a database user's assignment to a database role
sp_grantdbaccess	Grants permission to access the current database to a server login name
sp_helpdbfixedrole	Returns information about one or all predefined database roles
sp_helpntgroup	Returns information about those Windows NT, Windows 2000, or Windows XP user groups for which there are permissions defined in the current database
sp_helprole	Returns information about one or all database roles
sp_helprolemember	Returns information about one or all of the database role's members
sp_helpprotect	Returns information about the user permissions for a database object or specific database commands
sp_helpuser	Returns information about one or all database users
sp_revokedbaccess	Revokes a database user name

frmUserAndRoles Example Form

The example form *frmUserAndRoles* consists of several list boxes. The top half returns information about server login names and server roles, and the bottom half displays data about database users, database roles, and permissions (see Figure 20-13).

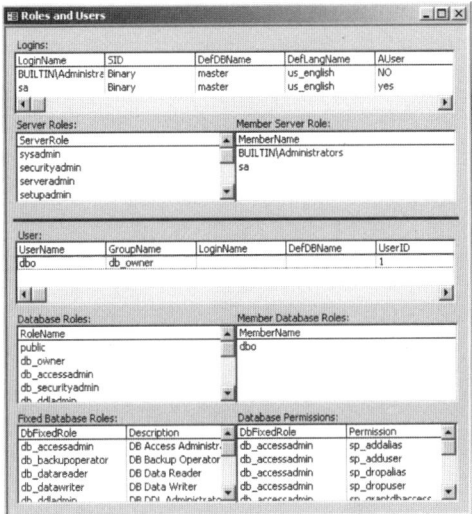

Figure 20-13   Example form with roles and users

You cannot use a system stored procedure directly as the *Record Source* for a list box. Instead, you must use the SQL *EXEC* command, as shown in Figure 20-14 for the *lstUser* list box.

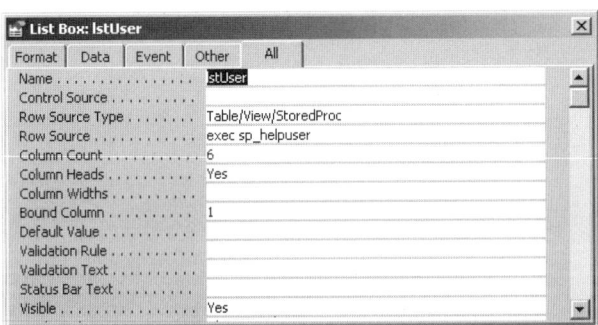

Figure 20-14   List box settings

System Functions for Security Functions

With views and stored functions, you can also use the system functions described in Table 20-7 in addition to the system stored procedures introduced earlier to request information about SQL Server/MSDE users, roles, and permissions.

Table 20-7 **System Functions**

Function	Description
CURRENT_USER	Returns the current user. This function is the same as *USER_NAME()*.
IS_MEMBER (['group' | 'role'])	Shows whether the current user is a member of the specified Windows NT, Windows 2000, or Windows XP group or SQL Server role.
IS_SRVROLEMEMBER ('role' [, 'login'])	Shows whether the current user name is a member of the specified server role.
PERMISSIONS([objectid [, 'column']])	Returns a value with a bitmap, which shows the statement, object, or column permissions for the current user.
SESSION_USER	This is a function that allows a system-supported value to be inserted for the user name of the current session in a table if no default value has been specified. The function also permits the use of the user name in queries, error messages, and so on.
SUSER_SID(['login'])	Returns the security ID (SID) for the user name of the user.
SUSER_SNAME([server_user_sid])	Returns the user name from the SID of a user.
SYSTEM_USER	Allows a value, which is provided by the system, to be inserted for the current system user name in a table when no default value is specified.
USER	Allows a value, which is provided by the system, to be inserted for the database user name of the current user in a table when no default value is specified.
USER_ID(['user'])	Returns the database ID of the user.
USER_NAME([id])	Returns a database user name via a specific ID.

21

Data Backup Functions

Data backup functions for Microsoft SQL Server/MSDE databases differ from normal data backups in that the data for all database users is saved simultaneously and the database backup is usually performed during normal system operation. Most backup programs are not capable of backing up files that are open, so SQL Server and Microsoft Data Engine (MSDE) must be closed during a backup. SQL Server and MSDE therefore have their own backup and restore components to allow these operations.

SQL Server and MSDE are designed so that power outages, hardware failure, and other problems have a minimal effect on the database. Every database operation is logged in the transaction log file. When an error occurs, the log file is used to restore the database to its condition before the error occurred.

In this book we do not describe the options provided with SQL Server for backing up large databases. This chapter explains only the basic functions for this area.

The following sections introduce the different options for performing backup and restore operations using Access projects, SQL Server Enterprise Manager, and SQL. The final section describes the SQL Server/MSDE mechanisms for restoring data after an error has occurred.

Basics

We should first define the terms *data backup* and *data restoration* as they apply to SQL Server/MSDE.

Data Backup and Restoration

The backup and restore functions in SQL Server/MSDE correspond to those you might be familiar with from other applications in all but one significant respect. During a normal backup operation, files and folders are saved. These objects can then be reimported fully or partially for individual users. Files that are open when the backup is made are not backed up.

When a database is backed up, even if it is still in active use, the current status is backed up to files or tape. This status can then be restored from the backup, although data for individual users cannot be reconstructed.

Recovery: Restoring Data After a System Crash

Recovery entails the restoration of the database after a system crash. This process is run automatically after a system crash. The transaction log is used to re-create the last consistent database status.

If the server hardware is defective and SQL Server/MSDE needs to be installed on another computer, then the corresponding backup must be imported.

Transaction Log

Every database operation is logged by SQL Server/MSDE in a transaction log file. This file makes it possible to restore data when an error occurs because the system performs all database operations listed in the log that are not stored in the database.

In larger database systems, full system backups take a great deal of time, so these are carried out at less frequent intervals (for example, once a week). For daily or hourly backups, only the transaction log is saved. The database can then be restored using both the full system backup and the saved transaction log. Each time a transaction log is backed up, the log is truncated (that is, it is restarted for each backup).

The following database operations are not logged: *SELECT INTO*, *CREATE INDEX*, text operations with the SQL commands *WRITETEXT* and *UPDATE-TEXT*, and bulk copy operations with SQL Server's bulk copy (BCP) program.

Data Backup Functions

When performing a backup, you can apply the corresponding functions for Access projects, SQL Server Enterprise Manager, SQL, or the Distributed Management Objects (SQL-DMO) library.

To perform any data backup or restore functions, you must be a member of the database roles *db_owner* or *db_backupoperator* for the database that you want to back up or restore.

Backing Up in Access Projects

To create a data backup, select Tools, then Database Utilities, then Backup SQL Database (see Figure 21-1). Only the database currently linked to the .adp file is saved, and only if the database is administered on SQL Server/MSDE, which must be set up on the local computer. This means that the Access project must run on the same computer as SQL Server/MSDE.

Figure 21-1   Creating a backup copy

By default, the backup is saved with the name of the Access project and the file extension .dat.

Note   You cannot create backup copies using Microsoft Access 2000 if you have installed Microsoft SQL Server 2000 locally and have set up your connection to the server and database with the integrated security option (select File, then Connection, then Use Windows NT Integrated Security). An error message appears that reports a failed logon attempt by a user.

The data backup function of Access projects plays a minimal role because SQL Server/MSDE is usually installed on a network server for which user access is required only for administration purposes. It also makes sense to automate data backups as much as possible so that they do not rely on a user or administrator remembering to carry them out.

Another use of data backup is for a one time transfer of data from one SQL server or MSDE computer to another.

Using SQL Server Enterprise Manager

SQL Server Enterprise Manager provides a much broader and higher performance function for performing data backups. The following sections describe its most important options and configuration settings.

Activating Data Backup

To activate the data backup function, select the database to be saved from the left pane in the Enterprise Manager window, shown in Figure 21-2. You can then either click Backup Database in the right pane, select Backup Database on the Tools menu, or select Backup Database from the database shortcut menu.

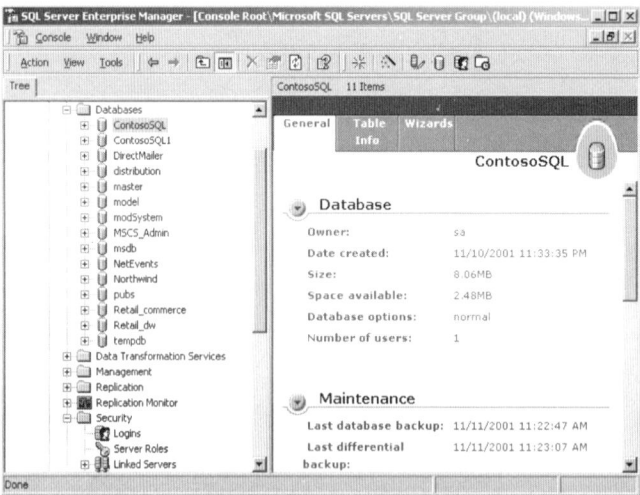

Figure 21-2 SQL Server Enterprise Manager

In the SQL Server Backup dialog box, shown in Figure 21-3, you can define the backup type and additional settings.

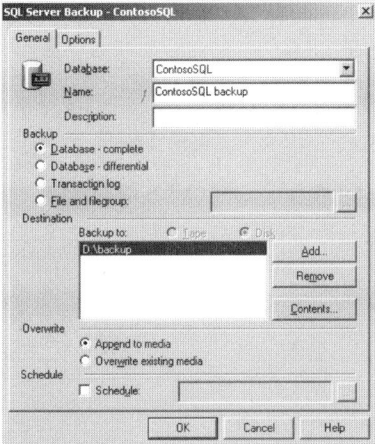

Figure 21-3.   Backup settings

Backup Variants

There are four basic backup variants, as follows:

■ **Database–complete.** The database selected in the Database field is saved completely. A complete backup saves all data.

■ **Database–differential.** The database selected in the Database field is saved on a differential basis. A differential backup only saves the data that has changed since the last full backup.

■ **Transaction log.** This option is used to save the transaction log.

■ **File and file group.** The system saves the actual files in a database that can be grouped into different file groups.

> **Note**   If Microsoft SQL Server 7 or SQL Server 2000 is installed on Microsoft Windows NT, Microsoft Windows 2000, or Windows XP, you can save directly to tape.

Destination

In the Destination section (see Figure 21-3), you can determine where the backup is saved. Click Add to activate the Select Backup Destination dialog box, shown in Figure 21-4.

Figure 21-4   Backing up to file

Either enter the name of the file to which you would like to back up, or define a backup medium, which can be a file or a tape.

If you click the button with the ellipses (...), a Backup Device Location dialog box appears in which you can define the drive, the folder, and the filename for the backup. Remember that the dialog box only displays the drives for the computer on which SQL Server/MSDE is installed. No network drives are displayed.

> **Note**   You can specify any network share as the backup destination by specifying the filename in the Universal Naming Convention (UNC), for example, \\SERVER\SHARE\FOLDER\FILE.BAK.

The file extension for the backup file is freely definable. In some dialog boxes, SQL Server/MSDE proposes the extension .bak.

If you select the Backup Device option, you can select a given backup device, which can represent either a file or a tape. To define a new backup device, select New Backup Device from the combo box. The Backup Device Properties dialog box appears, as shown in Figure 21-5.

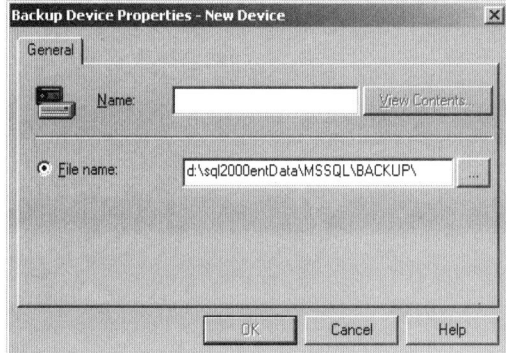

Figure 21-5   Defining a backup device

If your server has a tape drive, then the option to select a tape drive also appears in the dialog box.

Scheduled Backups

Backups are only effective if they are carried out fully and at regular intervals. You can use the Schedule section to define at which times and intervals the backups are to be performed (see Figure 21-6).

> **Note**   A scheduled backup only works if the SQL Server Agent service has been started. You can start the service using the Service Manager by selecting Start, then Programs, then Microsoft SQL Server, and then Service Manager and configure it so that the service is activated automatically when Windows starts.

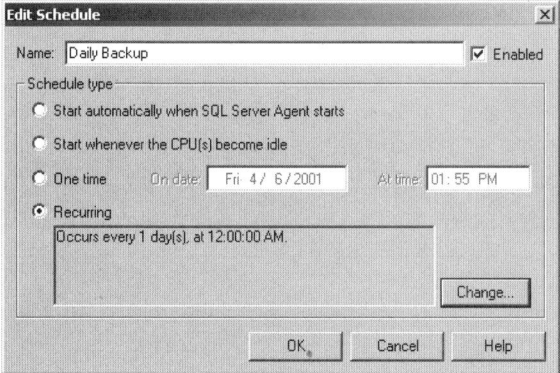

Figure 21-6   Defining a schedule

Backup Options

In the Options tab of the SQL Server Backup dialog box, displayed in Figure 21-7, you can define additional settings that refer mainly to backups to tape. You can assign media set names to backup tapes. Before the backup, the program checks whether the tape has been created with the correct name.

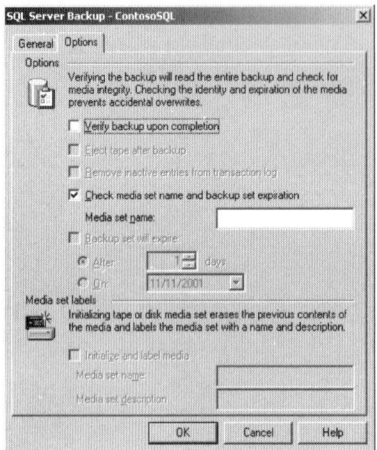

Figure 21-7 Configuring backup options

Performing the Backup

When you confirm the dialog box displayed in Figure 21-3, the backup is started. If you defined a schedule, the backup is carried out at the specified time. During the backup, users can continue to work with the database.

Backup Using SQL

You can also perform a backup using a stored procedure. Transact-SQL provides the *BACKUP* command with the following syntax:

```
BACKUP DATABASE { database_name }
TO < backup_device > [ ,...n ]
[ WITH
  [ DESCRIPTION = { 'text' } ]
  [ [ , ] NAME = { backup_set_name } ]
]
```

There are many other options that we have not specified, especially for tape drives.

Enter the database to be backed up as the *database_name*. For *backup_device* you can enter either the name of the predefined backup device (see Figure 21-7) or use the supplements *DISK=* or *TAPE=* to specify the name of a file or tape directly.

The following listing creates a procedure that saves the database *ContosoSQL* (data and log) to a file:

```
CREATE PROCEDURE spContosoBackup

AS

  SET NOCOUNT ON

  BACKUP DATABASE ContosoSQL TO DISK =

    'C:\mssql\backup\ContosoSQL.bak'

RETURN
```

Predefined Backup Devices

If you want to use a predefined backup device for the backup, then the *BACKUP* command becomes

```
BACKUP DATABASE ContosoSQL TO ContosoBackup
```

The backup device *ContosoBackup* used in this example can be defined using the following command:

```
sp_addumpdevice [@devtype =] 'device_type',

    [@logicalname =] 'logical_name',

    [@physicalname =] 'physical_name'

    [, { [@cntrltype =] controller_type | [@devstatus =]
    'device_status'}]
```

You can specify *DISK*, *TAPE*, or *PIPE* (for a named pipe connection) as the *device_type*. You can use *logical_name* to define the name of the backup device. In the preceding example, this is *ContosoBackup*. The *physical_name* is used to specify the name of the file to which the backup is to be saved. If you are saving to tape, then you could enter \\.**TAPE0**, for example, for the first tape drive on the server. The *controller_type* parameter is not currently used. The *device_status* can have the values *SKIP* or *NOSKIP*, which control whether tape names are read or not.

Furthermore, *sp_dropdevice* can be used to delete a defined backup device.

Backup Using SQL-DMO

Chapter 23, "The SQL-DMO Library," describes how to use the SQL-DMO Library. The library provides a *Backup* object that you can use to perform backups. The *Backup* object allows you to set all the same settings available in SQL Server Enterprise Manager.

As an example, we have created a form with which you can save the current database in a file, as shown in Figure 21-8. Enter the name of the backup file in the Backup File field in UNC notation as \\Computer\Share\Folder\File.

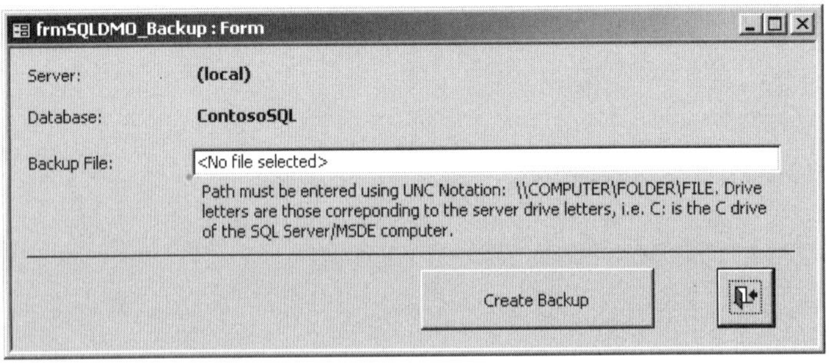

Figure 21-8   Form for data backup

If you enter only a filename rather than a path, the file is created in the default SQL Server installation folder \MSSQL7\Backup with SQL Server 7 or \Programs\Microsoft SQL Server\Backup with SQL Server 2000. If you use a drive letter for the data backup file path, this letter refers to the drives on the computer of the SQL Server/MSDE computer (therefore, C is the first drive on the corresponding computer).

The following listing belongs to this form:

```
Option Explicit
Option Compare Database


Const conNoFile = "<No file selected>"


Dim mdmoServer As SQLDMO.SQLServer
Dim mdmoDatabase As SQLDMO.Database


Private Sub Form_Load()
  Dim strServer As String
```

```
Dim s As String


Set mdmoServer = New SQLDMO.SQLServer
' Retrieve server
strServer = CurrentProject.Connection.Properties("Data Source")
' Windows- or SQL Server-security?
If CurrentProject.Connection.Properties("Integrated Security") = _
  "SSPI" Then
  mdmoServer.LoginSecure = True
  ' Connect to server
  mdmoServer.Connect strServer
Else
  Dim strUser As String
  Dim strPassword As String


  ' Retrieve user and password
  strUser = CurrentProject.Connection.Properties("User ID")
  strPassword = CurrentProject.Connection.Properties("Password")
  ' Connect to server
  mdmoServer.Connect strServer, strUser, strPassword
End If
' Show server name
lblServer.Caption = strServer


' Current database
s = CurrentProject.Connection.Properties("Initial Catalog")
lblDatabase.Caption = s
Set mdmoDatabase = mdmoServer.Databases(s)


' Initialize text control
```

```
      txtBackupFile = conNoFile


End Sub


Private Sub cmdClose_Click()
   DoCmd.Close
End Sub


Private Sub cmdBackup_Click()
   If txtBackupFile <> conNoFile Then
     DoCmd.Hourglass True
     ' Create backup
     BackupDatabase txtBackupFile
     DoCmd.Hourglass False
   End If
End Sub


Sub BackupDatabase(strDestinationPath As String)
   Dim dmoServer As SQLDMO.SQLServer
   Dim dmoBackup As SQLDMO.Backup


   On Error GoTo err_:
   Set dmoBackup = New SQLDMO.Backup
   dmoBackup.Database = Trim(CurrentProject.Connection.Properties
   "Initial Catalog"))
   dmoBackup.Files = strDestinationPath
   dmoBackup.SQLBackup mdmoServer


   MsgBox "Backup of database " & dmoBackup.Database & " to file " &
   dmoBackup.Files
```

```vba
    Exit Sub
err_:
  ErrorHandler
End Sub


Private Sub ErrorHandler()
  Dim errADO As ADODB.Error
  Dim strErr As String


  strErr = "VBA-error information" & vbNewLine & vbNewLine
  strErr = strErr & "Number: " & Err.Number & vbNewLine
  strErr = strErr & "Description: " & Err.Description & vbNewLine
  strErr = strErr & vbNewLine
  If CurrentProject.Connection.Errors.Count > 0 Then
    For Each errADO In CurrentProject.Connection.Errors
      strErr = strErr & vbNewLine & "ADO-error information (ADO V." & _
              CurrentProject.Connection.Version & ")" & _
              vbNewLine & vbNewLine

      strErr = strErr & "NativeError: " & errADO.NativeError & _
      vbNewLine
      strErr = strErr & "Number: " & errADO.Number & vbNewLine
      strErr = strErr & "Description: " & errADO.Description & _
      vbNewLine
      strErr = strErr & "Source: " & errADO.Source & vbNewLine
      strErr = strErr & "SQLState: " & errADO.SQLState & vbNewLine
      strErr = strErr & "Source: " & errADO.Source & vbNewLine
    Next
  End If
  MsgBox strErr
End Sub
```

Restoring Data

To reimport a backup, use the following restore procedures. To restore databases, you need the same authorizations as for the backup.

Restoring Data in Access Projects

To reimport a backup, activate the relevant function by selecting Tools, then Database Utilities, then Restore SQL Database. Remember that the function only works with SQL Server/MSDE if it is installed on the same computer as Microsoft Access. When you are importing the data backup, no other users can work on the database.

Using SQL Server Enterprise Manager

This section describes the most important settings and options available in Enterprise Manager for restoring databases.

To activate the data restore function, select the database to be restored from the left pane of the Enterprise Manager window. You can then either click Restore Database in the right pane, select Tools, then Restore Database from the menu, or select Restore Database from the database shortcut menu. This activates the Restore Database dialog box shown in Figure 21-9.

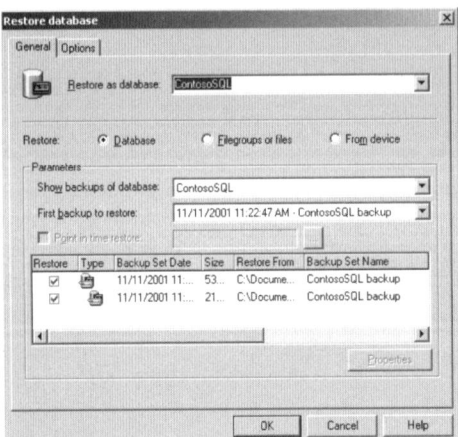

Figure 21-9   Restoring a database

In the Restore As Database combo box, enter the name of the database to be restored. If you specify a new database name, this database is created with the contents of the data backup. If you define an existing database as the target, then the backup must have been created from this database. In the Parameters section, you can use the Show Backups Of Database combo box to view the backups of the different databases. During restoration, the database and the backup must match; otherwise the warning message shown in Figure 21-10 appears.

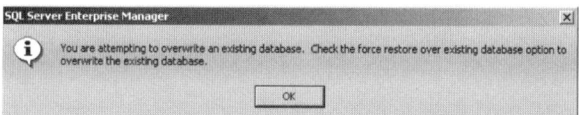

Figure 21-10   Warning message with existing databases

The backup information contained in the Restore Database dialog box displayed in Figure 21-9 is also copied by SQL Server/MSDE during every data backup. If you want to import a backup that has been created on a different server, for example, your server will have no information about this backup. In this case, you must select the From Device option and click Select Devices to select the relevant backup device (see Figure 21-11).

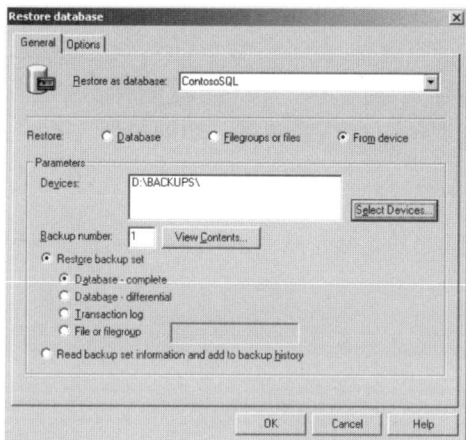

Figure 21-11   Selecting a backup device

Remember that every backup contains information about the path and name of the physical files in the database. During data restoration, the system attempts to re-create the files in the same place. You can change the path in the Options tab of the Restore Database dialog box (see Figure 21-12).

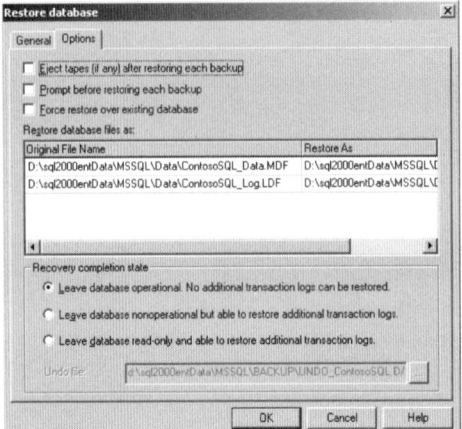

Figure 21-12   Data restoration options

Restoration Using SQL

Data restoration can be performed with the *RESTORE* SQL command. For the most important options, the syntax for the command is as follows:

```
RESTORE DATABASE { database_name }

[ FROM < backup_device > [ ,...n ] ]

[ WITH

  [ MOVE 'logical_file_name' TO 'operating_system_file_name' ]


     [ ,...n ]


  [ [ , ] REPLACE ]

]
```

The database that is currently linked to your Access project cannot now simply be reimported because a database that is being restored, including your Access project, cannot be accessed by any user.

The routine displayed in the following listing circumvents this problem by terminating the current connection and then sets up a connection to the *master* database to execute the *RESTORE* command. It then activates the original connection to the restored database. The routine takes on the name of the backup file.

```
Sub Restore(strBackupfile As String)

  Dim cnn As ADODB.Connection

  Dim strBaseConnection As String
```

```
        Dim strMasterConnection As String

        Dim strDatabase As String

        Dim strTmp As String

        Dim strUser As String

        Dim strPassword As String

        ' Save current connection string

        strBaseConnection = CurrentProject.BaseConnectionString

        ' Current database

        strDatabase = CurrentProject.Connection.Properties(
        "INITIAL CATALOG")

        ' Replace name of current database with MASTER

        strMasterConnection = Replace(strBaseConnection, _

                "INITIAL CATALOG=" & strDatabase, _

                "INITIAL CATALOG=Master")

    With CurrentProject

        If Not .Connection.Properties("Integrated Security") = "SSPI" Then

            ' Username and password

            strUser = .Connection.Properties("User Id")

            strPassword = .Connection.Properties("Password")

        End If

        ' Close connection to current database

        .CloseConnection

        ' New connection to database MASTER

        .OpenConnection strMasterConnection, strUser, strPassword

        ' Restore Backup

        .Connection.Execute _

            "RESTORE DATABASE " & strDatabase & _

            " FROM DISK = '" & strBackupfile & "'"

        ' Connection to restored database

        .OpenConnection strBaseConnection, strUser, strPassword

    End With

End Sub
```

You can use *BACKUP* and *RESTORE* to copy databases from one SQL Server/MSDE computer to another. Remember that the paths to the database files (.mdf/.ldf) are also included in the backup file. If you want to reimport a backup, but it cannot or must not be created in the same path, then you can use *MOVE* statements in the *RESTORE* command to specify where the files are to be stored. The *REPLACE* statement overwrites any existing database with the same name:

```
RESTORE DATABASE ContosoSQL
    FROM DISK='C:\mssql7\backup\ContosoSQL.dat'
WITH MOVE 'ContosoSQL_Data' TO
              'F:\data\Contoso_data.mdf',
    MOVE 'ContosoSQL_Log' TO
              'F:\data\Contoso_log.ldf',
    REPLACE
```

In a standard Access project you cannot determine which physical files are behind a database. If you are working with SQL Server Enterprise Manager, you can use the properties of a database to view a dialog box displaying the dates and log files. A database can be distributed over several data and log files, which can be stored on different drives.

You can use the stored procedure *sp_helpdb*, contained in the Microsoft *master* database, to view the details for a database. The procedure returns several resultsets, the second of which lists the names of the files. Access always displays the first resultset for a stored procedure. To receive the following resultsets, you must create Microsoft Visual Basic for Applications (VBA) programs as described in the following listing. The procedure *DatabaseFiles* outputs all filenames that are determined with the function *DatabaseFilename()*.

```
Function DatabaseFilename(strDB As String) As String()
' set up An Array of Strings, filename returned
    Dim rec As New ADODB.Recordset
    Dim rec2 As New ADODB.Recordset
    Dim strResult() As String
    Dim i As Integer
    ' Stored procedure returns two resultsets
    rec.Open "sp_helpdb '" & strDB & "'", CurrentProject.Connection
    ' Assign next recordset
    Set rec2 = rec.NextRecordset
```

```
    ReDim strResult(rec2.RecordCount)

    Do While Not rec2.EOF

        strResult(i) = rec2.Fields("filename").Value

        i = i + 1

        rec2.MoveNext

    Loop

    DatabaseFilename= strResult

End Function

Sub DatabaseFiles()

    Dim i As Integer

    Dim strResult() As String

    ' Fill field with database names

    strResult = DatabaseFilename("ContosoSQL")

    ' Show all database names

    For i = LBound(strResult) To UBound(strResult)

        Debug.Print strResult(i)

    Next

End Sub
```

Restoration Using SQL-DMO

You can also use the SQL-DMO library to reimport a data backup. The routine described in the following listing uses the data backup file transferred as a parameter to re-create the current database that is linked to the current Access project. Remember, just as for the previous example with the *RESTORE* command, the connection between the Access project and the database must be closed before the data is restored.

SQL DMO provides the *Restore* object for the restoration of backed up data:

```
Sub RestoreDatabase(strBackupFile As String)

' Current Database Project

    Dim dmoServer As SQLDMO.SQLServer

    Dim dmoRestore As SQLDMO.Restore

    Dim strBaseConnection As String

    Dim strUser As String
```

```
    Dim strPassword As String

    On Error GoTo err_:

    ' Retrieve current connection string

    strBaseConnection = CurrentProject.BaseConnectionString

    If Not _CurrentProject.Connection.Properties("Integrated Security")
    = "SSPI" Then

      ' User and password

      strUser = CurrentProject.Connection.Properties("User Id")

      strPassword = CurrentProject.Connection.Properties("Password")

    End If

    ' Current server

    Set dmoServer = New SQLDMO.SQLServer

    ConnectServer dmoServer

    Set dmoRestore = New SQLDMO.Restore

    ' Current database name

    dmoRestore.Database = _

        Trim(CurrentProject.Connection.Properties("Initial Catalog"))

        ' Backup file

    dmoRestore.Files = strBackupFile

    ' Close connection to current database

    CurrentProject.CloseConnection

    ' Execute restore

    dmoRestore.SQLRestore dmoServer

    ' Reconnect

    CurrentProject.OpenConnection strBaseConnection, strUser,
    strPassword

    MsgBox "Database '" & dmoRestore.Database & "' restored."

    Exit Sub

  err_:

    ErrorHandler

  End Sub
```

```vb
Private Sub ConnectServer(dmoServer As SQLDMO.SQLServer)
  Dim strServer As String
  On Error GoTo err_
  strServer = CurrentProject.Connection.Properties("Data Source")
  If CurrentProject.Connection.Properties("Integrated Security") = _
    "SSPI" Then
    dmoServer.LoginSecure = True
    dmoServer.Connect strServer
  Else
    Dim strUser As String
    Dim strPassword As String
    strUser = CurrentProject.Connection.Properties("User id")
    strPassword = CurrentProject.Connection.Properties("Password")
    dmoServer.Connect strServer, strUser, strPassword
  End If
  Exit Sub
err_:
  ErrorHandler
End Sub
```

22

Data Transformation Services

Data Transformation Services (DTS) is a comprehensive package for importing and exporting data. DTS allows transport of data between two data sources using open database connectivity (ODBC) or object linking and embedding database (OLE DB). It also allows the data to be converted and transformed during import or export. You can also use DTS packages to carry out complex, multilevel data transfers that can be started at specified points in time.

Microsoft SQL Server Enterprise Manager provides the DTS Editor, which you can use to create and process DTS packages. This feature is described later in this chapter.

Microsoft Data Engine (MSDE) includes only the DTS Import/Export Wizard. Retroactive processing of DTS packages created using the DTS Import/Export Wizard is only possible with Transact-SQL, system stored procedures, and SQL Distributed Management Objects (SQL-DMO) programming.

The DTS Wizard

To start the DTS Import/Export Wizard, select Start, then Microsoft SQL Server, then Import and Export Data, which activates the DTS Import/Export Wizard, click next, and the Choose A Data Source wizard screen appears, as shown in Figure 22-1. This is where you determine the data source by using the Source combo box to choose the required OLE DB, ODBC, or Indexed Sequential

Access Method (ISAM) driver. Depending on the source chosen, the corresponding fields in that group are displayed. The following example uses the *ContosoSQL* database on the local server.

> **More Info**   The DTS Import/Export Wizard can be activated through various context menus within the SQL Server Enterprise Manager console as Import Data or Export Data tasks.

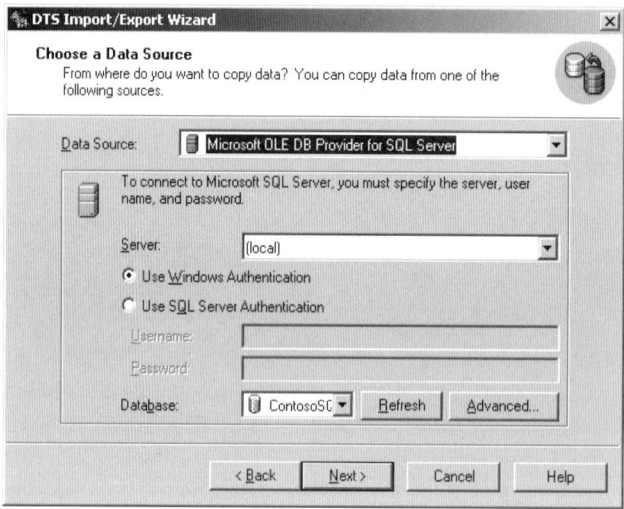

Figure 22-1   Selecting the data source

In the Choose A Destination wizard screen, shown in Figure 22-2, you define the destination. In this example, an Access mdb is to be created using the name CONTOSO.MDB. You use the Destination combo box to select the required OLE DB, ODBC, and ISAM driver from the list.

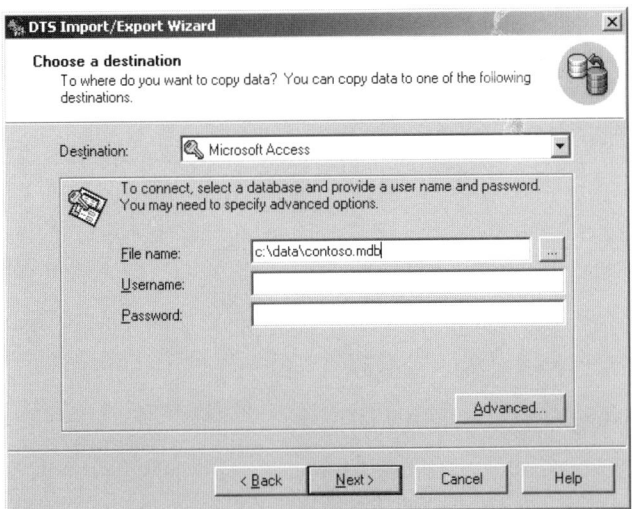

Figure 22-2   Selecting the destination

> **Note**   If you want to use DTS to transfer data between two SQL
> Server/MSDE-based databases, you must pay special attention to a
> peculiarity in Microsoft's licensing policy. If you want to transfer data
> between a SQL Server Desktop or an MSDE Edition from or to a non-
> Desktop SQL Server Edition (Standard, Enterprise, Small Business
> Server), then the license on the non-Desktop SQL Server must be
> defined as a Per Seat license, not as a Per Server license. Otherwise
> DTS will issue an error message.
>
> For the Per Seat configuration, all SQL Server users must have
> their own licenses. The licensing system is set up so that all users with
> a Per Seat license can install SQL Server Desktop Edition on their
> computers. The Desktop Edition comes as a component of one of the
> larger SQL Server versions and it cannot be purchased separately.

You use the next wizard screen, Specify Table Copy Or Query (see Figure 22-3) to define the type of transfer. Select the Copy Table(s) And View(s) From The Source Database option to define one or more tables to be transferred to the destination database.

Figure 22-3 Select what you want to transfer

The second option, Use A Query To Specify The Data To Transfer, allows you to create a query for the data to be transferred. The third option, Copy Objects And Data Between SQL Server Databases, is activated if SQL Server/MSDE is specified as both source and destination. This also allows the transfer of database objects such as views, stored procedures, and other SQL Server objects.

In this example, the first option is selected, activating the Select Source Tables And Views wizard screen, shown in Figure 22-4, in which you can select the tables to be transferred. The destination table can be an existing table, or you can create a new one.

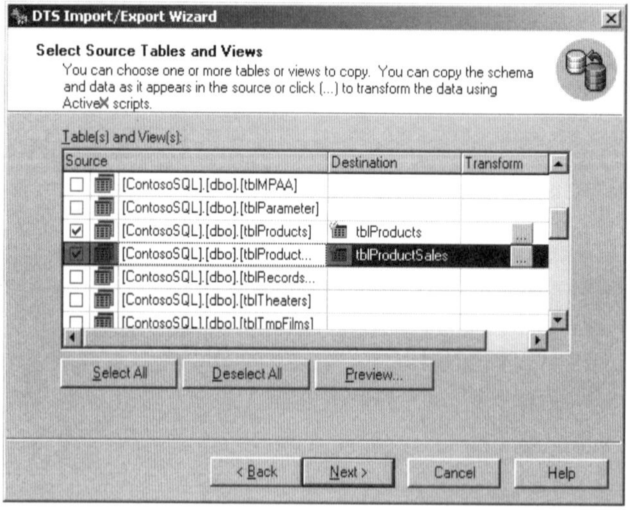

Figure 22-4 Selecting the source tables

In the *Transform* column, you can use the ellipses buttons (…) to bring up the Column Mappings And Transformations dialog box, shown in Figure 22-5, in which you can influence the manner of the transfer in detail.

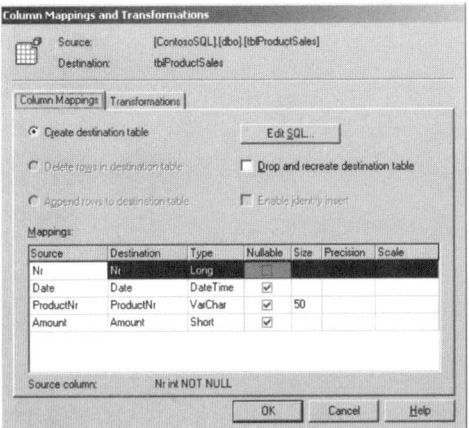

Figure 22-5   Column mappings and transformations

In this example, the Create Destination Table option is selected because the Microsoft Access destination databases have been re-created and are therefore empty. When you transfer the data to an existing table, you can determine whether the data for the destination table is deleted first and then replaced by the new data, or whether the new data is added to the existing data. It is also possible to completely delete the destination table and then re-create it.

Special Features of Identity and Timestamp Fields

You are provided with several options for transferring columns for which an identity is specified. If a new table is being created in the destination database, then the identity column there is created as a column without identity. If the data is being added to an existing table, then the default setting is for the identity column in the destination table to be write-protected. If you are using the *Activate IDENTITY_INSERT* option, you can also write data to the identity field. When the data is being inserted, the destination identity column is not counted, but the values of the source table are inserted.

Also, when transferring timestamp fields, you must bear in mind a series of special features (for further information on the *timestamp* data type, see the corresponding sections in Chapter 5, "Tables in Access Projects"). If you copy a table with a *timestamp* data type column to a new table, then the data type of the *timestamp* column will be created as *binary* (or a similar data type, depending on the destination database). If the destination table already exists, then the *timestamp* column cannot be changed.

Transformations

You can use the Transformations tab in the Column Mappings And Transformations dialog box, shown in Figure 22-6, to program additional data transformations during data transfer using an ActiveX script. DTS provides different script languages for the creation of ActiveX scripts like Microsoft JScript and Microsoft VBScript.

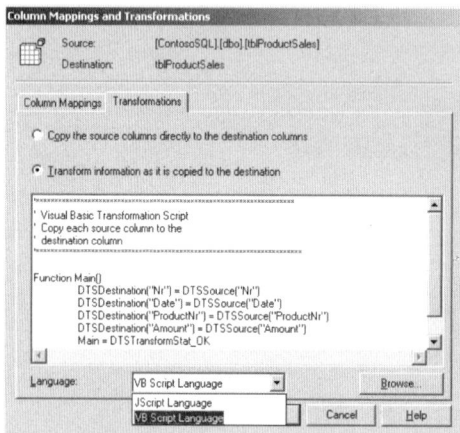

Figure 22-6   Transformation using script

The "Advanced Transformations" section of this chapter contains further information on using scripts for transformation.

You use the Save, Schedule, And Replicate Packge screen displayed by the wizard, and shown in Figure 22-7, to specify the time at which the DTS package is executed and to create a corresponding schedule, if necessary.

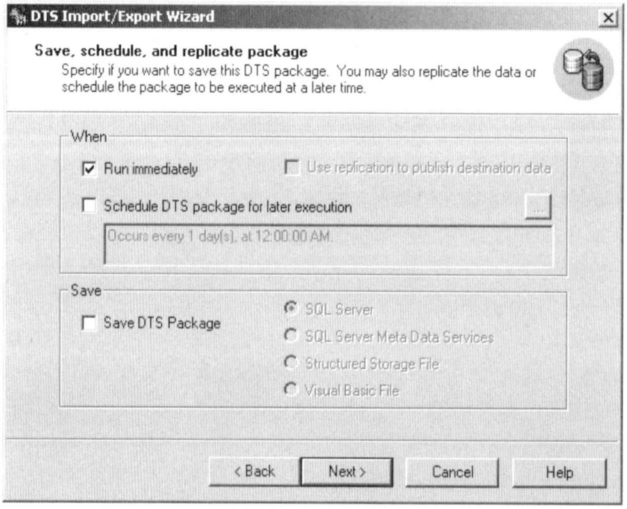

Figure 22-7   Execution time and saving

If you select the Save DTS Package check box, you can save the DTS package definition in the specified location. Microsoft SQL Server 2000 also provides the Visual Basic File option, which is used to create a Microsoft Visual Basic program that can be integrated with your Visual Basic programs.

DTS in Enterprise Manager

The DTS Wizard is provided with both SQL Server and MSDE. The Enterprise Manager in SQL Server also provides additional options for creating and processing DTS packages using the DTS Package component.

The next section describes how the DTS Package option can be used to create a DTS package that manipulates data in the *tblProductSales* table and exports it to an Access database.

DTS Package

DTS Package, displayed in Figure 22-8, is launched in SQL Server Enterprise Manager from the branch of the active SQL Server by right-clicking Data Transformation Services, then New Package.

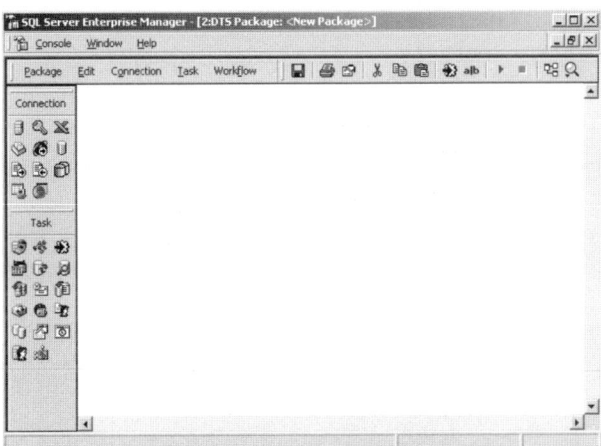

Figure 22-8   DTS Package designer window

To transfer data, DTS Package needs at least three pieces of information:

■   The data source (in this case, the SQL Server database *ContosoSQL*)

■   The data destination (in this case, an initially empty Access database PRODUCTSSALES.MDB)

■   The data to be transferred

Determining the Data Source

From the toolbar, drag the Microsoft OLE DB Provider For SQL Server (SQL Server) icon from the Connections tab into the work area. The Connection Properties dialog box opens, containing the connection properties (see Figure 22-9). In the New Connection field, enter a name you might want to call the connection, for example, **ContosoSQL**. From Data Source option, make sure that **Microsoft OLE DB Provider For SQL Server** is selected. Then choose the database *ContosoSQL* from the Database combo box after you specify the server and the authentication method.

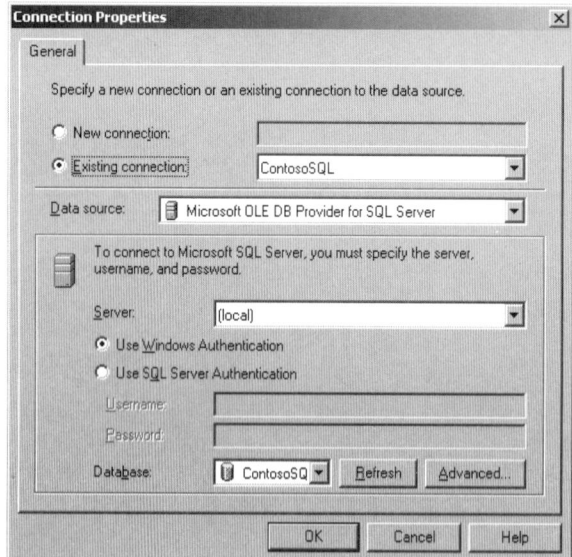

Figure 22-9 Determining the data source

When you click OK, the system displays the new ContosoSQL data source in the form of an icon in the DTS Package work area.

Determining the Data Destination

Next, you create the data destination. Create an empty Access database with the name PRODUCTSALES.MDB. Drag the Microsoft Access icon from the Connection toolbar into the work area. The Connection Properties dialog box opens again, as shown in Figure 22-10.

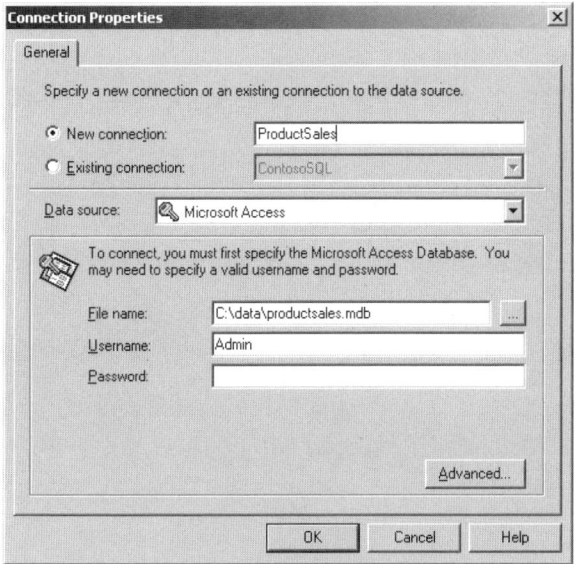

Figure 22-10   Determining the data destination

In the New Connection field, enter **ProductSales**. In the File Name text box, specify the path and the name of the Access database you just created, or select it using the ellipses button (…).

Determining the Data Transformation

Click and drag the mouse to draw a rectangle around the two connection icons. When both icons are selected, click the Transform Data Task (yellow cog) icon in the Task toolbar. DTS Package draws an arrow between the data source and the data destination and then creates a Transform Data Task.

In the Transform Data Task, you define the data transfer and possibly also data processing. Double-click the gray arrow. The Transform Data Task Properties dialog box appears, containing the data transformation properties. The Source, Destination, and Transformations tabs must be processed in that order. Use the Lookups tab to retrieve data from other connections.

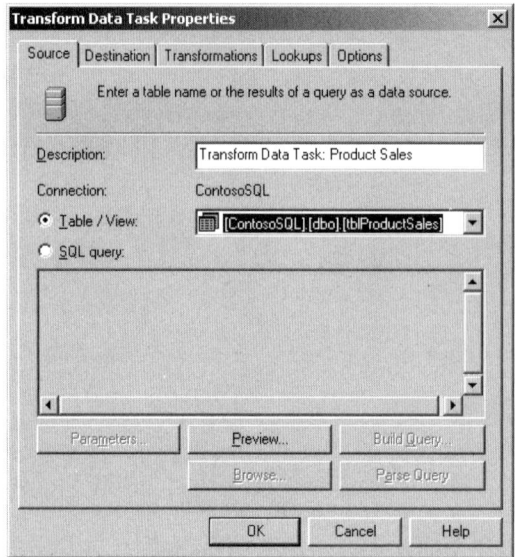

Figure 22-11   Transform Data Task between source and destination

In the example, the articles stored in table *tblProductSales* need to be transferred to the Access database *PRODUCTSALES.MDB*. The table in the Access database is to be used to determine which single product has sold the best for each individual day and how much money was made.

First, define the data transformation in Transform Data Task: ProductSales. There are several options for actual data selection:

■   You can select the Table/View option to select the data source from the combo box for a table or to select a query as the data source.

■   In the SQL Query text box, you can type a SQL command directly.

When creating the SQL query, you can click Build Query to open the Data Transformation Services Query Designer, which is similar to the other designers in SQL Server Enterprise Manager or Access. It facilitates interactive creation of a SQL query. Figure 22-12 displays a query that has been generated for our example.

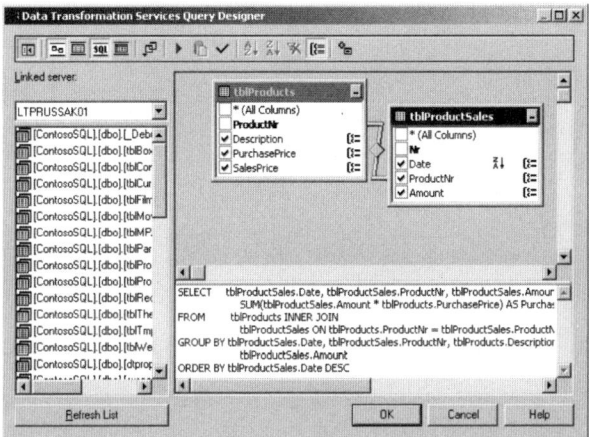

Figure 22-12   Creating the query in DTS Query Designer

The full text of the SQL query is as follows:

```
SELECT
  tblProductSales.Date,
  tblProductSales.ProductNr,
  tblProductSales.Amount,
  tblProducts.Description,
  tblProducts.PurchasePrice,
  tblProducts.SalesPrice,
  SUM(tblProductSales.Amount * tblProducts.PurchasePrice) AS Purchase,
  SUM(tblProductSales.Amount * tblProducts.SalesPrice) AS Sale
FROM tblProducts INNER JOIN tblProductSales
  ON tblProducts.ProductNr = tblProductSales.ProductNr
GROUP BY
  tblProductSales.Date,
  tblProductSales.ProductNr,
  tblProducts.Description,
  tblProducts.PurchasePrice,
  tblProducts.SalesPrice,
  tblProductSales.Amount
ORDER By
  tblProductSales.Date desc
```

If the result of the query is as you expected, then you can proceed to the next step. To do this, click the Destination tab. If there are no tables in the destination database, then the Create Destination Table dialog box appears immediately (see Figure 22-13). Otherwise, you can select an existing table from a combo box, or you can call the Create Destination Table dialog box by clicking Create.

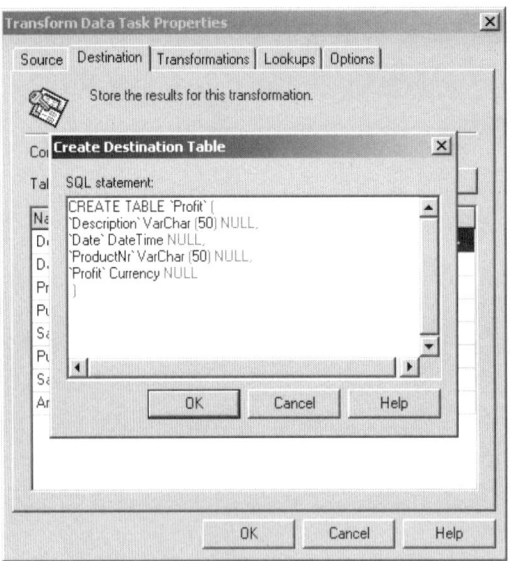

Figure 22-13 SQL definition of the destination table

The SQL command for creating the new table is displayed automatically, but you can edit the statement. Instead of `New Table` type **Profit**. Delete the columns *Purchase*, *Sale*, and *PurchasePrice*, and add the column `Profit` *Currency NULL*. This is where the calculated earnings will be saved. If you want to change the default data types for the columns, do so now. Later on, it will not be possible to change this setting without re-creating the table.

> **Note** Remember that the delimiter of the field names is an accent (`), and not a single quotation mark.

Advanced Transformations
Now click the Transformations tab. As you can see in Figure 22-14, the source fields are displayed on the left and the destination fields are displayed on the right. The lines between the fields represent the mappings for transferring the data.

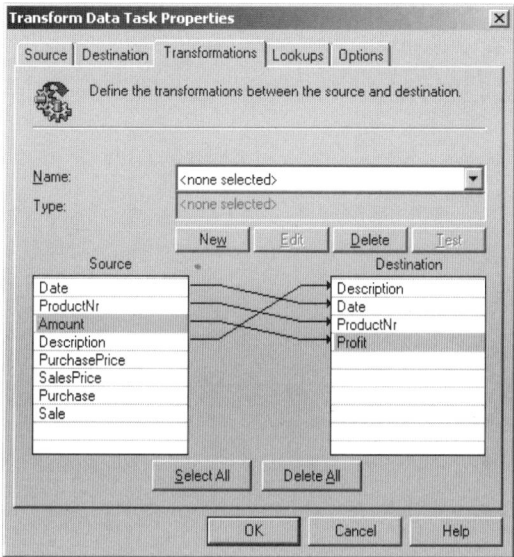

Figure 22-14   Transformations tab

The mapping between Amount and Profit does not, of course, make much sense. You will now learn how to use an ActiveX script to set up the mapping to Profit.

First, delete the connecting line between Amount and Profit. Select the connecting line and click Delete. Next, select Purchase and Sale on the left and Profit on the right by clicking while holding down the Ctrl key. The fields are now highlighted in gray. Click New.

In the Create New Transformation dialog box, shown in Figure 22-15, select ActiveX-Script and click OK.

Figure 22-15   Create new transformation

The Transformation Objects dialog box, displayed in Figure 22-16, shows the transformation options.

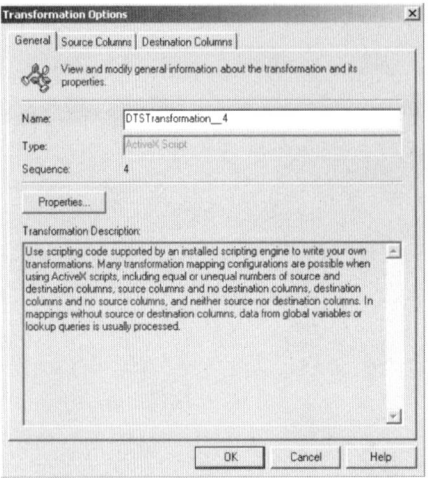

Figure 22-16   SQL definition of the destination table

Click Properties to show the ActiveX Script Transformation Properties dialog box, shown in Figure 22-17. Transformation scripts can be created in different programming languages: JScript, VBScript, Perl Script (if installed), or other scripting languages. The default is VBScript. Click Auto Gen. to re-create the script.

Figure 22-17   Transformations

The Profit is then determined from Sales − Purchase, so modify the script to read as follows:

```
Function Main()
  DTSDestination("Profit") = DTSSource("Sale") - DTSSource("Purchase")
  Main = DTSTransformStat_OK
End Function
```

You can click Parse to check whether your script is syntactically correct. Click Test to check whether your script works.

We are aware that the underlying query could also have been used to calculate earnings, but we wanted to keep the example for an ActiveX transformation as simple as possible. We have used ActiveX scripts for complex formatting of destination columns or to propose values in other tables on the basis of certain conditions because ActiveX Directory Objects (ADO) database accesses are also possible in ActiveX scripts.

The Transform Data Task Properties dialog box, displayed in Figure 22-18, shows the new transformation line.

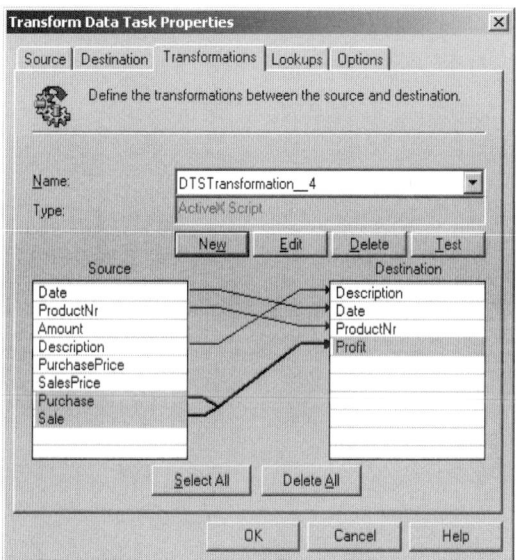

Figure 22-18   Visual Basic transformation script

In the Lookups tab, shown in Figure 22-19, you can define values to be retrieved from additional connections.

Figure 22-19 New transformation line

All required settings for the package have now been assigned. You can use the options in the Options tab, shown in Figure 22-20, to determine, for example, how many errors are allowed during the transfer due to incorrect data (Max Error Count), in which file the errors are to be logged (Name), whether *Null* values are transferred (Keep NULL Values), and whether destination table constraints are considered (Check Constraints).

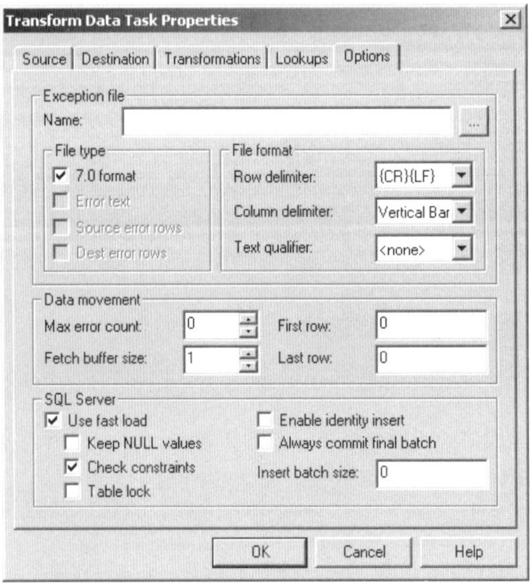

Figure 22-20 Advanced options

Starting the Transformation

After the data pump properties have been determined, you can select Package, then Execute to start the transformation, displayed in the Executing Package dialog box (see Figure 22-21).

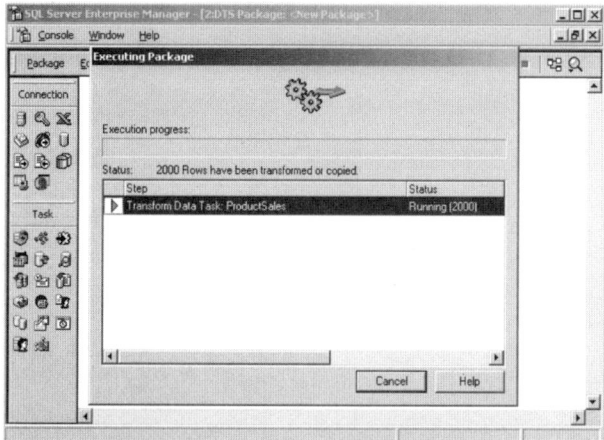

Figure 22-21   Executing the transformation

Saving the Package

DTS Package Designer had some stability issues in SQL 7 that have been fixed in SQL 2000. In any case, it is always smart to save a newly created package as soon as possible. Select Package, then Save As to open the Save DTS Package dialog box, shown in Figure 22-22. Enter a name for the package in the Package Name field. You can save the package on the SQL server or as a file. You can also save to another SQL server on the network.

> **Note**   If you save the package to another computer, a user account must exist for your user on that computer, or it will not be possible to execute it on the destination computer!

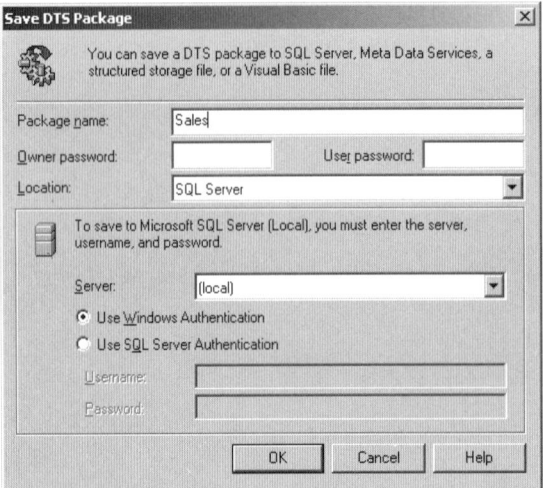

Figure 22-22 Saving the package

Note Remember that when you resave a DTS Package on the SQL server after making changes to it, the existing package is not replaced by the new one with the same name; rather the package is saved as a new version. If, in the Enterprise Manager, you select the name of a DTS package by right-clicking it and then select Versions from the shortcut menu, a dialog box appears, displaying all versions of that package. You can edit or delete old versions.

Executing the Package

To open a stored package, go to the branch of the active SQL server in the SQL Server Enterprise Manager and navigate to the saved package through by selecting Data Transformation Services, then Local Packages, then Sales, and then Execute Package.

On the same menu, you can select Schedule Package to specify regular times at which the package can be executed. The date specified creates a task in SQL Server Agent, which can only be changed there.

Executing Packages Step by Step

A package can include several steps that are executed depending on the success of the preceding step.

In this example, we assume that the product sales table is re-created every day. On completion, an e-mail is to be sent to the system administrator, containing either a success message or a warning if an error has occurred.

Open the *Sales* package, then click the Send Mail Task icon in the Task toolbar to call the Send Mail Task Properties dialog box, as seen in Figure 22-23.

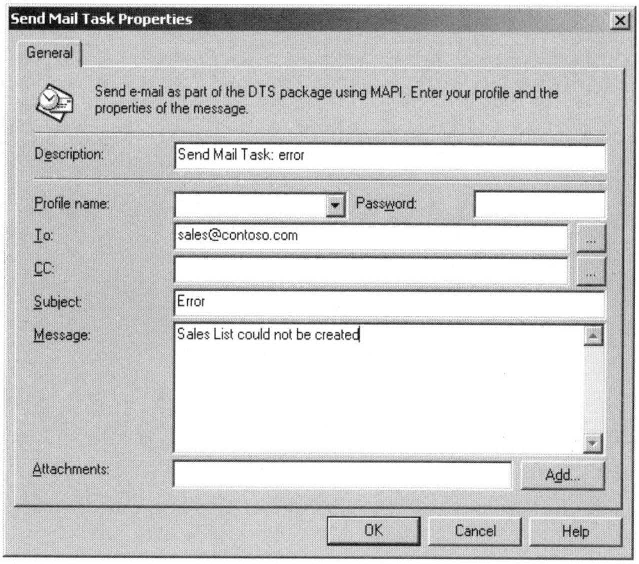

Figure 22-23   Sending e-mail

Specify a recipient, a subject, and a message. Create another e-mail for a success notification message. Next, hold down the Ctrl key and select first the icon for the destination of transformation *ProductSales* and then the new e-mail icon specified for an error message. On the Workflow menu, select On Failure. The *ProductSales* and *Send Mail Task: Error* icons are now connected with a red and white arrow, as shown in Figure 22-24.

Note   In order for the Send Mail task to work, you must configure the SQL Server Agent Mail Profile.

To set the mail profile for SQL Server Agent, expand a server group, and then expand a server. Expand Management, right-click SQL Server Agent, and then click Properties. Under Mail session, select a profile in the Mail profile box. If no profiles are listed, enter the name of the profile to use.

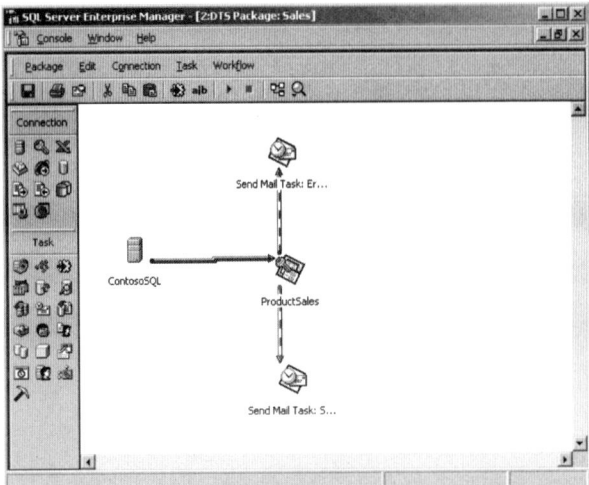

Figure 22-24 E-mails confirming success and failure

Repeat the process for the other e-mail message and select Workflow, then On Success. The *ProductSales* and *Send Mail Task: Success* icons are now connected with a green and white arrow.

You can connect any number of steps. Pay attention to the sequence in which you select objects, as this determines the direction of the workflow arrows.

23

The SQL-DMO Library

Microsoft uses the SQL Distributed Management Objects (SQL-DMO) library to administer Microsoft SQL Server/MSDE. The library provides a program interface to all SQL Server/MSDE functions and components that you can use from your programs.

The default SQL Server/MSDE installation includes SQL-DMO. If you want to use the library on any client of your choice, it must be installed and registered on that client. You can do this in a few small steps, which we describe at the end of this chapter.

To execute the examples in this chapter, you must set up a reference to the library in the corresponding .adp file. Activate the Microsoft Visual Basic editor and select Tools, then References. Select Microsoft SQLDMO Object Library from the list of options.

Object Model

The SQL-DMO library's object model, shown in Figure 23-1, contains all SQL Server/MSDE objects. SQL Server 2000/MSDE 2000 SQL-DMO library is more comprehensive than the library distributed with SQL Server 7/MSDE.

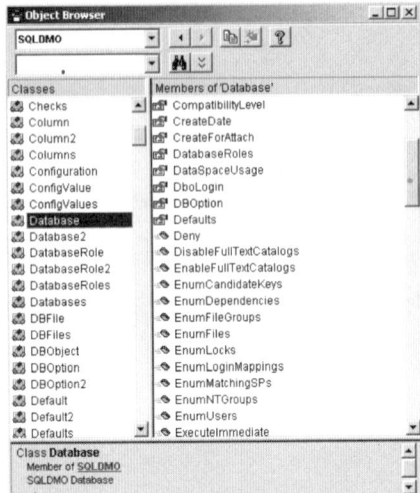

Figure 23-1 SQL-DMO object model

You can use the Microsoft Visual Basic for Application (VBA) editor's object catalog to look up the different collections, objects, methods, and properties.

In this chapter, we are using the object *SQLServer*, which is the root object in the hierarchy and contains basic data for a given server. The *SQLServer* object's *Databases* collection returns an object for every database created on SQL Server/MSDE. Use the *Database* object to access tables (*Tables*), views (*Views*), and other elements.

The following sections provide you with a few examples of the SQL-DMO object use.

Information About a Database

The following routine, *ServerInformation*, opens a message box that displays information about the server to which the current Access project is connected. The object's extended property provides you with the information about the linked server and information about users (*User ID*), passwords (*Password*), or use of the integrated Windows security (*Integrated Security*).

```
Sub ServerInformation()

    Dim dmoDB As SQLDMO.Database

    Dim dmoServer As SQLDMO.SQLServer

    Dim strServer As String

    Dim s As String
```

```
Dim strTmp As String


Set dmoServer = New SQLDMO.SQLServer
' Retrieve current server
strServer = CurrentProject.Connection.Properties("Data Source")
' Windows- or SQL Server-security?
If CurrentProject.Connection.Properties("Integrated Security") _
                                            = "SSPI" Then
    dmoServer.LoginSecure = True
    ' Connect to server
    dmoServer.Connect strServer
Else
    Dim strUser As String
    Dim strPassword As String
    strUser = CurrentProject.Connection.Properties("User id")
    strPassword = CurrentProject.Connection.Properties("Password")
    ' Connect to server
    dmoServer.Connect strServer, strUser, strPassword
End If
' Retrieve versions data
s = dmoServer.VersionString & vbNewLine
' For all databases
s = s & "Database" & String(30 - Len("Database"), " ") _
            & vbTab _
            & "Size" _
            & vbTab _
            & "Space available " _
            & vbNewLine
For Each dmoDB In dmoServer.Databases
    'Name, size and space available
```

```
        s = s & dmoDB.Name & String(30 - Len(dmoDB.Name), " ") _
            & vbTab _
            & Format(dmoDB.Size, "#,##0.00") _
            & vbTab _
            & Format(dmoDB.SpaceAvailableInMB, "#,##0.00") _
            & vbNewLine

    Next
    ' Display the Information
    MsgBox s, vbOKOnly, strServer


    Set dmoServer = Nothing
End Sub
```

When compiling information about the server's databases, the system uses the *SQLDMO.SQLServer* object's *Databases* collection.

Generating Scripts

When you are using SQL Server/MSDE, views and stored procedures are frequently transferred from the development server to the production server, or you must create new tables, triggers, or constraints on the production server. Because the development server and production server are usually not connected to the same network, the simplest transmission method is the creation and import of SQL scripts. A SQL script lists all the SQL commands needed to create a table, view, and so forth.

The SQL Server Enterprise Manager provides you with the option to create corresponding SQL scripts for all the objects in a database. The newly created script is a simple text file that can be imported to another SQL Server/MSDE. You can use the SQL Server Query Analyzer or the command prompt-based OSQL for this purpose. If you are using MSDE only, you cannot use these options for generating and executing SQL scripts.

The form *frmSQLDMO_GenerateScripts* uses SQL-DMO library objects and methods to display the objects (tables, triggers, views, and stored procedures) that are currently connected to the .adp file (see Figure 23-2).

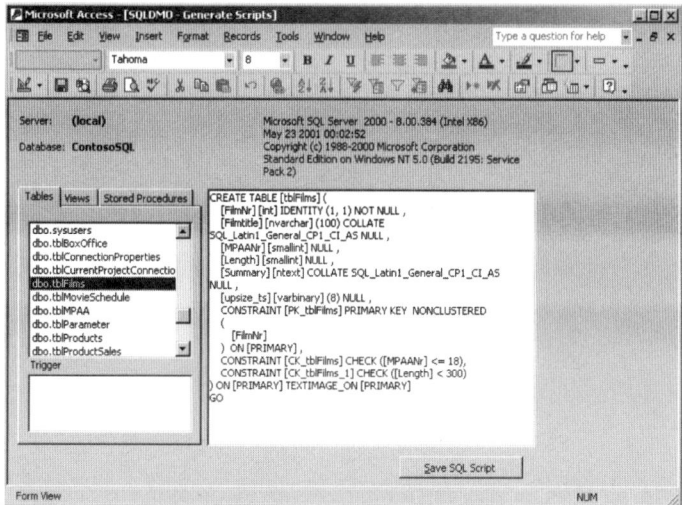

Figure 23-2   *frmSQLDMO_GenerateScripts* form

If you select the desired tab on the left and then click an object name, the text box on the right displays the associated SQL text. The Tables tab has a special feature: If you select a table, the system not only shows the SQL text, but the list box below the tables also displays the triggers defined for the selected table. If you click a trigger name, the SQL text appears.

The list boxes for the objects of the tab control element's individual tabs in the left half of the form are all defined with the Value List option entered as the Origin Type. When you open the form for all list boxes, the routine *Form_Load* uses the corresponding SQL-DMO commands to assemble a string with entries that are separated by semicolons. The system assigns this string to the *Row Source* of the respective list box.

One event routine named *OnClick* is defined for every list box. This routine uses the *Script* method to create the SQL code for the selected object and displays the code in the text box. The *Script* method is defined for all database objects. You can edit the script generated with *Script* in the text, and then click Save SQL Script to save it.

```
Option Compare Database

Option Explicit


Dim mdmoServer As SQLDMO.SQLServer

Dim mdmoDatabase As SQLDMO.Database
```

```
Private Sub Form_Load()
    Dim dmoProc As SQLDMO.StoredProcedure
    Dim dmoView As SQLDMO.view
    Dim dmoTable As SQLDMO.Table
    Dim dmoTrigger As SQLDMO.Trigger
    Dim strServer As String
    Dim s As String


    txtScript = ""


    Set mdmoServer = New SQLDMO.SQLServer
    ' Retrieve current server
    strServer = CurrentProject.Connection.Properties("Data Source")
    ' Windows- or SQL Server-Security?
    If CurrentProject.Connection.Properties("Integrated Security") _
                                        = "SSPI" Then
        mdmoServer.LoginSecure = True
        ' Connect to server
        mdmoServer.Connect strServer
    Else
        Dim strUser As String
        Dim strPassword As String


        strUser = CurrentProject.Connection.Properties("User ID")
        strPassword = CurrentProject.Connection.Properties("Password")
        ' Connect to server
        mdmoServer.Connect strServer, strUser, strPassword
    End If
    lblServer.Caption = strServer
    ' Retrieve version information
```

```
' and remove returns/tabs
s = Replace(mdmoServer.VersionString, Chr(10), " ")
s = Replace(s, vbTab, vbNewLine)
lblServerVersion.Caption = s


' Retrieve current database
s = CurrentProject.Connection.Properties("Initial Catalog")
lblDatabase.Caption = s
Set mdmoDatabase = mdmoServer.Databases(s)


' Tables
s = ""
For Each dmoTable In mdmoDatabase.Tables
    s = s & dmoTable.Owner & "." & dmoTable.Name & ";"
Next
lstTables.RowSource = s
' Views
s = ""
For Each dmoView In mdmoDatabase.Views
    s = s & dmoView.Owner & "." & dmoView.Name & ";"
Next
lstViews.RowSource = s
' Stored procedures
s = ""
For Each dmoProc In mdmoDatabase.StoredProcedures
    s = s & dmoProc.Owner & "." & dmoProc.Name & ";"
Next
lstProcs.RowSource = s
End Sub
```

```vb
Private Sub lstProcs_Click()
    Dim dmoProc As SQLDMO.StoredProcedure


    Set dmoProc = mdmoDatabase.StoredProcedures(lstProcs.Value)
    txtScript = Replace(dmoProc.Script, vbTab, "    ")
End Sub


Private Sub lstTables_Click()
    Dim dmoTable As SQLDMO.Table
    Dim dmoTrigger As SQLDMO.Trigger
    Dim s As String


    Set dmoTable = mdmoDatabase.Tables(lstTables.Value)
    txtScript = Replace(dmoTable.Script, vbTab, "    ")
    ' Trigger
    For Each dmoTrigger In dmoTable.Triggers
        s = s & dmoTrigger.Name & ";"
    Next
    lstTriggers.RowSource = s
End Sub


Private Sub lstTriggers_Click()
    Dim dmoTrigger As SQLDMO.Trigger


    Set dmoTrigger = _
        mdmoDatabase.Tables(lstTables.Value).Triggers( _
        lstTriggers.Value)
    txtScript = Replace(dmoTrigger.Script, vbTab, "    ")
End Sub
```

```vb
Private Sub lstViews_Click()
    Dim dmoView As SQLDMO.view


    Set dmoView = mdmoDatabase.Views(lstViews.Value)
    txtScript = Replace(dmoView.Script, vbTab, "    ")
End Sub
Private Sub cmdSaveScript_Click()
    Dim strFilter As String
    Dim strRet As String
    ' Open file dialog
    strFilter = "*.sql|SQL Script (*.sql)|*.*|All Files (*.*)"
    strRet = ChooseFile(Me.Hwnd, _
                    "Save script", _
                    "&Save", _
                    strFilter, _
                    "script.sql", _
                    "c:\", _
                    1, False)
    ' if is not empty
    If Len(strRet) <> 0 Then
        Dim f As FileSystemObject
        Dim ts As TextStream


        ' Create new file
        Set f = New FileSystemObject
        Set ts = f.CreateTextFile(strRet, True)
        ts.WriteLine txtScript.Value
        ts.Close
        Set f = Nothing
    End If
End Sub
```

Clicking Save SQL Script activates the *cmdSaveScript_Click* routine, which uses objects and methods from the Microsoft Scripting Runtime library to save the SQL script as a text file. The library's File System Object (FSO) advantage is that it takes only one command to write the entire text box to a file without having to use the somewhat obsolete VBA commands for writing text files. By default, the Microsoft Scripting Runtime library is included with newer versions of Microsoft Windows. The Microsoft Scripting Runtime is included as a reference in the project.

Use the *ChooseFile* function to select the filename and path name. This function is defined in the VBA module *basFileOpen*. The *ChooseFile* function uses one of the Access library's internal functions to activate the Windows general file dialog box that makes it easy to select folders and filenames.

> **Note**   You can also use the stored system procedure *sp_helptext* to output the script on which a SQL Server/MSDE database object is based. The system passes the name of an object to this procedure.

A Script for All Database Objects

The form *frmSQLDMO_GenerateAllScripts,* shown in Figure 23-3, is an extension of the form described earlier. Here the system does not display and save the scripts of individual objects, but instead creates a script for all database objects. This process also includes the database object's rules (*Rules*), defaults (*Defaults*), user-defined data types (*UserDefinedDatatypes*), and so on.

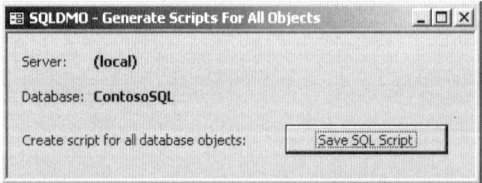

Figure 23-3   *frmSQLDMO_GenerateAllScripts* form

The following listing shows the routine the script creates. In the process, the *Script* method is applied to the respective objects and for every *Script* command the name of the file to which the script will be written is specified. The value *intScriptingOptions* is passed to the *Script* method as well. This value contains predefined constants that are linked with *Or* in a bit-wise manner. The constants control the format in which the script will be generated. Table 23-1 lists a selection of key constants within the *SQLDMO_SCRIPT_TYPE* enumeration. The SQL-DMO version installed with SQL Server 2000 contains additional constants within the *SQLDMO_SCRIPT2_TYPE* enumeration. Both enumerations are further documented in SQL Server Books Online.

Table 23-1   Script Constants

Constant	Description
SQLDMOScript_AppendToFile	Appends script output to an existing file.
SQLDMOScript_Bindings	Generates the commands *sp_bindefault* and *sp_bindrule.*
SQLDMOScript_ClusteredIndexes	Generates clustered indexes within the script.
SQLDMOScript_DatabasePermissions	Outputs all permissions as well.
SQLDMOScript_Default	Corresponds to *SQLDMOScript_PrimaryObject.*
SQLDMOScript_DRI_All	Corresponds to linking all *SQLDMOScript_DRI_* constants with *Or.*
SQLDMOScript_DRI_AllConstraints	Corresponds to linking *SQLDMOScript_DRI_Checks*, *SQLDMOScript_DRI_Defaults*, *SQLDMOScript_DRI_ForeignKeys*, *SQLDMOScript_DRI_PrimaryKey*, and *SQLDMOScript_DRI_UniqueKeys* with *Or.*
SQLDMOScript_DRI_AllKeys	Corresponds to linking *SQLDMOScript_DRI_ForeignKeys*, *SQLDMOScript_DRI_PrimaryKey*, and *SQLDMOScript_DRI_UniqueKeys* with *Or.*
SQLDMOScript_DRI_Checks	Generates all check constraints for tables.
SQLDMOScript_DRI_Clustered	Generates all clustered indexes for tables.
SQLDMOScript_DRI_Defaults	Generates all column default values for tables.
SQLDMOScript_DRI_ForeignKeys	Generates all foreign key relationships for tables.
SQLDMOScript_DRI_NonClustered	Generates all nonclustered indexes for tables.
SQLDMOScript_DRI_PrimaryKey	Generates all foreign key constraints for tables.
SQLDMOScript_DRI_UniqueKeys	Generates all unique key constraints for tables.

continued

Table 23-1 Script Constants *(continued)*

Constant	Description
SQLDMOScript_DRIIndexes	Generates all indexes for tables.
SQLDMOScript_DRIWithNoCheck	Generates all constraints for tables without checking existing data.
SQLDMOScript_Drops	Inserts a *DROP* command for every object, so that you can first delete the object and then create it. Be careful when working with *Table* objects, because the *DROP* command deletes the table's content.
SQLDMOScript_IncludeHeaders	Inserts a comment with the date of creation, and so forth.
SQLDMOScript_IncludeIfNotExists	Inserts a check for the object's existence. As a result, the object can be created only if it does not yet exist.
SQLDMOScript_Indexes	*SQLDMOScript_ClusteredIndexes*, *SQLDMOScript_NonClusteredIndexes*, and *SQLDMOScript_DRIIndexes* combined using an OR logical operator
SQLDMOScript_NoCommandTerm	The SQL commands are not separated from each other by a special password. The default password is *GO*.
SQLDMOScript_NoIdentity	Do not include definition of identity property, seed, and increment.
SQLDMOScript_ObjectPermissions	Outputs all object permissions as well.
SQLDMOScript_OwnerQualify	Outputs the owners for all objects as well.
SQLDMOScript_Permissions	Corresponds to the following: *SQLDMOScript_ObjectPermissions* or *SQLDMOScript_DatabasePermissions*
SQLDMOScript_PrimaryObject	This is the default setting for creating all objects.
SQLDMOScript_TimestampToBinary	Causes *timestamp* fields to be created in *binary(8)* format.
SQLDMOScript_ToFileOnly	Writes the script to a file only. The *Script* method then returns an empty string.
SQLDMOScript_Triggers	Generates Transact-SQL defining triggers.
SQLDMOScript_UseQuotedIdentifiers	Causes the object identifier to be enclosed in quotation marks.

All other parts of the form's program correspond to those of the form *frmSQLDMO_GenerateScripts* described previously.

```
Sub ScriptDB(strPath As String)
    Dim intScriptingOptions As Long
    intScriptingOptions = _
                    SQLDMOScript_Drops Or _
                    SQLDMOScript_Bindings Or _
                    SQLDMOScript_IncludeHeaders Or _
                    SQLDMOScript_Default Or _
                    SQLDMOScript_AppendToFile
    ' Script User Defined Data Types
    Dim dmoUserdef As SQLDMO.UserDefinedDatatype
    For Each dmoUserdef In mdmoDatabase.UserDefinedDatatypes
        dmoUserdef.Script intScriptingOptions, strPath
    Next
    ' Script Tables and Triggers, ignoring system
    ' tables and system generated triggers
    Dim dmoTable As SQLDMO.Table
    Dim dmoTrigger As SQLDMO.Trigger
    For Each dmoTable In mdmoDatabase.Tables
        If Not dmoTable.SystemObject Then
            dmoTable.Script intScriptingOptions, strPath
            For Each dmoTrigger In dmoTable.Triggers
                If Not dmoTrigger.SystemObject Then
                    dmoTrigger.Script intScriptingOptions, strPath
                End If
            Next
        End If
    Next
```

```
    ' Script Rules
    Dim dmoRule As SQLDMO.Rule
    For Each dmoRule In mdmoDatabase.Rules
        dmoRule.Script intScriptingOptions, strPath
    Next


    ' Script Defaults
    Dim dmoDefault As SQLDMO.Default
    For Each dmoDefault In mdmoDatabase.Defaults
        dmoDefault.Script intScriptingOptions, strPath
    Next


    ' Script Stored Procedures, ignoring system sprocs
    Dim dmoSP As SQLDMO.StoredProcedure
    For Each dmoSP In mdmoDatabase.StoredProcedures
        If Not dmoSP.SystemObject Then
            dmoSP.Script intScriptingOptions, strPath
        End If
    Next


    ' Script Views, ignoring system views and informational schemas
    Dim dmoView As SQLDMO.view
    For Each dmoView In mdmoDatabase.Views
        If Not dmoView.SystemObject Then
            dmoView.Script intScriptingOptions, strPath
        End If
    Next


End Sub
```

> **Note**   The preceding routine does not output the scripts for the new objects of Microsoft SQL Server 2000, such as user-defined functions (UDF), and so on. To include these objects in the script, you must use the SQL-DMO library delivered with SQL Server 2000. This library includes a new object (*Database2*) for accessing SQL Server 2000 databases that support the new objects and new constants within the *SQLDMO_SCRIPT2_TYPE* enumeration.

Executing Stored Scripts

To re-import the scripts created in the preceding form to other SQL Server/ MSDE systems, use the SQL Server Query Analyzer, OSQL, or the form introduced in this section. When executing scripts, note that the generation process does not only create SQL commands, but also partly creates command sequences consisting of several commands that are separated from each other by the text *GO*. *GO* is not a regular SQL command. Instead, in the SQL Server Query Analyzer or in OSQL, *GO* is used to separate T-SQL commands from each other and to initiate execution of the commands until *GO*.

The *GO* separator strings, in turn, make it impossible to execute a T-SQL script with a *Connection* or *Command* object's *Execute* method. To process a T-SQL script, you must use the *SQLDMO.Database* object's *ExecuteImmediate* method.

You can use the example form *frmSQLDMO_ExecuteScripts,* shown in Figure 23-4, to load a T-SQL script, view it in the text box, and edit it, if needed. Click Execute Script to execute the script.

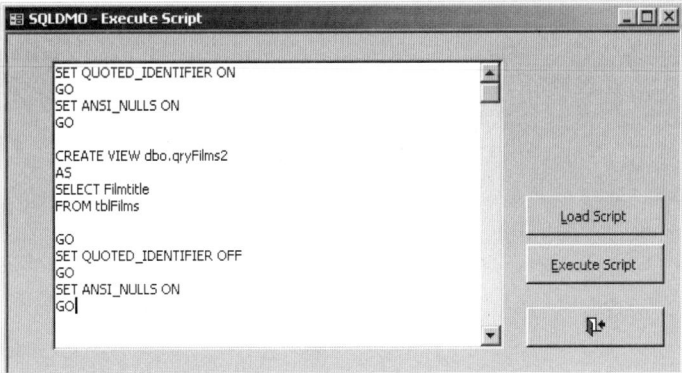

Figure 23-4   Executing T-SQL scripts

Note that a *FileSystemObject* object is used to load the script, as shown in the preceding example. This object makes it possible to read the entire script with a single command (*ReadAll*):

```
Option Compare Database
Option Explicit
Private Sub cmdClose_Click()
    DoCmd.Close
End Sub
Private Sub cmdExecute_Click()
    Dim dmoServer As SQLDMO.SQLServer
    Dim dmoDB As SQLDMO.Database
    Dim dmoQryResult As SQLDMO.QueryResults
    Dim strMsg As String
    Dim strServer As String
    On Error GoTo ErrorHandler
    If txtScript.Value <> "" Then
        ' Execute script
        Set dmoServer = New SQLDMO.SQLServer
        ' Retrieve current server
        strServer = CurrentProject.Connection.Properties("Data Source")
        ' Windows- or SQL Server-security?
        If CurrentProject.Connection.Properties("Integrated Security") = _
        "SSPI" Then
            dmoServer.LoginSecure = True
            ' Connect to server
            dmoServer.Connect strServer
        Else
            Dim strUser As String
            Dim strPassword As String
            strUser = CurrentProject.Connection.Properties("User id")
```

```vb
        strPassword = CurrentProject.Connection.Properties("Password")
         ' Connect to server
         dmoServer.Connect strServer, strUser, strPassword
        End If


        ' Current database
        strMsg = CurrentProject.Connection.Properties("Initial Catalog")
        Set dmoDB = dmoServer.Databases(strMsg)


        ' Execute script
        dmoDB.ExecuteImmediate txtScript.Value


        Set dmoServer = Nothing
    End If
Exitsub:
    Exit Sub


ErrorHandler:
    ErrorHandler
    Resume Exitsub
End Sub


Private Sub cmdLoad_Click()
    Dim f As FileSystemObject
    Dim ts As TextStream
    Dim strFilter As String
    Dim strRet As String


    On Error GoTo ErrorHandler
```

```vb
' Open file dialog
strFilter = "*.sql|SQL-Scripts (*.sql)|*.*|All Files (*.*)"
strRet = ChooseFile(Application.hWndAccessApp, _
                 "Open script", _
                 "&Open", _
                 strFilter, _
                 "script.sql", _
                 "c:\", _
                 0, False)


' If not cancelled
If Len(strRet) <> 0 Then
    ' Read file
    Set f = New FileSystemObject
    Set ts = f.OpenTextFile( _
            Filename:=strRet, _
            IOMode:=ForReading, _
            Format:=TristateUseDefault)
    ' Write to text control
    txtScript = ts.ReadAll
    txtScript.SetFocus

    ts.Close
    Set f = Nothing
End If
Exitsub:
    Exit Sub


ErrorHandler:
    ErrorHandler
    Resume Exitsub
End Sub
```

```vba
Sub ErrorHandler()

    Dim errADO As ADODB.Error

    Dim strErr As String

    strErr = "VBA-error information" & vbNewLine & vbNewLine

    strErr = strErr & "Number: " & Err.Number & vbNewLine

    strErr = strErr & "Description: " & Err.Description & vbNewLine

    strErr = strErr & vbNewLine

    If CurrentProject.Connection.Errors.Count > 0 Then

        For Each errADO In CurrentProject.Connection.Errors

            strErr = strErr & vbNewLine & "ADO-error information (ADO V." _
                    & CurrentProject.Connection.Version & ")" _
                    & vbNewLine & vbNewLine

            strErr = strErr & "NativeError: " & errADO.NativeError & _
                    vbNewLine

            strErr = strErr & "Number: " & errADO.Number & vbNewLine

            strErr = strErr & "Description: " & errADO.Description & _
                    vbNewLine

            strErr = strErr & "Source: " & errADO.Source & vbNewLine

            strErr = strErr & "SQLState: " & errADO.SQLState & vbNewLine

        Next

    End If

    cmdErrorOK.Visible = True

    cmdErrorOK.SetFocus

    cmdExecute.Enabled = False

    cmdLoad.Enabled = False

    txtScript.Visible = False

    txtError.Visible = True

    txtError = strErr

End Sub

Private Sub cmdErrorOK_Click()
```

```
        cmdExecute.Enabled = True

        cmdLoad.Enabled = True

        cmdLoad.SetFocus

        txtScript.Visible = True

        txtError.Visible = False

        txtError = ""

        cmdErrorOK.Visible = False

End Sub
```

The form includes an additional text box (*txtError*) and a button (*cmdErrorOK*) for error handling. The commands at the end of the *ErrorHandler* routine and those in *cmdErrorOK_Click* let you show, hide, or activate control elements when an error occurs.

Processing Information

In Chapter 19, "SQL Server Tools," we described how you can use SQL Server Enterprise Manager to view the current processes on the SQL server. Sometimes, it is necessary to abort processes, if, for example, an infinite loop occurs in a stored procedure, a deadlock occurs, or a procedure remains unfinished for any reason. If you are running MSDE only, you will not have access to SQL Server Enterprise Manager.

You can use the SQL-DMO library to determine the SQL server's active processes or you can abort them, as illustrated in the example form *frmSQLDMO_Processes*, shown in Figure 23-5.

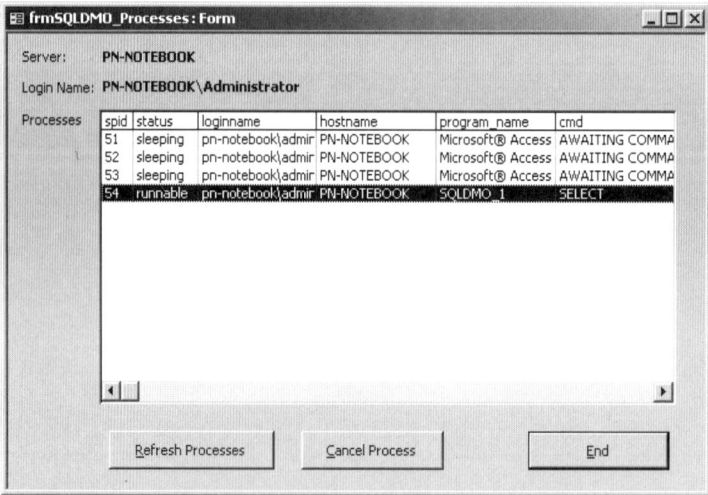

Figure 23-5   *frmSQLDMO_Processes* form

> **Warning**   Aborting processes means that you are interfering with the
> server's internal procedures. You should do so only in case of emer-
> gency and you should always proceed with the utmost caution, other-
> wise an irreversible loss of data may occur!

The following is the form's listing:

```
Option Compare Database
Option Explicit
Dim mdmoServer As SQLDMO.SQLServer
Private Sub Form_Load()
    Dim strServer As String
    Set mdmoServer = New SQLDMO.SQLServer
    ' Retrieve current server
    strServer = CurrentProject.Connection.Properties("Data Source")
    ' Windows- or SQL Server-security?
    If CurrentProject.Connection.Properties("Integrated Security") = _
    "SSPI" Then
        mdmoServer.LoginSecure = True
        mdmoServer.Connect strServer
    Else
        Dim strUser As String
        Dim strPassword As String
        strUser = CurrentProject.Connection.Properties("User ID")
        strPassword = CurrentProject.Connection.Properties("Password")
        mdmoServer.Connect strServer, strUser, strPassword
    End If
    lblServer.Caption = strServer
    ' user name
```

```
        lblLoginname.Caption = mdmoServer.TrueLogin

        ' Show all processes

        RefreshProcesses

End Sub

Private Sub cmdClose_Click()

        ' Close form

        DoCmd.Close

End Sub

Private Sub lstProcesses_Click()

        ' Activate button

        cmdKillProc.Enabled = True

End Sub

Private Sub cmdKillProc_Click()

        ' Is a process selected?

        If Not lstProcesses.Selected(lstProcesses.ListIndex) Then

            Exit Sub

        End If

        If MsgBox("Kill process " & lstProcesses.value & "?", _

                    vbYesNo, _

                    "Kill Process ") = vbOK Then

            ' Kill process

            mdmoServer.KillProcess lstProcesses.value

            RefreshProcesses

        End If

End Sub

Private Sub cmdRefresh_Click()

        RefreshProcesses

End Sub
```

```
Sub RefreshProcesses()
    Dim dmoQry As SQLDMO.QueryResults
    Dim strTmp As String
    Dim i As Integer
    Dim j As Integer
    ' Retrieve all processes for current login name
    ' and place in QueryResults
    Set dmoQry = mdmoServer.EnumProcesses(mdmoServer.TrueLogin)
    strTmp = ""
    ' Show column titles
    lstProcesses.ColumnHeads = True
    lstProcesses.ColumnCount = dmoQry.Columns
    ' Column heads
    For i = 1 To dmoQry.Columns
        strTmp = strTmp & dmoQry.ColumnName(i) & ";"
    Next
    ' For all rows
    For i = 1 To dmoQry.Rows
        ' For all columns
        For j = 1 To dmoQry.Columns
            strTmp = strTmp & Trim(dmoQry.GetColumnString(i, j)) & ";"
        Next
    Next
    ' Assign string as value list
    lstProcesses.RowSource = strTmp
End Sub
```

Setting Up the SQL-DMO Library

Two options are available for setting up the SQL-DMO library on a client. You can either install the SQL server client components on the server or you can copy the SQL-DMO library components to the client, as described next.

> **Note**   The SQL-DMO library is not part of the Microsoft Data Access Components (MDAC) that are usually installed on clients and that also include, for example, ActiveX Data Objects (ADO) and the object linking and embedding (OLE DB) provider for the SQL server.

Installing the SQL Server Client Components

Start the SQL Server or MSDE installation program on the client and select the option Client Tools Only. See Chapter 3, "Installation," for a detailed description of the installation program.

Copying the SQL-DMO Components

Follow these steps to manually copy the SQL-DMO library:

■ Copy the files SQLDMO.DLL, SQLSVC.DLL, SQLWOA.DLL, SQLRESLD.DLL, SQLWID.DLL, and W95SCM.DLL into the Windows system folder \Windows\System or \Winnt\System32.

■ Copy the files SQLDMO.RLL and SQLSVC.RLL into the folder \Windows\System\Resources\1033 or the folder \Winnt\System32\Resources\1033. If the folder does not exist, you must create it.

■ Select Start, then Run and type the command **Regsvr32 C:\Windows\system\ sqldmo.dll** or **Regsvr32 C:\Winnt\system32\ sqldmo.dll**. If execution is successful, the message "DLLRegisterServer in SQLDMO.DLL succeeded" should appear.

24

External Data Sources

Using Access mdb databases, it is easy and uncomplicated to link tables from other database programs or servers, where links to these tables are created using Indexed Sequential Access Method (ISAM) or open database connectivity (ODBC) drivers. In the mdb, select File, then Get External Data, then Link Tables, and then select the required data source. In Microsoft Access adp projects, this simple link to other data sources is no longer available. In the project, it is only possible to use tables from Microsoft SQL Server/MSDE. There are, however, three different options if you still want to use other data sources:

- Access the data sources directly using the Microsoft Visual Basic for Applications (VBA) program with ActiveX Data Objects (ADO) connection objects.

- Create linked servers within a SQL Server/MSDE server.

- Create an ad-hoc link with Transact-SQL commands.

In Microsoft Access 2002, the Table Connection Wizard is provided for the creation of linked servers and ad-hoc connections with Transact-SQL. This wizard is described at the end of this chapter.

Setting Up a Linked Server

In simple terms, a SQL Server/MSDE linked server can be regarded as a connection to an external data source in the same way that they are created in an Access mdb.

Setup in SQL Server Enterprise Manager

In SQL Server Enterprise Manager, you set up a new linked server by selecting Linked Servers under Security in the left pane, as shown in Figure 24-1.

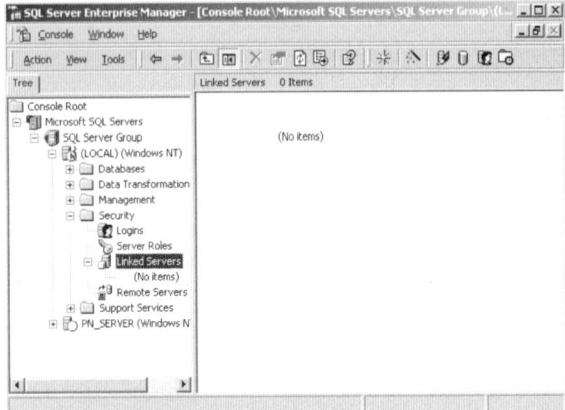

Figure 24-1 Setting up a linked server

You can select Action, then New Linked Server to open the Linked Server Properties dialog box, shown in Figure 24-2, which is used to define a linked server. As an example, we have set up a link using the Microsoft Jet 4 object linking and embedding database (OLE DB) provider to the Access database *CONTOSO.MDB*. To do this, the corresponding provider name has to be selected and the name of the database specified with the full path in the Data Source field.

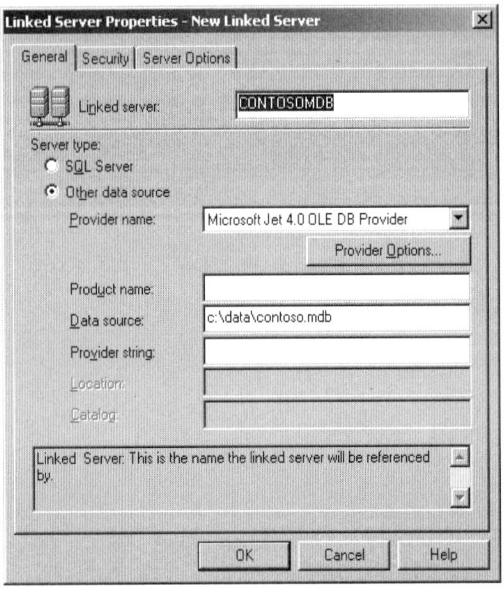

Figure 24-2 Basic data for the linked server

You then map the SQL Server users who are allowed to use the linked server in the Security tab to the Access mdb user names (see Figure 24-3).

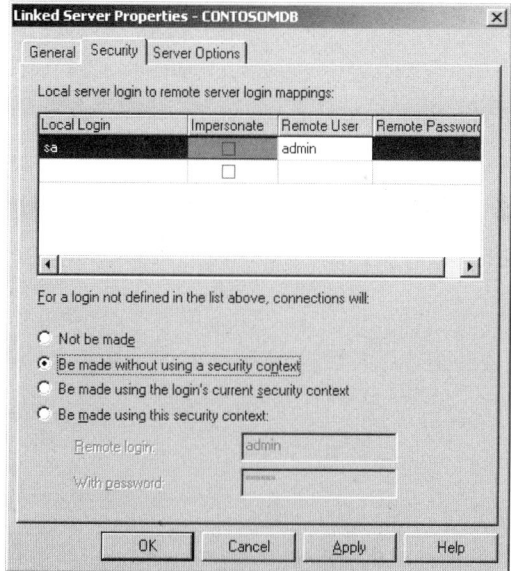

Figure 24-3   Security settings

In an unsaved Access .mdb file, only the user *admin* is created (that is, the remote user *admin* is assigned to every SQL Server user, as shown for a user in Figure 24-3).

> **Note**   If you are defining a linked server for a protected Access mdb database, you must define where the system database for the protected database is stored. To do this, set the following registry key for the server: *HKEY_LOCAL_MACHINE\SOFTWARE\Microsoft\Jet\ 4.0\ Engines\SystemDB* with the path and the name of the system database.

For all users that are not defined in the list box in the lower section of the dialog box, you can choose one of the four available options. If you select Be Made Without Using A Security Context, these users will be logged on to the linked server with their name and password. If you select Be Made Using The Login's Current Security Context, then all users not created in the list box will use their user definition to access the linked server. Select the Be Made Using

This Security Context option to assign all users not listed in the list box to the user names and passwords defined here for access to the data source. Select the Not Be Made option to deny access to users not explicitly listed in the list box.

Note   SQL Server 7 Security options are named differently than SQL Server 2000 options.

Settings for Different Data Sources

Table 24-1 displays the required entries for the different data sources. The simplest variant is a link to other SQL servers. To do this, select the SQL Server option in the Server Type section of the Linked Server Properties dialog box (see Figure 24-2), and enter the name of the SQL server as the name of the linked server.

Table 24-1   Specifications for Different Data Sources

Data Source	Server Type	Product Name	Provider Name	Data Source	Location	Provider Character Sequence	Catalog
SQL Server	SQL Server	—	—	—	—	—	—
SQL Server	Other data source	—	Microsoft OLE DB provider for SQL Server (SQLOLEDB)	Name of the SQL Server	—	—	Database name (optional)
Jet (Access)	Other data source	—	Microsoft Jet 4 OLE DB provider (Microsoft.Jet .OLEDB.4)	Path and name of the Access .mdb file	—	—	—
Oracle	Other data source	—	Microsoft OLE DB provider for Oracle (MSDAORA)	SQL*Net alias for Oracle database	—	—	—

continued

Table 24-1   Specifications for Different Data Sources   *(continued)*

Data Source	Server Type	Product Name	Provider Name	Data Source	Location	Provider Character Sequence	Catalog
ODBC data source	Other data source	—	Microsoft OLE DB provider for Oracle (MSDASQL)	System DSN of the ODBC data source	—	—	—
ODBC data source	Other data source	—	Microsoft OLE DB provider for Oracle (MSDASQL)		—	ODBC link character sequence	—
Microsoft Excel worksheet	Other data source	—	Microsoft Jet 4 OLE DB provider (Microsoft.Jet .OLEDB.4)	Path and name of the Excel file	—	Excel 5	—
IBM DB2 database	Other data source	—	Microsoft OLE DB provider for Oracle (DB2OLEDB)	—	—	See documentation of OLE DB provider for DB2	Catalog name of DB2 database

Configuration with System Stored Procedures

You can also manage linked servers using system stored procedures. The following procedure creates a new linked server:

```
sp_addlinkedserver

[@server =] 'server'

[, [@srvproduct =] 'product_name']
[, [@provider =] 'provider_name']

[, [@datasrc =] 'data_source']
[, [@location =] 'location']

[, [@provstr =] 'provider_string']
[, [@catalog =] 'catalog']
```

The parameters for the procedure are defined according to Table 24-1. Remember that the internal names must be used for the provider names (that is, the names that are listed in parentheses in the Provider Name column of Table 24-1).

For a linked server, assignment of the SQL Server users to the data source user IDs must be defined. To do this you use the following procedure:

```
sp_addlinkedsrvlogin

[@rmtsrvname =] 'rmtsrvname'
[,[@useself =] 'useself']
[,[@locallogin =] 'locallogin']
[,[@rmtuser =] 'rmtuser']
[,[@rmtpassword =] 'rmtpassword']
```

The stored procedure *sp_linkedservers* lists all linked server definitions. To delete a linked server, use the following:

```
sp_dropserver

[@server =] 'server'

[, [@droplogins =]{'droplogins' | NULL}]
```

Use this stored procedure to delete linked server logins:

```
sp_droplinkedsrvlogin

[@rmtsrvname =] 'rmtsrvname',
[@locallogin =] 'locallogin'
```

Configuration with SQL-DMO

You can also create, view, and delete linked servers and corresponding security information using the SQL Distributed Management Objects (SQL-DMO) library (described in Chapter 23, "The SQL-DMO Library").

We have created the form, shown in Figure 24-4, that displays the definitions of the linked servers created on the server specified. When you click one of the definitions, the user assignments are displayed in the lower list box.

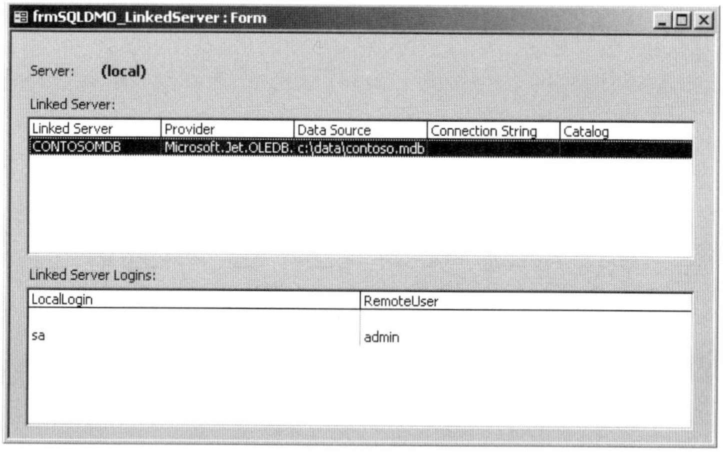

Figure 24-4   Linked servers

The following listing displays the VBA code of the form:

```
Option Compare Database

Option Explicit

Dim mdmoServer As SQLDMO.SQLServer

Private Sub Form_Load()

 Dim strServer As String

 Set mdmoServer = New SQLDMO.SQLServer

 strServer = CurrentProject.Connection.Properties("Data Source")

 If CurrentProject.Connection.Properties("Integrated Security") _

         = "SSPI" Then

  mdmoServer.LoginSecure = True

  mdmoServer.Connect strServer

 Else

  Dim strUser As String

  Dim strPassword As String

  strUser = CurrentProject.Connection.Properties("User ID")

  strPassword = CurrentProject.Connection.Properties("Password")

  mdmoServer.Connect strServer, strUser, strPassword

 End If
```

```
    lblServer.Caption = strServer
    Dim dmoLinkedServer As SQLDMO.LinkedServer
    Dim strTmp As String
    strTmp = "Linked Server;Providername;DataSource;" & _
             "Provider String;Catalog;"
    For Each dmoLinkedServer In mdmoServer.LinkedServers
      strTmp = strTmp & dmoLinkedServer.name & ";"
      strTmp = strTmp & dmoLinkedServer.ProviderName & ";"
      strTmp = strTmp & dmoLinkedServer.DataSource & ";"
      strTmp = strTmp & dmoLinkedServer.ProviderString & ";"
      strTmp = strTmp & dmoLinkedServer.Catalog & ";"
    Next
    lstLinkedServer.RowSource = strTmp
    lstLinkedServer.Value = lstLinkedServer.ItemData(1)
    lstLinkedServer_Click
End Sub
Private Sub lstLinkedServer_Click()
  Dim dmoLinkedServer As SQLDMO.LinkedServer
  Dim dmoLinkedServerLogin As SQLDMO.LinkedServerLogin
  Dim strTmp As String
  Set dmoLinkedServer = mdmoServer.LinkedServers(lstLinkedServer.Value)
  strTmp = "LocalLogin;RemoteUser;"
  For Each dmoLinkedServerLogin In dmoLinkedServer.LinkedServerLogins
    strTmp = strTmp & dmoLinkedServerLogin.LocalLogin & ";"
    strTmp = strTmp & dmoLinkedServerLogin.RemoteUser & ";"
  Next
  lstLinkedServerLogins.RowSource = strTmp
End Sub
```

Data Access to Linked Servers

To access tables, views, and other objects, if necessary, the following four-part syntax is used:

```
linkedserver.catalog.user.object
```

All four parts of this convention are not always available for linked server definitions (that is, in many cases, the name is abbreviated as in the following examples).

If you have defined a linked server for accessing another SQL server, you can access the objects on the remote server with

```
linkedserver.database.user.Object
```

For example:

```
SERVER2.Marketing.Bob.Customer
```

If the linked server is set up for an Access mdb, you do not need the *Catalog* and *User* parts. Access can be made using *linkedserver...table* and/or *linkedserver...query*.

When accessing an Oracle database system, you need the following three parts:

```
linkedserver..user.object
```

For example:

```
ORASRV..RALF.tblProducts
```

Linked Servers in Access Forms

Tables (and views and queries) from data sources that are accessed with linked servers can also be used in forms and reports, as demonstrated in Figure 24-5. Here, the form's *row source* was determined with a SQL command that uses the linked server *SERVER3* to access the table *Authors* from the SQL Server/MSDE example database *pubs*.

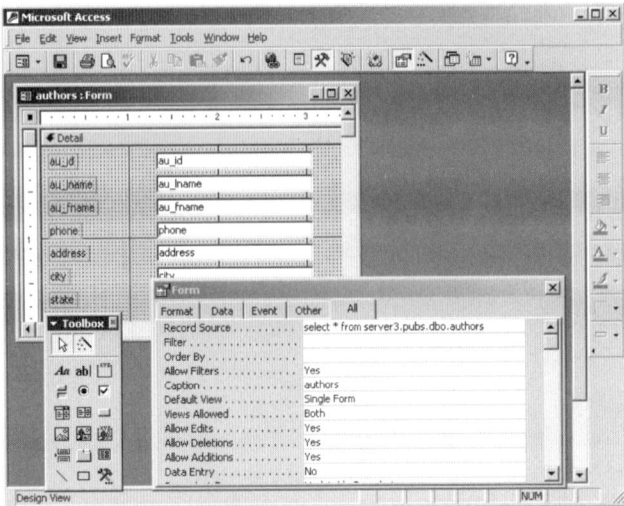

Figure 24-5 Example form

Remember that tables, views, and queries accessed with a linked server are displayed in linked forms as read-only elements (that is, no changes can be made to the data). Unfortunately it does not seem possible to access a linked form because even the assignment of an ADO recordset (with read and write permission) to the form property *Me.Recordset* is unsuccessful: the form remains read-only.

Accessing Using Views

Because the four-part syntax is rather time-consuming, it can make sense to access the linked server using a view. This allows the linked server to be "hidden" from the user so that the user does not need to work with this four-part syntax. Furthermore, you can assign detailed access rights for the view within SQL Server/MSDE. In many cases, for example, access to the data source by way of the linked server is established using a special user account so that all users of the view can access the data source with the same user names.

Figure 24-6 displays a view containing all the columns of an Oracle table accessed using a linked server.

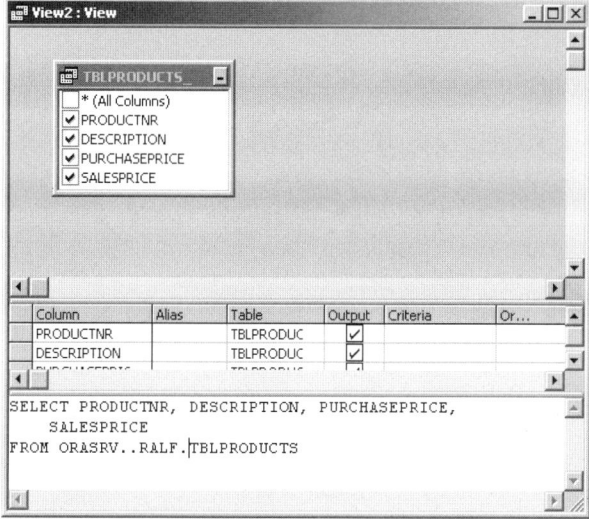

Figure 24-6   View for accessing a linked server

Ad-Hoc Accesses

SQL Server also enables ad-hoc or pass-through accesses to external data sources. Two SQL commands are available for these purposes: *OPENQUERY* and *OPENROWSET*. In an ad-hoc query, a command is transferred and processed directly at the data source. This allows the transfer of not only SQL commands, but also specific commands for a data source.

> **Note**   The ad-hoc or pass-through queries (*OPENQUERY* and *OPENROWSET*) function in a similar manner to pass-through queries in Access mdb databases.

OPENQUERY for Accesses with Linked Servers

You can use the *OPENQUERY* function to transfer a command or a query to a linked server. The function returns a resultset. It only returns one resultset, even if the transferred command returns several resultsets. *OPENQUERY* can be used in *SELECT-*, *INSERT-*, *UPDATE-*, and *DELETE* commands.

The command takes the following standard form:

```
OPENQUERY(linked_server,'query')
```

The following example transfers a query to the *Orasrv* linked server:

```
SELECT * FROM OPENQUERY(Orasrv,
      'SELECT Description FROM tblProducts ORDER BY Description
      DESC')
```

OPENROWSET for Accesses without Linked Servers

You can also access external data sources without defining a linked server if you use the *OPENROWSET* function for the access. *OPENROWSET* works along the same principles as *OPENQUERY*, except that instead of the name of a linked server, it transfers the parameters for the creation of a link to a data source. The function is defined as follows:

```
OPENROWSET ( 'provider_name'

  , { 'datasource' ; 'user_id' ; 'password'
  | 'provider_string' }
  , { [ catalog. ] [ schema. ] object
  | 'query' }

  )
```

The following example collects all lines and columns in table *USER.TBLPRODUCTS* that are managed by an Oracle server:

```
SELECT Products.*

FROM OPENROWSET('MSDAORA',

'ORASRV.PN1';'USER';'password', 'select * from USER.TBLPRODUCTS')

  AS Products
```

Linked Tables in Access 2002

In Access 2002, the creation and linking of linked servers and ad-hoc links have all been simplified. Access 2002 provides the Link Table Wizard for creating table links (see Figure 24-7). This wizard can be started by selecting File, then Get External Data, and then Link Tables. The wizard does, however, have a significant restriction: Table links can only be created with the wizard if the Access project is linked to a local SQL Server and/or MSDE (that is, the database must run on the same computer as the project). This restriction is easy to explain because, as described earlier, OLE DB or ODBC information is used for linked servers or ad-hoc links. This information must be present on the computer running SQL Server/MSDE. For this reason, the wizard can only determine this information for a local SQL Server/MSDE server.

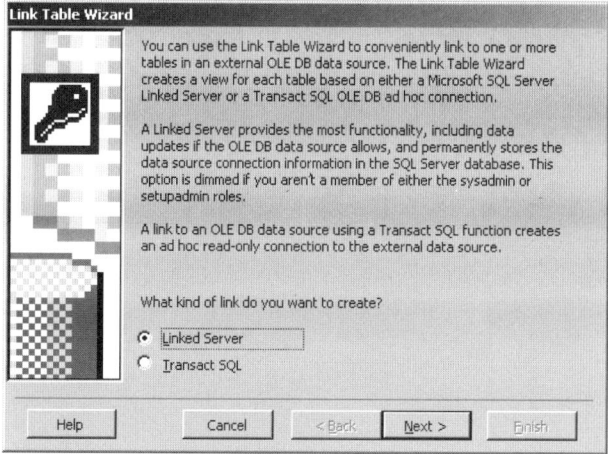

Figure 24-7   LinkTable Wizard

In the first wizard screen, define whether you want to create a linked server or an ad-hoc link using Transact-SQL.

Setting Up a Linked Server

First we demonstrate how to create a linked server. The system displays the Select Data Source dialog box in which you select the required data source. In the example shown in Figure 24-8, we choose +Connect to New Data Source. Selecting +New SQL Server Connection opens dialog boxes that you use to connect to another SQL Server/MSDE server in your network.

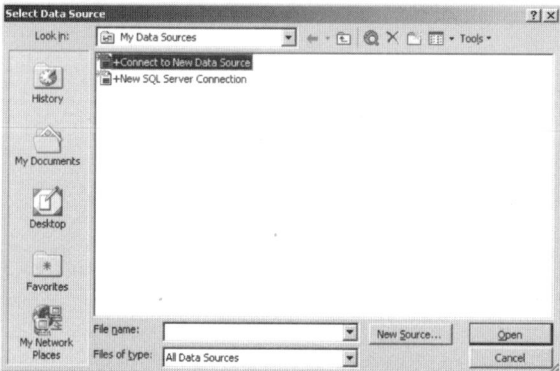

Figure 24-8   Selecting the data source

The system then calls the Data Connection Wizard, which helps you define an ODBC data source. In this example, we choose Microsoft Access Database, as shown in Figure 24-9.

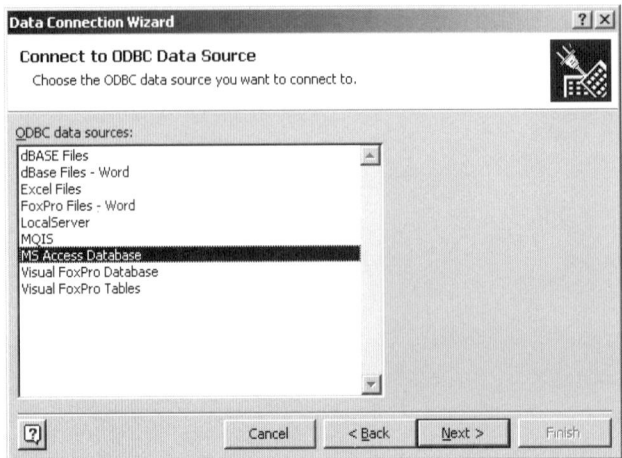

Figure 24-9 Data Connection Wizard

In the subsequent dialog box, the required Access mdb database is selected. In our example, the database is called *CONTOSO.MDB*. The Select Database And Table wizard screen, shown in Figure 24-10, provides you with additional selection options, depending on the data source. If you choose an Access database, then the list box cannot be selected.

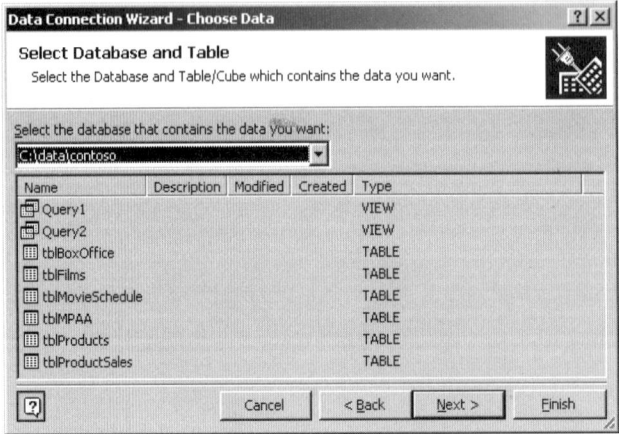

Figure 24-10 Selecting database and table

The data source information created is now saved to a data connection file with the extension .odc, as shown in Figure 24-11. You can also enter an additional description and key words.

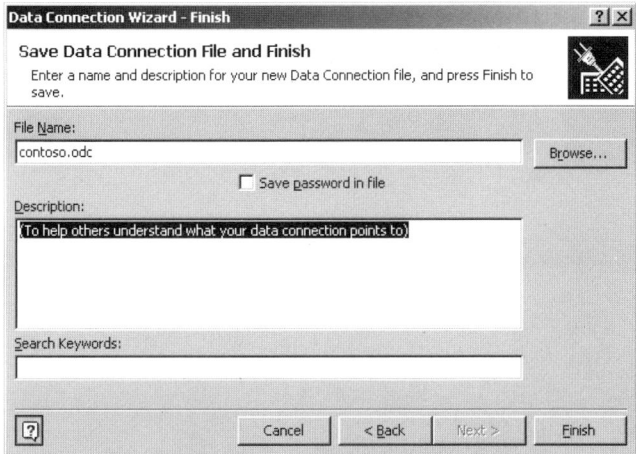

Figure 24-11   Saving the data connection file

At this point, the wizard only checks the table to determine whether you are trying to create the linked server for a remote SQL Server/MSDE server. Because the wizard can only create linked servers to a local SQL Server/MSDE server, the wizard displays an error message, as displayed in Figure 24-12, and then terminates. This is inconvenient, because you cannot now use the data source definition just defined.

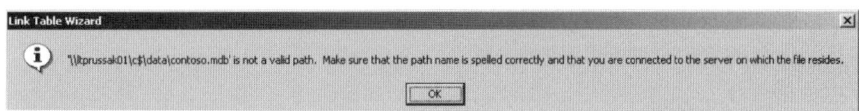

Figure 24-12   Error message when linking to tables

If no error message is displayed, then a dialog box appears displaying the possible Access database tables and queries for the link, which are accessed earlier in the data source definition. We have selected some tables for the link in the example shown in Figure 24-13.

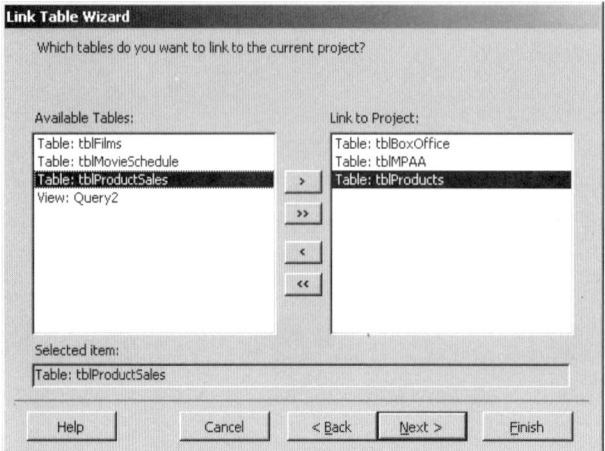

Figure 24-13 Selecting tables and queries

The tables and queries selected for the link are displayed in the database window of the Access project as query objects, as displayed in Figure 24-14. Query names are prepended with the name of the database connected to the project.

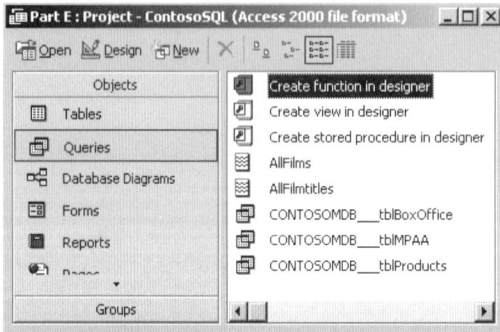

Figure 24-14 Linked tables and views in the database window

The wizard automatically creates views that use the defined linked server to access the Access database and the corresponding tables and queries. Figure 24-15 displays one of these views in design mode.

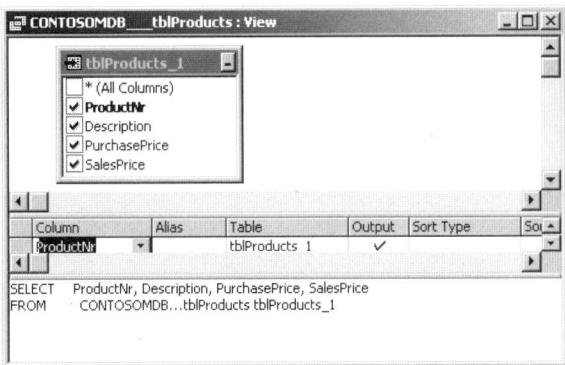

Figure 24-15   View in design view mode

In the SQL area of the design view, you will recognize the four-part syntax. Here, only the first and fourth parts of the name are required to access the Access mdb linked server. If, for example, you had defined a linked server to access another SQL server, then you would need to use all four parts of the syntax (that is, *SERVER.database.user.table*).

The Table Connection Wizard uses the four-part name to define the names of the views, where the periods in the name are replaced by underscores; this creates names such as *Contoso___tblProducts*.

Setting Up an Ad-Hoc Link

If, in the first screen of the Table Connection Wizard (Figure 24-7), you choose to create an ad-hoc link using Transact-SQL, then you must complete the same series of screens to select and define a data source. Rather than creating a linked server to SQL Server/MSDE, however, the system creates a view in which the link to the data source is created using the Transact-SQL command *OPENDATASOURCE* for Microsoft SQL Server 2000/MSDE 2000 or *OPENROWSET* for Microsoft SQL Server 7/MSDE 1.

Figure 24-16 displays the definition of the ad-hoc link using the *OPENDATASOURCE* command. Remember that when using *OPENDATASOURCE*, you must enter all parameters and passwords required for access to the data source. Every user who can view the design view can therefore also view any passwords that may be entered. Stored procedures and views can be encrypted in SQL Server using the With Encryption option.

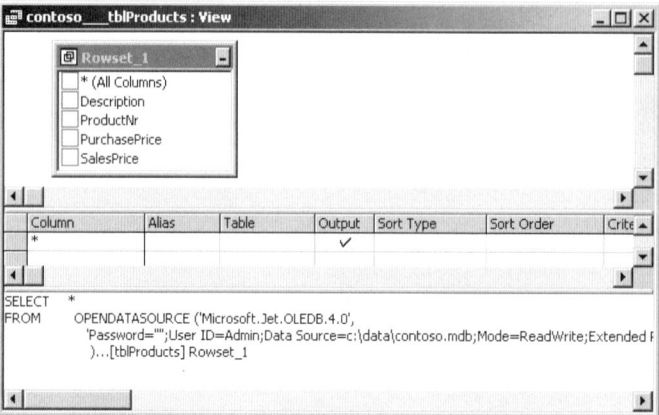

Figure 24-16 View with ad-hoc link in design view mode

25

System Stored Procedures

This chapter contains an alphabetical list of the most important procedures in Microsoft SQL Server 7 and Microsoft SQL Server 2000, together with their parameters. To help you quickly find the system stored procedure you are looking for, the alphabetical list is preceded by a table in which the system stored procedures are grouped by function.

Detailed information about all system stored procedures can be found in the SQL Server Books Online. The online help, incidentally, does not ship with Microsoft Data Engine (MSDE). However, the latest version can be downloaded from *www.microsoft.com/sql/productdoc*.

All system stored procedures are stored in SQL Server/MSDE in the *master* database. The names of the system stored procedures all begin with *sp_* or *xp_* (extended stored procedure). You should make sure that the names of the user stored procedures created by database programmers do not begin with these prefixes because SQL Server first looks in the *master* database for these procedures.

Grouped by Function

The system stored procedures listed in Table 25-1 are used to run and set up SQL Server/MSDE.

Table 25-1 General Procedures

sp_addmessage	sp_detach_db	sp_helpserver
sp_addtype	sp_dropdevice	sp_helpsort
sp_addumpdevice	sp_dropmessage	sp_helptext
sp_attach_db	sp_droptype	sp_helptrigger
sp_bindefault	sp_executesql	sp_monitor
sp_bindrule	sp_help	sp_recompile
sp_configure	sp_helpconstraint	sp_rename
sp_datatype_info	sp_helpdb	sp_renamedb
sp_dbcmptlevel	sp_helpdevice	sp_unbindefault
sp_dboption	sp_helpfile	sp_unbindrule
sp_dbremove	sp_helpfilegroup	sp_validname
sp_depends	sp_helpindex	sp_who

With catalog procedures, listed in Table 25-2, you can get data about databases, tables, and other elements that might have been created locally or on a connection server.

Table 25-2 Catalog Procedures

sp_column_privileges	sp_pkeys	sp_table_privileges
sp_columns	sp_server_info	sp_tables
sp_databases	sp_statistics	
sp_fkeys	sp_stored_procedures	

You can use the system stored procedures listed in Table 25-3 to add linked servers and get data about linked servers to perform distributed queries.

Table 25-3 Distributed Queries Procedures

sp_addlinkedserver	sp_droplinkedsrvlogin	sp_linkedservers
sp_addlinkedsrvlogin	sp_foreignkeys	sp_primarykeys
sp_catalogs	sp_indexes	

The system stored procedures given in Table 25-4 can be used to manage the security of a SQL server.

Table 25-4   Security Procedures

sp_addlinkedsrvlogin	*sp_denylogin*	*sp_helprole*
sp_addlogin	*sp_droplinkedsrvlogin*	*sp_helprolemember*
sp_addremotelogin	*sp_droplogin*	*sp_helprotect*
sp_addrole	*sp_droprole*	*sp_helpsrvrole*
sp_addrolemember	*sp_droprolemember*	*sp_helpsrvrolemember*
sp_addsrvrolemember	*sp_dropserver*	*sp_helpuser*
sp_adduser	*sp_dropsrvrolemember*	*sp_password*
sp_approlepassword	*sp_grantdbaccess*	*sp_revokedbaccess*
sp_changedbowner	*sp_grantlogin*	*sp_revokelogin*
sp_change_users_login	*sp_helpdbfixedrole*	*sp_srvrolepermission*
sp_dbfixedrolepermission	*sp_helplinkedsrvlogin*	*sp_validatelogins*
sp_defaultdb	*sp_helplogins*	
sp_defaultlanguage	*sp_helpntgroup*	

The procedures listed in Table 25-5 can be used for SQL Mail administration, to send status or error messages, for example.

Table 25-5   SQL Mail Procedures

sp_processmail	*xp_readmail*	*xp_stopmail*
xp_deletemail	*xp_sendmail*	
xp_findnextmsg	*xp_startmail*	

Alphabetical List

Table 25-6 contains an alphabetical list of the most important system stored procedures and short descriptions of their parameters. The SQL Server Books Online help contains detailed information and practical examples as well as complete information about the possible parameters. It also contains information about other system stored procedures not listed in Table 25-6.

Table 25-6   System Stored Procedures and Descriptions

Procedure Name	Description and Parameters

sp_addlinkedserver	Defines a linked server, which allows access to object linking and embedding database (OLE DB) data sources. Furthermore, stored procedures on the linked server can be executed. Linked servers are covered in detail in Chapter 24, "External Data Sources."
	
	```sp_addlinkedserver [@server =] 'server'```
	``` [, [@srvproduct =] 'product_name']```
	``` [, [@provider =] 'provider_name']```
	``` [, [@datasrc =] 'data_source']```
	``` [, [@location =] 'location']```
	``` [, [@provstr =] 'provider_string']```
	``` [, [@catalog =] 'catalog']```

sp_addlinkedsrvlogin	Maps a user name on a local server to a user name on a linked server. In other words, an assignment is made between a user of the SQL server and a user of the data source on the linked server. Linked servers are covered in detail in Chapter 24, "External Data Sources."
	
	```sp_addlinkedsrvlogin [@rmtsrvname =] 'rmtsrvname'```
	``` [, [@useself =] 'useself']```
	``` [, [@locallogin =] 'locallogin']```
	``` [, [@rmtuser =] 'rmtuser']```
	``` [, [@rmtpassword =] 'rmtpassword']```

sp_addlogin	Creates a SQL Server login (see Chapter 20, "Security").
	
	```sp_addlogin [@loginame =] 'login'```
	``` [, [@passwd =] 'password']```
	``` [, [@defdb =] 'database']```
	``` [, [@deflanguage =] 'language']```
	``` [, [@sid =] sid]```
	``` [, [@encryptopt =] 'encryption_option']```

sp_addmessage	Creates a new error message in the *sysmessages* system table.
	
	```sp_addmessage [@msgnum =] msg_id ,```
	``` [@severity =] severity ,```
	``` [@msgtext =] 'msg'```
	``` [, [@lang =] 'language']```
	``` [, [@with_log =] 'with_log']```
	``` [, [@replace =] 'replace']```

sp_addremotelogin	Creates a new user name for a remote server.
	
	```sp_addremotelogin [@remoteserver =] 'remoteserver'```
	``` [, [@loginame =] 'login']```
	``` [, [@remotename =] 'remote_name']```

continued

Table 25-6   System Stored Procedures and Descriptions   *(continued)*

Procedure Name	Description and Parameters
sp_addrole	Adds a new database role in the current database. ``` sp_addrole [@rolename =] 'role' [, [@ownername =] 'owner'] ```
sp_addrolemember	Creates a security account for a database role in the currently used database. ``` sp_addrolemember [@rolename =] 'role' , [@membername =] 'security_account' ```
sp_addsrvrolemember	Adds a user name to a fixed server role. ``` sp_addsrvrolemember [@loginame =] 'login' , [@rolename =] 'role' ```

sp_addtype	Creates a user-defined data type.
	
	``
	sp_addtype [@typename =] type,
	   [@phystype =] system_data_type
	   [, [@nulltype =] 'null_type']
	   [, [@owner =] 'owner_name']
	``

sp_addumpdevice	Adds a dump device to create a backup for the different parts of a database.
	
	``
	sp_addumpdevice [@devtype =] 'device_type' ,
	   [@logicalname =] 'logical_name' ,
	   [@physicalname =] 'physical_name'
	   [, { [@cntrltype =] controller_type
	
		[@devstatus =] 'device_status'
		      }
		   ]
		``

sp_adduser	Adds a user; the procedure was used until Microsoft SQL Server 6.5. *sp_grantdbaccess* should be used with Microsoft SQL Server 7 and later versions.
	
	``
	sp_adduser [@loginame =] 'login'
	   [, [@name_in_db =] 'user']
	   [, [@grpname =] 'group']
	``

sp_approlepassword	Changes the password for an application in the current database. ``` sp_approlepassword [@rolename =] 'role' , [@newpwd =] 'password' ```
sp_attach_db	Adds data (.mdf) and log (.ldf) files, which can then be addressed as a database. ``` sp_attach_db [@dbname =] 'dbname' , [@filename1 =] 'filename_n' [,...16] ```

continued

Table 25-6 **System Stored Procedures and Descriptions** *(continued)*

Procedure Name	Description and Parameters
| *sp_bindefault* | Binds a default to a data field or user-defined data type. Use of *DEFAULT* constraint is preferred.<br><br>```
sp_bindefault [ @defname = ] 'default' ,
   [ @objname = ] 'object_name'
   [ , [ @futureonly = ] 'futureonly_flag' ]
``` |
| *sp_bindrule* | Binds a rule to a data field.<br><br>```
sp_bindrule [ @rulename = ] 'rule' ,
   [ @objname = ] 'object_name'
   [ , [ @futureonly = ] 'futureonly_flag' ]
``` |
| *sp_catalogs* | Shows a list of the catalogs (databases) on the specified linked servers.<br><br>```
sp_catalogs [ @server_name = ] 'linked_svr'
``` |
| *sp_change_users_login* | Changes the relationship between a SQL Server user name and a user of the current database.<br><br>```
sp_change_users_login [ @Action = ] 'action'
   [ , [ @UserNamePattern = ] 'user' ]
   [ , [ @LoginName = ] 'login' ]
``` |
| *sp_changedbowner* | Changes the database owner of the current database.<br><br>```
sp_changedbowner [ @loginame = ] 'login'
   [ , [ @map = ] remap_alias_flag ]
``` |
| *sp_column_privileges* | Shows the privileges for columns of a table in the currently used database.<br><br>```
sp_column_privileges [ @table_name = ] 'table_name'
   [ , [ @table_owner = ] 'table_owner' ]
   [ , [ @table_qualifier = ] 'table_qualifier' ]
   [ , [ @column_name = ] 'column' ]
``` |
| *sp_columns* | Shows column information for tables and views of the current database.<br><br>```
sp_columns [ @table_name = ] object
   [ , [ @table_owner = ] owner ]
   [ , [ @table_qualifier = ] qualifier ]
   [ , [ @column_name = ] column ]
   [ , [ @ODBCVer = ] ODBCVer ]
``` |
| *sp_configure* | Shows or modifies global configuration settings for the current server.<br><br>```
sp_configure [ [ @configname = ] 'name' ]
   [ , [ @configvalue = ] 'value' ]
``` |
| *sp_databases* | Returns a list of the databases on the server.<br><br>```
sp_databases
``` |

continued
```

Table 25-6   System Stored Procedures and Descriptions *(continued)*

Procedure Name	Description and Parameters
sp_datatype_info	Returns a list of all data types (without an argument). You can also specify a data type as an argument.
| | ```
sp_datatype_info [ [ @data_type = ] data_type ]
    [ , [ @ODBCVer = ] odbc_version ]
``` |
| *sp_dbcmptlevel* | Determines the SQL Server version with which the specified database has to be compatible. |
| | ```
sp_dbcmptlevel [ [ @dbname = ] name ]
    [ , [ @new_cmptlevel = ] version ]
``` |
| *sp_dbfixedrolepermission* | Returns the permissions for all fixed database roles or of a selected role. |
| | ```
sp_dbfixedrolepermission [ [ @rolename = ] 'role' ]
``` |
| *sp_dboption* | Lists or modifies all database options . |
| | ```
sp_dboption [ [ @dbname = ] 'database' ]
    [ , [ @optname = ] 'option_name' ]
    [ , [ @optvalue = ] 'value' ]
``` |
| *sp_dbremove* | Removes a database. This command is outdated and *sp_detach_db* should be used in SQL Server 7 and later versions. |
| | ```
sp_dbremove [ @dbname = ] 'database'
    [ , [ @dropdev = ] 'dropdev' ]
``` |
| *sp_defaultdb* | Assigns a default database to a SQL server login. |
| | ```
sp_defaultdb [ @loginame = ] 'login' ,
    [@defdb =] 'database'
``` |
| *sp_defaultlanguage* | Changes the default language for a SQL Server login. |
| | ```
sp_defaultlanguage [ @loginame = ] 'login'
    [ , [ @language = ] 'language' ]
``` |
| *sp_denylogin* | Prevents connections from being made to a SQL server. |
| | ```
sp_denylogin [ @loginame = ] 'login'
``` |
| *sp_depends* | Shows the dependencies of a database object. |
| | ```
sp_depends [ @objname = ] 'object'
``` |
| *sp_detach_db* | Detaches a database from a server. The .mdf and .ldf files are not deleted by this. |
| | ```
sp_detach_db [ @dbname = ] 'dbname'
    [ , [ @skipchecks = ] 'skipchecks' ]
``` |

continued

Table 25-6 System Stored Procedures and Descriptions *(continued)*

Procedure Name	Description and Parameters
sp_dropdevice	Detaches a database or backup medium by deleting the relevant entry from the table *master.dbo.sysdevices*.
| | ```
sp_dropdevice [ @logicalname = ] 'device'
   [ , [ @delfile = ] 'delfile' ]
``` |
| *sp_droplinkedsrvlogin* | Clears the connection between a user name on the local SQL server and the linked server. |
| | ```
sp_droplinkedsrvlogin [ @rmtsrvname = ]
'rmtsrvname' ,
   [ @locallogin = ] 'locallogin'
``` |
| *sp_droplogin* | Removes a SQL Server login. |
| | ```
sp_droplogin [ @loginame = ] 'login'
``` |
| *sp_dropmessage* | Removes an error message from the *sysmessages* table. |
| | ```
sp_dropmessage [ @msgnum = ] message_number
   [ , [ @lang = ] 'language' ]
``` |
| *sp_droprole* | Deletes a role from the current database. |
| | ```
sp_droprole [ @rolename = ] 'role'
``` |
| *sp_droprolemember* | Deletes a computer or domain security account from a role in the current database. |
| | ```
sp_droprolemember [ @rolename = ] 'role' ,
   [ @membername = ] 'security_account'
``` |
| *sp_dropserver* | Removes the link to a linked server. |
| | ```
sp_dropserver [ @server = ] 'server' [ ,

[ @droplogins = ] { 'droplogins' | NULL} ]
``` |
| *sp_dropsrvrolemember* | Removes a SQL Server login or security account from a fixed database role. |
| | ```
sp_dropsrvrolemember [ @loginame = ] 'login' ,

[ @rolename = ] 'role'
``` |
| *sp_droptype* | Removes a user-defined data type. |
| | ```
sp_droptype [ @typename = ] 'type'
``` |
| *sp_executesql* | Executes one or more Transact-SQL statements and can contain parameters. |
| | ```
sp_executesql [@stmt =] stmt
[
   {, [@params =] N'@parameter_name data_type
   [,...n]' }
   {, [@param1 =] 'value1' [,...n] }
]
``` |

continued

Table 25-6   **System Stored Procedures and Descriptions**   *(continued)*

Procedure Name	Description and Parameters
sp_fkeys	Returns information about foreign key relationships.
| | ```
sp_fkeys [ @pktable_name = ] 'pktable_name'
   [ , [ @pktable_owner = ] 'pktable_owner' ]
   [ , [ @pktable_qualifier = ] 'pktable_qualifier' ]
   { , [ @fktable_name = ] 'fktable_name' }
   [ , [ @fktable_owner = ] 'fktable_owner' ]
   [ , [ @fktable_qualifier = ] 'fktable_qualifier' ]
``` |
| *sp_foreignkeys* | Returns the foreign keys that point to primary keys in a table on the linked server. |
| | ```
sp_foreignkeys [ @table_server = ] 'table_server'
   [ , [ @pktab_name = ] 'pktab_name' ]
   [ , [ @pktab_schema = ] 'pktab_schema' ]
   [ , [ @pktab_catalog = ] 'pktab_catalog' ]
   [ , [ @fktab_name = ] 'fktab_name' ]
   [ , [ @fktab_schema = ] 'fktab_schema' ]
   [ , [ @fktab_catalog = ] 'fktab_catalog' ]
``` |
| *sp_grantdbaccess* | Creates a security account on the current database for a SQL Server login or a Windows NT user or group. |
| | ```
sp_grantdbaccess [@loginame =] 'login'
   [, [@name_in_db =] 'name_in_db' [OUTPUT]]
``` |
| *sp_grantlogin* | Allows a Windows NT user or group account to log in to a SQL server as a Windows NT-authenticated user. |
| | ```
sp_grantlogin [@loginame =] 'login'
``` |
| *sp_help* | Provides information about database objects with the exception of triggers. |
| | ```
sp_help [ [ @objname = ] name ]
``` |
| *sp_helpconstraint* | Provides information about a table's constraints. |
| | ```
sp_helpconstraint [ @objname = ] 'table'
   [ , [ @nomsg = ] 'no_message' ]
``` |
| *sp_helpdb* | Provides information on all databases or specified databases. |
| | ```
sp_helpdb [ [ @dbname= ] 'name' ]
``` |
| *sp_helpdbfixedrole* | Provides information on all database roles or a fixed database role. |
| | ```
sp_helpdbfixedrole [@rolename =] 'role'
``` |
| *sp_helpdevice* | Provides information on SQL Server database files. This procedure is provided to ensure backward compatibility. |
| | ```
sp_helpdevice [ [ @devname= ] 'name' ]
``` |

continued
```

Table 25-6 System Stored Procedures and Descriptions *(continued)*

Procedure Name	Description and Parameters
sp_helpfile	Returns the physical names and attributes of the files that are assigned to the current database. You can use this stored procedure to determine the names of files that are to be appended to or detached from the server.
	`sp_helpfile [ [ @filename = ] 'name' ]`
sp_helpfilegroup	Returns the names and attributes of file groups that are assigned to the current database.
	`sp_helpfilegroup [ [ @filegroupname = ] 'name' ]`
sp_helpindex	Returns information on the indexes in a table or view.
	`sp_helpindex [ @objname = ] 'name'`
sp_helplanguage	Returns information on all languages or on a specific alternative language.
	`sp_helplanguage [ [ @language = ] 'language' ]`
sp_helplinkedsrvlogin	Provides information on the defined user name assignments for a specific linked server, which are used for distributed queries and remote stored procedures.

	`sp_helplinkedsrvlogin [[ @rmtsrvname =]`
	`'rmtsrvname' ]`
	`  [ , [ @locallogin = ] 'locallogin' ]`

sp_helplogins	Provides information about SQL Server logins and the associated users in the databases.
	`sp_helplogins [ [ @LoginNamePattern = ] 'login' ]`
sp_helpntgroup	Returns information about Windows NT groups with accounts in the current database.
	`sp_helpntgroup [ [ @ntname = ] 'name' ]`
sp_helprole	Returns information about the roles in the current database.
	`sp_helprole [ [ @rolename = ] 'role' ]`
sp_helprolemember	Returns information about the members of a role in the current database.
	`sp_helprolemember [ [ @rolename = ] 'role' ]`
sp_helpprotect	Returns a report with information about user permissions for an object in the current database.

	`sp_helpprotect [ [ @name = ] 'object_statement' ]`
	`  [ , [ @username = ] 'security_account' ]`
	`  [ , [ @grantorname = ] 'grantor' ]`
	`  [ , [ @permissionarea = ] 'type' ]`

continued

Table 25-6   System Stored Procedures and Descriptions   *(continued)*

Procedure Name	Description and Parameters

sp_helpserver	Returns information about remote or replication servers.
	
	```sp_helpserver [[@server =] 'server']```
	``` [, [@optname =] 'option']```
	``` [, [@show_topology =] 'show_topology']```

sp_helpsort	Displays the sort order and the character set. ```sp_helpsort```
sp_helpsrvrole	Returns a list for all SQL Server roles or for a fixed server role. ```sp_helpsrvrole [[@srvrolename =] 'role']```
sp_helpsrvrolemember	Returns information about all members or one member of a fixed server role. ```sp_helpsrvrolemember [[@srvrolename =] 'role']```
sp_helptext	Prints the text of a rule, standard, stored procedure, user-defined function, trigger, or view. ```sp_helptext [@objname =] 'name'```

sp_helptrigger	Returns the trigger types defined for the specified table.
	
	```sp_helptrigger [@tabname =] 'table'```
	``` [, [@triggertype =] 'type']```

sp_helpuser	Returns information about users, NT users, and database roles in the current database. ```sp_helpuser [[@name_in_db =] 'security_account']```

sp_indexes	Returns index information for the specified remote table.
	
	```sp_indexes [@table_server =] 'table_server'```
	``` [, [@table_name =] 'table_name']```
	``` [, [@table_schema =] 'table_schema']```
	``` [, [@table_catalog =] 'table_db']```
	``` [, [@index_name =] 'index_name']```
	``` [, [@is_unique =] 'is_unique']```

sp_linkedservers	Returns the list of linked servers, which is defined on the local server. ```sp_linkedservers```

continued

Table 25-6 System Stored Procedures and Descriptions *(continued)*

Procedure Name	Description and Parameters
sp_makewebtask	Creates a task that fills a Hypertext Markup Language (HTML) document with data returned by the executed queries.

```
sp_makewebtask [@outputfile =] 'outputfile',
[@query =] 'query'
  [, [@fixedfont =] fixedfont]
  [, [@bold =] bold]
  [, [@italic =] italic]
  [, [@colheaders =] colheaders]
  [, [@lastupdated =] lastupdated]
  [, [@HTMLheader =] HTMLheader]
  [, [@username =] username]
  [, [@dbname =] dbname]
  [, [@templatefile =] 'templatefile']
  [, [@webpagetitle =] 'webpagetitle']
  [, [@resultstitle =] 'resultstitle']
  [
    [, [@URL =] 'URL', [@reftext =] 'reftext']
    | [, [@table_urls =] table_urls, [@url_query =]
    'url_query']
  ]
  [, [@whentype =] whentype]
  [, [@targetdate =] targetdate]
  [, [@targettime =] targettime]
  [, [@dayflags =] dayflags]
  [, [@numunits =] numunits]
  [, [@unittype =] unittype]
  [, [@procname =] procname]
  [, [@maketask =] maketask]
  [, [@rowcnt =] rowcnt]
  [, [@tabborder =] tabborder]
  [, [@singlerow =] singlerow]
  [, [@blobfmt =] blobfmt]
  [, [@nrowsperpage =] n]
  [, [@datachg =] table_column_list]
  [, [@charset =] characterset]
  [, [@codepage =] codepage]
```

| *sp_monitor* | Displays statistics about SQL Server. |

```
sp_monitor
```

| *sp_password* | Adds or modifies a password for a SQL Server user name. |

```
sp_password [ [ @old = ] 'old_password' , ]
  [ @new =] 'new_password'
  [ , [ @loginame = ] 'login' ]
```

continued

Table 25-6   System Stored Procedures and Descriptions   *(continued)*

Procedure Name	Description and Parameters
sp_pkeys	Returns primary key information for a single table.

	``sp_pkeys [@table_name =] 'name'
	    [, [@table_owner =] 'owner']
	    [, [@table_qualifier =] 'qualifier']```

sp_primarykeys	Returns the primary key columns for the specified remote table.

	``sp_primarykeys [@table_server =] 'table_server'
	    [, [@table_name =] 'table_name']
	    [, [@table_schema =] 'table_schema']
	    [, [@table_catalog =] 'table_catalog']```

sp_processmail	Processes incoming mail queries on the SQL server. The result of the query is returned to the sender by mail.

	``sp_processmail [[@subject =] 'subject']
	    [, [@filetype =] 'filetype']
	    [, [@separator =] 'separator']
	    [, [@set_user =] 'user']
	    [, [@dbuse =] 'dbname']```

sp_recompile	Causes stored procedures and triggers to be recompiled the next time they are executed.
	```sp_recompile [@objname =] 'object'```
sp_rename	Renames an object created by the user in the current database (for example, table, column, user-defined data type).

	``sp_rename [@objname =] 'object_name',
	    [@newname =] 'new_name'
	    [, [@objtype =] 'object_type']```

sp_renamedb	Renames a database.
	```sp_renamedb [@dbname =] 'old_name' , [@newname =] 'new_name'```
sp_revokedbaccess	Removes a security account from the current database.
	```sp_revokedbaccess [@name_in_db =] 'name'```
sp_revokelogin	Removes the user name entries in SQL Server for Windows NT users or groups, which were created with *sp_grantlogin*.
	```sp_revokelogin [@loginame =] 'login'```
sp_runwebtask	Runs a previously defined Web task (*sp_makewebtask*) and creates the HTML document.
	```sp_runwebtask [[@procname =] 'procname'] [, [@outputfile =] 'outputfile'```

continued

Table 25-6 **System Stored Procedures and Descriptions** *(continued)*

Procedure Name	Description and Parameters
sp_server_info	Returns a list of information about the server.
	`sp_server_info [[@attribute_id =] 'attribute_id']`
sp_srvrolepermission	Returns the permissions applicable to a fixed server role.
	`sp_srvrolepermission [[@srvrolename =] 'role']`
sp_statistics	Returns a list with all the indexes and statistics for a specific table or indexed view.

	`sp_statistics [@table_name =] 'table_name'`
	`[,[@table_owner =] 'owner']`
	`[,[@table_qualifier =] 'qualifier']`
	`[,[@index_name =] 'index_name']`
	`[,[@is_unique =] 'is_unique']`
	`[,[@accuracy =] 'accuracy']`

sp_stored_procedures	Returns a list of the stored procedures in the current environment.

	`sp_stored_procedures [[@sp_name =] 'name']`
	`[,[@sp_owner =] 'owner']`
	`[,[@sp_qualifier =] 'qualifier']`

sp_table_privileges	Returns a list of table privileges.

	`sp_table_privileges [ @table_name_pattern = ]`
	`'table_name_pattern'`
	`[, [@table_owner_pattern = ] 'table_owner_pattern' ]`
	`[, [@table_qualifier = ] 'table_qualifier' ]`

sp_tables	Returns a list of objects that can be queried in the current environment.

	`sp_tables [ [ @table_name = ] 'name' ]`
	`[ , [ @table_owner = ] 'owner' ]`
	`[ , [ @table_qualifier = ] 'qualifier' ]`
	`[ , [ @table_type = ] 'type' ]`

sp_unbindefault	Removes a default from a column or user-defined data type.
	`sp_unbindefault [@objname =] 'object_name'` `[, [@futureonly =] 'futureonly_flag']`
sp_unbindrule	Removes the rule from a column or a user-defined data type.
	`sp_unbindrule [@objname =] 'object_name'` `[, [@futureonly =] 'futureonly_flag']`
sp_validatelogins	Provides information about lost Windows NT users and groups that no longer exist in the Windows NT environment but for which there are still entries in the SQL Server system tables.
	`sp_validatelogins`

continued

Table 25-6   System Stored Procedures and Descriptions   *(continued)*

Procedure Name	Description and Parameters
sp_validname	Checks for valid SQL Server names.
	`sp_validname [@name =] 'name'` `[, [@raise_error =] raise_error]`
sp_who	Provides information about the current SQL Server users and processes.
	`sp_who [[@login_name =] 'login']`

Table 25-7 displays extended system procedures.

Table 25-7   Extended System Stored Procedures

Procedure Name	Description and Parameters
xp_cmdshell	Executes a given sequence of commands as an operating system command shell and prints the output as lines of text.
	`xp_cmdshell {'command_string'} [, no_output]`
xp_deletemail	Deletes a message from the SQL Server in-box.
	`xp_deletemail {'message_number'}`
xp_findnextmsg	Accepts a message ID as an entry and returns the next message ID as the output.

	`xp_findnextmsg [[@type =] type]`
	`[,[@unread_only =] 'unread_value']`
	`[,[@msg_id =] 'message_number' [OUTPUT]]`

xp_logevent	Logs a user-defined message in the SQL Server log file and in the Windows NT or Microsoft Windows 2000 Event Viewer.
	`xp_logevent {error_number, 'message'} [, 'severity']`
xp_readmail	Reads an e-mail message from the SQL Server in-box.

	`xp_readmail [[@msg_id =] 'message_number']`
	`[, [@type =] 'type' [OUTPUT]]`
	`[,[@peek =] 'peek']`
	`[,[@suppress_attach =] 'suppress_attach']`
	`[,[@originator =] 'sender' OUTPUT]`
	`[,[@subject =] 'subject' OUTPUT]`
	`[,[@message =] 'message' OUTPUT]`
	`[,[@recipients =] 'recipients [;...n]' OUTPUT]`
	`[,[@cc_list =] 'copy_recipients [;...n]' OUTPUT]`
	`[,[@bcc_list =] 'blind_copy_recipients [;...n]' OUTPUT]`
	`[,[@date_received =] 'date' OUTPUT]`
	`[,[@unread =] 'unread_value' OUTPUT]`
	`[,[@attachments =] 'attachments [;...n]' OUTPUT])`
	`[,[@skip_bytes =] bytes_to_skip OUTPUT]`
	`[,[@msg_length =] length_in_bytes OUTPUT]`
	`[,[@originator_address =] 'sender_address' OUTPUT]]`

continued

Table 25-7 **Extended System Stored Procedures** *(continued)*

Procedure Name	Description and Parameters
xp_sendmail	Sends a message to the specified recipients. The resultset from the SQL query is attached to the mail. ```xp_sendmail {[@recipients =] 'recipients [;...n]'} [,[@message =] 'message'] [,[@query =] 'query'] [,[@attachments =] 'attachments [;...n]'] [,[@copy_recipients =] 'copy_recipients [;...n]' [,[@blind_copy_recipients =] 'blind_copy_recipients [;...n]' [,[@subject =] 'subject'] [,[@type =] 'type'] [,[@attach_results =] 'attach_value'] [,[@no_output =] 'output_value'] [,[@no_header =] 'header_value'] [,[@width =] width] [,[@separator =] 'separator'] [,[@echo_error =] 'echo_value'] [,[@set_user =] 'user'] [,[@dbuse =] 'database']```
xp_startmail	Starts an SQL Mail client session. The Messaging Application Programming Interface (MAPI) profile needs to have been created beforehand. ```xp_startmail [[@user =] 'mapi_profile_name'] [,[@password =] 'mapi_profile_password']```
xp_stopmail	Stops an SQL Mail session. ```xp_stopmail```

Part VI

Transactions and Locks

26   Transactions and Locking

This part of the book explains how several individual commands can be combined to make transactions. A transaction can either be run in full or not at all to ensure data consistency.

In multiuser mode, locking is essential to ensure that the users do not conflict with each other, for example, several users changing the same data simultaneously.

26

Transactions and Locking

Transactions

Microsoft Access allows you to combine several database operations in a single transaction. The changes to the database are only valid when all suboperations for a transaction have been processed successfully. If this is not the case, then the database is returned to its original status before the transaction was commenced.

The basic rules for processing of transactions can be described with the acronym *ACID*:

- *Atomicity* means that a transaction cannot be subdivided further; it represents the smallest possible unit.

- *Consistency* means that the system must always have a consistent status after a transaction has been completed.

- *Isolation* means that different transactions running simultaneously are not allowed to interfere with one another.

- *Durability* means that the changes that are brought about by a transaction are permanent.

The following sections demonstrate how to program transactions in Transact-SQL and with ActiveX Data Objects (ADO).

Transactions in Transact-SQL

Transact-SQL distinguishes between two types of transactions: implicit and explicit.

Implicit Transactions

Every Transact-SQL command that changes data is treated as a transaction by default. This means that changes made with an *UPDATE*, *INSERT*, or *DELETE* command, for example, are either executed fully or not at all.

If, for example, you execute an *UPDATE* operation that changes 1000 records and only one of these records cannot be modified for some reason (for example, due to a missing foreign key dependency), the entire *UPDATE* action is reset and none of the records are changed. Termination and resetting of the *UPDATE* command does not cause termination of the stored procedure, which then continues to execute the commands subsequent to the *UPDATE*.

Implicit transactions are carried out for the following commands: *ALTER TABLE, CREATE, DELETE, DROP, FETCH, GRANT, INSERT, OPEN, REVOKE, SELECT, TRUNCATE TABLE*, and *UPDATE*.

Explicit Transactions

When using explicit transactions you can use the Transact-SQL commands *BEGIN TRANSACTION, COMMIT TRANSACTION*, and *ROLLBACK TRANSACTION* to combine and control your own transactions. For all commands, *TRANSACTION* can be abbreviated to *TRAN*.

In the following example procedure, all data for table *tblProductSales* that exists before a specified date is copied to table *tblProductSalesArchive*. The data is then deleted in *tblProductSales*. The two commands required for this procedure (*INSERT* and *DELETE*) have been included in a single transaction to avoid problems such as data being deleted even though it has not been copied.

```
CREATE PROCEDURE "ArchiveProductSales"

        @Date DATETIME

AS

        SET NOCOUNT ON

        DECLARE @Err INT

        BEGIN TRANSACTION

        INSERT tblProductSalesArchive

            SELECT * FROM tblProductSales WHERE Date < @Date

        SET @Err = @@ERROR

        IF @Err > 0 GOTO ErrorHandler

        DELETE tblProductSales WHERE Date < @Date

        SET @Err = @@ERROR

        IF @Err > 0 GOTO Errorhandler

        COMMIT TRANSACTION
```

```
ErrorHandler:

        ROLLBACK TRANSACTION

        RAISERROR ('Failure',16,1)

        RETURN
```

Transactions with ADO

The ADO *Connection* object contains three methods for executing transactions. You can use

```
Connection.BeginTrans
```

to start a transaction. After this command, you can specify database operations that belong to the transaction. The command

```
Connection.CommitTrans
```

completes the transaction. To reset a transaction, you use

```
Connection.RollbackTrans
```

The transaction consists of database operations, to each of which a record is to be added:

```
Sub TransactionsTest()

  Dim conn As ADODB.Connection

  Dim rstProducts As New ADODB.Recordset

  Dim rstProductSales As New ADODB.Recordset

  Dim fInTransaction As Boolean

  Set conn = CurrentProject.Connection

  rstProducts.Open "select * from tblProducts", conn, _
      adOpenStatic, adLockOptimistic

  rstProductSales.Open "select * from tblProductSales", conn, _
      adOpenStatic, adLockOptimistic

  On Error GoTo err_TransactionsTest

  conn.BeginTrans

  fInTransaction = True

  With rstProducts

    .AddNew
```

```
        !ProductNr = "0000"
        !Description = "TestProduct"
        .Update
    End With
    With rstProductSales
        .AddNew
        !ProductNr = "0000"
        !Amount = 5
        .Update
    End With
    conn.CommitTrans
    fInTransaction = False
exit_TransactionTest:
    rstProducts.Close
    rstProductSales.Close
    conn.Close
    Exit Sub
err_TransactionTest:
    MsgBox "Error: " & Err.Number & " "" & Err.Description & """"
    If fInTransaction Then
        conn.RollbackTrans
    End If
    Resume exit_TransactionsTest
End Sub
```

ADO allows nesting of transactions (that is, transactions can be executed within transactions). The *CommitTrans* commands must be called in the correct sequence, from the innermost transaction to the outermost.

Remember that a *RollbackTrans* is executed automatically if you use

```
Connection.Close
```

to close the connection without calling the *CommitTrans* method.

Transactions in Multiuser Environments

Transactions can also be used when several users are accessing the same table simultaneously. You should remember, however, that the records concerned are locked during the entire transaction. This can negatively affect performance, because the lock can last for considerable periods. For this reason, you should make transactions as small as possible.

User Actions During Transactions

You should always avoid using commands that require a user entry in a transaction. While the system waits for the user entry, all locks set up to this point remain active. In a multiuser environment, this can lead to an extreme restriction of performance.

Locking Records

This section describes the procedure used by Access projects and Microsoft SQL Server/MSDE for locking records in multiuser environments. A record is locked so that it cannot be edited by more than one user at the same time.

In Access mdb environments, two procedures are provided for locking records: optimistic and pessimistic locking. In Access projects and SQL Server/MSDE, you can only use optimistic locking. During pessimistic locking, the data is locked at the point at which you start processing.

Optimistic Locking in Forms

During optimistic locking the data is locked just as the changed record is about to be updated. If the record is also changed by another user during the processing period and before the update, you receive the message displayed in Figure 26-1. You then have to decide what to do with the changes you made.

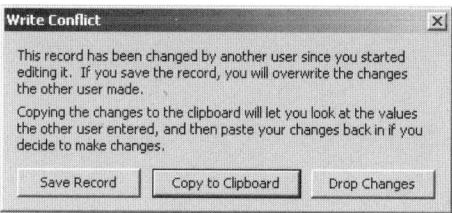

Figure 26-1   Error message

Optimistic Locking in VBA Programs

The following example displays optimistic locking for an ADO recordset using the *adLockOptimistic* parameter:

```
Sub LockTest()

  Dim rst As ADODB.Recordset

  Set rst = New ADODB.Recordset

  rst.Open "SELECT * FROM tblFilms", _

    CurrentProject.Connection, adOpenKeyset, adLockOptimistic

  On Error GoTo err_LockTest

  ' ...

  rst!Filmtitle = rst!Filmtitle

  ' ...

  rst.Update

exit_LockTest:

  rst.Close

  Exit Sub

err_LockTest:

  MsgBox "Error: " & Err.Number & " :" & Err.Description & ":"

  Resume exit_LockTest

End Sub
```

Part VII

Internet

If you would like to publish Microsoft Access data on the Internet or on an intranet, Access provides a range of features, such as the creation of static Hypertext Markup Language (HTML) files, dynamic creation with the help of Active Server Page (ASP) files, or deployment with Access data access pages. The HTML and ASP pages created by Access allow read-only data access, so you cannot make changes to the data. If you want to add, change, or delete records, you have to use different software tools, program ASP pages manually, or use Access data access pages.

Unfortunately, data access pages have decided disadvantages: Due to Microsoft's licensing policy, a Microsoft Office license must be set up for each client that wants to call a data access page. Moreover, Office Web components that are normally part of the standard Office installation have to be set up on the client. Because data access pages in an Access project do not differ from those in an Access mdb database, data access pages are not covered further in this documentation.

Chapter 27, "Web Publishing with SQL Server," provides an introduction to the Internet capability of Microsoft SQL Server/MSDE. There is an explanation of how to create time- or data-driven HTML pages with SQL Server/MSDE.

Extensible Markup Language (XML) is a document-handling standard that has been used increasingly for many applications, particularly Internet and intranet applications. Microsoft is promoting the use of XML and has built in support for it in Microsoft Access 2002 and Microsoft SQL Server 2000. Chapter 28, "XML with Access 2002 and SQL Server 2000," provides an overview of the XML functions.

27

Web Publishing with SQL Server

This chapter describes the options provided by Microsoft SQL Server for generating Web sites. This involves the creation of static Hypertext Markup Language (HTML) pages, the generation of which can be time- or data-dependent. When controlling data-dependent creation, SQL Server monitors specified tables and fields to automatically update the HTML pages when these tables and fields are changed.

For many Internet or intranet applications, static HTML pages that are regularly filled with new data are sufficient. They are easier to create and maintain than dynamic solutions, in which Active Server Pages (ASP) programs, for example, fetch the required data from the database when it is needed. Static pages are loaded significantly more quickly than dynamically generated pages and the load on the database server is reduced.

Generation of HTML pages is carried out with system procedures such as *sp_makewebtask* and *sp_runwebtask* (see Chapter 25, "System Stored Procedures"). You can also use these system procedures directly in your stored procedures.

The SQL Server Web Assistant Wizard

SQL Server provides the Web Assistant Wizard, with which you can define generation of HTML pages. Start SQL Server Enterprise Manager and connect with the SQL server containing the database that will be used to generate HTML pages.

To publish specific data, select the Wizards from the Tools menu. In the Select Wizard dialog box, shown in Figure 27-1, select the Management subgroup, and then double-click Web Assistant Wizard.

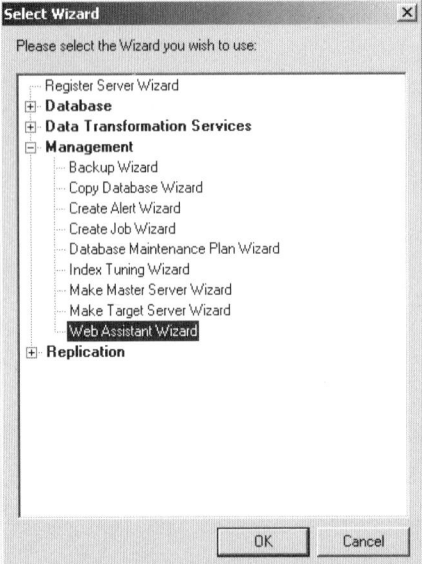

Figure 27-1   SQL Server Web Assistant Wizard in the Select Wizard
dialog box

The wizard first asks you to specify a database from which to fetch the
data using the Start A New Web Assistant Job screen. As shown in Figure 27-2,
we selected the *Contoso* database. In the next step, you enter a name for this
job and define whether the data comes from a table, a procedure, or a Transact-
SQL application.

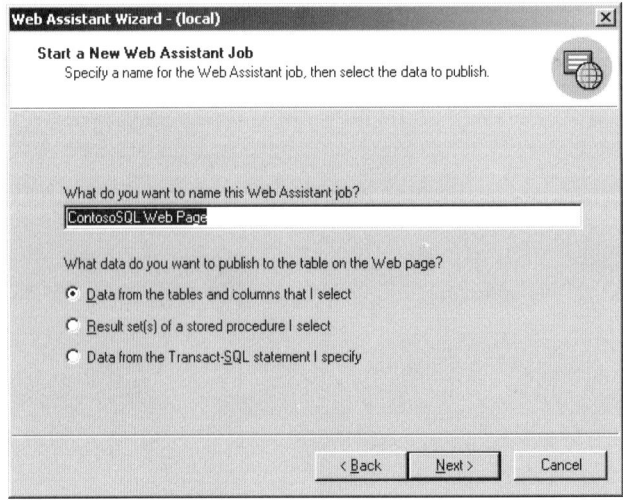

Figure 27-2   The SQL Server Web Assistant Wizard in action

If you choose the first option, the next wizard screen provides an overview of the available tables. If you choose the second option, you must select from the available procedures. If you choose the third option, the system asks you to enter your own Transact-SQL statement. For our purposes, we chose the first option, Data From The Tables And Columns That I Select.

This provides you with an overview of the available tables in the database, from which we chose the table *tblFilms*, as shown in Figure 27-3. Next, select the columns that you would like to include on the Web page.

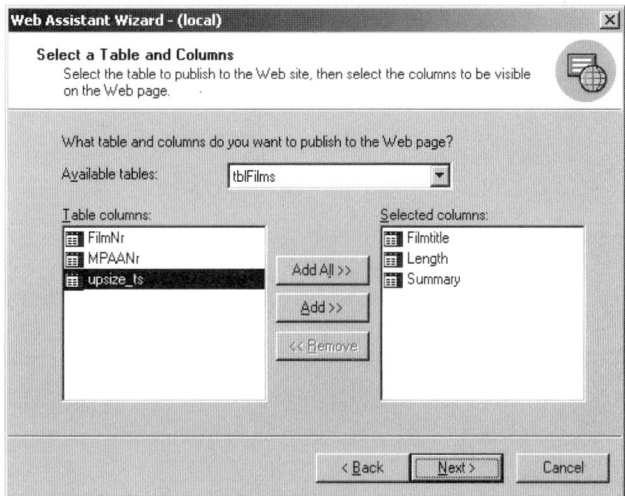

Figure 27-3   Selecting the table and columns to be included on the Web page

In the Select Rows wizard screen, displayed in Figure 27-4, you can enter some additional criteria to delimit the records or specific data. Select the All Of The Rows option if you do not want to set any restrictions. Otherwise, you can set criteria using the second option or by entering a SQL *WHERE* clause in the third input box. Because this example deals with the creation of an overview of all the films in the database, we chose the first option.

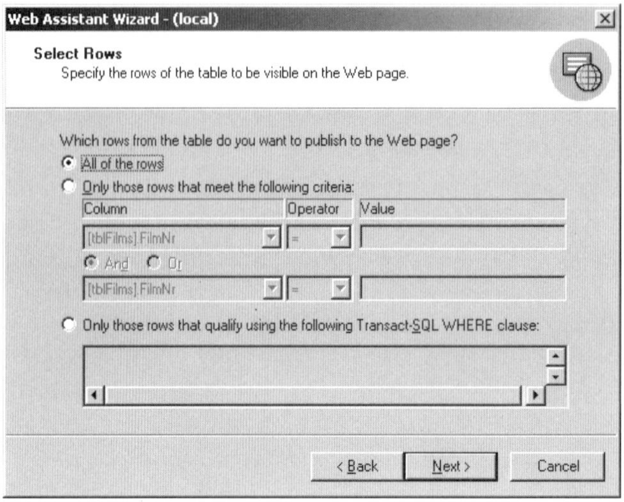

Figure 27-4   Specification of criteria for selecting records

After clicking Next, you come to what is probably the most important screen in the wizard. In the Schedule The Web Assistant Job screen, shown in Figure 27-5, you define the extent to which the page created is to be dynamic or static.

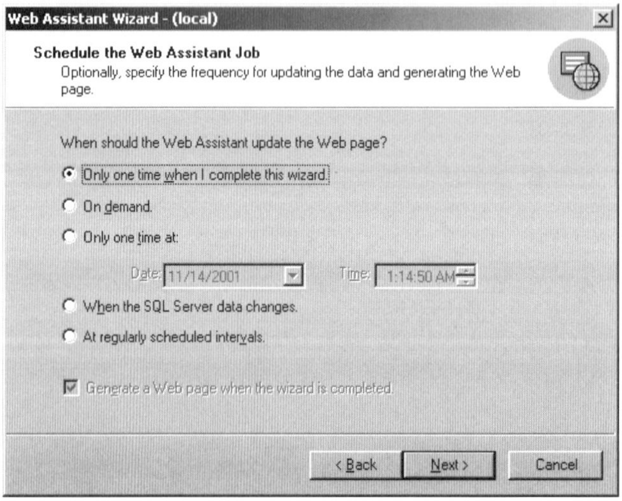

Figure 27-5   Frequency of data update

The Only One Time When I Complete This Wizard option corresponds to the creation of static pages. The Web page is created only once with all the latest data immediately on completion of the wizard. The HTML pages created can then be copied into any required directory (for example, into the Web directory of a Web server) or a virtual directory can be mapped to point to the location of the saved file.

When the On Demand option is selected, the data is updated on demand. The administrator can define when he or she wants to execute the job again and therefore re-create the Web page. There is no automatic update. The third option, Only One Time At, creates a one-time only output of the data at the time specified. This is useful if you know that after a given point in time, the data cannot be changed in any case.

Finally, you can use the wizard's last two options to update the Web page either at regular intervals (for example, every Sunday at 12:00), or whenever changes are made to the data. These variants guarantee that the data is up-to-date, but they also place additional demands on the database server.

Remember that the SQL Server Agent utility must be started to implement time-dependent Web page generation.

You can use the Generate A Web Page When The Wizard Is Completed check box to determine whether the wizard always creates the pages on completion. This check box is not available if you have selected the first option.

Select When The SQL Server Data Changes. When you click Next, the wizard asks you to define the columns to be monitored in the Monitor A Table And Columns wizard screen, shown in Figure 27-6. This is where you define which columns you want the job to monitor for changes (that is, which data changes trigger an update to the Web site).

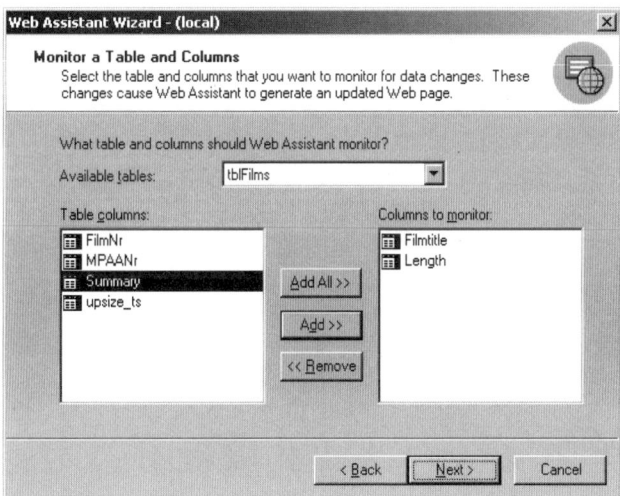

Figure 27-6   Selecting tables and columns to be monitored

If, for example, the film title is changed in a column that has been defined for monitoring, then the stored procedure created by the wizard will be executed by a trigger again and the Web page will be updated. If, however, the film number (*FilmNr*) or the Summary field is changed, then the Web page will not be updated because these columns are not monitored.

In the next wizard screen, you define where SQL Server writes the HTML files. This can be a local directory on the server hard drive, a connected network directory (for example, the directory of the Web server), or a File Transfer Protocol (FTP) directory. It is possible, for example, to save the HTML pages to a local directory and then copy them to the Web directory on the Web server by FTP upload. Select the directory to which the completed HTML pages (and also, later, the regular updates) are to be saved. Remember that the default directory to which SQL Server writes the files is the local hard drive on which SQL Server is physically installed.

In the next step you define whether or not you want to use a predefined template file, so that the Web site is generated accordingly. Then, in the next wizard screens you can define headers and formats for the page.

The system then asks you to define the hyperlinks required for the page (for example, to return to the start page). You can also take the hyperlinks directly from a table on the SQL server. The advantage to this is that you only need to enter changes to hyperlinks in the tables. At the next update to the SQL server, the correct hyperlinks are inserted.

You can use the Limit Rows wizard screen, shown in Figure 27-7, to delimit the number of records returned.

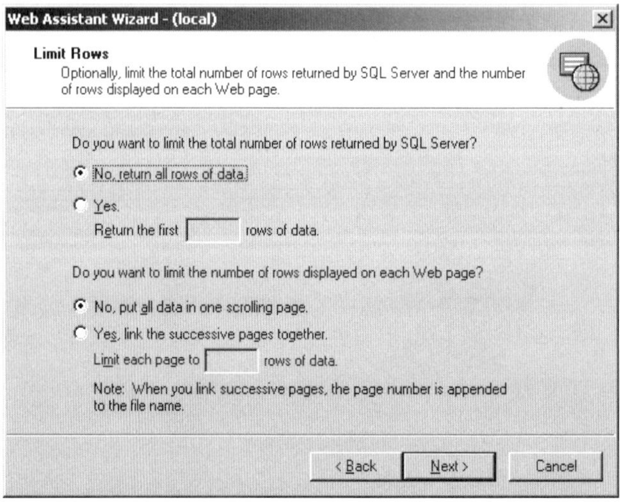

Figure 27-7   Define number of records

To ensure a better overview, you can restrict the number of records per page. The SQL Server Web Assistant Wizard then creates several Web pages with the records and connects them with hyperlinks.

The final wizard screen displays the most important settings for you to check. The Transact-SQL command created on the basis of your definitions can also be saved in a separate file. When you click Finish, the Web Assistant Wizard creates the job and generates the Web sites. The result is shown in Figure 27-8.

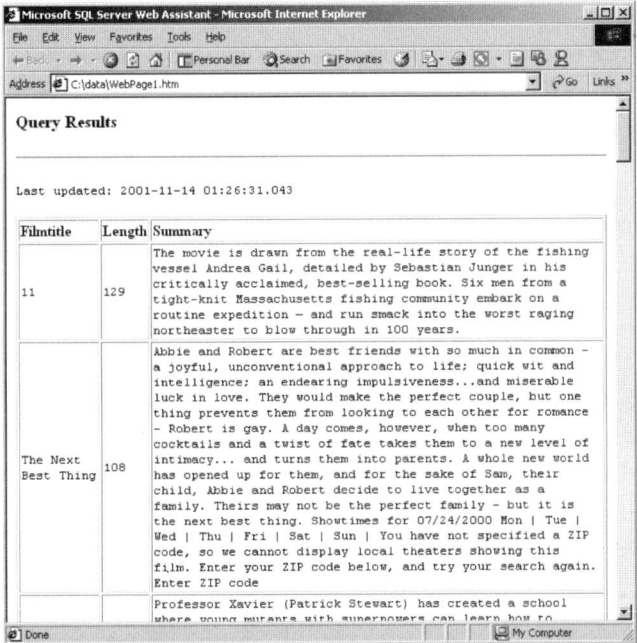

Figure 27-8   The result of the Web Assistant Wizard in Microsoft Internet Explorer

The job can be found again later in Enterprise Manager in the corresponding database under the stored procedures, such as *ContosoSQL Web Page* in this example. Note that the wizard can create additional triggers if you choose the When The SQL Server Data Changes update.

28

XML with Access 2002 and SQL Server 2000

In recent years, Extensible Markup Language (XML) has established itself as a standard for describing data and data structures. XML is a data exchange format that makes it possible to transmit data between different systems and applications.

XML utilizes the concept of self-explanatory documents that contain all the information needed to process the documents within their application environments. The World Wide Web Consortium (W3C), the same organization that defined Hypertext Markup Language (HTML), has standardized XML and related standards.

For the efficient use of XML in practice, a number of accompanying standards have been developed, such as, for example, XHTML, XML Namespaces, XML Schema, XPointer, XLink, XslT, and XPath.

Like HTML, XML is based on Standard Generalized Markup Language (SGML), which is a very sophisticated and complex language. SGML provides an architecture you can use to write any document. XML continues the SGML concept, albeit with a much simpler structure. Many exceptions and abbreviations, for example, have been eliminated.

A *tag* is a block enclosed by the characters < and >. An *element* is a block enclosed by a start tag and an end tag; for example:

```
<Filmtitle>The Perfect Storm</Filmtitle>
```

A tag can have additional attributes, such as, for example:

```
<Filmtitle Language="DE">Der Sturm</Filmtitle>
```

Tags can also enclose multiple lines and include other tags, as shown in this example:

```
<Film>

<Filmtitle>The Next Best Thing</Filmtitle>

<Length>107</Length>

</Film>
```

Note that tags are case-sensitive, which means that *<FILMTITLE>*, *<Filmtitle>*, and *<FilmTitle>* are three different tags.

In addition, in XML you can specify processing commands that are defined with *<?name data?>*, such as, for example, *<?xml version="1.0"?>*, a command that specifies the XML file's version number.

In HTML, the available tags, such as *<HTML>* ... *</HTML>* or ** ... ** are predefined, whereas you can define your own tags in XML.

If you follow the fundamental rules for using tags, you will create "well-formed" XML documents that follow these fundamentals:

■ There must be exactly one element (root element) that contains all the others.

■ All elements must have start and end tags, or the elements must be marked explicitly as empty in the tag.

■ All tags must be nested correctly.

■ All attributes must have a value enclosed by single or double quotation marks.

■ The encoding you are using must be defined at the beginning of the document, unless it is Unicode Translation Format-8 (UTF-8) or UTF-16.

The following sections describe the Microsoft Access 2002 and Microsoft SQL Server 2000 XML functions, including a short overview of the structure of XML files and their possible uses.

XML with Access 2002

You can export data in XML format from tables, views, stored procedures, forms, and reports, and you can import existing data saved in XML format. You can use Microsoft Internet Explorer, which supports XML, to view the output of the export procedure directly.

Exporting Data in XML

For the following example, we have created a view named *vwFilms* that sorts the *tblFilms* table's columns *FilmTitle* and *Length* by *Film Title*. To export the data in XML format, select the view under Queries in the Access database window, and then select File, then Export. In the Export dialog box, shown in Figure 28-1, in the Save As Type combo box, select XML Documents (*.xml).

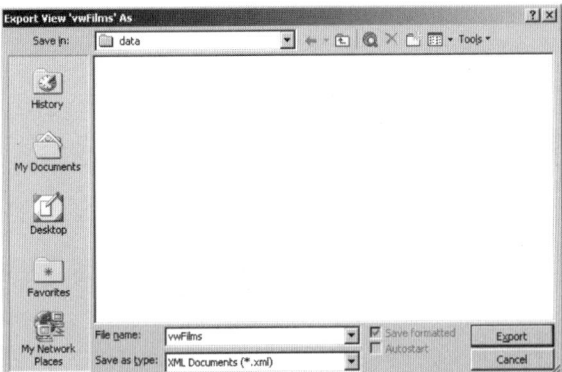

Figure 28-1   Exporting the table *tblFilms*

Once you have confirmed the dialog box, proceed to the next step and specify which information is to be exported in the Export XML dialog box, shown in Figure 28-2. The table's data is exported to an XML file, and the table structure (that is, the schema of the data) is saved to an XSD file. You can also save information about the presentation of your data to an XSL file.

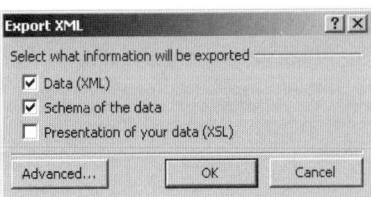

Figure 28-2   Selecting formats for export

Click Advanced to open the Export XML dialog box shown in Figure 28-3, which provides you with additional options.

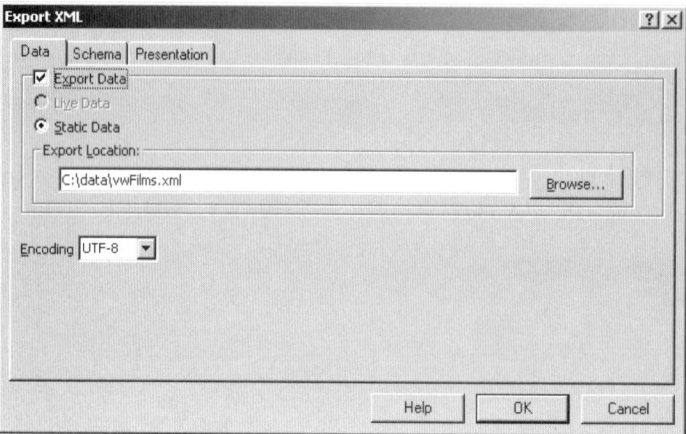

Figure 28-3   Additional export settings

Use the Data tab to define the XML file's settings. The Export Data check box specifies whether or not the system creates an XML file. If you select the Static Data option, the system generates the XML file with the data that is currently available for export in the data source. The Live Data option is available only if you are exporting a form or a report. See the section later in this chapter entitled "Live Data" for more information.

Use the Schema tab, displayed in Figure 28-4, to define if and how to write an XSD file. You can specify whether the XSD file should contain information about the data source's primary keys and indexes. Alternatively, you can also opt to embed structure information in the XML file.

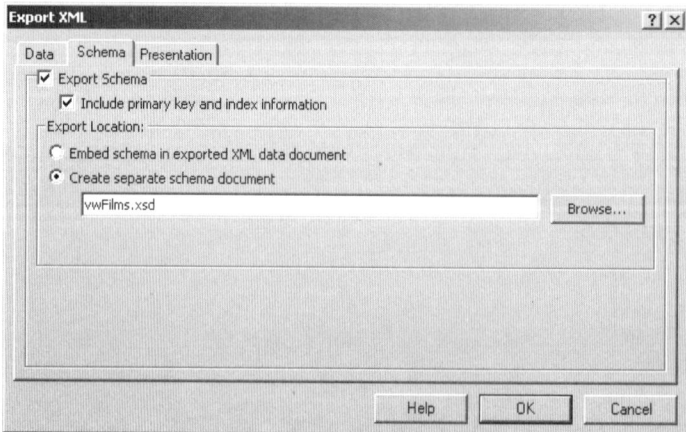

Figure 28-4   Settings for schema information

The third tab, Presentation, which is shown in Figure 28-5, lets you define information about the XML data's presentation. You can also specify whether the system analyzes the data on the client (HTML) or on the server (ASP) by selecting one of those options.

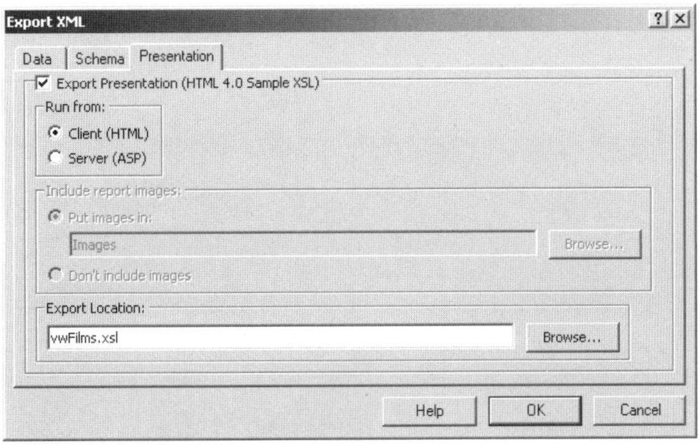

Figure 28-5   Presentation settings

The XSL file contains information about the data's display and layout. Thus, the system builds program sections in the VBScript programming language into the file. Internet Explorer analyzes these program sections when viewing the associated XML file.

The XML File

The following listing excerpt shows the contents of the XML file exported for the view *vwFilms*. The three dots in the file are not part of XML, but are intended to denote that there is more data in the actual file.

The XML file begins with the specification of the version number and encoding type. Next, the *dataroot* tag defines, among other things, the associated XSD file with the structure information:

```
<?xml version="1.0" encoding="UTF-8"?>

<dataroot xmlns:od="urn:schemas-microsoft-com:officedata"
xmlns:xsi="http://www.w3.org/2000/10/XMLSchema-instance"
xsi:noNamespaceSchemaLocation="vwFilms.xsd">

<vwFilms>

<Filmtitle>Alice and Martin</Filmtitle>

<Length>0</Length>

<MPAANr>4</MPAANr>
```

```
</vwFilms>

<vwFilms>

<Filmtitle>Fantasia 2000</Filmtitle>

<Length>74</Length>

<MPAANr>1</MPAANr>

</vwFilms>

<vwFilms>

<Filmtitle>Pokemon, the Movie 2000</Filmtitle>

<Length>80</Length>

<MPAANr>1</MPAANr>

</vwFilms>

<vwFilms>

<Filmtitle><![CDATA[Big Momma's House]]></Filmtitle>

<Length>90</Length>

<MPAANr>3</MPAANr>

</vwFilms>

...

...

...

<vwFilms>

<Filmtitle>Sunshine</Filmtitle>

<Length>180</Length>

<MPAANr>4</MPAANr>

</vwFilms>

</dataroot>
```

Figure 28-6 displays the XML file in Internet Explorer, which can analyze the XML file and output it in a structured manner.

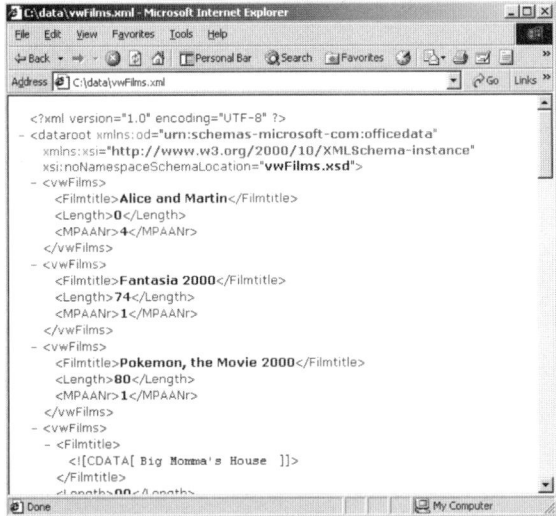

Figure 28-6   Display of the XML file in Internet Explorer

Structure Information in the XSD File

The XSD file saves the information about the XML file's structure in the same notation that is used in the XML file:

```
<?xml version="1.0" encoding="UTF-8"?>
```

```
<xsd:schema xmlns:xsd="http://www.w3.org/2000/10/XMLSchema"
xmlns:od="urn:schemas-microsoft-com:officedata">
```

```
<xsd:element name="dataroot">
```

```
<xsd:complexType>
```

```
<xsd:choice maxOccurs="unbounded">
```

```
<xsd:element ref="vwFilms"/>
```

```
</xsd:choice>
```

```
</xsd:complexType>
```

```
</xsd:element>
```

```
<xsd:element name="vwFilms">
```

```
<xsd:annotation>
```

```
<xsd:appinfo/>
```

```
</xsd:annotation>
```

```
<xsd:complexType>
```

```
<xsd:sequence>

<xsd:element name="Filmtitle" minOccurs="0" od:jetType="text">

<xsd:simpleType>

<xsd:restriction base="xsd:string">

<xsd:maxLength value="100"/>

</xsd:restriction>

</xsd:simpleType>

</xsd:element>

<xsd:element name="Length" minOccurs="0" od:jetType="integer"
type="xsd:short"/>

<xsd:element name="MPAANr" minOccurs="0" od:jetType="integer"
type="xsd:short"/>

</xsd:sequence>

</xsd:complexType>

</xsd:element>

</xsd:schema>
```

XSL File-Based Presentation

During export, the system inserts HTML commands and a VBScript program into the XSL file for the display of the XML data. The following listing shows an example that displays the XML data in three columns of a table, but this script is significantly abbreviated. You should attempt to export a test form or report in XML and then view the created XSL files to familiarize yourself with the display options.

In addition to the XSL file, the export function creates HTML or Active Server Pages (ASP) code, which is attached to the XSL file's listing:

```
<?xml version="1.0"?>

<xsl:stylesheet xmlns:xsl="http://www.w3.org/TR/WD-xsl"
language="vbscript">

<xsl:template match="/">

<HTML>

<HEAD>

<META HTTP-EQUIV="Content-Type" CONTENT="text/html;charset=UTF-8" />

<TITLE>
```

```
vwFilms

</TITLE>

<STYLE TYPE="text/css">

</STYLE>

</HEAD>

<BODY link="#0000ff" vlink="#800080">

<TABLE BORDER="1" BGCOLOR="#ffffff" CELLSPACING="0" CELLPAD
DING="0"><TBODY>


<xsl:for-each select="/dataroot/vwFilms">

<xsl:eval>AppendNodeIndex(me)</xsl:eval>

</xsl:for-each>

<xsl:for-each select="/dataroot/vwFilms">

<xsl:eval>CacheCurrentNode(me)</xsl:eval>

<xsl:if expr="OnFirstNode">

<TR><TH style="width: 1in">

Filmtitle

</TH>

<TH style="width: 1in">

Length

</TH>

<TH style="width: 1in">

MPAANr

</TH>

</TR>

</xsl:if>

<TR><TD>

<xsl:eval no-entities="true">Format(GetValue("Filmtitle", 202),""
,"")</xsl:eval>

</TD>

<TD>
```

```
<xsl:eval no-entities="true">Format(GetValue("Length", 2),"" ,"")
</xsl:eval>

</TD>

<TD>

<xsl:eval no-entities="true">Format(GetValue("MPAANr", 2),"" ,"")
</xsl:eval>

</TD>

</TR>

<xsl:if expr="OnLastNode">

</xsl:if>

<xsl:eval>NextNode()</xsl:eval>

</xsl:for-each>

</TBODY></TABLE>

</BODY>

</HTML>

<xsl:script>

<![CDATA[

    'variable declaration

    dim cNodes

    dim iCurrNode

    dim rgNodes()

    dim objCurrNode

    dim sizeIncrement

    dim objGroupNodes

    dim rgFields()

    dim rgRowsources()

    dim rgGroupOn()

    dim rgGroupInterval()

    dim rgfGroupBoundaries()

    dim cGroups

    dim cGroupBoundaries

    dim rgGroupRowsources()
```

```
'variable initialization
sizeIncrementGroup = 10
sizeIncrementNode = 100
cNodes = 0
cGroups = 0
cGroupBoundaries = 0
iCurrNode = 0
objCurrNode = null
objGroupNodes = null
ReDim rgNodes(sizeIncrement)
ReDim rgFields(sizeIncrementGroup)
ReDim rgRowsources(sizeIncrementGroup)
ReDim rgGroupOn(sizeIncrementGroup)
ReDim rgGroupInterval(sizeIncrementGroup)
ReDim rgfGroupBoundaries(sizeIncrementNode)
ReDim rgGroupRowsources(sizeIncrementGroup)

function SetGroupFilter(iLevel, strField, strRowsource, strGroupOn, _
 strGroupInterval)
   if (cGroups Mod sizeIncrementGroup) = 0 then
       ReDim Preserve rgFields(sizeIncrementGroup+cGroups)
       ReDim Preserve rgRowsources(sizeIncrementGroup+cGroups)
       ReDim Preserve rgGroupOn(sizeIncrementGroup+cGroups)
       ReDim Preserve rgGroupInterval(sizeIncrementGroup+cGroups)
       ReDim Preserve rgGroupRowsources(sizeIncrementGroup+cGroups)
   end if
   dim Field
   dim Rowsource
   dim GroupOn
   dim GroupInterval
   rgFields(cGroups) = strField
```

```
            rgRowsources(cGroups) = strRowsource

            rgGroupOn(cGroups) = strGroupOn

            rgGroupInterval(cGroups) = strGroupInterval

            cGroups = cGroups + 1

            SetGroupFilter = ""

        end function
...

...

...


]]>
</xsl:script>
</xsl:template>
</xsl:stylesheet>
```

HTML for Execution on a Client

The export function has generated the following HTML code to provide a formatted display of the XML data with XSL. The integrated script loads the XML and XSL files.

Note that the export function creates HTML code you that can execute only with Internet Explorer, although an .asp template can be used to generate HTML code with an Active Server Page (ASP) instead, as shown in the following sample:

```
<HTML xmlns:signature="urn:schemas-microsoft-com:office:access">

<HEAD>

<META HTTP-EQUIV="Content-Type" CONTENT="text/html;charset=UTF-8"/>

</HEAD>

<SCRIPT event=onload for=window>

  objData = new ActiveXObject("MSXML.DOMDocument");

  objData.async = false;

  objData.load("vwFilms.xml");

  if (objData.parseError.errorCode != 0)

    alert(objData.parseError.reason);
```

```
objStyle = new ActiveXObject("MSXML.DOMDocument");

objStyle.async = false;

objStyle.load("vwFilms.xsl");

if (objStyle.parseError.errorCode != 0)

  alert(objStyle.parseError.reason);


document.open("text/html","replace");

document.write(objData.transformNode(objStyle));

</SCRIPT>

</HTML>
```

ASP for Microsoft Internet Information Services

If you want to run the XML/XSL solution on Microsoft Internet Information Services (IIS), select the Server (ASP) option in the Export XML dialog box (see Figure 28-5). The following listing shows the content of the file VWFILMS.ASP. If you open the file from a client with *http://localhost/vwFilms.asp*, for example, the ASP file is processed on the server. This means that the script is executed and the result is sent to the client in HTML code for display. The client supports all browsers, not just Internet Explorer.

```
<%

Set objData = Server.CreateObject("MSXML.DOMDocument")

objData.async = false


if (false) then

        Set objDataXMLHTTP = Server.CreateObject("Microsoft.XMLHTTP")

        objDataXMLHTTP.open "GET", "", false

        objDataXMLHTTP.setRequestHeader "Content-Type", "text/xml"

        objDataXMLHTTP.send

        objData.load(objDataXMLHTTP.responseBody)

else

        objData.load(Server.MapPath("vwFilms.xml"))

end if
```

```
Set objStyle = Server.CreateObject("MSXML.DOMDocument")

objStyle.async = false

objStyle.load(Server.MapPath("vwFilms.xsl"))


Response.ContentType = "text/html"

Response.Write objData.transformNode(objStyle)

%>
```

The *ExportXML* and *ImportXML* Methods

The *Application* object's *ExportXML* and *ImportXML* methods are available to execute the XML export or import from a Microsoft Visual Basic for Applications (VBA) program.

ExportXML
This is the definition for *ExportXML*:

```
Application.ExportXML(ObjectType, DataSource, DataTarget,

        SchemaTarget, PresentationTarget, ImageTarget,

        Encoding, OtherFlags)
```

You can enter one of the following constants, which specify the type of object to be exported, for *ObjectType*: *acExportTable*, *acExportQuery*, *acExportServerView*, *acExportStoredProcedure*, *acExportFunction*, *acExportForm*, *acExportReport*, or *acExportDataAccessPage*.

Enter the name of the object to be exported under *DataSource* and the target file under *DataTarget*.

If you want to create an XSL file with structure information in addition to the XML file, you must enter a filename under *SchemaTarget*. If you do not specify a filename, the system embeds the schema information in the XML file.

You can control the file's presentation from an XSL file. Enter the filename under *PresentationTarget*. If you need images for the presentation, you can use *ImageTarget* to specify a path name for the images to be exported.

Use *Encoding* to specify the text-encoding format for the file to be exported. The default format is *acUTF8*, and other possible values are *acEUCJ*, *acUCS2*, *acUCS4*, or *acUTF16*.

The parameter *OtherFlags* is a bitmap that can also help control the XML format export procedure. Refer to Access Help for more information.

ImportXML

You can use this method to import XML data. The method's complete definition is as follows:

```
Application.ImportXML(DataSource, ImportOptions)
```

DataSource specifies the name of the XML file to be imported. The name of the target table is defined in the XML file or the associated XSD file. During the import process, you can convert the XML data with an XSL file designated as *DataTransform*. You can pass one of the following constants to the *ImportOptions* parameter: *acStructureAndData*, *acStructureOnly*, or *acAppendData*.

ADO Recordsets and XML

If you are programming with ActiveX Data Objects (ADO), you can save an ADO recordset as an XML file. For more information, read the section entitled "Saving Recordsets" in Chapter 13, "Recordset Objects."

XML with SQL Server 2000

XML support is one of the new features of SQL Server 2000 (and Microsoft Data Engine [MSDE] 2000). The supported XML functions include the following:

■   The option to access SQL Server queries and procedures using Hypertext Transfer Protocol (HTTP) with a uniform resource locator (URL). The system returns the results in XML.

■   The option to read and generate XML data with commands such as *OPENXML*.

■   Support of XML Data Reduced (XDR), a proprietary Microsoft XML schema standard environment (also known as XSD). W3C has recommended XML schema since May 2001.

■   Support for XSD with SQLXML 2.0 download.

■   The SQL Server 2000 object linking and embedding database (OLE DB) provider and ADO were expanded, so that the system can now process XML data.

■   With a SQL Server 2000 extension (available for download at *www.microsoft.com/sql*) you can use *updategrams*. Their purpose is the insertion, update, and deletion of tables using XML data in SQL Server.

> **More Info**   As XSD and XML implementations are being developed, SQL Server integration with these standards is continuously improving. For more information and the latest downloads, including support for XSD, you can visit *http://msdn.microsoft.com/sqlxml*.

The following sections explain how to use a URL to query SQL Server data using HTTP and describe a possible use in Access. The scope of this book does not permit the inclusion of a complete description of SQL Server 2000 XML capabilities.

Configuration

A few preparations are necessary before you can use a URL to query a SQL Server's data using HTTP. The following sections assume that you have a computer running Microsoft Windows 2000 Server, IIS, and SQL Server 2000.

Setting Up a Virtual Directory

First, create a folder named Contoso in the \Inetpub\Wwwroot folder. Next, create a virtual directory. Select Start, then Programs, then Microsoft SQL Server, and then Configure XML Support In IIS, which displays the screen shown in Figure 28-7.

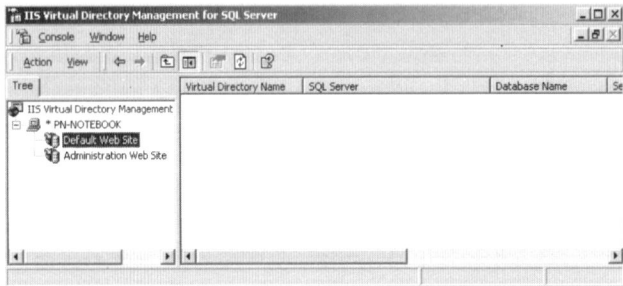

Figure 28-7   Administration program for virtual directories

Select Default Web Site. Select Action, then New, then Virtual Directory to open the New Virtual Directory Properties dialog box shown in Figure 28-8.

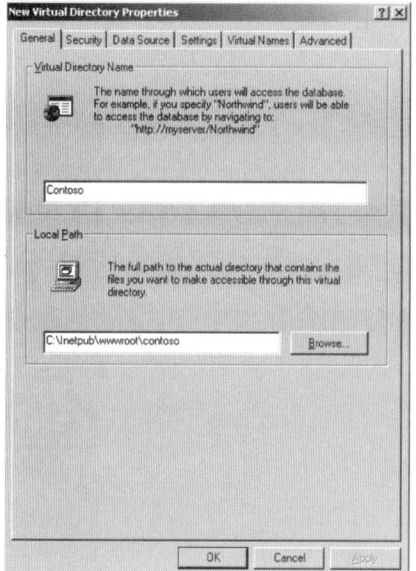

Figure 28-8   Dialog box for creating a virtual directory

In our example, the virtual directory name is *Contoso*. The specified local path name is c:\Inetpub\wwwroot\Contoso.

You can use the Security tab to select security information settings. There are three available options. If you select the first option, the system executes all database operations with the specified user name, regardless of who submitted the query. This option uses Windows authentication, which means that the user must be entered as a Windows user. The last option uses SQL Server security.

Use the Data Source tab to specify the SQL server and database.

You can use the Settings tab to specify which query variants you want to allow. It is safest to allow template queries only, which is the default setting. We want to introduce you to the easier-to-use variant of URL queries, which is why the Allow Sql = ... Or Template =... URL Queries check box is also selected, as shown in Figure 28-9.

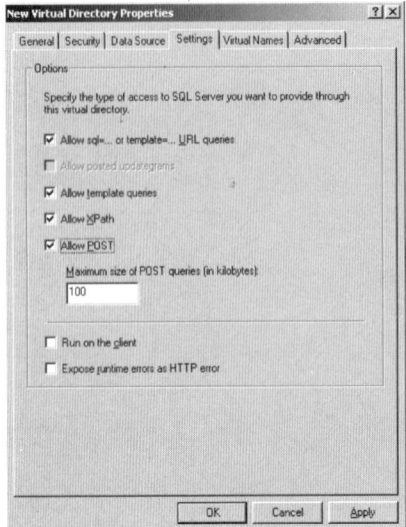

Figure 28-9   Allowing query variants

> **Note**   Depending on the versions of the SQL XML tools you have installed, the dialog boxes may be slightly different. Additionally, you may require a network connection on your computer in order to configure IIS support for SQL Server. If you are working on a stand-alone computer, you may add a Microsoft Loopback Adapter using the Add/Remove Hardware Wizard.

Next, use the Virtual Names tab to define settings needed for XPath queries or XML templates, for example. The Advanced tab lets you assign additional settings that we are not using in this context.

Executing URL Queries

You can now query SQL Server with Internet Explorer. This process takes advantage of the SQL Server 2000 feature that returns query results directly in XML code. You can do this with the supplement *FOR XML*, for example:

```
SELECT * FROM tblProducts FOR XML AUTO
```

The *AUTO* parameter returns the XML query result in the form of embedded elements. Note that the query result is an XML fragment only and not a well-formed XML document.

To run a URL query, enter a URL in Internet Explorer's address line, for example:

```
http://localhost/contoso?sql=select+*+from+tbl
Films+for+xml+auto&root=root
```

You must enter the name of your server under *servername*. Figure 28-10 shows the result. Alternatively, use *localhost* if your IIS server is installed on your local computer.

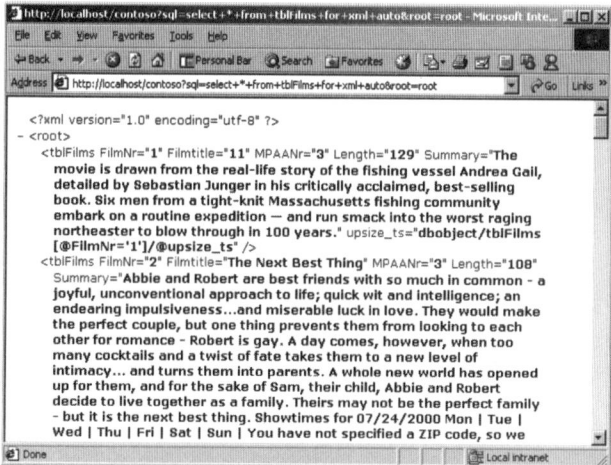

Figure 28-10   Result displayed in the browser

Note that plus signs are used instead of spaces in the SQL command. *&root=root* was appended to the SQL query to instruct the SQL server to generate a tag <root> ... </root> that encloses the query's resultset. This ensures well-formed XML output.

If you do not append *&root=root*, Internet Explorer displays the message shown in Figure 28-11.

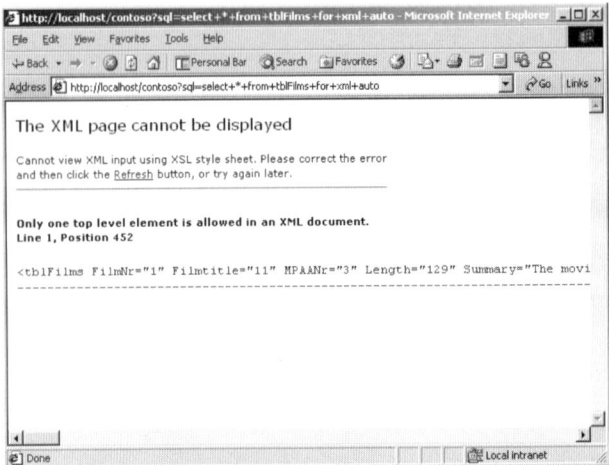

Figure 28-11   Error message shown because the XML document is not well-formed

Activating a Stored Procedure with a URL

You can use a stored procedure to generate a well-formed XML document directly. The procedure *FilmsXML* shown in Figure 28-12 adds root tags to the query.

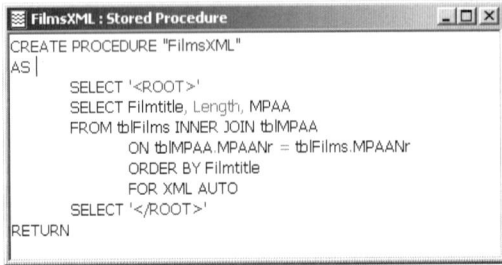

Figure 28-12   The stored procedure *FilmsXML*

Enter the URL *http://localhost/contoso?sql=exec+FilmsXML* to activate the query.

Now you can also use queries with parameters. The following listing extends a parameter named *@FilmNr*.

```
CREATE PROCEDURE FilmsXML2 @FilmNr INT

AS

        SELECT '<ROOT>'

        SELECT Filmtitle, Length FROM tblFilme

            WHERE FilmNr = @FilmNr
```

```
        ORDER BY Filmtitle
        FOR XML AUTO
     SELECT '</ROOT>'
RETURN
```

The activation *http://localhost/contoso?sql=exec+FilmsXML2+1* of the stored query returns the data for the film with the film number 1 as the result.

This method of querying data with URLs is not suitable for the end user, because it is not easy to compose the query, and the query result's display is not reader-friendly. The following section describes a case for using URL queries.

Programming with the Microsoft XML Library

Imagine the following scenario: A company's branch office uses Access. One of the Access applications occasionally requires data that is administered by a SQL server at the company headquarters. All employees at the branch office have Internet access, and the SQL server at the company's headquarters is accessible through the Internet with IIS. A form that uses a URL query that returns data from the central server through the Internet is now added to the branch office's Access application. In this context, we are overlooking the issue of data security, but in practice you should always implement appropriate security measures.

We have transferred this scenario to our example and we are using a form to request film data through the Internet. The system fetches the film titles using a URL query and displays them in a list box, as shown in Figure 28-13. If you select a film title, a second URL query returns the film's rating and length.

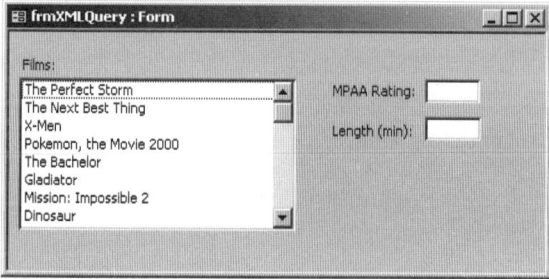

Figure 28-13   Example form *frmXMLQuery*

The URL queries are activated from a VBA program that the system executes when loading the form, for example. We use the Microsoft XML library, which is included with Internet Explorer, to enable a VBA program to send HTTP queries through the Internet and to receive XML. You must define a reference to the Microsoft XML library in the VBA editor, as shown in Figure 28-14.

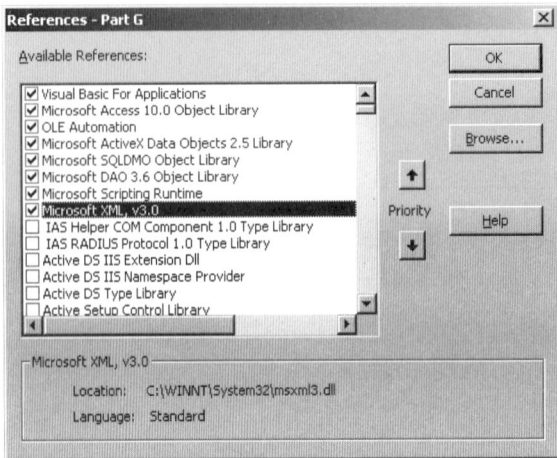

Figure 28-14   Integrating the Microsoft XML library

The example form's program shows the following listing:

```
Option Compare Database
' Object for HTTP-connection
Dim mHTTP As XMLHTTP
Private Sub Form_Load()
  Set mHTTP = New XMLHTTP
  ' Retrieve film title
  AllFilmtitles_XML_via_HTTP
End Sub


Private Sub Form_Unload(Cancel As Integer)
  Set mHTTP = Nothing
End Sub


Private Sub lstFilms_Click()
  ' Retrieve movie data
  Filmdata_XML_via_HTTP lstFilms.Value
End Sub


Private Sub AllFilmtitles_XML_via_HTTP()
```

```
Dim dom As DOMDocument

Dim child As IXMLDOMNode

Dim att As IXMLDOMAttribute

Dim strURL As String

Dim strFilmNr As String

Dim strFilmtitle As String

Set dom = New DOMDocument


' Query

strURL = "http://localhost/Contoso?sql=exec+FilmtitleXML"

' Open HTTP-connection

mHTTP.Open "GET", strURL, False

' Send data to server

mHTTP.send

' If result

If dom.loadXML(mHTTP.responseText) Then

  ' dom.childnodes(0) = <tblFilms>-element

  For Each child In dom.childNodes(0).childNodes

    ' Retrieve FilmNr and Filmtitle

    strFilmNr = child.Attributes.getNamedItem("FilmNr").nodeValue

    strFilmtitle =
    child.Attributes.getNamedItem("Filmtitle").nodeValue

    ' add to list box

    ' Column width for FilmNr is 0

    lstFilms.AddItem strFilmNr & ";" & strFilmtitle

  Next

End If

Set dom = Nothing

End Sub
```

```
Private Sub Filmdata_XML_via_HTTP(lngFilmNr As Long)


    Dim dom As DOMDocument

    Dim child As IXMLDOMNode

    Dim att As IXMLDOMAttribute

    Dim strURL As String


    Set dom = New DOMDocument


    ' Query with parameter

    strURL = "http://localhost/Contoso?sql=execute+FilmsXML2+" &
    lngFilmNr


    mHTTP.Open "GET", strURL, False

    mHTTP.send

    If dom.loadXML(mHTTP.responseText) Then

        ' dom.childnodes(0) = <tblFilms>-element

        txtFSK = dom.childNodes(0).childNodes(0).Attributes(1).nodeValue

        txtLength =
        dom.childNodes(0).childNodes(0).Attributes(2).nodeValue

    End If

    Set dom = Nothing

End Sub
```

Updategrams

The XML extensions for SQL Server 2000 provided by Microsoft extend the XML functions with updategrams, which are special XML files that can be used to add, edit, and delete data in SQL Server tables. You can download the XML extension on the Internet from *msdn.microsoft.com/sqlxml* and *msdn.microsoft.com/xml*. In the download area, look for XML for SQL Server 2000 Web Release 2 or later and SQLXML 2.0. The download includes documentation for the updategrams.

Live Data

The Access 2002 XML export function we introduced in the earlier section "Exporting Data in XML" lets you define the Live Data option for exporting forms and reports (see Figure 28-2). If you select this option, the system does not create a static XML file with the data on which the form or report is based. Instead, a URL query is added to the XML file that updates the data when you open the XML file in the browser. The following listing exemplifies such an XML file:

```
<?xml version="1.0" encoding="UTF-8"?>

<!DOCTYPE dataroot [

 <!ENTITY livedata SYSTEM

"http://localhost/ContosoSQL?sql=SELECT+*+FROM

+%22tblFilms%22+for+xml+auto,elements">

]>

<dataroot xmlns:od="urn:schemas-microsoft-com:officedata">&livedata;
</dataroot>
```

Part VIII

Appendices

Appendix A

Naming Conventions

When working in the Microsoft Access development environment, you should use a naming convention that defines guidelines on how to name variables, objects, and components in Microsoft Visual Basic for Application (VBA) programs, forms, reports, and so forth. Naming conventions allow users to determine information about the properties of an object (for example, a variable) just by looking at its name. Naming conventions are also intended to make programs easier to read and improve cooperation among programming teams.

Microsoft Office 2000 Developer Tools, available at *http://www.microsoft.com*, includes "Naming Guidelines for Visual Basic" from Microsoft Consulting Services. You can find these guidelines in the MCS NAMING CONVENTIONS.DOC file in the folder \Odetools\V9\Samples\Opgappendixes on the corresponding CD-ROM. Unfortunately, the naming conventions date from 1997, which means that they do not contain naming conventions for ActiveX Data Objects (ADO) objects, for example.

Microsoft Office XP Developer Tools does not contain any naming convention documents.

One of the guidelines used by many programmers is the Reddick VBA (RVBA) naming convention. Greg Reddick worked on the Microsoft Access development team for four years and is president of Xoc Software, a company that develops software in Microsoft Visual Basic, Microsoft Access, C/C++, and software for the Internet. His naming conventions can be downloaded from the Xoc software Web site (*http://www.xoc.net*).

The Microsoft guidelines and the RVBA naming convention contain many similarities, partly because both are based on the *Hungarian notation* developed by Charles Simonyi at Microsoft. Simonyi was in charge of the early development of Microsoft Word.

Neither the naming guidelines from Microsoft nor the RVBA naming conventions meet all the requirements for the programming of Access, especially Access projects. The following text is a summary and reworking of both guidelines. In his text, Reddick wrote, "These conventions are intended as a guideline. If you disagree with a particular part of the conventions, simply replace that part with what you think works better. However, keep in mind that future generations of programmers may need to understand those changes, and place a comment in the header of a module indicating what changes have been made. To be concise, the conventions are presented without rationalizations for how they were derived although each of the ideas presented has a considerable history to it."

The following text is intended to serve as an impetus for you to develop your own naming conventions or adapt existing naming conventions to your own requirements.

Hungarian Notation

The purpose of Simonyi's Hungarian notation is to express information for an object concisely and efficiently. Hungarian notation takes some getting used to, but it quickly becomes second nature. The format of an object name created using Hungarian notation is as follows:

```
[Prefix]tag[Basename[Suffixes]]
```

The brackets indicate the optional sections of the object name. The individual components are described next.

The *prefix* provides additional information for the tag. The prefix is written in lowercase. Prefixes are usually taken from an existing list described later in this appendix.

The *tag* consists of a short series of letters that indicate the object type. The tag is written in lowercase. A standardized list of tags is provided later in this appendix.

The *base name* consists of one or more words that describe what the object represents. The first letter of each word is written in uppercase.

The *suffixes* provide additional information about the base name. The first letter of each word of the suffix is written in uppercase. A standard list of suffixes is provided later in this appendix.

Remember that the word *Object* in later text refers to simple variables and VBA objects, as well as to objects that are provided by Access and other applications.

Tags

The tag describes the data type for an object, and it is the only part of an object name that is actually needed. At first glance, it seems strange that the base name is not the most important part of an object name. However, consider an integrated procedure that works within a form, for example. In this case, the fact that the routine works within the form is important, rather than what the form represents. Because the routine could work within many different types of forms, you do not necessarily need the base name. If, however, you use more than one object of a certain type in a routine, you must use a base name for all but one of the objects to differentiate between them. The base name also contains information on the variable, which should always contain a base name.

Tags for Variables

Use the tags for VBA data types listed in Table A-1.

Table A-1   Tags for VBA Variables

Tag	Variable Type
bool {f, bln}	Boolean
byte {byt}	Byte
cur	Currency
date {dtm}	Date
dec	Decimal
dbl	Double
int	Integer
lng	Long
obj	Object
sng	Single
str	String
stf	String (fixed length)
var	Variant

Here are some examples:

```
lngCount

intValue

strText
```

You should declare all variables explicitly in a single line. Do not use the old basic declaration for variables (such as %, &, and $). This is unnecessary if you are using the naming convention. Also, no symbol is defined for some data types, such as *Boolean*. Declare all variables of the data type *Variant* with *As Variant*, even if the data type *Variant* is the standard data type:

```
Dim intCount As Integer

Dim varField As Variant

Dim strName As String
```

Tags for Collections

Collections contain special tags that are defined by adding an *s* to the data type for the collection. A collection with data type *Long*, for example, would have the tag *lngs*. The tag for a collection of forms is *frms*. Although a collection of theoretical objects can contain different data types, in practice all data types in a collection are the same. If you want to use different data types in a collection, use the tag *obj*:

```
intsSupplierNo

frmsAddresses

objsDummy
```

Tags for Constants

VBA constants always have one data type. Because VBA will define the data type for you if you do not do so yourself, you should specify the data type for constants. Constants that are contained in the general declarations section should have the keyword *Private* or *Public*, and should be given the prefix *m* or *g*. The constant is indicated by adding the letter *c* to the tag:

```
Const intcStandard As Integer = 3

Private Const mdblcPi As Double = 3.14159265358
```

Explicitly specifying constants using the data type is considered by many programmers too time-consuming. If you want to name constants more quickly, use the *con* tag:

```
Const conPi As Double = 3.14159265358
```

Menu Elements

Names of menu elements should reflect their position in the menu hierarchy. All menu elements should use the tag *mnu*, and the base name should indicate the position of the menu element within the menu hierarchy. Use *Sep*, followed by an ordinal number in the base name, to indicate a separating hyphen in a menu.

- *mnuFile* (in the menu bar)

- *mnuFileNew* (New command in the File menu)

- *mnuFileNewForm* (Form command in the flyout menu for File, New)

- *mnuFileSep1* (first separation hyphen in the File menu)

- *mnuFileSaveAs* (Save As command in the File menu)

- *mnuFileSep2* (second separation hyphen in the File menu)

- *mnuFileExit* (Exit command in the File menu)

- *mnuEdit* (in the menu bar)

Creating Data Types

VBA enables you to create three categories of new data types: *Enum* types, classes, and custom types. In each case you must devise a new tag to describe the new data type that you have created.

Data Type *Enum*

Groups of constants for the data type *Long* should be combined in a single *Enum* type. Invent a new tag for the data type, append a *c* to it, and define the *Enum* constants with the tag. Because the name that is defined in the *Enum* line is represented in the object browser, you can use the base name to describe the abbreviation that is defined by the tag, as shown here:

```
Public Enum ervcErrorValue
   ervcNoError = 0
   ervcADOError
   ervcValueOutOfBounds
   ervcInvalidType = 205
End Enum
```

Define the base name in the singular: The enumerated type should be called *ervcErrorValue* and not *ervcErrorsValues*. You can then apply the tag that you invented for the *Enum* type to variables that contain values of this type, for example:

```
Dim erv As ervcErrorValue
```

Tags for Classes and Custom Types

A class defines a custom (user-defined) object. Because this creates a new data type, you must invent a new tag for the object. You can use the base name to describe an abbreviation of the tag. Custom types are treated as a simple class that only contains properties, but are otherwise used in the same way as class modules.

Creating Procedures

VBA procedures require names for different objects: the procedures themselves, parameters, and markers. These objects are described in the following section.

Creating Procedure Names

Event procedures are named by VBA, and you cannot change these names. You should use the uppercase proposed by the system. When writing custom procedure names, write the first letter of each word in uppercase, for example:

```
cmdOK_Click
```

```
GetTitleBarString
```

```
PerformInitialization
```

For procedures, you should always specify the validity range using *Public* or *Private*, if they are being declared:

```
Public Function GetTitleBarString() As String
```

```
Private Sub PerformInitialization()
```

Naming Parameters

You should use the supplement *ByVal* or *ByRef* for all parameters, even if *ByRef* is optional and therefore redundant. Parameters for procedures are named in exactly the same way as simple variants of the same type, except that arguments that are transferred "by reference" receive the supplement *r*, as in:

```
Public Sub TestValue(ByVal intInput As Integer, ByRef rlngOutput As Long)
```

```
Private Function GetValue(ByVal strKey As String, ByRef rgph As Glyph)
As Boolean
```

Very few programmers use *ByVal* and *ByRef* consistently. The parameters are mostly used by procedures without supplements so that they are transferred in the standard manner "by reference." This process actually makes little sense, because the parameter transfer by reference can cause errors that are difficult to detect if changes to a procedure have consequences for the calling program.

Naming Markers

When naming markers, uppercase letters indicate the first letter of each word:

```
ErrorHandler:
```

```
ExitProcedure:
```

Prefixes

A prefix is intended to change an object name so that more information is available for that object.

Prefixes for Data Fields (Arrays)

For data fields, use the prefix *a*, for example:

```
aintFontSizes
```

```
astrNames
```

Prefixes for Validity Ranges and Lifetimes

VBA has three validity levels for every variable: Public, Private, and Local. A variable also has a lifetime for the current procedure or the length of the program. Use the prefixes displayed in Table A-2 to indicate the validity level and lifetime.

Table A-2   Prefixes for Validity and Lifetime

Prefix	Object Type
(none)	Local variable, lifetime at procedure level, is declared with *dim*
s	Local (static) variable, lifetime at program level, is declared with *Static*
m	Private (modular) variable, lifetime at program level, is declared with *Private*
g	Public (global) variable, lifetime at program level, is declared with *Public*

The prefixes *m* and *g* are not used to represent the validity levels of other objects (for example, constants):

```
intLocalVariable

mintPrivateVariable

gintPublicVariable

mconConstant

mdblcPi
```

Suffixes

Suffixes change the base name of an object and provide additional information about a variable. You will probably create your own suffixes that are specific to your own developments. Table A-3 contains some general VBA suffixes.

Table A-3 Frequently Used Suffixes

Suffix	Object Type
Cnt	This is used with database elements to indicate that a counter is being used.
First	The first element that is used in a field or a list during the actual operation.
Last	The last element that is used in a field or a list during the actual operation.
Lim	The upper limit for elements that are used in a field or a list. *Lim* is not a valid index. *Lim=Last+1* usually applies.
Max	The absolute last element of a field or a list.
Min	The absolute first element of a field or a list.

See the following examples:

```
iastrNamesMin

iastrNameMax

iaintFontSizesFirst

lngCustomerIdCnt

varOrderNrCnt
```

Tags for Access

Every application with VBA and every component that can be installed has many objects that can be used. This section defines tags for the objects in the different host applications and components.

Access Objects

Table A-4 lists the tags for Access object variables. In addition to being used in programming code to refer to the corresponding object types, these same tags are used to name these objects in forms and reports.

Table A-4   Tags for Access Object Variables

Tag	Object Type
aob	AccessObject
aop	AccessObjectProperty
aops	AccessObjectProperties
app	Application
bas	Module
bfr	BoundObjectFrame
brk	PageBreak
cbo	ComboBox
chk	CheckBox
cmd	CommandButton
ctl	Control
ctls	Controls
dap	DataAccessPage
dcm	DoCmd
fcd	FormatCondition
fcds	FormatConditions
fra	OptionGroup (frame)
frm	Form
frms	Forms
grl	GroupLevel
hyp	Hyperlink
img	Image
lbl	Label
lin	Line
lst	ListBox

continued

Table A-4   Tags for Access Object Variables   *(continued)*

Tag	Object Type
ocx	CustomControl
ole	ObjectFrame
opt	OptionButton
pal	PaletteButton
prp	Property
prps	Properties
ref	Reference
refs	References
rpt	Report
rpts	Reports
scr	Screen
sec	Section
sfr	SubForm
shp	Rectangle
srp	SubReport
tab	Tab Control
tgl	ToggleButton
txt	Textbox

Table A-5 lists the tags that identify the object types in a database.

Table A-5   Tags for Access Database Objects

Tag	Object Type
bas	Module
cls	Class module
dap	DataAccessPage
frm	Form
mcr	Macro
qry	Query
rpt	Report
sp or *proc*	Stored procedure
tbl	Table
vw	View

Do not use spaces when naming objects in a database. Instead, write the first letter of each word in uppercase.

Tags for ADO

Table A-6 contains proposed tags for ADO. Many ADO object names correspond with those of Data Access Objects (DAO). For this reason you should make sure that you enter the name of the object library in all references, to avoid confusion. Use *Dim rst As ADODB.Recordset* rather than entering the object type without the name of the library. This avoids confusion about the source of an object and allows your program to run more quickly.

Table A-6   ADO Object Tags

Tag	Object Type
cmd	Command
cnn	Connection
err	Error
errs	Errors
fld	Field
flds	Fields
prm	Parameters
prms	Parameters
prp	Property
prps	Properties
rst {rec}	Recordset

Tags for SQL Server Objects

Table A-7 lists tags for Microsoft SQL Server and Microsoft Data Engine (MSDE) objects.

Table A-7   SQL Server/MSDE Object Tags

Tag	Object Type
def	Default
dgm	Database diagram
fk	Foreign key
idx	Other index
pk	Primary key
proc or *sp*	Stored procedure
qry or *vw*	View
rul	Check constraint
tbl	Table
trg	Trigger

Appendix B

Internet Addresses

Commonly Used Resources

You can get more information from Microsoft about Microsoft Access and Microsoft SQL Server at the addresses in the following sections.

Microsoft Office and Microsoft Access

http://www.microsoft.com/office
http://www.microsoft.com/office/ork/2000
http://www.microsoft.com/office/ork/xp

Microsoft SQL Server

http://www.microsoft.com/sql
General information about application development with Microsoft products can be obtained from these Web sites:
http://msdn.microsoft.com/
http://msdn.microsoft.com/office
http://msdn.microsoft.com/officedev
http://msdn.microsoft.com/sqlserver
http://msdn.microsoft.com/library/techart/acaccessprojects.htm
The latest downloads from Microsoft, such as service packs, can be found at this Web site:
http://msdn.microsoft.com/downloads

Information on SQL Server

http://www.mssqlserver.com/
http://www.sqlmag.com

General Information

http://www.advisor.com/home

Newsgroups

Many answers about Access and SQL Server can be found in the following newsgroups:

news://msnews.microsoft.com/microsoft.public.access

news://msnews.microsoft.com/microsoft.public.access.adp.sqlserver

news://msnews.microsoft.com/microsoft.public.sqlserver

news://msnews.microsoft.com/microsoft.public.sqlserver.programming

news://msnews.microsoft.com/microsoft.public.sqlserver.xml

Appendix C

SQL Server/MSDE Specifications

Table C-1   SQL Server 7 and SQL Server 2000 Specifications

Specifications	SQL Server 7	SQL Server 2000
Bytes per column of data types *varchar* or *nvarchar*	8000	8000
Bytes per column of data types *text*, *ntext*, or *image*	approximately 2 GB	approximately 2 GB
Bytes per *GROUP BY*, *ORDER BY*	8060	8060*
Bytes per index	900	900**
Bytes per foreign key	900	900
Bytes per primary key	900	900
Bytes per row	8060	8060
Grouped indexes per table	1	1
Nongrouped indexes per table	249	249
Columns per index	16	16
Columns per primary key	16	16
Columns per foreign key	16	16
Columns per base table	1024	1024
Columns per *SELECT* statement	4096	4096
Columns per *INSERT* statement	1024	1024
Database size	1,048,516 TB; 2 GB for MSDE	1,048,516 TB; 2 GB for MSDE
Databases per SQL Server (with SQL Server 2000 per instance)	32,767	32,767
Instances per computer	Not possible	16
File groups per database	256	256
Files per database	32,767	32,767
File size of a data file	32 TB	32 TB

continued

Table C-1 SQL Server 7 and SQL Server 2000 Specifications *(continued)*

Specifications	SQL Server 7	SQL Server 2000
File size of a log file	4 TB	32 TB
Nesting levels of stored procedures	32	32
Nested subqueries	32	32
Nesting levels for triggers	32	32
Parameters per stored procedure	1024	1024
Tables per *SELECT* statement	256	256

* There is no limit to the number of items, but there is a limit of 8060 bytes for the row size of intermediate worktables.

** The maximum number of bytes in any key cannot exceed 900 in SQL Server 2000. You can define a key using variable-length columns whose maximum sizes add up to more than 900, provided no row is ever inserted with more than 900 bytes of data in those columns.

Index

Numbers and Symbols

Spur Gear

The simplest *gear* is the spur gear, a wheel with teeth cut across its edge parallel to the axis. Spur gears transmit rotating motion between two shafts or other parts with parallel axes. In simple spur gearing, the driven shaft revolves in the opposite direction to the driving shaft. If rotation in the same direction is desired, an idler gear is placed between the driving gear and the driven gear. The idler revolves in the opposite direction to the driving gear and therefore turns the driven gear in the same direction as the driving gear.*

At Microsoft Press, we use tools to illustrate our books for software developers and IT professionals. Tools are an elegant symbol of human inventiveness and a powerful metaphor for how people can extend their capabilities, precision, and reach. From basic calipers and pliers to digital micrometers and lasers, our stylized illustrations of tools give each book a visual identity and each book series a personality. With tools and knowledge, there are no limits to creativity and innovation. Our tag line says it all: *The tools you need to put technology to work.*

*Microsoft ® Encarta ® Reference Library 2002. © 1993-2001 Microsoft Corporation. All rights reserved.

The manuscript for this book was edited and prepared by nSight, Inc. using Microsoft Word 2000 for Windows. Pages were composed by nSight, Inc. using Adobe FrameMaker+SGML 6.0 for Windows, with text in Garamond and display type in Helvetica Condensed. Composed pages were delivered to the printer as electronic prepress files.

Principal Compositor:	Donald Cowan
Editor:	Sarah Kimnach Hains
Copy Editor:	Teresa Horton
Technical Editor:	Piotr Prussak
Indexer:	Jack Lewis

Get a **Free**
e-mail newsletter, updates,
special offers, links to related books,
and more when you

register on line!

Register your Microsoft Press® title on our Web site and you'll get a FREE subscription to our e-mail newsletter, *Microsoft Press Book Connections.* You'll find out about newly released and upcoming books and learning tools, online events, software downloads, special offers and coupons for Microsoft Press customers, and information about major Microsoft® product releases. You can also read useful additional information about all the titles we publish, such as detailed book descriptions, tables of contents and indexes, sample chapters, links to related books and book series, author biographies, and reviews by other customers.

Registration is easy. Just visit this Web page and fill in your information:

http://www.microsoft.com/mspress/register

Microsoft®

Proof of Purchase

Use this page as proof of purchase if participating in a promotion or rebate offer on this title. Proof of purchase must be used in conjunction with other proof(s) of payment such as your dated sales receipt—see offer details.

Microsoft® Access Projects with Microsoft SQL Server™
0-7356-1002-9

_____

CUSTOMER NAME

Microsoft Press, PO Box 97017, Redmond, WA 98073-9830

MICROSOFT LICENSE AGREEMENT
Book Companion CD

IMPORTANT—READ CAREFULLY: This Microsoft End-User License Agreement ("EULA") is a legal agreement between you (either an individual or an entity) and Microsoft Corporation for the Microsoft product identified above, which includes computer software and may include associated media, printed materials, and "online" or electronic documentation ("SOFTWARE PRODUCT"). Any component included within the SOFTWARE PRODUCT that is accompanied by a separate End-User License Agreement shall be governed by such agreement and not the terms set forth below. By installing, copying, or otherwise using the SOFTWARE PRODUCT, you agree to be bound by the terms of this EULA. If you do not agree to the terms of this EULA, you are not authorized to install, copy, or otherwise use the SOFTWARE PRODUCT; you may, however, return the SOFTWARE PRODUCT, along with all printed materials and other items that form a part of the Microsoft product that includes the SOFTWARE PRODUCT, to the place you obtained them for a full refund.

SOFTWARE PRODUCT LICENSE

The SOFTWARE PRODUCT is protected by United States copyright laws and international copyright treaties, as well as other intellectual property laws and treaties. The SOFTWARE PRODUCT is licensed, not sold.

1. **GRANT OF LICENSE.** This EULA grants you the following rights:

   a. **Software Product.** You may install and use one copy of the SOFTWARE PRODUCT on a single computer. The primary user of the computer on which the SOFTWARE PRODUCT is installed may make a second copy for his or her exclusive use on a portable computer.

   b. **Storage/Network Use.** You may also store or install a copy of the SOFTWARE PRODUCT on a storage device, such as a network server, used only to install or run the SOFTWARE PRODUCT on your other computers over an internal network; however, you must acquire and dedicate a license for each separate computer on which the SOFTWARE PRODUCT is installed or run from the storage device. A license for the SOFTWARE PRODUCT may not be shared or used concurrently on different computers.

   c. **License Pak.** If you have acquired this EULA in a Microsoft License Pak, you may make the number of additional copies of the computer software portion of the SOFTWARE PRODUCT authorized on the printed copy of this EULA, and you may use each copy in the manner specified above. You are also entitled to make a corresponding number of secondary copies for portable computer use as specified above.

   d. **Sample Code.** Solely with respect to portions, if any, of the SOFTWARE PRODUCT that are identified within the SOFTWARE PRODUCT as sample code (the "SAMPLE CODE"):

      i. **Use and Modification.** Microsoft grants you the right to use and modify the source code version of the SAMPLE CODE, *provided* you comply with subsection (d)(iii) below. You may not distribute the SAMPLE CODE, or any modified version of the SAMPLE CODE, in source code form.

      ii. **Redistributable Files.** Provided you comply with subsection (d)(iii) below, Microsoft grants you a nonexclusive, royalty-free right to reproduce and distribute the object code version of the SAMPLE CODE and of any modified SAMPLE CODE, other than SAMPLE CODE, or any modified version thereof, designated as not redistributable in the Readme file that forms a part of the SOFTWARE PRODUCT (the "Non-Redistributable Sample Code"). All SAMPLE CODE other than the Non-Redistributable Sample Code is collectively referred to as the "REDISTRIBUTABLES."

      iii. **Redistribution Requirements.** If you redistribute the REDISTRIBUTABLES, you agree to: (i) distribute the REDISTRIBUTABLES in object code form only in conjunction with and as a part of your software application product; (ii) not use Microsoft's name, logo, or trademarks to market your software application product; (iii) include a valid copyright notice on your software application product; (iv) indemnify, hold harmless, and defend Microsoft from and against any claims or lawsuits, including attorney's fees, that arise or result from the use or distribution of your software application product; and (v) not permit further distribution of the REDISTRIBUTABLES by your end user. Contact Microsoft for the applicable royalties due and other licensing terms for all other uses and/or distribution of the REDISTRIBUTABLES.

2. **DESCRIPTION OF OTHER RIGHTS AND LIMITATIONS.**

   • **Limitations on Reverse Engineering, Decompilation, and Disassembly.** You may not reverse engineer, decompile, or disassemble the SOFTWARE PRODUCT, except and only to the extent that such activity is expressly permitted by applicable law notwithstanding this limitation.

   • **Separation of Components.** The SOFTWARE PRODUCT is licensed as a single product. Its component parts may not be separated for use on more than one computer.

   • **Rental.** You may not rent, lease, or lend the SOFTWARE PRODUCT.

   • **Support Services.** Microsoft may, but is not obligated to, provide you with support services related to the SOFTWARE PRODUCT ("Support Services"). Use of Support Services is governed by the Microsoft policies and programs described in the user manual, in "online" documentation, and/or in other Microsoft-provided materials. Any supplemental software code provided to you as part of the Support Services shall be considered part of the SOFTWARE PRODUCT and subject to the terms and conditions of this EULA. With respect to technical information you provide to Microsoft as part of the Support Services, Microsoft may use such information for its business purposes, including for product support and development. Microsoft will not utilize such technical information in a form that personally identifies you.

- **Software Transfer.** You may permanently transfer all of your rights under this EULA, provided you retain no copies, you transfer all of the SOFTWARE PRODUCT (including all component parts, the media and printed materials, any upgrades, this EULA, and, if applicable, the Certificate of Authenticity), **and** the recipient agrees to the terms of this EULA.

- **Termination.** Without prejudice to any other rights, Microsoft may terminate this EULA if you fail to comply with the terms and conditions of this EULA. In such event, you must destroy all copies of the SOFTWARE PRODUCT and all of its component parts.

3. **COPYRIGHT.** All title and copyrights in and to the SOFTWARE PRODUCT (including but not limited to any images, photographs, animations, video, audio, music, text, SAMPLE CODE, REDISTRIBUTABLES, and "applets" incorporated into the SOFTWARE PRODUCT) and any copies of the SOFTWARE PRODUCT are owned by Microsoft or its suppliers. The SOFTWARE PRODUCT is protected by copyright laws and international treaty provisions. Therefore, you must treat the SOFTWARE PRODUCT like any other copyrighted material **except** that you may install the SOFTWARE PRODUCT on a single computer provided you keep the original solely for backup or archival purposes. You may not copy the printed materials accompanying the SOFTWARE PRODUCT.

4. **U.S. GOVERNMENT RESTRICTED RIGHTS.** The SOFTWARE PRODUCT and documentation are provided with RESTRICTED RIGHTS. Use, duplication, or disclosure by the Government is subject to restrictions as set forth in subparagraph (c)(1)(ii) of the Rights in Technical Data and Computer Software clause at DFARS 252.227-7013 or subparagraphs (c)(1) and (2) of the Commercial Computer Software—Restricted Rights at 48 CFR 52.227-19, as applicable. Manufacturer is Microsoft Corporation/One Microsoft Way/Redmond, WA 98052-6399.

5. **EXPORT RESTRICTIONS.** You agree that you will not export or re-export the SOFTWARE PRODUCT, any part thereof, or any process or service that is the direct product of the SOFTWARE PRODUCT (the foregoing collectively referred to as the "Restricted Components"), to any country, person, entity, or end user subject to U.S. export restrictions. You specifically agree not to export or re-export any of the Restricted Components (i) to any country to which the U.S. has embargoed or restricted the export of goods or services, which currently include, but are not necessarily limited to, Cuba, Iran, Iraq, Libya, North Korea, Sudan, and Syria, or to any national of any such country, wherever located, who intends to transmit or transport the Restricted Components back to such country; (ii) to any end user who you know or have reason to know will utilize the Restricted Components in the design, development, or production of nuclear, chemical, or biological weapons; or (iii) to any end user who has been prohibited from participating in U.S. export transactions by any federal agency of the U.S. government. You warrant and represent that neither the BXA nor any other U.S. federal agency has suspended, revoked, or denied your export privileges.

DISCLAIMER OF WARRANTY

NO WARRANTIES OR CONDITIONS. MICROSOFT EXPRESSLY DISCLAIMS ANY WARRANTY OR CONDITION FOR THE SOFTWARE PRODUCT. THE SOFTWARE PRODUCT AND ANY RELATED DOCUMENTATION ARE PROVIDED "AS IS" WITHOUT WARRANTY OR CONDITION OF ANY KIND, EITHER EXPRESS OR IMPLIED, INCLUDING, WITHOUT LIMITATION, THE IMPLIED WARRANTIES OF MERCHANTABILITY, FITNESS FOR A PARTICULAR PURPOSE, OR NONINFRINGEMENT. THE ENTIRE RISK ARISING OUT OF USE OR PERFORMANCE OF THE SOFTWARE PRODUCT REMAINS WITH YOU.

LIMITATION OF LIABILITY. TO THE MAXIMUM EXTENT PERMITTED BY APPLICABLE LAW, IN NO EVENT SHALL MICROSOFT OR ITS SUPPLIERS BE LIABLE FOR ANY SPECIAL, INCIDENTAL, INDIRECT, OR CONSEQUENTIAL DAMAGES WHATSOEVER (INCLUDING, WITHOUT LIMITATION, DAMAGES FOR LOSS OF BUSINESS PROFITS, BUSINESS INTERRUPTION, LOSS OF BUSINESS INFORMATION, OR ANY OTHER PECUNIARY LOSS) ARISING OUT OF THE USE OF OR INABILITY TO USE THE SOFTWARE PRODUCT OR THE PROVISION OF OR FAILURE TO PROVIDE SUPPORT SERVICES, EVEN IF MICROSOFT HAS BEEN ADVISED OF THE POSSIBILITY OF SUCH DAMAGES. IN ANY CASE, MICROSOFT'S ENTIRE LIABILITY UNDER ANY PROVISION OF THIS EULA SHALL BE LIMITED TO THE GREATER OF THE AMOUNT ACTUALLY PAID BY YOU FOR THE SOFTWARE PRODUCT OR US$5.00; PROVIDED, HOWEVER, IF YOU HAVE ENTERED INTO A MICROSOFT SUPPORT SERVICES AGREEMENT, MICROSOFT'S ENTIRE LIABILITY REGARDING SUPPORT SERVICES SHALL BE GOVERNED BY THE TERMS OF THAT AGREEMENT. BECAUSE SOME STATES AND JURISDICTIONS DO NOT ALLOW THE EXCLUSION OR LIMITATION OF LIABILITY, THE ABOVE LIMITATION MAY NOT APPLY TO YOU.

MISCELLANEOUS

This EULA is governed by the laws of the State of Washington USA, except and only to the extent that applicable law mandates governing law of a different jurisdiction.

Should you have any questions concerning this EULA, or if you desire to contact Microsoft for any reason, please contact the Microsoft subsidiary serving your country, or write: Microsoft Sales Information Center/One Microsoft Way/Redmond, WA 98052-6399.